The Archaeology
of Anglo-Saxon
England

The Archaeology of Anglo-Saxon England

edited by David M. Wilson

Methuen & Co Ltd

First published in 1976
by Methuen & Co Ltd
11 New Fetter Lane, London EC4P 4EE
© 1976 Methuen & Co Ltd
Printed in Great Britain by
Butler & Tanner Ltd, Frome and London

ISBN 0 416 15090 X

Distributed in the USA by
HARPER & ROW PUBLISHERS, INC
BARNES & NOBLE IMPORT DIVISION

Contents

Acknowledgements

A book of this sort makes great demands on the patience of the contributors. Delays are inevitable and chances of revision almost impossible. I hope, however, that this series of studies, some of which were prepared as much as three years ago, will justify all the patience expended on them in difficult circumstances – both financial and editorial. I would like to thank all who contributed to its eventual appearance, and particularly my secretary, Hilary McKeon, for constant and varied aid at all times, my daughter for her help with the index and my wife for much trouble in redrawing some of the text figures (but not those in chapters 1, 2, 3, 5 and 7 which were drawn or provided by the authors).

The sources of many of the text illustrations are acknowledged in the list of figures. The copyright of the following photographs is acknowledged: The British Museum pls I, IIIb, IV, V, VI, VII, VIII, IX; The Bodleian Library, Oxford, pl. XIII; Bridget Cherry pls XXIb and d; The Courtauld Institute pls XVIIIa and b, XXIa and c; F. H. Crossley pl. XXa; *The Illustrated London News* pl. Xa; The Ipswich Museum pl. XV; Professor A. W. Lawrence pl. XIXb; David Leigh pl. XIV; The National Monument Record pls XVIIa and b, XVIII; Holger Schmidt pl. XVI; University of Southampton (Dept. of Archaeology) pl. XI; University College London pl. II; Professor D. M. Wilson pl. IIIa; David Yaxley pl. Xb.

David M. Wilson
May 1976

List of figures

x   List of figures

List of plates

The plates appear between pages 272 and 273

Introduction

David M. Wilson

It is seventy years since the first volume of Baldwin Brown's *The Arts in Early England* was published. For the best part of this century his volumes have been a cornerstone of the study of Anglo-Saxon archaeology. Although still useful, they need to be replaced because of the shift in emphasis in Anglo-Saxon studies since he started to write and because of the vast quantities of new material since excavated. Baldwin Brown attempted to cover the whole period and all the material; he was as interested in pagan graves as he was concerned with Christian churches. He had a broad knowledge of the comparative continental material, and the extent of his travels and of his forceful personality is shown by the many photographs which he took in museums as far apart as Stockholm and Budapest. He was writing in a period before settlement archaeology had reached any kind of maturity and before the full potentialities of the archaeological discipline had been appreciated by historians; and although his book remains a quarry of inestimable value to the professional, it no longer fulfils the needs of students in many disciplines who need to know in some detail about both the method and content of Anglo-Saxon archaeology. This book is intended to provide an authoritative source for at least part of the archaeology of the Anglo-Saxon period. It is not conceived on the scale attempted by Baldwin Brown, nor does it follow the lines he laid down; modern archaeology demands a different approach which we now try to provide.

Archaeology has more potential than any other discipline for adding to our knowledge of the Anglo-Saxon period in that new material is being uncovered daily. It has not fulfilled this potential and to that extent this book must be considered as a preliminary report on work in progress; but the material considered here cannot be ignored by any student of the period, for in many fields it provides the sum of our knowledge. The archaeologist, like all students of the early medieval period, must work with specialists in other disciplines; in this book we have combined to produce a summary of our discipline, make available our sources and explain our methods to students of other disciplines – historians, philologists, literary historians, geographers and sociologists. The book cannot summarize completely the whole material of Anglo-Saxon archaeology, it merely attempts to point to certain salient features which seem to the editor and to the authors important in the present state of study of the Anglo-Saxon period. The subject is constantly changing, new disciplines are used in interpreting the evidence produced by the archaeologist, new techniques are introduced in the field and in the museum, and old and tried disciplines, long out of fashion, are tested again and brought back into the discussion. In ten years' time this book may be considered out-of-date in relation to new approaches of technique, but it must be written because there is no summary of the period which will at once advise and warn scholars about the limits and strength of the archaeological evidence. This is a synthetic work – avowedly so – which attempts to provide a true and documented estimate of the present state of certain aspects of Anglo-Saxon archaeological studies.

The limits of the evidence

Although archaeology uses the methods of the natural and social sciences in building up a picture of man's past, it is not itself an exact science and is not governed – as is, say, chemistry – by natural laws. The tendency on the part of some American archaeologists[1] to force it within certain philosophic boxes quite at odds with the loose methods of induction often needed to deal with the archaeological material must be ignored. In its approach it is akin to formal history: by studying the content of the human past the archaeologist hopes to build up a picture of the period with which he is concerned; the facts which he uses are as subjective or objective as the facts used by the historian. From these facts– from his material – the archaeologist attempts to write history and, in a period where literary evidence is available, he has to combine his evidence with that provided by books and documents. In the Anglo-Saxon period his material is as thin, as one-sided, as full of gaps as the historian's material; fortunately, however, archaeological and historical evidence often complement each other. Thus the historian identifies a royal palace site at Yeavering (pp. 65ff.) and the archaeologist reconstructs by excavation its appearance. But the interpretation of the document that records the site is just as open to re-interpretation as is the archaeologist's interpretation of the site plan.

In using the archaeological material there may be a tendency to stretch the evidence. To take the example of Yeavering again, a structure found at this site was in plan shaped like the segment of a circle (fig. 2.8). A perfectly valid study of archaeological evidence enables it to be reconstructed in the form of a segment of an amphitheatre with a small platform at the apex of the plan. This has been interpreted as an Anglo-Saxon place of assembly – a reasonable enough interpretation – but the tendency to go beyond the evidence has occasionally proved too tempting and it has been dignified with a name (a *moot*) and wilder spirits have imagined that it was at this very structure that the missionary Paulinus preached to the king of Northumbria. Any one of these suggestions is possible but none of them can be proved. It could equally well be suggested – in an only slightly more ludicrous vein – that it was a place for open-air board games or for pagan rites of unmentionable character. The job of the student of the period is to test these hypotheses. Suggestions must be made (it would indeed be an arid subject which simply recorded archaeological material in the most objective manner possible), but the suggestions must be questioned and examined again and again.

It is impossible through archaeology alone to enter far into the workings of the human mind. It is clear, for example, that Saxons were fond of a certain type of animal ornament as embellishment, but the meaning of these motifs either to a single person or to a community cannot be recaptured from the archaeological material and it is, in my view, worthless to try and interpret it in the light of the surviving literature, which was written down long after the inception of the style. By the fact that the Anglo-Saxons buried their dead (before the coming of Christianity) with grave goods, by the fact that food is found in graves, and by the fact that there is a strong possibility that human sacrifice was occasionally practised,[2] we may postulate some sort of belief in the after-life. But from the archaeological material it is impossible to name the religion practised, the gods worshipped or the ritual which preceded burial.[3]

Indeed much of our knowledge of the religion of pagan Anglo-Saxon England is based on a handful of facts drawn from later literary sources. We know little of Anglo-Saxon heathendom, and that little is more in the nature of slight hints and minute snippets of information than an ordered and coherent account of the religion.[4]

If there is little information about religion in archaeology there are practically no clues to political structure, to national boundaries, to marital practices or to the rights of the individual. Occasionally a very rich grave may give an idea of social structure and the wealth of a particular person, but such indications are rare. For such evidence the historical sources are more useful, but archaeology has more value for certain more tangible material.

From archaeology it is possible to produce a considerable body of material relating to the daily life of the Anglo-Saxon people – their houses, their jewellery, their crafts, their Christian buildings, their towns, their fortifications, their domestic animals. This is the evidence which is discussed in this book. At all stages of our study we must turn to the historical sources for aid, but often the archaeologist has more to tell than the historian. A subject which is on the borderline between archaeology and history – numismatics – is also considered here (ch. 8) because of its importance to both disciplines and because it is difficult to see it in context due to its complicated terminology and elaborate method. There are gaps in this book: matters such as physical anthropology, burial customs, diet and national distinctions – for which there is a fair amount of evidence available – have been omitted because of the lack of competent studies, or because existing studies are not yet available for synthesis. Likewise certain matters, such as style history, are dealt with in this introduction, although in the past they have often taken up a fair proportion of the archaeologist's attention. This is done intentionally as there is a distinct need to emphasize modern trends in archaeological thought about the Anglo-Saxon period. This is not to deny the validity of such subjects – style history is still one of the most commonly used methods of dating in the period – but it is rather to reduce the role of such studies to a level similar to that held by excavation and to that held by botanical and geological sciences in the study of prehistory.

The Anglo-Saxon archaeologist is a true archaeologist in that he uses most of the methods of the prehistorian; that he must also use the methods of the historian and philologist sets him in some measure apart from his colleagues in the prehistoric field. Indeed, it is often rather dangerous for one man to teach both prehistory and Anglo-Saxon archaeology in view of the large spectrum of methods which must be covered. But although the Anglo-Saxon archaeologist uses all these methods – from dendrochronology to textual criticism, from the carbon-14 method of dating to numismatics – such inter-disciplinary aids are simply a means to an end, just as the technique of excavation is a means to an end. The archaeologist is interested in the whole effect of human activity on the environment, in the product of man's labours and of his hands, and it is his job to recreate as best he can a coherent story from this material. There are plenty of books on archaeological method and, since it is not our job to consider such generalities here, the reader is referred to them. Here we present our picture of the Anglo-Saxon people.

The people and the land

The settlement of England by the Anglo-Saxons took place gradually, in the simplest of historical terms, between 400 and 600. Between 800 and 1066 the Anglo-Saxons were subjected to raids and sometimes conquest and settlement by the Scandinavians. At all times there was contact – sometimes friendly, sometimes unfriendly – between the English and their British neighbours to the west and the north. The story of these movements and contacts of people is told in the historical sources with varying degrees of reliability. The archaeological material tells something of these events, but the story it tells is often rather thin, especially in relation to the Scandinavian settlement and to the contact with the British peoples. A few cultural traits transferred from one people to another – as for example stylistic elements in the art of a handful of major monuments or finds – but this is practically the sum total of archaeological evidence about these two latter contacts. But the coming of the Anglo-Saxons is well documented in the archaeological evidence, even though the story that is told is often obscure.

The clear distinction of material culture and political organization between the Anglo-Saxons and the Romano-British population of England is the main reason for the clarity with which one can draw a distinction between the two groups in the archaeological record. The Anglo-Saxons came from a Germanic stock who, although they had considerable contact with the Roman peoples, had never had a Roman civilization grafted onto their way of life. They knew nothing of masonry buildings, of municipal organization, of imperial estates, of well-disciplined standing armies. They were not interested in imitating Roman dress (which was in any case more suited to the mediterranean climate than to northern Europe), they did not initially try to retain a monetary economy (with all that this implies) and they appear to have struggled actively to suppress the naturalistic side of Roman art and to have retained their own goals. The Britons of the west and north never had more than a marginal effect on the culture of the Anglo-Saxons, although they were in almost continuous contact with them. The reason for this may well be that the economies of the two peoples were similar, being based on agriculture and other rural pursuits, with little emphasis on town life or international trade; both had a building tradition which owed nothing to the Romans. Although for some periods of the pagan Anglo-Saxon age there were British enclaves – around Leeds, for example – which were truly British in population, language and polity, the Anglo-Saxons mostly came into contact with the British in the west and the north.

Here, however, it is difficult to isolate archaeological evidence which is at all meaningful. There are, for instance, only eight sites in Bernicia which have produced pagan Anglo-Saxon graves and only one of these (Howick Heugh) can in any sense be called a cemetery.[5] At both Yeavering and Bamburgh recent excavation has produced royal sites – the latter interpreted in a preliminary lecture by Hope-Taylor as a mercantile centre. The only other definite settlement of the pre-Christian period in this important area of Northumbria is the site at Doon Hill, Dunbar (which might suggest a British origin for certain Anglo-Saxon building techniques).[6] To discuss British influence here is, at the moment, hardly meaningful and even in the south-west of England intense work by Alcock, Rahtz and others[7] has yielded very little real evidence in the archaeological record of that long sought after Arthurian twilight. It must, however, be recognized that the native British population was not exterminated by Anglo-Saxon incomers. Intermarriage between members of the aristocracy and royal families is recorded fairly frequently in the literature and there are hints of the same practice at other social levels. But although the two nationalities coalesced, it was the Anglo-Saxons who emerged as the dominant element in society and who basically produced the English culture.

The new invaders came as mercenaries to help the Romans and Romanized Britons left behind after the withdrawal of the Roman administration. Traces of their presence are to be seen in the graves – many of them found in close relation to Roman towns – which display the equipment of *comitatenses* or auxiliaries,[8] or the burial habits of the Germanic nations (as for example the Germanic cremation burials found in a Romano-British cemetery at York).[9] But with the gradual collapse of the Roman administration and the attempts by the British to preserve the old ways, many towns appear to have been deserted (see pp. 103ff.) and (where the Anglo-Saxons continued to use the old sites) there was a tendency to occupy them on a reduced scale. The newcomers had no use for the great public buildings of the Empire, buildings like the basilica of York[10] which later was gradually covered by the great complex of the Christian minster. Alcock[11] has rightly pointed out that there is little evidence of deliberate sacking or destruction of Roman towns from archaeological sources.

The decay of Roman institutions is also seen in the countryside. The villa system broke down gradually; squatters or the impoverished original owners are occasionally seen occupying parts of Roman buildings or adapting them to a different use.[12] The land cultivated by the Romans was, however, useful land, cleared and in good heart. In a countryside of fen, scrub and forest this land would not be ignored in an economy built up by the successors of the Romans. The fields and pastures of the Romans would undoubtedly have been adapted to the new economic and social conditions. The apparent continuity between Romano-British and Anglo-Saxon agriculture may not be due so much to a continuity of economy as to a continuity of land utilization; the Anglo-Saxon settlers would tend to take land previously occupied rather than clear virgin land. It is possible then that many of the field shapes recognized in the later Anglo-Saxon period, which are not satisfactorily explained by parallels in the Germanic homelands, may merely be the shapes imposed by boundaries created in the Romano-British period. Recent suggestions by Bonney[13] propose that the parish boundaries of the later middle ages were already established as meaningful boundaries (presumably of estates) in the pagan Anglo-Saxon period. (The suggestion is based on the fact that a high proportion of the pagan burial sites are closely related to parish boundaries and on the fact that such late linear earthworks as Wansdyke bear no relation to the shape of parish boundaries.) Bonney attempts to go beyond this and place the origin of some of the boundaries of later estates and parishes in the Roman period and even earlier. The validity of his arguments is open to question, but the possibility stands and underlines the argument that existing land utilization had considerable influence on the Anglo-Saxon settlement pattern.

As more Anglo-Saxons joined their relations who had come as mercenaries and invaders so they turned to the land and founded villages of which many traces have been recovered (pp. 31ff.). The villages are represented in the archaeological record by the vast number of Anglo-Saxon pagan cemeteries scattered throughout the country, which tell much about the origins of the invaders, about their mode of life, their dress, their wealth and their social condition. The cemeteries have provided a vast body of material concerning the pagan Anglo-Saxons, but the very size of these remains tends to unbalance the picture; too much attention can be paid to brooches, pots and swords, but at the same time these objects provide us with a scale by means of which we can set the archaeological evidence in some sort of chronological sequence. The settlement pattern begun in the first years after the end of Roman rule in Britain developed through the Anglo-Saxon period with only minor modifications until the village and farming structure recorded in Domesday Book was gradually built up.

Towns developed, at first slowly, as administrative centres, as markets (both local and national) and as places of defence and refuge in times of trouble. When all three functions coalesced in one place a town was the inevitable result, for only a large unit could carry the complicated economic structure that all these functions implied. When the three elements did not coalesce – as with some of the towns founded specifically by Alfred for defence against the Danish invaders – then the town failed to mature, to such an extent that the sites of some towns of the ninth century are not now known.[14]

With the towns developed the industries and specialized crafts which produced the goods for the markets. The foundations of the English trade and industrial economy of the later middle ages were laid at this time. Within the landscape, both in town and country, the Church made its presence felt with the first formally built stone structures to be erected in this country since the Romans had left. Monasteries (ch. 5) and churches (ch. 4) were built, and from some of these later churches sprang the indigenous style of vernacular stone building which we glimpse rarely before the Conquest.[15]

Communication in Anglo-Saxon times was both easy and difficult. Difficult because of such impassable barriers as the undrained fens of Somerset and East Anglia and the great forests like Selwood and the Weald[16] traversed by few roads or tracks, which were the haunts of robbers and outlaws and were in any case in a much more primeval state than the pleasant park-like remnants that survive today. But at the same time communication was easy along the great network of roads left by the Romans and the series of prehistoric trackways, like the Icknield Way, which were also presumably in use at this time. The Roman roads may in some cases have fallen into disrepair, but many remained and we must remember that this same network was still in use long after the Reformation and that in the Anglo-Saxon period the roads were probably often in better repair than they were in the later middle ages. The speed of communication is glimpsed occasionally in the historical sources which record the passage of armies and of messengers up and down the country. The roads did not necessarily teem with life, but they were in constant use and were presumably a considerable feature of the landscape. For the rest, navigation up and down rivers and along the coast also allowed easy communication: finds in archaeological contexts of imported goods or materials like stone transported for only a few miles tell of the use of rivers and roads, just as do records of the travels of bishops, monks and soldiers.

The roads were not the only features of the countryside left by the Romans. They also left the ruins of their buildings. Ruins which left such an impression on the minds of the Anglo-Saxons that their poems tell of it:

> Wonderful is this wall of stone, wrecked by fate.
> The city buildings crumble, the bold works of the giants decay
> Roofs have caved in, towers collapsed,
> Barred gates have gone, gateways have gaping mouths, hoar frost clings to mortar.[17]

At no place are these 'bold works of the giants' more evocatively recalled than at York Minster where under the late Anglo-Saxon cemetery a fallen pillar lay shattered at full length.[18] The Anglo-Saxons seem to have avoided in large measure the stone buildings of their Roman predecessors. Throughout the countryside villas and forts must have stood as mute testament to the difference between the mediterranean and Germanic invaders of this island. With the coming of Christianity these sites were used as quarries for building stone[19] for the new churches, or became the sites of monastic communities. The stone walls of the Roman towns were used as fortifications as late as the eleventh century[20] and occasionally the buildings may have served as temporary refuges for the incoming population. At one Roman fort – Portchester – an Anglo-Saxon settlement has been found within the walls, and at a latish period of its development it seems to have functioned as a place of refuge in the control of an aristocrat who lived within a single building complex – as did his feudal successor.[21] But in general the Anglo-Saxons avoided these sites and developed their own settlements in rural surroundings.

Chronology

The period covered by this book is – in historical terms – more than six and a half centuries. The generalizations made here are to a certain extent valid in that the rate of cultural development in the Anglo-Saxon period was obviously slow. The people who lived in an Anglo-Saxon village in 1050 probably lived a life little different from that of their predecessors 500 years earlier. But in the course of the Anglo-Saxon period there was inevitably a development in material culture as there was in language and institutions. These changes must be calibrated chronologically.

In building up this chronology the archaeologist relies on the well-tried techniques of his discipline: by the use of stratigraphy and typology, and by the use of natural historical dating methods (both comparative and absolute), it is possible to build up an overall dating framework. The chronology provided by coins is extremely important in the later Anglo-Saxon period, and the methods used by the numismatist are discussed at some length elsewhere (pp. 349ff.), as are the potentialities of dating by pottery (p. 253ff.). But the greatest potentiality for dating in the Anglo-Saxon period remains the much-criticized method of dating by means of the ornament – usually zoomorphic – which appears on metal objects and (in the later Anglo-Saxon period) the ornament on stone sculpture. In general terms such a study makes it possible to date a decorated object to within a century and sometimes to within fifty years. Such dating is sufficient for most archaeological purposes and, when a group of objects dated in such a way is found in an excavation, it is possible to postulate the general chronological situation of the level or of the site in which they are found. A single find cannot of course provide more than a *terminus ante quem*, but the more datable objects found on a site, the more likely it is that the site can be dated with some validity. An example of such dating is provided by the finds in the earliest phase of the Cheddar site (pp. 65ff.). An account, in all simplicity, of the sequence of Anglo-Saxon ornament is therefore essential to any understanding of the period. Further, the methods by which this sequence is reached are also of some importance in any understanding of the archaeological approach to the period.

The earliest ornament of the Anglo-Saxon period is dominated by a semi-naturalistic animal motif (fig. 0.1a) and is known as the quoit-brooch style – named after the type of object (pl. 1b) on which the ornament appears. The style occurs on metal brooches, buckles, earrings and other incidental pieces of jewellery. It gives a polychrome impression, as the metal surface of the objects tends to be embellished with parcel gilding, silver plating and niello, and is occasionally inlaid with blue glass studs. The motifs of this style have their origin in late Roman ornament and passed into the Germanic repertoire by way of ornamented imperial military equipment produced, presumably, in provincial workshops in Gaul. The basis for the dating of this style rests on two factors. Firstly, the objects on which it appears occur in well-recognizable Anglo-Saxon graves, and secondly, in one case at Mucking, Essex,[22] the ornament is found on a buckle of the type used by the late Roman auxiliary troops (pl. 1a and fig. 0.1a). The style must, therefore, have appeared in England at the beginning of the fifth century, and is unlikely to have lasted into the second half of the century.

Figure 0.1 Animal styles in pagan Anglo-Saxon art (scale 1 : 1):
a Animal from the Mucking buckle (pl. Ia)
b Style I ornament from a drinking horn mount from Taplow, Berks.
c Style II ornament from a buckle from Faversham, Kent
d Ornament from a silver disc from Caenby, Lincs.

The quoit-brooch style is peculiar to England, but a similar group of styles was gradually being evolved in southern Scandinavia, just outside the northern boundaries of the Roman Empire, at approximately the same time. These styles were to develop into another style which was universal in north-west Europe in the late fifth and first half of the sixth century, a style labelled by Bernhard Salin as Style I.[23] The basic motif of the style – which is almost certainly Danish in origin – consists quite simply of an animal, the body of which has been broken up into its component parts (fig. 0.1b). These may be related in a logical fashion one to another or may be scattered throughout the area available for decoration in a seemingly haphazard jumble. The ornament may originally have been developed for use on wood (presumably the commonest medium for ornament in the Anglo-Saxon period), but is found almost exclusively on metal mounts and jewellery, normally of bronze or silver and often gilded (pl. 1c). Although the ornament is usually cast (occasionally impressed) the technique used is a woodworking one – chip-carving. The surface of the object as a consequence generally appears to be faceted, each surface catching the light at different angles to produce a glittering effect. The chronological position of this style is difficult to gauge as there are few absolute dates against which it can be checked, but it is usually said to have flourished in the hundred years following the middle of the fifth century.

During the third quarter of the sixth century this style was gradually replaced by Salin's Style II, which perhaps had its origin in Scandinavia. This is also basically a zoomorphic style – the animals are now much more snake-like (fig. 0.1c) and more coherent in their anatomy, twisting and interlacing with their own bodies (Style II). At some stage in the seventh century (arguably in the second quarter) a rather more elaborate animal made its appearance; its body is of more naturalistic proportions, although the tendency to interlace remains (pl. 1d and fig. 0.1d).

The coming of Christianity had little immediate effect on the ornamental motifs used by the Anglo-Saxons, for the inherent love of animal ornament continued to be felt until the end of the ninth century. But the introduction of two new media – stone sculpture and manuscript illumination – from the mediterranean world provided a new impetus to the art. In the third quarter of the seventh century new motifs, plaited band and vine-

Figure 0.2   The ornament of a silver bowl from Ormside Lancs. (after Bruce-Mitford)

scroll ornament particularly, first appear in the Anglo-Saxon ornamental corpus. These motifs of classical origin were at first reproduced, sometimes perhaps by imported craftsmen, with great faithfulness (pl. 2). But soon the Germanic tendency to ignore naturalism asserted itself and the ornament became less classical. The animals which sometimes appear within the vine-scrolls (fig. 0.2), for example, became less naturalistic, and ultimately the bodies became incorporated in the tendrils of the vegetal ornament (pl. 3a). By the middle of the eighth century the true classical motifs seem to have disappeared, surviving only on very few objects – mostly on stone crosses in the north of England and in manuscripts produced in the monastic *scriptoria* of Northumbria. In this period the manuscripts provide the major dating evidence for the English styles. Sometimes the manuscripts can be dated on internal evidence with some accuracy, and co-operation between palaeographers, style historians and textual scholars can often isolate a group of manuscripts and date it closely and in sequence.[24] The validity of dating other objects by comparison with objects of known date (especially objects executed in different media) is one of the nice problems which exercises all style historians. From the middle of the eighth century until about 900 Anglo-Saxon ornament seems to develop slowly on the

Figure 0.3   Ornament from ninth-century metalwork (scale 1 : 1):
a and b From a hoard from Trewhiddle, St Austell, Cornwall
c From the Fuller brooch

lines already laid down in the first years of the manuscript tradition (fig. 0.3). It is interesting, however, that the chronological fixed points are more often provided in this period by the metalwork. By means of inscribed objects and objects laid down in hoards of coins it is possible to build up a coherent picture of the art of this middle period of Anglo-Saxon England, although there are always marginal considerations which affect the judgement of date.[25] About 900 a new factor made itself felt in the art of those parts of England which were now settled by the Scandinavians (see pp. 393–402), for the newcomers introduced their own taste to the sculpture, particularly of the north.[26] Occasionally their ornamental influence is to be seen in other media, metalwork for example,[27] but such occurrences are rare and relatively unimportant. This new influence is important in understanding the chronological sequence of Anglo-Saxon art. The motifs introduced by the Scandinavians were related in many respects to the animal ornament of the Anglo-Saxons – the art of England and the art of Scandinavia had a common origin – but the more barbarous elements of the animals' bodies and certain distinctive interlace patterns were quickly assimilated into northern English ornament (pl. 3b).

Meanwhile a new art style was developing in the south. This last major Anglo-Saxon style is known as the Winchester style. It makes its first positive appearance in the embroidery of the stole and maniple found in St Cuthbert's tomb (pl. 4b), which was made between

909 and 916 at Winchester (a fact known from the inscription).[28] The style developed from two main sources, the figural art of the eastern Empire and the lush acanthus-bound ornament of the Ottonian Empire. The acanthus ornament is the most diagnostic feature of this style outside manuscripts (although figural elements are seen in both ivory[29] and stone-sculpture).[30] The acanthus motif itself combines occasionally in the early years of the eleventh century with the Scandinavian Ringerike style (introduced presumably under the influence of the Danish conqueror, Knut) to produce singularly successful eclectic ornaments.[31]

This simple account of the ornament of the Anglo-Saxon period is presented as a background to the contents of this book. The chronology used in this book often depends on the evidence provided by the style historian, and the problem of the validity of the dating of the Anglo-Saxon art styles must obviously exercise every archaeologist. There is general agreement concerning the stylistic sequence; however much the style historians may disagree concerning minor points there will not now be any great revolution in the relative chronological sequences of the different styles. Although there is a strong temptation for style historians to talk in terms of absolute dates, such dates are only to be considered as ciphers: for much of the Anglo-Saxon period it would be unwise to date any object within a margin of fifty years (often, indeed, to within a century) on the basis of the ornament with which it is decorated. When an archaeologist dates an object stylistically, however, he is merely dating the time of manufacture of that object, he is not providing the date of its deposition, nor even the date of the deposit in which it occurs.

If an object is made in year Y, it cannot be dated before Y, but it could have been deposited at any time after Y. If the object is fragile and cheap to produce (a pot for example) and is found in a broken state in a deposit, the deposit may well date to a period soon after Y. If it is found in the same deposit as a number of similar objects, and with nothing recognizably later, there is even more of a likelihood that the deposit is to be dated closely after Y, say within ten years of manufacture ($Y+10$). If the object is not fragile, the formula for the date of the deposit may be $Y+50$ or even $Y+100$; it is the archaeologist's job to reduce this margin as much as possible. The archaeologist, by means of a series of interlocking dates of objects, can gradually build up a reasoned argument for the laying down of a particular deposit. For example, a deposit containing a group of three objects all manufactured in the first half of the ninth century, together with one eighth-century object and no later material, should probably be dated to the late ninth century. Dates for archaeological deposits are for the moment (until, for example, dendrochronological methods are more thoroughly tabulated) largely provided by style-historical studies, combined naturally with other methods, such as coin-dating (the more coins found in a deposit the more valid is a dating judgement based on them) and the normal natural historical methods used by the archaeologist.

The stylistic dating outlined above is paralleled by the use of typological sequences. For the pagan Anglo-Saxon period particularly such sequences are of considerable importance, and scholars like Åberg[32] have built up a major part of their chronology of the

Anglo-Saxon period on a typological study of certain objects, particularly brooches. To a certain extent this method is valid; cruciform brooches particularly can be set in a chronological sequence and the date of later examples cross-checked by reference to the animal ornament on some of them. The sequence of saucer brooches is a less happy chronological tool,[33] as it is often difficult to tell whether the ornamental differences are chronologically of great significance. The method of counting the number of spirals on these objects and setting them in sequence on this basis would certainly not stand up to modern critical judgements.

Probably the most intractable material in chronological terms is pottery (see below, pp. 283–346), particularly the pagan cremation vessels upon which in some areas our complete knowledge of more than a century of the Anglo-Saxon period depends. The remarkable typological study of this material by Myres[34] has provided a notional framework for a ceramic chronology of the pagan period; but this is possibly more reliable for the fifth century than it is for the sixth and seventh centuries, as it is based on apparently firmer continental dating evidence. Such qualifications of statement are necessary, as much of the dating evidence is based on typological studies of material from north Germany and Denmark, where absolute dates are unknown. For the later period dating on the basis of ceramic types is not refined enough to answer questions raised by a site for which there is other datable material.

Natural historical methods of dating are sometimes used in the study of Anglo-Saxon archaeology. Two methods, archaeomagnetism and dendrochronology, will ultimately prove to be of some value in the study of this period. The former method of dating pottery kilns[35] is at present little used due to lack of support. Recent work in the field of dendrochronology (tree-ring dating), on early medieval sites on the Continent and in Ireland, holds out hopes that this method will in future be used more often on sites which produce timber. Absolute dates are not yet available, but floating chronologies for the early medieval period are beginning to emerge. The method has particular application in relation to distinguishing different building phases on the same site, a method that has been particularly used outside England at Hedeby[36] and Dublin.[37]

A third scientific method of dating – radiocarbon determination – is of limited value in the Anglo-Saxon period. The margin of error due to the fluctuation of the atmospheric radiocarbon content and other causes is so great that the method can only be used for very coarse dating, when there is no other evidence available. A recent ninth-century date for part of a clinker-built ship found at Graveney, Kent, demonstrates the use of the method.[38]

The brutal life

It has often been emphasized that life in the Anglo-Saxon period was filled with danger, was nasty and was full of trouble.[39] Life was cheap, and illness, plague and famine were never far from the surface. The threat of violent death was very real: the heroic society is celebrated by poets. The glorious deeds of the warrior in battle, the picture of vengeance, loyalty to one's lord, the single-handed fight, these and many more actions and ideas, celebrated in chronicles and stories, hide a violent undertow in Anglo-Saxon history. It is, however, impossible to tell how the wars with the British population or with the Scandinavian invaders affected the everyday life of the ordinary English family, and one looks in vain for such information in archaeology.

Traces of warfare are of course found. The fortification of the towns and the use of certain hill-top sites as fortifications tell part of the story. The great linear earthworks, Offa's Dyke[40] and Wansdyke,[41] and the many minor ditches of the Cambridge region, give hints of strategic thought. The siting of a royal fortress on the great rock of Bamburgh, Northumberland, shows an appreciation of the military value of natural features. But more tangible and personal traces of warfare can only really be seen in the graves of the pagan period. Rarely do we find any trace of a documented raid or pillaging (see for example the discussion of the Scandinavian presence, p. 393); there is, for example, no cemetery which can definitely be related to a battle. Occasionally traces of death by violence are found.[42] The feature which gives the clearest picture of the warlike nature of Anglo-Saxon society is undoubtedly the presence of weapons in the graves. A large proportion of male graves of the period contain weapons or the remains of weapons.

The most prestigious weapon was the sword. In the pagan period swords are found in the graves of men, and in the Viking Age are also found in rivers. Similar river finds occur in Europe and may be related to some common German religious or sacrificial practice.[43] Swords (pls 5 and 6) have received considerable attention from literary historians and archaeologists in the course of the last few years,[44] partly because of their literary importance and partly because of the frequency with which they occur archaeologically. Basically they are fairly uncomplicated objects which change little in form over the period, the only major functional change being in the development of the fuller down the length of each face of the blade – a feature which was probably introduced in the course of the eighth century, by which time the sword had also become a heavier weapon. All other features are by way of embellishment. The typical sword is a two-edged weapon, about 90 cm long, with a hilt which fits the normal clenched hand of a man. The sword blade is often pattern-welded (pp. 265–6) and the grip and mounts of the hilt are frequently missing, presumably because they were originally made of perishable material such as horn, bone, wood or leather. The blade occasionally has the maker's mark or name towards the hilt, but such a name does not necessarily imply that the sword came from the workshop of that craftsman, certain makers apparently being much sought after. The hilt is built up round a narrow tang and can be very elaborate. It has been used – with some validity – as the basis of a typological system for the material. The typology commonly used is that of Behmer[45] (for the early Germanic period) or Petersen[46] (which only deals with the Viking Age); a revised typology devised by Wheeler[47] is unsatisfactory.

Basically the earliest swords (pl. 5) have straight pommel bars and guards, the guard only slightly broader than the heel of the blade and the pommel capped by a mount in the shape of a cocked hat. In the ninth century the Anglo-Saxon pommel and pommel bar became slightly longer and were given a curved form, the classical type being Type L of Petersen (pl. 6), of which a typical example is the Abingdon sword.[48] This type continued in use with certain modifications until the end of the Anglo-Saxon period. The sword hilt was the subject of much embellishment, the pommel and guard were decorated, inlaid or gilded; sometimes they were treated most elaborately, embellished with runes,[49] or given a loose ring.[50] Occasionally traces of the grip survive, most notably on a sword-hilt from Cumberland,[51] but the form is well demonstrated in the late eighth century by the plates of the upper half of a sword-grip from Fetter Lane, London.[52] The sword was carried in a wooden scabbard, occasionally with a metal chape and covered with leather,[53] sometimes lined with fleece so that the natural oils should keep it free from rust.[54] The scabbard appears to have been slung from a baldric (occasionally from a belt), but evidence for this is based on manuscript illumination, and other representations,[55] although there is a little evidence from British Viking Age graves that this was at least one method of carrying a sword in the ninth century.[56] The baldric (or belt) was fastened to the scabbard by means of a loop or clasp and (in the case of Sutton Hoo) by means of buttons.[57]

A few swords were single-edged, such as that from Little Bealings, Suffolk,[58–59] or the three from the Thames.[60] While common in Norway,[61] these one-edged swords are probably to be related to the daggers of similar form which are sometimes identified by the Frankish term *scramasax*. The most famous examples are those from Sittingbourne, Kent, and from the Thames at Battersea (pl. 4a),[62] but they are a universal form in England, dating from as early as the late sixth century and known until the Conquest and beyond.[63] Such daggers or scramasaxes are often decorated below the back, some, like the two examples quoted, being inlaid in a most elaborate fashion with precious and semi-precious metals (pl. 4a). The form of the scramasax is very close to that of the knife and it is often difficult to distinguish between the two functions – perhaps there was little distinction in the minds of the Anglo-Saxons.

Swords, although fairly common in Anglo-Saxon graves, seem to have been buried only with the wealthy. Indeed many cemeteries have produced none.[64] The commonest weapon, however, was the spear, which would presumably have been owned by every Anglo-Saxon male. It is the commonest piece of male equipment (other than knives) found in the pagan Anglo-Saxon graves, where it is represented by the iron point or head. Some spears presumably had no head, the point consisting merely of the sharpened end of the shaft.[65] A convenient published survey of pagan Anglo-Saxon spearheads is now available.[66] The normal Anglo-Saxon spear had a shaft of ash[67] (as would be expected from the literary sources)[68] and an iron head usually of a slightly lozenge-shaped section and a socket which, after the immediate settlement period, was split at one side (fig. 0.4d). The spearhead was riveted to the tip of the shaft through the socket. The proportions and form of the head vary greatly, depending probably more on the availability of material, local fashion, the skill of the craftsman and the demand of the customer, than on any

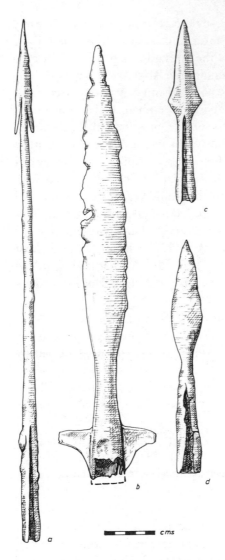

Figure 0.4
a Angon from Abingdon, Berkshire, grave 69
b Winged spearhead from the Thames at Twickenham
c Spearhead from the Thames at Chiswick Eyot
d Spearhead from Dover, Kent, grave 15b

distinct typological development. In the pagan period the Northumbrians seem to have favoured – but not used exclusively – spearheads with leaf-shaped blades (fig. 0.4d); a form not found, for example, in East Anglia where the blade takes a variety of forms which have been typologized by Swanton. It is difficult to place the spearheads of the pagan period in any rational chronological series. It is clear, however, that in the sixth century the angular, concave-sided blade became typical (fig. 0.4c). In the seventh century elegant narrow-bladed spearheads were produced in some quantity, but these were soon to be replaced by heavier weapons. Later in the Anglo-Saxon period, probably in the ninth century, a number of spearheads, either made in this country or imported from the Continent, have wings welded to the socket (fig. 0.4b), presumably to act as a stop when the spear was used. Spearheads are occasionally decorated very simply with, for example, a single inlaid ring of copper wire at the base of the socket. More elaborately decorated sockets were produced in Scandinavia and found their way to England,[69] but apart from spearheads with moulded sockets[70] and a rather strange gilded spearhead found in a possibly post-Conquest grave in Durham Cathedral,[71] finely decorated sockets of English manufacture are unknown. A small group of spearheads with fullered, semi-lunate incisions on either side of the central keel are clearly of Anglo-Saxon date.[72] Occasionally the ferrule of a spear is found.[73]

Closely related to the spear was the *angon*, a weapon first mentioned by Agathias[74] in describing the weapons used by the Franks and Alamenni at the battle at Casilinum in 554. He describes them as light javelins and mentions that they were barbed. Whether

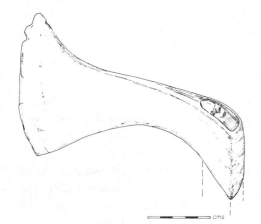

Figure 0.5   Francisca from Howletts, Kent

the long-shafted, barbed spears (fig. 0.4a), of which a handful have been found in Anglo-Saxon contexts,[75] are related to the angon described in this Byzantine source can never be proved, but there seems some likelihood that they are: they certainly have a very different appearance to the more solid spearhead. It is, however, archaeologically impossible to decide whether either the angon or the spear (or indeed both) were used as javelins, or whether they were used for hunting or for war, for private defence or as walking sticks.

The axe had a double function in Anglo-Saxon society, as a weapon and as a tool. The axe as a tool is dealt with elsewhere (pp. 255–7), but the primitive nature of warfare at this period may well have made the distinction between the two functions minimal. Some axes have decorated sockets, and can hardly be considered as tools.[76] The same is presumably also true of the iron-shafted axe found at Sutton Hoo,[77] although Bruce-Mitford thinks of it as a tool.[78] One specific type of axe, which may be a throwing axe, has been dignified by the name *francisca* (fig. 0.5), and because it is common in Frankish graves it is considered to be Frankish in origin. Again the equation of object and name is doubtful, but it has none the less passed into the archaeological vocabulary. It is found in a number of Anglo-Saxon graves[79] and in form consists of a light axe-head with the cutting-edge set well above an imaginary line at right angles to the shaft. The head has a graceful curve and would seem to be ideally suited to throwing. How long throwing axes continued to be used in England is unknown; certainly axes of francisca type are not found in non-pagan contexts.

Axes were certainly used in battle by the Anglo-Saxons in the eleventh century,[80] and are often taken by scholars to be weapons used by the housecarles. But the only axes of this period which can really be taken as weapons are those which have decoration at the socket.[81]

The last offensive weapon to be considered is the bow. This is recorded in only one Anglo-Saxon context – at Chessel Down[82] – although it is known abroad.[83] Arrowheads are, however, occasionally found and hazelwood shafts of arrows have been recorded at Chessel Down.[84] How far they were used in battle and how far for hunting is unclear, although they were certainly used at Hastings. An archer's bracer is postulated by Evison from a barrow at Lowbury Hill, Berkshire.[85]

Machines of war, such as those recorded as having been used in the siege of Paris by the Scandinavians in the ninth century,[86] have left no trace in the archaeological remains of the Anglo-Saxons, but the presence of the defence walls around towns and the use of such machines on the other side of the Channel might suggest that they were used in England.

The shield is the commonest weapon of defence and seems to have remained relatively unchanged until the last years of the Anglo-Saxon period, when the kite-shaped shield with rounded top was introduced, perhaps from the Continent.[87] It seems probable that for the greater part of the period the Anglo-Saxons used the round shield common to the whole of northern Europe. The shield (fig. 0.6) consisted of a wooden board with a central flanged iron boss. Behind the boss was the grip, originally bound with leather or cloth, but basically consisting of a bar the same length as the diameter of the rim of the boss. (Occasionally the grip was extended as an iron bar across the board.)[88] The board of the shield was pierced behind the boss to take the fist; it was of wood and may have measured as much as 90 cm in diameter but was rarely more than 1.5 cm thick. The wood is frequently said to be lime in the literature (indeed the word *lind* is often cognate with shield),[89] but to my knowledge no identification has been made of the wood of English shields, although quite substantial remains of what has been identified (possibly wrongly) as a shield board were found, for instance, at Caenby, Lincs.[90] At Petersfinger, Wilts., Atkinson examined the make-up of the shields in some detail.[91] He showed that the board of the shield was built up of at least two laminations of wood set at right angles to each other (as in modern plywood). This structure was only noticed on one of the shields and, as the grip of this object suggested that the shield was concave,[92] it has been suggested that laminated wood, curved by soaking or steaming, would be the easiest method of achieving this shape. Shields were rarely bound at the rim,[93] but were sometimes covered with leather, as in graves xx and xxi at Petersfinger,[94] where Atkinson has suggested that the leather may well have been moulded by the *cuir bouilli* technique. Not all shield boards were covered in leather, but the exact proportion is not known. They were sometimes decorated with appliqués, as possibly at Caenby,[95] but only rarely have such mounts been identified with the actual board of a shield (pl. 7).[96] One such example is the radiating iron bars on a shield from the London Road cemetery at Thetford, Norfolk.[97]

The form of the boss is of some chronological interest. Unfortunately there are few surviving shield bosses of the period after the cessation of the pagan burial rites, but from the earlier period a considerable number of shield bosses are known. The earliest recorded Anglo-Saxon boss was found at Richborough, Kent, and may have belonged to one of the late Roman mercenaries. It is of conical form with a slight carination towards the

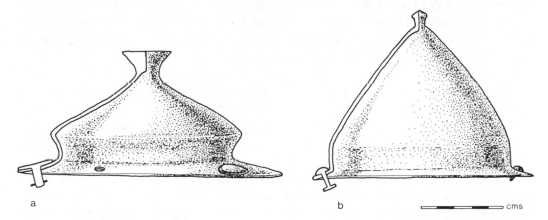

a

b   cms

Figure 0.6   Shield bosses:
a from Winall, Hants., grave I
b from Alton, Hants., grave 16

flange which is slightly angled. The tip has a tendency to be pointed.[98] In the fifth and sixth centuries the boss (fig. 0.6a) became squatter (sometimes concave or convex sided) and the carination tends to be more emphasized. Towards the end of the pagan period the bosses become much taller and are distinguished as 'sugar-loaf' (fig. 0.6b) bosses (from the German *Zuckerhut*).[99] Through most of the period the bosses were attached to the shield by five rivets, the heads of which may be tinned. The tip of the boss is ocasionally embellished with a stud, which is sometimes decorated with animal ornament.[100] Traces of paint on the face of shields has not been recorded in Anglo-Saxon contexts, although shields from Scandinavia and the western areas of the British Isles in the ninth century have traces of surviving paint.[101] Not until the Bayeux Tapestry do we have direct evidence of painted or ornamented shields.

Helmets are rarely found in Germanic Europe and only two examples, one of them probably imported, are known from England. The imported object is the closely studied

Sutton Hoo helmet (pl. 8) which has recently taken a new form in the British Museum.[102] This helmet with its neck and cheek guards was 'probably either made in Sweden itself or by armourers, fresh from Sweden, working in Suffolk, exclusively in their traditional manner and using Swedish dies, moulds and other equipment'.[103] The other helmet, from a rich barrow burial at Benty Grange, Derbyshire, is almost certainly made in this country and in form is unique in Europe.[104] It has a crest in the form of a boar (with eyes of garnets set in gold and decorated with silver studs and plates cut from Roman silver), the cap consisting of plates of horn fastened together with bands of iron to which the plates were riveted with ornamental silver heads of double-axe shape. The helmet has a nose-guard decorated with a silver cross. It is usually dated to the seventh century. It seems likely that helmets were quite common in the late Anglo-Saxon period – at least in the wealthy or professional warrior class – if we are to judge by the evidence of the Bayeux Tapestry,[105] but for some reason they are rarely found in the pagan period graves and it is possible – although not in any way supported by evidence – that poorer members of society protected their heads with leather caps.

Also from Benty Grange come traces of what might be chain mail,[106] which is only paralleled in England at Sutton Hoo.[107] X-ray examination reveals that the latter is made up of rows of rings alternately riveted and welded (not, as originally stated, butted together).[108] The form of the garment is in neither case certain, although they are usually said to be byrnies or mail shirts like those recorded in the Bayeux Tapestry.[109] This and the helmet are the only type of body armour recorded archaeologically.

These weapons tell of the ever-present threat of death by violence. Life was cheap and provisional examination of skeletal material showed that life expectancy was not high, although it would be unwise to generalize on the basis of the material at present at our disposal.[110] But disease also took its toll, and in only a few cases does the record of this make itself felt in archaeology.

Notes

1 E.g. Watson *et al.* (1971).

2 Cf., for example, Wilson and Hurst (1960) 137, and Meaney (1964) 18.

3 The storing of dead bodies or their decapitation comprise but details of the stranger aspects of burial ritual practised by the pagan Anglo-Saxons. Such rites, presumably to protect the living, have most recently been discussed by Audrey Meaney, cf. Meaney and Hawkes (1970) 30ff.

4 Page (1970) 27.

5 A recent summary of this evidence appears in the Archaeological News Bulletin of the Council for British Archaeology, Regional Group 3, for September 1972, pp. 2–4.

6 Wilson and Hurst (1966) 175–6.

7 Summarized in Alcock (1973).

8 Cf. Hawkes and Dunning (1961) *passim*.

9 Stead (1958). Other cemeteries found in relation to Roman towns are found, for example, at Malton, Ancaster, Cambridge and Caistor-by-Norwich: for the latter see Myres and Green (1973).

10 Hope-Taylor (1971).

11 (1973) 181ff.

12 The archaeological evidence of this decay in the countryside is best summarized by Applebaum in Finberg (1972) 253ff. For a villa site with apparent continuity into the Anglo-Saxon period, cf. Shakenoak, near Wilcote in Oxford-

shire, where excavations in progress seem to indicate a direct continuity: Brodribb *et al.* (1972).

13 Bonney (1972) 171ff.
14 Cf., for example, Brooks (1964).
15 Seen, for example, at Porchester and Sulgrave.
16 Cf. Finberg (1972) 402ff. for forests.
17 Quoted from Mitchell (1965).
18 Hope-Taylor (1971) pl. 15.
19 Taylor and Taylor (1965).
20 Anglo-Saxon Chronicle, C, *sub anno* 1006.
21 Cunliffe (1969).
22 Evison (1968).
23 Salin (1904); the most recent discussion of its origins in Haseloff (1973).
24 Cf., for example, the Lindisfarne group of manuscripts, Kendrick *et al.* (1960).
25 For the dating of Anglo-Saxon ornamental metalwork see Wilson (1964) 5ff., and for a general discussion of the limits of such chronologies see Wilson (1959).
26 Cf. Wilson and Klindt-Jensen (1966) 100ff.
27 Cf., for example, Wilson (1964) pl. xliv, 154 and 155.
28 Battiscombe (1956) 376–432.
29 Beckwith (1972) *passim.*
30 E.g. Kendrick (1949) pl. xxxvii.
31 E.g. ibid., pl. lxxiii.
32 Aberg (1926).
33 Cf., for example, Leeds (1912).
34 Myres (1969), modified slightly in Myres and Green (1973).
35 A convenient description of archaeomagnetism as a technique is Cook (1969).
36 Eckstein (1969); and Eckstein and Lisse (1971).
37 Information from Mr B. O'Riordain.
38 Evans and Fenwick (1971) 94.
39 Most virulently by Page (1970).
40 Fox (1955).
41 Fox and Fox (1958).
42 E.g. Meaney (1964) 247, 248, 250.
43 Cf. Wilson (1965) 52.
44 Cf., particularly, Davidson (1962).
45 Behmer (1939).
46 Petersen (1919).
47 Wheeler (1927) fig. 13.
48 Hinton (1974) 1–7.
49 Hawkes and Page (1967).
50 Listed ibid., 10.
51 Behmer (1939) pl. II, 3.
52 Wilson (1964) pl. xxiii, 41.
53 Davidson (1962) 88ff.

54 Ibid., 88.
55 E.g., ibid., pl. xvi.
56 Bersu and Wilson (1966) 55f.
57 Bruce-Mitford (1972) pl. D.
58–59 Davidson (1962) fig. 16.
60 Wheeler (1935) pl. xiii, 4–6.
61 Gjessing (1934) 69ff.
62 Wilson (1964) pl. xxii, 36, and xxx, 80.
63 Baldwin Brown (1903–37) 225ff.
64 This complicated matter is partially discussed by Davidson (1962) 8ff. There seems to be no rule about the number of weapon graves in a given area, although they seem commoner in Kent and Yorkshire than elsewhere in the country. It is possible that the practice of handing swords down from father to son may account for the lack of swords in graves. Weapons achieved virtue by age and some remarkable pedigrees are recorded concerning specific examples in literature. Cf., for example, the sword bequeathed in 1015 by the Atheling Æthelstan to his brother Edward, which was 200 years old or more, having belonged to King Offa: Whitelock (1955) 549.
65 There may be some evidence of this from the elaborate Oberflacht graves in Germany, where they are described as wands: Wylie (1855) pl. xxxvi.
66 Swanton (1973).
67 Information from tests made from M. J. Swanton.
68 E.g. *æsc* (ash=spear) *Beowulf*, 1.1772.
69 E.g. Wheeler (1927) fig 5A.
70 E.g. Wheeler (1935) pl. xi.
71 Kendrick (1938a) pl. XVIII, 2b.
72 Swanton (1973) figs 45–8.
73 Ibid., figs *passim.*
74 For a recent review of this passage, cf. ibid., 29f.
75 Ibid., 33f.
76 Cf., for example, Wheeler (1927) fig. 3.
77 Bruce-Mitford (1972) fig. 17.
78 Ibid., 36.
79 Baldwin Brown (1903–37) iii, 231f.
80 E.g. Florence of Worcester, i, 195.
81 E.g. Wheeler (1927) fig. 3.
82 Hillier (n.d.) 30.
83 E.g. Veeck (1931) pl. 5b. A long bow was recently found during excavations at Hedeby.
84 Hillier (n.d.) 30. For arrowheads cf. Baldwin Brown (1903–37) iii, 241f. For an illustration of Alamannic arrows from Oberflacht, cf. Veeck (1931) fig. 9.
85 Evison (1963) 46n.

86 Abbo, 88 (Waquet, 1942).
87 Cf. Stenton (1957) plates *passim*.
88 E.g. Leeds and Shortt (1953) fig. 8.
89 Cf. Bosworth and Toller (1898) *s.v.*
90 British Museum, see note below.
91 Leeds and Shortt (1953) 55ff.
92 A feature also noted at Sutton Hoo (cf. Bruce-Mitford (1972) 26).
93 The Sutton Hoo shield is atypical in this respect but may well be an import.
94 Leeds and Shortt (1953) 56f.
95 *British Museum, Guide to Anglo-Saxon and Foreign Teutonic Antiquities*, London 1923, fig. 104.
96 The Sutton Hoo shield is again an exception as it may have been imported. A note of caution must also be struck with regard to the Caenby shield. This was excavated in 1850 and it is quite possible that Jarvis misinterpreted the finds, especially as there was no apparent trace of a shield boss in the barrow. Cf. Jarvis (1850). A number of possible appliqués are listed by Baldwin Brown (1903–37) iii, 199ff.
97 Evison (1963) fig. 3.
98 Ibid., fig. 11.
99 Ibid., for the best summary of the evidence with regard to bosses and especially sugar-loaf bosses.
100 E.g. Kendrick (1938) pl. xxix, 4.
101 Nicolaysen (1882) frontispiece and p. 63; Bersu and Wilson (1966) 60 and fig. 37.
102 Cf. Bruce-Mitford (1972a) and Bruce-Mitford (1972) 30f. and pl. 17.
103 Ibid., 80.
104 *The City Museum, Sheffield, Annual Report 1955–6*, 13–15 and pl. 4.
105 It should be remembered that the *fyrd* – unencumbered by defensive armour – may be represented in the Bayeux Tapestry. Cf. Stenton (1957) pls 67 and 73. The heavily armoured soldiers so widely represented in this much-used source may be the semi-professional element of the army.
106 Bateman (1861) 32. The illustration here does not entirely convince one that this is the right interpretation.
107 Bruce-Mitford (1972) 37.
108 Stenton (1957) 62.
109 Ibid., plates *passim*.
110 Brothwell (1972) 83 quotes an average life-span of skeletal material of 36.0 for men and 29.9 for women town-dwellers and 34.7 and 33.1 for country-dwellers – but the sample is small and these figures should not be confused with life expectancy, which was probably under 20.

1

Agriculture and rural settlement

P. J. Fowler

Introduction

'Agrarian history becomes more catastrophic as we trace it backwards;'[1] it also seems to disintegrate as we move forwards out of the Roman period. The direct archaeological and documentary evidence on this topic between the fifth century and Domesday Book is limited and, for the first four centuries of that period, almost non-existent. This remains true over the country as a whole, even taking into account the late Saxon land charters and the recent and current archaeological excavation programme. Until the last decade, this fact has tended to be glossed over in general histories either by ignoring it or by adhering to an implicit 'model', with roots in nineteenth-century Germanic scholarship, which is no longer acceptable.

Our prime concern here is archaeological and topographical, but the historical nature of the inquiry must be made explicit. We are dealing, particularly in the second half of our period, with a documented phase of English history, however defective the written evidence for its agrarian history. This documentary evidence, the translation and inter- pretation of which has become a specialist field of scholarship in its own right, includes both contemporary material from the Saxon period and all that post-Conquest material up to the present which has been variously used to extrapolate back to the centuries between Roman and Norman. It cannot be reassessed here, nor is there a need to do so: many of the basic contemporary documents are published[2] and a vast literature of comment and interpretation is easily consulted. Several recent historical studies in English discuss our topic in the context of early medieval Europe with behind them a great corpus of original work in numerous languages.[3] Of the insular works, Loyn's[4] is an exceptionally good synthesis of the archaeological and documentary approach to and evidence for our subject up to a decade ago, building on three-quarters of a century of deep historical scholarship in which topography has always been present to a greater or lesser extent. Vinogradoff,[5] Maitland, Gray[6] and Seebohm,[7] though all concerned with the major issues of institutional and legal origins, realized, at best explicitly, the value of particularization, of detailed local studies of a single area or community. Their realization of the need for the topographical detail links them with a traditional element underlying the development of English archaeology, the practice of fieldwork,[8] which has matured this century in the work of such students of the landscape as Crawford,[9] Hoskins,[10] Bowen,[11] Taylor,[12] and Beresford and Hurst.[13] Starting with the particular – an air photograph, a flight of lynchets, a settlement deserted or otherwise – scholars like these have separately assembled a body of evidence denied to the Maitland generations and indeed even to historians such as Hodgkin, Myres and Stenton up to the 1940s.[14] Yet this topographical evidence is cumulatively of direct relevance to the problems at the core of the historical issues which the great historians of two or three generations ago sought to illuminate.

More recently, and especially in the last twenty years, archaeological excavation has become an important factor too, although much of the new evidence is not yet accessible and its published results are understandably by no means comprehensive. It appears however, perhaps surprisingly, that little direct agrarian evidence, other than that implied by the existence of the excavated settlements themselves, has so far come from this increase in excavation. The dynamic and fluid nature of this situation nevertheless must partly explain why, in contrast to the topographical developments, little work of archaeological synthesis, let alone of archaeological and historical synthesis, has yet been attempted on the agrarian theme. Beresford and Hurst[15] have laid the foundations and started the assessment in the light of much recent work, and Finberg has now contributed an authoritative discussion. The following essay repeats the author's contribution to Finberg's work[16] but otherwise consciously seeks to complement it by concentrating on material and topographical considerations. Despite these two recent works we start from a position in which, archaeologically, we still know less about the context and practices of the Anglo-Saxon 'village' than we do about the Iron Age farm and the Roman villa.

Anglo-Saxon agriculture was presumably a mixed agriculture, variations in the emphases on crop and animal husbandry being partly the result of regional factors.[17] The arable fields produced a familiar range of crops, though we lack good statistics to indicate accurate proportions. Barley was nevertheless far and away the most important quantitatively, and was of course used for brewing; both naked and hulled types are known and, with oats for animal feed and porridge, would have been a spring-sown crop. Wheat and rye were planted in autumn; other known field-crops were hemp, flax and woad, possibly beans and certainly vines. All of these varieties could have been inherited from Roman Britain, and the same may well be true of the wide range of fruits and vegetables attested in that period. Grass for grazing and haymaking must also be accounted a major crop, reminding us, though it is not our prime concern here, that the Anglo-Saxon rural economy depended to a considerable extent on livestock, partly for traction and partly for a great variety of both essential and luxury products.

The nature of the arable field, its ownership and its methods of working are crucial to any understanding not only of agriculture but also of the basis of rural life in the period over much of England and Wales, yet archaeology can only indirectly throw light on these aspects. But unless we assume, as has often been the case, that Saxon settlers brought with them a completely new type of arable farming, for example the 'open field' system, totally replacing whatever previously existed in southern and eastern England, or unless we assume that arable farming did not exist in those areas when the Saxons arrived, an understanding of developments can use three main approaches. First, the archaeological approach can look at the relatively good cultural evidence from the first half of the first millennium A.D. and then review the millennium as a whole; second, the historical approach can assess the documentary evidence, most of which comes from late in the period; and third, the 'theoretical' approach can discuss numerous 'models' representing what could have happened, testing them against such evidence as exists and, equally important, stimulating new work. These approaches are of course closely interrelated and any synthesis must involve all three. The next sections, however, discuss the archaeological and theoretical approaches only, since there is no need to repeat Finberg's work on the documentary evidence.[18] Throughout this study our discussion relates to the two themes of continuity and topography.

Agricultural practices and techniques

Archaeologically, farming is well attested in Roman Britain,[19] and though many problems remain we can at least outline what could have been part of the background to Anglo-Saxon agriculture, if we assume that something less than a complete break occurred in the centuries on either side of A.D. 500.[20] On the question of arable fields themselves, we can see that basically one tradition, that of the native field system, persisted throughout the Roman period, and we can suspect that another (the imported field system associated with *colonia*, *vicus* or villa estate) also existed.[21] The limited archaeological evidence for such a Roman development need not necessarily mean that it was insignificant, although it is tempting to think that such was the case.

The native tradition is represented by the so-called 'Celtic' fields, conventionally regarded as mainly of Roman date[22] even though the tradition (and probably many more of the field systems themselves than has been suspected) go back to the second and third millennia B.C.[23] Even so, there can be no doubt that over many parts of Britain tillage was being carried out in small and nearly always rectangular fields making up networks of irregular chequer patterns on the landscape. This is true on the uplands of the west and on the Pennines, on the chalk of Wessex and Sussex, on the midland gravels and in the Fens (fig. 1.2, 3).[24] One of the characteristics of this 'system' was the frequency of small settlements, often 400–800 m apart, set along droveways or tracks between the fields. The physical remains of these Roman landscapes have been widely studied, but we do not know the basis on which they were operated: whether they were farmed in common, whether they were in effect all demesne land controlled from an estate centre, or whether their use was rotated and, if so, on what basis.[25]

Two advances in our knowledge of this background over the last decade could be relevant to what happened in the Saxon period. Within the mass of native field systems a particular type of field has been recognized as belonging specifically to the Roman period. Fields are much longer than wide, up to a ratio of 5:1, and they are grouped together and laid out in blocks of parallel fields. They can be seen on the chalk in Wessex and Sussex, on limestone in Wharfedale and Somerset, and in the Fens – apparently in association with 'peasant' farms rather than villas or bigger units.[26] Their form implies that a one-way plough rather than a scratch ard was being used, and that, however remotely, some idea of Roman mensuration was being applied in land-allotment.

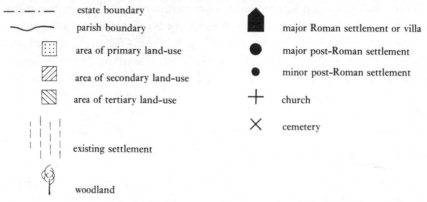

Figure 1.1   Key to the conventions used in figs. 1.2–1.9

Similar arrangements, though specifically in villa contexts, have also now been recognized, providing some supplement to the long-known Ditchley example with its hint of a field system more regular than that characteristic of the native farm. Examples are still too few to generalize reliably, but it appears from Brading, Isle of Wight, Lye Hole, Somerset (fig. 1.2), and Barnsley Park, Glos., where visible field remains have been planned in close association with villas, that the field systems owed more to the native tradition than to centuriation or other mediterranean ideas of how land should be divided up.[27] Nevertheless, there is now some sort of background in the Roman period to provide for at least the possibility of continuity, in arable practices if not institutions, into the Saxon period.

It must be said immediately, however, that there is little direct archaeological evidence of such continuity. Archaeologically, the gulf between the Roman villa and the Saxon settlement (pp. 33–6) remains, despite hints from several contexts of continuity in farming and even of community. Although the evidence for late occupation at many villas (not only into the late fourth century but into the earlier fifth century) has accumulated recently,[28] the fact is that none seems to exist as a habitation by 600. Their farming procedures and not least their fields presumably continued to be used until occupation ceased, but the abandonment of the villa did not necessarily mean the abandonment of its associated farmland. Conceivably that continued to be used, albeit from another centre and perhaps even by other people.

This brief archaeological background is written on the assumption that one of the basic problems of the Anglo-Saxon period concerns the origin and dissemination of the

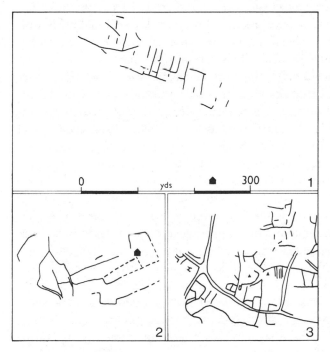

Figure 1.2 Field systems and Roman settlements:
1 Brading, Isle of Wight (after Bowen 1969)
2 Lye Hole, Wrington, Somerset (after Fowler 1970)
3 Ashtree Farm area, Fenlands (after Phillips 1970)

'open field' system of communal agriculture. The Anglo-Saxon introduction of the three-field system, grouped neatly around a nucleated village with church, manor house and villeins' cots, is now recognized as a back-projection of an essentially medieval picture. We must doubt too the early Anglo-Saxon introduction of the heavy plough: in the Roman period, along with the oblong fields, were ploughs with large, sometimes asymmetrical iron shares and big coulters, though the importance and indeed presence of the vital mould-board is still a matter of debate.[29] It has been argued that a mould-board plough is not in fact essential for the production of strip fields, i.e. fields much longer than they are wide, and that such fields, communally cultivated, existed over much of Roman Britain and beyond.[30] But whatever the discussions about the plough in Roman Britain, at least it is a discussion based on surviving models and parts of ploughs, whereas virtually no such evidence exists for the period A.D. 500–900 in England. Plough shares, and other agricultural implements, are known chiefly from non-Anglo-Saxon western Britain, and principally from Ireland, between late-Roman and late-Anglo-Saxon times.[31]

It is from the west also that the only excavated evidence of early medieval fields in Britain comes. In contrast to the field systems of the 500 years or so on either side of the beginning of our era, little evidence has survived on the ground from the next half millennium – or at least, though many more examples of present-day enclosed fields with Anglo-Saxon origins may exist than has been appreciated, little has so far been recognized as surviving as earthworks, i.e. abandoned fields. This curious fact seems to imply, firstly, that prehistoric and Roman fields were much the more extensive, spreading widely over what subsequently became marginal land on which they survived into the twentieth century; and secondly, that the arable of the early centuries of the English settlement was more narrowly confined to land which by and large has been much cultivated since and has not therefore preserved earthwork evidence. Such an argument, however, makes two assumptions: firstly, that the pre-Anglo-Saxon 'Celtic' fields were no longer cultivated after the settlement, and secondly, that such field arrangements as were in use would have been sufficiently permanent and distinctive to have left their recognizable mark on the landscape had they not been obliterated by subsequent ploughing. The dearth of Anglo-Saxon earthworks is a curious phenomenon, and applies to settlements as well as fields (see p. 31). It may indeed be that some existing or traditional arable areas (around villas for example) were cultivated, even if the established 'Roman' field patterns were ignored: in either case, their Anglo-Saxon use would be difficult to recognize. With regard to the second assumption, is there possibly a similarity to the earliest prehistoric farmers whose field systems have not been recognized (almost certainly because their arable practices did not require or produce them)? Behind such arguments at the moment must lie the fact of defective evidence, for it is only recently that excavators of Anglo-Saxon sites have been conscious of the need to look for traces of fields.[32]

The best chance of visible evidence of early post-Roman agriculture surviving on the ground is then on marginal land and particularly in the west, though in neither case is any such chance survival necessarily immediately relevant to what was happening in the main areas of Anglo-Saxon settlement and colonization to the east. Claims have indeed been made for the high antiquity of some existing field patterns in Wales and the south-west. While some have been demonstrated as representing piecemeal enclosure in the later medieval period, localized arrangements of small enclosed fields for both arable and pasture probably existed in the west in our period and a few of them may have survived intact to the present, incapsulated perhaps in later systems.

In only two cases, however, can surviving ridge-and-furrow be quoted as dating from before the Norman Conquest, and both probably belong to the tenth or eleventh centuries rather than earlier (figs 1.3; 1.5, 6). The first, at Gwithian in west Cornwall, is dated primarily by pottery similar to that from the appropriate occupation layer in an adjacent settlement. It exists as narrow, parallel undulations in part of a contemporary field bounded by a headland, a ditch and a marsh.[33] The second, very similar, example has been recorded beneath and outside the bailey bank of the castle at Hen Domen, Montgomeryshire, built by Roger de Montgomery, first earl of Shrewsbury.[34]

Obviously little can be adduced from only two examples, although their similarity could imply something of wider import. It suggests that in two areas of western Britain

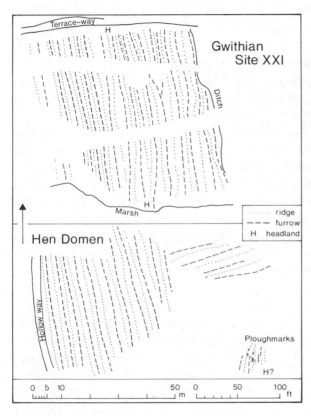

Figure 1.3 Comparative plans of pre-Norman ridge-and-furrow at Gwithian, Cornwall, and Hen Domen, Montgomeryshire (after Fowler and Thomas 1962 and Barker and Lawson 1971)

towards the end of the Anglo-Saxon period a plough capable of turning a furrow was in use, that it was being used deliberately to create the form of seed-bed known to us as ridge-and-furrow, and that the process was repeated a sufficient number of times for the land-surface to be permanently marked (the slightness of the evidence, however, bears out the point, above p. 28, that such traces could very easily be destroyed by later activity). It must be stressed that the field evidence from Gwithian and Hen Domen is primarily of a technique of cultivation and in itself carries no implications of 'open' or any other type of field system. It is argued for Hen Domen, however, that the ridge-and-furrow there probably represents part of the permanent arable in an 'infield-outfield' system that was put out of use by the building of the castle.

Two other types of relevant archaeological evidence come from excavation, although at the moment neither is particularly helpful for this period. Ploughmarks are a well-known phenomenon in the study of early agriculture, consisting of the grooves or lines, sometimes scratched into the subsoil surface, sometimes represented only by changes in soil consistency or colour, made by the plough (or ard) during cultivation. There are only three directly relevant instances for this period and again they are in the 'Celtic west'. The best example is once more at Gwithian, but this time in a phase earlier than (and located differently from) the ridge-and-furrow discussed above. Its date is within the sixth and ninth centuries. Because of the unusual circumstances of a ploughsoil lying immediately on and sealed by windblown sand, it was possible to see here that the 'ploughmarks' retained traces of the sod that the plough had inverted. The clear implication is that the implement employed a share, a coulter and, probably, a mould-board. If this interpretation is correct, the possibility of there having been such a plough in the far south-west, probably before the West Saxon conquest of that particular area, is of considerable interest.[35]

The same point is made by the second, probably later, example, recorded beneath a Viking barrow at Cronk Moar, Isle of Man. Here the ploughmarks lay parallel not only to one another, as at Gwithian, but also to a probably contemporary boundary ditch and to the existing alignment of field boundaries.[36] Ploughmarks also lay directly beneath the Hen Domen ridge-and-furrow, the only example of such an association in our period.[37]

In all three cases, the ploughmarks or furrow-tips lay parallel to one another in one direction only, forming a pattern much less complicated than the criss-cross pattern of earlier examples. The implication is that cross-ploughing was not practised, presumably because an improved type of plough made it unnecessary. Unfortunately, this scanty field evidence is not yet supplemented by parts of ploughs from post-Roman/pre-Viking contexts in Britain and so, archaeologically, as with documentary evidence, it is only possible to speculate on the origin, development and continuity of such a plough in the west. Point is given to the possibility by the recent argument that some of the ridge-and-furrow in north-west England is also Roman.[38] The same is in effect true of the implements used by the Saxon farmers further east in the seventh and eighth centuries.[39] Particularly in view of the scarcity of relevant evidence on the Continent, it is tempting to look back to Roman Britain, but until archaeology produces parts of ploughs from contexts indisputably dated to the four centuries after A.D. 400, little or no progress can be made. Overall, the evidence could hardly be more defective, and hence the tendency in the past to project backwards concepts, techniques and descriptions based on later sources.

Such a tendency has rather coloured historical writing, but it has now been argued that the 'mature' common field system did not appear in England until the *later* middle ages.[40] The definition of 'common field system' is the crux. For our purposes, however, the main point is that the incidence and chronological development of the 'open field system' have been queried on the basis of historical evidence, the inevitable consequence of Hilton's blunt statement, echoing Maitland: 'Beyond (i.e. before) the 11th century (or in some cases even before the 13th century) the amount of evidence on the subject of field systems in operation is so scanty as to be virtually non-existent. This total lack of any evidence at all is certainly no proof that the open field system existed at the time.'[41]

Settlement patterns and the rural economy

The general area (fig. 1.4) occupied by the early Anglo-Saxons has conventionally been indicated by the distribution of their cemeteries.[42] This distribution has not significantly

Figure 1.4 The Anglo-Saxon settlement as indicated by fifth–sixth-century pottery, here plotted on a grid of 15 mile squares (i.e. 225 sq. miles):
1 areas without 'pagan Saxon' pottery
2 areas with non-Saxon fifth–sixth-century pottery e.g. imported mediterranean wares

altered in the course of this century, despite new discoveries; although now, as the Ordnance Survey[43] and Rahtz[44] demonstrate, there is much other evidence, not least being that of settlements, to supplement the incidence of cemeteries. Clearly, however, a distribution map of archaeologically attested Saxon settlements is of a different order from, for example, a distribution map of Roman villas. In the latter case, the map represents in spatial terms all that we know, and inferences drawn from such a map are based on the best available evidence even though we know it is incomplete; in the former case, however, we know not only that the archaeological evidence is incomplete, as with villas, but also that its incidence is largely the result of chance disturbance through activities such as ploughing and gravel-extraction. It is obvious too that a far greater relevant body of evidence must be drawn on to present a map showing anything like a complete distribution of Anglo-Saxon settlement. Such evidence would include in particular place- and field-names, land surveys, maps and indeed, for many rural areas, the present topography and distribution of settlement. As Rahtz (p. 55) points out, however, much of the excavated archaeological evidence is of Anglo-Saxon settlements *which were deserted*, sometimes within the Anglo-Saxon period and without a legacy of documented or place-name evidence. As a result, we must beware of thinking in terms of *the* Anglo-Saxon settlement pattern: the Anglo-Saxon landscape was not static. It saw, and the present landscape bears witness to, a dynamism within those 600 years which demonstrates an irregular ebb and flow of human endeavour as settlements multiplied and disappeared, expanded and contracted.

Unfortunately, no alternative comprehensive model is available as substitute and probably never will be.[45] Local studies tend to show different stories and different patterns in each area: while we may now glimpse the complexities, it is difficult to perceive the generalities. Perhaps a clearer picture will emerge, but at this stage we can only illustrate the variety in settlement patterns by briefly reviewing some recently published work.

In spatial terms, little can be added to points already well known: that early settlement tended to be along rivers and to avoid Roman roads (fig. 1.5). Both Leeds[46] and Fox[47] elaborated on these points, the latter particularly so when discussing the pagan settlement of the Cambridge region. There are doubtless many localities where the generalization does not hold, but nationally the Anglo-Saxon settlement was related to river valleys rather than anything else and excavated examples bear this out. Nevertheless, there must be qualifications and additions to this well-established generalization. In the first place, some of the very earliest incomers were settled (rather than settled themselves) specifically in relation to Roman sites, not a surprising fact when it was apparently to protect such places that they were brought into the province. Since Hawkes and Dunning[48] identified these incomers from their equipment, the archaeological evidence has accumulated for such settlement in relation to towns like Winchester,[49] and rural settlements like Shakenoak, Oxon.,[50] and Mucking, Essex.[51] An isolated military-type buckle was recently found in the field system around the Barnsley Park villa in Gloucestershire.[52] Such examples perhaps allow us to think in terms of 'rural military *émigrés*'. The places where such newcomers lived, however, would almost by definition not be new settlements; and even if their dwellings were new, even if they were not actually on top of a Roman settlement, their situation would relate to an existing focus or 'central place'. We are therefore here envisaging new settlers indeed but occupying a 'niche' in an existing settlement framework, as is now argued for the West Stow Anglo-Saxon village (fig. 1.5, 2).[53]

The same could be true too of one of the obvious exceptions which must qualify the generalization about Anglo-Saxon settlers and Roman roads. In many cases, settlements are known where such a road crosses a river. Perhaps the coincidence is of converging but different patterns meeting at such points, but that settlements existed in such places in the Anglo-Saxon period cannot be doubted. This is not to say either that they

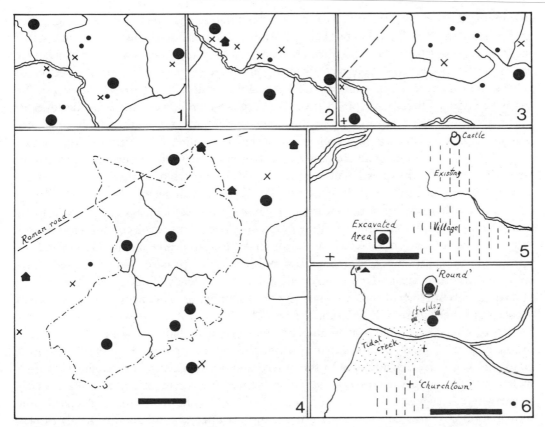

Figure 1.5 Some excavated Anglo-Saxon settlements and their archaeological contexts
(scale: 1–4, 1 mile, 5, 1 mile; 6, 1 mile):
1 Cassington, Oxon. (after Kirk 1956)
2 West Stow, Suffolk (after Selkirk 1973)
3 Salisbury area, Wilts. (after Leeds and Shortt 1953)
4 Shakenoak, Oxon. (after Brodribb *et al.* and Gelling 1967)
5 Maxey, Northants. (after Addyman 1964)
6 Gwithian (after Fowler and Thomas 1962)

were new Anglo-Saxon settlements or that they were occupied solely by Anglo-Saxons.
Roman settlements, from cities to hamlets, are known to have existed at many such points
and the likelihood of a British community continuing in at least some cases cannot be
dismissed.

It is also legitimate to wonder just how many of the other ostensibly Anglo-Saxon
settlements set back from the lines of Roman roads did in fact begin *de novo* in the fifth
to seventh centuries. The pattern along the Fosse Way in north-west Wiltshire is typical,
but we only assume the Anglo-Saxon origin of the settlements from their mainly Old
English names.[54] Such evidence, however, provides only a *terminus ante quem* when first

documented. More importantly, we can see from different parts of the country, e.g. north Oxfordshire (fig. 1.5, 4) and central Hampshire,[55] that Roman settlements up to villa status were also set back from the main through-roads. This arrangement is not then exclusively an Anglo-Saxon settlement characteristic, a point recently emphasized by the cutting of the M5 motorway through Gloucestershire roughly parallel to and 400–800 m east of the main Sea Mills–Droitwich Roman road. No Anglo-Saxon settlements were discovered, perhaps because the new route avoided existing settlements, but a string of Roman sites was noted during constant archaeological surveillance along some 80 km of the motorway.[56] There is obviously no Roman–Saxon continuity here in settlement location, but the M5 results raise the question of whether the similar pattern of settlements with Anglo-Saxon names along the Fosse Way is quite as 'English' as it seems.

The whole question of the location of Anglo-Saxon settlements is now seen to be a much more complex and indeed subtle nexus of relationships, choices and determinants than has often been envisaged. The traditional, geographically inspired, riverbank or spring-line explanation of settlement location[57] in effect emphasizes but one factor which in reality may have been no more important than the incidence of other natural resources such as different types of soil, minerals and food supplies as represented by woods, open water and other identifiable habitats.[58] Lines of communication too were a factor, either to be exploited or avoided, but in any case considered, perhaps more in relation to the arable and other local resources than to through routes represented by derelict Roman roads or even older 'hardways'. On the other hand, major existing settlement foci, such as Roman towns or river crossings, surely influenced the emergent pattern – even if only negatively, as suggested in the Verulamium[59] and Silchester[60] areas. An economic explanation is suggested for the pattern which developed around another Roman town, Chichester.[61]

The possibility of deliberate plantation should also be allowed, perhaps under British direction in the fifth century and by Anglo-Saxon leaders in the sixth century. Plantation was apparently a factor in some areas in the Roman period – the Fens[62] and Northumbria,[63] for example – in the Scandinavian settlement of eastern England,[64] and in Norman and later times.[65] The formative phases of the early English settlement pattern around places like Canterbury, Winchester and Chichester could certainly be examined in this light.

Unfortunately little is known about the significant factors and influences in the formation of the settlement pattern in the fifth and sixth centuries, nor indeed in its later development, even though we can then identify new elements – Christian centres, markets, royal residences, fortifications – which stimulate further change in the rural landscape. A new church, for example, may embrace an existing community, but the church itself, an abbey or a monastery, may well have unconsciously created a new nodal point in the settlement pattern although the conscious reason for placing it at x rather than y may have been precisely to move outside the existing pattern. In fact, such a foundation is, in settlement terms, simply a rather specialized form of secondary or tertiary settlement developing from the primary phase. Such 'colonization' is of course more usually considered in terms of new farms, hamlets, and villages – sometimes with appropriate evocative names like 'Welpley'[66] or 'Newton' – filling up in post-Conquest times the lands of the settlement around the 'church town' or primary settlement. But a similar process was certainly operative in Anglo-Saxon England too, and any model of settlement pattern in the country-side must allow both for the formation of new settlements additional to the primary one and even for the relocation of the primary one itself. The primary settlement too may itself either be overtaken in importance by a 'secondary' settlement – as the maps on fig. 1.5 suggest – or, in some cases, may actually disappear. Deserted medieval villages appear in the English landscape long before 1066, as every air photograph of Anglo-Saxon settlement crop-marks along river gravel terraces demonstrates. And all the time, in all parts of England, there remain the fundamental questions of whether the primary Anglo-Saxon settlement, however indicated by archaeological, place-name or documentary evidence, really was 'new' or developed from a place with Roman origins or, even if physically separate from a Roman site, whether it was established within an earlier settlement framework.

Such questions of continuity are complex yet basic; and the concept of 'continuity' must be defined for useful discussion. In this context, we are discussing settlement location and settlement patterns in the period 400–1000 (settlement form is discussed on p. 58). Continuity, in the first place, must be examined as a factor influencing both individual settlements and their collective distribution in the sense that what existed in pre-Anglo-Saxon times could have persisted, or at least been influential, in the Anglo-Saxon period as well. We must at the same time distinguish between physical juxtaposition of settlements and physically separate settlements existing, perhaps even shifting around, in the same basic land-unit. The social or communal dimension can also provide a continuum, even though tangible evidence is difficult to recognize, and so too can the institutional, even legal, factor which depends for its observance, then as now, on the written word.[67]

Straightforward archaeological contiguity or even association need not, of course, mean continuity of location or community, though the evidence for physical links of this sort is cumulatively impressive. Roman objects in pagan Anglo-Saxon graves, for example, are commonplace if ambiguous in meaning:[68] while they can usually be recognized as deliberately placed grave-goods (even when, in a funerary context, not being used for their original purpose), Roman objects in post-Roman graves can also be derived and accidentally included in the grave rather than associated with the burial.[69] This material does not necessarily provide evidence of any sort of continuity. Where the association is good, however, its significance is not in the grave group itself but in the implication of living contact between Briton and Anglo-Saxon. It has often been remarked that fifth- and sixth-century cemeteries relate to Roman ones and, as at Dorchester, Dorset, not only in a pagan Anglo-Saxon context.[70] On the other hand, the majority of pagan Anglo-Saxon cemeteries and other burial places seemingly occur in non-Roman contexts.[71]

Physical contiguity also occurs at settlements (fig. 1.5, 2 and 4), although again most early Anglo-Saxon settlements are not on Roman sites (Rahtz, p. 54, stresses that archaeologically we know more of early settlements than those after *c.* 700 simply through the accident of discovery and excavation). Rahtz's gazetteer (pp. 405ff.) instances several Saxon settlements on Roman sites; in Wiltshire nearly 15 per cent of the known Roman settlements are beneath later settlements;[72] and there are more instances than are perhaps appreciated of churches overlying Roman structures, as, for example, Woodchester and Frocester, Glos.,[73] and Wimborne Minster, Dorset.[74] It would not be surprising if further examination of ecclesiastical substructures produced enough evidence overall to dismiss such relationships as coincidence only.[75]

Superimposition of sites is, however, no proof of continuity of community or even of habitation; and indeed both can occur (might even be more likely to occur) if successive settlements are not on the same spot. Just how complex continuity can be as expressed archaeologically is now becoming apparent after a decade of excavation at Shakenoak, Oxon. (fig. 1.5, 4),[76] where, significantly perhaps, the break arguably comes in the eighth or ninth century, not in the fifth or sixth century (see p. 42). Physical juxtaposition is indeed present in the form of fifth-century burials in an abandoned fourth-century building, and so too is contiguity in the form of a sixth- to eighth-century ditch across an extensive Roman settlement.[77] Much relevant material supports a story of continuity in the use of the site from the Roman and through the early Anglo-Saxon centuries, even though the functions of the sites are not yet clear. The evidence also suggests a continuity of community, despite the clear indication of a small number of intrusive, probably military, newcomers. Of exceptional interest are the hints that all this was taking place within a fixed tenurial framework which, when it emerged as a written statement, was already old and included memories, very real to a local community, of land-use several centuries previously.

Such striking evidence, all the stronger for the way in which it supports the suggested significance of the place-name element *wīchām*,[78] takes the continuity discussion into a broader spatial context where we can consider it in terms of the land-unit rather than just the settlement site. The idea, first, that the Roman villa estate existed, and second, that it persisted despite the demise of the villa buildings themselves, is an old and attractive one, explored by Seebohm[79] and, more recently, by Finberg[80] and Applebaum.[81] The Gallic evidence on the point[82] has always held out the prospect that something similar could have occurred in Britain and has raised the acute problem of why, if it did not, Britain was so different. As long as the English local land-unit, be it called estate, parish or manor, was seen not only through medieval eyes but as a creation of medieval or, at best, Anglo-Saxon times, following a complete break with Roman and British culture, then the possibility of even earlier origins for it could not reasonably be considered. Indeed, it was conceptually impossible.

Now, however, three factors have changed the historical climate. Much of the relevant documentary evidence (the Anglo-Saxon land charters), has been re-examined, leading some scholars to remark on their Roman form and, in some cases, on their specialized use of legal terms and underlying 'classical' concepts of land-tenure.[83] Secondly, numerous local studies (fig. 1.6) have sought to identify early (pre-Domesday) 'estates' and, in some cases, have argued for their pre-Saxon origins, a move which has prompted thought again about villa 'estates' and, indeed, under the influence of early Welsh scholars, about 'estates' generally.[84] Thirdly, the increasing, albeit still scrappy, amount of archaeological evidence not so much supporting the possibility of continuity as undermining the traditional view of discontinuity has to be taken into account (see p. 36).

It is the second of these factors which can be summarized here. At best these local topographical studies have involved an intimate knowledge of the area – producing that unscientific but all-important 'feel' for a locality which Vinogradoff[85] recognized but could

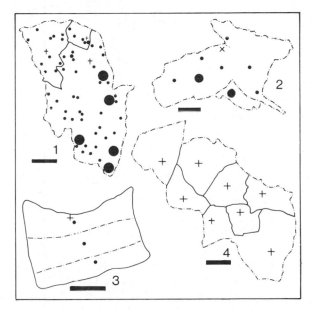

Figure 1.6 Examples of Saxon estates in relation to parish boundaries (scale: 1 mile):
1 Sampford, Devon (after Hoskins 1963)
2 Blockley, Glos. (after Finberg 1957)
3 Piddletrenthide, Dorset (after Taylor 1970)
4 Parishes in East Leics. (after Hoskins 1957a)

not hope to attain – together with a combination of documentary and archaeological interpretation (fig. 1.7). In the West Riding, for example, without excavated archaeological evidence, Glanville Jones[86] has argued for the identification of a British settlement pattern persisting strongly through the Anglo-Saxon period to form an influential element, based on 'estates' appearing not only in Domesday Book but in later medieval documents. In East Anglia Wade-Martins,[87] while studying settlement location and dating in the first millennium A.D. in considerable detail, has also argued for the antiquity of the basic land-units later formalized as parishes, seeing them in some cases as parts of a Roman framework in a landscape which has been continuously used. Hoskins[88] in the east midlands has also pointed to places where the outlines of the settlement framework also certainly go back to Anglo-Saxon and possibly earlier times (fig. 1.6, 4), and in the different context of Devon has argued more generally for a similar interpretation of the many smaller land-units.[89]

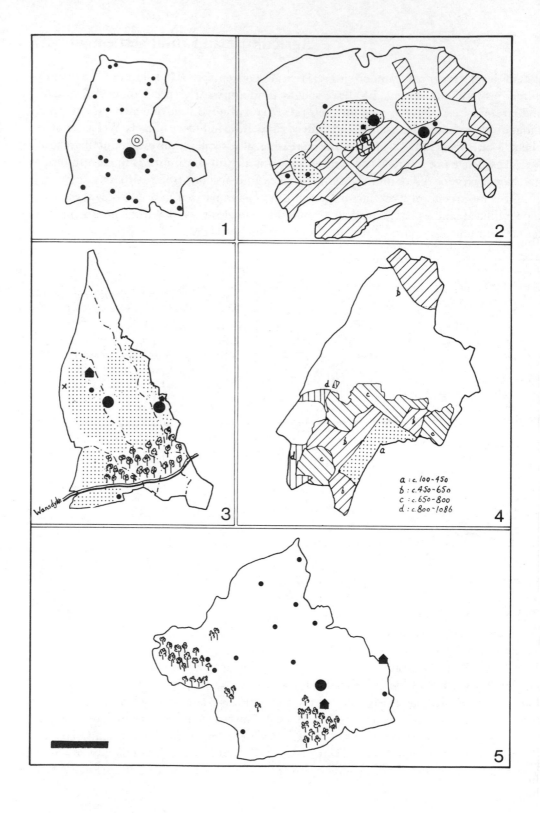

a : c. 100-450
b : c. 450-650
c : c. 650-800
d : c. 800-1086

Wansdyke

1

2

3

4

5

He has consistently expressed his belief in the widespread incidence of the 'ancient estate'[90] and, in this respect, his ideas have converged from a different starting point with those of Glanville Jones.

Hoskins' main contribution in this respect has, however, been in identifying the existence of such pre-Domesday estates without necessarily demonstrating their pre-Anglo-Saxon origins (fig. 1.6, 1). The most recent and boldest attempts to bridge the hypothetical gap have been made in Wessex. Bonney[91] showed a positive correlation between pagan Anglo-Saxon burials and ecclesiastical parish boundaries in Wiltshire, thereby suggesting that the boundaries already existed when the burial sites were chosen. If the argument is accepted, it does not necessarily follow that the land-units were therefore Roman or earlier, since most Wiltshire pagan Anglo-Saxon burials are of the sixth or seventh rather than the fifth century:[92] theoretically, there would have been time for the 'parishes' to be laid out by the British or by very early Anglo-Saxon incomers in the fifth century. While this is possible and would indeed fit in well with traditional ideas about Anglo-Saxon settlement, it is hardly a satisfactory way of avoiding the clear implications of Bonney's argument. It seems even less likely now that he has followed up his initial work by demonstrating, convincingly, that in three areas of Wiltshire where 'parishes' relate to linear earthworks (and notably in the north-west of the county along Wansdyke) the boundaries are earlier than, or at latest contemporary with, the earthworks.[93] The Wansdyke evidence is crucial and, whatever the date of that earthwork, there can be little doubt that it crossed an area already divided up into economically viable land-units, best envisaged as Roman 'estates' (fig. 1.7, 3). This is not to say that every medieval parish was such an 'estate' or indeed existed as a separate land-unit in Roman times; but the basic framework must be allowed at that date, and so too must its persistence through the next fifteen hundred years.

That this is not so unlikely is suggested by other examples, though the dangers of a circular argument are appreciated. In the Vale of Wrington, Somerset, a pattern of elongated north/south parishes adjacent to and divided by an east/west river recalls a symmetry well known not only in the chalk country but, as the Orwins pointed out,[94] much further afield. Charter evidence in the Vale is just sufficient to demonstrate that all these 'parishes' were in existence as Anglo-Saxon estates before Domesday Book, thereby filling up the landscape in an orderly and efficient manner in terms of 'direct agricultural consumption'.[95] This in itself is of some interest (see p. 37), but its relevance here is that the Roman settlement pattern has also been established in outline, producing an apparent

Figure 1.7 Parishes as land-units with their Anglo-Saxon elements such as primary arable areas and primary and secondary settlements (scale 1 mile):
1 Cadbury, Devon (after Hoskins 1967)
2 Whiteparish, Wilts. (after Taylor 1967a)
3 West Overton and Fyfield, Wilts. (after Fowler, 1969)
4 Laughton, Sussex (after Moore 1965)
5 Withington, Glos. (after Finberg 1959)

positive correlation between Roman settlements, mostly villas, on the valley floor and the Anglo-Saxon estates spanning the valley. The implication that the latter originated in Roman (or earlier) times as villa 'estates' is clear but unproven – and probably unprovable.[96]

The most positive assertions of agrarian continuity have recently come from Dorset, based on thorough fieldwork and documentation.[97] Two arguments are particularly relevant here. First, the general one that in certain areas, notably Cranborne Chase and the Isle of Purbeck, some extant settlements represent the sites of continuous occupation since the Roman period; second, that in certain places definable medieval 'estates' were in existence in Anglo-Saxon times and probably represent an even older land-organization (fig. 1.6, 3). It is only fair to say that much of the work reviewed here has been consciously stimulated by the single seminal example of Withington (fig. 1.7, 5):[98] much of what has

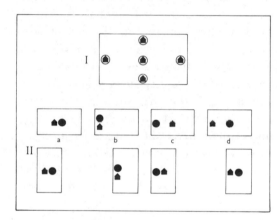

Figure 1.8 Settlement units and continuity: replacement models of Roman villas by main post-Roman settlements within settlement units

been said here was anticipated there, in method, in results and in discussion, the main difference being that now there is more evidence to support the basic thesis.

Granted that in some cases it is reasonable to think in terms of an agrarian continuity from Roman to Anglo-Saxon times within individual land-units (fig. 1.7, 4), it is perhaps appropriate to postulate a way in which the process could have occurred. For the sake of discussion, we shall assume as constants the land-unit and one focal settlement in it at any one time; we shall also assume that the focal Roman settlement was responsible for an area of arable which continued to be cultivated even after that settlement had ceased to function. In fact, it is the existence of the arable which is seen as the main continuous attraction, the other major assumptions being that the land-unit was basically self-sufficient and that the needs of the local agrarian community remained constant in range, albeit changing in quantity with population change and other factors like taxation and range wars. The land-units are shown as rectangles without prejudice to the actual shape of real units (fig. 1.8).

Within the unit, there are only two possible permutations for the relationship between successive foci, i.e. that the later was on the same site as the earlier (Type I) or that it was not (Type II). The Type I diagram with superimposed symbols simply indicates a range of possibilities for the place where the successive foci could have been situated in relation to the unit.

Four variants are shown for Type II, two (a and b) where the foci are adjacent to

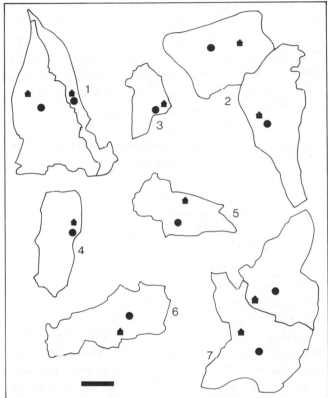

Figure 1.9   Parishes as settlement units in relation to Roman villas and main existing 'nucleated' settlements (scale: 1 mile):
1 West Overton and Fyfield, Wilts. (after Fowler 1969)
2 Bramdean, Hants. (O.S.)
3 Wigginton, Oxon. (O.S.)
4 Chart Sutton, Surrey (O.S.)
5 Barnsley, Glos. (after Fowler 1975)
6 Halstock, Dorset (O.S.)
7 Candover, Hants. (O.S.)

each other, and two (c and d) where they are separated. In IIa, the Roman focus is central to the 'estate' and is replaced by a later focus nearby; in IIb, the principle is the same but the original focus is situated peripherally to the 'estate'. In IIc a central Roman focus is replaced by a peripheral later focus; and in IId the reverse happens.

The model, it might be said, is not casual; it was suggested, with its variants, by a quick sample taken across the country from Ordnance Survey one-inch maps of parishes containing Roman villas. Some of them are illustrated in fig. 1.9 without in any way suggesting that all the parishes and their boundaries are Roman, though for the sake of illustration it is assumed that the 'villa' marked on the Ordnance Survey map is the Roman focus and that the 'church-town' of the parish is the Anglo-Saxon focus (but see below). Doubt-less some of the examples chosen are unfortunate due to lack of local knowledge, but it will be more useful to test the model against new work in detailed local studies than to 'disprove' the examples here. It seemed from the sample, for instance, that villas *are* either approximately central to, or near the edge of, existing parishes; but is this in fact generally the case and, whether so or not, what are the implications? Or, to take another question, Type IIc could be interpreted as a case where a villa lay surrounded by its fields but was replaced, when it fell into disuse, by a subsequent focus at the edge of the arable fields which were too precious to build on: is there evidence for such an interpretation? Could such a later focus have grown from a subservient 'native' settlement originally con-temporary with the Roman focus? This particular suggestion stems from recent fieldwork and excavation at Barnsley, Glos. (fig. 1.9, 5), where grass-tempered pottery in the villa fields indicates some sort of fifth- to sixth-century activity, possibly the manuring of arable, after the villa itself had ceased its domestic functions. The medieval (and existing) village lies beyond the traceable extent of the 'Roman' field system around the villa.[99]

Where the above examples are likely to be wrong is in the assumption that the existing 'church-town' of the parish was the primary Anglo-Saxon settlement (if such is not the case, it will not affect the theory, only the accuracy of the examples). Such an assumption has of course long been basic to early English history, but recent work, particularly excava-tion, has tended to raise doubts about its validity. Two points are immediately relevant: firstly, that most excavated Anglo-Saxon settlements have been investigated precisely because they do not lie beneath an existing settlement (fig. 1.5). They are in fact *deserted* Anglo-Saxon settlements and may not be typical for that reason (p. 60). Secondly, the great increase in the number of excavated deserted medieval (i.e. post-Conquest) settle-ments has failed to show a corresponding increase in the number of underlying earlier Anglo-Saxon settlements.[100] There is little correlation in placement between early and pagan (and later, see p. 61, for all we know) Anglo-Saxon settlements and the distribution of settlements as witnessed by Domesday Book. Fox[101] demonstrated this for the Cam-bridge region and subsequent research has tended to confirm the dichotomy. We must, therefore, be more precise – as archaeologists have had to be in distinguishing their pottery and brooches – in talking about things Anglo-Saxon: we need to qualify the adjective by 'early', 'middle' or 'late', or by the century, in discussing incipient settlement studies just as much as in dealing with more conventional archaeological material.

The likelihood that East Anglian settlements shifted from place to place has for long been postulated because of the isolated churches characteristic of the region; it seems likely that existing, supposedly 'Anglo-Saxon', villages are in some cases medieval or, at the earliest, late Anglo-Saxon creations rather than developments from migration period foot-holds.[102] As with the countryside so with towns, the last one to two centuries of the Saxon period, and not the fifth to sixth centuries, seem to be the crucial time when many 'medieval' settlements were created or took root (although many subsequently suffered vicissitudes ranging from total desertion to engulfment in Victorian cities).[103]

One way in which a significant change in settlement pattern could occur by the late Anglo-Saxon period has been suggested recently at Chalton, Hants.[104] One of a number of settlements on the top of the downs has proved to be Anglo-Saxon, probably dating from the sixth to seventh centuries and containing numerous large rectangular buildings. Surface scatters of pottery suggest other Anglo-Saxon settlements in similar positions in the neighbourhood. Their position high on the downs, surrounded by 'Celtic' fields, adds interest to these sites, for previously the Wessex downs have been regarded as deserted after the Roman period.[105] Meanwhile, other settlement evidence has come from the adjacent valleys, notably at Manor Farm, Chalton – evidence indicating occupation from late Anglo-Saxon times onwards but not earlier. Although the sequence is not yet complete, there is strong evidence from this one area that the existing, and recognizably medieval, pattern of nucleated settlements strung along the river valleys does not represent primary Saxon colonization in the fifth to seventh centuries, but rather a much later development (albeit still a break) from a long-continued downland occupation. This demonstration of the probable chronology and movement at Chalton raises many questions, not least those about how generally such an explanation might apply in Wessex. It is not completely general since both archaeological and documentary evidence combine to provide examples of valley-bottom settlement before the tenth century elsewhere in that region. Nevertheless, while it may be premature to say so, it could well be that a major alteration in settlement location, and possibly pattern, took place in the late Anglo-Saxon period, so that Domesday Book represents developments which took place mainly in the previous two centuries and not the previous five. The question of continuity may, in the event, relate as much to the ninth and tenth centuries as to the fifth or sixth.

Continuity apart, two major results of the local topographical studies of the last decade have been the recognition and delineation of Anglo-Saxon estates, often subdivided into their component parts, and the increase in our appreciation of the processes, human and environmental, which went into their documentary emergence as dynamic production units in 1086 or in the twelfth and thirteenth centuries. We can now in part detail the generalizations about Anglo-Saxon forest clearance, the extension of arable and the distribution of secondary settlements.[106] Fig. 1.6 shows some estates and fig. 1.7 gives some examples of colonization within a 'parish'. Even if the samples are fair and the individual examples accurate, the problem of dating remains. It is impossible to state how slow or continuous were the processes, whether there were static periods or even phases of retraction, or whether the processes happened relatively quickly in the late Anglo-Saxon period.

Population, nationally and in a given locality, is a crucial and insoluble question. One view[107] is that, despite the Anglo-Saxon immigration, the population dropped catastrophically in the sixth and seventh centuries (from two million plus to under a million? – have we in fact already discovered a reasonable sample of the pagan Anglo-Saxon settlements?), and only began to rise slowly again in the seventh and eighth centuries (hence our relative lack of middle Saxon settlements?), before increasing with the Scandinavian settlement and the relative peace of the tenth century. If so, Domesday may represent a point on a rising population graph untypical of earlier centuries. Settlement evidence could fit such a view, allowing a greater element of British influence in the immediately post-Roman centuries, compared with a sparse element in the later documented period, with its suggestions of an increasing population and its depiction of a rural settlement pattern now recognizably English.

The future of agrarian archaeology in Anglo-Saxon England

To say that the origin and development of 'open field' farming is the major problem of Anglo-Saxon agrarian studies is perhaps to be over-influenced by the historical model. That it is a basic problem is undeniable; but it is largely so as a result of a defective documentary record. The problem might be restated more objectively as, 'What were the methods and techniques of tillage in the Anglo-Saxon period?' Archaeologically, we cannot excavate a field, 'open' or otherwise, in the legal or institutional sense: as with villas and their fields, we can recognize and excavate the settlement and the physical remains of the fields, but we cannot dig up the tenurial arrangements, although our evidence could well tempt us to infer them. Even if we can prove archaeologically that a field was being ploughed in the seventh century, we cannot prove that it was being cultivated in common or that its crop was rotated – two essential elements of common field agriculture. We can, however, obtain more evidence concerning the date at which 'Celtic' field systems were last used; and we can discover more about villa field systems. With a clearer idea of fourth-century agriculture, we would at least have a firmer basis for an understanding of what was being cultivated, and how, in the fifth to seventh centuries. In the process of tackling the problems from the Roman end, we might even demonstrate that some of the Roman fields continued, not just after 400 but after 500 as well.

From the medieval side, it should become standard practice to give thought and resources to the exploration of the agricultural setting of Anglo-Saxon sites. It would, for example, be a great step forward to have some indication of the shape of the associated fields or at least of the potential field areas. As with barrow excavations, it is insufficient to examine only the obvious earthworks and visible structures: we also need to know what lay outside them. The type of plough, and perhaps, therefore, the field shape, could be adduced by firmly associated ploughmarks, such as are known in prehistoric and Roman contexts.[108] This is not just a matter of technical skill in exposing such slight evidence, nor does the slightness of the evidence reflect its importance. If White,[109] for example, is correct in interpreting his philological evidence, a pagan Anglo-Saxon settlement in this country should be associated with scratch cultivation producing only grooves in the subsoil and perhaps, one would imagine, a criss-cross pattern of ploughmarks (unless, that is, such a settlement borrowed immediately the superior techniques and implements from a Roman villa). Strip fields, communally cultivated or otherwise, would be extremely unlikely in these circumstances. And, if the Anglo-Saxons brought or borrowed a heavy plough, its use should be reflected in ploughmarks regular and parallel only and possibly, as at Gwithian, associated with evidence of inverted furrows.

Nor should this approach be confined only to ostensibly Anglo-Saxon sites. Evidence of such phenomena – fields and plough techniques – is worth searching for at medieval settlements since it may well, though not inevitably (see p. 42), have originated long before Domesday Book. Field boundaries themselves, and certainly internal divisions such as existed within 'open fields', probably changed with time, so that evidence of earlier cultivation such as ploughmarks might exist beneath later boundary banks – even beneath settlements, since settlements too may have moved on to, or simply expanded over, former arable. Conversely, the ridge-and-furrow around some deserted medieval villages may well mask earlier settlement remains, as is patently the case on the gravels, where air photography reveals precisely such a relationship.[110] Nor need the desertion of a medieval settlement mean that the associated fields were also abandoned contemporaneously – the farmers may simply have moved elsewhere. Steensberg[111] makes the same point concerning Borup Ris, and it is of course directly relevant both to Roman villas and all deserted early Anglo-Saxon settlements in southern and eastern England. Similarly, one field system may mask another one, not only in the obvious sense of ridge-and-furrow overriding 'Celtic' fields,[112] but also in the sense of similar and near contemporary systems being laid out on different axes or altered to accommodate new access-ways or even an intrusive secondary farm.

Excavation is, however, not the only, nor even the most important, method of tackling the problem of early fields. It is impressive how frequently reference is made to the work of English local historians in their topographical studies. Finberg[113] demonstrated the method and its possibilities, and he has been followed by others (see p. 37). Probably much time could more profitably be spent in such work than in the expensive and laborious work of excavation. Bonney's suggestion,[114] arising from such an approach, that land-units subsequently fossilized as ecclesiastical parishes were in existence in pagan Anglo-Saxon Wiltshire, is a case in point (see p. 39). If correct, what are the implications of the suggestion in terms of land-use and especially of field systems? Do the arrangements relate to a Roman background or to a Saxon colonizing phase? This sort of archaeological/topographical study promises to hold out more hope, as Finberg said of Withington, of bridging the gap in the agrarian history of the first millennium of our era than the always chancy and inevitably limited incidence of excavated evidence relating directly to fields and land-use.[115]

Nevertheless, it is excavation which has so far provided the earliest dating evidence for two of the most obvious types of agricultural earthwork which are often ascribed to the Anglo-Saxon period. Ridge-and-furrow and strip lynchets have been much discussed by geographers, historians and archaeologists.[116] The meagre excavated archaeological evidence of ridge-and-furrow for the period has been discussed above (p. 28). Ridge-and-furrow is not of course necessarily in itself evidence of 'open field' cultivation and we must in any case distinguish ridges of different width and from different contexts: the 'narrow rig' of eighteenth-century cultivation in Wessex[117] has about the same width as

Gwithian field XXI,[118] yet neither is evidence of 'open field' arable. As the Hen Domen example illustrates,[119] we must hope that further examples will come to light before the development of all our marginal land where, almost alone, they can be expected to survive from pre-Conquest times.

Strip lynchets have not been dated by excavation alone, and in any case are likely to have originated at different times in different places. A post-Roman date can be assumed until proved otherwise: there is, as yet, no evidence that any are Roman or earlier. Two important points to emphasize in view of all the confusion are: first, that strip lynchets are not a third type of field to be set beside or between 'Celtic' fields on the one hand and 'open' fields on the other;[120] and secondly, that the great majority of strip lynchets can be shown to fit into the layout of the local medieval strip-field pattern as, for example, impressively at Worth Matravers, Dorset.[121] We can only echo Bowen and Taylor in saying that strip lynchets occur simply where strip cultivation of medieval times has spread on to sloping ground. Doubtless excavation can tell us more of their structure, but it is doubtful whether excavation will produce good dating evidence except by chance, simply because medieval manuring practice did not normally involve spreading domestic midden material on fields in the same way as was done in prehistoric and Roman times.

Nevertheless, it is only from excavation that certain evidence can come. Agricultural implements, above all parts of ploughs, will have to be dug up – a mould-board from a pagan Saxon context in south-east England, for example, would be useful, as indeed would be a *Donnerup* ard. The same is true of scythes, sickles and axes,[122] and of various pieces of horse equipment. The basic importance of such items is clear, for example, from the various arguments advanced about the development of proper harness. This has been regarded as of fundamental importance in the evolution of the medieval economy in enabling plough-teams to exert a more efficient traction, and the horse to become an agricultural beast instead of just a fighting machine. Current opinion is that such developments occurred from *c*. 800 onwards: for example, the long-handled scythe, new types of woodman's axes for more efficient forest clearance, and horseshoes for common use.[123] Any items of an agricultural function in pre-Norman contexts are almost certainly going to be of significance well beyond the particular site on which they are found.

Such items, however, are unlikely to be numerous (cf. twenty-five iron objects at Maxey; fig. 1.5, 5).[124] An entirely different approach is necessary to study what often constitutes the most bulky material from a settlement, namely animal bones (see p. 373). Their value has been recognized in other periods, but their full import has yet to be felt in Anglo-Saxon studies;[125] some evidence has been put forward from defended, non-Anglo-Saxon, sites in the west.[126] It is from this source that we may eventually obtain a clearer idea of fundamentals of Anglo-Saxon economy: was it more arable-based than in Roman times? Did it change with time between the seventh and the eleventh centuries? Did animal breeds develop? Did diet change? How important was over-wintering? And what were the animal diseases facing the Saxon herdsmen? Answers to these questions are not going to come from documents;[127] like so much still to be learnt of the agricultural economy of the period, progress is most likely to come from new evidence excavated in controlled circumstances. The same is true of crops and indeed of palaeo-environmental matters generally. Most of the techniques now standard in prehistoric, and to a large extent post-Conquest medieval, excavations have yet to be widely applied in the Anglo-Saxon period.[128] Although such work may not directly answer the problem of the 'open fields', it could well in the next few decades reveal more about life in the Anglo-Saxon countryside than any amount of further attention to the finite and known documentary evidence.

Notes

1 Maitland (1897) 425.
2 Whitelock (1955).
3 White (1965); Slicher van Bath (1963); Postan (1966) and Stevens (1966).
4 Loyn (1962).
5 Vinogradoff (1892).
6 Gray (1915).
7 Seebohm (1905).
8 Fowler (1972).
9 Crawford (1953).
10 Hoskins (1955), (1959) and (1967).
11 Bowen (1961).
12 Taylor (1970).
13 Beresford and Hurst (1971).
14 E.g. Beresford and St Joseph (1958).
15 Beresford and Hurst (1971).
16 Finberg (1972) 417–20.
17 Thirsk (1967a).
18 Finberg (1972).
19 Applebaum (1966) and (1972).
20 Myres (1969) ch. viii.
21 Bowen (1969); Applebaum (1972); and Fowler (1974).
22 Ordnance Survey 1956.
23 Fowler (1971).
24 Bowen (1961); R.C.H.M. (1960); and Phillips (1970).
25 Applebaum (1972) ch. iii.
26 Bowen and Fowler (1966) fig. 4; Applebaum (1972) fig. 12; St Joseph (1973) pl. xii; Fowler (1970) fig. 27; and Phillips (1970).
27 Bowen (1969); Applebaum (1972) ch. vi; and Fowler (1974).
28 Webster (1969a).
29 Payne (1957); and Manning (1964).
30 Stevens (1966); and White (1965).
31 Wilson (1971) 73–80; Wilson (1962); Thomas (1971) 120–22.
32 The next five paragraphs are documented in Finberg (1972) 418–20.
33 Fowler and Thomas (1962).
34 Barker and Lawson (1971).
35 Fowler and Thomas (1962).
36 Bersu and Wilson (1966).
37 Barker and Lawson (1971).
38 Jones (1975).
39 Wilson (1971) 73–80.
40 Thirsk (1967b).
41 Hilton (1955).
42 E.g. Leeds (1913) fig. 1, and Myres (1969) map 1.
43 Ordnance Survey (1966).
44 See fig. 2.21.
45 Cf. Taylor (1972) 112.
46 Leeds (1913).
47 Fox (1923).
48 Hawkes and Dunning (1961).
49 Biddle (1970) 313–14.
50 Brodribb et al. (1968) 96–101 (note especially p. 99) and (1972) 74–7.
51 Jones (1968).
52 Webster (1969b).
53 Selkirk and Selkirk (1973) 152.
54 Gover et al. (1939).
55 Ordnance Survey (1956).
56 Fowler and Walthew (1971); Fowler and Bennett (1973), (1974) and (1976).
57 E.g. Crawford (1928), cf. Bonney (1972).
58 Note especially ch. VI of Chisholm (1968).
59 Branigan (1972) 854.
60 O'Neil (1944).
61 Ellison and Harris (1972) 944–7.
62 Phillips (1970).
63 Jobey (1966) 106.
64 Stenton (1947) 517.
65 Beresford (1967); and Hurst (1972).
66 Taylor (1967a).
67 Cf. John (1964) ch I.
68 Myres (1969) ch. v.
69 Rahtz and Fowler (1972) 199–202.

70 Green (1971).
71 Meaney (1964): but there are significant exceptions, e.g. Myres (1969) 74–7, for cemeteries related to Romano-British towns.
72 Bonney (1968) 38.
73 Gracie (1958).
74 Farrar (1962).
75 Cf. the continuing excavations at Deerhurst, Glos. – Rahtz (1971).
76 Brodribb *et al.* (1968), (1971), (1972) and (1973).
77 Cf., however, Brown (1972) on the dating of these features.
78 Gelling (1967).
79 Seebohm (1905).
80 Finberg (1959).
81 Applebaum (1972) ch. 13.
82 Postan (1966), cf. particularly 186–8.
83 John (1964).
84 Cf., for example, Applebaum (1972); Bonney (1966), (1972); Finberg (1959); Fowler (1970), (1975); Jones (1971), (1972); and Taylor (1970).
85 Vinogradoff (1892) preface.
86 Jones G. (1966).
87 Wade-Martins (1975).
88 Hoskins (1957a) 6–11.
89 E.g. Hoskins (1954) ch. iii.
90 E.g. Hoskins (1963) ch. ii.
91 Bonney (1966).
92 Bonney (1973).
93 Bonney (1972).
94 Orwin and Orwin (1967) 24–8.
95 Slicher van Bath (1963) 29.
96 Fowler *et al.* (1970) and (1975).
97 Taylor (1970).
98 Finberg (1959).
99 Webster (1967); Fowler (1975).
100 Hurst (1972) 539.
101 Fox (1923) map v.
102 Wade-Martins (1975).
103 Beresford and Hurst (1971).
104 Cunliffe (1972); Addyman *et al.* (1972).
105 Crawford (1928).
106 E.g. Hoskins (1957b); Moore (1965); Spufford (1965).
107 Russell (1969).
108 Fowler and Evans (1967).
109 White (1969).
110 R.C.H.M. (1960) pls 11 and 12.
111 Steensberg (1968).
112 Bowen (1961) pl. v.
113 Finberg (1959).
114 Bonney (1966).
115 Cf. Beresford and Hurst (1971) 135–7; Hurst (1972) 540.
116 Taylor (1967b).
117 Bowen (1961) 47.
118 Fowler and Thomas (1962).
119 Barker and Lawson (1971).
120 This is the basic mistake that many writers have made until recently; cf. Wilson (1962) and Macnab (1965).
121 R.C.H.M. (1970).
122 Wilson (1971).
123 White (1965) and (1969).
124 Addyman (1964) 60–62.
125 Beresford and Hurst (1971).
126 Alcock (1963) 191–4; Fowler *et al.* (1970).
127 Finberg (1972) 407–11.
128 Cf. now West Stow – Selkirk and Selkirk (1973); Beresford and Hurst (1971) 144.

2

Buildings and rural settlement

Philip Rahtz

Introduction

This is a survey of the archaeological evidence for Anglo-Saxon secular buildings, primarily those of rural settlements, with some discussion of settlement form. It is limited to England and south-east Scotland, and includes no evidence of the 'Celtic west', Norse settlements or fringe areas where the use of 'Anglo-Saxon' might be questionable. It does not include defensive structures, churches or monastic buildings (see chs 3, 4 and 5), but does describe some structures associated with pagan cemeteries. There is only slight reference to continental parallels, evolution of building types, and regional and international influence. Literary, place-name and historical evidence are only considered in passing. There is some discussion of the principles on which buildings may be reconstructed on paper or on the ground; although some unpublished reconstructions are included, there is little mention of roof structures or other architectural problems – the buildings are considered mainly on the evidence of their plans.

The survey includes a gazetteer of 187 sites (Appendix A), which does not claim to be exhaustive, but includes the better-known sites. (This total does not include those added after 1972, which bring the total nearer to 200.) Only those with evidence of buildings or settlement-features are included; a pottery scatter, for instance, may well indicate the presence of a settlement site, but could be the result of muck-spreading, or of the disturbance of a cemetery. All references to named sites will be found in the gazetteer or on p. 407f., linked to the list of sources on pp. 405–52. Plans are included of most of the important 'framed' buildings up to 1972 and some of minor buildings such as those with sunken features; these are reproduced at uniform scales.

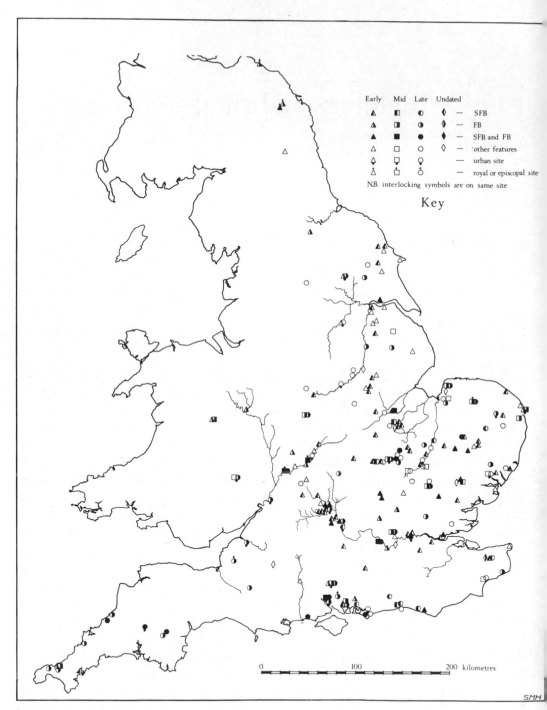

Key

	Early	Mid	Late	Undated	
	▲	◨	◐	◊	— SFB
	▲	◨	◐	◊	— FB
	▲	■	●	◆	— SFB and FB
	△	□	○	◊	— other features
	⬠	⬠	⬠		— urban site
	△	⬠	⬠		— royal or episcopal site

N.B. interlocking symbols are on same site

0   100   200 kilometres

SMH

Figure 2.1   Anglo–Saxon secular buildings

Settlement form is discussed, though the evidence is as yet slight; outline plans of the most important sites are included. The wider problems of settlement pattern, topography, parochial or other relationships, and economy are dealt with in ch. 3.

Some town buildings are included, but their contexts are to be found in ch. 3; no attempt has been made to record all pre-Conquest building traces in urban contexts. The list of sources is only of publications before 1972, though some more recent discoveries are mentioned in the text and gazetteer.

BACKGROUND OF STUDY

There are few subjects in which such progress has been made in recent years as Anglo-Saxon settlement. Earlier settlement studies were almost wholly based on cemetery evidence,[1] though there were notable exceptions.[2] The only excavation reports which were at all wide in their scope were those on Sutton Courtenay and the St Neots area.[3] The beginning of the present era of settlement studies was marked by two important papers, suitably published in the first number of *Medieval Archaeology*. Radford[4] drew attention to the view then current that the buildings with sunken features represented the dwellings of the Anglo-Saxons, however much the 'squalid' character of these 'hovels' was at variance with the riches and technical ability shown by the cemetery evidence and stone-built churches; he pointed to the continental evidence of framed three-aisled long-houses and other substantial buildings, and suggested that similar structures ought to exist in the areas in England to which such communities emigrated. The absence of such structures in the archaeological record was due, he suggested, to excavation techniques which were inadequate to recover the less obvious traces of framed buildings, by comparison with the clearly defined outlines of the sunken-featured buildings. Leeds had found such traces at Sutton Courtenay, but had dismissed them as of secondary importance (see below, p. 91). In the same volume of the journal, Cramp[5] discussed the literary evidence for substantial halls with particular reference to *Beowulf*, and Hope-Taylor contributed a preliminary note on the great buildings at Yeavering.

Since 1957 there have been many discoveries, mostly as a result of rescue excavations arranged by what is now the Directorate of Ancient Monuments of the Department of the Environment. Publication has lagged behind excavation, but there is now a considerable body of evidence available which can be reviewed. Phillips was able to list sixty-four settlement sites as against eighteen on the first edition of the Ordnance Survey Dark Age map.[6] Hurst[7] was recently able to increase this to over a hundred, including only rural (i.e. deserted medieval village) sites. The most recent survey of the subject is that by Addyman,[8] which necessarily covers a similar field to that of this chapter. I am grateful to him for showing this to me in advance of its publication, and to the many people who have made helpful suggestions or supplied details of unpublished sites, especially Margaret Gray, Margaret Jones and John Hurst.

Recent excavation has amply supported Radford's contention that framed buildings would be found if techniques were improved. Work has been on varying scales: many excavations have continued, like most of the pre-war work, to be concerned with single buildings or small areas; but there have also been several excavations as large as Sutton Courtenay, and these have inevitably yielded the most important results. Two more 'palace' sites have been discovered, the complete plan of an episcopal settlement has been recovered, area excavations have been attempted on two rural settlements, and there has been important work in towns and medieval villages. There is still, however, no clear resolution of the conflict between the continental evidence and that from this country in the period of early settlement.[9] Framed buildings of major scale have been found on the palace sites, and many smaller framed buildings on rural sites; but there are still no 'three-aisled long-houses' of the types well known in 1957 and since so well documented at Wijster, until much later centuries. Indeed it seems at present that the evidence in England relates more to the extremes of society, the palaces and sunken-featured buildings, than to the 'middle class', the prosperous farmer. Or is this a misinterpretation of the archaeological evidence, or of Anglo-Saxon society?

The importance of this growing body of settlement evidence has not been fully appreciated. Since Radford's paper it has still been possible to read papers on Anglo-Saxon settlement which only mention burial evidence.[10] Although Hurst gave ample space to Anglo-Saxon excavations in his 1971 gazetteer,[11] their implications had clearly not been realized by another contributor who in the same book[12] could still speak of Anglo-Saxon peasant houses as 'little better than holes in the ground', by comparison with the (superior) 'flimsy structures' of medieval peasant houses. What appear to be the cellars of quite sophisticated and large town houses in London were described as recently as 1968 as 'hovels'.[13]

The evidence is still insufficient to enable a serious analytical study to be made; the critical information from Yeavering, Dunbar and Old Windsor is still unavailable except in summary form. The points that can be made in this chapter are neither original nor other than tentative, but it may encourage a wider appreciation of the recent evidence, and indicate directions in which future work is likely to move.

SOURCES OF EVIDENCE

Evidence for buildings and settlements may be derived from sources other than archaeological excavation. The understanding of written sources depends on close collaboration between textual scholars and archaeologists, which is difficult to achieve: the former often do not appreciate the archaeological significance of words which they are therefore unable to translate meaningfully; archaeologists are rarely able to master early texts, or even to be aware of the kind of information that written sources contain. Only occasionally are attempts made to correlate the two.[14] There must be many useful references such as those which appear to describe post-pits and sill-beam construction (p. 84).

Pictorial sources (painting, sculpture and embroidery) are more readily accessible to archaeologists. They may not, however, appreciate the pitfalls inherent in their use, such as the use of non-contemporary or foreign models, or the degree of realism intended by the artist.[15] For the Anglo-Saxon period there is some detail on early manuscripts, tombstones and caskets,[16] and crosses, which may help our understanding of buildings. One of the most useful sources, the Bayeaux Tapestry, lies right at the end of, if not beyond, our period. The importance of the exact dating to be applied to the structures in the tapestry, which may not be that of its execution, has been clearly demonstrated with reference to castles,[17] and the same arguments may be used about the domestic buildings shown. These have been the subject of two studies[18] and will not be reiterated in this chapter.

Place-name studies are in the hands of a small group of scholars. Their importance in the study of Anglo-Saxon settlement is well known but is mostly correlated with cemetery evidence, even in recent studies.[19] A notable exception is the recent paper relating *wicham* names to roads and Roman *vicus* settlements adapted to later use[20] which has proved very relevant to the important site at Shakenoak.[21]

There is a dramatic contrast between what is usually called Anglo-Saxon architecture,[22] that is to say stone churches, and the buildings described in this chapter, which with very few exceptions do not use stone in their construction. It is possible, nevertheless, that certain features of church architecture may be related to timber buildings; the possibility of pilaster strip framing being related to timber-framing has long been well known[23] and other such features may prove equally relevant to this study. Another aspect of church archaeology may however prove to be of much greater importance: that is the evidence of timber churches. A few pre-Conquest examples are known, for example at Potterne,[24] and there must be thousands more awaiting discovery.

The Bayeux Tapestry provides a link of some kind between pre- and post-Conquest buildings. We may extrapolate backwards from it into the earlier eleventh and possibly tenth centuries; and in the same way we may learn much about late Saxon buildings from their twelfth- and thirteenth-century successors. Sequences which extend either side of the Conquest are rare, but can be discerned at Cheddar, Hound Tor and North Elmham. Although this chapter is concerned with pre-Conquest buildings, it is clear that any definitive study must cover the much longer period, at the end of which there are visible structures which can be studied in three dimensions. Even post-medieval buildings must be taken into account since they embody techniques based on local material (clay-lump in Norfolk, for example) which were possibly of equal importance in the local vernacular architecture of a millennium earlier.

Finally, tools indicate the range of carpentry techniques. The 'sophistication of the Anglo-Saxon carpenter's toolbox' has been discussed by Wilson.[25]

Archaeological site evidence is of poor quality, derived for the most part from excavations which were done either in ignorance of the potentialities of the ground evidence when properly observed and recorded, or under conditions of haste when only the obvious could be recovered. Hurst has coined the useful blanket word 'investigation' for all excavations and observations, good and bad.[26] The tendency towards 'area excavation', the exposing of one layer at a time over a large area, has been more than any other single factor responsible for the recovery of many of the plans of buildings described in this chapter.[27] This method, originating on the Continent, and adapted in this country by many workers,[28] encourages the observation and recording of subtle soil changes or stone patterns which may be the only evidence for the location of a major building. No less important are the techniques of dissection of timber features so brilliantly employed by Hope-Taylor at Yeavering and Dunbar. We cannot hold earlier workers responsible for their failure to employ such methods, but it must make us wary of believing that the features recorded by them comprise everything that was present either in an individual structure or in an area. Sometimes the record is much worse – some of the single-line entries in the gazetteer represent all we know of a whole settlement which has been totally destroyed. The excavation and its field recording may in some circumstances have been of higher quality, but our knowledge of them is hindered by limited or non-publication. Of the recent excavations of Anglo-Saxon settlements, only a few such as Maxey, Treworld and Tresmorn have received definitive publication, though others such as Chalton, North Elmham, Portchester, West Stow and Winchester have had exceptionally full interim reports.

Most of the archaeological evidence consists of soil differences, enabling the excavator to detect the shape of post-holes, stake-holes, post-pits, post-trenches, sill-beam trenches, slots or impressions, or the limits of a floor or exterior level. Not often is even the contemporary ground or floor level preserved, unless it has been protected by some agent, as the sand-drift at West Stow. Few of the sites mentioned below are in waterlogged levels, which preserve the form of at least the foundation of the structure. When such a site is discovered, such as at Tamworth (pl. 12a), it is most salutary to see not only the substance that lies behind the ghosts of soil-marks, but also the high quality of timber-dressing and the wide variety of joints employed (p. 93). Only in these circumstances do we suspect not only that the English buildings are in no way inferior to their continental counterparts, but that even the ubiquitous sunken-featured buildings may be something very different from 'hovels'.

The understanding of the archaeology of Anglo-Saxon settlements can only be achieved by very large-scale, preferably total, stripping of whole sites. Attempts have been made to do this at several sites, such as Mucking, West Stow and currently Catholme and Chalton, but we are still a long way from such enterprises in excavation and publication as Wijster or Feddersen Wierde, or that currently being undertaken by Van Es at Dorestad.

One difficulty in comparing buildings or settlements in different parts of the country is the uneven distribution of excavations (fig. 2.1). The density of settlement sites on sand and gravel may reflect the settlers' preference for these subsoils; but it may equally reflect the density of observations on air-photographs or areas of gravel extraction; a sunken-featured building in clay (New Wintles, for example) is a rare phenomenon! Rescue conditions largely dictate the locality of excavation; in the present circumstances of British archaeology the gaps in the record will be filled only by accident.

A final point may be made about excavated sites of rural settlements. Anglo-Saxon settlements are excavated because they have been abandoned at an early date; they did not survive to develop into medieval villages, 'deserted' or otherwise. There are certainly some Anglo-Saxon settlements under medieval villages, but most of the excavated ones are not; they may therefore be 'failed' settlements, or ones whose population has migrated to a new site under pressures other than failure. In either case, they are perhaps in no way 'typical', in either their layout or buildings.

The archaeological evidence is thus unsatisfactory, incomplete and largely unpublished; one of the reasons for these deficiencies is that it is also very expensive to obtain.

The continental background to the English settlement has been summarized by Radford,[29] and discussed by Parker.[30] Since then the familiar pattern of the settlement complexes of a variety of long-houses, ancillary buildings, sunken-featured buildings, pits and wells has been confirmed by the large-scale excavation at Wijster, which has provided plans of eighty-six major buildings (one is shown in fig. 2.2) and 147 sunken-featured buildings. There is also much evidence of the changing plan of this compact 'village' settlement, on an inland sandy site which forms a useful comparison with the raised 'terp' and 'wurt' settlement mounds such as Feddersen Wierde. The inhabitants of the Wijster settlement, of second- to fifth-century date, may well have migrated to England, where we might expect them and their descendants to build similar houses or settlement layout, and have a similar economy. Settlement sites of later centuries are not common.[31] The evidence from the Merovingian village of Brebières is obviously relevant to any discussion of contemporary settlements in south-east England, lying as it does well within the Gallo-Roman province. Demolon[32] suggests that this is not a typical village, but a settlement of peasants dependent on the nearby royal estate of Vitry-en-Artois. Only thirty sunken-featured buildings were found, with a few other features, but no larger framed buildings. Of rather later date is the site of Warendorf, with its wide repertoire of framed buildings. With this may now be compared the recent excavations at Dorestad, where dozens of building plans are now being recovered in an urban context centring on the ninth century; the general impression is that of building types not unlike those of Warendorf. However, there are insufficient sites of this period for these to be typical in the same way as we may be confident that Wijster and Feddersen Wierde are essentially typical of Dutch and German settlements of at least some of the people whose descendants emigrated to England. There is in any case more validity in making comparisons between ancestral settlements and those of adopted land, than in looking for more than general similarities between settlements developing over the centuries in countries of such possibly diverse natures as for instance Carolingian Germany and Alfredian England. Any ultimate study of buildings and settlement must be on a northern European basis, but the time has not yet arrived for this to be profitable except as a matter of general interest.

In reviewing a period of six or seven centuries, precise dating may not be important. Even if it were, the limitations of archaeological dating in this period would make it impossible. Coins and other precisely dated objects are rare by comparison with earlier sites. Written reference to levels or structures which can be identified archaeologically are equally elusive, by comparison with the medieval period. Only in fortunate cases, like at Yeavering or the Cheddar sequence, do coins and/or written evidence combine to allow a dating of some precision. As these two instances suggest, such evidence is more likely to be available for palace sites than for other rural settlements. Neither the dating of pottery, nor that obtained by scientific methods such as radiocarbon or dendrochronological determination, allow of a dating closer than a hundred years at the best. Conventionally, the Anglo-Saxon period is divided into three, 'pagan' (up to *c.* 650), middle (*c.* 650–850), and late (*c.* 850–1066) Anglo-Saxon, and this division will be followed in these pages, with the substitution of 'early' for pagan. Where a closer dating can be given, especially in the gazetteer, the dates are given in years A.D., or in a century expressed as a Roman numeral V–XI. To the three periods may be prefixed a fourth, 'very early', to signify, where evidence exists, the settlements or buildings which are either associated with 'Germanic elements' in late and sub-Roman Britain, or with those that are so nearly related to their continental origins that the pottery and finds are indistinguishable, at any rate in form. A conventional dating for 'very early' would be pre-*c.* 450.[33]

Sites

EARLY 'GERMANIC' SITES

It is now clear that the origins of the English settlement must be sought in the third and fourth centuries in contexts which are wholly Roman; the presence of 'Germanic' elements is usually explained in terms of mercenaries or other officially settled groups; they have so far been recognized mainly in towns, villas and forts. There can be little doubt, however, that some of the 'very early' settlements and buildings (West Stow, Mucking), to be described later, although newly founded on non-Roman sites, also have their origin in a 'late Roman' context. They may be the homes of people similar to those found in the vicinity of Roman sites.

Many of the buildings on these Roman sites are sunken-featured, similar to those found in the new settlements (see below, p. 70); examples are known from Canterbury, possibly aligned on the Roman streets; and from the Saxon shore fort of Portchester, with a finely carpentered well. Addyman[34] suggests that on this site and elsewhere the sunken-featured buildings may have been in spaces between surviving Roman buildings of the fourth century. More substantial buildings have also been claimed as possibly 'Germanic' in 'late Roman' contexts. At Latimer, on the edge of the villa courtyard, were two buildings (fig. 2.2); one was a six or eight-post setting, possibly a granary; the other (possibly of cruck construction) is, with the 'granary', compared by Branigan to buildings at Wijster; the 'cruck'-building is, however, probably too narrow (3.4 m) to be a farmhouse or byre. At Dorchester unmortared stone footings, probably for timber-framed buildings, make their appearance only in very late fourth- or fifth-century levels; they are suggested by Frere to be housing for military units. At Catterick there is also a stone building with a 'grandiose' entrance, and a timber building with posts in the ground or on stone

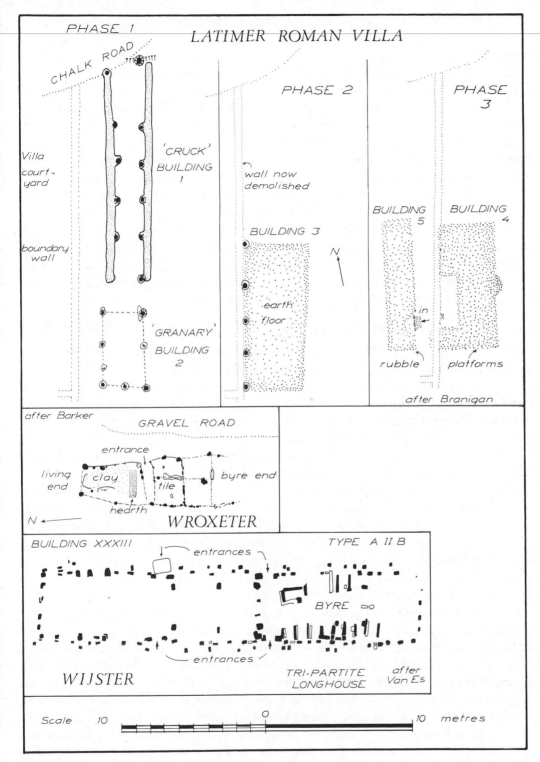

Figure 2.2 Late and sub-Roman buildings

pads, of fifth-century date; from the former came 'Germanic' military metalwork. Evidence of ceramics, metalwork, and burials suggests that similar settlements will be found at Winchester, and at the Shakenoak villa site.

There are obvious difficulties in recovering plans of buildings in such late Roman levels, lying as they do in the higher levels which used to be removed in order to reach the Roman 'floors'. Only the most meticulous techniques enabled Barker to recover the plans of possible long-houses (fig. 2.2) and other remarkable structures at Wroxeter; it would be rash to claim these as 'Germanic', in spite of their plan; but they appear to be of late fourth- or fifth-century date, and may well also be 'military', even if 'Irish'.

Whether or not these early 'Germanic' settlements on Roman sites are military, they are the precursors in some cases of later occupation of the villa estate, as at Shakenoak, or of the town, as at Canterbury and Dorchester where there are buildings (including sunken-featured buildings) or finds of later centuries. Biddle has claimed that at Winchester and elsewhere[35] the settlement is no less than the very foundation of the importance of the town which is demonstrable by the seventh century.

EARLY RURAL SETTLEMENT FORM (fig. 2.3)

Most of the known Anglo-Saxon settlements are rural ones and are on sites which had not previously been occupied, at least in Roman times; this is not to say that the land on which they arose was not, originally at least, closely associated with Roman towns or estates, a point especially relevant in the later fourth and fifth centuries. In many cases, Roman finds are numerous, unweathered and closely associated with Saxon finds and buildings. They are often dismissed as 'residual', or from grave-robbing activities, or even looted from a nearby Roman house (Bourton-on-the-Water); but it seems more likely that they represent contact with neighbouring late Roman groups.

Few sites have been explored on an adequate scale or with an adequate technique to be able to assess their morphology. Understanding of their layout depends very largely on the nature and function of the sunken-featured and framed buildings, which will be discussed later. In no case is anything like a nucleated or 'green' village plan in the medieval sense discernible.[36] The buildings with sunken features at Sutton Courtenay are apparently arranged on the sides of a large open space, which may have been empty or may have contained large buildings. West Stow appears to be at least a dense settlement, but the site is relatively constricted (c. 2.5 ha) and it is not yet certain how much of the palimpsest existed at any one time; West suggests that there are discrete groups of framed and sunken-featured buildings (halls, outhouses, workshops and sheds) representing individual farmsteads, though later sunken-featured buildings are more haphazard in their arrangement. There are also what have been interpreted as animal pens and a pit area. A similar grouping of framed and sunken-featured buildings is apparent at New Wintles with other features such as pits, pens and burials. Although some unity is given to the plan by paths linking different areas and by some grouping of features (fig. 2.3), the settlement has no boundaries and may be merely part of a very much larger area of dispersed

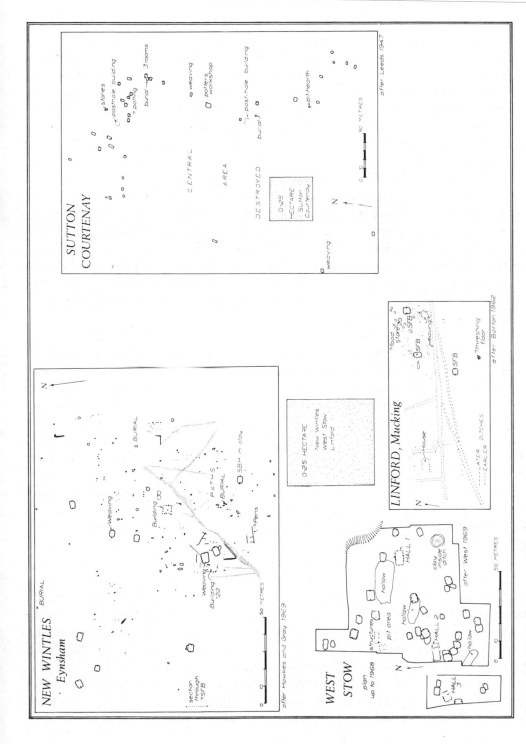

Figure 2.3 Early Saxon rural settlements

settlement, which seems to be characteristic of the whole Oxford region, as at Cassington. It should be emphasized that the recovery of such a relatively complete plan as that of 3 ha at New Wintles was only made possible by the skill of the excavators in clearing a very large area swiftly enough to appreciate it all at one time, in, it must be added, exceptionally favourable humid but not rainy weather conditions. No plan is yet available of Mucking except that part earlier excavated at Mucking-Linford. Here there were sunken-featured and framed buildings with ditches, but on the main site (Mucking-Orsett) more than a hundred sunken-featured buildings and ditches were found; the two associated cemeteries imply that these are some type of individual settlement. Jones does not believe there were framed buildings here, as some Roman and prehistoric post-holes were found (though one framed building has recently been located on the edge of the excavated area); if there were framed buildings they must have been on foundations whose plans were not recoverable at subsoil level. The relationship of the main site to Mucking-Linford and the cemeteries may be more meaningful when further excavation is done and a plan is available. It has been suggested by Myres[37] that the Mucking complex housed mercenaries guarding the Thames approach to late fourth- and fifth-century London.

The settlements so far excavated on an adequate scale are few, and may not be representative, especially since they are settlements which did not survive; the true Anglo-Saxon 'villages' may lie under deserted villages or, more probably, under settlements which continue to this day. It may be that further discoveries will confound this view. The most promising recent site is that of Chalton, a downland area where Saxon pottery is found over 5 ha; preliminary excavations here have located a dense area of framed buildings (fig. 2.15, pl. 9), now in 1976 much more extensive, but there were only a few sunken-featured buildings. This is now one of the government's main Saxon settlement excavations, and there is every chance that a complete plan will be obtained, under conditions of high-quality excavation. The site is also one of the rare ones which can be assigned to the South or West Saxons.

The contrast between these early settlements in layout, building function and building type and those of the ancestral homelands is radical and requires explanation. The excavated settlements may not be typical: orderly plans of farmhouses and ancillary buildings may yet be found, and are indeed currently postulated at Catholme and Chalton. The passage to England may have resulted in drastic changes in the economy. New settlement areas may have allowed more space than the rather restricted confines of at least the settlement mounds such as Feddersen Wierde; this may have made close planning unnecessary. Different or smaller social groupings, such as pioneering families (cf. American pioneers), or a lower population density may have encouraged individual or dispersed settlement. In some of the very early settlements the settlers may in any case have been bands of mercenaries or farm-workers rather than organized 'village' groups.[38]

An equally radical difference, however, is the apparent absence in the English settlements of the very large long-houses so familiar at Wijster, for example (fig. 2.2). Some of the framed buildings known may indeed be comparable with the living-end of such buildings. What is absent is the lower end of the long-house, the animal accommodation, specifically for cattle. The lack of such byres may be related to a greater concentration on sheep farming on the more spacious English pastures (there is plenty of archaeological evidence for spinning and weaving). However, cattle are not absent from Anglo-Saxon food bones: adequate statistics are not yet available,[39] but there is no clear indication that sheep outnumbered cattle to any extent. Indeed at Cassington the opposite is true (52 per cent cattle, 14 per cent sheep[40]). It can only be assumed therefore that cattle no longer needed such accommodation, because of the milder winter climate of England.[41]

Such discussion is not yet very useful: not only are there insufficient settlement plans available, but there is also much ambiguity about the buildings themselves (see below). Such evidence as is available from north-west France (for example, Brebières) is for settlements of similar type to those in England.

LATER SETTLEMENTS

There are even fewer large-scale excavations of middle and late Saxon rural settlements (fig. 2.4). The large areas cleared at the middle Saxon site of Maxey contained several framed buildings and many pits and post-holes which seem to have been set around a fairly empty central area; but none can be identified as definite living-houses, and there was no typical building with a sunken feature, a type which is clearly more characteristic of settlements of the fifth to seventh centuries. Addyman[42] suggests that the framed buildings there may be 'peasant dwellings in a vill, or specialised structures of an estate'; he emphasizes, however, that only one-eighth of the site was excavated, so no firm conclusions could be drawn. Little Paxton was destroyed before proper excavation could take place, but the features were plotted. Pits, wells, querns, ovens, palisade trenches and ditches were dated to the late Anglo-Saxon period. There seem to have been large enclosures, one of them circular, and one with a triple-post gateway; there was also a droveway and field boundaries. Addyman suggests that there must here have been 'individual farm units with ancillary buildings, homefields, and droveways leading to the village centre'.

In the St Neots area the dangers of drawing conclusions from one excavated area are clearly shown. Earlier excavations had disclosed only sunken-featured buildings, but more recent work by Addyman in a different area located only framed buildings of similar late date, in ditched or fenced areas with access ways and possibly a boundary ditch. Larger clearance here might have revealed a layout more akin to that of a 'medieval' village; the site was of eight or more hectares in extent, on a gravel terrace overlooking a tributary of the Ouse.

It is difficult to assess the character of the other sites included in the gazetteer. Some may indeed have been single isolated 'cots' or workshops; others may have been part of farmsteads or hamlets, of dispersed settlement patterns rather than extensive communal 'village' or estate settlements. The buildings at Grimstone End were presumably associated with the pottery production centre there. Those under deserted medieval village sites may reasonably, though not certainly, be seen as the antecedents of their medieval successors,

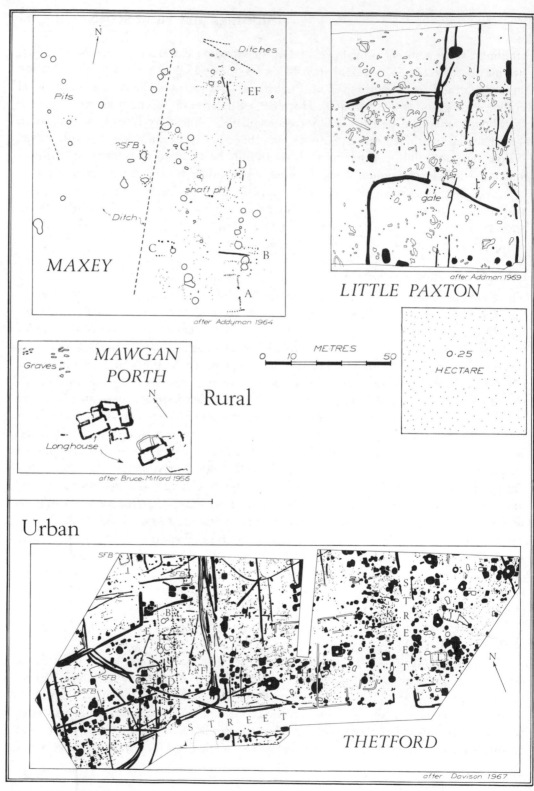

Figure 2.4 Mid–late Saxon settlements

though it is by no means true that there need be any relationship in settlement form between the two.[43] The same argument applies even more strongly to those under moated sites like Northolt or Milton.

In south-west England the late Anglo-Saxon settlements are clearly ancestral to those of later centuries. Mawgan Porth is related not only to Scandinavian settlements, but to the linked building clusters of Dartmoor and Bodmin Moor. It is exceptional in being of stone construction, and seems to have been a coastal hamlet of three or more farmsteads with long-houses and its own cemetery; no church has yet been found. The sites at Hound Tor, Hutholes and other places (fig. 2.14) seem to have been hamlets like their medieval successors; a few of the buildings had sunken features, but most are long-houses built in a distinctive technique, of as many as ten phases.

ARISTOCRATIC SITES

Two sites, Sulgrave and Portchester (fig. 2.5), appear to represent an upper stratum of late Saxon society; no such sites are known either of early or middle Saxon date, though they may, of course, have existed as the nuclei or controlling element of many of the sites so far described. The second lies in the *burh*, within the walls of the Saxon shore fort; the *burh* itself may, however, have extended beyond these walls to the outer earthwork. At Sulgrave, which Davison believes to have been a thane's residence, there was a remarkable stone and timber hall, a kitchen and a freestanding building, at first thought to be a stone tower but now clearly seen to be a rectangular structure. The latter was incorporated into a Norman ringwork as a covered entry, the hall being rebuilt at the same time.

At Portchester, Cunliffe has recovered the plan of a series of buildings which again comprise both timber structures, including an aisled hall, and what is possibly a stone tower; in this case graves may suggest a partly religious function for it. There are also wells, cesspits and a boundary fence. This may be one of several such complexes within the *burh*, and not necessarily the *halla* of Domesday Book.

Another possible defended thane's residence was that at Dunbar, where Hope-Taylor excavated a hall inside an octagonal palisaded enclosure with a plank façade. The site is dated to the early seventh century by its similarity to a hall of that date at Yeavering.

EPISCOPAL SITES

The only thoroughly explored site of this type is North Elmham (fig. 2.6), though Mrs Le Patourel is currently excavating a late example at Otley in Yorkshire. Wade-Martins has cleared a large area near the cathedral, and has skilfully disentangled four periods of pre-medieval occupation, and the plans of some thirty buildings which show a continuous architectural sequence. The prompt publication of the evidence and its interpretation stands almost alone in the sites described in this chapter. Period I is thought to represent the planned layout of a pre-Scandinavian cathedral community; there were three

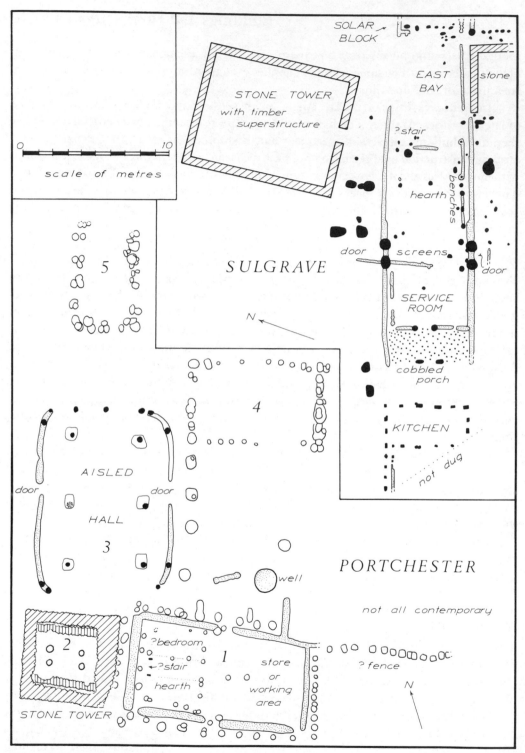

Figure 2.5 Late Saxon aristocratic complexes

ditched enclosures, in each of which were substantial buildings and other features. Period II is interpreted as the episcopal palace of the tenth century; three major buildings surround a courtyard, and the richest finds belong to this phase. In Period III, in the early eleventh century, the area was replanned; the cathedral cemetery spread over part, and the remainder was divided up into three individual fenced areas, each with ancillary buildings. In a further replanning in the late eleventh century more major buildings were erected; the site was abandoned by *c*. 1175.

The only other site which may prove to be part of an episcopal estate is Fladbury, where a remarkable sunken-floored bread oven of the ninth century was found, with a framed building close by; this site could historically be part of either an episcopal or a monastic estate.

ROYAL PALACES

We are fortunate in having in England two royal sites, Yeavering and Cheddar (fig. 2.7) which have been extensively excavated, and which provide us with plans of buildings of the highest level of Anglo-Saxon society. Nor does their detail disappoint: the size and constructional techniques of their halls fulfil the expectations aroused by *Beowulf*.[44] Yeavering was perhaps the finest excavation that has ever taken place in this country. Hope-Taylor, working under conditions of considerable difficulty, worked out construction and destruction sequences in soil in which the fillings of the foundation trenches were described by him as 'a yellow-buff colour in a buff-yellow subsoil', a distinction which disappeared in dry weather! In spite of this, we have the plan of some twenty buildings originally under the shadow of a great timber fort. It is difficult to appreciate the full complexities of the site until it is published; reproduced here is the only published plan of the layout in the time of King Edwin (616–32); apart from the buildings shown here, there were other great halls of different dates in the seventh century, and a line of minor halls extending to the north-west in echelon from the great hall, at intervals of eighty 'Yeavering feet' (see below). Another building may have been a temple, converted to a church when the royal court at Northumbria was converted. The timber 'grandstand' focused on a platform, presumably a place of assembly, may have been the scene of Paulinus' preaching in 627.

Yeavering represents the early supremacy of Northumbria; a similar site is known from air photographs at nearby Millfield. At the other end of England, Cheddar may be representative of a rural palace of the kings of Wessex; it was certainly so in the tenth century, in the reigns of Edmund, Edwy and Edgar, when charters were drawn up and witnessed at Cheddar; the site is referred to in these documents as *villa celebris*, *palatium regis* and *sedes regalis*. There is good reason to believe that it was also a palace in Alfredian and earlier times, though the only ninth-century reference, in Alfred's will, is ambiguous.

The area excavated in 1962–3 was clearly only the nucleus of the palace complex, comprising in each phase a hall and outbuildings. There was clearly no accommodation here for the hundred or more people who are likely to have attended the king at his court,

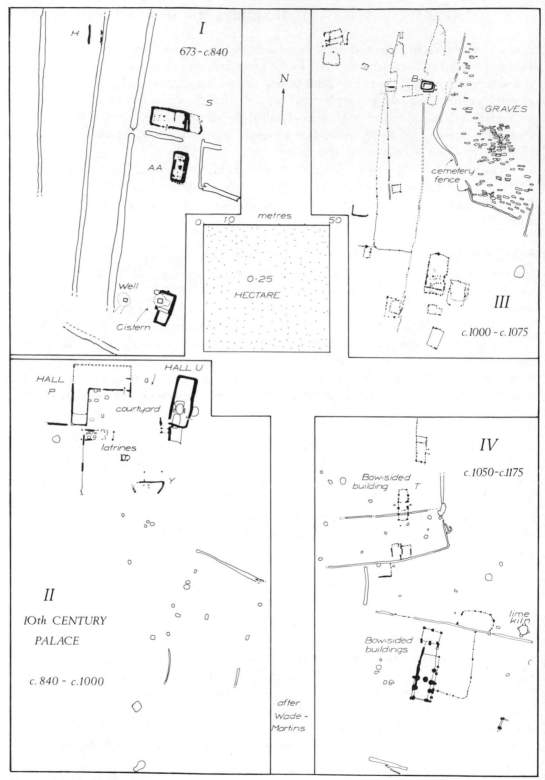

Figure 2.6 North Elmham mid–late Saxon episcopal settlement 1967–71

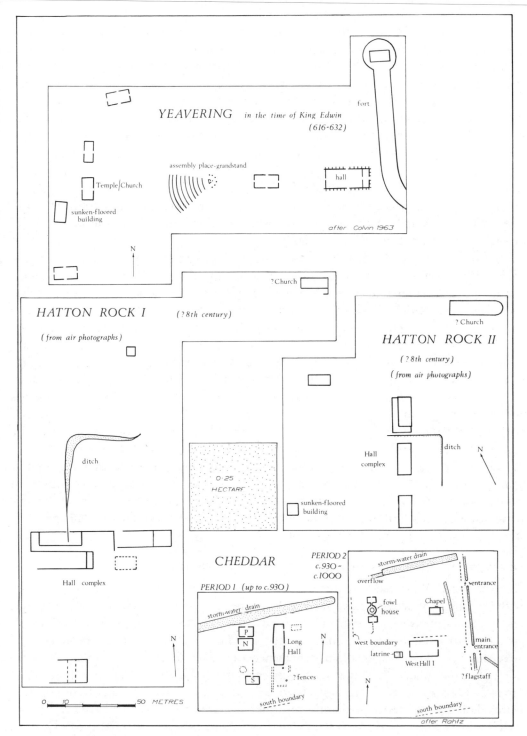

YEAVERING *in the time of King Edwin*
(616-632)

fort

assembly place-grandstand

Temple/Church

sunken-floored
building

hall

after Colvin 1963

N

?Church

HATTON ROCK I   *(?8th century)*

(from air photographs)

?Church

HATTON ROCK II

(?8th century)

(from air photographs)

ditch

Hall
complex

ditch

N

0·25
HECTARE

sunken-floored
building

Hall complex

N

CHEDDAR

PERIOD 2
*c.930 –
c.1000*

storm-water drain

overflow

?entrance

PERIOD 1 *(up to c.930)*

storm-water drain

P

N

Long
Hall

fowl
house

Chapel

west boundary

main
entrance

S

?fences

latrine

West Hall I

N

N

south boundary

?flagstaff

south boundary

after Rahtz

0   10   50   METRES

Figure 2.7   Saxon rural palaces

or for their horses. Before *c*. 930 the long hall, with its outbuildings and small fenced areas, was protected from flood-water by an elaborate drainage scheme to the north. This yielded much occupation débris, especially food bones and floor-cleanings. After *c*. 930, there was a much more elaborate layout; apart from the new west hall and its (now clean) storm-water drain, there was now added a small stone chapel for the use of the king and his family. Other minor buildings included what may merely be the nearest of many service or agricultural buildings lying further to the west, the fowl-house and store. The whole complex was approached through empty ground to the east by an elaborate entrance in a stockade and ditch; just to one side of this was a 'flagstaff' or carved wooden pole set in a carefully prepared hole, with a plinth of Roman brick. The layout remained substantially the same in the eleventh century, though the storm-water ditches were levelled off, and an iron-working building with stone footings was built over them; the west hall and chapel were rebuilt at this time (*c*. 1000).

Midway between Cheddar and Yeavering, both geographically and in time, a palace complex has been located at Hatton Rock, near Stratford-upon-Avon. The plans reproduced here are not reliable since they were drawn out from oblique air-photographs, but they clearly represent halls, possibly a church, minor building and ditch complexes on two distinct orientations closely comparable to Cheddar and Yeavering. A radiocarbon date obtained from a sunken-featured building cut by a pipe trench suggests an eighth-century date, of the period of the supremacy of Mercia. A further Mercian palace of the eighth century is hinted at by the discovery of stone and timber building material in a ditch and an elaborate timber watermill close by, at Tamworth. Topographical evidence has suggested the possible site of an East Anglian palace at Rendlesham.[45] Stone buildings with glazed windows and a major watermill at Old Windsor are probably also part of a palace complex of mid–late Saxon date; no plan is yet available of their layout.

All these, however, are rural palaces; impressive though they are, they may appear minor if and when a major urban palace complex can be excavated at some important centre like Oxford, Gloucester or (more realistically) Winchester.[46] Some hint at the ultimate scale of such buildings may be got from the size of Westminster Hall (fig. 2.8), if indeed its plan originated before 1066.

CEMETERY BUILDINGS AND OTHER PAGAN RELIGIOUS STRUCTURES

Excavations of Anglo-Saxon cemeteries have been with some exceptions little concerned with buildings. Before area excavation of cemeteries was practised trenching was the rule, and it was not therefore surprising that few post-holes of shrines, temples or other possible cemetery structures were recorded. It was also formerly the practice, encouraged by government and other sponsors of cemetery excavations, to cease excavation where the graves began to thin out, so that fences, gates, entrance buildings, mortuary-houses and other exterior structures were unlikely to be discovered. Earlier records have not been combed, and the cemetery structures recorded here are only those that have come to the writer's knowledge in recent years. None is well authenticated or published. Those at

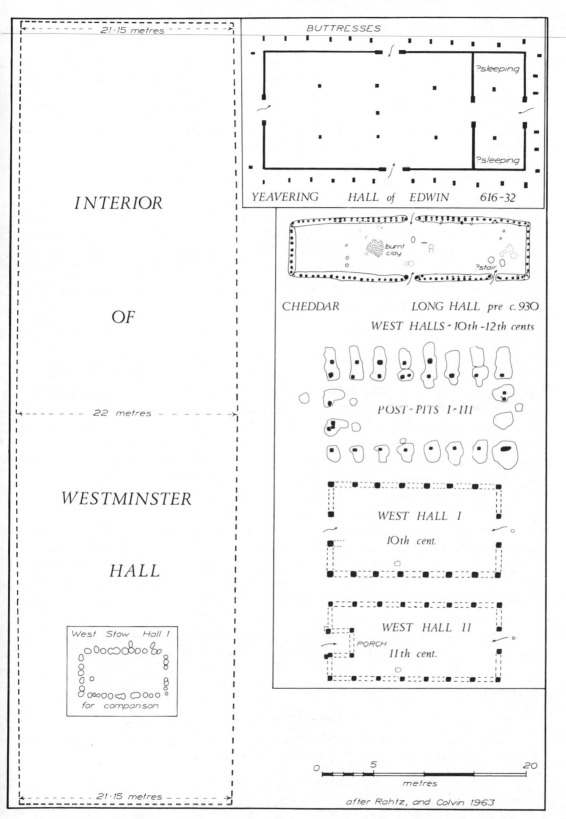

BUTTRESSES

?sleeping

?sleeping

YEAVERING   HALL of EDWIN   616-32

INTERIOR

OF

WESTMINSTER

HALL

21·15 metres

22 metres

21·15 metres

burnt clay

?stair

CHEDDAR   LONG HALL pre c.930

WEST HALLS - 10th -12th cents

POST-PITS I-III

WEST HALL I

10th cent.

WEST HALL II

PORCH

11th cent.

West Stow Hall 1

for comparison

0   5   20

metres

after Rahtz, and Colvin 1963

Figure 2.8 Saxon royal halls

Broadstairs are apparently directly associated with graves; they include palisade ditches, sub-rectangular slots, and stone 'walls'. At Sewerby and Stretton-on-the-Fosse there were, respectively, circular and rectilinear features within the cemetery, though possibly of an earlier date. At Loveden, there was a rectangular stone structure in the cemetery. The most positive are those at Bishopstone; here was a building in a grave-free area within the cemetery, with a burial across its entrance; a trapezoidal building adjacent to the cemetery may be something akin to a lych-gate.

Temples, sanctuaries or shrines not associated with cemeteries are so far known only from place-name studies; they may of course be represented only by groves of trees, which would be difficult for the archaeologist to find; or by pits full of ox skulls (cf. the ox skull on a spearhead at Butley), which should be obvious. The recent discovery of a possible sanctuary at Blacklow Hill, Warwick, is therefore of the greatest interest. Here settings of arcs of what may be post-pits, although not independently dated, seem to be associated in plan with two early graves; the hill-top position, looking east, seems appropriate to the identification of the hill as a pagan religious site.

BUILDINGS IN TOWNS

These are from two kinds of sites. On open sites, like Thetford, the excavation problems are similar to those on other settlements; the problem here in the recent excavations by Davison were those of the decipherment of a palimpsest (fig. 2.9), though there was vertical stratification as well. On lightly developed sites such as Dorchester, Lydford or Southampton (Hamwih) later occupation has been slight enough to have destroyed only a small part of the Saxon evidence, at least that below subsoil level. In most towns, however, the problem is formidable. The comparatively few Saxon buildings known from such important towns as London, Oxford or Norwich may be due partly to inadequate excavation techniques or resources compared with those so brilliantly developed in recent years by Biddle at Winchester; but they are at least as much due to the almost total destruction of the stratification by medieval and later pits and building foundations. Often only pits survive and it is still a matter of discussion as to whether those at Oxford, for example, were cellars of buildings or latrines. Only fortuitously are reasonably complete plans of buildings recovered, either in islands, among seas of destruction, or where waterlogging has preserved them, as at London, Tamworth or York, and has encouraged later occupants to build up rather than dig down.

The relationship of Saxon buildings to their urban environment is discussed in ch. 3. The individual buildings are dealt with in the ensuing sections.

Structures

SUNKEN-FEATURED BUILDINGS (figs 2.10 and 2.11)

This term has been chosen in preference to those previously used – viz. Grubenhaüser, cabanes, sunk(en) huts, pit-huts – because such structures are not necessarily huts or

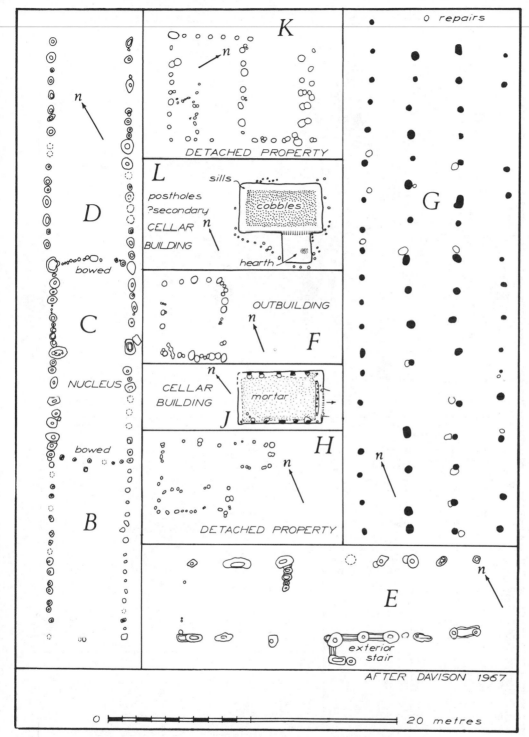

Figure 2.9 Thetford late Saxon town buildings

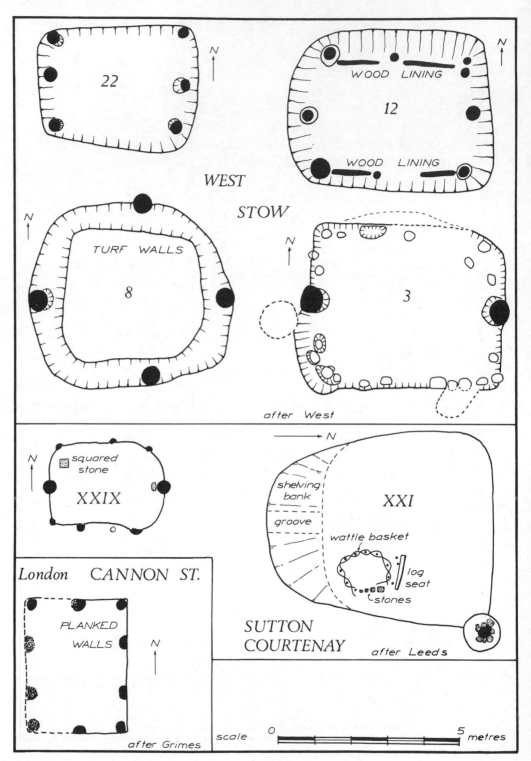

Figure 2.10 Sunken-featured buildings I

houses, in the sense that those words are normally used, nor are they always dug out, or pits. The new term accommodates those structures whose floor was at ground level, the sunken area being a sub-floor space, a store, a cellar, or something akin to an undercroft.

It will be seen from the gazetteer that these buildings predominate in the archaeological record; this is because, unlike framed buildings, they are obvious even to the least experienced excavator in almost any conditions, but especially in gravel or sand, in which most of the excavated examples have been found. It is sometimes thought that sunken-featured buildings are really all rather alike, and collectively dismissed as 'hovels'. Yet even at the site where they were first adequately recorded and described, Sutton Courtenay, nearly fifty years ago, they vary considerably in size, depth, structure and function. Although some general points will be made in this section, it is not the place for a full-scale analysis of such buildings in England,[47] which is a badly needed study.

Sunken-featured buildings first appear in the earliest 'Germanic' contexts of the late fourth or early fifth centuries and are clearly derived from their counterparts abroad. They are common features of most, though not all, English settlements in the early period; they become less common in middle and late Saxon contexts and appear only occasionally in twelfth- to fourteenth-century contexts in England[48] and into recent times in Somerset[49] and Ireland.[50]

The depths of the sunken areas are not all known; where recorded, the excavator does not always specify whether he is referring to the depth below present ground level or to the subsoil – a depth of a few centimetres from the former may in fact be no more than the finding of a firm bed for the 'sunken' floor, and some are certainly no more than this. Even where the sunken area does penetrate the subsoil, the depth may be no more than will have resulted from repeated cleaning and subsequent erosion of the floor. In these cases the structure may not be essentially different from buildings constructed at 'ground' level. Where the depth is demonstrably greater than (say) 0.25 m into the subsoil, then the problem is whether the living or working surface was really at that depth or at a higher level, i.e. that of the contemporary ground surface or higher. Certain criteria that have been used to settle this problem seem invalid. The presence of more than one layer in the sunken area has been interpreted as evidence of 'occupation' dirt (or that accumulating in a sub-floor space) and secondary filling; they may in fact be fills of different date. Similarly dead dogs or even human beings in the fill are not evidence of 'squalor' on or under the floor, but only perhaps of the purpose to which the abandoned hollow has been put. Post-holes visible in the filling do not prove that it accumulated during the lifetime of the building, but only that posts were still there when the fill was deposited. Only in certain cases can we be sure that the sunken level was used; for example, where there is a definite constructed used floor or hearth (not 'burnt area' or 'ashes'), or where there are structures or other features at the lower level. A sloping entrance ramp or steps are sometimes quoted as evidence of the working surface being sunken (as it certainly was, for example, at Dorchester, fig. 2.11); but this may equally be giving access to a sub-floor store or cellar as at Great Dunmow. It is perhaps easier to prove that there was

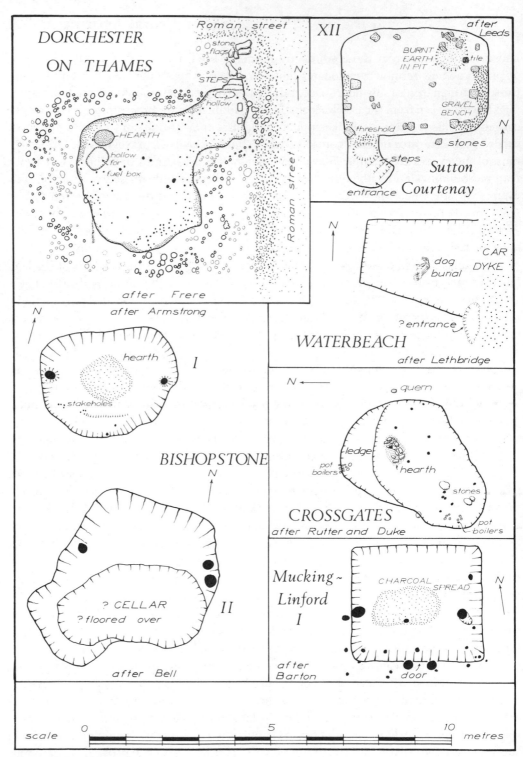

Figure 2.11 Sunken-featured buildings II

a floor at a level higher than the bottom of the sunken area. West[51] has recently listed criteria for believing that some if not all of such buildings at West Stow had wooden floors at or near ground level, as Leeds suggested for at least one of the Sutton Courtenay buildings (fig. 2.11).[52] West lists these as follows: (1) that dead dogs had been deposited in an empty space on a 'grey' primary fill (the head in one case had rolled away from the body): this sounds convincing, but these events could have taken place in an empty abandoned hollow; (2) that there were no entrances to the hollows: if there had been the sand sides of the pit would have collapsed – if there was access it must have been by trap-door; (3) that in one case (hut 15), the hut being burnt, there was clear evidence that the hut had a plank floor, pieces of which were found both above *and below* the loom-weights, though the latter were found in rows.

There were also internal clay hearths which extended over the edge of the fill, showing that they had originally been on wooden floors. West considers that the sub-floor spaces if deep were for storage, especially if lined; or if shallow, to provide air-space to give longer life to the wooden floors. He has made a convincing case for the structures at West Stow at least having had higher floors. The whole evidence from sunken-featured buildings needs to be reviewed in the light of his observations, which have by no means met with universal support.

Structural supports consist of posts or sill-beam slots in the sunken floor, in the sides, in the ground around the hollow, or in 'walls' around the edges. These may be giving support to the sides of the hollow (as lining or revetment), to the floor above, to the walls, or most probably to the roof.

The commonest form is the two-post type, one at each end, usually interpreted as having supported a simple ridge-pole. In many cases such post-holes are shown in the hollow, hard against each edge; but in some cases one or both are outside. It may be possible, at least in some cases, that the posts were placed outside, but subsequent erosion has extended the ends of the hollows so that the post is exposed, weakened and eventually gives way; a third post in line with these two or elsewhere is often recorded and may have been an attempt to prop up the structure when this happened; the weakening of the twin supports may perhaps be the reason for the abandonment and replacement of the building, a circumstance which seems very common (but see Athelney, fig. 2.13, where the posts were inside).

The size of sunken-featured buildings ranges from 1.8 by 1.5 m (St Neots) to 9.1 by 5.5 m (Upton, Northants., fig. 2.12) but averages *c*. 3 by 2 m. Clearly these represent very different ranges of floor area, the largest being twenty times the smallest in area. In the larger examples it seems probable that this was their true size as a building, but the smaller ones may be only the sunken component of a larger building;[53] this may be true even of two-post types with the posts in the hollow, as a glance at the Athelney hut (fig. 2.13) will show. If post-holes, outer structural supports, or traces of walls are looked for by excavators, it is only on the perimeter of the pit (where indeed many have been found). Such traces may, however, be found a metre or more from the edges; only if the whole area around the sunken part is stripped meticulously can it be certain that any such evidence for a larger building has not been missed. The clearest case where such a larger building has been found is Puddlehill (fig. 2.13), where sill-beam slots and post-holes delimit a large area, in the middle of which is a sunken area with a hearth. An even larger example is being excavated at Great Dunmow, where there was a floor over a space 1.50 m high.

Internal hearths certainly exist in some buildings with sunken floors at a lower level, or on floors above the sunken part (cf. West Stow); but there are many sites where 'external' hearths have been found; in this case one may look for evidence of the hearth being in fact within the wider limits of the building defined at ground level (as, for example, the Mucking-Linford 'pit-hut' and hearth).

The plans of these structures are normally sub-rectangular, but there are square, sub-circular, trapezoid, irregular and multiple or two-level examples.

The following functions have been ascribed to sunken-featured buildings in this country,[54] but not always with the strictest regard for the evidence:

1 living-houses with or without cellars, the former especially in towns (e.g. London);
2 barns;
3 byre (Wykeham);
4 weaving sheds (Upton, Northants., West Stow, etc. – see fig. 2.12);
5 spinning huts;
6 store-houses;
7 bake-houses (Fladbury);
8 pottery workshops;
9 loom-weight manufactories (Mucking, Sutton Courtenay VII);
10 ? iron-working, lead-working, antler-working (Mucking).

Many sunken-featured buildings are believed to be weaving-sheds, -huts or -shops; this is usually on the basis of rows or groups of loom-weights which are found lying in such a way as to suggest that they have fallen from looms; the latter are assumed to be situated in the sunken area, sometimes with post-holes for the loom uprights, and even with a seat for the operator (Bourton-on-the-Water, fig. 2.12). While in some cases this may be true (as Holden claims for Old Erringham, fig. 2.12), West has shown that at West Stow the loom was on a wooden floor above the hollow space, and other examples may on reconsideration also perhaps be of this type. At Upton, Northants., for instance, the most remarkable of these weaving-buildings (fig. 2.12), the charred remains found on the 'floor' may be the remains of a raised floor; it may be noted that the loom-weights were threaded on sticks (cf. Grimstone End) and had fallen from racks or cupboards rather than from looms. Nor are post-holes necessarily for a loom; the loom may be sloping, with the loom-weights hanging down behind, the loom leaning against the wall or roof.[55] It is thus shown in the example reconstructed in the Weald and Downland Open-Air

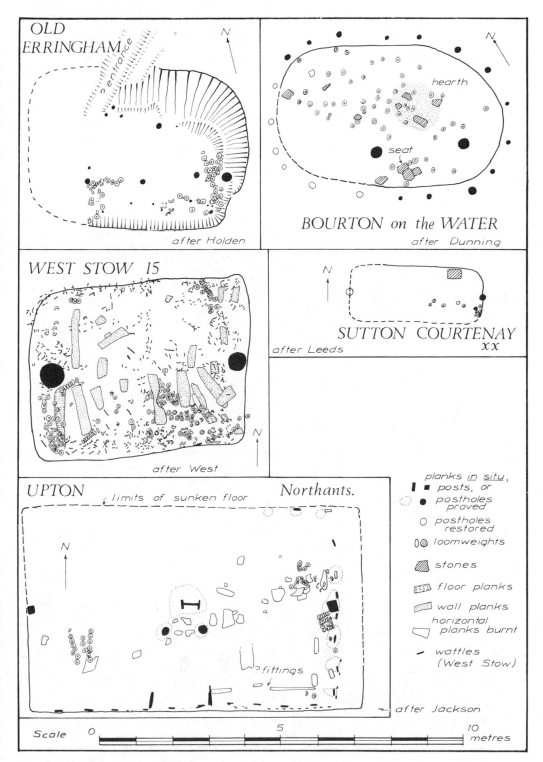

OLD ERRINGHAM

entrance

N

after Holden

BOURTON on the WATER

hearth

seat

after Dunning

N

WEST STOW 15

N

after West

SUTTON COURTENAY

N

xx

after Leeds

UPTON

limits of sunken floor

Northants.

N

?fittings

after Jackson

planks *in situ*, posts, or postholes proved

postholes restored

loomweights

stones

floor planks

wall planks

horizontal planks burnt

wattles (West Stow)

Scale   0   5   10 metres

Figure 2.12   Weaving buildings

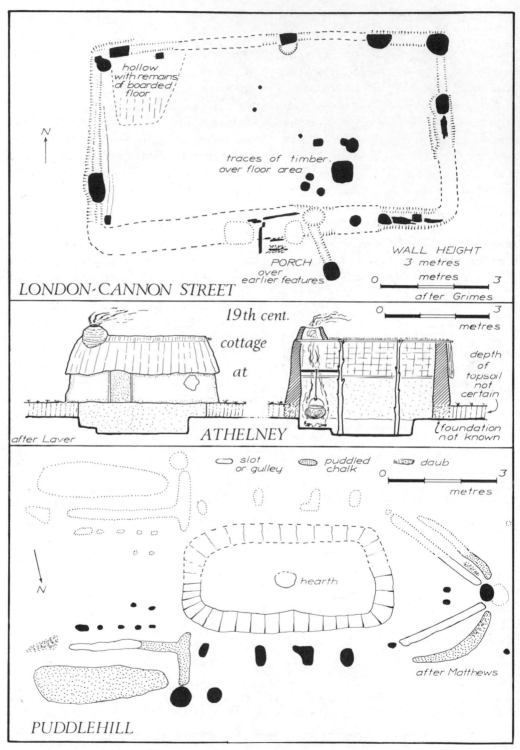

LONDON·CANNON STREET

hollow with remains of boarded floor

traces of timber over floor area

PORCH
over earlier features

WALL HEIGHT
3 metres

0   metres   3

after Grimes

N

19th cent. cottage at

after Laver

ATHELNEY

0   3
metres

depth of topsoil not certain

foundation not known

slot or gulley

puddled chalk

daub

0   3
metres

hearth

N

after Matthews

PUDDLEHILL

Figure 2.13 Larger buildings with sunken areas

Museum.[56] Upton is the largest of English weaving-buildings; it can perhaps be regarded as equivalent to the Carolingian *genicium*[57] but is still rather smaller than continental examples such as the *Tuchmachereien* at Tilleda.[58]

Many types of construction were used for the hollow lining, floors, walls and roofs of sunken-featured buildings, including posts, sill-beams, wicker-work, stakes and planks; some of the more elaborate examples are shown in fig. 2.10. The walls were of wattle and daub, clay, turf, planks or boards, sometimes perhaps on a low footing as at Salmonby; they were either founded at ground level or rose directly from the sides of the hollow (see above). There is little evidence for roof material; thatch or turf seem most probable, though shingle or board roofs cannot be ruled out.

The wide variety in size, function, and construction of sunken-featured buildings must prohibit the generalizations which have been perpetuated about them in the past, especially those which relegate them universally to the status of 'squalid hovels' for the 'lower classes'. In many cases they were clearly spacious and well-appointed residences (Dorchester, fig. 2.11, and see now the reconstruction recently erected at West Stow). The smallest may have been quite comfortable, even with a sunken floor, as a visit to the Weald and Downland Open-Air Museum will soon demonstrate. Excavation of one of the comfortable cottages at Athelney (fig. 2.13) might be very informative.

This discussion of sunken-featured buildings merely introduces the problems which any larger study must take into account. This would be important not only for any understanding of the sunken-featured buildings themselves, but also for that of their relationship to framed buildings in any settlement. These latter are usually regarded as being more 'important' (cf. their description as 'halls' at West Stow). Their presence is taken as a criterion for determining whether or not a particular settlement is likely to be other than the lower orders or workers of Anglo-Saxon society. There may be a lot in this view, which is obviously influenced by continental evidence. Agglomerations of buildings with sunken features like Mucking-Orsett may not be complete; 'normal' settlements like Chalton (fig. 2.15) may prove to be so, but there is at present insufficient evidence for a positive judgement. Finally attention may be drawn to the rural dwellings shown on the Bayeux Tapestry (pl. 12b), perhaps regarded by the designer as typical of eleventh-century England; they are neither long-houses nor halls, but simple, well-constructed, single-cell buildings; there is nothing in their depiction which precludes their identification as sunken-featured buildings. Are the walls on sill-beams, or bedded in the upcast from the sunken area?

Analysis of the English examples may lead to conclusions similar to those reached by continental scholars. They seem generally to assume that such buildings were of similar size to that of the sunken area, and that the working or living surfaces were below ground level. Guyan's[59] typology was based on whether there was evidence of posts and, if so, how many there were (two, four, six or more). Ahrens[60] would prefer a typology based on the position and function of the posts rather than their number, and suggests that the commonest two-post type should be thought of as a 'gable-post house' (*Giebelpfostenhaus*),

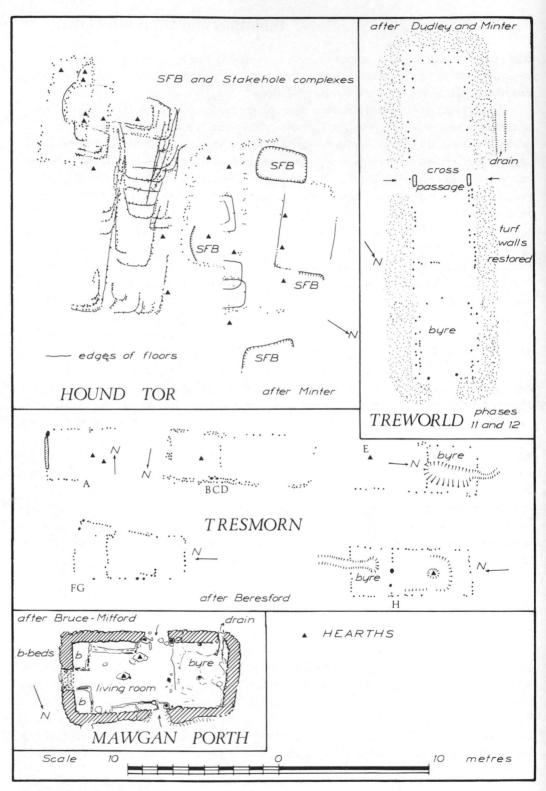

Figure 2.14 Late long-houses in the South-West

the four-post as a 'corner-post house' *(Eckpfostenhaus* – as, for example, West Stow 22, fig. 2.10), and those with six or more posts as 'wall-post houses' *(Wandpfostenhäuser)*. He discusses the structural implications of each type. Demolon's typology[61] like Guyan's is based on numbers of posts; he has some interesting comments on the method of construction of the two-post types, which include the suggestion that the posts were put in position before the sunken area was dug.

Ahrens[62] considers that sunken-featured buildings may have been used for living in, but other functions may include temporary shelters (cf. Ezinge), animal houses, apiaries, granaries, barns or weaving-sheds. He suggests that the last function might be assisted by the increased humidity of a semi-underground structure, perhaps increased by the use of turf or dung roofs. Storage is indicated by finds of grain and other materials. Demolon[63] thinks that the Brebières examples were too small (averaging 3 by 2 m) to be used for anything except sleeping and shelter in bad weather.

Typologies such as these German and French examples have not yet been attempted for England; although some correlation is clearly possible, the English examples seem to include a greater variety of types, which will make any simple groupings difficult.

FRAMED BUILDINGS (figs 2.15 and 2.16)

This term is adopted for all timber buildings other than those with sunken features, though these too may have had a 'framed' superstructure. The adjective 'framed' is not a very suitable blanket label, implying a fully framed structure, the strength of which lay in its inherent stability rather than in the depth or size of its foundation holes or trenches; all timber buildings, however, have some element of framing, even if it is no more than a wattle-and-daub panel, a hurdle, a tie-beam or a wall-plate.

Framed buildings are with very few exceptions a recent addition to the repertoire of Anglo-Saxon buildings, mainly because of larger-scale excavation and improved excavation techniques. They are arranged here in groups according to the technique in which the foundations were laid, which is usually all the evidence that archaeology can recover. Most of the important framed buildings are illustrated at least in outline in figs 2.15 and 2.16; additional detail, including dimensions, will be found in the gazetteer.

Over fifty buildings are known which appear to have been wholly of post-hole construction. In most cases the post-holes are simple holes, which are presumed to have held vertical posts. Some evidence of outer sloping ones, for buttresses, has been recorded at Bishopstone and Portchester (figs 2.15 and 2.16). The size of the post-hole is usually that of the hole dug for the post. The size of the actual timber can in some cases be determined, either by its survival, by a 'core' of different character (usually darker or looser), or by the space within packing stones. Recorded depths range from a few centimetres to half a metre; posts deeper than this are usually in post-pits. Post-hole buildings are represented in all periods, though they may be representative of a particular phase of construction as at North Elmham. Only in a few cases is it possible to determine what materials there

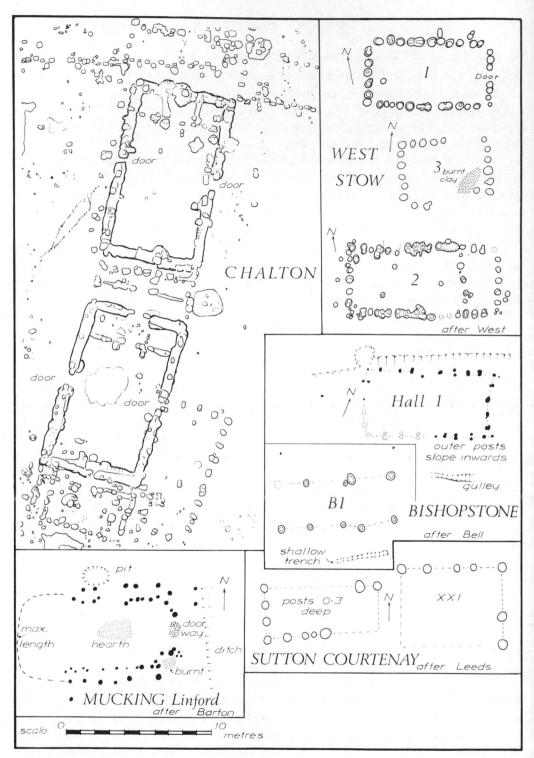

Figure 2.15 Early Saxon framed buildings

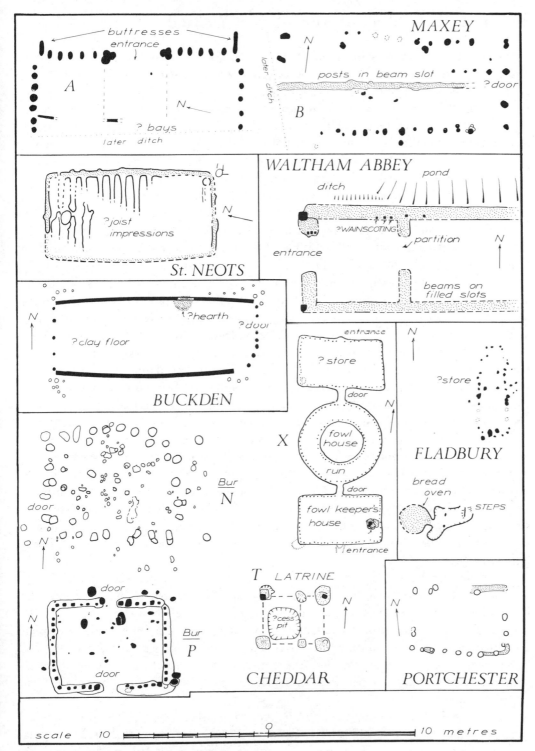

Figure 2.16 Mid–late Saxon framed buildings

were other than posts, or what kind of superstructure they supported. Most post-hole buildings are rectilinear or square, some are very irregular, but a few, such as at Shepperton, and possibly Burgh Castle, were circular.

Attempts have been made to determine the degree of architectural competence and sophistication represented by a post-hole building, on such criteria as the regularity of the plan, the straightness of the lines of holes, or the extent to which they 'matched' or 'paired'; these will be discussed further below (pp. 88–93). Entrances are indicated by gaps in the lines of post-holes, often flanked by larger or multiple post-holes.

Other buildings of simple post construction may not be represented by post-holes but by stone blocks or pads, as at Catterick (though here possibly sub-Roman), or by nothing, where the post-holes have not entered the subsoil, as at Goltho (C, fig. 2.17) where there was other evidence of buildings of this type. A selection of post-hole buildings is shown in figs. 2.14 and 2.17, which indicate the range of size.

Stake-holes are usually distinguished from post-holes in that the posts, of smaller size, are driven into the ground rather than put into holes; in practice it may not be easy to distinguish one from the other, especially in soft ground. Stake-holes are common in or around sunken-featured buildings in the early and middle periods, but their use as the main structural elements seems to be restricted to the late Saxon period. They are normally interpreted as the framework for walls of wattle and daub, as at Cheddar (N); or supporting a revetment for turf walls. This is especially characteristic of a number of rural sites in Devon and Cornwall such as Hound Tor (fig. 2.14), but also in the urban context of Lydford. They are seen here in double or single lines for hurdle-like frames, acting as revetments for walls of turf *c.* 1.5 m wide; in some cases the stake-holes are set in shallow U-shaped trenches as at Hound Tor and Tresmorn. The life of such buildings might be short or as long as twenty or thirty years; it is on the longer assumption that the stake-hole sequences on these sites are extended backwards as early as the tenth century, where there is no other dating evidence. The stake-holes are succeeded by stone revetments, and by cob and stone in the eleventh and thirteenth centuries. All these are rectilinear structures; the only circular stake-hole buildings recorded are those at Cheddar and Wyueling.

Post-in-trench buildings are those in which a continuous trench is dug for the upright posts rather than separate holes. This is clearly a more advanced technique, allowing as it does for more controllable alignment and foundation of the bases of the posts in the course of construction, probably to facilitate the integration of posts with the wall-plate. The posts may be in the middle of the trench, or close to one side (Cheddar long hall, figs 2.16 and 2.20) to use the stability of the undisturbed natural. In these buildings the posts are closely set and normally load-bearing, the spaces between them being filled with planks or other material.

Most of the known examples are late, and from urban (Dorchester) or aristocratic contexts (Cheddar, pre-*c.* 930, North Elmham, Portchester: figs 2.5 and 2.6), though there are earlier examples in rural settlements at Maxey and Chalton (fig. 2.15). The technique may be derived both from Roman examples and from the long-established palisade trenches; indeed, at Water Newton the structure may be a palisade rather than a building.

Sill-beam construction is usually shown by the presence of continuous or interrupted slots in which were placed horizontal beams; on or in these are erected the walls themselves, of variable materials. In some cases it can be demonstrated (Tamworth, pl. 12a) that the posts were morticed into the sill-beams, giving a stability that would be impossible to achieve in simple post-hole or post-hole-in-trench construction; differential indications of the uprights and the beam may cause these to be interpreted as post-in-trench structures. Most known structures with sill-beams are those in which the beam has been placed deeply enough into the subsoil, or in distinctive material, to enable its shape to be recorded; there must be many more cases where it was placed on or in the original ground surface so that no traces survive: only other evidence may indicate its former presence. Normally the slot contains the sill-beam, but in some cases (Waltham Abbey, fig. 2.16) it was filled with compact material and acted as a bedding for the sill-beam.

Early examples are known, in sub-Roman contexts (Wroxeter, fig. 2.2), in and around many early buildings with sunken features (Puddlehill, fig. 2.13), and in the major early building of Great Dunmow. There is little doubt, however, that it is primarily a late Saxon technique, over thirty examples being known from urban (London, York, Hereford, Bristol), aristocratic (North Elmham, Period 3, Portchester, Sulgrave) or (more rarely) rural contexts (St Neots, Buckden).

The technique is apparently a stage in the development of fully framed buildings. It is regarded as standard practice in the eleventh century in Byrhtferth's manual.[64]

Post-pits are used where the posts need to be founded deeply. They are also necessary to give manoeuvring space for the erection of uprights which may often have exceeded ten metres in length. The pit needs to be large not only in order to be able to dig it to the depth needed (a metre or more at Yeavering A4 and Cheddar) but to enable the material around the post to be rammed thoroughly. Appropriately the technique is found only in major buildings; it is the last of the pre-Conquest techniques at North Elmham (Period 4), occurs in the pre-Saxon hall at Dunbar, at Yeavering for the buttresses of A4 (fig. 2.7), at Cheddar in the west halls (fig. 2.7), and for the arcade posts or other major timbers at Portchester, Tamworth and elsewhere. It is obviously needed also for free-standing posts, such as the Cheddar 'flagstaff', or those at Blacklow Hill.

What may be a contemporary reference to such pits is to be found in the *Life of Æthelwold*, the subject of which was saved from a falling beam by being knocked into a pit which protected him.[65]

Timber-in-trench construction may, like the post-hole technique, be derived from palisade construction, especially from such massive constructions as that at Dunbar. A deep trench is dug for the reception of squared baulks of timber, sometimes at different levels. The trenches at Yeavering were up to 3 m deep. Such massive foundations are known in detail only from Yeavering and Dunbar, though they may exist also at Millfield and at Hatton Rock. They must be expected on other palace sites, though the technique is not represented at Cheddar.

Stone construction is surprisingly rare, in spite of the familiarity with this material shown in hundreds of churches. For non-structural purposes, it is used for 'walls' round graves (Broadstairs), hearths in several sunken-featured buildings, floors (Pagham, for example) or pavements (Sutton Courtenay, Normanby-le-Wold). As building material in a humble sense, it is used for what may be dwarf walls at Salmonby, as a pad supporting a floor-post at Great Dunmow, as roof-post pads at Catterick, as revetments for turf walls at Hound Tor etc., or as post-hole packing at Upton, Glos., and elsewhere, or delimiting circular huts at Grimstone End.

As material for foundations, it is not surprisingly found in late or sub-Roman contexts such as Catterick, St Albans or Wroxeter; though it seems to be a military innovation at Dorchester in the fifth century. As re-used Roman material packed with clay it is found in the early or possibly mid Anglo-Saxon corn-dryers at Hereford, or for the fort gate of Portchester. A structure in the Loveden cemetery had stone foundations.

With these exceptions, stone is found only in important secular contexts in the late Saxon period, anticipating its fuller use in the twelfth and especially in the thirteenth centuries, the latter even in peasant contexts. While it is not surprising to find it used for tower-like structures (Portchester, possibly a church, fig. 2.5, or at York) it is clearly in normal use as foundations supplanting the more perishable sill-beams, in royal contexts at Old Windsor and Cheddar, in urban buildings at Dover, Gloucester and Winchester, (under St Mary in Tanner St); and in domestic buildings at Sulgrave and in the south-west at Mawgan Porth (fig. 2.4) and Gwithian. The displacement of wood by stone may be due to timber shortage. The use of Roman tile is known (as at Cheddar) and other Anglo-Saxon tile and brick is known from some other sites such as Hamwih, Oxford, Winchester, Thetford, Southoe and Old Windsor.

Building form, construction, function and detail

Most of the buildings listed are rectilinear. The varying proportions and areas may prove relevant if analysed statistically. A few are square (New Wintles, fig. 2.3) and some circular. The latter do not seem to be in any particular area, such as the west, which might suggest that there was some survival of prehistoric or British tradition. They are, however, well authenticated from Cheddar, Shepperton and Wyueling. The excavators of Wykeham claim a series of circular sunken buildings up to eight metres in diameter, continuing the local 'native' Roman building tradition. Other 'huts' described as circular may in fact be roughly circular buildings with sunken floors.

Aisled buildings are known only from the late Anglo-Saxon period, with the possible exception of some of the Yeavering halls. They do not occur in the representative sequences at North Elmham or Cheddar (where the form begins in the twelfth century). The known examples are those of the eleventh century at Portchester (fig. 2.5) and Bishops Waltham,

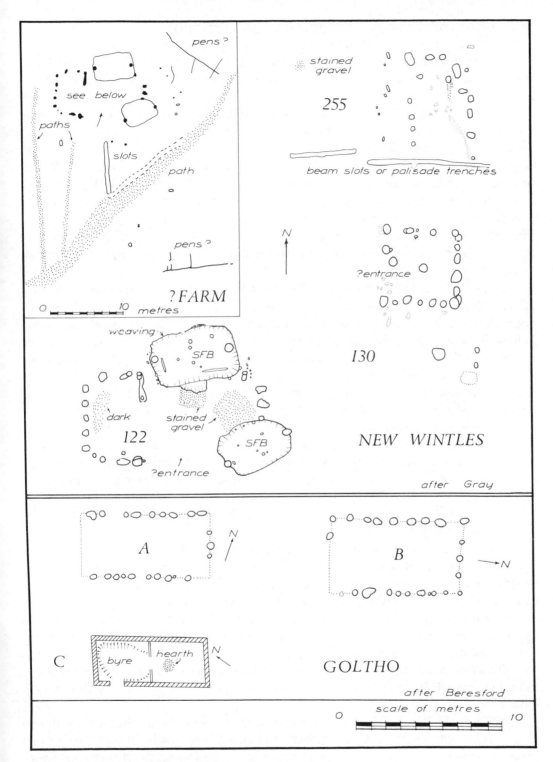

Figure 2.17 Early and late buildings

in aristocratic contexts, and possibly in urban Thetford (G in fig. 2.9). It seems likely that the possibly pre-Conquest span of 22 m at Westminster Hall (fig. 2.8) must have been aisled.

Long-houses in the sense of buildings with combined human/animal/work accommodation under one roof, usually with entrances in the middle of the long sides and cross passage, are similarly wholly of late date, even though they are so well known earlier in Holland and Germany (p. 55, above). The only possible early examples are those at Wroxeter (oddly in a late or sub-Roman context), which is hardly 'Germanic'. When they do appear, it is not in the areas facing the European mainland but in the west, in the relatively remote and lately anglicized area of Devon and Cornwall, at Hound Tor and Tresmorn etc., and at the coastal site of Mawgan Porth (fig. 2.14), where the building clusters and courtyard houses are in any case reminiscent of Scandinavian rather than English examples.

Bow-sided buildings, often mis-called boat-shaped buildings, have been a subject of some discussion in their European context, where they have an ancestry possibly extending back to the fifth century, or even into prehistoric times.[66] Hope-Taylor[67] suggested in his comments on Buckden (fig. 2.16) that their design was related to the need to reduce the chance of collapse, by the adoption of an aerodynamic design; it was the deliberate convexity of the ridge which determined the plan, rather than that the need for more space in the middle of the building determined the roof-type. Even if the origins of the type are pre-Viking it seems likely that their introduction into England is related in some way to Scandinavian influence; all the known examples are either in Scandinavian areas or in late contexts and in eastern and northern areas; the latter are also the area of the 'hog-backed' tombstones and house-shaped caskets which appear to reflect a building tradition of this type.[68] An exception is Cheddar (the long hall, fig. 2.8) which is pre-*c*. 930 in Somerset. Other examples are those at St Neots, Thetford,[69] North Elmham (Period 4 only) and possibly now Catholme. The largest of all is Westminster Hall (fig. 2.8), even if it was of aisled plan (see above).

Cruck construction has been discussed by Smith and Charles,[70] using data derived from surviving examples, whose distribution is not necessarily meaningful in discussing origins. Sloping post-holes (Cheddar long hall, fig. 2.8) or inner posts (Latimer, fig. 2.2) can be explained in other ways, and true crucks may leave no evidence at foundation level.

Entrances in most framed buildings are in the middle of the long sides, sometimes opposed, in both sides, or in the ends; it was through the latter that Bede's[71] well-known sparrow made his entrance and exit.[72]

Divisions into compartments, annexes or rooms are seen in several of the illustrated examples, though the function of such subdivisions is not usually clear (North Elmham, Chalton).

Window glass has been found in non-monastic contexts only in urban and royal contexts, at Hamwih, Thetford, Old Windsor and possibly Tamworth. In both the last two cases the windows seem to have been in a mill or some building closely connected with it. There is no evidence of actual glass among the semi-melted lead masses at Tamworth, but possibly diamond-shaped cames of H-section imply some translucent material. Nothing is known of windows from other sites.

Walls can only be defined in favourable conditions, usually where the structure has been burnt (Eaton Socon, Sedgeford) or its remains preserved as at Tamworth (fig. 2.19, pl. 12a). The mill walls there were horizontal planks or boards slotted into sill-beams.

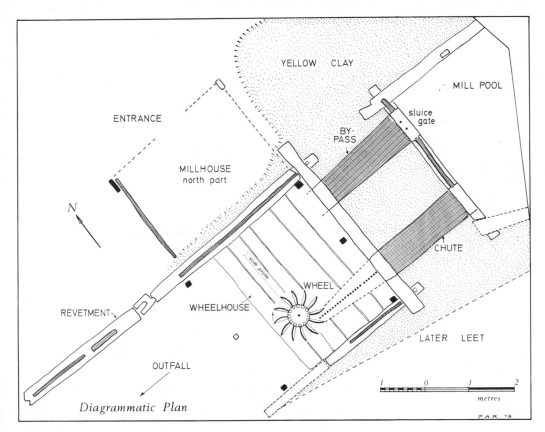

Figure 2.18   Tamworth Saxon water mill

Burnt boards were found at West Stow (fig. 2.15) and Upton, Northants. (fig. 2.12). Planks have been claimed from other evidence at Bristol, London, Thetford, Maxey and Medmerry. Wattle and daub, clay, or turf are often assumed, especially in relation to stakehole structures. The case for one kind of wall material or roofing rather than another is one that can only be discussed in connection with the whole architectural consideration of a particular building from its ground plan and other evidence, as Smith has done for Cheddar buildings.[73]

Floors of clay, cobbles, stone or earth are known from several sites; the evidence for wooden floors in sunken-featured buildings has been discussed above; they seem very likely to be used in many other cases, though apparently direct evidence like the joist-impressions at St Neots are rare. The rarity of hearths in framed buildings may also imply wooden floors, on which there were braziers, or heating structures on a clay base. Sometimes the ground-floor hearths may have been destroyed by later cultivation (as at Cheddar west halls), but in other cases where this has not happened (Cheddar long hall) the excavated evidence makes it clear that the heating structure was on an upper floor, a feature

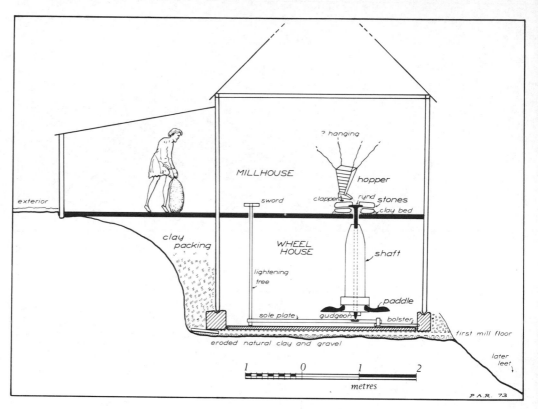

Figure 2.19   Tamworth Saxon water mill (diagrammatic section N–S)

indicated by other evidence from this building, notably the inward sloping post-holes on the inner side of the main wall-posts (figs. 2.16 and 2.20). There is a well-known reference in the Anglo-Saxon Chronicle (*s.a.* 978) to the upper floor of a tenth-century hall at Calne, which collapsed, killing several of the assembly. Evidence of staircases is also known from Portchester (fig. 2.5).

Evidence for roofs is limited to the turf roofs indicated at Mawgan Porth and Puddlehill.

Evidence for furniture and fittings is rare; seats and other loom fixtures have been discussed for sunken-featured buildings, especially for Upton, Northants.; stone structures at Mawgan Porth (fig. 2.14) have been interpreted as cupboards and box-beds; wooden remains at Upton, Northants. (fig. 2.12), were suggested to be box-beds, shelving, racks for loom-weights and other furniture; post-holes at Waltham Abbey (fig. 2.16) may have been for wainscoting.

The function of buildings has been discussed indirectly many times in the foregoing pages. At the highest level are the royal halls, for assembly and possibly for royal residence; the main examples are shown in fig. 2.8; the episcopal equivalents at North Elmham are shown in fig. 2.6, and other aristocratic halls in fig. 2.5. There is a considerable gap between these buildings and those from other sites. West has given the title 'hall' to the framed buildings from West Stow, to emphasize their similar function in a rural setting; but they are small indeed (see West Stow hall, fig. 2.15, 2). They may be, as Leeds believed one of the Sutton Courtenay post-hole buildings (xxi, fig. 2.12) to be, no more than ancillary sheds or barns to the sunken-featured buildings, whose possible improved status has been hinted at above (p. 79). The same may be true of the framed building at New Wintles, while it is perhaps implied by Addyman for the Maxey buildings. Each case must be considered on its own merits; much will depend in this argument on the relationship of the framed buildings at Chalton to the rest of the site. Minor residential buildings are known at royal level, including the 'echelon' range at Yeavering. Those adjacent to the Cheddar long hall (N, P, S) (figs 2.8 and 2.20) are each interpreted as a *bur*, a building like that in which (with a single entrance) Cynewulf was killed at Meretun (Anglo-Saxon Chronicle *s.a.* 757). The stone building beneath St Mary's Church at Brook St, Winchester, may also be of similar character in an urban estate. Other buildings and features in royal complexes are interpreted as latrine-buildings (Cheddar T), a fowl-house with adjacent store and fowl-keeper's dwelling (Cheddar X, fig. 2.8), grandstand (Yeavering, fig. 2.8), iron-working building (Cheddar L), temples, churches or chapels (Yeavering, Cheddar, Hatton Rock) and a 'flagstaff' (Cheddar). The mills at Old Windsor and Tamworth are both likely to be parts of palace complexes, and perhaps also the corn-dryers at Hereford. Cemetery structures are discussed on p. 68.

At a humbler level, the functions suggested for sunken-featured buildings have been listed above (p. 76). Examples of functions suggested for framed buildings and features include: byres (Goltho), threshing floors (Linford, Bishopstone), animal-pens (New Wintles), barns, sheds, outbuildings, fenced yards, latrines, iron-working buildings, military buildings (Catterick, Dorchester), granaries (Dunstable, Latimer), pottery clamp kilns (Cassington-Purwell, Grimstone End, Thetford), charcoal-burners' huts (Wyueling), industrial features (Hereford), wells, ovens, weaving buildings (fig. 2.12), merchants' houses or warehouses (Norwich) or booths (Hamwih), barrel-standing (Southoe), kitchen (Sulgrave), timber roads (Tamworth), potter's workshop (Thetford), potter's house (Torksey), clay-store (West Stow), working hollows (West Stow), and a fish-processing building at York. The majority of buildings which have been excavated, however, are not given specific names by their excavators. In the absence of evidence that the buildings were for

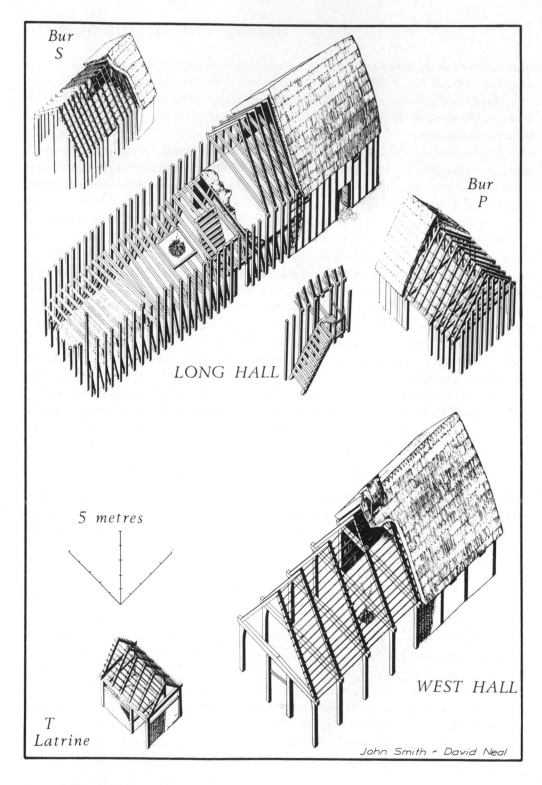

Bur
S

Bur
P

LONG HALL

5 metres

WEST HALL

T
Latrine

John Smith ~ David Neal

Figure 2.20   Cheddar reconstructions

agricultural or industrial use, they use the words 'hall', 'house' and 'hut' to imply no more than that the buildings are for living in at more than one social level.

Techniques of timber construction and carpentry (see p. 53) can likewise only be inferred by a close study of individual buildings, which is facilitated if the remains are burnt or waterlogged. The shape of soil marks can give precise information on the size and finish (i.e. squared or dressed, or left rough) of the timbers below ground, but this does not necessarily give any guide to what they were like above foundation level. Where timbers are preserved, high-quality work is usually evident, as in the carefully shaped and fitted timbers of the wells at Portchester and North Elmham, or the burnt planks at Upton, Northants., or West Stow (fig. 2.15). Perhaps the best illustration of the quality of timber construction comes from the Tamworth mill. Daryl Fowler, who recorded the structure, has contributed the following summary of the techniques which were used (fig. 2.19 and pl. 12a).

The timber of the mill pool, facing the wheel space, is taken from a piece at least 430 by 350 mm and shows the marks of adze dressing. The poolface is finished vertically whereas the opposite face, towards the wheel space, is battered. The joint between this timber and that forming the north side is a half lap, accurately cut to take the batter into account.

The timbers forming the base to the mill undercroft are jointed by a type of mortice and tenon; the shoulders are rebated into the receiving timber and the tenon passes through, held by a stout peg. This would have tightened the joint, drawing the shoulders into the rebate, increasing its mechanical strength and making it less liable to erosion.

REGIONAL STYLES, INFLUENCES, DATING, SEQUENCES

With certain exceptions, such as the bow-sided buildings, mainly of northern and easterly distribution, and the stake and turf long-houses in south-west England, there is at present insufficient data, in very uneven distribution, to suggest regional styles or dating for particular features. Certain sites, however, do have internal development which does suggest temporal sequences in their area. It would be premature to attempt to discuss that from Yeavering and Dunbar in advance of Hope-Taylor's definitive publication; that from North Elmham (fig. 2.6) shows a progression through post-in-trench, individual post-holes, sill-beam slots and post-pits, the latter also marking the advent of bow-sided buildings on the site; a number of sequences of this quality would do much towards the establishment of wider patterns. Smith will suggest in the final report[74] that the buildings at Cheddar show a logical sequence which indicates increasing mastery of the problems of major timber construction. The progression there is post-in-trench to post-pits; the west hall was twice rebuilt in this last technique in the eleventh century, though its width was scaled down from that of West Hall I, where the 8.5 m width may have been too ambitious. The sequence is continued after the Conquest with an aisled hall wholly of timber in the twelfth century, a smaller aisled hall with stone footings for the outer walls in the early thirteeth century, and finally a building wholly constructed in stone. Other sites suggest local changes such as that of sunken-featured buildings at West Stow, where six-post types gave way to two-post types, or Chalton, where post-in-trench construction succeeded that of individual post-holes. Finally there is a consistent sequence in the south-west on several sites where the earliest structures are possibly of sunken-featured type, succeeded by long sequences of stake and turf construction (fig. 2.14); in the final phases stone replaces the hurdles as revetment for turf; in the twelfth and thirteenth centuries the walls change to cob (Tresmorn) or to stone.

RECONSTRUCTION

In the excavation reports will be found a number of reconstruction drawings, such as those of Maxey, which stimulate, while at the same time inhibiting, the imagination of the reader. They embody the ideas which derive from a close study of the evidence; the form of the superstructure and roof should, Hope-Taylor believes, be constantly in the mind of the excavator while he is digging, so that he may not miss the slender but vital clue which is observed as a result of formulating hypotheses and looking for evidence to support or reject them. The present writer would prefer a more objective approach, in which the excavator records exactly what is in the ground, and subsequently considers what it implies in terms of superstructure, or provides the data from which an experienced architectural historian may do so. Obviously it is preferable if the excavator and the interpreter are the same person, as no one understands the evidence quite so well as the person who recorded it; but this is rarely possible, without a degree of historical and technical specialization which is increasingly difficult to maintain.

This being said, to draw a reconstruction, or better still to make a model to scale or make a full-scale reconstruction (such as the Trelleborg building, or more humbly the sunken-featured building at the Weald and Downland Open-Air Museum), is obviously the best way to think about the meaning of the ground evidence. If alternative reconstructions are given,[75] this encourages the reader to keep an open mind.

Smith, in considering the reconstructions of Cheddar, of which some are shown in fig. 2.20, has set out at length principles on which such work should be based.[76] He stresses the need to stick closely to the evidence and the level of craftsmanship that it implies; and to use every possible analogy, English or European, standing or excavated, to arrive at the possible range of what is, and just as important what is not, possible to reconstruct on the foundations of the excavated evidence. He also suggests that the more detailed the drawings the more quickly will the defects of reasoning and inadequacies of analogy be revealed.

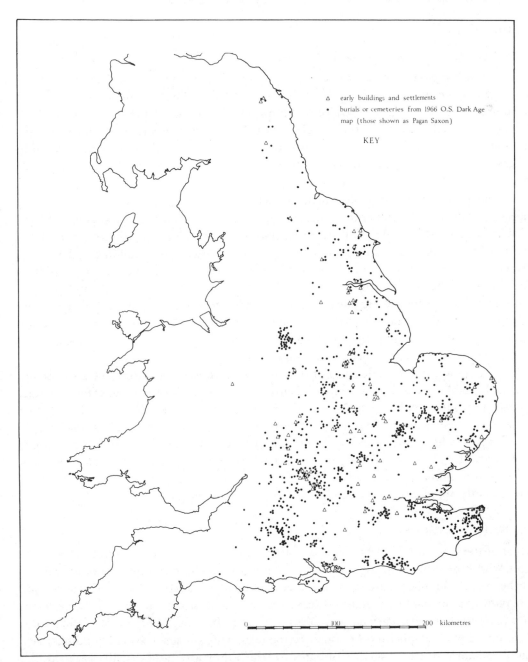

Figure 2.21   Early settlements and pagan burials

Future work

ANALYSIS OF SIZE, ORIENTATION AND MODULE

This is not the place in which to attempt this; we may merely suggest the principles on which it may be attempted, as more data become available. The need for a statistical study of sunken-featured buildings has already been stressed, and a similar study would be worth while for framed buildings, which would incorporate all the evidence from other sources. This should include the (rare) information from objects, such as the Sutton Hoo cauldron chains; the new reconstruction of these gives a minimum height for the beam of the building in which it was suspended of 4.3 m.[77]

One of the most remarkable conclusions which Hope-Taylor has arrived at, by a study of the Yeavering and Dunbar buildings, is that the builders employed a module, multiples of which were used not only for the dimensions of the buildings themselves, but for the width of their door-jambs, entrances and the spaces between one building and another. At Yeavering the module was a 'foot' of 11.05 ins (c. 28.1 cm), at Dunbar one of 10.0 ins (c. 25.4 cm). The Dunbar building which was dated by its similarity to one at Yeavering would, with the slight scaling down that the different 'feet' implied, fit into the Yeavering foundation trenches. Such extraordinary conclusions can only be arrived at by very careful surveying, and excavation. It is doubtful whether the combination of accurate surveying and precise soil-marks has been met with on any other excavated site.

Orientation may be relevant not only in determining what features of a site layout are likely to be contemporary (Wijster, Hatton Rock, fig. 2.7), or to what extent the relationship of buildings is a planned one (Yeavering, Cheddar, fig. 2.8), but also whether it has any constructional significance. Jones notes that all the Mucking sunken-featured buildings are aligned along the axis of the slope of the ground; is this fortuitous, or related to factors of light or shelter for the doorways? Are the orientations of major buildings chosen to minimize wind-pressure, by aligning them to the prevailing wind, especially the possibly aerodynamically designed bow-sided buildings?

SCIENTIFIC TECHNIQUES

Most of the evidence described in this chapter has been derived from empirical observation, with little or no help from scientific techniques which, in common with other facets of the 'new archaeology', are more in evidence in prehistoric rather than medieval studies. Air photography has been vital in discovering sites, assessing their potential importance and planning their excavations, as at Yeavering and Mucking. Many more of the indications on air photographs may be Anglo-Saxon (especially sunken-featured buildings) than the prehistoric or Romano-British dates to which they are more usually assigned. Air photographs may also help in assessing the whole of the topography of areas which is essential to the understanding of any settlement. New techniques in air photography may locate settlements on areas other than those based on gravel or sand, which at present dominate the archaeological record. Geophysical and other prospecting techniques may help to locate sites, or those parts of them which would most repay large-scale excavation. Objective recording of excavated structures will be made easier by photogrammetric techniques now being developed. Analysis of soils,[78] floor sediments, pit contents and objects may help to determine the use of different areas of settlements, and the functions of particular buildings or features. The 'development' of soil differences by chemical means may assist in the discovery of timber features otherwise invisible or amorphous. Study of grain impressions, animal bones and food residues will expand the information available on diet and the economy. Geographical techniques such as location analysis will help in the understanding of settlement patterns. The development of dendrochronology[79] will assist in the dating of preserved timber structures and that of climatic changes and events. Radiocarbon determinations have already indicated likely dating for structures for which no other dating evidence is available (Hereford, Tamworth).

These are only the most obvious of many applications of scientific and analytical techniques.

SETTLEMENT STUDIES

It will be clear from this chapter that it is mainly from the large excavations that the most significant kinds of information emerge, though isolated buildings like Puddlehill or Upton, Northants., are also very informative. Excavations like West Stow, Mucking and Chalton must be our aim in future, preferably on the scale and with the resources of their continental counterparts like Wijster and Dorestad, especially in the matter of full and scientifically supported publication.

As already mentioned, such sites as are available for large-scale excavation are failed settlements, a fact which needs investigation. There are advantages in excavating a site whose occupation was short-lived; even more can be learnt by studying successive occupations of the same site, though the process is more difficult and time-consuming. Most informative of all, perhaps, are those sites in which occupation began in the Anglo-Saxon period and continued into medieval times; the sites here described, with some notable exceptions such as Goltho or those in the south-west, are not the result of large-scale work on medieval village sites, on which substantial pre-Conquest remains are still rare,[80] though their importance was stressed long ago by Hawkes.[81]

Excavations of sites or area studies should be objective and unprejudiced by the evidence from textual studies, which have bedevilled the archaeology of the earlier period. The historical significance of the Wijster settlement is not discussed until the archaeological evidence has been exhaustively dealt with at the end of Van Es's classic monograph.[82]

It may finally be stressed that our ultimate objective must be total area and interdisciplinary studies, in which the Anglo-Saxon settlements, their history, their buildings, their art, their cemeteries, their fields and their environment, are seen as part of the settlement pattern from the earliest prehistoric times to the present day. Such an approach was recommended by Wilson ten years ago.[83] Significant studies of this type include those of Wade-Martins[84] or those recently done by Cunliffe in the Chalton area, Ford in the west midlands, Freda Berisford in the Thames valley and Fowler in north Somerset. They are the only basis on which we may hope ultimately to understand the history of the English settlement.

Notes

1 Cf. Parker (1965).
2 E.g. Phillips (1934).
3 Lethbridge and Tebbutt (1933).
4 Radford (1957).
5 Cramp (1957).
6 Ordnance Survey (1966).
7 Beresford and Hurst (1971) 146–68.
8 Addyman (1972).
9 Cf. Radford (1957).
10 E.g. Cook (1958) 76–81, or Ozanne (1962–3).
11 Beresford and Hurst (1971).
12 Ibid., 174.
13 Grimes (1968) 160.
14 E.g. Cramp (1957); Hamilton (1968).
15 Wilson (1962) 75f.
16 Walton (1954); see now Schmidt (1973).
17 Davison (1967b).
18 Holmes (1959) and Brown (1965).
19 E.g. Smith (1956) and Dodgson (1966).
20 Gelling (1967).
21 Gelling in Brodribb et al. (1972) 134–40.
22 Taylor and Taylor (1965).
23 Cf. Taylor (1970a).
24 Davey (1964).
25 Wilson (1968).
26 Beresford and Hurst (1971).
27 Cf. ibid., 85f.
28 Cf. Barker (1969).
29 Radford (1957).
30 Parker (1965).
31 Cf. van Es (1965–6) 65f.
32 Demolon (1972).
33 Cf. Myres (1969).
34 Addyman (1972).
35 Biddle (1971) 394–6.
36 Contra Thorpe (1961).
37 Jones et al. (1968).
38 Cf. Wilson (1962) 74.
39 Ryder (1961); Wilson (1962).
40 Beresford and Hurst (1971) 139.
41 Cf. Grundy (1970).
42 Addyman (1972).
43 Beresford and Hurst (1971) 117–21ff.

44 Cramp (1957).
45 Bruce-Mitford (1948).
46 Cf. Biddle (1971) 399–402.
47 Cf. Guyan (1952); Ahrens (1966); Stjernqvist (1967); and Demolon (1972).
48 Beresford and Hurst (1971) 103.
49 Laver (1909).
50 Reference in Beresford and Hurst (1971) 103n.
51 West (1969a) 4–8.
52 House xxi, Leeds (1947) 83.
53 Cf. Dannheimer (1973) 159, Abb. 5.
54 Cf. Guyan (1952); Ahrens (1966).
55 Hoffman (1964).
56 Armstrong (1971).
57 Cf. Radford (1957) 37.
58 Grimm (1968) 97 and fig. 24.
59 Guyan (1952).
60 Ahrens (1966).
61 Demolon (1972).
62 Ahrens (1966).
63 Demolon (1972).
64 Smith (1957).
65 Whitelock (1955) 835.
66 Capelle (1969); Schmidt (1973).
67 Hope-Taylor (1962).
68 Walton (1954); Schmidt (1973).
69 Knocker (1950).
70 Smith (1964) and Charles (1967).
71 HE, II. 13.
72 Cf. Addyman (1972) 304.
73 In Rahtz forthcoming.
74 Ibid.
75 As for Maxey in Addyman (1972).
76 Rahtz forthcoming.
77 Bruce-Mitford (1972) 39, fig. 17.
78 Cf. Whitworth (1968).
79 Schove and Lowther (1957) 80–82.
80 Cf. Beresford and Hurst (1971).
81 Hawkes (1947).
82 Van Es (1967) 545ff.
83 Wilson (1962) 77–9.
84 Wade-Martins (1971).

3

Towns

Martin Biddle

There could scarcely be a more difficult moment at which to attempt a survey of the town in Anglo-Saxon England. The legal and historical discussions which marked the forty years up to 1936 were brought to a point by James Tait's magisterial survey published in that year. For more than three decades the debate rested and only in the last few years have historians turned again to fundamental inquiry in this field. In the meantime an entirely new approach has been opened up by the application of archaeological methods and by a return to topographical evidence rendered more precise by the results of archaeology and detailed analysis of the documents. Nowhere more than in the study of the Anglo-Saxon town has the so-called 'anti-urban bias' in English history delayed progress until recent years. The archaeological approach itself is barely twenty years old; the concept of urban archaeology as a rounded inquiry into the origins and growth of urban settlement is a product of the early 'sixties. No account can in these circumstances be more than an interim statement, marked by hypotheses and suggestions rather than by deduction from a solid and extensive basis of observed fact. It must be hoped that subsequent editions of this book will provide an opportunity for revision as a result of the now burgeoning activity in all aspects of the study of the Anglo-Saxon town.

What is a town?

When M. W. Beresford asked this question of the medieval town in his pioneering work of 1967 he proposed to accept

> any place that passes *one* of the following tests: had it a borough charter? did it have burgages? was it called *burgus* in the Assize Rolls, or was it separately taxed as a borough? did it send members to any medieval Parliament?[1]

'The tests', he added, 'are lawyers' tests rather than economists', but the selection is dictated by the nature of the surviving documents … it would be difficult to think of any important town in medieval England, however, that would pass none of the prescribed tests.'[2] We have emerged at once at the heart of our problem, for the fact that these questions are inapplicable and unappliable to the Anglo-Saxon town must not be allowed to obscure the fact of its existence. It is evident that we must seek different criteria.

The question has had to be tackled in recent years under the practical stimulus of the need to define medieval urban places in the face of the destruction of their archaeological evidence by modern development. Since there is no basic agreement on what a town was or is, a conceptual definition was adopted according to which a place was accepted as a town if it possessed or fulfilled more than one of the following criteria:[3]

1 defences	7 a relatively large and dense population
2 a planned street-system	8 a diversified economic base
3 a market(s)	9 plots and houses of 'urban' type
4 a mint	10 social differentiation
5 legal autonomy	11 complex religious organization
6 a role as a central place	12 a judicial centre

These critieria are clearly of differing importance. The possession of one or even more of them does not prove urban status, but merely provides an indication which has to be considered more closely in each case. With hindsight it can perhaps be suggested that a place needs to fulfil not less than three or four of these criteria to merit serious consideration as a town. With all its drawbacks, this list does provide a reasonably objective basis on which to define urban character.

Edith Ennen has stressed the need to focus on the typology of a town if urban history is to be brought out of 'the bewilderment of controversy'.[4] In a recent work she has defined precisely the dangers and advantages of the use of such a bundle of criteria (*Kriterienbündel*): 'the possession of a bundle of criteria, whose composition varies with time and place, allows us to distinguish chronological stages and regional differences and to define the unchanging individuality which each town possesses. We need a conceptual view of the town *(Stadtbegriff)* if urban history is not to devolve into a series of town histories *(wenn sich Stadtgeschichte nicht in eine Summe von Stadtgeschichten auflösen soll)*.'[5] The need for such a pragmatic approach is especially evident in dealing with a period and a place such as Anglo-Saxon England where towns were emerging from a post- or non-urban background and where every stage in urban development is encountered, from 'pre-urban' or 'proto-urban' settlements to fully fledged and highly developed towns.

The study of the early medieval town

The development of historical thought in relation to the Anglo-Saxon town was dealt with explicitly and implicitly in the 'thirties by Stephenson and Tait in their debate over its

very existence,[6] a debate Tait settled irrevocably in favour of the town.[7] 'We are all Tai-
tians now.'[8] Subsequent developments were surveyed in 1971 by Henry Loyn in a characteristically wide-ranging account[9] that appeared fittingly enough in a volume dedicated
to Dorothy Whitelock and was accompanied by a paper by Nicholas Brooks on the development of military obligations that showed how much may still be learnt of urban origins
by a return to the documents.[10] It is perhaps important to stress this point, for the long
quiescence since Tait's book of 1936 might almost seem to suggest that the documentary
materials have little more to offer. Nothing could be further from the truth. The evidence
of the Anglo-Saxon charters[11] for urban history has scarcely been touched: the urban
charters have not been listed under their respective towns, let alone analysed and compared. This must remain the greatest single requirement. The new series 'Anglo-Saxon
Charters' will provide well-founded texts, but the first volume is a disappointment, for
its handling of the charters relating to the town of Rochester is incomplete and otherwise
unsatisfactory.[12] Even a document as well known and important as the Burghal Hidage
has had to wait until 1969 for the establishment of a full text,[13] while the Winton Domesday, possibly the most important single document relating to any one pre-Conquest town,
has only now been studied in detail,[14] although first published in 1816.

The study of urban place- and street-names has much to offer the student of pre-
Conquest towns, especially now that greatly increased attention is being given these names
in the publications of the English Place-Name Society and elsewhere.[15] An allied problem
is that of terminology, in this case the words used at different dates and by different sources
to describe the varying kinds of urban place. This inquiry has long been pursued abroad,[16]
but it has been little followed in England despite the great wealth of the sources. The
contrast between the use of *wih* and *mercimonium* for Anglo-Saxon Southampton and
civitas and *urbs* for Winchester reflects essential differences in the nature of those places
in the eighth and ninth centuries;[17] it also emphasizes the need for an investigation into
the uses and perhaps varying meanings of these and similar words.

The archaeological study of the Anglo-Saxon town is a recent phenomenon, but the
topographical approach which archaeology has now subsumed is a good deal older. As
early as 1871 E. A. Freeman was attempting sketch reconstructions of the early medieval
layouts of Cambridge, Chester, Exeter, Lincoln and York, efforts now long forgotten.[18]
Stephenson in 1933 tried again, and with greater if still primitive success, publishing
sketches of early medieval York, Lincoln, Nottingham, Norwich, Cambridge and Bristol,
accompanied by plans of Ghent and Cologne.[19] As Stephenson realized well enough, his
sketches suffered from a lack of archaeological evidence and the imprecision of such as
was available.[20] It is curious that the study of urban topography had so long remained
the preserve of the amateur and local patriot. It was by this time and has remained a
well-established, sometimes even over-developed, branch of continental urban history,
and in England as long ago as 1898 Maitland had recognized the Ordnance Map, 'that
marvellous palimpsest, which ... we are beginning to decipher', as a fundamental source
for the history of the rural landscape.[21] Its value as a source for the evolution of the urban

landscape was more slowly appreciated. Tait's reply to Stephenson in 1936 made no use of the physical evidence,[22] and this has remained historical practice, with the exception of an occasional essay on a specific town, until quite recently.[23] It is only with the foundation and progress of the Historic Towns Atlas, the first volume of which appeared in 1969,[24] that the historical study of urban topography in Britain has at last caught up with and even surpassed the work being carried out elsewhere in Europe.

The archaeological study of the Anglo-Saxon town was begun by an historian. When the late Helen Cam published her study of the origins of Cambridge in 1933 as a reply to Stephenson's theories, she included a map of Cambridge showing churches, ditches, watercourses and finds of what was supposed (with some reason, as it turned out) to be late Anglo-Saxon pottery.[25] Two years later R. E. M. (later Sir Mortimer) Wheeler issued his study of Anglo-Saxon London which made full use of the archaeological and historical evidence then available displayed in a series of distribution maps in which certain categories of finds were plotted against their archaeological and historical background.[26] The use of such maps was greatly developed by E. M. Jope in studies of Norwich[27] and Oxford,[28] and has been followed by others working on York[29] and Cambridge.[30] The method consists in plotting all the geographically locatable archaeological and historical facts in relation to the natural setting of soil, relief and rivers (fig. 3.1). The results can be used to discover the exact location, extent and setting of the earliest town as well as the course of its subsequent territorial development, the growth of suburbs and the incorporation of previously distinct settlements.

Such distribution studies could be and usually were built up from records of chance finds and small excavations. The application of planned excavation to the solution of specific problems of pre-Conquest urban development was a much slower growth and most early results in the later 'forties and 'fifties were incidental to other programmes, usually directed at major medieval buildings or Roman deposits.[31] These apart, it was probably E. M. Jope's work at Oxford over some fifteen years from the early 'forties which demonstrated most clearly the value of problem-oriented excavation in the study of the medieval town, notably his excavation under Oxford castle mound in 1952.[32] F. T. Wainwright sectioned Anglo-Saxon burghal defences at Cricklade from 1953 onwards[33] and at Tamworth in 1960,[34] while the Royal Commission on Historical Monuments (England) excavated on the defences at Wareham in 1952–4.[35] This work led to P. V. Addyman's excavations at Lydford in 1963–7, undertaken initially at the instigation of E. M. Jope and C. A. R. Radford as part of a more general investigation of the West Saxon *burh*.[36] Meanwhile the programme begun at Winchester in 1961 set out deliberately to apply to the overall problems of urban development the problem-oriented approach which had characterized the investigation of Romano-British towns since the 1930s.[37]

In the second half of the 'sixties urban sites became a major field of British archaeological activity and a good deal of this effort has been directed to pre-Conquest problems. Much of the work on which the present survey is based has taken place in the decade since 1965. Major advances have been secured, but there has been little attempt so far at generalization. Except for the West Saxon *burhs* of the later ninth century, which are becoming reasonably well-charted territory,[38] most of the field is still relatively unknown. Pre-Conquest urban studies are at present highly particular and it seems likely that it will be some time yet before they move from the descriptive to the comparative stage. Contrasts and comparisons are vital for an understanding of urban development as a whole. They are also essential to any serious estimate of the specific character and changing role of individual settlements. It is essential therefore to frame our descriptive statements as far as possible in a way which will facilitate future comparisons, and this will inevitably mean the use of a quantitative approach.

Meanwhile much that is important to study of the Anglo-Saxon town is appearing in the essentially ephemeral form of the so-called 'implications surveys' now being produced in many towns where archaeological evidence is threatened with destruction by proposed development. These surveys frequently provide the most up-to-date statements that are available.[39]

The Romano-British foundations

The break between Roman Britain and Anglo-Saxon England had long seemed so absolute that the 'continuity question' scarcely arose in insular archaeology before the 'sixties.[40] Even now, when evidence for continuity is appearing in very various guises, the question has scarcely received the attention it has long enjoyed on the Continent, notably in the territories along the Rhine and Danube frontiers of the empire.[41] As long as the problem as a whole seemed of such little moment, the question of the continuity of settlement in towns remained undefined. It was bedevilled by an imprecision of concepts, for urban continuity seemed to imply continuous occupation of urban character. Since there was no evidence that towns as such had survived, the question was shelved, whereas it might have been rephrased to ask whether occupation had been continuous even if non-urban in character. The growing realization that towns could revert to non-urban settlements before re-emerging as urban places in later centuries opened the way for an entirely fresh approach to problems of urban continuity.

It used sometimes to be claimed that medieval towns occupying the sites of Roman towns had emerged from the re-settlement of long-deserted but commercially and geographically desirable positions, the potential of which had been obvious to Roman surveyor and medieval merchant alike. In default of documentary or archaeological evidence to the contrary, this may have seemed a reasonable view, but it implied a high degree of coincidence and suggested that English towns of Roman origin had evolved in ways quite different from towns of Roman origin on the Continent. This was of course the nub of the matter, for it was believed that in England, unlike the Continent, the break had been total. The thread of continuity may indeed have been tenuous, but the absence of settlement must be proved before desertion and re-occupation can be accepted. Continuity is inherently more likely.

Three factors have defined our emerging views of urban continuity: the evidence that Romano-British towns were materially equipped to withstand barbarian attacks; the demonstration that they did survive, albeit greatly changed, as focal points in a new pattern of settlement and administration; and the realization that survival might take different forms paralleled by the variety of contemporary experience elsewhere in the former empire.

The ability of Romano-British towns to survive into the fifth century rested in the first place on their defences. Sometimes after the middle of the fourth century (perhaps as a result of Count Theodosius's reorganization of Britain in 369) these defences were strengthened by the addition of external towers designed to carry artillery and by the modification of the ditches to break up enemy concentrations within range of the *ballistae* and other machines.[42] Towns now looked much more like the purely military forts of the period, with their high curtains and projecting bastions. The epithet *castrum* may even have been applied to them and have given rise to the Old English *ceaster* which appears in the names of so many towns of Roman origin.[43] If this were so, it would emphasize another aspect of the problem, for the provision of such sophisticated plant implies the presence in towns of a military force trained to man the defences.[44] Whether this was a local trained band or an element of the field-army of the *Comes Britanniarum* cannot yet be decided.[45] In the present context it is the ability of towns to defend themselves which is central to the problem. If, indeed, as has recently been suggested, Honorius's famous rescript of 410 telling the towns of Britain to look to their own defence was less an abdication of imperial authority than a directive in the exercise of that authority, then it was in the context of defensible and defended towns that it was issued.[46] What is now abundantly clear is that the towns of Britain were materially equipped to survive long into the fifth century, and were certainly no less well provided for in this respect than the towns of Noricum Ripense on the upper Danube with whose dying years Frere drew some years ago an evocative and elegant parallel.[47] The towns *could* survive; in what ways did they survive?

The archaeological evidence for the latest stages of Romano-British town life and for continuity of settlement within walled places in the fifth to seventh centuries rests at present essentially upon the study and interpretation of certain kinds of late Roman metalwork and upon the distribution and date of finds of early Anglo-Saxon pottery, especially when derived from cemeteries close to the towns. Evidence for the continued use of intramural sites and buildings, and for the replacement of Roman structures by Anglo-Saxon buildings, is increasing but is still thin by comparison with the overall picture derivable from the metalwork and the pottery. The situation as it was understood down to the end of 1963 was fully described by Sheppard Frere with particular reference to his work at Canterbury, Dorchester on Thames and Verulamium.[48] The picture was reviewed again by Leslie Alcock up to 1970[49] and has recently been reconsidered in detail in relation to Hampshire, the area from which many of the most recent discoveries have come.[50]

The metalwork and the pottery are reflections, it seems, of two aspects of the same problem, the need to provide troops for the defence of the towns, at first under imperial control and later under local arrangements. The identification of the metalwork as late Roman military equipment and specifically as the bronze mounts from official belts marked a major advance in our knowledge of the fourth and early fifth centuries and provided a positive indication of the presence of the forces needed to man the new defences.[51] While some of this equipment may have been used by locally recruited forces, other pieces, especially those with continental parallels, suggest the actual presence of foreign troops whether *laeti* or units of the regular field army. It is perhaps a moot point whether these alien elements must necessarily be regarded as Germanic, but it is clear from Winchester at least that Germanic soldiers were being buried in the cemeteries of the town in the second half of the fourth century.[52] On the evidence of the metalwork and related material of the so-called *laetenhorizont*, it must now be clear that the population of the late Roman towns of Britain was already mixed with alien and perhaps specifically Germanic elements before the end of the fourth century.

Sporadic finds of early Anglo-Saxon pottery in Romano-British towns and the occurrence of surprisingly early pagan Anglo-Saxon cemeteries in close proximity to their walls had long been known. It was the discovery of this material in stratified contexts within towns and other walled places, notably at Canterbury[53] and Dorchester on Thames,[54] and now latterly at Colchester,[55] Portchester[56] and Winchester,[57] which made it necessary to relate the cemeteries specifically to the towns. Meanwhile work on the pottery from the cemeteries led to a growing perception of their early date and relatively frequent occurrence in relation to the towns, and this gave rise in due course to an entirely fresh appreciation of their significance.[58] Beginning perhaps before the end of the fourth century, these cemeteries suggest that the imperial practice of stationing military detachments in the newly strengthened towns was continued in the fifth century under local arrangements by the employment of Germanic bands who were settled within, or in the immediate vicinity of, the walled area.

Far from there being a complete break between Roman Britain and Anglo-Saxon England, the new evidence shows that the roots of the English settlements were planted while Britain was still part of the empire and were strengthened for as long as the *civitates* remained in being. The implications for the history of towns are considerable. Since Germanic peoples had been settled in and around the towns specifically for defence against further barbarian attack, they must have been well acquainted with town ways and have become identified with them.[59] With the collapse of the economy and the decay of urban life and institutions, political authority seems to have passed naturally into the hands of those who exercised military power and were no longer paid to wield it in the interests of their employers. By some such process Romano-British towns might become Germanic settlements.[60]

This model, which cannot at present claim to be more than a hypothetical reconstruction from a very scattered and incomplete set of facts, does at least provide a possible explanation of the facts we do know and a background to the evidence which is now accumulating for the long-continued use of some buildings inside former Roman towns.

Most striking so far is the evidence from York where buildings in both the fortress (notably the *principia* and the *colonia*) can now be shown to have survived in use long after the end of the Roman period.[61] The case of the *principia* is especially important, for the continued use of an official building of this importance should perhaps be compared with the use down to the Carolingian period of the Roman *praetorium* in Cologne as a residence for the Frankish kings[62] and the adoption of both the *horrea* and the *aula palatina* in Trier as Frankish royal residences.[63] In London there seems a good case for locating the Anglo-Saxon royal residence inside the former military fort at Cripplegate,[64] an official property that by continental analogy might have passed direct from sub-Roman control into Anglo-Saxon royal or princely hands some time in the fifth or sixth century. In Winchester there is a striking coincidence between the site of the Roman forum, perhaps specifically its basilica, and the location of the Anglo-Saxon royal palace.[65] At Gloucester, the siting of the Anglo-Saxon palace at Kingsholm in the area of the first-century legionary fortress might perhaps be explained by the survival of the fortress site in official possession down to the end of the Roman and through the sub-Roman period, after which it could have passed direct into Anglo-Saxon royal hands.[66] The discovery of an important fifth-century military burial at Kingsholm underlines the exceptional interest of the site.

Usually of course Roman buildings survived as uninhabited ruins and no more.[67] They might subsequently be re-used, or incorporated in other structures and eventually robbed,[68] but this is quite different from their survival in continuous use and must be sharply distinguished from it. The fields that had once been Roman towns must long have been scattered with the standing fragments of the past. It is only the intensive use and re-use of our land and its materials that has for the most part removed these traces. But just because they have now vanished, it is not possible to neglect the influence they may once have exercised on the evolving topography of subsequent settlement within the walls of former Roman towns. Such an influence might derive from continuity of land-use, but it could quite as well result from the way in which major structures condition later patterns long after ceasing to serve their own original function and even after periods of total abandonment. The role of such relict features is admirably demonstrated by the amphitheatres whose outlines can still be read in the plans of French and Italian cities – Tours, Périgueux, Lucca, Assisi, Arezzo, for example – although the actual fabric of the original structure may now be entirely invisible. Although Romano-British buildings may never have exerted on subsequent patterns an influence comparable to that of the colonnaded streets of Roman Syria seen today, for example, in Damascus in the Street-called-Straight,[69] it would be unwise to ignore the role they may once have played in conditioning the topography of Anglo-Saxon occupation.

Romano-British town and fortress defence exercised, by contrast, a pervasive and enduring control over later developments on the same site. One has only to consider places like London, Colchester, Lincoln, Canterbury, Winchester, Chichester and Exeter, where the medieval walls followed precisely the course of their Roman predecessors, or York, Chester, Gloucester and Rochester, where the Roman circuits were partially lost only when the medieval towns expanded beyond their former limits, to perceive the dominant role played by Romano-British defences in conditioning later patterns. This role was essentially passive. The Roman defences – ditch or ditches, wall and earthen rampart – presented even in decay a massive physical barrier. Even if the walls were not maintained, it was easier to go round them, or to enter by the sites of the original gates, than to level whole stretches or to pierce new entries. These considerations must account in part at least for the notable continuity of use demonstrable in the sites of the principal gates of medieval towns of Roman origin. This continuity was certainly encouraged in some cases by the continued use of the Roman long-distance roads leading to the gates and also on occasion by the survival of the gate structures themselves. Roman gates still stand in whole or in part at Lincoln,[70] Colchester[71] and Canterbury,[72] and others are known or suspected to have survived into the post-medieval period, for example, the south gate at Exeter.[73] It cannot be doubted that many others were still in existence in the early middle ages and by their very presence encouraged continued use of these entries through the defences. Even when they were demolished or had collapsed, traffic would still make for the gap in the defence where the gates had stood, as excavation of the south gate of Winchester has vividly shown, with street surfaces laid down in the post-Roman period over the fallen rubble of the former gate.[74]

The obstacle provided by the defences and the resultant tendency to ensure the continued use of the gates or their sites must inevitably have had its effect on the internal pattern of the walled areas. The shortest route between two opposing gates continued in use and, given the regular planning of most Romano-British towns, a later route might inevitably follow more or less the line of a Roman street. As a result the streets of some medieval towns seem to show the survival of elements of the Roman street plan. York (within the area of the legionary fortress), Gloucester, Chester and Lincoln are among those towns where this situation has been noted.[75] It occurs also at Winchester (fig. 3.1), where the principal thoroughfare of High Street runs from the site of the Roman gate at West Gate downhill to leave the city at East Gate, some sixteen metres north of the site of the Roman east gate. The medieval street lies over the line of the Roman street for the western third of its course, but then diverges to run the rest of the distance with its whole width just to the north of the Roman street. This alone would suggest that Roman property boundaries had been entirely lost; indeed, Roman buildings have often been recorded below the present High Street. Moreover, in the western third of High Street, where the ground slopes downhill to the east, traffic has cut a wide hollow into the hillside. The limits of this hollow lie far behind the medieval frontages to north and south of the street, and demonstrate that the hollow was formed before these frontages became fixed in the tenth or eleventh century. Similarly, the limits of the hollow far exceed the Roman frontages to either side of the Roman street which here occupies approximately the same position as High Street. It must be concluded that traffic using this route in the post-Roman period was able to ignore the former limits of the Roman street and has eroded over the centuries, by constant minor divergences in bad conditions, the kind of hollow

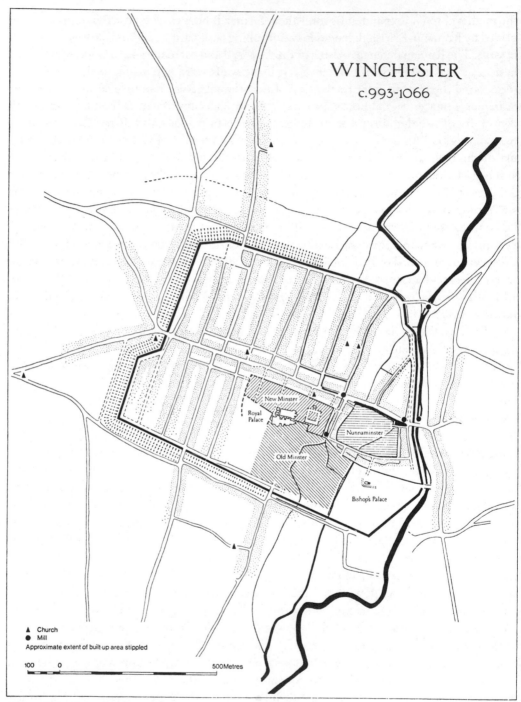

WINCHESTER
c.993-1066

New Minster
Royal Palace
Old Minster
Nunnaminster
Bishop's Palace

▲ Church
● Mill
Approximate extent of built-up area stippled

100   0   500 Metres

Figure 3.1   Late Anglo–Saxon Winchester, *c.* 993–1066

way which is characteristic of unsurfaced medieval routes in hilly country and which can be seen on all the medieval approach roads to the city.[76] This example suggests that the apparent survival of a Roman street in a medieval pattern needs to be closely examined if its true significance is to be established. In Winchester this apparent survival demonstrates in reality the complete absence of any importance attached to the buildings and properties lining one of the most important streets of the Roman town. Nothing could emphasize more clearly the breakdown of the urban order of *Venta*. If there is any evidence for continuity here, it is for the continued importance of a through route from the west gate to the east gate. And the position of this route appears to be conditioned entirely by the obstacles and channels formed by the defences, the gates and the crossing of the river.

This is not to say that there was no settlement within the walls of Winchester, or of the other places mentioned, which required the passage of these routes through the walled areas and ensured their continued importance. It is simply to emphasize that the apparent survival of Roman streets is a very uncertain guide to actual continuity of settlement, and no indication at all that Roman urban conditions, buildings or property boundaries had survived in any recognizable form. Arguments for continuity of settlement must normally be based on indications other than the apparent survival of fragments of a street plan.

The loss of even the major elements of the Roman street plan is emphasized in those towns where the Roman through routes do not always pass through opposed gates, but are for some reason diverted within the town to pass out of the walled area by a gate or gates not directly opposite the point of entry. Canterbury provides a case in point; the medieval and modern east–west streets now run diagonally across the grain of the Roman pattern.[77] London presents much greater difficulty. Almost the entire Roman street pattern has been lost, but there are some notable exceptions.[78] The survival of the internal plan of the Cripplegate Fort suggests that its defences exercised some control over the development of this area in the early middle ages and thus that the fort itself survived as a distinct and possibly still defensible enclosure into the Saxon period.[79] Elsewhere, lengths of the two most important streets of the Roman town have remained in use, while along intervening stretches of the same streets, the medieval and modern courses have wandered away from the earlier lines. It is remarkable that the great street markets of medieval London – Westcheap (Cheapside) and Eastcheap – both occupy approximately the lines of Roman streets. There may be topographical controls here of which we are ignorant, but the possibility that some London streets did actually survive in continuous use with properties along them cannot be entirely ignored. They would provide the exception which emphasizes the general lack that has been stressed here of the demonstrable continuity of streets as built-up routes.

The scattered evidence that the sites of Romano-British towns continued in use cannot yet be fitted into a coherent pattern varying with location and historical situation such as Böhner has proposed for the upper Danube, the Rhineland and the Trier region.[80] It must nevertheless be clear that in Britain too there were many different ways in which the thread of continuous settlement might be kept intact. A great deal is sometimes made of the Roman towns which seem to have failed. Silchester, Verulamium and Wroxeter are the cases most often mentioned, and of these only Silchester is an acceptable example, a failure due to changing political frontiers in the fifth and sixth centuries.[81] Verulamium and Wroxeter, the former certainly, the second less clearly, are cases of settlement shift (*Schwerpunktverlagerung*), a phenomenon of exceptional and to date little regarded importance in the evolution of English towns.[82] Far more remarkable is the number of Roman towns which are still towns today. In defining the principal factors that led to the survival of these places on however reduced a scale, discussion is limited by the few detailed case studies that have yet been undertaken. Moreover, the situation in the west, in areas not conquered by the Anglo-Saxons until the later sixth or seventh century, may be quite unlike that in regions further east which came early under Germanic control. Too much should not perhaps be made of this apparent contrast. Given that some towns in the east may have remained Romano-British enclaves until a late date, and that both in these towns and in those to the west that lay outside the areas of primary Anglo-Saxon settlement there may already have been a significant Germanic mercenary presence, the differences in their development may not have been great. Unfortunately we do not yet know enough to decide either way.

The stages by which *Durovernum Cantiacorum* became Canterbury may never be known in detail, but the take-over of power by Germanic mercenaries in the mid-fifth century and the existence of the Canterbury of Æthelbert as a royal and episcopal centre by the end of the sixth are undisputed facts.[83] There may have been little within the walls of Canterbury except a royal residence during much of the fifth and sixth centuries, but such a residence would express the underlying reason for the continued importance of the site – the exercise of an acquired authority from its traditional centre. Winchester may have survived for the same reason,[84] and Addyman has recently pointed out that a similar explanation would fit the currently known facts at York.[85] The survival of these cities and their emergence as important royal centres would thus be due to the operation of basic political factors and not to chance. The importance of residence as the common denominator cannot be overstressed: it is clearly paralleled in continental patterns of continuity.[86]

The survival of Christian cult centres has played an important role in the discussion of urban continuity in Germany, Switzerland and Austria.[87] It has been comparatively little discussed in relation to English towns. Christian centres must have survived in the western areas of England which did not come under Anglo-Saxon control until after the conversion of Mercia and Wessex in the mid-seventh century,[88] and they probably survived also in the British enclaves in the east.[89] St Albans is the one case of central importance in the present discussion. All the evidence supports the probability that the present abbey occupies the traditional site of St Alban's martyrdom in A.D. 209.[90] This site lies about 100 m from a minor Roman road to the south-east, in an area from which Roman burials have been recorded.[91] An important royal centre existed from at least the eighth century at Kingsbury north-west of the abbey and the medieval town grew up or was created at the abbey gates in the tenth century.[92] No archaeological evidence is yet available from the site of the abbey itself. There seems a strong possibility, however, that St Albans provides a close parallel to the Rhineland towns of Xanten and Bonn. At Xanten – *ad sanctos* – the medieval town grew up not on the site of the Roman *colonia*, but around a church that marked a martyr-tomb beside the road in an extra-mural cemetery some distance from the walls.[93] At Bonn the development was similar.[94] The evidence for the survival of a British enclave in the Chilterns until the battle of Bedcanford in 571 is well known, as is the archaeological evidence for the survival of a degree of civilized life in Verulamium until at least the mid-fifth century.[95] The cult of St Alban could have survived into the sixth century and need not have been interrupted for more than a generation following 571, if at all. Bede apparently believed that the church which marked the site in his day was of Roman origin, and that it had been in continuous use since its construction.[96]

St Albans may provide the only example of this kind of continuity in England. Future excavations may, however, be expected to reveal some cases where medieval urban churches, whether intra- or extra-mural, have preserved the sites of Romano-British Christian centres. Examples are most likely to occur in the west, in areas that were only conquered by the Saxons after their conversion, but some cases may be found in the east. Suburban churches are vital for the study of continuity in continental towns.[97] The case of St Martin's at Canterbury shows, for all its difficulty, that this approach cannot be ignored in England.[98] The churches of St Bride, Fleet Street, St Andrew, Holborn, and St Martin's in the Fields may suggest the possibility of Christian continuity or at least the later preservation of once abandoned Christian centres in the suburbs of early London.[99]

Political factors may have kept the settlement of some towns just alive in the fifth and sixth centuries. Christian continuity may have helped in a few highly speculative cases. For most of these examples there has been at least some written evidence on which to draw; for the majority of settlements there is none at all. Yet many of the walled towns of Roman Britain are on sites still occupied today. Is much of this to be explained by the re-occupation of suitable locations? Or do the lines of continuity dimly perceived in the better documented and more extensively excavated places provide indications of some general relevance for the continuity of settlement in other towns? The discussion cannot be restricted to places which were urban both in the Roman period and in the middle ages. A Roman town such as Great Casterton may be represented today by a village (not always on exactly the same site, as in the case of Irchester), or a modern town like Doncaster may have been no more than a fort in the Roman period. In either case the continuity question may be as relevant as for a Lincoln or a York. The stone-walled forts that became the sites of villages, with a medieval church often occupying a corner of the defences, are common enough to raise the question whether in some cases the connection is not causal rather than casual.[100]

Some places did not survive. Others, like Silchester, survived only for a time.[101] In a surprising number of places settlement was continuous, or was re-established at an early date, but there is no good evidence that *urban* conditions as such survived anywhere unbroken. London remains the one possible exception, but even there, in a city which was by the early eighth century 'a mart of many nations coming by land and sea',[102] the hard evidence remains stubbornly elusive.[103]

Almost all the work on this difficult question remains to be done. A clue to the reason why some places survived while others did not may lie in the varying administrative status and functions of the Roman walled places. If the reality of the transfer of authority and territorial lordship from Romano-British to Germanic hands can be accepted,[104] then this, rather than conquest by battle and the imposition of entirely new patterns, will have conditioned at least in some areas the survival of settlements. The accumulating evidence for the survival of Romano-British and even pre-Roman boundaries into the post-Roman period,[105] and in particular the indications that suburban territories passed with their towns into the framework of Anglo-Saxon estates,[106] shows that this view cannot be lightly set aside. If this is so, the clue to survival or failure may possibly be found in the administrative divisions of the late Roman diocese of the Britains,[107] in the hierarchy of Romano-British walled places[108] and in their various types and functions.[109] In this, as in much else, early Anglo-Saxon history and archaeology are inextricably involved with the Roman world. *Ignoramus*, to paraphrase Levison, *sed non ignorabimus*.

The rise of the Anglo-Saxon town

The earliest large-scale Anglo-Saxon settlements recognizable as towns seem to have been the coastal or riverine trading and industrial centres of the seventh century and later, of which Anglo-Saxon Southampton, Hamwih, provides at present the best-known example.[110] There have been three settlements at Southampton (fig. 3.2). The Roman site of *Clausentum* at Bitterne, fortified in the late fourth century; the open settlement on the opposite side of the River Itchen in the neighbourhood of St Mary's Church, occupied from the late seventh or early eighth down to the tenth century; and the medieval town of Southampton on the western shore of the same promontory overlooking the River Test, first occupied apparently in the tenth century. The sequence provides the clearest case of settlement shift *(Schwerpunktverlagerung)* yet investigated in detail in this country. The second site, around St Mary's Church, is to be identified as *illud mercimonium quod dicitur Hamwih* ('that mart called Hamwih') from near which at the Hamble mouth St Willibald set sail across the Channel in about 721.

Discoveries made during digging for brick-earth in the nineteenth century, and latterly in excavations conducted since 1946, and on an increasing scale since 1968, have shown that Hamwih covered an area of some 30 ha (72 acres) to the east of the gravel terrace which forms the spur of land at the confluence of the Itchen and the Test. The eastern side of the settlement bordered what seems to have been a shallow lagoon on the western shore of the Itchen. Although all trace of the original arrangement has long disappeared, older observations and recent excavations have shown that Hamwih originally possessed a regular layout of gravelled roads running parallel and at right-angles to the Itchen shore. Repeatedly repaired, these roads lasted throughout the lifetime of the settlement.[111] Properties were laid out along the roads and within individual plots the buildings

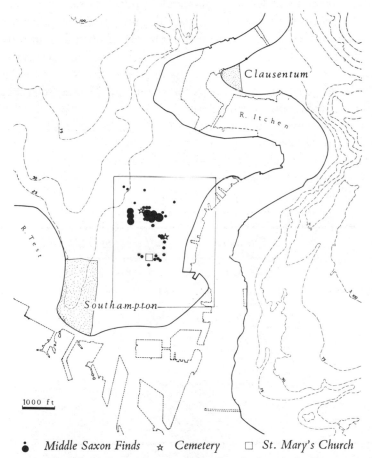

•   Middle Saxon Finds   ★   Cemetery   □   St. Mary's Church

Figure 3.2   Anglo-Saxon Southampton in relation to the Roman and later medieval settlements (after Addyman and Hill (1968) fig. 25)

tended to be set on the road front, with areas behind them separately reserved for latrines, wells, rubbish pits and industrial purposes. Once established, these arrangements persisted as long as occupation continued. In the earlier phases of the town's existence there were several small cemeteries, each possibly with its own wooden church, but these were later abandoned, perhaps at a time when burial was being concentrated at the main church, presumably on or near the site of the later St Mary's, traditionally the mother church of Southampton.

The very extensive finds derived mainly from the wells and pits, of which over a thousand have been excavated, provide evidence of intensive industrial activity and far-flung market contacts. Iron, bronze, lead and silver were worked, and it is a safe deduction that Hamwih was the minting place of the so-called Southampton sceatta series, the majority of known specimens of which have been found there. Pottery was produced, wood, bone and antlers were worked and loom-weights and spindle whorls from every part of the site show the dominant role of textile production. The imported finds illustrate the extent of Hamwih's insular hinterland, stretching north into Mercia, but demonstrate above all the range of its contacts with the Continent: from Germany, fine glassware, pottery of Badorf and Pingsdorf type, Tating ware, lava millstones from the Niedermendig area; from France, pottery similar to that from Beauvais and Saran in the Loire, and other types not yet identified, but probably also of French origin.

As for chronology, renewed discoveries support H. R. Loyn's suggestion that Hamwih probably owed its foundation to the increased prosperity of Wessex under Ine.[112] But we can now go further and draw a comparison between Hamwih and its ancient neighbour 18 km up the Itchen at Winchester.[113]

Winchester and Southampton in the later seventh to ninth centuries

	Winchester	*Southampton* (Hamwih)
Nomenclature	*civitas, urbs*	*mercimonium, villa, pagus* *wih, wic, tun*
King	×	?[114]
Bishop	×	—
Private estates of high social rank	×	?
Mint	?	×
Elements of regular plan	—	×
Long-distance trade	—	×
Intense industrial activity	—	×
Relatively dense population	—	×

Clearly these are two complementary settlements, the one royal, ecclesiastical, ceremonial, heir of an ancient and still lively dignity; the other bustling, crowded, commercial, out-ward-looking, from which the shire was named. Whether Winchester should be regarded as an urban community is doubtful and a point to which we shall return. What seems certain is that they were intimately related. The presence of a royal centre in Winchester, the establishment of a bishop's see there about 662, and its unification with the see transferred from Dorchester in the 670s, provide the context and the impetus for the emergence of Hamwih during Ine's reign (688–726).[115]

A comparable rationale may lie behind the appearance of other trading centres at this period in similar riverine or coastal situations. It seems possible that there was at least one such centre in each of the major kingdoms, Southampton (Hamwih eighth century) for Wessex; Fordwich (*Fordeuuicum* 675), Sarre (*ad Serrae, Seorre* 761), Dover (*Dofras* 696–716) and possibly Sandwich (*Sondwic* 851) for Kent; London (*Lundenwic* 673–85(?)) for Kent, Essex and later Mercia; Ipswich (*Gipeswic* 993) for East Anglia; and York (*Eoforwicceaster* 644 (ninth century)) for Northumbria. The force of *wic* in these names may appear to be that of 'market-town', comparable to Quentovic, Bardowick, *Sliaswich* (Schleswig) or Wijk bij Duurstede (Dorestad), as older writers have accepted,[116] but it seems doubtful now if such an interpretation can be maintained. The question is not so much, it seems, of towns getting the suffix -*wic*, as of some places called -*wic* eventually becoming towns.[117] It is not entirely clear that this distinction is valid for Anglo-Saxon England,[118] but it would be wiser at present to see what other evidence there is for the trading character of these places.

In Kent, toll-charters of 747 and 761 granted the monasteries of Reculver and Minster exemption from dues in the ports of Fordwich and Sarre where they were trading.[119] Fordwich at the head of the Great Stour estuary and close to the royal villa at Sturry may have been the port for Canterbury. Sarre served the Isle of Thanet and its importance is attested by a large Anglo-Saxon cemetery with an exceptionally high proportion of well-armed male burials. Sonia Hawkes has commented that the only truly comparable case in Kent is the Buckland cemetery at Dover and has suggested that these unusually well-armed communities in strategic positions close to known ports might represent for the sixth to seventh centuries the military establishments which the king's port-reeves may have maintained for the execution of their duties in the eighth century.[119] None of these sites has yet produced evidence of occupation comparable to that at Hamwih, but their function seems to have been broadly similar and their number may have been a reflection of the wealth of Kent and its close involvement with continental trade. The relationship between Fordwich and Canterbury seems not unlike that between Hamwih and Winchester.

There is no early documentary evidence for Ipswich, but the extent of middle Saxon occupation is attested by the distribution of pottery of the period *c.* 650–*c.* 850 (Ipswich Ware) over an area of some 12 ha (30 acres) on the north bank of the Orwell.[120] Pottery was made in the town,[121] but there is no other evidence for industry, probably because of the very limited investigation which has so far taken place.[122] Imports of glass and of pottery of Badorf type and relief-band amphorae testify to cross-channel trade.[123] In its situation, and in the large extent and early date of the occupied area, Ipswich is comparable to Hamwih.

These places were, so far as one can tell, new settlements; at least, they did not occupy former Roman walled places. They lay on the coast or beside rivers, seem to have been undefended, and appear to have been related to some other settlement or settlements inland: Hamwih to Winchester; Fordwich, Dover and perhaps Sarre and Sandwich to Canterbury; Ipswich to an East Anglian centre or centres less easy to define.[124] These insular trading places thus belong to the general type as Quentovic, Domburg and Dorestad on the continental side of the channel.[125]

London and York were the two other major trading places in England in the seventh, eighth and ninth centuries. Both occupied their former sites and were therefore defended by what remained of their Roman walls. In both cases king and bishop formed an element in the community. They thus combined the functions that might elsewhere be divided between a Hamwih and a Winchester and in this they are to be compared with Cologne[126] rather than with the new, undefended sites such as Dorestad.

London was a bishop's see from 604 and the Kentish kings had a hall there by the third quarter of the seventh century, if not long before.[127] The issue about 640 of gold tremisses with the legend LONDVNIV suggests that the city's commercial importance was already established and this impression is confirmed by the law code of Hlothhere and Eadric of 673–85(?) which is partly concerned with Kentish men trading in London. Transactions were regulated by the king's reeve (wīc-gerēfa), and the place itself was *Lundenwic*. By the 720s, when Bede was writing, the city was 'a mart of many peoples coming by land and sea' *(multorum emporium populorum terra marique uenientium)*.[128] During the eighth and ninth centuries Mercian and Kentish kings served incidentally to record the importance of London's sea-borne trade by granting to bishops and the heads of monastic houses the right to send ships into port free of dues. It was described in 811 as 'a famous place and royal town' *(in loco praeclaro oppidoque regali Lundaniae vicu)*,[129] and seems to have been the principal trading-town of the Mercian kingdom, the probable route, for example, of the contacts between Offa and Charlemagne.[130]

The archaeological evidence for this period of London's history is negligible, despite the clear indications of its importance given by the documents. The excavation of the Thames waterfront may eventually remedy this situation, but meanwhile no survey has yet been published of the imported objects of this period, glass, pottery, querns and so forth, found in the city. The 'London inscribed' silver sceattas with the legend LVNDONIA which may have been issued as late as *c.* 730 gave rise to the 'London derived' and 'London connected' series, as well as to a number of copies. The derivative types are not necessarily from a London mint, and some were certainly imitated in Frisia. It is indeed probably not by chance that three of the great continental trading towns of this period, Quentovic, Dorestad and Domburg, lie opposite the Thames estuary. Although much of their importance undoubtedly derived from the coastal trade, the cross-channel route to and from London and Mercia undoubtedly played a major role in their activity.

London, within the 133.5 ha bounded by its Roman wall, can never have approached the 240 ha of contemporary Dorestad. But it would be surprising if it were smaller than the 30 ha of Hamwih. It may have contained as many as nine churches and may have had more than one centre, as the markets of Westcheap (Cheapside) and Eastcheap suggest. The current poverty of archaeological evidence relating to seventh-, eighth- and ninth-century London should not obscure the indications that it was among the most important north-west European centres of this period.

The evidence for York suggests a picture rather similar to that of London.[131] Paulinus, the first bishop of York, was consecrated in 625 and a small wooden church was
in existence by 627. Edwin of Deira's baptism in the church that Easter may suggest that
there was already a royal residence in the city and that, as in Winchester,[132] the church
was established in the first instance to serve the residence. There is good evidence both
from documents and archaeology that some of the buildings of Roman York survived into
this period and even down to the twelfth century. On the site of the Minster, for example,
the *principia* of the legionary fortress continued to be used and repaired into the late Saxon
period.[133] It does not seem likely that the royal palace was there, at least at this late date,
for there is some evidence that the Danish palace of the ninth century and later made
use of the south-east gatehouse of the fortress, when the rest of the defences on that side
had been pushed further out.

The emergence of commercial life at York is poorly documented. Three gold
tremisses – the so-called York thrymsas – suggest a gold coinage of the seventh century
parallel to that known from the south, for example from London. But it is not until the
later eighth century that we have a description by Alcuin of a populous town inhabited
by men of many nations including, as Altfrid makes clear, a colony of Frisian merchants.[134]
The archaeological evidence for York before the Danish conquest in 867 is still very thin,
but the most striking result of recent work has been the demonstration that the defences
were refurbished in this period, perhaps as early as *c.* 650, and strengthened by the addition
of a stone tower on the line of the legionary fortress wall between the western angle and
the north-west gate.[135] No other place in the country has yet produced structural evidence
for the reconstruction and strengthening of Roman defences in this period and it is a notable testimony to the importance of seventh- and eighth-century York. Although the
north-west and north-east sides of the fortress defences remained in use, the other two
sides were gradually lost, probably by the encroachment of the Anglian buildings on to
them and eventually by the expansion of settlement beyond their limits. It is not yet known
how these sides of the growing community were protected. It is possible that the addition
of the tower on the north-west side took place before the legionary defences were breached,
and that once this had happened, the city remained essentially undefended until after the
Danish conquest, as Asser may imply when he says that in 867 'the city did not possess
strong and well-built walls'.[136]

By the early ninth century, if not before, settlement had extended to both banks of
the Ouse; there were four or more churches and the defences of the old legionary fortress
were beginning to disappear beneath buildings that were pushing out both north-west
towards Marygate and south towards the site of the later castle. The commercial success
of this burgeoning community is attested both by its size, which must have been at least
33 ha (80 acres), and by the hoards of coin which its citizens deposited in the middle of
the ninth century.[137]

The presence of king and bishop in London and York should not obscure the commercial importance of these cities from the seventh century onwards. They combined in

themselves the functions that seem elsewhere at this date to have been divided among two or more settlements. But whereas the royal authority, to which the Church had adhered, was in some sense founded in the past, the commercial activity seems to have been a rebirth. In this respect London and York were comparable to the new-born trading places at Hamwih and Ipswich, and around the Kentish coast. These bare half-dozen settlements represent the real beginnings of the Anglo-Saxon town and now that we can locate them and can discern, however faintly as yet, their character, functions and contacts, we can see that they reflect both in their distribution and in their chronology similar trends on the continental shores of the Channel and the North Sea.

If the thesis argued here for a certain continuity of settlement in former Roman places can be maintained, then it is the emergence of trading places in the seventh century that marks the real break with the past. This view in some ways confirms, in others modifies, Pirenne's theses as they affect north-west Europe and England in particular.[138] Pirenne argued that the Germanic invasions caused no substantial break in the continuity of economic development in the fifth and sixth centuries. Loyn and others have shown with obvious truth that Britain remained an exception to this rule. In economic terms this is clear enough. And yet in terms of the transfer of control over walled towns and other official land, perhaps especially military sites, and in the context of the exercise of authority from the traditional seats of power, this exception is beginning to look less and less justifiable. There was, it seems, an underlying continuity of *romanitas*, even if *civiltas* and *commercium* had disappeared. Of Pirenne's view that the break when it came was the result of the Mohammedan conquests in the Mediterranean, the English evidence has little to say, although the interruption of the Atlantic trade through the Straits of Gibraltar has sometimes been called in evidence to explain changes in the overseas contacts of the Celtic west.[139] That the break, whatever its cause, came in the late seventh century seems broadly to be supported by the evidence recited here for the emergence at just this period of Anglo-Saxon and continental trading-places, often on new sites and reflecting new patterns of commerce. Pirenne's further thesis, that the break led to economic decline in western Europe, finds no support in an Anglo-Saxon context. Perhaps because the disruption of the Romano-British economy had been so complete, the re-establishment of a commercial basis came as a greater contrast in Anglo-Saxon England of the seventh and eighth centuries than it appeared on the north-western coasts of the Continent. Be that as it may, the evidence is for economic growth rather than decline. Of that growth, the new trading-places are a distinctive sign, and one which Anglo-Saxon England shared with the neighbouring Channel coasts.

Even before the new trading-places came into being, the older centres had in some cases received a fresh impetus from the Church. The establishment of episcopal sees in the former towns of Roman Britain has sometimes been seen as the result of policy formulated by Pope Gregory in Rome on the basis of long-outdated imperial lists. However much truth may lie behind this view, it is certain that such a policy would not have succeeded except in so far as it could be related to the realities of contemporary politics.

Such realities decreed the ecclesiastical dominance of the see of Canterbury (founded 597) in preference to that of London (604) or York (625); they marked out such places as Lindisfarne (635), Lichfield (669; ? *c*. 656),[140] Hereford (676) and Hexham (678), to name only four of the bishoprics on non-Roman sites; and we may suspect that it was contemporary realities too which saw the setting up of sees in Rochester (604), Dorchester (634), Felixstowe (*c*. 630),[141] Winchester (662), Leicester (679) and Worcester (680), places none of which was in the first rank of Romano-British towns. By contrast, with the exception of Worcester,[142] these former Roman places were all at the centre of or adjacent to notable concentrations of Anglo-Saxon cemeteries of the fifth to seventh centuries.[143] It was pastoral and political factors which led bishops to work from these centres, not antiquarian lore.

Not a great deal is yet known of the character of these erstwhile Roman towns, now bishops' sees, in the seventh to ninth centuries. But, by combining documentary and archaeological evidence, the main outlines can perhaps be drawn. Winchester, for example, seems to have displayed four main components during this period: a royal residence, a cathedral church and its community, an unknown but probably small number of private estates of high social status, and perhaps a street market and some service population along the eastern part of the main through route, *ceap strǣt*, by *c*. 900.[144] Canterbury is better known from the written sources. A royal residence there must have been, though its location is unknown; the cathedral inside the walls and four extra-mural churches date from the early seventh century, if not before, and at least three other churches were in existence by the early ninth century;[145] by this date the land inside the walls was divided up into a number of large enclosed holdings and a charter of 868 reveals the customary law that an eavesdrip of 2 ft had to be left between houses. There was a market-place and the community could be described as a *port*, a trading-place, its citizens as *portware* or *burgware*, dwellers in the *port* or *burh*, the defended place.[146] There was also among them some element of communal organization, for ninth-century Canterbury possessed a gild of *cnihtas* who, whether they were traders themselves or the resident servants of landed proprietors, 'have a distinguished place in social history as the founders of the earliest gild on record in England'.[147] Canterbury was also a mint[148] and it is altogether clear that by the ninth century it was a fully urban community.

Unfortunately the evidence for Canterbury is at present almost exclusively documentary and we have no means of telling the date by which truly urban conditions had come into being. The contrast that has already been drawn between Winchester and Southampton suggests that Winchester was not an urban community in the seventh to ninth centuries, for there is no evidence there of relatively dense population, intensive trading or industrial activity.[149] A community of limited size, restricted in essence to the upper levels of society, can scarcely be regarded as urban even if some trading element is present to serve the greater establishments. The documentary evidence that Rochester was divided into large enclosed holdings is not therefore by itself sufficient to demonstrate that it was an urban community, nor do the existence of the see and the presence of a mint confound this view.[150] The impression given by the Rochester charters is not an urban impression.[151] Here again, archaeological evidence is lacking as a control against which to test the possible interpretations of the documents.[152] As at Rochester, so too at Dorchester on Thames there is no reason to suggest an urban community, although the archaeological evidence is there, as at Winchester, becoming more readily available.[153]

The courses by which Anglo-Saxon England was moving towards urban life in the seventh and eighth centuries were basically two. The new trading towns in open, undefended sites on the coast or along the rivers were accompanied by the greatest surviving towns of Roman Britain, London and York, in which the urban air may never have entirely ceased to blow, and in which trade and industry were now re-emerging. Alongside these commercial centres there was a series of other erstwhile Roman places in which under royal and ecclesiastical impetus new life was on the move. Of these places, Canterbury at least was a town. Winchester and Southampton shared a dual role with complementary and contrasting functions; but Winchester was not yet truly urban. The remaining places of this kind, Rochester, Dorchester, Leicester and Worcester, would not emerge, if at all, as fully fledged towns until the tenth century. They were meanwhile ecclesiastical, and possibly like Winchester aristocratic. They were not urban.

Towns in Mercia before the tenth century

Excavations at Hereford between 1967 and 1972 revealed the most complex and certainly the best-preserved sequences of Anglo-Saxon town defences yet investigated.[154] The early tenth-century rampart, revetted with timber and strengthened with stone soon after its original construction, enclosed an area of about 21 ha (50 acres).[155] On the western side of the town this rampart was preceded by two earlier defences. The first bank and ditch was small, probably little more than a boundary,[156] but it was replaced on the same line by a gravel and clay rampart of some size.[157] These earlier defences have been observed only on the west side of the town, but their course on the north and east can probably be inferred from the line of the early tenth-century rampart and from the behaviour of the internal street plan. The rampart turned east at the junction of Victoria Street and West Street and ran east for 380 m on the line of West and East Streets. Close to the junction of St John Street and Offa Street with East Street it swung south-east to run parallel with East Street towards the easternmost point of the defences.[158] The earlier defences probably followed the tenth-century line as far as St John Street/Offa Street and then turned south on a course parallel to the western defences. The streets within this rectangular enclosure of some 13.6 ha (33 acres) formed a remarkably regular layout based apparently upon the intersection of a north–south route from the Wye ford, now partly surviving in Broad Street, with an east–west route over which the cathedral has encroached, but which still survives in St Nicholas Street, King Street and the westernmost end of Castle Street. The intersection of these routes falls in the centre of the reconstructed *enceinte*, which can thus be seen to have defended an occupied area astride an important route across the Wye and including the site of the Anglo-Saxon cathedral.

This arrangement probably went with the second of the defences investigated on the western side of the town.[159] The function of the first boundary cannot yet be established[160] and neither can it be satisfactorily dated within the general bracket of the eighth and ninth centuries.[161] The enclosure of a further 7.5 ha (18 acres) to the east in the early tenth century may suggest that a considerable suburb had formed here during the ninth century, which it was now thought advisable to include within the defences. The second enclosure could therefore be a work of the early ninth or even eighth century, but it is impossible at present to be more precise.

Excavations at Tamworth in 1960 and latterly since 1967 have traced the course and defined the character of an Anglo-Saxon defensive system enclosing a rectangular area of some 20 ha (50 acres) and probably to be identified as the *burh* erected by Æthelflæd in 913.[162] As at Hereford, these excavations have also revealed an earlier defence of slighter construction on the line of the later rampart. This earlier work may have been no more than a boundary, although possibly the boundary of the Mercian royal palace,[163] and there is nothing as yet to link it to the street pattern, nor to demonstrate that the latter is of pre-Æthelflædan date.[164]

It is striking that the two Mercian boroughs where relevant recent excavations have taken place should both have produced evidence of defence systems of a date earlier than the tenth century. However uncertain the character and exact date of the first work at Tamworth may be, the early *enceinte* at Hereford shows that Mercia played a central role in the creation of the Anglo-Saxon town. In a recent study of the development of military obligations in eighth- and ninth-century England, Nicholas Brooks showed that 'Mercian charters first refer to borough work from the middle of the eighth century, whilst in Wessex it was not until the middle of the ninth century that kings began to demand in their diplomas work on the building of fortifications'.[165] Since pre-Alfredian defence works have not been recognized in Wessex, the Hereford evidence provides a concrete example of the situation discernible in the written sources and greatly extends our understanding of their implications. A fortification enclosing over 13 ha is more than a military station.

The siting, size, internal layout and inclusion of the cathedral all show that Hereford was a town; the rectangular outline of its defences and the regularity of the street plan suggest that it was a deliberately planned foundation. 'Planned' in this context implies that the town had been laid out in a regular pattern at one moment in time with the purpose of dividing and apportioning the ground for permanent settlement.[166] It is the deliberate organization of space that is the critical factor, and defences, although they may exercise an important influence on the form of the planned layout and on the function of its individual components, are irrelevant to this definition.

The apparently sudden appearance of a planned and defended town on the marches of Mercia in the ninth or perhaps even the eighth century should not lead us headlong into a search for origins. The idea of the defended settlement is a commonplace. The walls and ramparts of Roman towns were visible then and are still visible today; in the post-Roman period there was a return to the defended hill-fort, at least in the west,[167] and this tradition was evident in early medieval Wales;[168] in Northumbria, the defences of York had been refurbished perhaps as early as the seventh century;[169] and Mercia itself was bounded on the west 'by the greatest public work of the whole Anglo-Saxon period', the dyke built by Offa perhaps between 784 and 796.[170] As for the internal layout of Hereford, it seems doubtful that a sub-rectangular[171] pattern of streets reflects in essence anything other than an efficient approach to the division of land and the provision of easy communication from point to point. It would not have come as a revelation to Englishmen whose fields had for generations been tilled in a regular fashion and whose administrators could think in the orderly patterns recorded, for example, in the Tribal Hidage.[172] If sources must be defined, Anglo-Saxon Southampton seems to have displayed, if not from the first then from some date well before 800, a regular semi-rectilinear layout of streets which served it as long as the settlement endured.[173] Such an example would not have been unknown in Mercia. The street behind the ramparts at Hereford, the wall-street,[174] presents perhaps a special case, if indeed it belongs to the pre-tenth-century arrangement. It might reflect a tradition of Roman military planning,[175] but it may be no more than a specific adaptation of the regular street layout to the need for communication on internal lines in an enclosed settlement where defence was a prime consideration.

Some may perhaps feel that this is an unduly pragmatic, excessively common-sense view of the emergence of the defended, planned *burh*, one of the most distinctive achievements of Anglo-Saxon society. It is for them to demonstrate alternative explanations and to show, for example, how the classical experience of civil or military planning might have directly and plausibly influenced Anglo-Saxon Mercia and the Wessex of Alfred.

Unfortunately, very little is yet known of these developments in Mercia before Æthelflæd's campaigns of the early tenth century. Hereford is the only clear example, for the pre-tenth-century enclosure at Tamworth, although it may have been nearly as large as the *burh* of 913[176] and thus perhaps larger than pre-Æthelflædan Hereford, seems too slight to be truly defensive and cannot, as we have seen, be satisfactorily related to the internal street plan.[177] Nevertheless, the evidence for a possible planned layout at Hereford in the eighth to ninth century emphasizes the role that Mercia may have played in the development of the Anglo-Saxon planned town.

Even less is currently known of the fortified centres established by the Danes in the eastern midlands in the second half of the ninth century. Much important work has been done in recent years in each of the Five Boroughs – Derby, Leicester, Lincoln, Nottingham and Stamford – but in none of them can the character and topography of the ninth-century Danish settlement be defined with any precision. The 'Anglian Burh' at Nottingham has been identified with the headquarters of the Danish army, in existence by 868 and repaired by Edward the Elder in 920, but the dating evidence is scanty and the situation has been complicated by the discovery of a yet earlier defence.[178] Stamford provides a similar problem.[179] In tracing the evolution of the pre-Conquest town it clearly makes a great difference whether the Five Boroughs were urban foundations of the Danish period or whether their urban element was created by Edward the Elder in the early tenth century, in the aftermath of the construction of the Wessex *burhs*. Were the Danish fortifications fortresses or towns?

At York there is no doubt about the answer. The city fell to the Danes in 867. In 876 one section of the Danish army 'restored the walls of York, settled the surrounding region, and stayed there'.[180] The defences on three sides of the Roman legionary fortress were restored by the addition of an earth rampart and on the fourth side the defended area was extended by the enclosure of an additional 15 ha (37 acres) south-east towards the Foss. The bank around the new area may not all have been of the same date. Along the Foss a bank of layers of brushwood and clay laced with stakes and piled on a raft of brushwood prevented the newly enclosed area from flooding and provided an embankment at which ships could unload, while from the south, and probably from the north angle of the fortress a defensive bank crowned by a stockade ran down to meet the Foss. The total area now enclosed was some 36 ha (87 acres) and by the early tenth century at the latest settlement was spreading over the Ouse into the Micklegate area of the city.

The Danish royal palace lay in the centre of the defended area and was probably constructed around the surviving remains of the south-east gatehouse of the legionary fortress.[181] The life of the cathedral and its community was interrupted for only a few years before Guthfrith, chosen king on Halfdan's death, became the first Christian Viking ruler of York in 883. By the tenth century the commercial success of the city is seen in the number of its churches, the importance of its coinage, and the range of its imports and manufactures, for which there is for the first time ample archaeological evidence.[182] The intensity of its occupation, notably in the newly enclosed area to the south-east, which became the commercial heart of the city, is suggested by the great depth of the ninth- to eleventh-century layers in this area, which reach a thickness of more than five metres.[183]

Unlike Hereford or the later West Saxon and Mercian *burhs*, Viking York displays no sign of a regular internal layout, even in the newly extended area between the fortress and the Foss. Nor can there be any question of the disappearance of some original layout, for the evidence suggests that the modern property divisions in this part of the city were already in existence in Danish times.[184] This contrast with Wessex and Mercia is heightened by a similar contrast between York and the contemporary Danish trading town at Hedeby (Haithabu).[185] There in recent years evidence has been accumulating to show that the settlement within the later *Halbkreiswall* was laid out from the early ninth century in rectangular parcels which persisted until the end of the occupation in the second half of the eleventh century, and were reflected in a roughly corresponding allocation of various parts of the area to different commercial or industrial activities.[186] Whatever differences there may be – and the contrasts are likely to be as informative as the similarities – there can be no doubt that Danish York was one of the greatest North Sea trading places of the Viking age and probably excelled them all in size and wealth. York in the tenth century covered an area of at least 40 ha, Hedeby less than 35, and Birka perhaps 20 ha. Because it was a Christian town, York has not produced the rich grave-goods which characterize Birka and to a lesser extent Hedeby, but its wealth is expressed as clearly in the number of its churches – more than twenty in 1100 and probably over ten by the year 1000. It is a curious tribute to England's academic insularity that York has found little place so far in discussion of the origins of the northern town.[187]

York is the only Viking town in England of which anything substantial is known. It would be foolish to extrapolate its evidence to the other Danish settlements of possibly urban character: we can only await the results of excavations in the Five Boroughs and elsewhere. The influence of Viking trade on towns which remained substantially English needs also to be defined. At Chester, where the surviving Roman defences were refurbished by Æthelflæd in 907,[188] there is ample evidence of the Viking trade with Ireland and a Norse–Irish trading enclave has been suggested between the southern defences and the Dee.[189] Here the evidence is mostly in the form of chance finds, and extensive excavations are needed in this area outside the Roman fortress.[190]

Whatever may be the true character and extent of the specifically Danish contribution to the development of the pre-Conquest town, it seems clear that a two-way process was involved. The influence of Mercian and subsequently of West Saxon practice on Danish settlements was probably as important as the reverse. The time has passed when one could believe that it was the Scandinavian invaders who 'taught the English the value of fortified towns'.[191]

The *burhs* of Wessex

In the middle of the ninth century England was divided among four independent kingdoms: Mercia, Northumbria, East Anglia and Wessex. By 879 Wessex alone survived intact and Alfred's immediate task was to defend his kingdom against further inroads. Defence had previously been hindered by a lack of fortified strongholds. The arrangements he now made ensured that no part of Wessex would in future be more than twenty miles from a fortified centre (fig. 3.3).[192] By 892 at the latest this scheme was reasonably complete,[193] and it seems probable that it was well advanced before the West Saxon occupation of London in 886, for that operation involved warfare on a scale unlikely to have been undertaken except from a secure base.[194]

Our knowledge of the fortified centres or *burhs* on which this 'planned scheme of national defence'[195] was secured is derived partly from a list known as the *Burghal Hidage* and increasingly from excavation and topographical study.[196] The principal result of this work has been to show that the term 'fortress' formerly used to describe these *burhs* is misleading. It suggests an exclusively military function and obscures the variety of places actually involved.[197] It conceals above all their true character – and in so doing has drawn a veil over one of the most remarkable achievements of the Anglo-Saxon state. For in the main these *burhs* were not fortresses, but fortified towns.

This conclusion is not without profound consequences for our understanding of pre-Conquest England and it is one which could only have been reached by combining the evidence of the written sources with the results of archaeological and topographical inquiry.[198] It was only when standard archaeological procedures, which had been used for at least thirty years in the elucidation of Romano-British defences and street plans, were at last extensively applied to the problems of the Anglo-Saxon town in the 'sixties, that advance was possible. It was realized almost at once that the regular street pattern displayed by some of the larger *burhs* was contemporary with the fortification or restoration of the

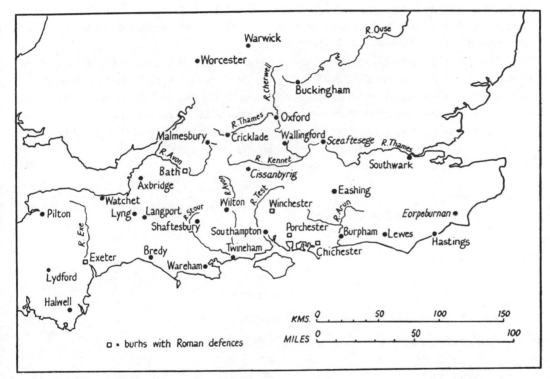

Figure 3.3   The *burhs* of Wessex

burh.[199] When this observation was related to the size of the area enclosed, it became apparent that these *burhs* were organized and apportioned for permanent settlement where military effectiveness was to be founded on economic viability and a growing population.[200] There seems to be no known parallel in contemporary Europe for a deliberate scheme of town foundation on such a scale. It provides the context for the later history of town plantation in England and in the English possessions in France,[201] and gives further expression, if expression is needed, to the administrative ability of the Alfredian kingdom. In the first decades of the tenth century, the reconquest of England and the eventual unification of the state was achieved by the gradual extension of *burh* foundation, first by Æthelred and Æthelflæd in Mercia and latterly by Alfred's son, Edward the Elder, and his grandson, Athelstan, in East Anglia and in Northumbria.

The *burhs* of Wessex are recorded in the document known as the *Burghal Hidage* which probably dates from the years between 914 and 918.[202] Thirty-three *burhs* are listed, thirty in Wessex and three (Buckingham, Warwick and Worcester) outside the borders of the kingdom. London is omitted – it belonged technically, and by Alfred's respect for tradition, to Mercia[203] – and also Kent. The number of hides belonging to each *burh* is quoted and the document ends with a statement showing the number of hides required to provide men to defend a given length of wall.[204] It reads like a summary of existing practice and may have been drawn up as a guide for use in the shiring of West Mercia towards the end of Edward the Elder's reign.[205]

The *Burghal Hidage* does not reveal the great variety of the *burhs* it lists. Situation, site, size, and hence function, differed widely and can best be revealed by an outline classification.[206] The basic distinction is between the burghal towns and the burghal forts. Both classes on occasion made use of pre-existing defences, but there the resemblance ended. Burghal towns were relatively large and even today their streets still display traces of an original planned layout.[207] Burghal forts were relatively small and do not seem ever to have been organized internally on regular lines.[208]

A *Burghal towns*

   (i) Re-used Roman walled towns

Winchester[209]	2,400 hides[210]	58.2 ha
Chichester[211]	1,500 hides	40.5 ha
Bath[212]	1,000 hides	9.5 ha
Exeter[213]	734 hides	?

   (ii) New towns on open sites: rectangular perimeter

Wallingford[214]	2,400 hides	41 ha
Wareham[215]	1,600 hides	37.2 ha
Cricklade[216]	1,500 hides	29.2 ha
Oxford[217]	1,400 hides	?

   (iii) New towns on promontory sites: irregular perimeter[218]

Wilton	1,400 hides
Lewes	1,300 hides
Malmesbury	1,200 hides
Bredy (? Bridport)	760 hides
Shaftesbury	700 hides
Langport	600 hides
Watchet	513 hides
Twyneham (Christchurch)	470 hides

Axebridge	400 hides
Lydford[219]	140 hides
Lyng[220]	100 hides

B *Burghal forts*

(i) Re-used Iron Age or Roman forts

Chisbury[221]	700 hides
Hastings[222]	500 hides
Portchester	500 hides
Pilton	360 hides
Halwell	300 hides
Southampton[223]	150 hides

(ii) New forts

Sashes[224]	1,000 hides
Burpham	720 hides
Eashing[225]	600 hides
Eorpeburnan[226]	324 hides

C *Unclassified*

Southwark[227]	1,800 hides

We are concerned here only with those places in category A. Of the remainder, Hastings and Southwark later became urban, but nothing certain is yet known of their probably very different burghal origins; while at Southampton, despite contrary views,[228] the *Burghal Hidage* fort seems most probably to have utilized the site and surviving defences of Roman *Clausentum*,[229] and thus to have lain apart and distinct from the urban centres of Anglo-Saxon Hamwih and medieval Southampton. This restricted view does not imply that the burghal forts are of little relevance to studies of the burghal town. Both in detail, as for example in the types of their defensive structures, and in general, in their tactical siting and underlying strategic purpose, they need to be studied together. But for present purposes, and with all too little yet known of the forts themselves, the towns may be taken alone.

The *defences* of the *burhs* have recently been reviewed at some length,[230] but it may be useful briefly to recapitulate the Wessex evidence available up to 1974. Excavations at the four Roman walled towns whose sites were re-used (group A (i) in the list above) have not so far produced evidence for a general refurbishing of their defences at this period.[231] The length of the defences examined has been minimal in relation to their total extent,[232] but it seems unlikely that traces of a major works programme of this date would not have been found, had it ever taken place. The Roman stone walls were probably still standing sufficiently high above ground to require no more than repairs to their stonework. Such repairs would have left no trace below ground and have so far not been identified in such parts of the standing walls as still survive and are unchanged by later medieval alterations.[233] The ditches outside the walls probably needed complete recutting as part of the restoration programme, but evidence of this may often have been destroyed by the much wider ditches of the later middle ages. There are traces at some of the *de novo burhs*, as we shall see, for a double ditch system. Both excavation and documentary evidence suggests that such a system once existed at Winchester, with an outer flat-bottomed ditch, 8.2 m wide and 1.7 m deep, some 40 m in advance of the wall, all trace of an inner ditch having been destroyed by the later city ditch.[234] Our current knowledge of the gates of these towns in the late ninth or early tenth century is almost equally un-informative. Roman gates may have survived in use, as the south gate of Exeter[235] and the east gate of Chichester;[236] but both may have been early medieval replacements, a possibility that is strengthened by the recognition of Anglo-Saxon stonework surviving to a height of 5 m in the west gate at Winchester.[237]

The situation at the newly created *burhs* (groups A (ii) and (iii) in the list above) is by definition entirely different and it is from these sites that most of our knowledge of Wessex fortifications of the late ninth and early tenth centuries is derived. The ramparts were initially of earth or earth and turves, of dump construction, with varying amounts of wooden reinforcement. Stone walls appear invariably to have been additions. The work was probably undertaken by gangs in successive lengths, but evidence for this has so far only been recorded at Lydford, where the sections were about 7 m long.[238] As might be expected, the banks seems to have been abruptly scarped at the front and gently sloped to the rear. A width of perhaps 12 m and an original height of 3 m seem to have been normal. The main problem concerns the amount and nature of the timber reinforcement. Although it was initially expected – on what now seem chronologically very uncertain if not positively anachronistic grounds – that the ramparts of these *burhs* would have been formed within massive timber frames of the kind typified by Danish forts of the Trelleborg type, evidence for this has not been forthcoming in Wessex. The vertical timbering found at Wallingford in 1965 seems to have formed only a rather slight and irregular reinforce-ment;[239] the very substantial upright timbers found at Lydford in the same year and in 1964 have not been shown to continue round the *enceinte* and may have indicated the emplacement of interval towers;[240] no such timbering has been found at Cricklade,[241] Wareham,[242] Wilton[243] or Twyneham.[244] Wood does seem, however, to have been used on occasion to provide a foundation of beams or planks at right-angles to the line of the defences, and to form a strapping of saplings or branches alternating with layers of soil and serving to bind the whole mass together.[245] Turves seem also to have been used for this purpose and to form the rear and perhaps front revetment of the ramparts.[246] Radford has suggested that the Cricklade bank was strengthened at the front by a massive timber revetment, but the limited extent of the individual cuttings through the bank does not seem to allow for any certainty.[247] Dump construction with some wooden strapping and turf revetment seems to be as far as we can go on present evidence. It is likely that the ramparts were crowned with timber palisades, but direct evidence for this has not so far been found.

Evidence for the ditches outside the ramparts is available from several sites, notably Wareham, Cricklade and Lydford. All three sites have provided suggestions of a double-ditch system with an outer ditch some 50 m or more in advance of the rampart.[248] There is no evidence that these outer ditches are contemporary with the initial ramparts, but the possible outer ditch at Winchester mentioned above was certainly silted up by the early twelfth century and at Cricklade the evidence suggested a similarly early date.[249] At Cricklade the inner ditch of the second phase was some 3 m wide and 1 m deep and was separated from the rampart by a berm 6 m in width:[250] the early ditch seems to have occupied the same position and can have been no larger. The ditch of this phase at Wareham had been removed by a later ditch, but may be represented by a truncated, flat-bottomed cut just outside the latter; if so, it must also have originally been separated from the front of the rampart by a berm of about 6 m.[251]

Little is yet known of the gates provided for the new *burhs*, but they were probably of timber, at least initially.[252] A feature of several of these places, and of the *burhs* of Roman origin, is the presence of churches or chapels close to or even over the gates. Although the structural evidence sometimes shows that these churches are of pre-Conquest origin,[253] we do not yet know if they were ever original features, nor the precise reason for this widespread and interesting relationship.

The defences of the late ninth- or early tenth-century Wessex *burhs* were thus major public works with earthen ramparts strengthened on occasion with turf and wooden strapping, presumably crowned with timber palisades, and fronted by a ditch system which on some sites at least recalls the sophisticated multiple-ditch systems of the Roman period, with their tactical purposes of breaking up and trapping enemy formations.

The internal arrangement of these defended places displays, not suprisingly, a comparable sense of purpose and underlying unity of concept. It has already been suggested in discussing the possibility of an early planned town at Hereford that the deliberate organization of space is the critical factor in any planned layout.[254] Those of the Wessex *burhs* of the late ninth century which were intended to develop as towns were apparently provided from the start with a regular arrangement of streets that served to divide the ground enclosed by the defences into blocks capable of being further divided for permanent settlement. At the same time the streets ensured ready access from and to each part of the town and secured an easy and rapid approach to any point of the defences in time of need.

The characteristic pattern of a Wessex street layout of this period can best be defined by examining the plan of Winchester.[255] The Winchester street system comprises the following components (fig. 3.1):

(i) a pre-existing east–west thoroughfare, High Street;
(ii) a single back street parallel to High Street on either side;

(iii) a series of regularly spaced and parallel north–south streets at right-angles to High Street;

(iv) an intra-mural or wall street running around inside the entire circuit of the walls, linking the ends of High Street and the north–south streets.

When this system was first described in detail in 1971, insufficient emphasis was placed on the wall-street which subsequent excavation has shown to be an integral and original element of the system.[256] Recent work has shown that the streets as a whole originally extended over the south-east quarter of the city but were later obscured by the foundation of New Minster in 901–3, and by the extension of the monastic precincts in the 960s and of the royal palace *c*. 1070.[257] A radiocarbon date of A.D. 880 $\pm$ 60 (HAR 295), recalibrated to A.D. 902 $\pm$ 60, for the occupation on the earliest of the eight successive street surfaces sealed by the construction of Winchester Castle in 1067, suggests that even at the periphery of the system the streets belonged to the original layout. This view is supported by the observation that the first surfaces of all the streets so far excavated were formed of small broken flints distinct from the varied materials used in later resurfacings. It looks as if flints were stockpiled and knapped for the initial laying of the 8.6 km of surfacing involved, a task which required something like 8,000 metric tonnes of flint cobbles.

The realization that the wall-street formed an original component of the whole layout shows that the defences and the street system cannot be seen in isolation, but must be regarded as part of a single operation designed to provide a large defended enclosure in which the internal area was logically subdivided for apportionment and ease of movement on interior lines. The wall-street is a constantly recurring feature of the street plans of the large rectangular *burhs*, whether these are of Roman origin or occupy essentially new sites (groups A (i) and (ii), above).[258] This feature is not found in Romano-British town plans, as distinct from those of forts or fortresses, and emphasizes the initially military purpose of the Wessex *burhs*.

The significance of the back streets also requires some comment. They have frequently been obscured by later development, but in Winchester where they are well preserved the back streets run parallel to the principal thoroughfare of High Street. It is possible that this may prove to have been a consistent feature elsewhere and thus serve to define the principal axis of the pre-Conquest town. The function of the back streets was perhaps to provide rear access to important properties lining the main street, for the latter probably served in most cases, as at Winchester, for a market.

Street plans of the Winchester type occur not only in walled towns of Roman origin (group A (i)), but also in the new foundations of Wareham, Wallingford, Cricklade and perhaps Oxford (group A (ii)). In the former Roman towns only the main thoroughfares reflect any aspect of the Roman system and these facts together with the dating evidence available for Winchester show that street plans of this type are new creations of the Alfredian period. Their possible antecedents in Wessex and Mercia have already been suggested in the discussion of Southampton and Hereford.

It is evident that some of the promontory *burhs* (group A (iii)) possessed street plans similar in all essentials to plans of the Winchester type just discussed. Archaeologically the best known of these is Lydford (fig. 3.4).[259] A main thoroughfare follows the spine of the promontory; remnants of a parallel back street can be seen to the north of the main street; there is archaeological evidence for property divisions and paths on the same alignment; and there is a surviving wall-street behind the eastern rampart cutting off the neck of the promontory. This rampart was probably once continuous around the town, but there is no indication that the wall-street continued beyond its present limits behind the most vulnerable defensive line. D. H. Hill's plan of Lyng shows a spine road, side-streets at right angles, and possible traces of a wall-street behind the cross-promontory rampart.[260] There is no trace of the back streets and their absence may prove to have been characteristic of the smaller places.

Those of the Wessex *burhs* of the late ninth century large enough to have been provided with a planned layout display a remarkably consistent pattern. Whatever the physical constraints of their site, whether within Roman walls, on a narrow promontory, or on an open and unencumbered area, the same elements occur. It is not therefore surprising that the adjustments made perhaps in Athelstan's reign, when Barnstaple and Totnes seem to have replaced Pilton and Halwell, and Dorchester was refounded, appear to have followed much the same lines. It has also been suggested that the shift of Anglo-Saxon South-ampton from Hamwih to a site on the western shore by the Test was marked by the setting out of a new plan some time in the tenth century.[261]

Our current knowledge of the archaeology of the burghal towns is a skeleton of streets and defences. We know very little yet of the way in which that skeleton was fleshed out with yards and gardens, houses, churches and other structures to form the living town. Our ignorance of these things during the tenth century is almost complete; only towards the end of that century and during the eleventh can we begin in a few places to see the outlines of a fuller picture. It is unfortunate that so much of our available information comes from Winchester, for that city was probably exceptional and may provide no sure guide to the situation elsewhere. By the end of the tenth century Winchester displayed a high degree of internal specialization. There was a sharp distinction between the royal and ecclesiastical area occupying the south-east quarter of the walled city on the one hand, and the areas of ordinary commercial and domestic occupation spreading over the remaining three-quarters of the city on the other (fig. 3.1). Within each area there were further subdivisions. By about 970 the three minsters in the south-eastern quarter had been enclosed by a single boundary wall or fence which separated them from the rest of the city and from the palaces of the king and bishop which each formed a separate enclosure.[262] In the commercial and domestic quarters there were already by the end of the century areas whose special character was sufficiently distinctive to have given rise during the preceding decades to descriptive street-names: Tanner Street, Fleshmonger Street, Shield-wright Street and Ceap Street, to mention only those whose names are recorded before *c*. 1000.[263] When a survey of royal rents and services was drawn up in Edward the Con-

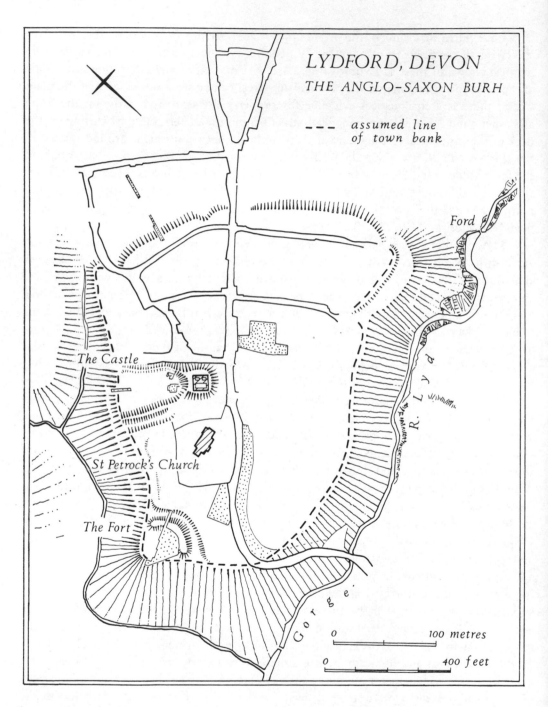

Figure 3.4 Lydford, Devon: plan of the Anglo-Saxon *burh* showing position of church and later fortifications (after Addyman in Radford (1970) fig. 35)

fessor's reign (perhaps *c*. 1056–9) this tendency towards the concentration of certain activities in specific areas of the city was even more marked.[264] A century later this tendency can be traced in some detail from information provided by the survey of 1148.[265] The location of some of these activities is conditioned by the availability of water, either as a source of motive power, or as a necessary element of such industries as tanning, dyeing or fulling; but the location of other activities was not governed, or need not have been, by any such precise control. The concentration of moneyers in the central areas of High Street, or of butchers near the church of St Peter *in macellis* – in the Shambles – seems to be the result of long-established custom, which can be traced in the case of the butchers back to the late tenth century and was then already old.

The existence of such specializations at so early a date suggests that the growth of population in the newly founded *burhs* was rapid. We know almost nothing about how this was achieved, but the inducements may have included security, tax concessions, low initial rents, and a freedom of tenure that gave rise before the Conquest to a class of burgesses (*burgenses*) who for all practical purposes operated a free property market, buying and selling, renting and leasing, with only small annual sums reserved to superior landlords from each property as a kind of ground-rent.[266]

The Winchester evidence suggests that the land along the new streets of the late ninth-century *burhs* may have been parcelled out to individual lay or ecclesiastical lords in large blocks of perhaps a half hectare each. Each lord seems to have exercised a degree of private jurisdiction over his own block or blocks and in several, perhaps even in many, cases erected a house and private church on one of these properties. In the course of time a block might be considerably subdivided to produce the 'typical' medieval urban pattern of long narrow tenements. From these tenements and from the profits of his private church, the lord would receive an income that would in the course of time decline in real value to the nominal 'landgable' ground-rents already mentioned. Several of these large early blocks can be identified in Winchester and their internal layout can on occasion be reconstructed (fig. 3.1).[267]

One of the striking facts about the English medieval town is the very large number of parishes and parish churches than can be found in towns which were already important in the Anglo-Saxon period. By the late eleventh century London seems to have had over a hundred churches, Norwich forty-six, Lincoln thirty-five, York as many, and Winchester perhaps as many as fifty. Many of these churches must have been founded as private, proprietary churches and have served initially a private residence, subsequently the families living in the properties developed on that tenement, and finally the tiny parishes which arose from such nuclei. There can be little doubt that the urban parish church is one of the most important indicators of the growing importance of towns in later Anglo-Saxon England.[268]

Growth may also be reflected in the emergence and expansion of suburbs outside the principal gates of a town.[269] Little archaeological evidence is so far available on this process until after the Conquest. But the existence of suburban churches of Anglo-Saxon date (such as St Bride, Fleet Street; St Andrew, Holborn; St Botolph, Bishopsgate; and St Botolph, Aldgate) outside the principal gates of London argues for the growth of pre-Conquest suburbs around that city for which there is little other evidence so far.[270] A considerable degree of suburban development at Winchester is suggested by the documentary evidence, and by a gradually increasing amount of archaeological information.[271] Outside West Gate this development was probably under way by the second quarter of the tenth century. It suggests that the walled area was by that time already relatively congested. Study of the origins, expansion and occasional contraction of such suburbs may eventually provide a valuable index to the economic fortunes of pre-Conquest towns. Excavation has a role to play in this inquiry, but the plotting of datable finds recovered from rescue observations, especially pottery, should be equally fruitful.[272]

The planned towns of Alfredian Wessex, as they have been defined by the research of the last fifteen years, mark a significant stage in the development of the English town. As far as we can see at present they were also a watershed in European urban evolution. Nowhere else north of the Alps at this date, or perhaps for another two centuries, was so extensive an effort of town plantation to be undertaken on royal initiative and on so clearly regulated a basis. It is therefore important to stress that the origins of this type of planned town may also be insular, and the examples of Southampton and Hereford have been quoted to show the experience which may have lain behind the developments of Alfred's reign. The very fact that the setting up of towns on this scale was then contemplated is an indication of the expectations men then held of their potential success.[273] Many of the Wessex *burhs* were in the event relatively successful, and some like Oxford and Winchester were spectacularly so. They provided also the pattern for the establishment of the Mercian *burhs* of the early tenth century and for Edward the Elder's foundations in the Danelaw. They appear as another reflection of the administrative ability of a community that was evolving a highly efficient coinage and was about to embark on the shiring of Mercia and the eastern midlands.

The extension of the burghal system

Between 907 and 915 Æthelred of Mercia and subsequently his wife Æthelflæd established a series of defended places for the protection of Mercia. Like the *burhs* of Wessex, these places cannot be described simply as fortresses for they included places like Chester (907), Tamworth (913), Stafford (913) and Warwick (914), which must on account of their size and subsequent development be regarded as town foundations.[274] The recorded works of 907–15 were not the only developments of this kind of the same general period in Mercia. Some time between 887 and 899 Æthelred and Æthelflæd had fortified Worcester at the bishop's request and the terms of the charter in which this is made clear show that an urban community was intended or was already in existence.[275] Archaeological evidence has yet to define the extent and character of this *burh*.[276] Gloucester was probably re-fortified at about the same time,[277] and here it was apparently the walls of the Roman *colonia* that were refurbished and within which a planned street system of 'Winchester' type was laid out.[278] At Hereford the earlier defended area seems to have been enlarged eastwards at this period,[279] the entire circuit of the defences remodelled, and the street layout extended over the 7.5 ha of the new enclosed area.[280] The new rampart enclosed a total area of about 21 ha. The rampart was constructed of clay strengthened with turf and strappings of branches, and was originally timber-faced, attaining a width of some 7 m and an original height of perhaps 3 m.[281] It was rapidly reinforced by the addition at the front of a massive stone wall which has been found intact up to a height of 2 m.[282] The method of construction of the rampart, and its subsequent reinforcement by a stone wall, are closely parallel to what is known of the ramparts of the new Wessex *burhs* of this period or slightly earlier.[283]

Of the ten *burhs* that were certainly the work of Æthelflæd, Chester and Tamworth have produced evidence for defences of this period.[284] At Chester, as at Gloucester, it was the Roman perimeter which was restored and within which at least the elements of a street layout were organized.[285] Excavation along the western defences of the legionary fortress in Linenhall Street in 1961–2 uncovered on the back of the Roman rampart a continuous narrow gully some 3 m from the inner face of the fortress wall and punctuated at intervals by deep square-cut pits.[286] Dating evidence was scanty: one sherd suggested that one of the post-pits, if that is what they were, had been filled up in the early thirteenth century at the earliest. This need only date the demolition or decay of the timbers, however, and the excavator suggested with some justification that the gully and pits were the emplacement for a palisade with massive vertical timbers at intervals. Since the defences on this line were perhaps out of use by the twelfth century, owing to the expansion of the city westwards to the Roodee, a late Saxon date for the timber refurbishing – and hence almost certainly its dating to Æthelflæd's work of 907 – becomes probable.

The Chester evidence must be compared with the results from Tamworth. These show quite clearly that the town was defended in the late Saxon period, probably as a result of Æthelflæd's works of 913, by a timber-framed turf rampart some 9 m wide, fronted by a 6 m berm beyond which lay a ditch 4 m wide and 2 m deep.[287] These defences enclosed three sides of a rectangular area some 20 ha (50 acres) in extent, the fourth side of which was formed by the River Anker.[288] Tamworth provides the clearest example so far known in England of a timber-framed rampart of the kind which it had once been expected would be normal for the late Saxon *burh*.[289] As we can now see, it is exceptional, the normal rampart being of dump construction with relatively slight wooden strapping, usually perhaps of branches, and turf or possibly timber revetment. Why Tamworth should appear exceptional is at present quite unknown. The wide berm, by contrast, is exactly paralleled by the available Wessex examples.[290]

The consolidation of the defences of Mercia provided the basis for Edward the Elder's reconquest of the rest of England south of the Humber in the years between 911 and 919, 'one of the best-sustained and most decisive campaigns in the whole of the Dark Age'.[291] Among the places Edward fortified were Bedford (915), Buckingham (914), Colchester (917), Hertford (912), Huntingdon (917), Maldon (916), Manchester (919), Nottingham (918, 920), Stamford (918), Thelwall (919), Towcester (917) and Witham (912).[292] As with the *burhs* of Wessex, so too the Edwardian *burhs* of the reconquest include places of very varied character. Stenton wrote that 'little is known about the plan or scale of the fortresses on which the war had turned', but that they 'were intended to be held by divisions of the national militia, and ... in area resembled the medieval town rather than the medieval castle'.[293] With a few exceptions, including the two unidentified sites, we may perhaps suspect that their size reflected rather the intention to establish places whose future, on the model of the larger Wessex *burhs* (my group A, above), was intended to be secured by the very fact of their being relatively populous places.

All too little is yet known of most of these places, but the Chronicle itself provides information of the first importance about their character. In five places we are dealing with double *burhs*, one to each side of a river. At Hertford in 912 boroughs were made north and south of the Lea.[294] At Buckingham in 914 'both the boroughs, on each side of the river' were built.[295] At Bedford the following year Edward obtained the existing borough and ordered another to be built on the south side of the river.[296] At Stamford in 918 a borough south of the river was again added to an existing northern borough.[297] At Nottingham the borough was captured and repaired in 918, and in 920 Edward ordered the building of 'the borough on the south side of the river opposite the other, and the bridge over the Trent between the two boroughs'.[298] The second boroughs cannot be siegeworks, for their construction is apparently always contemporary with their fellows, or is consequent upon Edward's capture of an existing place. It seems more likely that their purpose was to control the river by setting fortified works to either side which would be linked by a bridge as at Nottingham and thus command the passage up or down stream. That this could be the function of such double works is made clear by a vivid passage in the annal for 895:

> then one day the king rode up along the river [the Lea] and examined where the river could be obstructed, so that [the Danes] could not bring the ships out. And then this was carried out: two fortresses [*tu geweorc*] were made on the two sides of the river.[299]

Double fortifications linked by bridges played an important role in Frankish campaigns against the Northmen, for example in the siege of Paris in 885–6. Continental references to bridgeworks pre-date the known English examples and it has been inferred that these may reflect Frankish influence.[300] Whether or not this was the case, the use of bridgeworks or at least of double *burhs* was clearly an important element in Edward the Elder's campaigns. To the documented examples, London[301] and perhaps Cambridge[302] should probably be added.

Not all Edward's fortifications were on new sites: Colchester was repaired in 917[303] and Manchester in 919. This presumably refers to the Roman walls of Colchester and may refer also to the Roman fort at Manchester, rather than to a new site above the River Irwell, but if the latter was in existence before 919, then it may have been the work that was then repaired.[304] Certainly at Huntingdon in 917 and Nottingham in 918 the repairs must have been made to Danish works of no great age.[305] One reference in the Chronicle is of particular interest: the *burh* at Towcester was occupied and built in 917 and later in the same year, but perhaps as a continuation of the same operation, it was provided with a stone wall. As we have seen, the Wessex and Mercian *burhs* founded on new sites were as far as we can tell initially defended by earthen ramparts with turf or timber revetments; stone walls appear invariably as later additions and can rarely be dated with any precision.[306] Earthen defences, as Renaissance military engineers constantly found to their cost, decay with disconcerting suddenness. At Hereford the evidence suggested that the timber revetment of the early tenth-century rampart was replaced in stone relatively soon after its construction.[307] The Towcester reference may indicate that stone walls were becoming more usual by the second decade of the tenth century, although the very fact of its being mentioned at all can perhaps be taken to suggest that stone walls were still the exception.

Very little indeed is yet known of the internal arrangement of Edward the Elder's foundations. Elements of regular planning can perhaps be detected at Beford,[308] Stamford[309] and Colchester,[310] but at Nottingham the street layout may be an organic growth around a pre-existing east–west axis of very early origin.[311] Very few of these places are at all adequately documented in the pre-Conquest period and knowledge of their layout and growth can only come from excavation.

Later developments

The half century following 880 saw a rapid expansion in the number of English towns, from perhaps ten at the beginning of the period to some fifty urban settlements by about 930.[312] Most of the new foundations had been established for military as much as for commercial reasons, but these functions were intimately related, for only by securing a permanent population could towns of this size be effectively defended and their walls maintained. Some adjustments became necessary in the light of experience, the burghal forts at Pilton and Halwell being replaced, for example, by the commercially more effective situations of Barnstaple and Totnes; but on the whole the initial arrangements must have reflected real needs surprisingly well, for nearly all the towns (as opposed to the forts) founded in this period still exist today and include many of the southern and midland county towns.

Because of the conditions under which they came into being, these were defended towns, established by a single controlling authority, the king, or by a quasi-royal agent such as Æthelflæd, and having a clearly defined moment of foundation or refoundation. By contrast, the towns which came into being during the last century of the Anglo-Saxon state seem on the whole to have been the result of the general expansion of economic life and to have emerged more gradually. They were usually undefended and seem rarely to exhibit any degree of deliberate planning, as might indeed be expected given their essentially uncontrolled genesis.

The pressures which gave rise to these towns must have been gathering momentum by the middle of the tenth century, if not before, for nothing so clearly demonstrates their emergence as a comparison of mints at work before the reform of the coinage in 973 with those places in which coins were struck after that date.[313] Twenty-seven mints are known to have produced coins for Eadgar between his accession in 959 and the reform in 973. Of these, only Derby, Northampton, Shrewsbury and Thetford are not among the towns whose foundation or fortification is recorded earlier in the century, and in the case of the first three this is probably the result only of the silence of the records. Between 973 and Eadgar's death in 975 forty mints are known, a figure which is probably an underestimate due to the relatively low survival rate of coins of the 'Reform' type. Of these mints, twelve are places not earlier recorded as towns. A further thirty mints can be added from the last quarter of the tenth century. By the year 1000 there were thus some seventy mints in operation and it can be argued that this was broadly the pattern intended at the time of the reform of 973. Some eighteen further places may be added by way of changes and additions in the years up to 1066. There are 'a few mints which seem never to have been boroughs, and ... boroughs where coins seem never to have been struck',[314] but with this reservation the mints give a useful indication of the location and distribution of the boroughs. 'Of all the possible tests of borough status the possession of a mint is in many ways the most satisfying and complete.'[315] With these points in mind, the distribution of late Anglo-Saxon mints indicates the spread of urban places over the whole of lowland England south of a line from the Humber to Shrewsbury and to such a density that few areas were more than fifteen miles from a town.[316]

The documentary evidence for the institutional, legal and social development of the late Anglo-Saxon town was fully surveyed by Tait[317] and the whole field of recent research has been recently reviewed by Loyn.[318] We are concerned here with what is at present known of their physical character and development. It must be admitted at once that our knowledge is still very slight. The great increase in our understanding of the Anglo-Saxon town that has taken place in recent years has been concerned with the defences and street systems of the planned foundations, matters which are relatively easy to deal with compared with tracing the evolution of unplanned settlements or following the subsequent growth of the earlier planned foundations. Archaeologically the best known of these later settlements is Thetford.[319] The Saxon town lay on the south bank of the Little Ouse and was abandoned during the eleventh century when settlement shifted to the Norfolk side of the river. First recorded in 870, Thetford developed as a trading town and had a mint by the reign of Eadgar. It may have had a population of over four thousand and at least eight churches by the time of Domesday Book, but its expansion seems to have ceased by this date and it may already have been declining. The town was defended on the landward side by a line of bank and ditch which stretched for about a mile along the south bank of the river. Excavations undertaken between 1948 and 1958 demonstrated the extent of the town and revealed a peripheral area close to the defences with one large house and other small buildings straggling irregularly along narrow cobbled roads. There was considerable evidence for metalworking and other industrial activities. Much more important were the excavations of 1964–6 which uncovered a single block of rather more than a hectare in the western part of the town (fig. 2.4).

The growth of this area seems to have been sudden and the excavator thought that it might have been 'part of a programme of planned expansion. Large areas of open ground were apparently taken over and divided up into individual properties by narrow boundary ditches.'[320] Nevertheless the variations visible even within the excavated area makes it, in the excavator's own words, 'dangerous to generalize even about this one part ... In a town not conditioned by an inherited regular pattern of streets and walls [as at Winchester or Wareham], zoning may well have resulted in differing patterns of settlement through the town.'[321] Perhaps the most striking contrast between the Thetford layout as revealed by the excavated area and a town such as Winchester or York is the apparent lack of built-up street frontages. In this Thetford may be comparable to Anglo-Saxon Southampton, but the warning against generalization from this one area must be underlined.

When the difficulties of interpretation are so great on an open site with a largish area of actual excavation, it cannot be surprising that it is proving quite exceptionally difficult to elucidate the origins and early topography of a densely built-up, living city such as Norwich.[322] The general area of the late Saxon town has been known ever since the early 'fifties when E. M. Jope plotted the distribution of material of late Anglo-Saxon and Viking Age date, and churches known to have existed by the late eleventh century.[323] The bounds of this distribution are well defined by the twelfth- and thirteenth-century defences and it is clear that by 1066 Norwich may have occupied an area of as much as 200 ha. This is comparable to, if indeed it does not exceed, the entire walled area and suburbs of contemporary London, including Southwark.[324] It has been calculated that the population of Norwich was between five and six thousand at this date and that there were twenty-four churches.

It has long been recognized that early Norwich probably coalesced out of a number of separate smaller settlements, two to the north of the River Wensum and three or more on the south bank, close to the line of an east–west Roman road. The westernmost of the southern settlements, on the line of the later medieval defences between St Benedict's and Heigham Gates, has been partly excavated.[325] To the east lay the settlement later known as Westwick, probably focused on St Gregory's Church, and east again there was a fairly large settlement in the area of the present cathedral. Further to the south there may have been another settlement around St Etheldreda's Church. Of these, it was the settlement in the vicinity of the later cathedral, perhaps already specifically known as *Norðwic* by contrast, for example, with Westwick, which emerged as a town in the early tenth century and was the site of a mint by *c.* 930. Two or even three suburbs developed during this century: Pottergate, an ironworking and pottery-producing industrial suburb grew up to the west; the long, straggling suburb of Magdalen Street lay to the north of the river; while a trading suburb may have developed to the south around the church of SS Vaast and Amand, a Flemish dedication.[326]

So much seems a reasonable if partly hypothetical statement. The problems come with any attempt to define the exact location, boundaries and character of these agglomerating communities. Some of the difficulties involved have been raised in relation to Thetford, where there is also the possibility that the eleventh-century town represented a merging of several previously distinct settlements.[327] In these circumstances it is only possible to proceed by the formulation and testing of hypothetical reconstruction and the particular value of the current work of the Norwich Survey is that it is doing just this.[328] It is not necessary here to say more than that their work is proceeding from the observation that the form of the tenth-century settlement in the vicinity of the present cathedral may be preserved in eighteenth- and nineteenth-century maps of Norwich,[329] and may suggest a defended sub-rectangular enclosure in this area with a somewhat regular, although not necessarily planned, street layout. The testing of this hypothesis, and of further hypotheses relating to the location of the possibly defended boundaries of the various suburbs, is proceeding steadily, but has not so far produced confirmatory evidence of the postulated enclosures. A good deal of useful negative evidence has accumulated which conforms to the suggested depositions. The present stage of conjecture need not be detailed: the various hypotheses may have a quite transitory value, but this in no way lessens their importance as an example of the kind of methodology that is required if the evolution of the large, essentially unplanned, settlements like Norwich, Thetford and Ipswich[330] is ever to be properly understood.

Other settlements emerging to importance in this period include Bristol[331] and Northampton,[332] from which increasing information can be expected from work now in progress and the publication of earlier research. No less significant is the consolidation and expansion of the older centres such as London,[333] York and Winchester. Here a particular problem concerns the emergence of fully built-up street frontages, with the 'typical' medieval pattern of long, narrow tenements running back from the street, a process which is well under way in Winchester, for example, in the tenth century[334] and may be even older in York.[335] The foundation of urban churches appears to be a further guide to the intensification of both intra- and extra-mural settlement[336] and implies an historical importance for their investigation which transcends the interest of the structures themselves. The growth of suburbs around these towns is as significant for their status and economic condition in the late Anglo-Saxon period as research within the walls.[337] It is already clear that by this date the Anglo-Saxon towns of Roman foundation had far exceeded the extent of their Roman predecessors, a situation that can be demonstrated at Winchester,[338] York[339] and London,[340] and is probably definable elsewhere when the necessary detailed examination and above all the formulation of the necessary questions have been undertaken.

Defended places were established in the late Saxon period, especially in the troubled conditions of Æthelred's reign. Cadbury,[341] Cissbury[342] and Old Sarum[343] provide possible examples of this development and the recent excavations at Cadbury have produced detailed information about the stone defensive wall, as well as the plan of one of the entrance gates. Old Sarum became an important centre and was only abandoned with the move down into the valley to New Salisbury in the thirteenth century, but the other works were in the event of a more temporary nature. Yet the initial intention may have been different, for the stone defences of Cadbury seem to argue against the description 'emergency *burhs*' sometimes applied to these works.

By the end of the Anglo-Saxon period there were more than a hundred places with some claim to be regarded as towns.[344] The courses by which they had come into being were many and they were themselves places of very varied character. It has been calculated that some 10 per cent of the population lived in towns by the eve of the Conquest. The results of archaeological inquiry in the decades since the last war have provided something of the background for this situation; they have shown that there were many more towns in late Anglo-Saxon England than in Roman Britain and the minority of Anglo-Saxon towns that lay within former Roman walls were now beginning to spread far beyond their earlier limits. This complex network of places of ancient and more recent origin was the foundation upon which the burgeoning movement of town plantation in the Norman and later perods was to be based.[345] It was the heir to the ancient tradition.

Notes

1 Beresford (1967) 273.

2 Ibid.

3 Heighway (1972) § 3.8–10.

4 Ennen (1953) 121; cf. Schledermann (1970) for a wide discussion of the history and problems of urban definition.

5 Ennen (1972) 12.

6 Stephenson (1933) 3–21; Tait (1936) 1–138 *passim*, 339–58.

7 Tait (1936) 130–38.

8 Loyn (1971) 116.

9 Ibid.

10 Brooks (1971), on which see above, p. 121.

11 Sawyer (1968) provides the essential guide to the entire corpus and the bibliography of each charter.

12 Campbell (1973). The failure of this edition to take account of or even to refer to readily accessible work on the medieval topography of Rochester and the identification of its street- and place-names stresses the need to consider the content of the charters, along with their form, in future volumes of what is intended to be their definitive publication. Content in this context may be as decisive for adequate criticism as form, but is all too rarely considered.

13 Hill (1969).

14 Biddle (1975b).

15 Cf. Fellowes Jensen (1973) 6; Biddle (1975b) 231–9. For a study of the pre- and post-Conquest personal names of Winchester by Dr Olof von Feilitzen, see Biddle (1975b) 143–29.

16 Köbler (1973); Andersson (1971).

17 Biddle (1973) 247; see below, p. 114.

18 Freeman (1876) facing 153, 202, 212, 220 and 312 (first edn published 1871); J. R. Green made a similar attempt for Chester, London, Oxford and York in 1883: Green (1883) 437, 441, 451 and opp. 455.

19 Stephenson (1933) pls i–viii.

20 Ibid., 186–214.

21 Maitland (1960), 38–40.

22 Tait (1936).

23 Cf. e.g. Stenton (1970) on Norman London. The second edition of this essay, published by the Historical Association in 1934, was accompanied by a sketch map of London under Henry II prepared by Miss M. B. Honeybourne, but the text of this and subsequent editions made little use of the archaeological evidence, even to regret its poverty. The unwillingness of most English historians to consider the potential rele-

vance of archaeological evidence to their studies has undoubtedly delayed the emergence of archaeology as a central discipline in the study of the post-Roman periods and must partly account for the slow recognition of what I have elsewhere called 'the historicity of archaeology' (Biddle (1971) 392.)

24 Under the editorship of Mrs M. D. Lobel, vol. i (1969): Banbury, Caernarvon, Glasgow, Gloucester, Hereford, Nottingham, Reading and Salisbury; vol. ii (1975): Bristol, Cambridge, Coventry and Norwich; vol. iii (forthcoming): London; vol. iv (forthcoming): Edinburgh, Southampton, Winchester and York; and continuing.

25 Reprinted in Cam (1963) 8, cf. 17–18; see also Addyman and Biddle (1965) 90–100. For an outline of the development of urban archaeology in Britain, see Biddle (1968).

26 Wheeler (1935); see also Wheeler (1927).

27 Jope (1952) 318–22, fig. 1; cf. Green and Young (1968) maps 2 and 3.

28 Jope (1952–3) 106–10, fig. 39; (1956a) passim, fig. 53.

29 Waterman (1959) figs. 3–4; Cramp (1967) pls IV and VI; cf. Ramm (1971) fig. 28 and Ramm (1972) figs on pp. 229, 245 and 251.

30 Addyman and Biddle (1965) figs 12 and 13.

31 See e.g. Grimes (1968) passim, and the results of excavations in war-damaged Canterbury, e.g. Frere (1962b) and (1970).

32 Jope (1952–3).

33 Radford (1973).

34 Sheridan (1973b).

35 R.C.H.M. (1959).

36 Wilson and Hurst (1964), (1965), (1966), (1967) and (1968).

37 Summaries in Biddle (1973) and (1974).

38 Biddle and Hill (1971); Radford (1970).

39 General survey, ed. Heighway (1972), esp. § 3.17–26, 5.50–51, map 3, table 5, fig. 5; for specific towns, see Benson and Miles (1974) §§ 7.4, figs 17 and 18; Biddle and Hudson (1973); Down (1974); Heighway (1974); Shoesmith (1974); Simpson (1973); Tamworth Research Committee (1971); West (1973).

40 Charlesworth's Gregynog Lectures of 1947–8, in so far as they touch on this problem outside the Celtic west, are more in the nature of a catalogue of gains and losses than an inquiry into the processes by which certain features survived: Charlesworth (1949) 64–82.

41 Böhner (1966); Dollinger-Leonard (1958);

Doppelfeld (1970) and (1973); Ennen (1972) 27–45; Jankuhn (1970); Petri (1958) 232–47; Schindler (1973); Schönberger (1973); Vercauteren (1969); Von Petrikovits (1958); Weidemann (1968) and (1972). For a bibliography of work in the Rhineland 1945–72, see Janssen and Janssen (1973) nos 89–102 and passim.

42 Corder (1955); cf. Frere (1967) 255–7, 357–9 and fig. 12 to which Winchester as a town with external towers should now be added.

43 Alcock (1966–7) 231–2; Stevens (1937) 193–4. For the interesting OE glosses castra/fyrdwic, castrum/wic, oppida/heahcæstre (?), castela/wic, see Page (1973); the possibility that OE placenames in ceaster, cæster derive in some cases from a technical meaning or semi-technical usage of castrum, castra in relation to garrisoned towns clearly needs further investigation. A possibly cognate case may be the derivation of some occurrences of OE burgh, burh from late Latin burgus, 'fort, fortlet, fortified post', used in a technical sense. I am grateful to Dr Graham Webster for making this point to me.

44 Frere (1967) 359. See also B. R. Hartley in Wacher (1966) 52–3.

45 Martin (1969) esp. 419ff.; and cf. Frere (1971) 18–19.

46 Ward (1973) 255.

47 Frere (1966) 98–100; see now further Haberl with Hawkes (1973).

48 Frere (1966); cf. Frere (1960) and (1962a) for Verulamium and Dorchester respectively; and for Dorchester, see now also Dickinson (1973) and (1974) and Benson and Miles (1974) 91–4.

49 Alcock (1971) esp. 166–96.

50 Biddle (1975a).

51 Hawkes and Dunning (1961) and (1962–3); Hawkes (1974).

52 G. N. Clarke in Biddle (1970a) and Biddle (1975d).
    Roman Canterbury, see Frere (1962b), and for early Anglo-Saxon Canterbury, see Hawkes (1969).

54 Frere (1962a) 147–9.

55 Crummy (1974) 23–5.

56 Cunliffe (1970) 67–72.

57 Biddle (1973) 233–7.

58 Myres (1969) 62–99; for the Anglo-Saxon cemeteries outside the walls of Venta Icenorum (Caistor-by-Norwich), and for an important discussion of their significance, see now Myres and Green (1973) esp. 12–15, 31–4, 43–71.

59 The separateness of the contemporary Romano-

British and Anglo-Saxon communities at Caistor (Myres and Green (1973) 12–15) may be paralleled at Colchester (Crummy (1974) 24), but contrasts with their apparent fusion as seen in the Lankhills cemetery at Winchester.

60 Biddle (1973) 237–41; (1975a).

61 Ramm (1971) 185–7; cf. Hope-Taylor (1971).

62 Doppelfeld (1973) 118–21.

63 Schindler (1973) 146, 148.

64 Biddle and Hudson (1973) § 4.31.

65 Biddle (1973) 237–40, fig. 2, nos 1 and 4.

66 Heighway (1974) §§ 3.3–7, 17–22.

67 The evidence has been conveniently surveyed in Higgitt (1973). See now also Hunter (1974) (useful, but archaeologically out-of-date). For the wider background of the influence of Roman traditions on the Anglo-Saxons, see Deanesley (1943).

68 Cotton (1962) and Crummy (1974) 26–33, for the survival of buildings in Colchester; Biddle (1975) 303–10, for a Winchester example. For the exceptional case of Wroxeter, where the re-use may have followed immediately on disuse, see Barker (1973). For one among many examples of major Roman buildings robbed in the tenth or eleventh centuries, see Frere (1970) 108–11.

69 Elisséeff (1970) 170–3.

70 Thompson and Whitwell (1973).

71 Latest comment in Crummy (1974) 18.

72 Frere (1962b).

73 Fox (1968) 13.

74 Biddle (1975d).

75 Colvin (1958) 53, figs 13–16.

76 Biddle and Hill (1971) 70; Biddle (1975b) 260–68.

77 Frere (1962b); (1966) fig. 19; (1970) 83, fig. 1.

78 Biddle and Hudson (1973) § 4.31, 36.

79 Grimes (1968) 29, 39, 204n.; and cf. above, p. 106.

80 Böhner (1966), a fundamental paper of exceptional importance as a guide to the kinds of continuity that might be encountered in English towns.

81 Myres (1969) 89; Biddle (1975a); for the latest finds from Silchester, see Boon (1959).

82 Ennen (1972) 39; for a comment on the English evidence, see now Keen (1975) with particular reference to Southampton, a most movable place which has shifted four times if the post-World War II move to Above Bar is included.

83 Hawkes (1969), Biddle (1971) 394–6.

84 Biddle (1973) 237–42; Biddle (1975a).

85 *Interim*, i (1974), 20–23.

86 Böhner (1966) 314–15; Doppelfeld (1970), (1973); Schindler (1973).

87 Böhner (1966); Borger (1972); Ennen (1972) 38–9, 42; Haberl and Hawkes (1973); Weidemann (1968) and (1972).

88 Cf. e.g. Gould (1972–3).

89 The British kingdom of Elmet was not conquered by Deira until the second quarter of the seventh century, for example, so that a Christian tradition could have survived there unbroken. Thomas (1971) 13–20; Faull (1974) 1, 7–8, 21–25.

90 Levison (1941); for the date, see Morris (1968); for discussion and further references, see Painter (1971) 168, n. 3.

91 *Journal of the British Archaeological Association*, 1st ser., 3 (1848) 330–31.

92 Page (1920) 49–51.

93 Levison (1941) 338–9, 358, first made the comparison with Xanten and Bonn; for the bibliography of the Xanten excavations, see Hellenkemper (1972) 22.

94 Bibliography in Hellenkemper (1972) 21.

95 Frere (1960), (1966); for a general account of Verulamium, see Frere (1964a), (1964b).

96 Bede, *Historia Ecclesiastica*, i, 7.

97 Cf. Mainz and Metz: Weidemann (1968) and (1972).

98 Taylor and Taylor (1965) 143–5; Jenkins (1965); Grierson (1952–4) 41–2.

99 Biddle and Hudson (1973) § 4.18, 29.

100 This matter has never received any general study and a complete survey is needed. Cases can be found wherever stone-walled forts were constructed, e.g. Caerleon, Caer Gybi (Holyhead), Caerhun, Llandovery and Loughor in Wales; Bewcastle, Brampton Old Church, Burgh-by-Sands, Stanwix, on or close to the western part of Hadrian's Wall; Doncaster, Ebchester, Lancaster, Piercebridge, Ribchester and Scarborough in the northern area; and all the Saxon shore forts except Lympne and Brancaster. The examples are very varied and sometimes only a church seems to be involved. It is not suggested that its presence implies any Christian continuity, but only that we should ask why the church was built there in the first place. It may in some cases have served an existing community, itself the representative of continuous settlement; in other examples, the church may have been built on what was once official land granted by the authority into whose

hands it had passed; in some cases there may be no significant connection.

The problem is no less real in relation to the smaller towns, as the striking case of the church of St Edmund within the walls of Caistor-by-Norwich clearly shows (Myres and Green (1973) frontispiece and map 1). It is further illustrated by the small walled towns of Ancaster, Horncastle and Caistor in Lincolnshire, the two former with churches dedicated to St Mary, the latter (like Great Casterton in Rutland) with a church of St Peter and St Paul: Hawkes (1946a); and for Caistor particularly, Radford (1946), Rahtz (1960), Parsons (1973). These churches with potentially early dedications might instructively be compared with the association of fifth-century pagan cemeteries with the same walled places (see now Todd (1973) 126–37, esp. 134–3 and fig. 36; and Caistor from Parsons (1973); and cf. Myres (1969) 76, 81). These towns reflect a situation that would be regarded on the Continent, in the Middle Rhine for example, as an indicator of continuous settlement. They form a small and geographically restricted sample of a situation of widespread occurrence in England and Wales and emphasize the need for intensive further study.

101 Boon (1959); Myres (1969) 89; Biddle (1975a).
102 Bede, *Historia Ecclesiastica*, ii, 3.
103 Biddle and Hudson (1973), § 4.24–9.
104 I have argued this in Biddle (1971) 393–6; Biddle (1973) 237–41; and Biddle (1975a).
105 Bonney (1966), (1972).
106 Lombard-Jourdan (1972) surveys the Gallic evidence; for comment on *pomeria*, esp. London, see Rivet (1970); for Silchester in this context, see Biddle (1975a); and for Winchester, Biddle (1973) 240–41, and Biddle (1975b) 255–8.
107 Birley (1963); Mann (1961); cf. Frere (1967) 210–15.
108 Hodder and Hassall (1971); Hodder (1972); Dicks (1972).
109 Hassall (1972), Collingwood and Richmond (1969) ch. 6, Frere (1967) ch. 12, and Rivet (1964) ch. 4 (general); Richmond (1946) *(coloniae)*; Wacher (1966) *(civitates)*; Todd (1970) (small towns). For the late *civitates*, see Stevens (1937) and cf. Rivet (1966) 108–10. For *civitas*-names and their problems, Mann (1963) esp. 782.
110 The evidence available up to 1968–9 is fully reviewed in Addyman and Hill (1968), (1969);

for a more recent summary, see Addyman (1973a); the overall development of the urban settlement and its three sites is surveyed in Keen (1975).

111 The most recent excavations have shown that it cannot now be claimed (*pace* Addyman (1973a) 221–2, 224) that the road network was there in its entirety from the first. Roads excavated in 1973–4 have proved to overlie earlier Anglo-Saxon features including pits: inf. L. Keen.
112 Loyn (1962) 138.
113 Biddle (1973) 246–7 (revised).
114 A number of charters, including forgeries, were dated at Southampton: *in Omtune* 825, *in Homtune* 825, *in loco qui appelatur in Omtune* 826, *in villa regali quae appellatur Hamptone* 840, *in pago qui dicitur Hamtun* 901, 903, *in loco/in celebri loco qui dicitur Ha(a)mtun* 901, 903: Sawyer (1968) nos 273, 275–6, 288, 360, 366, 369 and 370. Making some allowance for forgeries, there may survive from this period three or four royal charters dated at Winchester and three dated at Southampton: Biddle (1975b) 466). There is no other tradition of a royal centre in Southampton at this time, but it seems likely enough that there was a residence in a place of sufficient importance to have a mint and to give its name to the shire. The area was already a point of embarkation (cf. St Willibald *c.* 721) and arrival, and this might partly account for the presence on occasion of the court.
115 A point made in Keen (1975).
116 E.g. Planitz (1954) 54–5.
117 Köbler (1973) 76.
118 Köbler (1973) 73–4, and cf. above, p. 142, n. 43. The OE compound *wīc-gerēfa* used to describe a royal official in London in 673–85 (?) suggests that OE *wīc* may early have acquired the connotation of market.
119 Hawkes (1969) 191–2.
120 West (1963) 233–7.
121 Ibid., 246–9; Smedley and Owles (1963).
122 West (1973) §§ 6.1–6, 7.4.
123 West (1963) 272, fig. 53, and G. C. Dunning, ibid., 279–86.
124 A good case can be made for attributing the origin and early importance of a trading settlement at Ipswich to the activities of the Wuffinga kings of East Anglia (Scarfe (1972) 98–102; Bruce-Mitford (1974) 80–82). In this case, the relationship of Ipswich on the River Orwell to a royal centre in the Woodbridge (Sutton Hoo,

Rendlesham) area would be comparable to the relationship between Hamwih and Winchester, with the difference that in the Suffolk case the bishop's see was established on a third site, probably the Saxon shore fort at Wallton near Felixstowe (see below, n. 141).

125 Ennen (1964) 800–9; Ennen (1972) 46–52; Jankuhn (1958) 463–72; Jankuhn (1970) 30–2; Jankuhn (1971) 12–13, 26–36; Petri (1958) 248–67; Van Es (1969), (1973).

126 Doppelfeld (1973).

127 For what follows, see Biddle and Hudson (1973) § 4.30–38, with further references and bibliography.

128 Bede, *Historia ecclesiastica*, II.3.

129 Sawyer (1968) no. 168.

130 For the circulation of coin in Offa's Mercia and its significance in commercial terms, especially in relation to the ports, see Metcalf (1967).

131 For what follows, see Cramp (1967) and Ramm (1972) 244–8; and for the current problems of archaeology in York, Addyman (1973b), (1974).

132 Biddle (1973) 239.

133 Hope-Taylor (1971) 39 corrects Ramm (1972) 246, written when the excavations were in an early stage.

134 For Alcuin's description, see *Monumenta Germaniae Historica, Epistolae IV* (1895) 42ff. Altfrid's statement is in his *Vita Liudgeri*, i, 11 (*M.G.H., Scriptores II* (1829) 408, translated in Whitelock (1955) 725), and relates to the period before *c*. 783 when Liudger and the Frisians were forced to leave York (for the date see Levison (1946) 141). The evidence of these two sources is sometimes wrongly conflated, as in Ramm (1972) 246.

135 Radley (1972); R.C.H.M. (England) (1972) 7–9, 58, 111–15 (Tower 19); cf. *Medieval Archaeology*, xvi (1972) 165–7, fig. 48.

136 R.C.H.M. (England) (1972) 7.

137 Dolley (1960a) 45–8.

138 Pirenne (1956), (1957); cf. Havighurst (1958); Latouche (1966) 97–175; and, especially for England, Loyn (1962) 67–79.

139 This view is not held by the more recent writers: Alcock (1971) 201–4 and Thomas (1971) 23–4 place the interruption of these contacts before the Arab seizure of the Straits in 711.

140 Gould (1972–3); and Gould (forthcoming).

141 For the location of the East Anglian see at the Saxon shore fort of Walton Castle, near Felixstowe, see Rigold (1961), (1974).

142 Barker (1968–9) 15–34, 39, esp. M. Wilson on 21–5 with fig. 4.

143 Ordnance Survey (1966). For a detailed consideration of the significance of this observation in relation to Winchester, see Biddle (1973) 237–41.

144 Biddle (1973) 242–7; see also above, p. 114; for the archaeological evidence for a private estate, see Biddle (1975a) 303–10.

145 Hawkes (1969), fig. 2; Taylor and Taylor (1965) 134–48; Urry (1967) 207–8.

146 Stenton (1971) 526–7; cf. Whitelock (1952) 126.

147 Stenton (1971) 527.

148 Brooke (1950) 2–5, 13–21; Dolley (1964) 14–20.

149 For a suggestion that there was no mint in Winchester before the end of the ninth century, see Dolley (1970).

150 Cf. Stenton (1971) 526, and see Ward (1949) for a discussion of the topography of the charters.

151 Campbell (1973) nos 1, 5, 7, 11, 13, 17, 21–4 and 26. The use of *Cæstruuaroualth* in no. 4 and *Cæstersætawalda* in no. 16 does no more than indicate that there were dwellers in the *cæster*; it does not necessarily imply an urban community.

152 Valuable work on the defences of Rochester, e.g. Harrison and Flight (1968); Harrison (1970), will make reconstruction of the Anglo-Saxon topography from the charter evidence more secure, but large-scale area excavation within the defences is needed if the nature of the early Anglo-Saxon community is to be understood.

153 For Dorchester, see now Benson and Miles (1974) 66–9 (map 36), 91–4; Dickinson (1973), (1974). The discovery that the north–south route into Oxford at St Aldate's was probably in use from at least the ninth century (Hassall (1972a), 147–9; (1972b) 10–11) raises the possibility of some relationship between Dorchester and Oxford comparable perhaps to that between Winchester and Southampton. The traditional centre at Dorchester (where the see, interrupted in the 660s, was re-established for Eahlheard in 869–88) and the emerging market centre at Oxford (where the great north–south route from Wessex into Mercia (now the A34(T)) crossed the Thames) were linked by the river. Their contrasting functions and character provide an interesting parallel to the Hampshire centres, a point made by T. G. Hassall in discussion after a paper given at the Council for British Archaeology Working Party on 'The Evolution

of Towns' held at Leamington Spa in November 1974.

154 Noble and Shoesmith (1967); Rahtz (1968a); Shoesmith (1968a), (1970–72), (1972). For a summary of the current situation and full references to earlier work, see now Shoesmith (1974), and for an historical survey and plans, Lobel (1969).

155 Rahtz (1968a) 'Period 5'; for details, see Shoesmith (1972).

156 Rahtz (1968a) 'Period 3'.

157 Rahtz (1968a) 'Period 4'; for what follows, see Lobel (1969) 3, and cf. Shoesmith (1974) n. 2.7 and map 1.

158 Where it was examined in detail in 1972: Shoesmith (1972).

159 The 1967 excavation in Victoria Street showed that a metalled surface ran parallel to the inside of the defences from a date prior to the construction of the tenth-century rampart (Noble and Shoesmith (1967) 55, fig. 2 following p. 70: 'Period II' metalling sealed by rampart of 'Period III'. The latter is the same as Rahtz (1968a) 'Period 5'. This metalling probably represents an intra-mural street along the defences, in which case at least one element of the street plan belongs to the pre-tenth-century layout. Further lengths of the intra-mural street survive as West Street and East Street (formerly 'Behyndethewall Lane', Lobel (1969) 3 and street-name map), but the eastern half of the latter is not earlier than the tenth century since it runs within the eastern extension of that date. See further above, p. 135.

160 It might relate to the boundaries of the king's 'fee', but there is too little evidence to allow speculation: cf. Lobel (1969) 3 and map of 'Anglo-Saxon *burh*'; Shoesmith (1974) § 3.6 (22).

161 Shoesmith (1972) 256 for radiocarbon dates derived from samples taken from the 1968 excavations (Rahtz (1968a)). The results were unsatisfactory and no closer dating is yet available.

162 Gould (1968–9); Sheridan (1973a), 1973b); see also Rahtz and Sheridan (1971–2) fig. 1.

163 Gould (1967–8), (1968–9), 37–8.

164 The passage of Lichfield Street through the western entrance of the Anglo-Saxon *burh* provides the only indication that the street plan is at least in part of Anglo-Saxon origin. The area south of Church Street gives the appearance of a regular layout into which the castle has been inserted, but the situation is complicated by the division of the town between Staffordshire and Warwickshire (Gould (1971–2) 17–18, 25–6, 41–2, fig. 1), and it is clear that only further excavation can now unravel its topographical evolution (cf. Tamworth Research Committee (1971)).

165 Brooks (1971) 82.

166 For a discussion of the concept and of Anglo-Saxon planned towns in general, see Biddle (1975d).

167 Fowler (1971a); Alcock (1971) 209–27; Jones (1972) 288–92.

168 Jones (1972) 358–65.

169 See above, p. 117.

170 Stenton (1971) 212–15. For defended places in early medieval Europe, esp. in the area of present-day Germany, see von Uslar (1964), reviewed in Thompson (1965).

171 I owe to Professor M. R. G. Conzen the suggestion that 'sub-rectangular' should be used, rather than 'rectilinear', to describe the characteristic slightly irregular layout of Anglo-Saxon planned towns.

172 Stenton (1971) 295–7.

173 See above, p. 113.

174 I owe to Professor Conzen the suggestion that 'wall-street' should be used, rather than 'intramural street', to describe the street running along behind the defences of a town. This suggestion finds added support in the use on occasion of the medieval and later street-name 'Wall Street', or variant, for this feature.

175 It is interesting to note that wall-streets do not normally occur in Romano-British towns, whereas the corresponding *intervallum* road is an almost invariable feature in the layout of fortresses and forts.

176 Excavation by C. Young in 1968 on the line of the eastern rampart revealed an early ditch below the late Saxon defences (*Medieval Archaeology*, 13 (1969) 239). If this is a continuation of the early ditch found in 1967 and 1968 on the west side of the town (Gould (1967–1968) 18; (1968–9) 33–5, 37–8), and this is by no means certain, the early enclosure followed the same course as the defences of 913 on the east and west. On the north, however, the early ditch does not appear to follow the same line: Sheridan (1973a), (1973b).

177 See above, p. 121.

178 The identification of the defences of the 'Anglian *burh*' is a classic example of urban topographical study: see Stephenson (1933),

196–7 with further references; Wildgoose
(1961); Barley and Straw (1969) 1–2. For
further discoveries and some indication of the
paucity of the dating evidence, cf. Dawe (1967)
and *Medieval Archaeology*, 15 (1971) 132; 16
(1972) 159–60. Excavation by C. S. B. Young
in 1972 appears to have confirmed the existence
of a defended settlement earlier than the *burh*,
thus opening up the whole question of the
authorship of the successive defences: see
Medieval Archaeology, 17 (1973) 147–8.
179 Mahany (1968). I am grateful to Christine
Mahany for confirming that the problem is still
as real in 1974 as at the time of her stimulating
article in 1968.
180 R.C.H.M. (1972) 8–9, and cf. esp. pp. 58 and
114–15. The R.C.H.M. volume is here (p. 8, n.
2) quoting from Cap. I of the anonymous *Historia Translationum Sancti Cuthberti*, ed. by I.
Hodgson-Hinde, *Symeonis Dunelmensis opera et
collectanea* (Surtees Society, li for 1867 (1868)
158). The *Historia Translationum*, a twelfth-
century source, is at this point entirely depen-
dent on the anonymous mid-tenth-century *Historia de Sancto Cuthberto*, the earliest surviving
MS. of which is of late eleventh-century date
(also in the Surtees edn, p. 144). The latter says
only *Eboracam civitatem reædificavit*, a phrase
less precise than the *Eboracae civitatis
mænia...restauravit* of the derivative *Historia
Translationum*, but probably with the same
meaning. Both texts were re-edited by Thomas
Arnold, *Symeonis Monachi Opera Omnia* (Rolls
Series, 1882–5) i, 204, 229, and their date and
relationship were discussed by Colgrave (1950).
181 R.C.H.M. (1972) 8, and Ramm (1972) 248–9;
for what follows, see Cramp (1967) 14–21;
Ramm (1972) 248–54; Radley (1971); Stenton
(1971) 542–3; and Waterman (1959).
182 Radley (1971) documents evidence for the
working of iron, copper, glass, amber, jet,
antler, bone, leather and wood, and the making
of cloth. For the coinage of York, see Brooke
(1950) 9–12, 33–40, and Dolley (1965) 19–26;
and for an outline of York hoards and their significance, Dolley (1960) 45–8.
183 *Antiquity*, xlviii (1974) 25; Radley (1971) 39–47.
184 Radley (1971) 43–5, fig. 7.
185 Jankuhn (1963).
186 Schietzel (1968), (1974).
187 See, e.g., Jankuhn (1958); Jankuhn (1963) 26–
46, 152ff.; Brøndsted (1965) 149–66; and cf.
Jankuhn (1971) which, although basically con-

cerned with the Baltic, is of wider relevance.
Nor have English scholars made much greater
use of its potential contribution: Sawyer (1971)
168–92; Foote and Wilson (1970) 217–24.
188 See above, p. 135.
189 Bu'lock (1972) 58–65 with further references.
190 The archaeology of post-Roman Chester has
not always received equal attention to that
accorded the legionary fortress. The situation
has shown signs of improvement in recent years,
but a distressing number of sections have been
published blank of all detail above the Roman
layers.
191 As was argued as recently as 1967 in relation to
York.
192 Stenton (1971) 255–7, 264–5.
193 Stenton (1971) 265.
194 Stenton (1971) 258–9; see also Biddle and Hill
(1971) 83, and cf. Biddle (1973) 251.
195 Stenton (1971) 264.
196 For summaries, see Radford (1970) (defences);
Biddle and Hill (1971) (street plans).
197 Stenton (1971) 264 fully realized this variety
but did not seek to define the functional differences which lay behind it. The Chronicle
(*s.a.* 894 (893)) used the word *burga*, which
Stenton (1971) 265 took as 'fortress', but
which can equally be translated 'boroughs':
Whitelock (1955) 185 *s.a.* Stenton also claimed
(loc. cit.) that Alfred's 'contemporary biographer [i.e. Asser] states that he was a builder
of fortresses'. Here Stenton was presumably
referring to the phrase *De civitatibus et urbibus
renovandis et aliis, ubi nunquam ante fuerat, con-
struendis* (Asser, cap. 91) which is best translated
'What of the cities and towns he restored, and
the others which he built where none had been
before?' (Whitelock (1955) 272).
198 Cf. Biddle (1971) 391–3, 397–8, 407–8.
199 Biddle (1964) 215–17.
200 Biddle and Hill (1971) 82–5.
201 Beresford (1967).
202 For a discussion of the manuscripts and the
establishment of the original text, see Hill
(1969). An edition and translation of the Nowell
transcript with variants from four of the other
six manuscripts was published by Robertson
(1939) 246–9, 494–6, but this must now only
be used in conjunction with Hill's reconstructed
text. For further discussion see Hunter Blair
(1956) 292–4; Kirby (1967) 251–3, 255; Loyn
(1962) 133–6; Loyn (1971) 117–18; Maitland
(1960) 577–81; Ordnance Survey (1974) 17–18,

55; Stenton (1971) 265; Stephenson (1933) 61–63, 74, 220; and Tait (1936) 15–20, 24–25, 35.

203 Stenton (1971) 259.

204 See list below.

205 Hill (1969) 92; cf. Stenton (1971) 337.

206 The number of hides allocated to each *burh* gives an indication of size, but is an imprecise guide by comparison with the site itself. See list below.

207 Biddle and Hill (1971).

208 Caution is needed here. Only Portchester has been excavated on any scale, and work in the other forts may yet reveal elements of deliberate military planning.

209 Summary in Biddle (1973) 248–52, with further references; see also Biddle (1974) and Biddle (1975b) 272–7.

210 The hidages follow the restored figures in Hill (1969) 87.

211 Biddle and Hill (1971) 81–2, fig. 2; Down (1974) n. 2.9, 10.

212 Biddle and Hill (1971) 81–2, fig. 3; Greening (1971).

213 Biddle and Hill (1971) 81–2, fig. 3. The hidage is such that only a part of the Roman walled area can have been involved.

214 Brooks (1965–6); Durham *et al.* (1973); Simpson (1973); cf. Biddle and Hill (1971) fig. 4.

215 R.C.H.M. (1959); Biddle and Hill (1971) fig. 4.

216 Radford (1973); cf. Biddle and Hill (1971) fig. 4.

217 Jope (1956); Hassall (1970) 15–18; Hassall (1971b) esp. 44–8; Hassall (1972b) 10–14. The extent of the original enclosure cannot yet be defined.

218 Areas are not given for the remaining *burhs*; their perimeters are too rarely defined, or defined with sufficient accuracy, to make useful comparisons possible at this stage.

219 Addyman (1964–8).

220 Hill (1967a).

221 Brooks (1964) 76–9.

222 The name *Hæstingaceastre* in the *Burghal Hidage* suggests that a Roman site, possibly a walled place, was re-used. If so, it has probably been lost by coastal erosion.

223 Hill (1967b).

224 Brooks (1964) 79–81.

225 Aldsworth and Hill (1971).

226 Brooks (1964) 81–6; Davison (1972).

227 Biddle and Hudson (1973) § 4.42, fig. 9.4.

228 Burgess (1964) 15–16.

229 So in Hill (1967b).

230 Radford (1970).

231 With the possible exception of the strengthening of the blocking of the south gate at Winchester, which could be of this date: Biddle (1975d).

232 Very few sections have been cut through the defences of Bath and Exeter; the Chichester defences have been examined to a greater or less degree at some twelve points: Down and Rule (1971) 7–17; Down (1974a) 33–7; and, casual observations apart, those of Winchester have been examined in some sixteen places.

233 Early re-facing in herringbone flint-work (broadly eleventh century?) has been recognized on the face of the wall at the Weirs in Winchester: Biddle (1975b) 273–4. Detailed structural record and analysis would probably provide further examples.

234 Biddle (1975b) 274–5; cf. Biddle (1975).

235 Fox (1968) 12–13.

236 C. Searle in Down (1974a) 72–4.

237 Biddle (1975b) pt IV.2, vi.

238 *Medieval Archaeology*, x (1966) 168.

239 Brooks (1965–6) 20; cf. *Medieval Archaeology*, x (1966) 168, and especially the informative account of the 1966 excavations in *Medieval Archaeology*, xi (1967) 262–3, 284.

240 *Medieval Archaeology*, ix (1965) 170–71; x (1966) 168–9.

241 Radford (1973) 100–102.

242 R.C.H.M. (1959) 125.

243 Excavations by D. H. Hill (1971).

244 Excavations by D. H. Hill (1971).

245 The clearest evidence is that provided by Lydford: Addyman (1964–8).

246 E.g. at Wallingford, see above, 239. Subsequent excavations have shown that in some areas the primary rampart was constructed almost entirely of turves: Durham *et al.* (1973); cf. Simpson (1973) fig. 8.

247 Radford (1973) 101–2, cf. 63–88.

248 For Wareham, see R.C.H.M. (1959) fig. 46, outside east rampart; Cricklade: Radford (1973) 68–9, 99–100, fig. 12; Lydford: P. V. Addyman, pers. comm.

249 Radford (1973) 68–9, 99–100.

250 Radford (1973) 105–6.

251 R.C.H.M. (1959) fig. 47.

252 A primary timber gate, tentatively suggested following the excavations at Wallingford in 1965 (Brooks (1965–6) 20, and rather more confidently in *Medieval Archaeology*, x (1960) 168), was apparently confirmed by subsequent

excavations: cf. Simpson (1973) 8; but no details have so far been published.

253 E.g. St Michael at the north gate at Oxford, and St Martin at the north gate of Wareham. At Winchester there was apparently a church or chapel dedicated to St Michael at or over the east gate by *c.* 994, and a church over this gate was going out of use by 1148: Biddle (1975) 276. There were also churches over the north gate, a church next to West Gate, and a church which still exists over King's Gate. A recent attempt to interpret the skew alignment of the north chapel of St Mary's Church, Cricklade, as arising from its adoption of the site of a late Saxon gatehouse or chapel at the west side of the north gate (Thompson and Taylor (1966)) is particularly interesting in this context, but has not been without its critics (Radford (1973) 106–8).

254 See above, p. 121.

255 For general accounts of the late Saxon planned town, see Biddle and Hill (1971); and Biddle (1975d). For Winchester in particular, see Biddle (1975b) 277–82, and for the archaeological evidence for the date of the streets, Biddle (1964) 242–3, pl. LXXXII; (1970) 285–289; and (1975d) forthcoming.

256 Biddle and Hill (1971) 73, 76; cf. Biddle (1970) 285–9; (1975d) forthcoming.

257 Biddle (1975b), pt IV.2, vii; cf. Biddle (1975c).

258 Biddle and Hill (1971) 76, figs 2–4. The report of the excavations at Cricklade shows that a wall-street was present there too, but the excavator does not comment upon it: Radford (1973) 102–3 and cf. figs 1–6 with fig. 12.

259 Addyman (1964–8); plan in Radford (1970) fig. 35, after Addyman.

260 Hill (1967a).

261 Addyman (1973a) 227–8.

262 Biddle (1975c).

263 For the early forms of these and other Winchester street-names, see Biddle (1975b) 231–5.

264 Ibid., 459–60 and 427–40.

265 Ibid., 427–40.

266 Ibid., 349–75.

267 Ibid., pt IV.4, ii.

268 Ibid., 329–35, 458–9, 485–6, 488–9; and cf. Rogers (1972).

269 Keene (1975) provides the first survey of suburban growth.

270 Biddle and Hudson (1973) § 4.45, cf. fig. 9.4 and map 3.

271 Biddle (1975b) 465–8.

272 Biddle (1968) 112; cf. Addyman and Biddle (1965) 90–100.

273 Keene (1975) forthcoming.

274 Convenient list in Ordnance Survey (1974) 55. For the political background, Stenton (1971) 324–7.

275 H. B. Clarke and C. C. Dyer in Barker (1968–1969) 28–30.

276 Barker (1968–9) 39.

277 Lobel and Tann (1969) 2.

278 Heighway (1974) paras 3.19–35; *The Antiquaries Journal*, iii, (1972) 67–8; (1974) 15.

279 Probably by 914 and thus an Æthelflædan work, although this is not recorded: Lobel (1969) 2.

280 See above, p. 120, nn. 154 and 158.

281 Rahtz (1968) 243, 'Period 5'; Shoesmith (1972) fig. on p. 258, 'Phase 1'.

282 Shoesmith (1972) 'Phase 2'.

283 See above, p. 128.

284 A recent attempt has been made to define the area and identify the street layout of Warwick: Klingelhöfer (1975). Excavations at Castle Ditch, Eddisbury, in 1935–8 revealed a rebuilding of the inner and outer ramparts and a re-cutting of the ditch that may be attributable to Æthelflæd's *burh* of 914–but we are dealing here with a 4 ha re-used hill-fort, comparable to the Wessex sites of group B (i) in the list on p. 127 above, and not with an urban site: Varley (1950) 2–3, 23–9, 59–63.

285 Bu'lock (1972) 58–64; Thompson (1969) 11–14, fig. 4, with further references; Webster (1951).

286 Thompson (1969) 2–3, 9, 11–14, figs 2 and 3.

287 Gould (1967–8), (1968–9); Sheridan (1973a), (1973b); see also *Medieval Archaeology*, ix (1965) 173, xiii (1969) 239.

288 Rahtz and Sheridan (1971–2) 10, fig. 1.

289 See above, p. 128.

290 See above, p. 129.

291 Stenton (1971) 335, and for an account of the campaign, 324–36.

292 I follow here the dates of the Anglo-Saxon Chronicle as given by Whitelock (1955) 193–99. The list in Ordnance Survey (1974) 55 is incomplete and the dates are erratic. In addition to the places listed here, Edward fortified unidentified sites at *Wigingamere* (917) and *Cledemutha* (921).

293 Stenton (1971) 335, 336.

294 Renn (1971) 3–4, cf. pp. 16–17 and fig. on p. 15.

295 Whitelock (1955) 195.

296 Hill (1970).
297 Mahany (1968).
298 Whitelock (1955) 199.
299 Whitelock (1955) 188.
300 Hassall and Hill (1970).
301 Biddle and Hudson (1973) para. 4.42.
302 Addyman and Biddle (1965) 100, fig. 12.
303 Crummy (1974) 25.
304 Bu'lock (1974).
305 For Nottingham, see above, p. 122.
306 E.g. Wallingford, Wareham, Cricklade and Lydford: see above, pp. 128–9. There may also have been a pre-Conquest wall at Oxford (see Hassall (1971) 46, fig. 5, site 1), but whether it was an addition to an earlier earthen rampart, or integral with it, is unknown.
307 See above, p. 135.
308 Hill (1970) 98.
309 Mahany (1968) fig. on p. 266.
310 Biddle and Hill (1971) 84, fig. 3; but see now Crummy (1974) 25–34.
311 Barley and Straw (1969) 2.
312 Map in Biddle and Hill (1971) fig. 1.
313 Dolley and Metcalf (1961) figs II and III and table 5.
314 Ibid., 147.
315 Loyn (1961) 131.
316 Dolley and Metcalf (1961) fig. III.
317 Tait (1936) 1–138.
318 Loyn (1971).
319 Davison (1967a).
320 Ibid., 194.
321 Ibid., 195.
322 For earlier work on pre-Conquest Norwich, see Jope (1952); Hurst (1963); and a general survey in Green and Young (1968) 8–10. For the recent campaigns of the Norwich Survey, see Carter (1972); Carter and Roberts (1973); and Carter (1974).
323 Jope (1952) 288–91, 318–22, fig. 1.
324 For comparative sketch plans to the same scale, see Biddle and Hudson (1973) fig. 2.
325 Hurst (1963).
326 I follow there the latest suggestions in Carter (1974).
327 Davison (1967a) 189.
328 Carter (1972); Carter and Roberts (1973).

329 See now Campbell (1975).
330 Little is yet known of late Saxon Ipswich, but see West (1963), (1973) paras 2.3, 7.4, 8.1–7.
331 See now Carus-Wilson and Lobel (1975).
332 For an attempt to explain its early topography, see Lee (1953). Recent excavations promise to provide a much firmer basis of evidence: J. Williams.
333 Stenton (1970); Biddle and Hudson (1973) paras 4.39–47, fig. 9.4.
334 Biddle (1975d) forthcoming; cf. Biddle (1973) 252–8 and (1975c) forthcoming.
335 Radley (1971) 40–5; for the general background to York in this period, see R.C.H.M. (1972) fig. on p. 58; Cramp (1957) 16–21; and Ramm (1972) 248–54.
336 See above, p. 133.
337 See above, p. 133–4.
338 Biddle (1974) diagrams on pp. 36–7 and cf. pp. 38–9; see also Biddle (1975d) fig. 21.
339 R.C.H.M. (1972) fig. on p. 58.
340 Biddle and Hudson (1973) fig. 9.
341 Alcock (1972) 194–201.
342 For the post-Roman re-fortification, see Curwen and Williamson (1931). This work is normally dated to the late Roman period, but the evidence appears quite inadequate for any certainty, and in view of the possibility that the earthwork is the site of the mint at SITH(M)ES-TEBYRI in use from c. 1009 to 1023, the case for a late Saxon re-fortification seems tenable: see Dolley and Elmore Jones (1955–7).
343 Dolley and Metcalf (1961) 153; Montgomerie (1947).
344 Heighway (1972) paras 3.17–20, 5.50–51, map 3, table 5 and Appendix I, passim.
345 Beresford (1967) passim. The remarkably regular town plans which have been attributed to the later eleventh century (e.g. Bury St Edmunds: Smith (1951); Ludlow: Archaeologia (1909)) are now no longer the surprising exception that commentators have found them.

4

Ecclesiastical architecture

Bridget Cherry

Part I

Past approaches: the major works

The realization that buildings from the pre-Conquest period are still standing grew slowly, and only after knowledge of later building periods of the middle ages had reached an advanced stage. In the eighteenth century and later, some buildings were described as 'Saxon' to distinguish them from what was obviously Gothic, but these cases almost always turned out on closer investigation to be Norman, that is eleventh or twelfth century in date. However, the name 'Saxon', no doubt through its romantic associations both with national origins and the beginnings of the English church, remained a popular label during the nineteenth century, even when more scholarly investigations had shown that an early date for a church was untenable. The emotional undertones of the study of Anglo-Saxon church architecture is still one of the difficulties with which the student has to contend.

The first serious attempt to distinguish Anglo-Saxon from Norman architecture was Thomas Rickman's *Attempt to discriminate the styles of architecture in England*, first published in 1817 and reprinted frequently throughout the nineteenth century.[1] But as late as 1896 J. T. Micklethwaite, the architect, restorer and enthusiastic student of early medieval architecture, could write (whilst giving credit to Rickman's work) that 'the long and short work, the turned baluster, the "triangular" arch and the rest are now admitted to be indications of a date earlier than the Norman Conquest. We have scarce got further than that.'[2] Micklethwaite's criticism was that identification of certain constructional techniques which are not characteristic of post-Conquest architecture, and which therefore by deduction must be Anglo-Saxon, did not necessarily lead to any clear picture of the chronological development of pre-Conquest architecture. He attempted to remedy this by classifying buildings according to plan, and showing how, by associating the buildings where possible with documentary evidence, conclusions could be drawn about the general development of types of buildings. While his principle was sound (and remains basic for any understanding of architectural development) his lack of appreciation of the complexities of individual buildings, and his almost total reliance on plans alone, produced an over-schematic pattern of development. From this he drew some generalized conclusions about the dating of constructional techniques.

This approach was criticized by Baldwin Brown, whose *Anglo-Saxon Architecture*[3] was the first attempt to tackle in detail both the presentation of a corpus of Anglo-Saxon buildings (total 182 in the first edition; nearly 240 in the second, listed in a gazetteer at the end of the book) and the discussion of both plans and constructional detail from a chronological point of view. One of Baldwin Brown's great merits was his observation of detail, which makes his book still valuable today, even though his drawings give a curiously amateurish atmosphere to his work. For the dating of buildings, Baldwin Brown relied primarily on documentary sources combined with comparison of constructional and ornamental detail, finding that Anglo-Saxon plans did not follow any systematic development.[4] Baldwin Brown was the originator of the terminology A, B and C for periods of churches. His use of these terms reflects the crucial realization that while there were far-reaching differences between Period A (seventh to early eighth century), Period B (late eighth to early tenth century) and Period C (later tenth century onwards), with the absence of documentary evidence for so many of the surviving buildings, and given the simplicity of architectural detail of so many of these examples, it was futile to try and assign precise dates to most Anglo-Saxon churches. His book in any event does not set out to be merely a typological survey of the development of Anglo-Saxon architecture. His classification of buildings rests on detailed observation combined with intuition, but the dating of buildings is only seen as a means to an end and he sought historical explanations for the changes in style which he describes. His attitude to architecture is summed up on p. 10, 'to inventory and label so many hundred specimens of Saxon masonry as if they were postage stamps or beetles is not the proper way to deal with them – they have a human and historical as well as an architectural value, and this is not to be measured by the number of stones that make them up'. However, (p. 11) 'nothing is really too small to notice'. Baldwin Brown's concentration on detail nevertheless produces a diffuse impression, although one which can be blamed very largely on the difficulty of the material. A. W. Clapman's *English Romanesque architecture before the Conquest* (1930), on the other hand, is a more straightforward and simplified account, where clarity of approach is achieved by the not wholly satisfactory method of separating discussion of general architectural development from descriptions of details, such as arches, doorways and decoration, which form the subject of later chapters. Instead of taking Baldwin Brown's approach of three main periods, Clapham avoided the problem of the controversial 'Period B' (for which hardly any firm dates are available) by calling everything after the period of the Heptarchy 'Carolingian Architecture'. Clapham's book is still the most useful summary in chronological order of the evidence both documentary and structural of the major buildings, given that certain aspects have to be modified in the light of recent research. But in his chapters on constructional and ornamental detail, features are often listed without detailed description and without being assigned a date, and are mentioned as occurring in churches which are not discussed elsewhere in the book. While this approach is reasonably useful for the much more limited period of post-Conquest Romanesque architecture, covered by Clapham's second volume,[5] it has considerable disadvantages for the pre-Conquest period spanning four centuries. Clapham's book is thus not much help for minor buildings, or for the dating of details.

The most recent major study of Anglo-Saxon architecture, by H. M. and J. Taylor,[6] is invaluable in that it fills the gaps left by Clapham, by providing a detailed gazetteer of all churches which can claim to have Anglo-Saxon fabric. In many cases the descriptions are supplemented by plans and measured drawings. The techniques of construction defined as Anglo-Saxon are described in an introductory chapter. The interpretation of the buildings takes into account the monographs and excavations which have added to our knowledge of the subject since the time of Baldwin Brown and Clapham. Chronological assessment, however, is confined to an attribution of A, B or C, in the manner of Baldwin Brown, to each building or part of building (in some cases amplified by A1, A2, etc.). More detailed discussion and justification for dating are promised in a third volume. Until this appears, the student must refer to a number of important recent articles by Dr Taylor and others which discuss various buildings and features in more detail.[7]

Recent approaches

There is thus no lack of raw material available. Apart from the books and articles already mentioned, numerous recent monographs have been devoted to detailed discussion of individual buildings,[8] much new information has come to light through excavation and through detailed surveys of existing buildings,[9] and the study of documentary evidence has been made easier by new publications.[10]

Yet when one surveys the present state of research, the results are depressing. Much effort has been devoted to rather arid arguments about chronology, which seem to be bedevilled too often by a predisposition towards early dating, with the result that more attention has been paid to the problems of the seventh and eighth centuries than to the later periods. While considerable energy has been expended on the study of individual buildings, in some cases the chief result has been the production of a series of personally antagonistic articles by different scholars, stressing special points, rather than a definitive study of a problematic building. Perhaps the greatest lack is any adequate study of the liturgical background to the development of architecture during this period, so that the functions of the different parts of churches are inadequately understood.[11] Only occasionally have recent studies been concerned with the internal arrangement of church furnishings, and with the liturgical requirements that conditioned their positions and consequently affected the planning of the building.[12] Similarly, the functions of western towers, with their many curious upper openings, remains obscure.[13] In some cases it is the lack of evidence rather than the lack of questions which is the difficulty, as in the case of the purpose of English crypts.[14] But it seems likely that the documentary evidence for the later period could be made to yield more information.[15] Comparative study of documents might, for example, throw light on the significance of relics and on burial practices, especially when the written material can be related to archaeological evidence, as in the case of Winchester.[16]

While numerous individual buildings have been studied, there has been very little effort until recently to investigate the relationship between churches, or to understand Anglo-Saxon architecture in the wider context of early medieval architecture in northern Europe as a whole. More work could be done, for example, on comparative studies on a regional basis, and on how far churches can be seen to reflect the ecclesiastical history of their area.[17] The evidence which pre-Conquest churches provide for the development of the parochial system could be explored further.[18]

No doubt one reason for the reluctance to embark on comparative studies is that the more one knows about the history of individual churches, the more chary one becomes of generalizing about the influence of one building on another. The redating of buildings previously dated late has confused traditional views on the development of certain types of plan and features (see below, e.g. Repton, p. 187), and the reappraisal of some of the constructional techniques characteristic of the pre-Conquest period has similarly called for a reconsideration of established views.[19] Yet although many aspects of Anglo-Saxon architecture remain obscure, the increasing attention given to the subject by the professional archaeologist and architectural historian is resulting in the development of new techniques which are beginning to change traditional approaches.

(a) ARCHAEOLOGY

The most dramatic additions to our knowledge of pre-Conquest church plans have been made through the excavations of previously unknown sites, as at Winchester and Cirencester (figs 4.7, 4.8b). Comparison between the two, however, shows that if detailed contemporary descriptions of the buildings are lacking, as is the case at Cirencester, it may be very difficult to assign a date to the archaeological evidence (except through stylistic comparisons), particularly if the stonework has completely disappeared. Even at Winchester, where the descriptions made it possible to date most of the stages of the Old Minster plan, St Martin's Tower can only be assigned to a date after c. 648 and before 971.[20] Perhaps the most influential new contribution that archaeology can make is the revelation of the sequence of development on a whole site over several centuries, even if the individual building periods cannot be precisely dated (e.g. see below, n. 42 and fig. 4.3). Such examinations can be of particular interest, for example, if they can establish whether there was any continuity of development between the Saxon churches and pre-Saxon buildings on the site. They may also throw light on quite small internal alterations of furnishings and fittings (see e.g. the excavations of the churches of St Mary and St Pancras at Winchester).

For the architectural historian, some of the most interesting recent information comes from the better understanding of surviving churches that can be achieved with the help of excavations. Even when these are modest in scale, results can be very instructive, as has been shown for example at Brixworth (fig. 4.8a), Escomb (fig. 4.4b), Deerhurst or Sherborne. The results often show how unwise it is to make assumptions about the plan or the date of standing buildings, if no excavations have been carried out, and if more investigations of this kind can be arranged, and planned in order to answer specific questions about problematic buildings, the familiar landmarks of the architectural historian's survey may soon appear in a very different light.[21]

(b) EXAMINATION OF STANDING BUILDINGS

Ideally, excavation should be linked to the detailed examination of standing structures. There is no doubt that the sophistication of current archaeological techniques has encouraged a more critical approach to the interpretation of surviving buildings. The importance of this 'archaeology above the ground', which Dr Taylor has called 'structural criticism', is only just beginning to be appreciated in this country.[22] So far it has often only been possible to investigate limited aspects of an existing church which is still in use, and the disadvantages of a series of partial excavations or examinations carried out by different people at different times are obvious. That meticulous examination of a standing building can produce important new interpretations has been demonstrated, for example, at Repton and Wing, where detailed measurements played a significant part in the investigations.[23] These two churches have received more attention than many others, and yet in both cases the history of the whole building has yet to be established. A particularly striking example of what structural analysis can reveal has recently been provided at Rivenhall, Essex,[24] where a substantial portion of the Anglo-Saxon fabric has been discovered in a church previously thought to have been rebuilt in the nineteenth century (fig. 4.3b). Clearly, if more churches could be made the subject of detailed scrutiny much new information could come to light. But if such investigations are to produce meaningful results, and not a mass of undigested detail, as with excavations, it is essential that there should be close co-operation between the architectural historian and the field worker, and that each should understand each other's discipline.

(c) THE STUDY OF DOCUMENTS

Two types of documents can be distinguished: (a) contemporary or near-contemporary descriptions and records of building activity, and (b) more recent evidence for buildings now destroyed or altered. The chief difficulty in dealing with the former category is that, although the material is extensive, it can only occasionally be definitively associated with excavated plans, and even more rarely with standing buildings. Consequently interpretations of descriptions of lost buildings rely heavily on surviving buildings of unproved relevance and uncertain date.[25] Discussion of documentary evidence can provide both a useful spur to excavate, and a greater understanding of sites previously examined, but the systematic presentation of all relevant documentary evidence is only just beginning.[26]

The study of more recent records, evidence, for example, of the appearance of churches before the restoration or demolition, and of archaeological observations made while such work was in progress, is a relatively new field of investigation, but one which can be extremely rewarding in its results, as Dr Taylor has shown in the cases of Repton, Hexham and Wareham.[27]

These thorough approaches to excavation, and to the examination of buildings and documents, have so far only been put into practice in a very limited number of cases. It must be realized that the majority of the studies referred to in the chronological survey below cannot be regarded as definitive; in some cases they present theories rather than facts, in other cases they add only a small piece of new evidence to what may be still an incompletely understood building. It is possible that new discoveries will soon make it desirable to rewrite the history of Anglo-Saxon architecture completely, but it would be premature to attempt this before more work has been done. The following survey can only endeavour to summarize how new evidence provided by recent research supports or refutes accepted views on the development of architecture of the period and to indicate some of the questions that remain open.

Part II Chronological survey

The pre-Anglo-Saxon centuries

A survey of the development of Anglo-Saxon ecclesiastical architecture must start by asking whether there were any older buildings in Britain which influenced the way in which churches were planned and built after the Augustinian mission. Although there is increasing evidence that Christianity had become well established in Roman Britain and continued until the mid-fifth century,[28] the archaeological evidence for this has so far been confined mainly to villa sites (e.g. Lullingstone, Hinton St Mary), and to a few small finds in towns, as at Cirencester. The only building that can be described as a Roman town church is the small fourth-century structure at Silchester.[29] This can be hailed as a prototype for early Anglo-Saxon churches, having an apse and side chapels, like the Kentish group, although it is not known how typical this building is of churches of this date. It is frustrating that at Verulamium, where there is evidence to suggest the existence of a cult around the grave of the martyred St Alban, no site has yet been discovered which displays the type of continuous development of a cult centre that has been investigated in Germany – notably at Bonn and Xanten,[30] where the later churches were found to have

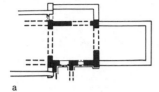

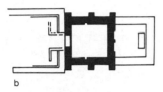

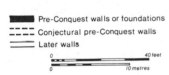

Figure 4.1 Anglo-Saxon churches incorporating Roman structures:
a St Martin Canterbury (after Jenkins)
b Stone-by-Faversham (after Meares)

▬ Pre-Conquest walls or foundations
---- Conjectural pre-Conquest walls
── Later walls

0   40 feet
0   10 metres

been built on the site of simple Roman memoria. It is not impossible that future excavations in this country may provide evidence for Roman origins of later churches. At Canterbury, Bede states that the church of St Martin was a Roman church used by Queen Bertha before the coming of St Augustine, and that St Augustine repaired an older church on the site of Christ Church.[31] There is no corroborative archaeological evidence available for the latter. The chancel of St Martin's has been interpreted as a Roman building, but the evidence is uncertain (fig. 4.1a).[32] So far the only English church where re-use of a Roman building can definitely be argued is at Stone-by-Faversham, Kent (fig. 4.1b),[33] although the evidence indicates that the building was not in continuous use between the Roman and Anglo-Saxon periods, and there is no indication of the original function of the roughly square Roman building which was converted into the chancel of the later church. Certainly some Roman Christian sites were completely abandoned, e.g. the cemetery at Cannington, Somerset, where there was a sub-Roman Christian shrine or mausoleum.[34] A problematic case is the small basilican building now incorporated in the later church at Lydd, Kent. Recent examination of this[35] indicates that it had an apse, a north arcade of three bays, and an elaborate west porch. The small scale of the building, and its regular arcades, do not fit with what is known at present about Anglo-Saxon churches (other arcaded buildings are larger, the smaller churches are simpler). A late Roman date for Lydd is a possibility, but there is no definite dating evidence.

The case for the influence of Romano–British ecclesiastical buildings on Anglo-

Saxon churches is not yet proved, although the conversion of Roman secular buildings or the re-use of building materials is indicated in several cases.[36]

On the other hand in the north and west of Britain there are indications of the continuous use of many ecclesiastical sites from the Celtic period into the Anglo-Saxon centuries.[37] This is of great importance in understanding the later development of a site, because the survival of early buildings often conditioned the siting and planning of later ones, particularly when, as at Glastonbury, the *vetusta ecclesia* was held in especial reverence (fig. 4.6, bottom).[38] On British sites which have been examined recently, the earliest churches (in some cases possibly replacing open shrines) appear to have taken the form of simple rectangular chapels (e.g. at Church Island, Kerry, Ireland, and Ardwall Island, Kirkcudbrightshire, Scotland: fig. 4.2a),[39] although literary descriptions, e.g. of the church at Kildare described in Cogitosus' *Life of St Brigit*,[40] suggest that more complex structures existed. But so far no definite evidence has been found to suggest that the Celtic Christian churches influenced the architectural form (as opposed to the siting) of Anglo-Saxon churches.

The early Saxon period

The traditional approach to churches of the seventh to eighth centuries has been to describe them as falling into two main groups: the Kentish group associated with St Augustine's mission, and the slightly later Northumbrian group centred round Benedict Biscop's activities at Wearmouth and Jarrow, and the work of Wilfrid at Hexham, Ripon and York.[41] There has been a temptation to assume that churches outside these areas must be seen as outlying members of one or the other group. However, as there are now an increasing number of scattered churches for which (with greater or lesser certainty) an early date has been claimed, it may be useful here to classify all these buildings by types of plan, where this is possible, although references to regional associations will be made where appropriate.

It is fairly clear that between the Augustianian mission and the arrival of the Scandinavians a wide variety of church plans existed. They can be summarized, in order of increasing complexity, as (1) single-cell buildings; (2) double-cell buildings (the E chamber sometimes apsed); (3) double-cell buildings, with or without an apse, with north, south or west adjuncts; (4) buildings of the basilican type (a category which in some cases overlaps with category (3); (5) centrally-planned buildings. In some cases the buildings may function on more than one level through the provision of crypts or upper chambers. Although there is some evidence that the first building on the site was usually small and simple, and was later altered and extended to become an increasingly elaborate structure,[42] an elaborate plan, as Baldwin Brown recognized,[43] does not *a priori* indicate a later date. Although recent research has thrown doubt on some of his examples, it has not changed this basic fact of Anglo-Saxon architectural development. Nor, as will be seen from the survey which follows, does the type of plan usually give any clear indication of the status of the church.

SINGLE-CELL BUILDINGS

The single-cell oratory, as has been mentioned, is the best-known type of church in the areas of Celtic Christianity, and on a site such as Glastonbury a chapel of this type survived into the Anglo-Saxon period, being supplemented rather than replaced by additional churches.[44] In important new foundations of the seventh century, it is known from documentary as well as structural evidence that there were frequently several churches rather than a single large one.[45] In some cases these monastic churches took the form of single-

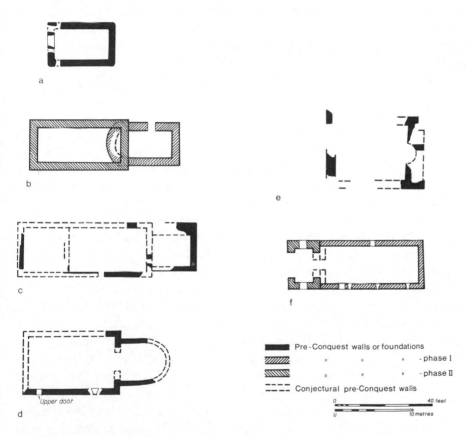

Figure 4.2 Comparative plans of small churches:
a Ardwall (after Thomas)
b Bargham (wall thickness largely schematic) (after Barr-Hamilton)
c St Alban Wood Street, City of London (after Grimes)
d St Mary Stoke d'Abernon (after Radford)
e Much Wenlock (after Jackson and Fletcher)
f Jarrow (present chancel) (after Taylor)

cell buildings. The eastern church (now the chancel) at Jarrow was probably originally such a case (fig. 4.2f).[46] At Much Wenlock remains excavated in 1901 and attributed to the seventh century indicate a rectangular building with the unusual feature of an internally apsed but externally straight east end (fig. 4.2c).[47] Another example of an early single-cell chapel is St Patrick's chapel, Heysham, Lancs., dated by Baldwin Brown to the eighth century, for which Celtic influence is suggested. The first two phases of the church excavated at Bargham, Sussex, appear to have been single-cell buildings (fig. 4.2b). Their date is uncertain.[48] The chancel of St Giles, Barrow, Shropshire, has also been claimed as a free-standing oratory of the eighth century, attached to St Milburga's monastery of Much Wenlock.[49] But this interpretation of the structural evidence has been disputed, and Dr Taylor gives reasons to suggest that the building is no earlier than the tenth century, and had a wooden nave attached.[50] The single-cell oratory may have remained popular in some areas throughout the pre-Conquest period and later. The type is found in the eleventh and twelfth centuries in and around York,[51] and a date as late as the twelfth century has recently been suggested for examples of this type in Ireland.[52]

DOUBLE-CELL BUILDINGS

The distinguishing feature of this very simple type of church, which continued to be built throughout the middle ages, is the provision of an eastern chamber for altar and priest, linked to a larger chamber for the laity. The type was widespread in northern Europe during the eighth century,[53] and the seventh-century church at Nivelles may pre-date English examples.[54] As with single-cell churches these buildings, whether of stone or wood, can be seen as an adaptation for religious functions of a traditional vernacular architecture, or they can be seen as very simplified instances of classical building traditions.[55] Many churches which now contain fragmentary Anglo-Saxon fabric probably began with this type of plan, but without excavation this cannot be proved. Recent investigations have, however, shown that several churches previously considered examples of simple two-cell buildings were in fact more complicated (e.g. Escomb, p. 164 and fig. 4.4b); and this indicates that it may be misleading to contrast churches in south-east England with more 'primitive' buildings elsewhere. Where excavations have revealed a very simple plan, a precise dating is often difficult.[56] An example of a surviving two-cell church with rectangular chancel, assigned on constructional grounds to the early period, is Kirk Hammerton, Yorkshire.[57] Excavations have suggested that at St Alkmund, Derby, there was a church with nave, chancel and something described as an 'E annexe', and at St Alban Wood Street in the City of London evidence for a nave and square chancel of different dates has been found (fig. 4.2c). Both these churches have been dated to the eighth to ninth centuries.[58] Evidence for a simple church with an apsidal east end survives at Stoke d'Abernon, Surrey (fig. 4.2d).[59] This church, suggested as the *Eigenkirch* or proprietary church of a local landowner, can be grouped, on account of its apse and its constructional details, with the early Kentish churches discussed below.

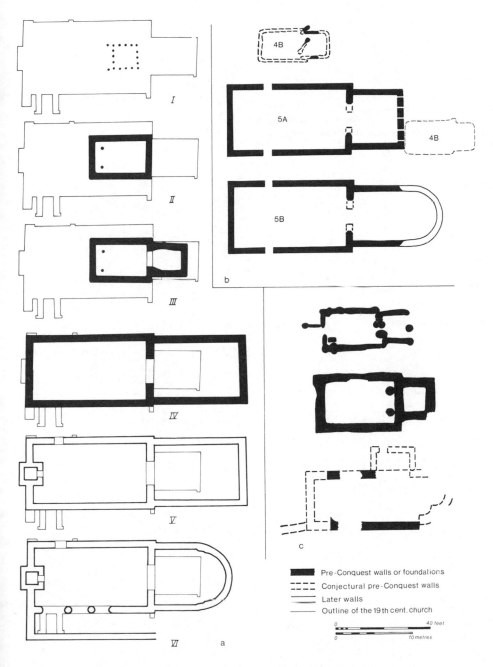

I

II

III

IV

V

VI

a

4B

5A

4B

5B

b

c

Pre-Conquest walls or foundations

Conjectural pre-Conquest walls

Later walls

Outline of the 19th cent. church

0   40 feet

0   10 metres

Figure 4.3 Comparative plans of the development of small churches:
a Wharram Percy (after Hurst)
b Rivenhall (after Rodwell)
c St Michael Thetford (after Davison)

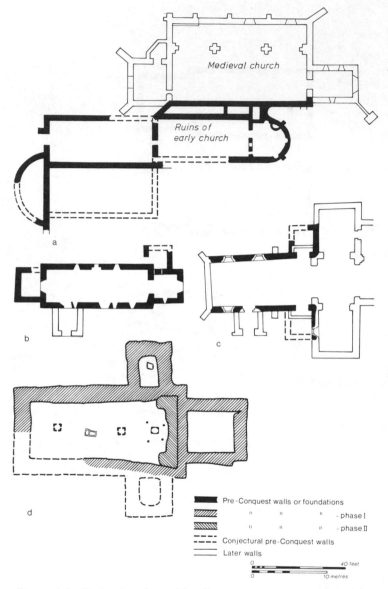

Medieval church

Ruins of
early church

a

b

c

Pre-Conquest walls or foundations

"   "   "   - phase I

"   "   "   - phase II

Conjectural pre-Conquest walls

Later walls

0   40 feet
0   10 metres

d

Figure 4.4 Early churches with adjuncts:
a Lyminge (see also p. 163, n. 70) (after Taylor)
b Escomb (after Pococke and Wheeler)
c Britford (after Taylor)
d Winchester Old Minster Phase I (after Biddle)

CHURCHES WITH NORTH, SOUTH AND WEST ADJUNCTS

North and south adjuncts

The use of lateral chambers (porticus) and apse are two of the most significant characteristics of the 'Kentish group' as defined by Peers and Clapham.[60] Recent research, however,
suggests that it is only the apse which is virtually exclusive to Kent (see also below,
p. 173). The chief Kentish buildings are St Peter and St Paul, and St Pancras (both within
the abbey founded by St Augustine at Canterbury; fig. 4.6, top); one of the churches
within the precincts of the cathedral at Rochester (founded 604); Lyminge (a double
monastery founded after 633; fig. 4.4a); Reculver (a minster founded in 669; fig. 4.5);
and finally Bradwell-on-Sea in Essex (a church identified as one built by the Northumbrian
missionary St Cedd *c*. 653; pl. 1a). Evidence for an apse has been found at St Pancras
(although its shape is disputed),[61] Lyminge, Reculver, Bradwell and perhaps Rochester.
At Reculver the foundations were semicircular, but the apse itself was polygonal on the
exterior. Evidence for north and south lateral chambers exists at St Peter and St Paul and
at St Pancras, Canterbury, as well as at Reculver and Bradwell. At Lyminge a northern
porticus is referred to by Bede and may be the one excavated in the nineteenth century.[62]
Other more fragmentary buildings which can be included in this group are St Martin,
Canterbury (evidence of a south porticus);[63] and St Mary in St Augustine's Abbey, Canterbury, built 620. Here only the west wall survives, but there is later documentary evidence for porticus, at least at the west end.[64]

     Both structural and documentary evidence indicates something of the internal appear-
ance and arrangement of these buildings. At Reculver, St Pancras, Bradwell (pl. 17a) and
Lyminge there is evidence that a triple arcade divided the apse from the rest of the church.
(The columns from the Reculver arcade, taken down only in 1805, are now in Canterbury
Cathedral crypt.) It used to be assumed that such an arcade formed a kind of chancel
screen, and that the altar stood east of it in the apse,[65] but a new interpretation of the
Reculver evidence suggests that the rectangular base west of the screen (hitherto inter-
preted as a base for the cross known to have stood within the church at a later date) was
originally the foundation of an altar.[66]

     The lateral chambers are known in certain cases to have been used as burial chapels –
the documentary evidence at St Peter and St Paul being strikingly confirmed by excavation.[67] The archbishops were buried in the north porticus, King Æthelbert and his wife
in the south porticus. Documentary evidence for burial in lateral porticus exists also for
Lyminge and Rochester.[68] In the case of St Martin, Canterbury, Bradwell, Reculver and
possibly Lyminge, there were porticus with an entrance from the chancel rather than from
the nave. This had led to the suggestion that such a porticus is derived from the Byzantine
diaconicon (or vestry), and the opposite chamber from the *prothesis* (the chamber designed
for the offerings of the faithful) which had to be accessible from the nave.[69] However,
only at Bradwell are there two chambers, one with an entrance from the chancel and
one entered from the nave, which corresponds with the Byzantine arrangement. At

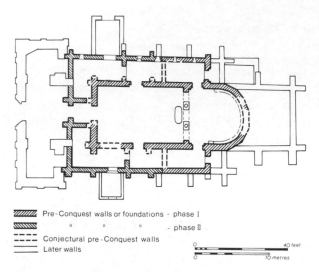

Pre-Conquest walls or foundations - phase I
"   "   "   " - phase II
Conjectural pre-Conquest walls
Later walls

0   40 feet
0   10 metres

Figure 4.5   Reculver (after Taylor)

Reculver both chambers open to the chancel. At Lyminge the north chancel porticus may have had a special function as the burial place of St Æthelburg.[70] Clapham's other example of lateral porticus adjoining the chancel – St Pancras at Canterbury[71] – is not universally accepted.[72] It has been suggested that it is possible to differentiate between the Kentish churches of the first half of the seventh century, with porticus adjoining the nave, and those of the second half (for example Bradwell and Reculver) which include a *diaconicon* attributable perhaps to new influences from Syria.[73] However, the precise function of these eastern lateral porticus cannot be taken as proved. There is some evidence that porticus were added to churches as required. At Reculver the church began with the two eastern chambers, which were later extended westwards until the nave was completely enclosed. Bede's reference to the burial chamber at Rochester also implies that it was added to an existing building.

The uses of lateral chambers in early churches was not confined to the Kentish group. In Northumbria one of the most interesting recent discoveries has been that of Escomb church (so often cited as the classic example of a two-cell church, fig. 4.4b),[74] where, it has now been shown, there was originally a northern porticus entered from the chancel. But no evidence was found for a porticus entered from the surviving Anglo-Saxon door in the north wall of the nave.[75] Other more tentative evidence for lateral porticus in buildings in northern England recently claimed as early has been put forward for Bywell St Peter[76] and Ledsham.[77]

Elsewhere excavations and some redating of known buildings have provided new evidence for early porticus. At Glastonbury the excavations of 1926–9 revealed King Ine's church of *c*. 700, which had northern and southern chambers (fig. 4.6, bottom).[78] At Winchester the recent excavations of the Old Minster have shown that the church attributable to the seventh century had a northern chamber flanking the nave (evidence for the south side was destroyed).[79] At Deerhurst, the formerly two-storeyed porticus flanking the nave

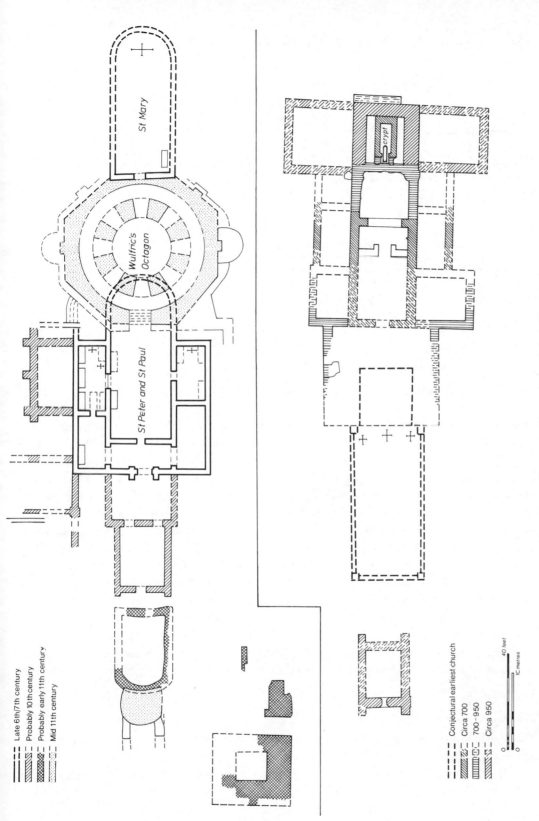

Figure 4.6 (top) St Augustine Canterbury (after Saunders); (bottom) Glastonbury (after Clapham)

Late 6th/7th century
Probably 10th century
Probably early 11th century
Mid 11th century

St Mary

Wulfric's Octagon

St Peter and St Paul

crypt

Conjectural earliest church
Circa 700
700 - 950
Circa 950

40 feet
10 metres

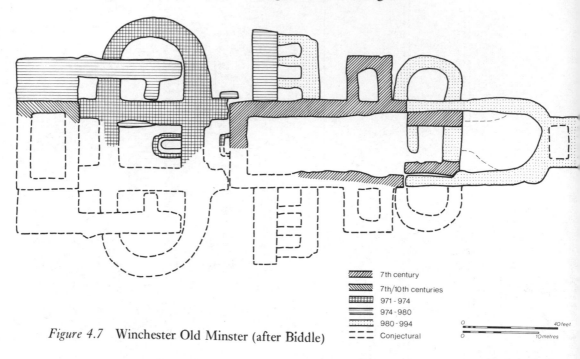

7th century	
7th/10th centuries	
971 - 974	
974 - 980	
980 - 994	
Conjectural	

Figure 4.7 Winchester Old Minster (after Biddle)

have been assigned to an early stage in the development of the building (although the precise dating is disputed).[80] Recent excavations have shown, however, that the sequence of development is more complicated than was previously thought,[81] and that the association with the early Kentish group may not have been as close as was suggested by Jackson and Fletcher. Britford, another building of problematical date but assigned by some authorities to the pre-Scandinavian period, has northern and southern arches at the east end of the nave, decorated with uniquely lavish ornament. Excavations have shown that these archways led into small porticus (fig. 4.4c).[82] Bishopstone, Sussex, has been claimed as an early building on the grounds that the south porch was formerly without an exterior entrance,[83] and that the subsequent history of the building suggests an original western entrance.[84] The same argument is one of those used to advance an early date for the plan and at least some of the structure of St Laurence, Bradford-on-Avon, Wilts., which has been identified by some authorities as the church built by St Aldhelm in the early eighth century.[85] Finally, early porticus may have existed at All Hallows, London, and at Prittlewell, Essex, where in both cases there are remains of an arch (for these buildings see below, p. 175).

West adjuncts

There are about ten churches with evidence for western annexes which are ascribed by various authorities to Period A, and several others dated tentatively to Period B (i.e. before *c*. 950). They will be considered together here.[86] In some cases these are buildings where

there are or were lateral porticus as well (St Pancras, Bradwell, Reculver, Escomb, Deerhurst and possibly Bywell-St-Peter). In other cases the evidence for the rest of the church
is not available (Bardsey, Brigstock, Corbridge, Monkwearmouth, Restenneth, Skepwith,
Titchfield). In only one case, Seaham, is it suggested that there was a western annexe
but no other porticus,[87] and here the early dating is not universally accepted. South Elmham, Suffolk, which has a western annexe and an apse, has been claimed as an early building, but recent excavations have disproved this.[88] Some of these western annexes seem
to be of the same build (e.g. Bardsey, Brigstock, Brixworth, Corbridge, Titchfield), but
others, especially in the cases of the earliest churches, can be shown to have been added,
although often soon after the nave was built. Probably the earliest example is St Pancras,
Canterbury, where the lower part of the western porch was not bonded into the west
wall, although the upper part was, implying a change of plan during construction.[89] At
Escomb (fig. 4.4b) the recent excavations have shown that there was a western annexe,
the south of which was not in bond with the nave, although the constructional techniques
of the foundations (which are similar to those of the nave) have been suggested as a reason
for not dating the western annexe much later (although of course there are no firm dates
for any part of this building).[90] Other seventh-century churches with added porches are
Reculver (fig. 4.5) and Monkwearmouth. The evidence for the complicated history of the
west end of the latter building has been much discussed recently.[91] The evidence suggests
that the church was originally built without a west porch. However, one existed by the
early eighth century, as Bede mentions that Abbot Eosterwine was buried in it (interesting
evidence of the function of such a porch). The first porch was soon afterwards extended
on the north and south sides to become a two-storeyed western annexe subsequently
altered on several occasions. It has been suggested that the small western annexe at Escomb
was also two-storeyed.[92] This was certainly the case at Brixworth (figs 4.8a, 4.9a), where
the porch had north and south annexes opening from it, as in the later stages of the Monkwearmouth porch.[93]

It has generally been assumed, as has already been noted in commenting on lateral
porticus, that in the early churches the entrance to the nave was from the west, and that
these western annexes had the function of an entrance porch or narthex. At Escomb, however, rather surprisingly no evidence for a door in the western annexe was found. At
Seaham there also does not appear to be any evidence of original doors in the western
porticus.[94] The other examples which do not conform in this respect are Bardsey (west
porch with north and south doors) and Ledsham (west porch with south door),[95] but
in both these cases an early dating is uncertain. The lower part of the tower at Restenneth,
Angus, which has been claimed in a carefully argued recent assessment as an outlying
member of the early Northumbrian group, associated with the activities of St Boniface
c. 715,[96] has an original south door, and a later western opening. Some sort of a western
structure – either an apse[97] or a west porch with upper storey[98] – has been suggested for
the cathedral at Canterbury, but as the interpretations depend on a much later description
there is no proof of the early date of any such structure.

The evidence for the nature of the opening between western annexe and nave varies; in many cases the doorway is not original. The exceptionally large opening at Corbridge (built of re-used Roman masonry), which used to be regarded as of the same date as the porch, has recently been interpreted as an insertion.[99]

Conclusions on early churches with adjuncts

It appears that churches with northern and southern porticus were built throughout England in the seventh and eighth centuries. They include churches on cathedral sites (Rochester, Winchester), churches in monasteries of different types (Glastonbury, St Augustine's at Canterbury), missionary churches (Bradwell) and lesser churches – perhaps minsters (Reculver) or churches of a proprietary nature (Escomb). There is some evidence to suggest that lateral chambers flanking the chancel may not be a feature of the first half of the seventh century, that west porches are less common in southern England than in the north and that they were sometimes later additions to an existing nave. These western adjuncts in several cases were not simply porches, but had flanking chambers and sometimes an upper storey. Lateral adjuncts are not unique to Britain. Early examples abroad which can be cited are the cemetery chapel of St German, Speyer, perhaps seventh century or earlier, the two earliest churches at Romainmoûtier, Switzerland (one of the fifth century and one built before 624), and Notre-Dame-sous-le-Bourg at St Maurice d'Agaune, Switzerland (sixth or seventh century).[100] A ruined church with a plan remarkably similar to the Kentish group, with side chambers and an apse, exists at Altenberg, South Tyrol.[101] All these examples, together with the evidence of Silchester, would suggest that the church with adjuncts is a very widespread simple type, existing already in late Roman times, and continuing in use during the seventh century and later both in England and on the Continent. The side chambers could be used for a variety of functions. Perhaps the most interesting aspect of the English churches is the provision of quite elaborate western adjuncts, foreshadowing the developed westwork of the Carolingian period.[102] The function of these, as of later westworks, is by no means clear; the most frequently indicated special use of the annexes flanking nave or chancel is for burials. It is interesting that at St Peter and St Paul, Canterbury, although the porticus functioned as mausolea for the archbishops and the royal family, it was not thought desirable to diverge from the standard plan, implying what must have amounted to a deliberate disregard by St Augustine of the architectural traditions of tomb buildings with which he must have been familiar in Rome.[103] Whether this attitude was accompanied, in the case of the Kentish churches, by a deliberate avoidance of architectural ostentation is impossible to say, as so little evidence exists for the appearance of the churches above ground. The use of a screen with columns at Reculver implies some architectural accomplishment on the part of the builders. Outside Kent, the most striking evidence that interiors of these churches could be ornamented with architectural sculpture is provided by the porticus entrances at Britford. No parallel has been found for any of the unusual features of these arches – the jambs with decorated panels above elaborate moulded plinths (fig. 4.2e), the north arch soffit faced with symmetrically arranged slabs. The function of the porticus has not been established and the status of the pre-Conquest church at Britford is not known.[104]

In some cases the porticus church may have had quite an elaborate exterior elevation with a two-storey porch and, as at Deerhurst, a two-storey lateral porticus as well (pl. 17b). At Monkwearmouth the entrance and the exterior of the upper part were decorated with sculpture. The tall proportions of these buildings, and particularly the Northumbrian examples, has frequently been emphasized.[105] These churches with adjuncts should not be dismissed as insignificant, especially when it is borne in mind how exceptional they must have appeared when compared with contemporary secular wooden buildings. However, they form only one of the architectural solutions, and one of the less ambitious ones, adopted for churches of the early Anglo-Saxon period.

EARLY BASILICAN BUILDINGS

There are only about a dozen pre-Conquest buildings which are known, from documentary or structural evidence, to have had aisles. In several of these, the aisles were not continuous passages, but were broken up by transverse walls, thus creating an arrangement analogous to a series of porticus. Only a few of these aisled buildings can be dated with any degree of certainly (the ones which are almost certainly late in date will be discussed below, p. 173). In most cases the structural evidence is incomplete and difficult to interpret. Thus any generalizations on the use of the basilican forms have to be made with great caution. Wilfrid's church at Hexham, built between 672 and 678 and added to by Acca in the early eighth century, is the earliest definitely datable church which had some kind of an aisled nave. The building is known from the account of it by Wilfrid's biographer Eddius Stephanus, and from later accounts, as well as from the archaeological discoveries made by C. C. Hodges at the beginning of this century when the present nave was built (finds which included massive foundations of three piers on the north side of the nave). The interpretation of all this evidence is difficult. Baldwin Brown postulated a basilica of Roman type, with transept and apse, with Wilfrid's crypt (which survives) lying beneath the crossing and eastern bays of the nave.[106] Baldwin Brown, however, admitted that it was difficult to make sense of all the evidence. 'As regards the actual discoveries a mere record of what has been seen or is reported would supply little more than a miscellaneous collection of facts in which no system is apparent, and it is essential that these should be brought into relation with some hypothesis for which they may seem to furnish a satisfactory groundwork.'[107] The Taylors' more recent careful examination of what Baldwin Brown unjustly called a 'miscellaneous collection', which includes the study of Hodges' original notes, has resulted in a very different interpretation; this has much less in common with a Roman basilica but is plausible in the context of other English buildings and of current knowledge of multiple churches on major ecclesiastical sites.[108] They suggest a church with a straight east end close to the eastern entrances of the crypt (thus siting the crypt below the high altar). The remains of the small apse further east are interpreted as belonging to a separate chapel; the walls taken by Baldwin Brown as evidence for transepts are explained as extensions to porticus, and, more doubtfully, as parts of the conventual buildings. The nave, which according to Baldwin Brown's plan was of eight bays with columns,[109] is suggested, in accordance with Hodges' evidence, as having four bays divided by broad rectangular piers. There remains the fact that neither Hodges' evidence nor the Taylors' suggested reconstruction throws light on certain aspects of Eddius' elaborate description, particularly the 'various winding passages with spiral stairs leading up and down', which imply some kind of upper storey. Eddius also refers to the building being supported by 'various columns and many side aisles'. This gave rise to Baldwin Brown's suggestion of arcades supported on columns,[110] an idea rejected by the Taylors, who however suggest that the surviving fragments of columns and of one half-column could have been used to decorate the soffit faces of the large rectangular piers.[111] The use of a single half-column against the centre of a pier would be highly unusual at this date, as it is a form of pier which became popular only in early Romanesque buildings of the eleventh century. A more relevant comparison may be the use of decorative angle columns in France and Italy, as found for example on the two tiers of wall arcading at St Pierre, Vienne, ascribed to the fifth century,[112] or in later buildings such as Germigny-des-Pres or San Stefano, Verona. It may well have been the use of late antique traditions of ornament, including columns, rather than close approximation to an Italian church plan or elevation, that inspired the admiration of Eddius and the later writers (just as the use of 120 columns in the church of St Martin, Tours, impressed Gregory of Tours). Surviving sculptural fragments indicate that Hexham also had carved string courses and figure sculpture.[113] The survival of small loose baluster shafts at Jarrow, and especially of paired shafts of the same type in the doorway of the west porch at Monkwearmouth, also suggests an ornamental rather than constructional use of 'columns' in Northumbria at this time.

The evidence for an early date for several other aisled buildings, at Jarrow, Brixworth, Wing and Lydd, is less precise. Lydd has already been discussed (p. 157). The nave at Jarrow was demolished in 1782 and the present nineteenth-century nave now stands on its site. An eighteenth-century plan and drawing show that the church then had a four-bay nave divided from the aisles by rectangular piers. This has been interpreted, by comparison with Hexham and Brixworth, as the church built by Benedict Biscop and dedicated in 684/5. The present chancel has been explained[114] as a separate pre-Conquest building. Excavations inside and outside the church have established the dimensions of the Anglo-Saxon nave.[115]

Brixworth (figs 4.8a, 4.9a) is one of the most complete pre-Conquest churches surviving. It has a nave, presbytery, apse (rebuilt in the nineteenth century on old foundations), remains of a ring crypt and a west porch later heightened to a tower. In addition there is evidence for aisles, and for northern and southern annexes to the west porch. Recent excavations have provided new evidence on the nature of the aisles and western narthex.[116] The north aisle had two cross walls at the east end (apparently added later) and evidence for one cross wall has been found on the south side. Thus Brixworth nave did not remain, and perhaps never was, a true aisled building, and the main features which distinguish the plan from the church with porticus is its considerable size and the regular pier-like treatment of the areas of wall between the arches in the nave. The narthex appears to have extended across the whole width of the 'aisles', being divided into five compartments, of which the centre one formed the porch.

The church was described by Clapham in a memorable phrase, since repeated with somewhat tedious frequency, as 'perhaps the most imposing architectural memorial of the seventh century yet surviving north of the Alps'.[117] Yet it has to be pointed out that the argument for dating the building to the foundation date of *c.* 670 of the monastery founded by monks from Peterborough rests entirely on stylistic evidence, and Clapham's argument depends chiefly on comparisons between Brixworth and the 'Kentish group'. Both date and connections now have to be reassessed. Recent examination of the Northumbrian evidence has shown that some features of Brixworth can be paralleled in the north. Apart from the (undated) evidence of Jarrow (which is a circular argument as Dr Taylor's early dating partly rests on a comparison with Brixworth) there is the two-storey west porch with side annexes at Monkwearmouth. Other distinctive features at Brixworth cannot be paralleled in Kent or in the north. These include the use of pilasters around a polygonal apse (although these have been attributed to a tenth-century rebuilding),[118] and the remarkable wall thickness of between 3 ft 4 ins and 4 ft.[119]

A date of *c.* 750–820, 'at the beginning of the Carolingian revival', has recently been suggested for Brixworth,[120] but this dating also does not rest on any firm evidence. Clapham's date was based partly on a comparison between Brixworth and Reculver (founded 669), both of which have polygonal apses, a triple arcade at the east end of the nave, and flanking chambers or aisles to the north, south and west. Gilbert reasonably points out that the western chambers at Reculver are agreed to be later additions, and also suggests, although without providing any proof, that the apse and triple arcade at Reculver could be a later rebuilding. He argues from the absence of the presbytery (i.e. the part of the building between apse and nave) in the early Kentish churches, that Brixworth is an example of a different type of church, which he calls the 'English basilica', which evolved from the Kentish type. However, his conclusions that 'English basilicas' were erected between 730 and 867 is far too categoric a statement, given the tenuous nature of the evidence; and his list of examples are too diverse in their plans to make this kind of typological argument convincing. Furthermore, the arguments are sometimes contradictory. Brixworth, as a basilican building with a ring crypt, is seen as a precursor, or early example, of the Carolingian revival,[121] but at the same time the suggestion is made that there may have been a tower over the east end of the church, an idea described by Gilbert as 'Gallic'. Some evidence for Merovingian towers in this position has been put forward,[122] but even if this is accepted as a hypothesis for Brixworth it does not prove a mid-eighth-century date.[123] All that the existence of the presbytery indicates is that (with the possible exception of St Martin's, Canterbury – not discussed by Gilbert – which may have been a three-cell church) Brixworth is different from the early Kentish churches. It must be admitted that, historically, a mid-eighth-century date for the church would fit conveniently with the period of Mercian supremacy[124] and would provide a satisfactory architectural counterpart to the Mercian sculpture ascribed to this time,[125] but the suggestion must remain a plausible but unproven hypothesis.[126]

The church at Wing (figs 4.8d, 4.9b, pl. 2b), whose status in the early pre-Conquest period is unknown and which was ascribed by Clapham and by Baldwin Brown to the tenth or early eleventh century,[127] has been re-examined by Jackson and Fletcher, who have argued that both the aisled nave and the foundations of the crypt are much older.[128] They suggest a seventh-century date, but do not provide any evidence to support their suggestion of an association with the mission of Birinus (635) or his successor Agilbert, or with the activities of Wilfrid later in the seventh century. The arcades at Wing are of three bays. As the walls are plastered, the details of the construction of the arches have not been fully investigated,[129] and whether the very wide chancel arch is of the same date as the arcades is uncertain.[130]

Interesting features at Wing are the upper doorways at the west end uncovered in 1954 which have plausibly been suggested as entrances to a wooden gallery.[131]

An early dating for the Wing nave depends partly on whether one accepts the argument that it is of the same date as the earliest crypt (for this see below). It is a building where detailed examination of the fabric might clarify the situation.

The problem of the date of Lydd has already been mentioned. From the evidence of recent excavations, this very small basilican building had some kind of elaborate western porch.[132] At York there is documentary evidence for a church built by Archbishop Albert (767–80) with porticus and upper chambers. This, and various interpretations of excavations below the minster, have been discussed fully by the Taylors,[133] who assumed a basilican building, but their suggestions have been invalidated by the recent investigations which have ascribed the herringbone masonry previously considered Saxon to the cathedral built by Archbishop Thomas after the Conquest.[134]

The pre-Conquest cathedral at Canterbury is another case where the documentary evidence can be interpreted as indicating an early building of basilican type with upper chambers. Recent interpretations have favoured a building of the Brixworth type rather than the more Roman basilican form suggested by older writers, but the whole matter is conjectural.[135]

Finally, two pieces of evidence for basilican buildings of uncertain date should be mentioned. The recently excavated church at Cirencester (fig. 4.8b) had a nave with aisles divided by lateral walls, and a narthex.[136] An apse and crypt were found, but whether these belonged to a very large single building (175 ft long) or whether there could have been two linked churches is unclear, as the centre of the site could not be excavated. At Lady St Mary, Wareham, Dorset (fig. 4.8c), there is evidence for an aisled pre-Conquest church which was destroyed in the nineteenth century.[137] Taylor suggests a late Anglo-Saxon date, but more recently the Royal Commission argued that on analogy with Brixworth and Jarrow the church might have been built in the last quarter of the seventh century.

One must conclude that the present state of knowledge on basilican buildings is very unsatisfactory. Apart from the uncertain dating, in several cases little is known about the total plan and arrangement of these buildings. The treatment of west ends varied and is not always known, but it is interesting that several of the east ends included a crypt of some form (see below). Recent views tend to discount the older suggestion that transepts are an early feature, and basilican buildings with transepts are generally dated late (see below, pp. 187ff.). But our knowledge of late Anglo-Saxon architecture is too incomplete to state categorically that basilicas without transepts must inevitably be early.[138]

It is possible to come to very different conclusions on the use of the basilican form in the seventh and eighth centuries. An extreme view is to assume that only in the seventh century was it likely that this Roman type of building would be adopted, and that Wilfrid is the key figure.[139] But against this argument for placing buildings of unknown date in the seventh century, is the fact that at least one aisled building was definitely constructed in the tenth century, the New Minster at Winchester.[140] The other extreme is to see the basilican form as one aspect of the influence of Carolingian architecture, an influence which might possibly have reached England already in the later eighth century, starting with Brixworth. Against this there is the Hexham evidence and the probably early date of Jarrow. A possible view is that the basilican form (probably in a version not very close to Roman buildings) was known throughout the Anglo-Saxon period, but only used occasionally. Why the type should have been chosen for some important churches but not for others has yet to be clarified.

CENTRALLY PLANNED CHURCHES

There is little new information that can be added to what is already known about early centrally planned churches. The evidence about this kind of building during the whole of the pre-Conquest period is almost entirely documentary.[141] It has been suggested recently that the second cathedral at York, described as built *per quadrum*, and surrounding the earlier church, should be interpreted as a centrally planned building of Armenian type,[142] but this seems to be reading too much into Bede's account. The earliest surviving centrally planned building appears to be the small mausoleum at Repton, later converted into a crypt, which is described below.

SPECIAL FEATURES IN EARLY SAXON BUILDINGS

The use of the apse

Preference for the apsidal east end must be seen as evidence of close contact with building traditions stemming ultimately from classical stone building techniques. As has been noted, in the early Anglo-Saxon period apses are found predominantly in churches associated with the Kentish group. There are few examples elsewhere: the apse at Hexham, now interpreted as belonging to a small chapel east of the main building;[143] the internal apse of the small building at Much Wenlock ascribed to the seventh century (fig. 4.2e);[144] the shallow western apse of the undated earliest structure at Bargham, Sussex;[145] and the two cases of larger polygonal apses at Brixworth (fig. 4.8a) and Wing (fig. 4.8d, pl. 18b), both associated with crypts (for the dating of these buildings see above, pp. 170–71). To these must be added two problematic documentary references: to the early church at Abingdon, described as 'round at either end', and which could thus have had a western as well as an eastern apse,[146] and to Canterbury Cathedral, where the twelfth-century description by Eadmer suggests that there was an eastern apse with a crypt as well as some kind of western structure. Several recent interpretations of these have been put forward.[147]

The problem of the immediate source of inspiration for the Kentish apses has not been solved. On the Continent eighth-century apsed aisleless churches have been attributed to the influences of the Kentish group through the mission of St Boniface,[148] but whether the original builders in Kent were imitating building in Gaul (as the connections with the Frankish court might lead one to expect), or were inspired directly by Italy or Byzantium, is still unclear. With regard to the polygonal form of the apse (Reculver, Brixworth, Wing) the rare continental parallels outside Italy seem either to be very early[149] or to date from the Carolingian revival. As has been mentioned, this is one of Gilbert's arguments for a mid-eighth-century date for Brixworth, and for the Reculver apse. In favour of an early date for polygonal apses are the Italian sources suggested by Clapham.[150]

Early crypts

The understanding of the fundamental importance of crypts in the development of early medieval architecture has considerably increased over the last few decades, and has made the European context of the few but diverse English examples more comprehensible.[151]

The English evidence has recently been fully surveyed and discussed by Taylor, with reference to continental comparisons.[152] The English crypts which have been attributed to the seventh or eighth century can be divided into those which appear to have started as independent or semi-independent structures later incorporated into a church, such as Repton, Glastonbury (fig. 4.6, bottom) and perhaps Sidbury,[153] and those which were built in conjunction with a major church, such as Ripon, Hexham, Brixworth (figs 4.8a, 4.9a) and – possibly early – Wing (figs 4.8d, 4.9b) and Cirencester (fig. 4.8b).[154] To the latter group must be added Canterbury Cathedral, known only from documentary evidence, and Abingdon Abbey, both of uncertain date.[155]

As Taylor has pointed out, as far as is known the English crypts all seem to have been created to house subsidiary relics; that is, they were not designed for the relics of the saint to whom the church was dedicated, and in this they differ from some of the most important continental examples. The originally independent buildings probably began as mausolea (independent burial chambers), a building type of classical origin, which continued into the early middle ages. This is particularly likely in the case of Repton, the place where King Æthelbald of Mercia is known to have been buried in 757. The crypt at Glastonbury has been interpreted as the intended burial place of King Ine.

The crypts designed as part of a major church are inspired by the next stage of the development of this feature on the Continent. An older mausoleum, or a chamber specially constructed, formed a subsidiary part of a larger church – usually lying beneath the main altar and accessible from the main building by stairs and passages, and perhaps sometimes directly in contact with the altar through a *fenestella*.[156] The earliest example of a crypt of this type is the ring crypt built beneath the apse at St Peter's in Rome, *c*. 600, to give access to the existing *memoria*.[157] The Ripon and Hexham crypts can thus be seen as early northern imitations of this arrangement, possibly created specially for relics brought back to England by Wilfrid. The details of the plans of the irregular angular passages of these two churches are, however, not very similar to the early Italian examples, but then medieval buildings frequently did not imitate their chosen prototypes very closely. The influence of St Peter's has also been argued in the case of the crypt known to have existed at Canterbury Cathedral. Eadmer actually compares the crypt to that at St Peter's in Rome, but his description is open to different interpretations and there is no certainty that the crypt was pre-Danish.[158]

MISCELLANEOUS EVIDENCE FOR EARLY ANGLO-SAXON BUILDINGS

Fragmentary evidence supporting an early date exists for a number of churches where not enough is known to classify them by plan. In many cases the only pre-Conquest fabric that survives is that of the upper parts of the nave walls, which survive above later arcades. As even very approximate dating cannot be attempted unless distinctive types of construction or decoration are found, it is easiest to consider here attributions to both Period A and Period B.

Arguments for early dating can be grouped under four main headings: constructional detail, decorative detail, evidence for two pre-Conquest building periods and documentary support for an early building on the site. In most cases the arguments cannot be considered conclusive on their own, but they suggest that further investigation of the buildings could be profitable. It is worth noting that several of these fragmentary examples provide unique instances of the use of certain types of architectural ornament.

The use of tiles for voussoirs (Brixworth; St Pancras, Canterbury) has been suggested as evidence for a date in Period A for arches at All Hallows, London (west end of south wall of nave), and at Prittlewell, Essex (north chancel wall), and more doubtfully at West Hampnett, Sussex (chancel arch, now destroyed).[159] But a suggestion of an early date for windows with tiled heads at St Nicholas, Leicester, has been rejected,[160] and there is no doubt that the use of tiles sometimes continued into the late Anglo-Saxon period.[161]

In the north, constructional details and proportions comparable to Escomb and Monkwearmouth have led to suggestions for early dates for churches at Heddon-on-the-Wall, Northumberland; Staindrop, Durham; Sockburn, Durham; and Hoddom, Dumfries.[162]

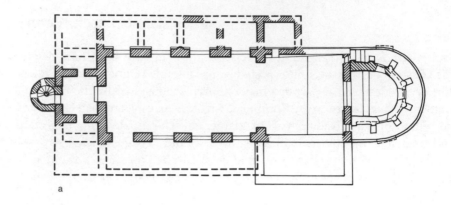

a

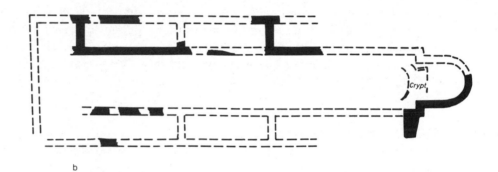

b

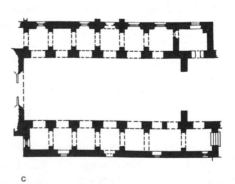

c

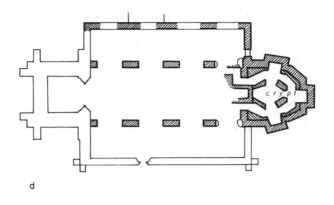

d

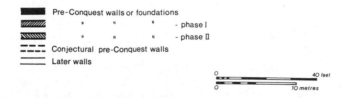

e

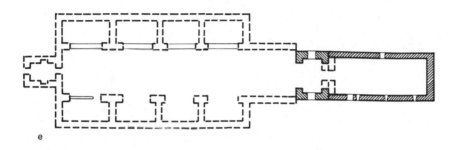

Pre-Conquest walls or foundations

"   "   "   "   - phase I

"   "   "   "   - phase II

Conjectural pre-Conquest walls

Later walls

0   40 feet

0   10 metres

Figure 4.8 Comparative plans of 'basilican' churches:
a Brixworth (see also section, fig. 4.9a) (after Taylor, with addition)
b Cirencester (after Brown and McWhirr)
c Lady St Mary, Wareham (after the plan of 1840) (after Taylor)
d Wing (see also section, fig. 4.9b) (after Taylor)
e Jarrow (after Taylor's reconstruction from 1769 drawings; but cf. p. 159, fig. 4.2f.)

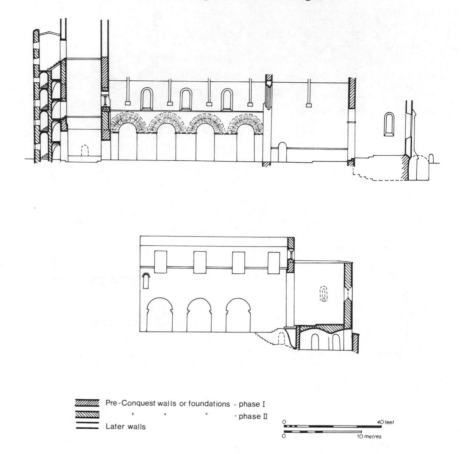

Pre-Conquest walls or foundations - phase I
"   "   "   - phase II
Later walls

0   40 feet
0   10 metres

Figure 4.9 Comparative elevations:
a Brixworth (after Taylor)
b Wing (after Taylor)

Other suggestions for early dating on constructional grounds are St Andrew's, Wroxeter,[163] and Atcham, Shropshire.[164]

Early dating of decorative sculptural detail has to depend very largely on the problematic question of the chronology of Anglo-Saxon sculpture. Isolated examples of architectural ornament surviving *in situ*, which have been dated early on stylistic grounds, are string courses at Masham, Yorks. NR (Period A), and at Edenham, Lincs. (Period B) (cf. the early use of a decorated string course at Monkwearmouth). A possible Period B dating is suggested for the imposts of the south door of Kirby Hill, Yorks. NR, which are decorated with Anglian vine-scroll.[165]

In cases where there is evidence for two or more pre-Conquest building periods the exact date for the earliest work must remain hypothetical, unless there is other evidence. Examples where the first period of work is claimed as early are the nave walls at Geddington, Northants., and at Billingham, Durham, and the nave and chancel of Whitfield, Kent.[166]

Finally, there are several instances where documentary evidence for an early church makes it tempting to suggest an early date for otherwise undatable pre-Conquest fabric. For example a Period A dating for the nave, walls and loose fragments at St Mary Magdalene, Hart, Durham, has been reinforced by the argument that this is known to have been the mother church of the double monastery of Hartlepool founded *c.* 650.[167] Similarly the pre-Conquest walls at Minster in Sheppey, Kent, have been associated with the double monastery founded by Queen Sexburga after 664.[168] More doubtfully parts of the pre-Conquest remains at Peterborough (fig. 4.10f) have been identified with the seventh-century monastery of Medehamstede,[169] and some very sparse evidence for a small early building at Langton Maltravers, on the Isle of Purbeck, has been associated with St Aldhelm (*c.* 700).[170] A late seventh-century date has also been assigned to the north door of Somerford Keynes, Glos., where land was granted to St Aldhelm in 685.[171] This door, recently unblocked,[172] was dated by Baldwin Brown to the eighth century because of the similarity of its ornament to Heysham. The most famous case where there is documentary evidence for an early church, and where structural evidence for more than one building period has been argued, is St Laurence's Church, Bradford-on-Avon, identified by some authorities as the church built by St Aldhelm *c.* 700, despite the apparently late Saxon character of the exterior decoration (pl. 21a). The evidence of the fabric has been interpreted in different ways, and has yet to be finally resolved.[173]

Attempts to associate churches with known individuals must be treated with caution. An early foundation date obviously does not prove that any of the surviving fabric dates from that time.[174] While in many of these cases precise dating may not be possible at present, evidence of an early site, combined with the existence of pre-Conquest fabric, suggests that excavations, or more detailed examination of the standing structure, could in some cases throw more light on the history and dating of some potentially interesting buildings.

CONCLUSIONS ON THE PRE-SCANDINAVIAN PERIOD: THE EUROPEAN SETTING

From the above summary it will be clear that the evidence for the pre-Scandinavian period indicates that most of the known churches of the seventh and eighth centuries were unambitious in their scale, and this holds true whatever their status. The exceptions, notably Brixworth and Hexham, do leave open the possibility that elsewhere some large early buildings may yet be revealed by excavation, although it is perhaps indicative that for instance at Winchester the first cathedral church was not basilican in plan. At Winchester, Glastonbury, and St Augustine's, Canterbury, the churches were altered, or increased in number, from an early period in some cases, rather than rebuilt on a grand scale. The existence of several small churches on a single ecclesiastical site, often developing rather haphazardly as need arose, seems to be comparable to the situation at both cathedral and monastic sites in Gaul.[175] In England, while we now have considerable evidence for early monastic churches, our knowledge of early cathedrals is much less satisfactory. Winchester is the only site where excavations have provided conclusive results. Interpretations of the first cathedral at Canterbury, resting solely on later descriptions, remain hypotheses. At Rochester there is only fragmentary evidence to suggest that there was a series of buildings of different dates. At Hexham Wilfrid is known to have built three churches.[176] At York also, the documentary evidence indicates that the seventh-century church was repaired and extended rather than replaced, and was supplemented in the later eighth century by an elaborate church dedicated (remarkably) to Alma Sophia.

When one turns to the more exceptional churches for which an early date is claimed, there is much greater difficulty in fitting them into a development which makes sense within the context of recent thinking on early medieval architecture in Europe as a whole. Despite the large number of excavations abroad, recent research on the Continent has not provided evidence for basilican buildings of the seventh or early eighth century comparable to Brixworth, or with early crypts analogous to the English ones for which an early date has been advanced (Hexham, Ripon and ?Brixworth and Wing). Thus the temptation is either to claim that various English buildings are 'in advance' of continental architecture,[177] which was the position Clapham put himself in over Brixworth, or one may try, with Gilbert, to date Brixworth to a period which would fit with continental evidence, thus rejecting the established English dating arguments. A similar situation exists with crypts, for as Taylor argues, if the ideas for Wilfrid's crypts came direct from Rome, several English crypts may pre-date the more elaborate examples found on the Continent during the Carolingian period. A third alternative is to disagree with the dating of the continental examples. But this is by no means easy to do, particularly as many excavation reports assign the evidence for successive buildings on a site to labelled phases, and do not attempt a precise chronology. It would be interesting to have the views of continental scholars on the recent research on Anglo-Saxon buildings: too often continental publications are based exclusively on the now rather out-of-date evidence of Clapham and Baldwin Brown.

Later Anglo-Saxon architecture

It is surprising, when looking at the pre-Conquest period as a whole, to find that while a considerable number of recent studies on buildings have been devoted to arguing the case for early dates, less attention has been paid to the much larger corpus of material which is generally agreed to be 'late Anglo-Saxon'. Possibly this is because despite the number of churches available for study (a much larger number than for the early period), and the intrinsic interest of many of them, an understanding of the development of English architecture from the ninth to the eleventh centuries is beset by peculiar difficulties.

Firstly, there is the problem of the connection between the 'early' and the 'late' Anglo-Saxon periods. The situation between c. 800 and 950 (Period B) is particularly obscure. The Viking raids and Scandinavian settlement in some places disrupted the ecclesiastical organization so completely that entirely new churches had to be constructed. These were at first on a modest scale, as at North Elmham and Stafford, where in both cases timber churches preceded stone ones in the post-Scandinavian period.[178] In other places, such as York, both the evidence for the relatively rapid conversion of the Scandinavian settlers and the survival of early Anglo-Saxon fabric in later churches suggests that the older churches may not have all disappeared.[179] However, although tombstones of Scandinavian taste survive,[180] there is little definite evidence at York of the kind of church building that went on during this period, and the situation is comparable in other areas settled by the Scandinavians.[181] If the recent suggestions for a dating of the important work at Repton and of Barnack tower (see below) into the first half of the ninth century are accepted, the implication would be that, despite the Danish disruptions, this period could have seen the construction of some progressive and ambitious buildings. But the case is not yet proved. Topographical studies of the type that have been undertaken abroad are badly needed.[182] Such work could clarify the extent of architectural activity and ecclesiastical continuity in particular localities during this problematic period. It is unwise to generalize about conditions in the country as a whole at this period, and an approach through regional studies of the historical background could be helpful.[183]

Secondly, perhaps the greatest difficulty in discussing the later Anglo-Saxon period is the lack of firmly documented and dated major surviving buildings. Although it is clear that the monastic revival of the later tenth and eleventh centuries led to the rebuilding of many major churches, all these have been replaced by later medieval buildings. In the few cases where structural or archaeological evidence for the pre-Conquest churches is available, it is by no means always certain that it can be identified with the building activity mentioned in the documents. When successive building periods, corresponding with the documentary evidence, are revealed solely by archaeology, as is the case at Winchester (fig. 4.7), the development of the ground plan is often the only aspect of the building that can be ascertained. Dated ground plans, although important in themselves, do not help in the dating of isolated architectural features such as arches, windows, capitals and such features which survive in minor standing buildings. If one wishes to concentrate on the visual evidence provided by these lesser buildings one is confronted by suggestions for dating which have to rely almost entirely on guesswork.[184] Furthermore, the status of these buildings often is not known, so that for the later Anglo-Saxon period it is very difficult to generalize about the type of plan or the quality of construction or detail that may be expected in churches of different rank. A comparison between the Taylors' gazetteer of churches including pre-Conquest fabric[185] and the list of pre-Conquest religious houses given by Knowles and Hadcock[186] (bearing in mind that some churches in the latter list are mentioned purely on the evidence of the architectural remains) will indicate not only how little we know about many important pre-Conquest monasteries, but also how we know nothing about the status of, for example, such notable late Saxon churches as Worth, Earl's Barton or Norton.

Dating of buildings in the late Anglo-Saxon period has been based very largely on the recognition of certain distinctive masonry techniques which, as has already been noted, were not used by the Normans (except when continuing Saxon practices). Although it is recognized that in the very early buildings (in particular the well-documented early Kentish group) certain 'characteristically Anglo-Saxon' constructional techniques, such as long-and-short working, do not appear, it is not clear how early some of these techniques developed. Recent suggestions (not all generally accepted) for early dates for a number of buildings would push back the introduction of some of these features to before the Scandinavian incursions, with the implication that certain constructional methods were established quite early, and continued in use throughout the pre-Conquest period. Examples are the use of pilaster strips (at Repton, *c.* 840),[187] other types of pilaster (Bradford-on-Avon; Brixworth apse);[188] stripwork around doorways (Ledsham, eighth century);[189] (cf. Britford[190]) and plinths (Atcham: ? Period A).[191]

The reassessment of dating of masonry techniques, and in particular of pilaster strips and related types of quoining, has to be considered in connection with Baldwin Brown and Clapham's emphasis on Carolingian influence on later Saxon architecture.[192] The whole problem is discussed with especial reference to pilaster strips by Taylor, who after examining both continental and English stripwork comes to the conclusion that the English examples have a functional and not purely a decorative purpose, and are not derived from continental sources.[193] It should also be noted that Taylor has argued for a much earlier development of the bell tower than has been accepted hitherto, suggesting that Barnack could be as early as the beginning of the ninth century.[194]

Dating buildings to the ninth rather than the tenth or early eleventh century does not preclude Carolingian influence;[195] it may simply indicate that English architecture may not have been so *retardataire* as has sometimes been thought. It is clear, however, that the whole question of the relationship between English and continental architecture during this period needs to be reconsidered. Recent excavations, especially in Germany, have vastly expanded the knowledge of the variety of the forms used in Carolingian architecture. Moreover it now seems over-simple to cite, as Clapham did, early ninth-century Carolingian buildings as precedents for the churches of the English monastic revival of the later tenth century, and not to take into account contemporary Ottonian buildings.[196]

It cannot be assumed that out of the wealth of continental comparisons now available, it will always be possible to discover close parallels for architectural forms current in England. Recent research has tended to underline the diversity of plans, and also the regional variations that existed in northern Europe during the pre-Romanesque period. While discoveries in England have produced further evidence that some of the basic characteristics of Carolingian and Ottonian architecture – the increasing complexity of the east end, the development of the westwork, and the general increase in scale of building – occurred in major English churches, in each case the detailed working out of the plan resulted in a very individual solution. No doubt one explanation of this, which is becoming increasingly clear from recent investigations, is that often the plan was conditioned by earlier buildings on the site. It is not until the Romanesque period that ruthless rebuilding becomes the general rule.

Recent work on later Saxon architecture has consisted almost entirely of studies of individual buildings. It must be hoped that in future there will be more excavations and detailed examinations of existing buildings (such as those now in progress at Deerhurst),[197] which will both clarify the internal history of problematic churches, and will eventually enable a reappraisal of the significance of individual buildings in the development of architecture during this period. Until more research has been done it would be premature to do more here than to note briefly the most important recent discoveries and observations which have altered or enlarged our knowledge of this period.

RECENT RESEARCH ON INDIVIDUAL BUILDINGS

Major buildings: ninth to early tenth century

Clapham discussed the documentary and structural evidence for eleven major churches of the later Saxon period.[198] When he wrote, in only four cases (Elmham, Peterborough, Glastonbury and Deerhurst) was any structural evidence available. Moreover almost all his examples dated from the period of the monastic revival or later. For the earlier period the situation is still not much clearer. The most important new consideration has already been mentioned: the suggestion of a ninth-century date for the later work at Repton, hitherto attributed to the late tenth or eleventh century.[199] The most recent study by Taylor, which takes up some of the ideas put forward by Gilbert, suggests that during the time of King Wiglaf of Mercia (827–40), who was himself buried at Repton, an older mausoleum of the eighth century was incorporated, in the form of the surviving hall crypt, below the chancel of a new church. There is evidence to show that this church had a central tower with north and south porticus opening from it through small arches decorated with columns.[200] The treatment of nave and west end is uncertain.[201] While it cannot be denied that a ninth-century date fits the documentary evidence very satisfactorily, it should be noted and reflected upon that Repton would thus provide the first known English example of a vaulted hall crypt with columns, and of a church plan with a central tower with salient eastern angles, with transept-like chambers attached. From a comparative point of view this early dating is less embarrassing than might appear at first sight. Hall-crypts are known in eighth- and ninth-century Carolingian buildings (e.g. at Fulda[202]). The treatment and the details in the crypt, with the spirally ornamented columns and the panelled respond pilasters, is harder to parallel.[203]

Transepts and crossings in various forms appear early in Carolingian architecture, the first known example being at St Denis (consecrated 775);[204] but the type of crossing which occurs at Repton and in other later Anglo-Saxon buildings where the crossing is wider than the attached northern, southern and eastern arms, so that its exterior angles project between chancel and transept, appears to be a particularly English feature. The development of the salient crossing in late Anglo-Saxon architecture is a complicated

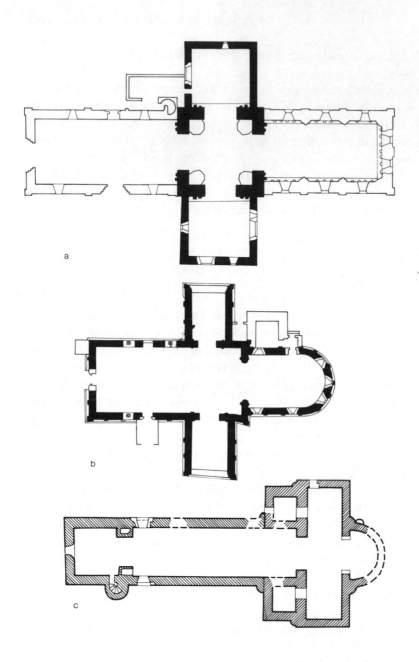

a

b

c

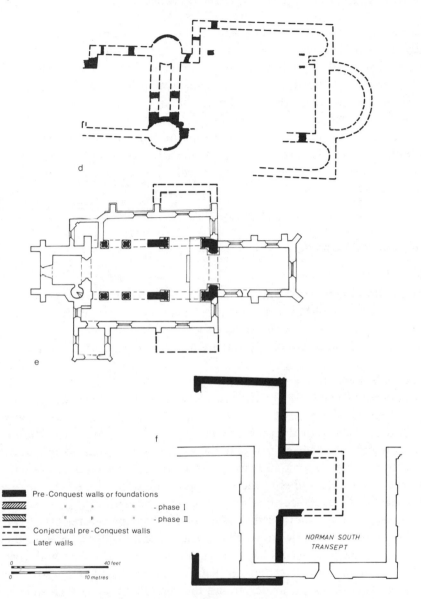

d

e

f

NORMAN SOUTH TRANSEPT

Pre-Conquest walls or foundations

    "   "   " - phase I

    "   "   " - phase II

Conjectural pre-Conquest walls

Later walls

0   40 feet

0   10 metres

Figure 4.10 Comparative plans of later Anglo-Saxon churches:
a Stow (after Taylor)
b Worth (after Taylor)
c North Elmham (after Rigold)
d Much Wenlock (after Jackson and Fletcher)
e Great Paxton (after Clapham)
f Peterborough (after Taylor)

problem which needs to be studied with reference to porticus or transepts in churches without central towers, where there may be a pseudo-crossing without a west arch (e.g. Worth, fig. 4.10b; Hadstock, pl. 20b), and also to salient central towers without lateral chambers (e.g. Langford).[205] Unfortunately none of the examples can be dated.[206]

Another piece of new evidence for the period before the monastic revival is provided by the trial excavations at Winchester which located the site of the New Minster. The evidence indicated a church with aisles and probably transepts, which it seems likely dates from the foundation of the New Minster in 903.[207] It must be hoped that there will be the opportunity to investigate this building further. It would be particularly interesting to know what type of crossing it had.

Major buildings: the late tenth and eleventh centuries

(i) Winchester Old Minster

The excavations of the Old Minster at Winchester have made the most important contribution to our knowledge of late Anglo-Saxon architecture. It is particularly satisfactory that the complex documentary evidence which was analysed lucidly and objectively before excavations started[208] could be convincingly related to the different building phases revealed.[209]

The plan (fig. 4.7) demonstrates how the seventh-century church was extended both to the east and west between 971 and 994. Firstly, a curiously shaped westwork with apsidal north (and presumed south) end was built over the site of St Swithun's grave, which was originally in front of the west end of the early church. This westwork links the church to the already existing tower of St Martin further to the west. It was subsequently altered so that it became a large rectangular structure incorporating St Martin's tower. Additional side chambers (or transepts) were added at the west end of the original church. Before 994 the small square east end was replaced by a much larger one, with a crypt and with a semicircular north (and perhaps south) side chamber. The unexpected results of the Winchester excavations are a salutary warning that it may be impossible to predict the eccentricities of plan that actually existed solely from the evidence of documents and from comparisons with other buildings. Now that the plan of the west end is known, the problematic passage in Wulfstan's poem describing the rebuilding by Æthelwold no longer appears quite so obscure.[210]

The robbed foundations of the Old Minster mean that little can be deduced about its construction or decoration. The find of a carved fragment of a frieze could thus be of especial significance if a pre-Conquest date is accepted. It has been suggested that it illustrates an incident from the *Volsunga saga*, and formed part of a frieze celebrating the ancestry of the royal house, thus expressing in visual terms the close connection that existed between the court and the Old Minster.[211] The original location of the sculpture is not known, but it seems plausible that it was used on the exterior of the building, in view of the evidence for exterior sculpture derived from the descriptions of the late tenth-century tower at the New Minster.[212]

(ii) Sherborne and other examples of westworks

Before the Winchester excavations, existence of westworks of the continental type depended chiefly on documentary evidence, although in his excellent discussion of this, Quirk also drew attention to the structural evidence at Sherborne and St Augustine's, Canterbury.[213] At St Augustine's (fig. 4.6, top) there does not seem to have been a fully developed westwork: a double narthex, narrower than the earlier church, is suggested. But at Sherborne (fig. 4.11) recent excavations have indicated that the pre-Conquest cathedral had not only a west tower but western side chambers, or transepts, extending beyond the line of the aisles of the Saxon church (fig. 4.11).[214] An examination of the existing church has suggested that the present crossing, which is wider than the nave and transepts, follows the lines of a pre-Conquest crossing.[215] The building has been associated with the introduction of Benedictine rule in 998.[216] The late Saxon church would correspond with the descriptions of the late tenth-century buildings at, for example, Durham or Ramsey, where there are references to both western and central towers. However, the recent evidence suggests that late Saxon Sherborne, like Winchester Old Minster, was a composite remodelling, the west end incorporating an older tower, and the west transepts perhaps only a rebuilding of an earlier structure which may have started as a separate church.[217]

The recent discussions of the interpretation of the documentary evidence for the pre-Conquest cathedral at Canterbury have already been mentioned.[218] The existence of some kind of late Anglo-Saxon westwork seems plausible, perhaps converted from an earlier porch.[219] Excavations at the priory of Much Wenlock have revealed a possible westwork with two circular turrets, belonging to a rather puzzling church (fig. 4.10d).[220] A pre-Conquest date has been suggested, but a post-Conquest one would also be possible.

(iii) North Elmham

Elmham was the see of the bishop of East Anglia, an area which was re-established as a single see c. 950. The site has now been identified as North Elmham (fig. 4.10c), but whether the surviving ruins, recently re-examined, are those of the chief church of the bishop, or of a subsidiary church in an ecclesiastical complex, is not entirely certain.[221] The excavations have shown that one peculiarity of the plan of this church, the siting of the small towers in the west angles of the transepts, may be explained by the existence of an earlier building with porticus on the site of the towers. The five floor levels pre-dating the standing walls, and the lack of any early finds, suggest that the present building was not erected before c. 1020. The only other pre-Conquest example of a continuous transept is at Peterborough (fig. 4.10f), for which Rigold suggests on stylistic grounds a similar date.[222] The remains of this, below the present Norman building, were excavated in 1883 by J. T. Irvine. It is generally assumed to be late Saxon, but it has been suggested that the transept was rebuilt on earlier foundations.[223]

(iv) Stow and Great Paxton

Stow (fig. 4.10a) is another example of a church with a crossing wider than the transepts, but in this case the four crossing arches are of equal height, although the arches are not of the fully developed Romanesque type as they do not take up the full width of the interior of the crossing.[224] The church has generally been dated to the eleventh century, although opinions vary on whether the crossing arches date from before or after the Conquest. The Taylors' examination of the building has led to the conclusion that the existing transepts incorporate earlier work. They tentatively date the earliest building to before the early eleventh-century collegiate foundation, and consequently suggest that the present crossing arches are early eleventh century. They support Clapham's argument that the palmette ornament of the western crossing arch and south transept window is of pre-Conquest character.[225] This type of ornament occurs in other churches in the Lincolnshire area, mostly members of the 'overlap' group of Lincolnshire towers,[226] but as the dating of these is also disputed, nothing is proved. On the western arch of the crossing, however, this palmette ornament appears on a hood mould which frames an arch of two orders with angle rolls. It is the latter feature that makes Professor Bony argue that the Stow crossing arches cannot be earlier than the Conquest[227] (this argument is referred to below, p. 191). The form of the original nave at Stow is uncertain. It has been suggested that there might have been aisles or porticus.[228]

The aisled and cruciform church of Great Paxton, Hunts. (fig. 4.10e, pl. 19a), must also be mentioned here. A date for this building in the mid-eleventh century is generally agreed, although again it is unclear whether the building should be placed just before or just after the Conquest.[229] Unlike Stow, the corners of the crossing do not project beyond the transepts, and the plan could thus be described as of a more developed type. On the other hand, the arches are not entirely regular, as the details of the transept arch responds are quite different from those of the chancel arch responds.[230] Although certain details, such as the use of compound piers in the nave, and the forms of the crossing responds (on which see below), appear exceptionally progressive in a Saxon context, these details are not Norman, and some aspects of the construction (e.g. the use of through stones laid in Escomb fashion) are definitely Anglo-Saxon. The church would repay more detailed examination: the size of the transepts has recently been ascertained,[231] but the original form of the east and west ends, and the construction of the nave arches (now covered with plaster), are as yet unknown.

(v) St Augustine's, Canterbury

The rotunda begun but never completed by Abbot Wulfric (1047–59) at St Augustine's Abbey as a link between the church of St Mary and that of St Peter and St Paul is an unusual and ambitious example of mid-eleventh-century English architecture which partly survives (fig. 4.6, top).[232] It can be compared with a group of centrally planned, polygonal buildings (although these were generally added at the east end of churches) which had a crypt and at least one upper storey. Many of these rotundae are known to have had a special funerary function (as was the case at Canterbury). Examples exist from the late eighth century to the twelfth century in France, Switzerland and Belgium.[233]

Minor churches of the later Saxon period: some recent discoveries

Several buildings and fragments dated tentatively to Period B have already been mentioned (see above, pp. 166–8 and 175–8). Although the Taylors' gazetteer includes a number of buildings attributed to Period C which were not discussed by Baldwin Brown or Clapham, some of these, as the authors admit by their definition of Period C3 (1050–1100), may be post-Conquest and thus can only be used with caution for deductions about pre-Conquest architecture.[234]

Archaeological discoveries have added to the known plans of lesser late Saxon buildings. One of the most interesting examples is the equal-armed cruciform building, apparently an uncompleted church, found at South Cadbury, and dated *c*. 1010–20.[235] Excavations have indicated that modest wooden churches continued to be built in the late Anglo-Saxon period, e.g. at North Elmham, Thetford (fig. 4.3c) and Stafford.[236] An interesting and so far unique discovery is the wooden building found at Potterne, Wilts., interpreted as a centrally planned church with attached baptistry.[237] Late Saxon stone buildings could still be very simple,[238] and sometimes it is only through archaeology that it can be established that a plan with archaic features is definitely late Anglo-Saxon.[239] The most common plan of surviving late Anglo-Saxon minor churches appears to consist of a chancel, nave and western tower, but more excavations are needed to establish, for example, whether side chambers continued to be a feature of the later Anglo-Saxon period. It would also be of interest to find out through excavation the plans of churches with exceptionally grand west towers (e.g. Earl's Barton, Sompting), some of which have sometimes been claimed as 'tower churches' (i.e. buildings where the tower forms the main vessel of the church), as may have been the case at Barton-on-Humber (pl. 18a).[240] There have been some excavations of lesser churches of this period,[241] and new evidence for Anglo-Saxon churches can still be revealed simply by careful study of existing buildings,[242] sometimes by deductions from the planning of a later church on the site. Here too archaeology can refute or confirm hypotheses.[243]

RECENT WORK ON SPECIAL ASPECTS OF LATE ANGLO-SAXON BUILDINGS

There are several ways in which the large numbers of surviving late Saxon churches would lend themselves to more detailed comparative analysis. Perhaps the most obvious characteristic of late Anglo-Saxon minor buildings is the tower, so far only inadequately studied.[244] Attention has been drawn to the use of staircase turrets,[245] and also to different types of belfry window, for which a chronological development, at least on a regional basis, can be worked out.[246] What is needed now is a discussion of the forms and functions

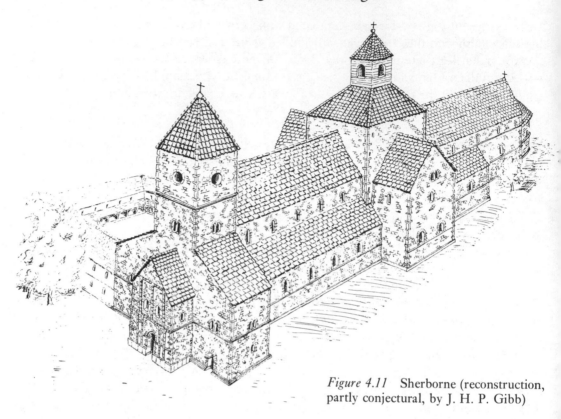

Figure 4.11 Sherborne (reconstruction, partly conjectural, by J. H. P. Gibb)

of towers of lesser buildings in relation to recent discoveries about major westworks and crossings. Another feature which would be worth studying in more detail is the development of arches on a monumental scale, both in towers (cf. Barnack, St Benet, Cambridge: pl. 19b) and as chancel arches (Worth, Wittering (pl. 21d), Bosham), and their relationship to buildings with developed westworks and crossings.

Late Anglo-Saxon towers provide some of the clearest indications that more regional studies of this period would be useful. The towers of Lincolnshire, East Anglia and Northumbria are all well known groups,[247] and in the first two cases, although the precise chronology is not clear, the groups definitely span the period before and after the Conquest. As has been suggested by Professor Bony,[248] more detailed comparative surveys of the evidence might provide a useful chronological sequence for methods of construction and ornament in a particular region. Other areas where buildings of the tenth to eleventh century could profitably be studied as a group are Sussex[249] and the churches of the midlands and eastern counties,[250] links between which may be explained by the Barnack quarries.[251] So far most of the regional studies that exist have been very general in scope, and have taken in the whole pre-Conquest period, providing local catalogues rather than comparative studies.[252]

It will be clear from the references for Stow and Great Paxton that in the later Anglo-Saxon period the treatment of architectural ornament becomes increasingly important, and many dating arguments rest upon these details. It is a subject on which very little recent work has been done, and it is made particularly difficult because so often the buildings with the ornamental details are ones about which very little is known historically. Some starting points have been provided, and there is a brief catalogue of architectural sculpture for the whole pre-Conquest period.[253] Reference should also be made to Okasha's thorough handlist of Anglo-Saxon inscriptions.[254] What would now be very useful would be a corpus of the simpler late Saxon capitals, or further discussion of architectural mouldings, e.g. of arches, string courses and imposts (see fig. 4.12, pls. 21b–c), not

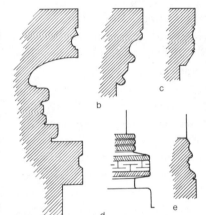

Figure 4.12 Anglo-Saxon mouldings (after Clapham):
a Barnack Tower arch
b Great Paxton
c Deerhurst, Odda's Chapel
d Reculver
e Britford

included in the Taylors' list of sculpture, or a discussion of the use of half-columns below arch soffits (Worth, Wittering: pl. 21d), of stripwork with half-round section (Wittering, Stow: pl. 20a) and of angle columns (Hadstock: pl. 20b). These are all features which indicate the growing interest in plasticity of treatment of surfaces and openings that characterizes early Romanesque developments both in England and on the Continent during the eleventh century.[255]

Professor Bony has suggested that the study of the 'overlap' is the approach most likely to throw light on the chronology of the eleventh century. As the development of arch mouldings and the use of the soffit roll and angle roll are reasonably well documented on the Continent, they could provide useful termini for the appearance of these features in England. On these grounds Bony suggests a post-Conquest date for a number of buildings included in the Taylors' book (e.g. Barholm, Corringham, Stoughton, Bosham). That more elegant mouldings were definitely beginning to appear before the Conquest is demonstrated by the chancel arch imposts at Odda's Chapel, Deerhurst, of 1056 (fig. 4.12c).[256] Elaborate moulded imposts are, however, a feature of Ottonian architecture (cf. also the respond imposts of Great Paxton and St Benet, Cambridge: pls 19a, b, fig. 4.12b), and the use of these must be distinguished from the Norman use of arches with angle rolls and soffit rolls. The two features do not usually occur together in 'overlap' buildings; an interesting exception is Strethall, Essex.[257]

An example of the retrospective approach to the overlap period is Professor Zarnecki's study of architectural sculpture of that period, where the contrasting approach of Anglo-Saxons and Normans to the use of sculptural decoration is emphasized.[258] On the principle that when both Anglo-Saxon and Norman features appear it is the latest one that is the best indication of date, a post-Conquest date is suggested for Milborne Port, Somerset,[259] interesting from an architectural point of view since this is a cruciform church with projecting crossing of the Anglo-Saxon type. Similarly, Sompting (which has many Anglo-Saxon characteristics) is dated to the post-Conquest period, on the grounds that it is built partly of Caen stone.[260]

The sources of late Anglo-Saxon architectural detail (as opposed to sculpture) have been little explored. The older authorities were tempted by the idea that late Anglo-Saxon masonry imitated details from wooden buildings.[261] An alternative approach has been to emphasize the contribution of Carolingian and Ottonian architecture, although Dr Taylor's recent article stresses the functional origins of stripwork and the dissimilarity between German *Lisenen* and English pilaster strips.[262] However, it is difficult to find a functional justification for the forms of arcading, either round- or triangular-headed, that appear on the late Anglo-Saxon towers of Barton-on-Humber (pl. 18a) and Earls Barton or around the apses of Wing and Deerhurst, and which suggest a superficial familiarity on the part of the builders with the appearance of continental buildings, even if an established type of native construction continued in use.[263]

Recently it has been suggested that the form of the Great Paxton piers (pl. 19a) could be derived from bundled wooden posts.[264] But it seems more likely that a wooden ancestry for such ideas, if it existed, was very remote. Comparable stone piers, with columns at the angles rather than in the centre of each face, can be found on the Continent.[265]

Much more work could be done on the interesting question of the variety of artistic contacts between England and the Continent on the eve of the Conquest. The indications are that Normandy was not the only source of ideas, and that the Confessor's church at Westminster, if it was as close to Norman buildings as has been suggested,[266] was rather exceptional. For the architectural historian of the twelfth century, the appearance of so many non-Norman features in English Romanesque architecture inevitably raises the question of what cultural contacts existed in England before the Conquest.[267]

It is not surprising that some Anglo-Saxon types of construction continued in use immediately after the Conquest.[268] What is more remarkable is the evidence for what appears to be a revival of Anglo-Saxon architectural detail in the 'second generation' buildings, from *c.* 1090 onwards, when Anglo-Norman architecture was becoming more sophisticated and ornate[269] – retrospective evidence that at least some aspects of pre-Conquest architecture contributed to later English architectural traditions.[270]

Notes

1 For comments on Rickman's approach, see Taylor (1961) 58–9.
2 Micklethwaite (1896) 293. See also Micklethwaite (1898).
3 G. Baldwin Brown, *The Arts in Early England*, vol. 2: *Anglo-Saxon architecture* (1st edn 1903, 2nd edn, much revised, 1925).
4 See his discussion of ground plans (1925) 327.
5 Clapham (1933).
6 Taylor and Taylor (1965).
7 See List of Sources, p. 463, below.
8 See e.g. the articles by Jackson and Fletcher, and by Gilbert. As the Taylors' work includes a full bibliography under each church for works published before 1965, this article will generally cite their book for further references, and will only refer to earlier studies directly when these are particularly important.
9 For new excavations see the annual summaries in *Medieval Archaeology*. For detailed surveys, see especially recent volumes of the Royal Commission on Historical Monuments.
10 Useful tools in this field are, for the early period, Bede's *Ecclesiastical History*, Colgrave and Mynors (1969), and for the later period, the extracts from Latin sources in Lehmann-Brockhaus (1955–60).
11 The need for research on this is stressed by Biddle (1971). The subject is highly problematic and controversial, not only in this country. For an important attempt to relate Carolingian architecture and liturgy on the Continent, see Heitz (1963). For some criticism of his approach, see Mathews (1971). On the mediterranean countries, see Peeters (1969).
12 See e.g. on Reculver, Taylor (1968a); on the Bishop's Throne at Norwich, Radford (1959).
13 On upper galleries, see below, n. 131. For some comments on the function of minor Anglo-Saxon towers, see Fisher (1969), especially 88ff.
14 On crypts, see Taylor (1969b).
15 A study by R. Gem of the documentary evidence for the architecture of the monastic revival is in progress.
16 See e.g. the problem of St Swithun's tomb, Quirk (1959) and Biddle (1970a). For a recent attempt to relate architecture and liturgy on the Continent during this period, see Sanderson (1971).
17 For examples of recent local studies of this kind in Germany (which demonstrate the extent of church excavation there), see Binding (1967) and (1971).
18 On this problem, see Addleshaw (1959) and (1963). For a discussion of minster churches of different types, see Radford (1973).
19 For summaries on constructional techniques, see Jackson and Fletcher (1944), (1949); Taylor and Taylor (1961b), (1964), (1965) 4ff.; Taylor (1969c) 192–3, (1970b); see also below, pp. 181–2.
20 Biddle (1970a) 316.
21 On the need for more thorough excavation of churches in England, see Biddle (1971) 404–5.
22 For a discussion of the technique, see Taylor (1972a).
23 Taylor (1971); Jackson and Fletcher (1962).
24 Rodwell and Rodwell (1973).
25 See e.g. the various recent interpretations of the pre-Conquest cathedral at Canterbury (see n. 135 below).
26 For exemplary discussions of the documentary evidence for the Winchester sites prior to excavation, see Quirk (1959) and (1961). For a discussion of all types of evidence including both medieval documents and unpublished excavations, see Biddle, Lambrick and Myres (1968) in their discussion of Abingdon Abbey.
27 See below, pp. 187ff.
28 For recent surveys, see Frend (1968); Radford (1971); and Morris (1973).
29 Frend (1968) 41; Wilson (1962) 185–6.
30 For a survey of recent continental material, with references, see Radford (1968).
31 *HE*, 86. Frend (1968) 49n., 81.
32 Jenkins (1965); Taylor and Taylor (1965) 143ff.
33 Fletcher and Meates (1969).
34 Rahtz (1968).
35 Jackson and Fletcher (1959), (1968).
36 Recent excavations at Deerhurst, see Rahtz (1971), have confirmed that there was a Roman building on the site of the church, but there is as yet no proof for Gilbert's hypothesis (1968) of a pre-Saxon rectangular church. Gilbert's suggestion that at Winchester there was a pre-Saxon rectangular church north of the present cathedral has been refuted: Biddle (1970b) and (1972). Other examples of churches built on Roman remains, recently confirmed by excavations, are St Nicholas, Leicester (Council for British Archaeology, *Report* (1971–2) 76) and St

Mary Bishophill Junior, York (R.C.H.M., *York*, iii, *The City of York*, 30).

37 For a full discussion of recent research, see Thomas (1971).

38 On Glastonbury, see Taylor and Taylor (1965) 250, with references to older literature.

39 Thomas (1971) 69–70, 72–3; Thomas (1967).

40 Thomas (1971) 145, 208.

41 Clapham (1930) 16–54. For a more recent survey of this period, see Taylor (1961).

42 Excavations have demonstrated sequences of this kind at e.g. Bargham, Sussex (fig. 4.2b): Barr-Hamilton (1961); Thetford, Norfolk (fig. 4.3c): Wilson and Hurst (1970) 173; Wilson and Moorhouse (1971) 135; Wharram Percy, Yorks. NR (fig. 4.3a); Wilson and Hurst (1969) 252–3; Wilson and Hurst (1970) 174; Wilson and Moorhouse (1971) 135; *Deserted Medieval Village Research Group Interim Report* (1971) 1–5; Winchester, churches of St Mary and St Pancras: Wilson and Moorhouse (1971) 153–4; Biddle (1972) 111–15; Webster and Cherry (1972) 165. On a much larger scale, extension of churches during the Anglo-Saxon period is illustrated by the development of Winchester Old Minster (fig. 4.4d, 7): Biddle (1970a); and St Augustine's, Canterbury (fig. 4.6, top): Taylor and Taylor (1965) 134–43.

43 Baldwin Brown (1925) 327.

44 See above, n. 38.

45 E.g. at Canterbury, Monkwearmouth, Jarrow, Hexham: see Taylor (1961a) 9 and (1969c) 197.

46 Taylor and Taylor (1965) 338–49. The church had a western annexe with gallery, suggested as a slightly later addition.

47 Jackson and Fletcher (1965); Taylor and Taylor (1965) 453–4.

48 For Heysham, see Baldwin Brown (1925) 187; Taylor and Taylor (1965) 312; for Bargham, see Barr-Hamilton (1961).

49 Jackson and Fletcher (1966a).

50 Taylor (1970a).

51 Royal Commission on Historic Monuments, *York*, iii, *City of York* (1972) xlii–xliii.

52 Harbison (1970). Cf. also the frequency of this type of church in Germany, Binding (1971a) esp. 11.

53 Boeckelmann (1956).

54 On Nivelles, see Oswald *et al.* (1966–71) 237. The church began as a simple rectangle to which a chancel was added in the seventh century.

55 On these alternative views, see Saalman (1962) 12–13.

56 E.g. at Thetford (fig. 4.3c; see n. 42 above), the first church, of wood, is dated to after the introduction of Thetford ware, i.e. after the Scandinavian settlement. Cf. also Rivenhall, where an Anglo-Saxon two-cell church has recently been discovered (fig. 4.3b). This was possibly preceded by a timber structure: Rodwell and Rodwell (1973).

57 Taylor and Taylor (1965) 361. But it has not been proved that porticus did not exist here.

58 For St Alkmund, Derby, see Wilson and Hurst (1969) 231. For St Alban Wood Street, see Grimes (1968) 204.

59 Radford (1961a).

60 Clapham (1930) 17ff.; Peers (1902). For more recent summaries of the Kentish evidence, see Fletcher (1965); Taylor (1969c).

61 Taylor and Taylor (1965) 147 interpret the apse as semicircular. Earlier authorities thought it was elliptical: see Peers (1901) 411; Peers and Clapham (1927) 205.

62 Bede, *HE*, V, 23; Taylor (1969d).

63 For a recent reassessment, see Jenkins (1965).

64 Taylor and Taylor (1965) 146.

65 Fletcher (1965) 25–6.

66 Taylor (1968a). There appears to have been a similar arrangement in the earliest form of Winchester Old Minster: see Biddle (1970a) 315. For comparative evidence, see a forthcoming article by Taylor in *Antiquaries Journal.*

67 Hope (1914–15); Clapham (1930) 18–19; Taylor and Taylor (1965) 135ff.

68 Jackson and Fletcher (1956) 2. Taylor (1969d) 258.

69 Clapham (1930) 26ff.

70 Jackson and Fletcher (1956) 2; Taylor (1969d). As has been observed recently by Rigold (1968: 35ff.) and Taylor (1969d) re-examination of the Lyminge evidence could be instructive. The nineteenth-century excavations revealed both Roman material and remains of buildings that may have belonged to the double monastery, and the identification of the structures shown on fig. 4.4a is difficult. Cf. also Cramp, p. 250, n. 9.

71 Clapham (1930) 19–20 and fig. 7.

72 Taylor and Taylor (1965) 147, fig. 64.

73 Fletcher (1965) 27–31.

74 See e.g. Saalman (1962) 12; Webb (1956) 4–5.

75 Pocock and Wheeler (1971). This contradicts the suggestion (Jackson and Fletcher (1956) 10) that this north door was not an exterior feature and that all early churches had western entrances.

76 Gilbert (1947) 140–70; Taylor and Taylor (1965) 122–6.

77 Taylor and Taylor (1965) 378–84.

78 Peers, Clapham and Horne (1930); Taylor and Taylor (1965) 253 and fig. 110. On the excavations at Glastonbury cf. Cramp, pp. 242–6.

79 Biddle (1970a).

80 Jackson and Fletcher (1961a); Taylor and Taylor (1965) 193–207. For other views, see Gilbert (1968).

81 Rahtz (1971).

82 Taylor and Taylor (1965) 106.

83 Jackson and Fletcher (1965) 5ff.

84 Taylor and Taylor (1965) 71.

85 Jackson and Fletcher (1956) 4; Taylor and Taylor (1965) 86. The date of the building is much disputed. See also n. 173.

86 In the south-east: Period A: Bradwell, Essex; St Pancras, Canterbury; and Reculver, Kent. In the north: Period A: Bywell St Peter, Northumberland; Corbridge, Northumberland; Escomb, Durham; Ledsham, Yorks. WR; Monkwearmouth, Durham; Restenneth, Angus; Seaham, Durham. Period B: Bardsey, Yorks. WR; Skipwith, Yorks. ER. Elsewhere: Period B: Brigstock, Northants.; Titchfield, Hants. Dating doubtful: Deerhurst, Glos., St Mary, Canterbury. In addition the basilicas of Lydd, Kent, and Brixworth, Northants., had west porches. A western annexe at St Martin, Canterbury, has also been suggested: Taylor and Taylor (1965) 143.

87 Taylor and Taylor (1965) 534–6.

88 Smedley and Owles (1970); the western annexe is interpreted as a late Saxon west tower.

89 Peers (1901) 412.

90 Pocock and Wheeler (1971).

91 Taylor and Taylor (1965) 432–46 (with references to earlier literature); Gilbert (1964); Colgrave and Cramp (1965). The rest of the plan of Monkwearmouth has not been established. No traces of a south aisle or porticus were found in recent excavations: Wilson and Hurst (1968) 156.

92 Pocock and Wheeler (1971).

93 Taylor and Taylor (1965) 112–13; Webster and Cherry (1972) 158.

94 Taylor and Taylor (1965) 534–6; Aird (1913).

95 Taylor and Taylor (1965) 39–40, 378–84.

96 Simpson (1963).

97 Taylor (1969a).

98 Gem (1971).

99 Parsons (1962).

100 Oswald et al. (1966–71) 317, 286, 298. For a discussion of these and other examples, referring to the varied uses to which such annexes were put, see Binding (1971b) esp. 130–33. See also the collection of plans in Hubert et al. (1969) figs 343ff. (some misleadingly schematic) and the continental comparisons in Taylor (1969c) fig. 4.

101 Oswald et al. (1966–71) 21.

102 On the possible relationship between the two, see Gilbert (1948).

103 A function as a mausoleum has been suggested for Bradford-on-Avon, although without any supporting evidence: Gilbert (1967). On other tomb buildings, see below, p. 147.

104 Taylor and Taylor (1965) 105–8; Clapham (1930) 49–50. Clapham suggested that there were transepts east of the porticus, but the evidence is not conclusive. Further investigation of the building would be worth while.

105 Clapham (1930) 41.

106 Baldwin Brown (1925) 160ff.

107 Ibid., 168.

108 Taylor and Taylor (1965) 297ff.

109 Baldwin Brown (1925) fig. 71.

110 Baldwin Brown (1925) fig. 71. Clapham (1930) fig. 15 suggests small square piers.

111 Taylor and Taylor (1965) 308.

112 Hubert et al. (1969) 27.

113 Taylor and Taylor (1965) 303–4; Taylor (1966). Surviving early fragments elsewhere in the north give some support to the theory of a tradition of architectural ornament. See e.g. the carved external string course on Monkwearmouth porch (see n. 91 above); the internal string course at Masham, Yorks. NR, compared to fragments at Ripon: Taylor and Taylor (1965) 734; and the external string course decorated with roundels, and ascribed to Period B at Edenham, Lincs.; Taylor (1963). For other aspects of the decoration of early Northumbrian buildings, see Cramp (1970).

114 Taylor and Taylor (1965) 338–49.

115 Cramp (1969) 42–5; Webster and Cherry (1972) 148ff. On the 1973 excavations inside the church, see Cramp (1973) 000 and fig. 0.

116 Jackson and Fletcher (1961); Burford (1967); Webster and Cherry (1972) 158.

117 Clapham (1930) 33.

118 Taylor and Taylor (1965) 109.

119 Noted by Taylor and Taylor (1965) 113.

120 Gilbert (1965).

121 For crypts, see below, p. 174.
122 Hubert *et al.* (1969) 32.
123 No structural evidence for a tower is suggested. The Taylors' measurements indicate that the presbytery walls are in fact thinner than those of the nave: Taylor and Taylor (1965) 113.
124 It has been suggested that Brixworth may have been the *Clofesho* at which ecclesiastical councils were held: Davis (1962).
125 Clapham (1928); Abbott (1963–4).
126 Taylor (1969c) 196 n. 12, suggests a date in the early eighth century.
127 Clapham (1930) 98 and 113; Baldwin Brown (1925) 321.
128 Jackson and Fletcher (1962).
129 Jackson and Fletcher (1962) 3.
130 See Taylor and Taylor (1965) 670 for a summary of different views.
131 Taylor and Taylor (1965) 669–70. For a discussion of western galleries here and elsewhere, with the suggestion that they may throw light on the obscure descriptions of the upper storeys at Hexham, see Taylor (1959) 138ff. Evidence for western galleries exists at Deerhurst, Jarrow, Tredington and Stoke D'Abernon. The suggested function of such galleries, as an elevated seat for the lay proprietor, or for a church dignitary, can be compared with the later development of western towers with upper rooms possibly used in this way: see Radford (1961a) 172–4. Whether the upper storeys of early western porches can be connected with such functions is disputed: cf. Taylor (1959) 141; Radford (1961a) 173.
132 Jackson and Fletcher (1968).
133 Taylor and Taylor (1965) 700ff.
134 Hutchison and Phillips (1972) 78–83.
135 For different recent views on plan and dating, see Taylor (1969a); Parsons (1969a); Gem (1970); Gilbert (1970).
136 Brown and McWhirr (1966), (1967).
137 Taylor and Taylor (1965), 634–7; Royal Commission on Historic Monuments, *Dorset South-East* (1970), xliii and 340ff.
138 On transepts, cf. Baldwin Brown (1925) 168ff.; on Hexham, and on the remains of the pre-Conquest transept at Peterborough which he interpreted as early. There is no firm dating for the latter; see also Taylor and Taylor (1965) 491–494.
139 Jackson and Fletcher (1961a) 11ff.
140 See below. This building probably had a transept.

141 Clapham (1930) 143–152. For later centrally planned buildings, see below.
142 *HE*, II, 14; Colgrave and Mynors (1969), 187. 'Very soon after his baptism he set about building a greater and more magnificent church of stone, under the instruction of Paulinus, in the midst of which the chapel which he had first built was to be enclosed. The foundations were laid and he began to build this square church surrounding the former chapel (*in gyro prioris oratorii per quadrum coepit aedificare basilicam*).' For the Armenian Theory see Gilbert (1964).
143 See above, p. 169, n. 108.
144 See above, p. 160, n. 47.
145 See above p. 160, n. 48.
146 Biddle, Lambrick and Myres (1968) 43.
147 See above p. 174, nn. 97, 98.
148 Boeckelmann (1956).
149 E.g. at Metz. Oswald *et al.* (1966–71) 214. An early sixth-century date is suggested for a polygonal apse, the ecclesiastical use of which is unproven. The building was converted, possibly in the early seventh century, into a church with rectangular east end.
150 Clapham (1930) 29ff. For a discussion of early polygonal apses on the Continent, see Verzone (1954).
151 For important summaries of the continental material, with further references, see Verbeek (1950) and Grodecki (1958) 219ff. For a brief, more recent account in English, with some useful references, see Saalman (1962) 14ff.
152 Taylor (1969b).
153 For Repton, see Taylor (1971) and Gilbert (1967a). For Glastonbury, see Peers *et al.* (1930). For Sidbury, see Taylor and Taylor (1965) 547–8.
154 For Ripon, see Taylor and Taylor (1965) 576–578. For the others, see pp. 169ff.
155 For Canterbury, see n. 135, above. The evidence for Abingdon depends on inadequate excavations: see Biddle, Lambrick and Myres (1968) 63.
156 The case for a *fenestella* used to be argued in the case of Wing, but this was not confirmed by recent examination: see Jackson and Fletcher (1962) 13–14.
157 Toynbee and Ward-Perkins (1956).
158 For different interpretations of this problem, see Taylor (1969a); Parsons (1969a); Gem (1970); and Gilbert (1970).
159 Taylor and Taylor (1965) 399, 499, 643.
160 Radford (1955); Taylor and Taylor (1965) 384.

161 For a late Saxon use of tiles, see e.g. Holy Trinity, Colchester: Taylor and Taylor (1965) 162–4.

162 For Heddon-on-the-Wall, see Taylor and Taylor (1965) 292, 'probably A'; also Gilbert (1948). For Staindrop: Taylor and Taylor (1965) 596, 'probably A2 or A3', following Romans and Radford (1954). For Sockburn: Taylor and Taylor (1965) 555. For Hoddom: Radford (1967) 116–17. St Mary Bishophill Senior, York, has been claimed as early: see Taylor and Taylor (1965) 699; but recent excavations have not supported this conclusion: see Royal Commission on Historic Monuments, York, iii (1972) 116–17.

163 Taylor and Taylor (1965) 694. The north wall is dated to Period A on the basis of a simple blocked window, despite a string course usually dated late.

164 Taylor and Taylor (1965) 31. The use of megalithic stones and an internal triangular head to a window is suggested as evidence for Period A. Fletcher (1966) objects that this would entail an early dating for a stepped plinth, a feature generally considered 'late'. But cf. Taylor's recent dating of the plinths at Repton (see below, p. 187).

165 For the string courses at Masham and Edenham, see p. 170, n. 113, above; for Kirby Hill, see Taylor and Taylor (1965) 354.

166 For Geddington: Taylor and Taylor (1965) 248. Period B is suggested for the triangular-headed exterior arcading, which is broken into by a later Saxon window. For Billingham, Gilbert (1948) suggests a ninth-century date for the nave walls. Taylor and Taylor (1965) 66 accept this date, but differ on the later history of the building. For Whitfield: Taylor and Taylor (1965) 655. A single-splayed window is suggested as evidence for a Period A building much altered in Period C.

167 Taylor and Taylor (1965) 287.

168 Taylor and Taylor (1965) 429. See also Rigold (1968).

169 Taylor and Taylor (1965) 491.

170 Jackson and Fletcher (1963).

171 Taylor and Taylor (1965) 556–8.

172 Taylor (1969c).

173 In support of an early date for part of the fabric, see especially Jackson and Fletcher (1953); Taylor and Taylor (1965) 86; Jackson and Fletcher (1966b); and using different arguments, Gilbert (1967a). In support of a late date

for the whole building, see Mercer (1966) who disputes Jackson and Fletcher's argument that the exterior pilaster strips were made later by cutting back older walls. H. M. Taylor also considers the fabric to be substantially of one date (Taylor 1973). On the important evidence recorded during the nineteenth-century restorations by J. T. Irvine, see Taylor (1972b).

174 At Hackness, Yorks. NR, for example, there was a monastery founded in 680, but the pre-Conquest fabric in the nave is dated to Period B1 on the basis of the carving on the chancel arch impost: Taylor and Taylor (1965) 268, following Baldwin Brown (1925) 203–4.

175 Hubert (1938) 39ff. and (1963), and more recently but more summarily, Hubert et al. (1969) i. See also Taylor (1969c) 197.

176 It is interesting that the description of Wilfrid's chapel dedicated to the Virgin at Hexham (Clapham (1930) 144–6) seems to correspond with the evidence produced by Hubert (see note above) that in Gaul a second church, dedicated to the Virgin, was sometimes added to an existing cathedral foundation (e.g. at Tours and Bordeaux, already in the sixth century). It is suggested that such a church was used as a kind of public church belonging to the bishop (as distinct from the bishop's private chapel).

177 This could lead to the conclusion that English architecture influenced later continental developments; Gilbert (1964) takes this approach.

178 Rigold (1962–3); Oswald (1955).

179 Cramp (1967) 14–15. See also Harrison (1962).

180 Cramp (1967) 19; Royal Commission on Historic Buildings, York, iii (1972) xli.

181 Wilson (1967).

182 E.g. Brozzi (1968) on Cividale; Weidemann (1968) on Mainz.

183 The need is not fulfilled by Fisher (1962). Recent volumes of the Victoria County History now provide useful summaries of the early ecclesiastical history of their areas: see e.g. Victoria County History, Stafford, iii (1970) 1ff.

184 It is significant that in Taylor's most recent list of buildings which he considers firmly datable from documentary evidence, only two standing buildings of the late Anglo-Saxon period are included: both are late, St Gregory, Kirkdale (rebuilt 1055–65), and Odda's chapel, Deerhurst (1056). Taylor (1973) Appendix I.

185 Taylor and Taylor (1965).

186 Knowles and Hadcock (1971) Appendix I.

187 Taylor (1970b).

188 Gilbert (1965); Gilbert (1967b).

189 Taylor and Taylor (1965) 382–3.

190 Clapham (1930) 50 and 112 suggested that Britford is the earliest example of this feature, *c.* 800.

191 Taylor and Taylor (1965) 31–2; cf. Fletcher (1966), where this dating is disputed. Cf. p. 178, n. 164.

192 Baldwin Brown (1925) 227–66; Clapham (1930) 77–97.

193 Taylor (1970b) 40. See also Jackson and Fletcher (1944), (1949), (1951).

194 Taylor (1968b). This, however, would imply a pre-Scandinavian date for the openwork panel in the tower. On the dating of towers, cf. Baldwin Brown (1925) 330ff.; Clapham (1930) 116.

195 Clapham (1930) 50 recognized this himself in the case of Britford.

196 For brief summaries in English with further references, see on Carolingian architecture: Hubert *et al.* (1970) 50ff., mainly on France; Thümmler (1960) mainly on Germany. On Ottonian architecture: Kubach (1965). For a more detailed discussion of Ottonian architecture (in French): Grodecki (1958). The evidence for individual churches in the Empire is now usefully summarized (in German) in gazetteer form with further references, in Oswald *et al.* (1966–71).

197 Rahtz (1971).

198 Clapham (1930) 85ff.: Canterbury Cathedral; Winchester Old Minster; Durham; North Elmham; Ely; Ramsey; Thorney; Peterborough; Glastonbury; Deerhurst; Canterbury, St Augustine's. To this list should be added Clapham's later discussion of Stow; Clapham (1946).

199 Gilbert (1967a); Taylor (1971).

200 Taylor (1971) 380 and fig. 22.

201 Taylor (1971) 385; cf. Gilbert (1967a) who suggests that there were aisles.

202 Oswald *et al.* (1966–71) 84ff.

203 Small decorative spiral columns appear in early Spanish churches, e.g. Santa Maria de Naranco of 848: Conant (1959) pl. 19 B. The idea in both cases derives from classical traditions. At Repton it has been suggested that the columns were intended to imitate those in St Peter's, Rome: Kidson *et al.* (1965) 31.

204 Crosby (1953) 51. On the revival of the transept in the Carolingian period, see Krautheimer (1942). On the use of different types of transepts during the Carolingian and Ottonian periods, see Grodecki (1958) 17–126.

205 On these different types of plan, see Clapham (1930) 99–104.

206 Well-known crossings with salient eastern angles (as at Repton) are Breamore, Hants., St Mary in Castro, Dover; cf. Bargham (Sussex): Carr-Hamilton (1961); and perhaps Canford Magna, Dorset, Royal Commission on Historic Monuments, *Dorset, South-East* (1970) 197–9. Examples of crossings with all four angles projecting, perhaps a later development of the previous type, are Norton, Durham; Sherborne, Dorset (fig. 4.11); Stow, Lincs. (fig. 4.10a); Milborne Port, Somerset (on the last three, see below, pp. 187ff.); and Tamworth, Staffs.: Sherlock (1963). Other types of crossing existed: one without salient angles occurs at Great Paxton (fig. 4.10e) (see below, p. 188) and perhaps existed at Bere Regis, Dorset, Royal Commission on Historic Monuments *Dorset, South-East* (1970), 11–12; a continuous transept (i.e. with no evidence of north and south arches) existed at North Elmham (fig. 4.10c) and Peterborough (fig. 4.10f) (see below, p. 187). There was a pre-Conquest transept of uncertain type at Rochester: Newman (1969) 454. Cf. also the evidence for a central tower at Abingdon: Biddle *et al.* (1969) 44–5.

207 Biddle (1964) 202–11.

208 Quirk (1959).

209 See Biddle (1970a) 311ff. for the final interpretation of the Old Minster plan. Earlier reports on the excavations are published in *The Archaeological Journal*, cxix (1964) 150–94, and in *The Antiquaries Journal*, xliv ff.

210 Quirk (1959) 44: 'He also added many chapels with sacred altars which keep the entry of the threshold doubtful, so that whoever walks in these courts with unfamiliar tread, cannot tell whence he comes or whither to return, since open doors are seen on every hand, nor does any certain path of a way appear.'

211 Biddle (1966) 329–32.

212 Quirk (1961); see esp. 29ff. for a comparative discussion of the uses of external friezes.

213 Quirk (1959) 53. On St Augustine's, see Taylor and Taylor (1965) 136, and Wilson and Hurst (1958) 186–7.

214 Gibb (1969), (1972) and (1976): I am grateful to Mr Gibb for letting me see his report in advance of publication; Royal Commission on Historic Monuments, *West Dorset*, Addendum (1974).

215 Royal Commission on Historic Monuments,

West Dorset, xlvii–1, 200. A similar history is suggested for the crossing of Wimborne Minster, Dorset.

216 Taylor and Taylor (1965) 543. For a discussion of the documentary evidence of the rebuilding, see the Appendix by R. H. D. Gem in Gibb (1976).

217 Gibb (1976). See especially his conclusion which differs from that in Royal Commission on Historic Monuments, *West Dorset*, Addendum. For documentary references to Durham and Ramsey, see Clapham (1930) 88, 90.

218 See pp. 167, 175.

219 See esp. Parsons (1969a), Gem (1970).

220 Jackson and Fletcher (1965).

221 Rigold (1962–3) esp. 68–70. The problem illustrates the need to excavate whole sites.

222 Rigold (1962–3) 107. Rigold also draws attention to the possibility, as yet unconfirmed by excavation, of the plan of a pre-Conquest transept of this type surviving at St Benet Hulme, Norfolk.

223 For a summary of the evidence, see Taylor and Taylor (1965) 491–3.

224 For comments on this, see Pevsner and Harris (1964) 380–81.

225 Taylor and Taylor (1965) 584–93; Clapham (1946). On the palmette ornament, see also Fisher (1962) 302.

226 Taylor and Taylor (1965) 587, n. 1.

227 Bony (1967) 76.

228 Taylor and Taylor (1965) 590–91.

229 Taylor and Taylor (1965) 484–8; Cobbett and Fox (1922–3).

230 See Taylor and Taylor (1965) 487, fig. 238.

231 Wilson and Moorhouse (1971) 126; Webster and Cherry (1972) 156.

232 Clapham (1930) 149–52. Taylor and Taylor (1965) 137, 141–2.

233 For an important discussion of this type of building, see Hubert (1954). To his list should be added St Pierre Louvain: Mertens (1963). For the possibility of a circular late Saxon addition at Abingdon, see Biddle *et al.* (1968) 64.

234 Taylor and Taylor (1965) xxv. Examples of such 'overlap' buildings are some of the 'Lincolnshire towers', e.g. Barnet by-le-Wold; also such buildings as St Mary, Bedford (on which see also below, n. 251), or Birchanger, Essex.

235 Alcock (1972).

236 Cf. Barrow: Taylor (1970a); and Rivenhall, fig. 3b: Rodwell (1973).

237 Davey (1964).

238 E.g. the chapel of St Ia, Camborne, Cornwall, dated to *c.* 1000: Wilson and Hurst (1964) 231. See also Wharram Percy, Wilson and Hurst (1970) 174; Wilson and Moorhouse (1971) 135; Deserted Medieval Village Research Group *Interim Report* (1971) 1–5.

239 E.g. South Elmham, see n. 88.

240 For this theory, see Fisher (1969) 43–6.

241 E.g. Beckery Chapel, Glastonbury: Wilson and Hurst (1969) 239; Flawford, Notts. (early eleventh-century tower, earlier nave): Webster and Cherry (1972) 159; Bristol, St Mary Port (late Saxon nave and chancel): Wilson and Hurst (1964) 249.

242 E.g. at Rivenhall, Essex (fig. 4.3b), where a church thought to have been rebuilt in the nineteenth century was found to be substantially a pre-Conquest building: Rodwell and Rodwell (1972) and (1973).

243 Royal Commission on Historic Monuments, *Dorset, South-East* (1970) 276–9: Studland (chancel, central tower, nave); 304: Wareham St Martin (nave and chancel); 394–5: Winterbourne Steepleton (nave). Also Royal Commission on Historic Monuments, *Cambridgeshire, North-East*, (1972) 65; Horningsea (church with porticus).

244 Fisher (1969).

245 Taylor (1959), Taylor and Taylor (1965 xxiv, 112–13, 113–16, 230–1, 322–3. See also, on this feature at North Elmham, Rigold (1962–3) 176; and on South Elmham, Smedley and Owles (1970).

246 Taylor (1959) 155–6; (1961) and (1968b).

247 On Lincolnshire and Northumbrian towers, see Taylor and Taylor (1961); also on Lincolnshire, Baldwin Brown (1925) 386ff.; Fisher (1962) 246–52; Fisher (1963). For the East Anglian towers, see Fisher (1962); also Rigold (1962–3) 107–8, for some pertinent comparisons with North Elmham.

248 Bony (1967) 77.

249 Fisher (1970) provides a new but inadequate catalogue. For a reappraisal of Bosham and Singleton by M. Hare, see Webster and Cherry (1972), 163.

250 E.g. Great Paxton; Wittering; St Benet, Cambridge; Peterborough.

251 On the use of Barnack stone, see Jope (1964). For interesting discussions of some late Saxon and overlap churches in Bedfordshire, referring to the availability of building stone, see Smith

(1966), Hare (1971). On St Mary's, Bedford, see Webster and Cherry (1972).

252 Examples of recent local surveys of this type are: Green (1951) on Hampshire; Taylor (1966b) on Staffordshire; Taylor (1963b) on Wessex; for some further comments on Wiltshire churches, see Ross (1967); Smith (1973) on Hertfordshire.

253 Taylor and Taylor (1966a). For some corrections to the inscriptions in the Taylors' list, see Okasha (1969). For Knook, Wilts., see further Taylor (1968c). The pre-Conquest dates of some of the Taylors' examples are not universally accepted: cf. on Knook, Pevsner (1963) 252; Zarnecki (1952); and on Milborne Port, Somerset: Zarnecki (1966) esp. 99–100. The Taylors' list excludes some architectural sculpture considered pre-Conquest by older authorities, e.g. the tympana at Southwell, Notts., Water Stratford, Bucks., and St Nicholas, Ipswich, Suffolk. On the arguments for a post-Conquest date for the Ipswich sculpture, see Galbraith (1968).

254 Okasha (1971).

255 For some remarks on these subjects, see Baldwin Brown (1925) 408–16; Clapham (1930) 122–6. There are some useful illustrations of architectural details in Fisher (1962) and (1969). On capitals, see Zarnecki (1955) and Zarnecki (1966). On angle columns and stripwork, see Bony (1965) esp. 101–3.

256 Bony (1967) 76–7. Bony points out that Clapham's profile of Odda's Chapel – Clapham (1930) fig. 38 – is more reliable than that in Taylor and Taylor (1965).

257 Taylor and Taylor (1965) 596–8.

258 Zarnecki (1966).

259 Zarnecki (1966) 98–9.

260 Zarnecki (1966) 91.

261 Clapham (1930) accepted this argument for Earls Barton.

262 See above, pp. 182, n. 193.

263 Attention has been drawn to two possible alternative early precursors of decorative late Anglo-Saxon stripwork; wooden openwork in furniture, as illustrated in an eighth-century manuscript, and the surprising appearance of triangular-headed arches carrying columns in the sixth-century church of Tigzirt in North Africa, see Schapiro (1959). For a general discussion of the problem, with reference to both classical practices and the problem of wooden origins, see Talbot Rice (1952) 52–4. For another attempt to use a manuscript illustration to interpret the appearance of a building (the treatment of doors), see Parsons (1969b).

264 Rigold (1962–3) 106. A post-hole suggesting a wooden post of this form was found at North Elmham.

265 Close parallels to the Great Paxton type of nave pier appears in the Essen-Werden group of churches of *c.* 1060, see Verbeek (1957). The same type of quatrefoil pier exists (re-used and undated, but probably eleventh century) at Stavelot. For the Great Paxton crossing responds, cf. the eleventh-century nave piers at St Remi, Reims.

266 Tanner and Clapham (1933).

267 On non-Norman features in English Romanesque, see Hearn (1971) esp. 200.

268 For a recently discovered example of Saxon type quoining definitely datable to after the Conquest, see Biddle (1970a) 290. A post-Conquest date for Anglo-Saxon type work has also been suggested at St Peter, Canterbury: Smith (1971).

269 E.g. the use of soffit rolls, see Webb (1956) 38, and for the monolithic column see Bony (1965) 105ff. On the whole question of the survival of Anglo-Saxon architectural ideas, see Kidson *et al.* (1965) 36–7. There is comparable evidence for a revival of Anglo-Saxon motifs in sculpture of the twelfth century: see e.g. Zarnecki (1951) 38–9, Zarnecki (1955b) esp. Zarnecki (1958) 12ff. and Galbraith (1968).

270 The author would like to thank Dr H. M. Taylor for his helpful suggestions made after reading this chapter in typescript. Every student of Anglo-Saxon architecture is greatly indebted to Dr Taylor's work, and it must be acknowledged here that many plans in this chapter are based on those in his publications. This chapter was written in 1973–4 and attempts to cover publications up to that date.

5

Monastic sites

Rosemary J. Cramp

The importance of monasteries within the post-Roman period is well summarized by Knowles when he says of their inmates, 'We may consider them as a social and economic phenomenon, as part of medieval society, as producers, farmers, capitalists, and consumers, or as a bulwark of the clerical as opposed to the lay institutions of their time. We may consider them as a great cultural force, as the greatest single agency in transmitting the legacy of the past... as patrons of architecture and sculpture, as the only artists in calligraphy and illumination during the greater part of the Middle Ages.'[1]

Not all of these considerations can be explored in this study, which is primarily concerned with the contribution which excavated evidence can make to the understanding of the monastic settlement. Nevertheless it would be perverse to ignore the contribution of textual evidence to the interpretation of this type of site, since the formal structure, the layout and the specialized activities of the inhabitants are determined by ideologies which are comparatively well documented. However, modern excavation has shown that it is dangerous to work on the assumption that there are clearly defined models which can be applied to the interpretation of excavated sites. Maps, such as Alice Ryan's compilation,[2] do not assist the archaeologist in determining the exact location of the monastery, although in many cases the monastic church survives to provide a clue.

By the time the Anglo-Saxons accepted Christianity the concept of monasticism had already engendered a variety of institutions, whose differing traditions of organization could have affected their appearance. By the end of the Anglo-Saxon period economic, liturgical and social changes in England had clearly brought about further development.

At the beginning of the period under consideration, the monastic institution con-

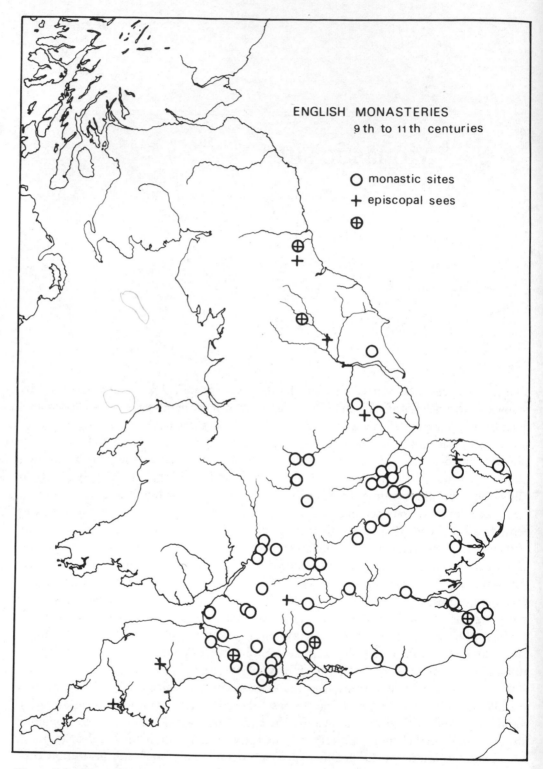

Figure 5.1 Map of monasteries in the late Saxon period (R. Cramp)

stituted something of a paradoxical reversal of its initial role. For the unsophisticated barbarian west, fragmented into small political units, it provided a stable environment linked with an international tradition which gave scope to the intellect and the arts, and ensured the survival of a more advanced technology than could be expected in contemporary secular society. The stimulus provided by these artificially created groups, which escaped in some measure from the secular ties of kinship and lordship, is easy to illustrate by the writings and the artifacts produced within the monastery. This is in fact the aspect of European monasticism which has been most explored. However, the context which produced such work has been singularly unexplored archaeologically. Of the hundreds of sites of this period which are known to have existed in Europe only a handful have received any consideration save in the analysis, and sometimes excavation, of the church. The Celtic west has perhaps the best record of archaeological survey and excavation, but in the area covered by this chapter (that area of the British Isles under the direct control of the Anglo-Saxon Church) the record is poor. Of the eighty-eight sites of the seventh to ninth centuries whose documentation is noted by Ryan, only ten sites have been excavated: Burgh Castle; Canterbury; Glastonbury; Glastonbury Tor; Hartlepool; Monkwearmouth and Jarrow; Tintagel; Tynemouth; and Whitby. Of the later reformed monasteries of the tenth and eleventh centuries for which the distribution is shown on fig. 5.1 only four have been excavated; Abingdon, Canterbury, Glastonbury and Winchester, and of these only Glastonbury and Winchester in large-scale modern excavations which can be compared with modern excavations of secular sites.

These sites do cover in some measure the different types of settlement that the documentary evidence would lead one to expect. Glastonbury and Tintagel belong to the Celtic west. Burgh Castle is a missionary centre of Irish monks, Whitby a double house, Monkwearmouth and Jarrow were founded under strong continental influence and Canterbury and Glastonbury were centres of the tenth-century reform movement.

The evidence for the hermitage site, the smallest settlement unit, is largely documented in England in relation to the early period, often specifically linked with the Celtic Church. The fullest description for a hermitage possibly derived from the Celtic type is that of St Cuthbert's on the Inner Farne. The writer of the *Anonymous Life*[3] describes a single group of buildings. He states that there was a wall, or enclosure of stone and earth, surrounding Cuthbert's dwellings (*domunculas*), and that he had a little latrine built outside over the cliff. Bede's account is more circumstantial. He describes the construction as almost round, measuring four or five poles from wall to wall. The area was excavated to a lower depth inside the wall, and the stones and earth quarried out were used in the construction of his dwelling. In the dwelling were two buildings – an oratory and a room for general purposes. They were both roofed with timber and straw. By the landing stage was a hospice and well.[4] These elements, together with a small area of cultivated ground, would be the essential components of the hermitage site.

Similar no doubt in appearance were the retreat houses of the early monastic bishops such as that which John of Beverley occupied from time to time near Hexham, or Chad near Lichfield. The former Bede describes as a *mansio secretior* surrounded by a *vallum*. The enclosure also contained a *clymiterium* 'oratory' dedicated to St Michael.[5]

The enclosure mentioned in all of these accounts seems to be an essential element of the insular monastic sites. In Irish monastic sites a substantial enclosure has proved an important identifying feature,[6] although it can also be a feature of secular sites in Ireland. In England the literary evidence suggests a variety of enclosure types, some of which like the thorn hedge at Oundle[7] might leave little archaeological trace. At Abingdon (see p. 216) there is evidence for a small circular enclosure of the Irish type, 120 ft (37 m) in diameter. However, at Bardsey or St Benet Hulme,[8] where the sites, as in Ireland, have remained comparatively undisturbed, air photographs show the very large rectilinear enclosures marked by a bank and ditch. Unfortunately, however, these have not been dated by excavation.

At Wimborne, Bede tells us, the double monastery was surrounded by high stone walls (see p. 206). Sometimes, however, the monastery seems to have been sited within an earlier enclosure, as on some Irish sites. These in England could be old hill-forts as at Breedon, Leics., or Roman stone-walled forts as at Reculver, Bradwell or Burgh Castle (see below, p. 212).[9] Sometimes natural features formed the enclosure on promontory or peninsula sites. Of Selsey, Bede says,[10] 'The place is surrounded by the sea on all sides except the west where there is an entrance about the cast of a sling.' Similar sites which were enclosed by a man-made structure on one side only are known from Tintagel (see p. 209), Hartlepool (p. 220) and Old Melrose.[11] Enclosures discovered by excavation are known at Glastonbury (see p. 244). Such enclosures would have defined the inner territory of the monastery and would have protected the privacy of the inhabitants, but there is no indication that they were meant to be defensive structures.

In fact the relationship of the world and the inmates of monasteries must have differed according to the foundation traditions of the individual house. From the earliest period these centres dispensed charity and provided hospitality. The poem *De Abbatibus*,[12] which throws some light on life in an eighth-century monastery, describes how Abbot Sigwine gave gifts at night to the paupers who, being shut out of the gates, laid their frozen limbs in the rubbish to keep warm. The duties of the guest-master at Lindisfarne included washing the blankets in the sea. However, it would seem that most communities were welcoming, and the hospice for visitors was usually by the outer enclosure. At Ripon when Cuthbert was guest-master he went out to the hospice '*de interioribus monasterii aedibus*' and found an angelic traveller.[13] The guest chamber where Wilfrid died at Oundle was attached by one corner to the enclosure of thorns, and so clearly was on the perimeter of the settlement.

Monasteries also provided convenient meeting places for noble or important visitors, and it seems in some houses there was no rigorous exclusion of the opposite sex as guests. Queen Osgyth met the Abbess Æthelhild at Bardney, a male community. Cuthbert met Abba at Coquet Island, another male community. In fact Bede implies that the feasting of important guests could be a strain on the economy when he says with approbation that the early community at Lindisfarne did not provide dwellings for the reception[14] of powerful seculars and did not provide special food to feast the king and his attendants. Some guests may have stayed for a length of time in or near the monastery, providing a service, and sharing to some extent in the liturgical life. It is recorded in the poem *De Abbatibus* that one of the brothers Cwicwine was a remarkable smith: after matins the sound of his hammer rang on the anvil and 'as it flew and smote the empty air, it decked the table of the brothers by beating out vessels'.[15] Bede mentions a dissolute brother in a Bernician monastery who was dedicated to drunkenness and other pleasures of a loose life, but the brethren bore with him because he was a skilful smith. 'He used to remain in his workshop day and night rather than go to church with the brothers.'[16]

It is difficult sometimes to know if the brothers mentioned were full members of the community, whether they were free tenants on the monastic lands which supported the community in the manner of the Celtic *manaig*,[17] or whether these were semi-servile tenants. Certainly some monastic land grants conveyed slaves with them—like those Wilfrid freed in his Sussex lands.[18]

In the *familia* of the Abbess Ælfflæd was a brother who is described in the *Anonymous Life of Cuthbert* as 'one of the bretheren in a shepherds' hut' and by Bede as 'one of the shepherds'.[19] The position of servants in these early monasteries is not quite clear. Wilfrid first went to Lindisfarne to look after an aged thegn, a friend of Queen Eanfled. Caedmon at Whitby was looked after by a 'thegn' just before his death. At Æthelhild's monastery there were both male and female servants,[20] and this seems in marked contrast to Wearmouth and Jarrow where some abbots, such as Eosterwine, took part in the manual labour of the farm. At Jarrow the building of the new monastery was carried out by twenty-two brethren, ten tonsured, twelve not. At Hexham some of the brethren built the church. It may be, however, that the community performed the tasks to which they were best suited and anyone unsuited to intellectual work would be expected to work with his hands. In the later reformed monasteries of the south it appears that building work was sometimes done by contract as in the building of Winchester; but even important ecclesiastics like Æthelwold or Dunstan could be skilful craftsmen.

The 'double' houses, in which a community of men and women were ruled over by an abbess, are a phenomenon of the seventh to ninth centuries in England, never to be revived with the same dominance. Although they were, as Professor Deansley[21] says, 'a Frankish institution transplanted to Britain', it is impossible to say how closely they were modelled on continental prototypes since none on the Continent have been fully excavated, and only one—Whitby—in England. Their distribution and organization have been fully discussed by Bateson and Rigold. Here I am only concerned with the buildings and layout.

Several of the monasteries such as Æthelhild's and Æthelburh's at Barking (founded 693) were sited near to a male relative's monastery. At Æthelhild's monastery the female establishment was enclosed and separated from the *locum virorum* by a gate. The guest-house of the monastery was separated from both sections and the abbess in visiting a sick traveller there took with her both a female attendant and one of the brothers. The small boy oblates were looked after in the female section of that monastery.

At Barking, Bede, drawing on a lost life of Æthelburgh, tells us[22] that there was a strict division between the male and female part of the establishment. There was a communal dormitory for the sisters but individual *cubiculi* for the aged and infirm nuns. There seems to have been a clear division between the cemeteries of the female and male communities, but no fixed tradition of where these should be located. The burial-place of the brothers seems to have been on the north of the church and the place of burial for the sisters was indicated by a miraculous light as on the south-west. The succeeding Abbess, however, decided because the site was very confined 'that the bones of the servants and handmaids of Christ should be taken up and buried in one place in the Church'. This decision to build over the site of the cemetery as the monastery expanded has by analogy relevance to the archaeological evidence from Whitby (p. 227), Monkwearmouth (p. 231) and Jarrow.

The description in Rudolf's *Life of St Lioba* of the double monastery at Wimborne supports the description of Barking as a community in which male and female inmates were rigidly divided. The writer says:

> Here two monasteries were of old founded by kings of that race surrounded with high and stout walls ... each of them was regulated by that rule of conduct that neither of them was entered by the opposite sex.[23]

Only the priest entered the nuns' church to celebrate mass and then left immediately. The mother of the monastery when having to give orders about the external affairs of the monastery spoke through a window, and Abbess Tate refused entry to the community to all clerics – even bishops. It is possible that some of the Northumbrian double houses did not maintain such rigid isolation. Certainly the abbesses seemed to eat and mix freely with visiting clerics. Hilda, in testing Cædmon's divine gift of song, called together the teachers of her monastery at Whitby, who were presumably men. At Coldingham the degree of mixing of the inhabitants became an occasion for scandal. Bede's description of Coldingham,[24] although often quoted as an example of a double monastery in which the inmates lived in individual cells (cf. Whitby, below, p. 225), can be considered differently. Bede tells how Adamnan and another brother approached the monastery and seeing its lofty buildings '*aedificia illius sublimiter erecta*' Adamnan burst into tears because, as he prophesied, all the buildings they could see, *publica vel privata*, would shortly be reduced to ashes. He then recounted a vision in which an angelic visitor stood beside him and congratulated Adamnan on his vigil and prayers. The visitor said, 'I have just visited every part of this monastery in turn : I have examined their cells and their beds (*singulorum casas ac lectos inspexi*).' The angel had found all the inhabitants either slothfully asleep or awake for the purpose of sin. 'And the little houses (*domunculae*) which were constructed for praying and reading have become haunts of feasting, drinking, gossip and other delights.'

The account clearly shows that there were both public and private buildings in the monastery, and that there were cells as well as small rooms or structures for reading and private meditation. This picture of a combination of the large communal buildings and individual cells is interesting in relation to Whitby and Jarrow. It is a feature of seventh-century monasticism also attested from Gaul in sites such as Lérins.[25] A similar picture is provided by Brie where Eorcengota on the day of her death went round the monastery, 'visiting the cells of Christ's infirm handmaids, and especially those who were of great age or distinguished for their virtuous lives'.[26]

The total impression of these early houses is of a variety of layouts within different types of enclosure. A common refectory, dormitory, guest house and domestic buildings seem normal, but even in such centres as Wearmouth and Jarrow which are some-times called 'Benedictine', there were obviously individual cells for the use of senior or sick monks, and it appears to have been normal for the abbot and prior to have had indivi-dual cells. Only at Abingdon (see below, p. 216) have we clear literary evidence for indivi-dual cells for the small early community.

We have at present little evidence for developments of the monastic plan in the period after the death of Bede and before the Viking invasions, although it is obvious they must have taken place (see below, p. 241). New houses were founded and old ones refurbished. The picture the literary records provide is of variation in organization, economic resources and spiritual and cultural importance. The poem *De Abbatibus* paints an attractive picture of a Northumbrian house founded *c*. 705–16 and still flourishing in the period 803–21. The heart of the monastery was of course the church, and this building was the one in which no doubt the most important changes were made in the occupation of any monastery. Here laymen and community could see for themselves the gifts they had given to glorify God's house.[27]

The church had long high walls, lead-covered roof and glass windows which softly diffused the sunlight. It was lit at night by rows of hanging torches and hanging bowls, which pious patrons had ordered to be made. The altars adorned with gold and jewels or silver reliefs are also witness to the generosity of donors. The generosity of kings, nobility and the monastic inmates themselves towards their institutions, together with the revival of technology and culture which such institutions encouraged, is one of the prepossessing features of pre-Viking England. Nevertheless the concentration of wealth in the form of precious artifacts made them the obvious target of envy from contemporary laymen, although their feelings could have been more influenced by the amount of land frozen in monastic possession. Bede's prophetic letter to Ecgberht of York in 734 points already to the seeds of corruption in the spread of false monasteries useful neither to God nor man.[28] The lack of secular will to refound monasteries in the north and the difficulties of the bishops and abbots in retaining their land grants in the south in the tenth and ele-venth centuries were no doubt because the Viking wars and settlement brought about a redistribution of this land comparable with the Dissolution. Many were no doubt founded in the first rush of religious enthusiasm and later, as their secular family lost its power to support them (or because of economic pressures), failed. Eadburga and Ean-gytha write to Boniface in the eighth century about the problems of the small community.

'We are tormented by our poverty, by the small size of our cultivated lands, and more still by the enmity of the king, who listens to all the accusations made to us by the envious; by the taxes laid on us for the service of the king, his queen, the bishop, the earl, and their satellites and servants. . . . To all these distresses must be added the loss of our friends and relations who formed almost a tribe, and of whom none remain.'[29]

In the reformed houses of the tenth century it seems that a formal claustral layout had been widely accepted. Dunstan is credited with having created such a cloister at Glastonbury (see p. 242) and Ælfric Bata's *Grammar*,[30] of the tenth century, describes the monastic buildings, some of wood and some of stone, in the following terms:

> *Dormitorium, refectorium, hospitium, (i. aula), vestiarium cellarium, horreum, molendinum; turris vel turres, triclinium coquina, pistrina, baluearium, ypodromum, promptuarium (i. cubicularium) hoc est cubicalum sermocinarium, solaria, multa latrina atque officina et cetera talia.*

Some of the words in the above list may have been culled from descriptions of more elaborate continental monasteries. However, the *Regularis Concordia*[31] mentions, besides the church, the common refectory, common dormitory, the cloister, a room set apart for the daily chapter meeting, a warming house, kitchen, bakehouse, guest house and *authitorium*. This may be presumed to constitute the normal tenth-century complex.

Such large communities with complex organization and major resources were not refounded in the north, however. For Northumbria indeed not one community which could have been recognized as monastic by the compilers of the *Regularis Concordia* survived into the late tenth century, and the distribution of late monasteries in England (fig. 5.1) makes an interesting contrast with the importance of the north in the pre-Viking period.

The archaeological evidence

British monasteries which were founded in the sub-Roman period but which could have survived as institutions in areas which were taken over later by the Anglo-Saxons have received some archaeological consideration. In the north-west, Whithorn (*Candida Casa*) was founded, according to Bede,[32] by Ninian in the time of the Romans. The church dedicated to St Martin must have been built or re-dedicated some time after his death in 397. The area came under Anglo-Saxon control possibly *c*. 700 and just before 731 an Anglo-Saxon bishop was established in the area. By 802 the written evidence for the site ceases. The early Christian occupation of the area is confirmed by inscribed memorial stones in the tradition of the Gallo-Roman church. The earliest of these was put up by one Borrovadus in the sixth century, in memory of his grandfather, Latinus, and his daughter. On the next peninsula to the west, at Kirkmadrine, memorial stones show a Christian settlement of some importance from the fifth to the seventh centuries.[33]

Despite a series of excavations at Whithorn the memorial stones provide the most unambiguous evidence for the early Christian community.[34] The first of these excavations revealed an early building 15 ft (4.57 m) wide with walls 3 ft 4 ins (1.02 m) thick.

> The walls of the early building were constructed of roughly split undressed blocks of local stone set in clay. Outside the masonry had originally been daubed with a cream coloured plaster, portions of which were found still adhering to the base of the wall face. The west end of the building was cut away by the end wall of the crypt and it is now impossible to establish its full size.

Radford considers that this justifies the deduction that it is indeed the White House named after St Martin.[35] Thomas, however, considers that this structure is a subsidiary chapel of seventh-century (or later) date constructed when the site at Whithorn had become a monastery under Irish influence.[36] The most recent excavations on the site (by P. R. Richie) have, however, revealed traces of an early cemetery disturbing what may be Roman cremations. The importance of such an early cemetery, which can later develop into a cemetery with a wooden chapel, and later still a stone chapel sometimes associated with a monastery, has been extensively discussed and convincingly demonstrated by Charles Thomas.[37]

Charles Thomas's excavation of Ardwall Island yielded a sequence of, firstly, an early lay cemetery focused around a possible slab shrine; secondly, a timber chapel with associated graves; and thirdly, a stone chancel. However, neither at Whithorn nor at Ardwall have the living quarters of a religious community been found.

The most completely exposed site claimed as a monastery in the British Isles is Tintagel, Cornwall, which is, strictly speaking, not within the Anglo-Saxon context. However, its layout, and the problems raised by the type of artifact discovered, are pertinent to later discussion (see p. 211). There is no documentary evidence to prove that this was a monastic site, and no continuing traditions of religious settlement. The excavator, Dr Radford, deduced that it was a monastery by analogy with monastic settlements in Ireland and Wales. The artifacts discovered appear to span a period from *c*. 350 to *c*. 850 and four constructional phases have been isolated. The end of the promontory is separated from the landward side of the headland by a deep natural cleft in the rocks, and this was bounded by a bank of piled stones 8 ft high and a broad ditch 25 ft wide.[38] The construction of this bank is dated by the excavator to *c*. 500 by fragments of imported pottery incorporated in the rampart. Within this enclosure eight scattered groups of rectilinear buildings have been located and six groups have been excavated.[39]

Site A comprises a complex of more than a dozen small rooms of four different periods cut by the later medieval chapel. This area, Radford suggests, could have surrounded the main monastic church, and he suggests a sequence whereby the two buildings of Period 1, which could have been a farmstead of the late fourth century, were superseded by a single cell. The building of Period 2 consisted of a long room—48 ft by 16 ft—with a small western annexe.[40] It was distinguished in its construction by courses of stone set herring-bone fashion. It had two entrances near the end of the west side, one of which was

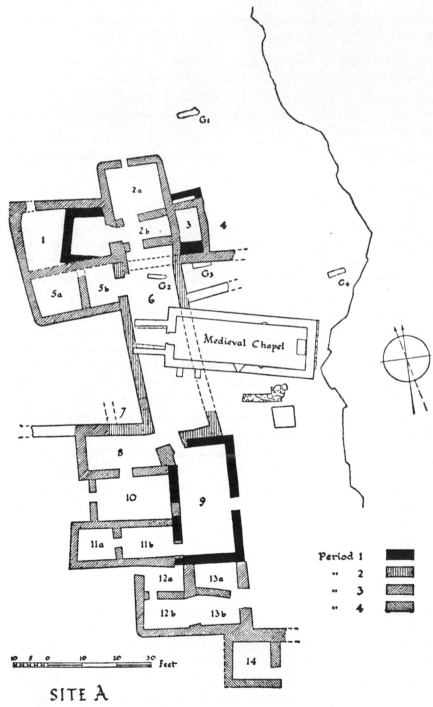

Period 1
" " 2
" " 3
" " 4

SITE A

Figure 5.2 Tintagel general plan (after C. A. R. Radford)

subsequently blocked. 'No similar building has been found on this site and as this appears to be the earliest part of the Celtic monastery it may represent the original cell.' Periods 3 and 4 showed a great extension of the site and the buildings were assumed to represent guest houses for the reception of visitors and pilgrims.

Site B is assumed to have comprised some of the living quarters of the monks. The irregular collection of buildings ran down the slope on artificially created terraces. The uppermost chamber was two-storeyed and could have been the living quarters of the superior. A low stone base runs along two sides of the interior. The next room, which belonged to a later period, consisted of a single rectangle with a door in the north side; this is large enough to be a refectory. Outside the seaward wall was a stone bench and, leading down from the space in front of the bench, were steps to the lower terrace. Here the excavator claims that a small stone structure, whose floors were heat-cracked and covered with wood ash, could have been a sweat house. From the lower end of Site B a path led down to an artificially created pool.[41]

Site C consists of three rooms set on a narrow man-made terrace. Originally the building consisted of one long room with a door in the centre of each of the short walls. Later two further rooms were added in ribbon development. Immediately above this area was a range of small rooms opening into a corridor (Site G). Radford suggests that the whole complex formed one of the main groups of cells.

Site D seems to have had a domestic function, since it contained a corn-drying kiln and some crudely built structures which could be connected with the farming activities of the community. No coherent plan was recovered for site E, but site F comprised an impressive group of structures. In its original form the upper terrace supported three rooms. One contained a living chamber from which hot air was carried in rock-cut channels under the paved floor of the central room. In the second period the heating chamber and its associated system were disused and the two surviving rooms reconstructed. The main lower room had in its earliest phase doors at each end and two doors on the lower side leading into small open-ended chambers. Radford supposes this could have been a library and *scriptorium* complex.

The clustered grouping of the buildings, and their ribbon development, is not unlike some of the early monasteries of the Middle East, and the differing functions of the groups – living quarters, domestic buildings, working areas and warmed rooms – fit well into a monastic context. However, as Radford has pointed out, the lacunae from the site are the failure to find an early church and the small extent of the cemetery,[42] both features central to any other monastic site discussed below. One could also add that a continuing religious tradition is also typical of other monasteries, as is evidence for literacy in the form of inscriptions or writing impedimenta.

The most noteworthy finds on the site were fragments of imported mediterranean pottery, in particular a fine red ware – Tintagel A – often impressed with a cross, and a pale buff type of combed amphora – Tintagel B.[43] It could be that a monastic community would need the Samian-type bowls and the amphorae which could have contained oil and wine for liturgical purposes. Alternatively any community who were so Romanized in their tastes as to construct a centrally heated building could equally have felt that pottery was not a luxury, but a natural concomitant of living. If the latter supposition were true then it would explain why otherwise in western Britain comparable pottery is found on royal and secular sites such as Dinas Powys.[44] A similar difficulty in distinguishing monastic artifacts is seen in other sites discussed below. The layout of Tintagel is not paralleled on other monastic sites in Anglo-Saxon England.

Glastonbury, the other excavated site which takes back the story of monasticism in Britain to the sub-Roman period, will be discussed below, since most of its buildings belong to later periods.

Monastic organization, as already stated, came to the Anglo-Saxons through two channels – the Celtic church of the west and the Continent, in particular Gaul. The physical distinctions one might expect from these two traditions are, however, difficult to determine and it seems best to examine the excavated evidence and then make interim deductions. The only missionary site of the Celtic Church which has been explored to the extent of providing evidence for living quarters is Burgh Castle in Suffolk.

BURGH CASTLE

Burgh Castle is a coastal site inside the enclosure of a massive Roman fort, six acres in area, with walls 9 ft thick. Bede describes the foundation when he tells how, some time after 630, 'there came a holy man from Ireland called Fursa. He was renowned in word and deed.'[45] After a time he received from Sigeberht, the East Anglian king, a site for a monastery: 'now the monastery was pleasantly situated close to the woods and the sea, in a Roman camp which is called in English *Cnobheresburgh*'. His successor King Anna and his nobles endowed it with still finer buildings and gifts. There is no record of the survival of the site after the eighth century.

Before Green's excavations in 1960–61 ploughing in 1957–8 had uncovered Anglo-Saxon plaster in the north-east angle and skeletons in the south-west angle of the fort. There had been some small trial excavations in 1855. The Norman motte in the south-west corner of the site was demolished in 1839 and at that time human bones were found.[46]

The cemetery, which was excavated in 1960, produced at least 144 interments as well as pits containing dumps of re-interred bones. Only on the south side did the excavator think he had the cemetery limit, in an area where he considered there was possibly a church. All the bodies lay supine and there was a variation in orientation between N.85° and N.121°. Green considered that this variation was derived less from different periods of burial than from burial taking place at different times of the year when orientation was fixed by the sun. In view of cases such as Jarrow (p. 236) where changes of orientation are combined with changes in corpse layout, and do seem to have some chronological force, I am inclined to disagree with this interpretation. Burial orientation on a Christian site seems likely to have been determined by a church or some other permanent focus, although its orientation would of course have been originally fixed by the sun on a certain day.

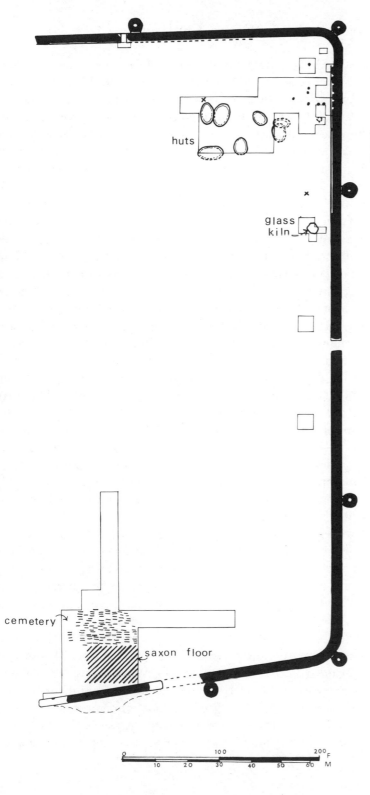

huts

glass kiln

cemetery

saxon floor

Figure 5.3 Burgh Castle, Suffolk, general plan (after Charles Green)

0   100   200 F
10 20 30 40 50 60 M

The layers in the area of the huts seem to be (i) a Roman floor lying on natural sand; above this, (ii) a destruction layer sealed by a layer of sandy clay, possibly a floor, since it was cut by post-holes and associated with a spread of fish débris, mainly oysters; above this, (iii) a smooth brown layer into which the hut footings were cut. In one place this layer sealed a pit associated with an Ipswich-ware sherd, above which was a layer of dark earth associated with later Anglo-Saxon material. It is not clear on the evidence I have seen whether this layer accumulated after the hut occupation. This layer was then covered by disturbed top-soil.

The huts were shown (fig. 5.4), by lateral and vertical association, to be of at least two periods: Hut 4 earlier than 5, and 3 than 1. However, there is apparently no significant change in their dimensions and construction. They vary in internal dimensions; for example, Hut 2 is 14 ft by 10 ft; 3 is 18 ft by 10 ft; Huts 4 and 7, 24 ft by 14 ft; and Hut 5, 20 ft by 10 ft. They appear to have had rammed clay floors, and their slots varied from 5 ins to nearly 1 ft in depth. The excavator concluded that they were 'wattle-and-daub bee-hives'. There were traces of carbonized wood adjacent to the structures, but no evidence for post-holes within the slots, although there were flint packings on either side of the slots. The Roman buildings are of concrete, the post-Roman builders, therefore, did not use local Roman stone, as they did for example at Jarrow. However, if they transplanted their own wooden building traditions, then in form and dimensions these can be compared with the round-ended wattle-and-plaster building at Monkwearmouth (p. 233) or the similar timber structure at Tynemouth (p. 219).

The material which came out of these huts can only be tentatively interpreted at this stage. However, there seems to have been no evidence for writing, indeed no inscriptions have been found anywhere on the site. Hut 2 produced a quantity of worked antler tines, as well as a spindle whorl and bronze key, while Hut 5 could well be a smithy, since this area produced slag fragments, nails, an iron spike, two horseshoes, an iron blade and two axes. (These finds are possibly from the later Saxon layer.)

The post-holes which were found to the north-east were associated with a floor level and a great deal of roughly painted plaster. This, Green supposed, could have been from a church, but in view of the painted plaster from Monkwearmouth (clearly not associated with the church) it could have been one of the public buildings of the monastery such as a refectory. There could be a multiplicity of churches on the site as elsewhere, but they are usually grouped together and associated, as is the south structure, with burials (fig. 5.3).

This cluster of oval huts is at present unique in the record of Anglo-Saxon monastic sites and one could interpret them as cells or workshops (cf. Whitby, p. 229). It seems premature, however, to relate them directly to Irish building traditions. In sites such as Cellwach in Killegrone,[47] or Kildrenagh,[48] there are oval huts of comparable form, as appears to be the case here. However, Anglo-Saxon monastic sites such as Tynemouth have also produced oval structures and the secular Germanic tradition of the sunken-floored building is not far divorced from these.

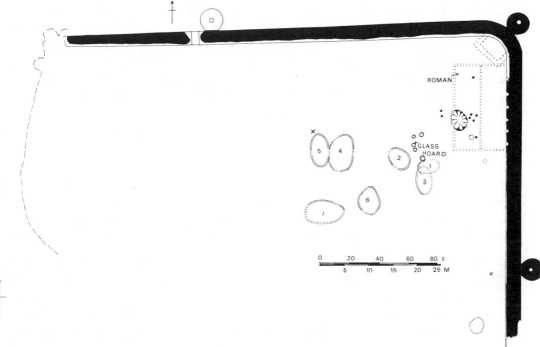

Figure 5.4 Burgh Castle, Suffolk (after Charles Green)

The extensive cemetery would seem to be an 'indicator' of religious settlement, but there is no other artifactal evidence such as inscriptions which could distinguish the type of site. However, there are other sites where separate huts are recorded; for example Abingdon, where the documentary evidence seems quite firm on this point.

ABINGDON

The monastery at Abingdon was possibly at one stage a double monastery, on an existing Romano-British site with a nearby pagan Saxon cemetery. Founded *c*. 675, it fell into decay and was refounded *c*. 954. Archaeological evidence only exists for the early period.

The three major manuscripts which comprise work of the *Chronicon Monasterii de Abingdon* have been subjected to considerable critical scrutiny.[49]

Medieval accounts of Abingdon clearly show two separate Christian foci: the site around St Helen's Church (in the confluence of the Thames and Ock), and the area around the present Abbey church; the heart of the medieval town lies between.

Mrs Lambrick has made out a good case for the fact that Abingdon was a centre for an ancient unit of royal administration, possibly dating back to Roman times. This is hinted at by the dedication to St Helen and by the legends of the Holy Cross later associated with this site. This ancient church of St Helen's could have been later converted into a nunnery connected with the monastery further north than the present Abbey. The two earliest histories[49a] both say that the seventh-century endowment of land was made to Hean and his sister Cilla; it may thus have been founded as a form of double monastery.

The earliest name for the area and for St Helen's, in the pagan Anglo-Saxon period, was according to some traditions *Seouechesham*: *Abbendun* II was originally an upland area on the south-east slopes of Boars Hill, about halfway between Oxford and Abingdon. The name *Abbendn* was thus transferred to the riverside site at the time when Hean was granted land to found a monastery by King Cedwall.

Certainly the antiquity of the lower site is confirmed by the archaeological evidence (see p. 217). The first Anglo-Saxon monastery in what is now the Abbey site is described in a manuscript which is not considered historically reliable.[49b] However, there seems no reason why the circumstantial account of the buildings need have been fabricated at a later date since, although the tradition it embodies may be somewhat distorted and is almost certainly selective in detail, the monastery of Abingdon which Hean, the first Abbot, constructed in that place could have been like this. In describing the church it is said:

> *Habebat in longitudine c et xx pedes, et erat rotundum, tam in parte occidentali, tam in parte orientali, Fundatum erat hoc monasterium in loco ubi nunc est cellarium monachorum, ita quod altore stetit ubi nunc est lauatorium. In circuiti hujus monasterii erant habitacula xii et totidem capellae et in habitaculis xii monachi ibidem manducantes et bibentes er dormientes; nec habebant clausam sicut nunc habent, sed erant circumdati muro alto qui erat eis pro claustro ... Habebant juxta portam domum pro locutorio.*[50]

A refectory is also mentioned twice in the records. The site was surrounded by a wall, and it seems that this was used instead of a cloister walk and that there were some regular gaps between it and the individual living quarters of the monks. The *habitaculi* in which the monks are said to eat, drink and sleep could each have had a chapel attached – as in Cuthbert's individual cell on the Farne (p. 203) or in Building B at Jarrow (fig. 5.13). Alternatively they could have been quite separate buildings, although there is no parallel for this.

The only comprehensive excavation report of any site at Abingdon is that of the pagan Anglo-Saxon cemetery to the south of the river excavated in 1934–5. Its evidence has recently been reassessed by Myres,[51] but it is not of central importance to this discussion save that it provides very early evidence of Saxon settlement in this area in the fourth to fifth centuries, and reinforces the supposition that Hean's monastery was sited on a well-developed royal *vill*.

In 1922 excavations were carried out on the site of the Abbey under the general direction of C. R. Peers and A. Clapham, apparently by hopefully cutting narrow trenches at right-angles across potential wall lines. No report of this excavation was published, although the records were preserved in the Berkshire Record Office. From these records twenty-five years later Martin Biddle produced a synthesized report, which has ably digested and interpreted the surviving evidence. A Roman occupation level was found below the crossing of the Norman church and perhaps over the whole area investigated.

The pottery dated from the second to the fourth century, and three coins, Tetricus, Constantine I and a very worn Valens, were discovered. No structures were recorded and Biddle surmises that the focus of the settlement is likely to be towards the Thames and the southern half of the town.[52]

A partial plan of an Anglo-Saxon church was discovered within the Norman abbey. On the evidence reconstructed by Biddle this would be at least 200 ft long and 57 ft wide. On the evidence so far provided one cannot be certain whether this is Æthelwold's church or a church of earlier date. Biddle is inclined to see it as a ninth-century type.

No pre-Conquest structures were encountered in the area investigated to the south of the Norman church, although many burials were found (apparently at different levels since some of the bodies appear to lie under the medieval cloister and adjoining ranges). Biddle reasonably supposes that there could have been an Anglo-Saxon cemetery between the Anglo-Saxon church or churches to the north and the tenth-century monastic buildings to the south, as at Glastonbury (see below, p. 245) and Winchester. This pattern also occurs at Wearmouth and Jarrow and, as in the latter sites, some of the burials could have been of a period between the occupation of the early and the late Saxon monastery. Other burials were found within the church and to the west, 50 ft from the north of the church.

NORTHUMBRIAN MONASTERIES

There has been some exploration of the monastic sites in Northumbria which were founded under the influence of the Ionan mission in the period between 635 and 664, and this has been more recently supplemented by excavations on two other monastic sites which were founded in the seventh century under strong influence from the Continent (Wearmouth and Jarrow). These sites have a particular bias in their history in that they are not subjected to the reforms of the tenth-century Benedictine revival as was the case of Abingdon, Canterbury, Glastonbury and Winchester, and so they constitute an early group, which may be considered together.

TYNEMOUTH

Tynemouth is a headland site[53] on the north side of the approaches to the Tyne. It probably spans the seventh to ninth centuries.

In the early records it is sometimes difficult to disentangle references to this site and to South Shields on the south bank of the river. The monastery was in existence in the time of Bede,[54] and was a royal burial-place in 792. A late tradition, however, maintained that King Oswin (d. 651), the patron saint of the monastery in the eleventh century, was buried there.[55] It could therefore have been a mid-seventh-century foundation.

Before the 1963 excavations[56] the only indications of the pre-Conquest monastery were two cross shafts and two cross-heads of the ninth and tenth centuries, one of which, 'The Monk's Stone', possibly stood on the outskirts of the monastic cemetery, and another

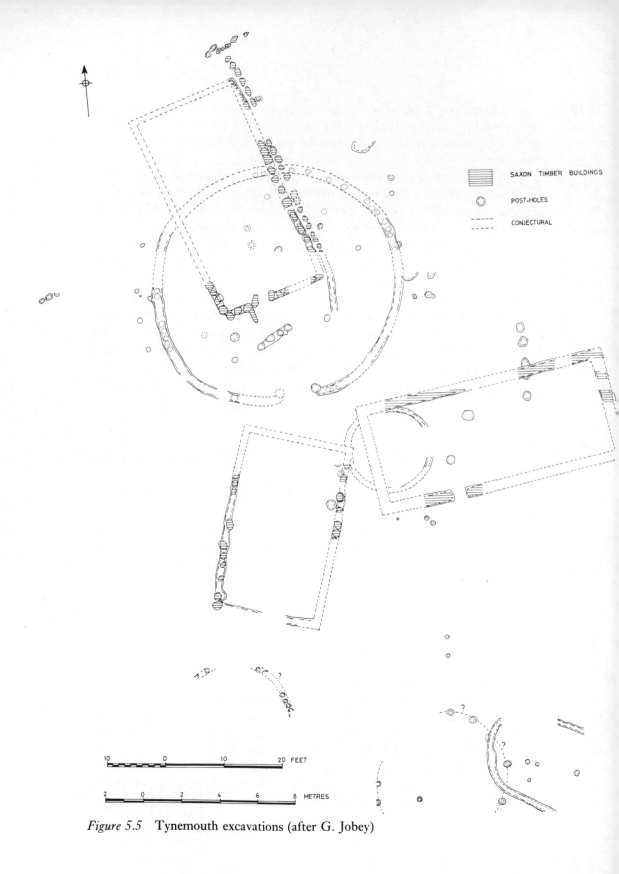

SAXON TIMBER BUILDINGS

POST-HOLES

CONJECTURAL

10 0 10 20 FEET

2 0 2 4 6 8 METRES

Figure 5.5 Tynemouth excavations (after G. Jobey)

fragment in the University Museum, Newcastle, was perhaps from the cemetery. Two other monuments were discovered in the course of the excavation.[57]

George Jobey's excavation took place in the winter of 1963, in advance of lowering the level of the modern road to the north of the priory church. A sequence of occupation from Iron Age huts to sixteenth-century defences was recorded.

Four timber buildings were discovered which are tentatively assigned by the excavator to a period between the second-century Roman occupation and the construction for the Norman church between c. 1050 and 1130 (fig. 5.5).

Building 1[58] was situated in the cemetery of the medieval church, partially overlaid by one of the foundations of the Norman piers. The area had been disturbed to below the potential floor-level of the building and the outline was indicated by a shallow groove 9 ins wide, with a maximum of 6 ins depth cut into the bedrock. The structure was aligned roughly east-south-east/west-north-west. Its internal width was 14 ft and it had a semi-circular west end and fairly straight sides.

Building 2 was situated under the medieval byre and aligned approximately south-south-east/north-north-west. No floor levels had survived. Its internal width was 17 ft and length about 30 ft:

> The irregularly formed construction trenches showed the remains of post-impressions for close-set uprights. The S.W. corner with its projecting post probably indicates that the timbers had not been squared off. A narrow doorway with the shallow trench for shelter-screen on its west side was placed off centre in the south side. Two conjoining sherds of second century Roman coarse pottery were found in the bottom packing of two of the post holes to the E of the doorway.[59]

Building 3 was under the sacristy. Although on a slightly different alignment, north-north-east/south-south-west, it was of the same type of construction as Building 2, with irregular post-impressions. Its internal width was 17 ft and its length, though uncertain, must have been between 26 ft and 31 ft.

An undecorated sherd of Samian ware was sealed in the packing of the wall trench. The excavator considered the building had been dismantled.[60]

Building 4, which may have been separated from 2 and 3 by a boundary fence, was constructed by a different technique with continuous trenches for sill-beams. Its alignment was approximately east and west. Its internal width was 16 ft and its length possibly about 39 ft. At least one off-centre doorway had existed in its south wall. This building cut through the Romano-British hut and was earlier than the medieval paths and the sacristy. Two fragments of second-century pottery were found in the packing used to level the sill-beams in their trenches. The excavator considered that there were signs of systematic dismantling of the buildings.

These timber buildings, as Jobey is at pains to point out, could be of any date from the late Roman to the Norman period, and, despite the convincing evidence for a monastery on the headland by the eighth century, there are few finds other than the sculpture which can provide evidence for an Anglo-Saxon occupation. However, a *stycca* of Æthelred II, 841–4, found in the disturbed levels above Building 4 is unequivocal evidence for mid-ninth-century occupation. The Roman pottery in the packing of the buildings is interesting in comparison with similar Roman finds at Jarrow.

A comparatively small area of this site was explored in these excavations, but the exclusive evidence for wooden structures in what seems to be the Anglo-Saxon period is interesting. There are, however, problems in identifying these buildings as 'monastic', rather than as secular, although the round-ended structure which is paralleled at Monkwearmouth and Knockea is not of a normal secular plan. The same problem of identification is to be found at Hartlepool.

HARTLEPOOL

Hartlepool is a double minster of the seventh to ninth centuries on a headland site which in the middle ages was cut off on the landward side by a wall and ditch. According to Bede[61] it was the first community for women in Northumbria. Founded by Heiu under the direction of St Aidan, *c.* 646, it was *c.* 650 taken over by Hild, who had been living with a small band of companions on the north bank of the Wear. The site of this last-mentioned monastery is unknown. It must have been very small, however, since it was only supported by one hide of land.[62] Hild had plenty of opportunity to know other monastic rules than those current in Northumbria since she had a sister in the monastery of Chelles, and had spent a year whilst waiting to go to Chelles herself in the court at East Anglia. It is clear from what is said of Whitby (at which she is said to have established the same rule as Hartlepool) that she maintained a coenobitical establishment in which 'no-one was rich, no-one in need for they had all things in common and none had any private property'. She also 'compelled those under her direction to devote so much time to the study of holy scriptures, and so much time to the performance of good works'. In fact her establishment seems to prefigure in many ways what we know from the literary sources of the conduct of life at Wearmouth and Jarrow.

Figure 5.6. The Hartlepool peninsula showing Anglo-Saxon and medieval sites investigated (after D. Austin):
  1 St Helen's Church: Norman
  2 Charles Street and Baltic Street School (attempts to find Wall): skeletons
  3 Back Gladstone Street: skeleton. ?Pre-Conquest
  4 Bank on Town Moor: ?Civil War defence
  5 Olive Street, late medieval burgages: late thirteenth/early fourteenth century kiln
  6 Friarage-structures (Friarage): *c.* thirty-six skeletons
  7 Lumley Street: medieval burgages, pre-Conquest timber buildings, prehistoric buildings
  8 Cross Field: Anglo-Saxon burials
  9 Church Walk: late medieval burgages, early medieval skeletons
 10 Middlegate: late medieval burgages, early medieval timber buildings
 11 Back Northgate: large timbers, ?medieval wharves
 12 Southgate: medieval burgages

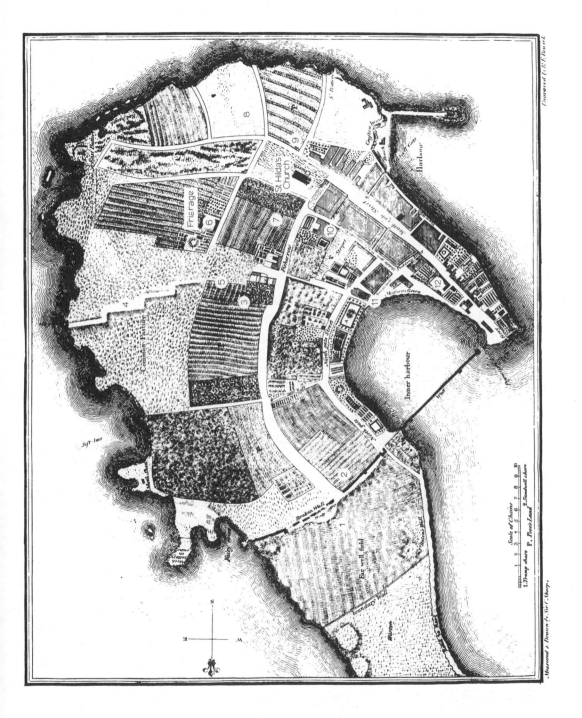

St Hilda's Church

Friarage

Harbour

Inner harbour

Common Pasture

Soft laer

Ear well field

boundary Wall

Broken Wall

Scale of Chains
1 2 3 4 5 6 7 8 9 10

1.Turnip share P.Poors Land 9.Backwell share

Measured & Drawn by Nic!.Wharp.

Engraved by R.E.Hawk

The history of the house after Hild's reign is obscure; it is not one of those refounded in the eleventh century.

In July 1833, excavations to construct a house in a field called Cross Close, about 135 yds to the south-east of the medieval church of St Hild, produced evidence for what is plausibly the monastic cemetery (fig. 5.6.8). The bodies, which were oriented north–south, were found lying on the natural limestone at a depth of about 3 ft. Associated with them were both plain and inscribed slabs, bearing the names of the dead and on some a request for prayers.[63] In 1843 and 1883 further work in the adjacent south terrace produced more burials and grave markers. In all, seven of the inscribed stones have survived and many more were obviously found and destroyed or lost.[64]

Small recumbent slabs such as these have been found singly in other nearby sites such as Billingham, Birtley and Monkwearmouth, and related monuments have recently been unearthed in the Minster excavations at York. However, only at Lindisfarne have such stones been found in comparable numbers to Hartlepool, unfortunately without proper association. It is interesting that at Whitby (although there were a number of funerary inscriptions as befits a monastic site) this type of grave marker has not been discovered. The exact extent of the Hartlepool cemetery has not been determined although an estimate of 15–20 yds long was made in 1838[65] and the bodies were said to be in two rows. The cemetery seems to have extended to the edge of the cliff. However, at least one skeleton found in the 1843 excavation had its head to the west;[66] it seems possible that there was an extension to the original group. In 1968 a large area in Lumley Street, earlier Fisher Gate, was mechanically stripped in advance of rebuilding and revealed in the sewer cuts a depth of stratification with, at the lowest level, extensive evidence of timber slots and ditches. Only a small area of this was excavated by the Department of Archaeology, Durham University. The work (fig. 5.6), which is as yet unpublished, was directed by Michael Griffiths, Susannah Spencer and Richard Lawless. Underlying the back buildings and a yard of a medieval house occupied in the fourteenth and fifteenth centuries was a layer of brown sand with pottery of the eleventh to fourteenth centuries, and below that a blown level of cleaner sand which covered the limestone bedrock. Cut into the bedrock were the foundations of rectangular timber buildings; four or five houses were of slot construction and three of individual post construction. The post-built structures seemed to be the earlier since in several cases the slots had cut through them. The post-holes and slots provided no dating evidence, and there were no occupation deposits associated with these buildings. There was, however, a scattering of pre-Conquest pottery outside the structures, and a large rubbish pit which was otherwise full of animal bones yielded one intermediate type loom-weight. No complete house plans were recovered, but the site presents similar problems as that at Tynemouth. It is clear that we have here buildings of what is now a common Anglo-Saxon type, but whether they are part of the monastery or part of a secular *vicus* is impossible to determine.

It is perfectly feasible that the early buildings on these monastic sites would, like the church and buildings at Lindisfarne, have been of wood, and that they would have resembled secular structures. There is unfortunately no hint that the excavators of Hild's second foundation at Whitby found timber buildings, although they do seem to have found an intermediate type of clay and stone foundations and wattle-and-daub partition walls.

WHITBY

Whitby is a monastery on a headland site and dates from the seventh to ninth centuries. It seems to be the place known to Bede and his contemporaries as *Streoneshalh*, which name Bede explains as *Sinus Fari*.[67] This has been interpreted by some as 'bay of light-house', by others as 'the corner of generation'.[68] No satisfactory explanation of the Old English name and of Bede's Latin translation has yet been found. Possibly the change of name to Whitby, which seems to have taken place after the destruction of the monastery in the ninth century,[69] was added because the significance of the earlier name had been lost. It seems probable that *Witebi* was originally the name of the harbour settlement, which then absorbed the hill-top settlement that in 1072 was known as *Prestebi*.[70]

The monastery was founded in 657 on an estate of ten hides donated by King Oswiu (apparently one of the twelve estates he gave to the church in thanksgiving for the victory at *Winwæd* in 655).[71] It is not clear from Bede's account whether its first abbess, Hild, took over an existing settlement or founded a monastery *de novo*, since his text is ambiguous: 'it happened that she undertook either to found or to set in order a monastery at a place called *Streanæshalch*'[72] (see below, p. 228). Under Hild's guidance the monastery became a famous training ground for ecclesiastics: five of her pupils became bishops.

It was important as a burial-place for the Northumbrian royal house, and Hild played a notable role in the politics of the time – witness the Council which took place there in 664.[73] This important political role was maintained by her successor Ælflæd, daughter of Oswiu, who ruled from 680–713/14. Part of her epitaph was recovered during excavation of the site.[74]

Mention of the monastic buildings at Whitby include a house for postulants and an infirmary, and, if its cell thickness was modelled on the same lines, a dormitory for the sisters.[75] There is no hint of any strict division between the male and female part of the monastery as at Wimborne. After 685 the ex-bishop of Whithorn, Trumwine, took refuge there with his community and lived there for the remainder of his life.

For the rest of the Anglo-Saxon period there is little documentation for the site. William of Malmesbury states that King Edmund pillaged St Hild's bones from Whitby to Glastonbury *c.* 944. However, between 1072 and 1078 the site was reoccupied by Reinfrid of Evesham. William describes the event in these terms:

> The aforesaid most powerful William de Percy gave them the most ancient monastery of St Peter the Apostle, with two carucates of land at Priestbi in perpetual alms. There were at that time, in the same place, as aged countrymen have informed us 'monasteria' or oratories to nearly the number of forty, whereby the walls and altars, empty and roofless had survived the destruction of the pirate-host.[76]

This seems to imply that many of the buildings were of stone.

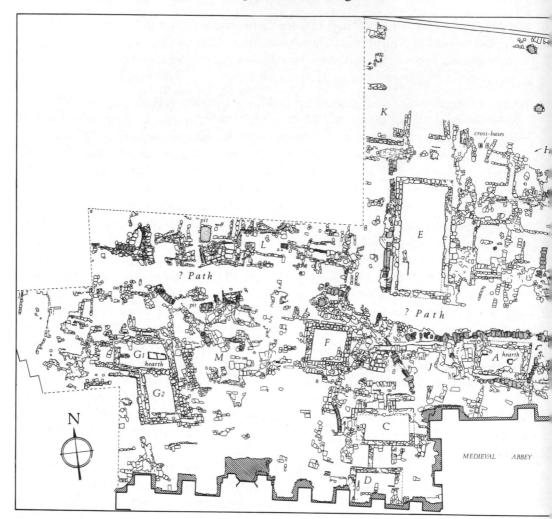

Figure 5.7 Whitby Abbey excavations redrawn by P. A. Rahtz

The account of the 1920–25 excavation as summarized by Sir Charles Peers was published in 1943,[77] a long time after the excavation. The abbey site was handed over to HM Office of Works in 1920 and, although the official guide book[78] only records excavation in the years 1924 and 1925, it is clear from further research that excavations began very soon after the site was taken into guardianship (see below, p. 453). The hazards of war destroyed part of the site record, and only one composite plan of the site now exists in the records of the Department of the Environment. Moreover, no indisputable account of the area explored exists, but a record of the finds and a gridded outline of the site are extant in the Department of Medieval and Later Antiquities, British Museum[79] (fig. 5.8). Radford kindly informs me that when he was writing up the finds from the site under

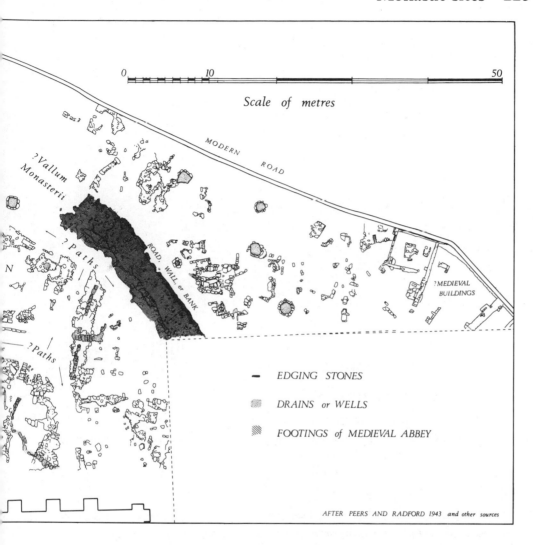

EDGING STONES

DRAINS or WELLS

FOOTINGS of MEDIEVAL ABBEY

AFTER PEERS AND RADFORD 1943 and other sources

circumstances of considerable difficulty during the war, he saw the foreman's diary of the excavation, but did not have access to any other plans or sections. No photographs appear to be extant, although there is a valuable supplement to those published in the 1943 report in a local guide book.[80]

The interpretation of the structures discovered followed a consideration of the model type to which it is supposed to have conformed – a model constructed from the scanty documentary evidence set out above, and the documentary account of Coldingham (see above, p. 206).

The excavators assumed that the church, or churches, of St Peter occupied the middle of the Anglo-Saxon monastic precinct. Only the northern part of this area was discussed,

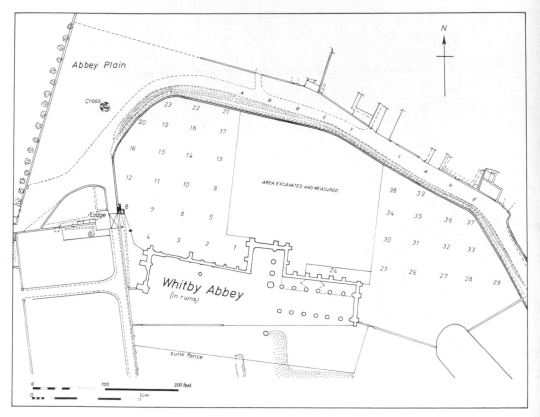

Figure 5.8 Grid plan of Whitby excavations (after the Department of the Environment)

although it had been noted that to the south of the medieval church were pre-Conquest buildings.

> The outer parlour is of late twelfth-century date, and beneath it, at a different angle to any other building was some rough stone foundation laid in clay and bits of fire reddened clay from a wattle and daub construction. These walls once recognised occurred in front of the west end of church, and were followed up on the north side till the greater part of the available area had been explored.[81]

No termination of the buildings was found to the north, a fact supported by excavations undertaken by Philip Rahtz in 1958, although the area to the north-east of the site, east of what is marked 'roadway' on the original plan, 'seemed to be definitely of late date, and it seems possible that the road preserves the outline of the original monastic boundary in this direction'.[82]

In the area which Peers gives as 300 ft east–west and 200 ft north–south he states:

Plans of seven buildings have been recovered and there is evidence of the former existence of many more. Only in a few places does any walling remain above foundation level and it is impossible to suggest any building sequence. All walls are of stone, the foundation courses seeming to be set in clay without lime, and not enough is left of the fair work to show whether, as is of course probable, lime mortar was used there. It can only be said that 2 feet seems to be the ordinary thickness of the walls, that any internal divisions were of timber filled in with wattle and daub and from the absence of any remains of tiles or slates, the roofs must have been thatched.

These general statements are supported by a detailed plan of the excavations in which seven structures are coloured red but not distinguished by numbering or lettering. Before describing them as shown on this plan it seems best to describe the research on this plan and the finds register which has produced fig. 5.7 and further commentary on the structures. Mr Rahtz and I independently tried to re-interpret the Whitby buildings, he from a new analysis and redrawing of the plan, and I by attempting to plot the finds from the notebooks and grid plan (fig. 5.8). The detail of this work is such that I have thought it best to include our contributions in appendices (p. 453ff.) and to summarize the conclusions in the text. Mr Rahtz has with great generosity allowed me to publish his plan here (fig. 5.7), and I follow his lettering of the buildings in subsequent discussion. Two structures, A and B, measured approximately 18 ft by 11 ft (5.5 m by 3.4 m). A stone hearth shows that there was a fire in the eastern half of the house and suggests a division into a living room 3.4 m (11 ft) square with a bedroom to the south-west and a lavatory at the north-west:

> each had a doorway in its South Wall, and a stone paved area about 4 ft square in the North West angle with a drain from it running north to an external drain which runs East and West along the North wall of each building.

These buildings are in the section of the plan (see p. 224) for which no finds can be located. The division into two rooms, paved, and with a sink or drain, can be compared with Jarrow Building B (p. 233). The excavator notes that the doorways 'seem to have had upright stone jambs in "long and short technique" resting on stone sills'.

Two other structures (fig. 5.7) C and D were also considered of the same type, but to the north a rectangular building (E), 47 ft by 19 ft (14.32 m by 5.79 m) internally, was tentatively thought to be 'a guest house or merely a store house'. It is not possible to confirm either of these suppositions by plotting the finds from this area (see p. 456) but as Rahtz points out, p. 461, the east wall of the building had been reconstructed when the range H was built.

The square Building F, 5.8 m (19 ft) square, was not discussed by the excavators. It is included in Section 5 on the grid plan, and the finds seem to imply (see Appendix, p. 455) that it was built over the northern limit of the Anglo-Saxon burial ground. The finds of styli, needles, pins and a quern indicate domestic activities here associated with the early ninth-century occupation.

The L-shaped building to the south-west was divided into two rooms, the northern (G1) 21 ft by 11 ft (6.4 m by 3.4 m), the southern (G2) 20 ft by 11 ft (6.1 m by 3.4 m). At the east end of G2 was 'a large stone hearth divided into two sections three feet wide by eight feet long suggesting that this was an industrial building perhaps a smithy'. This building is in Section 7. It seems curious to find a smithy among buildings so closely associated with female activities. Moreover the finds register gives no hint of metalworking. Two broken grave-covers in the lowest level may not be significant. The débris from the other levels seems consistent with other areas on the site (see Appendix, p. 456) and includes, besides dress fastenings, eighteen loom-weights and two styli. The group of buildings isolated by Rahtz (see p. 461) and marked H have at least one hearth (as in A) but are in the area for which no finds can be plotted. J, where Rahtz suggests that a wall (9.9 m (30 ft) long with a possible doorway) is the north wall of a house, is also a possible early structure. No finds can be plotted for this area.

Building L, which Rahtz noted as a large building with very small rooms, is in Section 9, and produced an interesting range of finds with some earlier evidence, such as the *sceatta*, and traces of spinning, writing and possibly copying or reading.

Perhaps the most important evidence that the location of finds produces is in confirming that buildings in Section 34–9, east of the path or *allum*, were used for the same purposes as elsewhere on the site (see Appendix, p. 457). In particular the area produced a very large number of coins and two book-clasps.

The area between the west wall of the present north transept of the abbey and the west wall of the nave, in Sections 1 and 4 on the gridded plan, clearly shows that it was the focus of important Anglo-Saxon burials; and it is just possible, since in Section 2 we find slabs which would best be inset in walls and an Anglo-Saxon baluster shaft, that part of the Anglo-Saxon church had once stood here (see Appendix, p. 455). However, some of the area had later been covered by buildings which in their turn were cut through by medieval structures. Rahtz's plan, by removing the burial evidence, does not in this place give a true picture of the site.

The composite plan of the site obviously shows structures of different periods: for example, E appears to be earlier than the building complex O to the east of it. Moreover many graves, of at least three different forms and alignments, are shown as sometimes cutting through the buildings and paths and disturbing their outline. In considering the building sequence it seems clear that some of the buildings overlaid part of the cemetery area, and this could be associated with a replanning of the site in which ranges of buildings seem to be aligned along paths as is shown in Rahtz's plan and commentary. Possibly at this time buildings were constructed outside the old enclosure in Areas 34–9 (see p. 457). It is interesting to note, however, that not only the late coins but *sceattas* were found here, and that as elsewhere there were finds from under the 'Saxon paving'. Rahtz (p. 461) makes the interesting suggestion that the wattle-and-daub found by the excavators could have been from an early building phase, and not from partitions within the stone structures. This theory cannot now be tested, and although plausible it is also possible that some of the clay and stone foundations carried wattle-and-daub superstructures.

The functions of the buildings excavated have not been much clarified by the finds register, save in a negative way to cast doubt on the identification of Building G1/G2 as a smithy. The rooms to which finds can be assigned seem to have been used for a variety of the domestic activities of the female inmates: spinning, weaving, sewing, book production and cookery. It is possible that this area comprised the *domunculae*, as described at Coldingham (see p. 206), and that elsewhere, perhaps to the south of the medieval church where foundations were noted, there could have been large communal buildings for both the male and female sections of the community.

There is no possibility of comparing the plan of this site with others such as Wearmouth and Jarrow, since the areas investigated in relation to the churches are different. One would not expect, however, to find the same plan for a single sex and double institution, but one can contrast the wealth of artifacts, and in particular the quantity of coins and imported pottery, with Benedict Biscop's two foundations.

WEARMOUTH

Wearmouth (now called Monkwearmouth) occupies a site at the mouth of the River Wear, and dates from the seventh century to the ninth century.

The sources for the foundation of this monastery and its twin foundation Jarrow are Bede's *Historia Ecclesiastica (HE)*, *Historia Abbatum (HA)*, and the *Historia Abbatum auctore Anonymo (HAA)*. The house was founded by a Northumbrian noble, Benedict Biscop, who during extensive continental travels in which he visited Rome four times had been professed as a monk on the island of Lérins, and had been temporarily abbot of St Peter and St Paul, Canterbury. According to Bede he was granted seventy hides of land from the royal estates to found a community according to the best practices he had seen in seventeen monasteries he had visited.[83] The building of the monastery seems to have begun in 674 and, not more than a year later, according to *HE* (or within the second year of the foundation, according to *HAA*), he went to Gaul to seek masons to build him a church of stone in the Roman manner. This was done within a year and dedicated to St Peter.[84] As the work neared its close Benedict again sent to Gaul to obtain glass makers '*ad cancellandas aecclesiae porticumque et caenaculurum eius fenestras adducerent*'. The mention here of refectories, and the mention elsewhere of a common dormitory,[85] indicate that this was envisaged as a fully coenobitical community; however, there were also *cubiculae* available for the abbot, prior and some senior members of the community. Mention is made of three churches on the site and of 'many oratories' added by Biscop's successor Ceolfrid. Also connected with the monastery were domestic and farm buildings which are mentioned casually by Bede.[86]

In 681 King Ecgfrith donated a further forty hides of land on which to build a second foundation at Jarrow of this 'one monastery in two places'.[87] The second site is similarly near to a great river mouth (the Tyne), but even today it appears more confined than

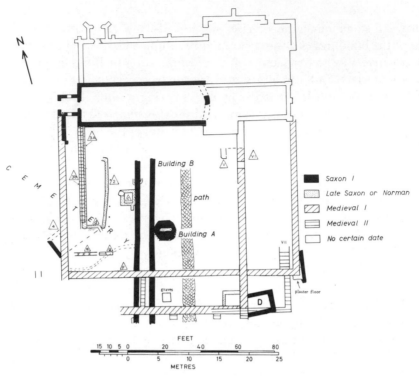

Figure 5.9 Monkwearmouth. Reconstruction plan, 1971 (R. Cramp)

Wearmouth, and the initial land grant, forty hides, was smaller. It appears that the Wearmouth community constructed various essential buildings for the monastery at Jarrow before the community there was finally established.[88] In 682 twenty-two of the brethren (seventeen according to Bede) began to build permanent structures, and in the third year from the foundation of the monastery they began on the church, which was consecrated and dedicated to St Paul in 685. In the early years of these foundations the king seems to have taken an active interest in them. His name appears on the dedication stone of the church at Jarrow, and Bede, in describing Lindisfarne, notes with some feeling that in the early days of that community when the king visited the island he only came with a few companions and was content with the simple food of the brethren.[89]

Bede provides us with one of the few contemporary references to the size of an Anglo-Saxon monastic community when he mentions that in 716 Abbot Ceolfrid left behind 600 brethren in the joint foundation and took eighty companions with him, many of whom must have been from the community. The reputation of the houses was enhanced by the fame of the works of Bede, who lived there between 680 and 735, but the establishments were also renowned for their stone masons whose services were sought as far away as the land of the Picts.[90] According to one rather doubtful source,[91] Jarrow was subjected to one of the early Viking attacks on Northumbria, and the two centres probably shared in the general decline of such sites in the ninth century. All record of them ceases in the ninth century, but in the period 1022–45 there is evidence of services being held at Jarrow.[92] It seems possible that the histories of the two sites had already diverged before the restoration of them both in *c.* 1072 (see below, p. 238).

When in 1959 the area to the south of St Peter's church was scheduled for redevelopment, only part of the church, the west wall and the west porch with a later tower superimposed, survived from the pre-Conquest period. Modern town development had encroached to within 20 ft of the south wall of the church, and limited trial excavations were undertaken in 1959, 1960 and 1961 in advance of replanning. In 1962 and 1964 more extensive excavations were possible while the sites were being cleared, and in 1966, 1967, 1969 and 1971 excavations were conducted in what has now been laid out as an open park.[93] Further excavation is planned, but in all of the area so far examined (figs 5.9, 5.10) modern town development has destroyed much of the stratification, and this, together with the paucity of datable pottery, has rendered the constructional sequence difficult to determine in an absolute manner.

The earliest feature on the site, possibly earlier than the earliest of the monastic buildings, is a Christian cemetery in which the bodies are orientated east–west, with heads to the west. The area had been intensively used for burial and many bodies were displaced by later graves. The lowest levels seem to be buried supine, and some had shadows of wooden coffins or biers. They all seem to have been buried in clean subsoil, although three had sherds of Roman pottery in their graves. To the west of Building B (fig. 5.10) the natural subsoil was sand with running spring lines and the burials extended as far as excavation has taken place to the west and south of the Anglo-Saxon church. The first group were overlaid by later burials which lay on their sides, and some of them underlay structures which are presumed to be pre-Conquest.[94] There seems to be a clear terminus to this phase of the cemetery to the west of Building B, just where the subsoil changes from sand to clay. No early burials have been found inside this latter structure, but like most of the other Saxon structures it has been cut through by later burials which seem to be of the post-monastic but pre-Conquest phase. Where it has been possible to determine the sex of the western burials it is clear that they form a mixed group of laymen, women, juveniles and infants. To the east of B there is a thin spread of primary burials in the supine position, some of which have been disturbed by Saxon buildings (such as Walls V1 and H) and where the sex of the first phase of interments is distinguishable, they all seem to be men. This is quite clearly the case in a group buried under a rectangle of small stones and cobbles in the south of the area investigated (fig. 5.10). It seems, therefore, that there was originally a large cemetery to the south of the church, and that at an early stage the area to the east of B was used as a monastic cemetery and to the west as a lay cemetery. A firmly cobbled path, running down the slope from the church, and areas of gravel paths seem to indicate that the possible monastic cemetery was traversed by paths. There also seem to have been shrines or *martyria* in this area. One such, Building

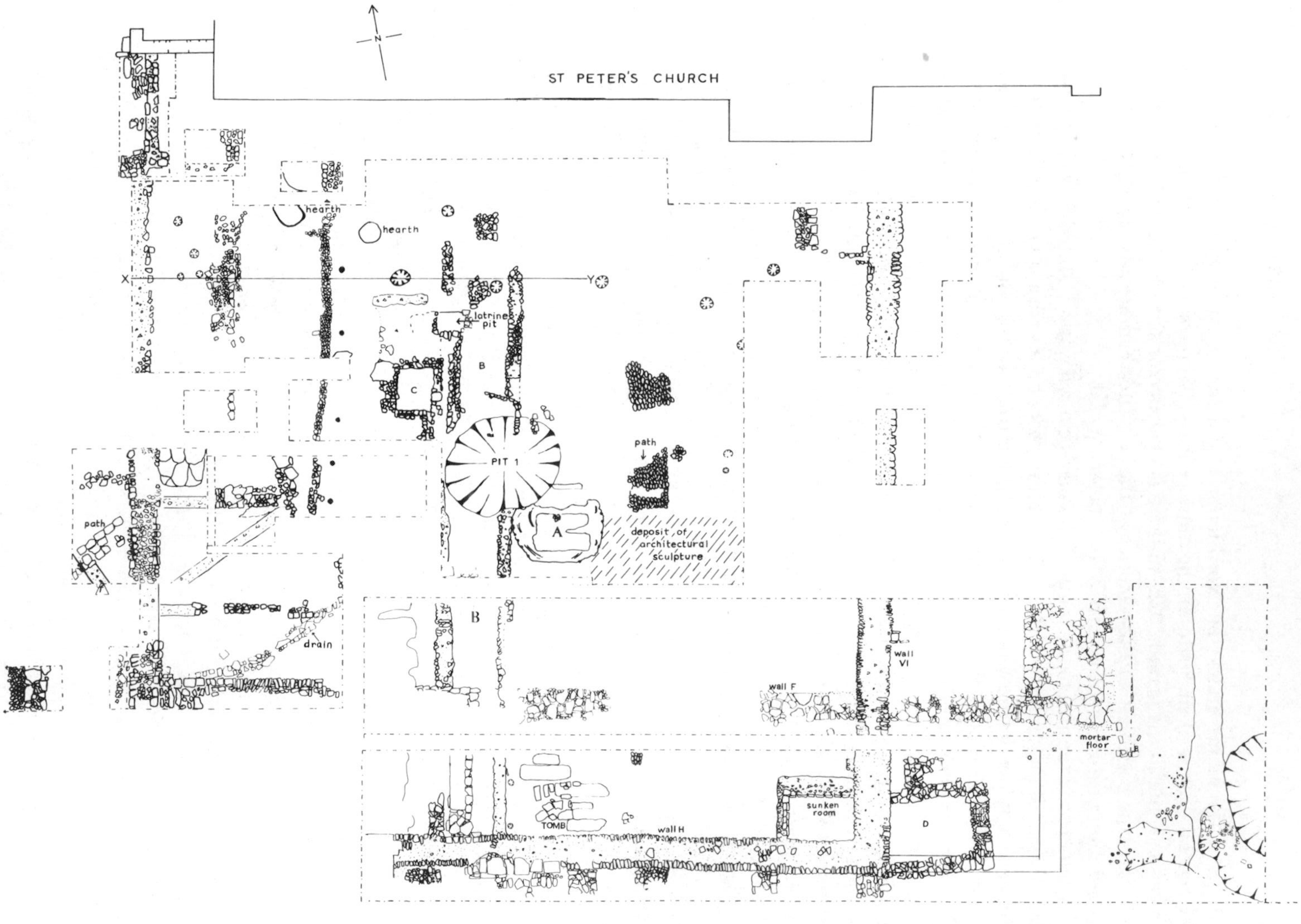

Figure 5.10 Monkwearmouth. Excavated features (R. Cramp)

A, was a round-ended structure, the floor of which measured 12 ft by 10 ft 6 ins (3.66 m by 3.20 m). The floor, which had been sunk about 1 ft (0.30 m) into the Saxon ground surface, was of a fine white concrete faced with a thin skim of powdered brick. It had carried a wattle-and-plaster superstructure, the main stake holes of which survived at 1 ft intervals in the curved ends. Débris from the superstructure showed clearly curved surfaces. In shape it has already (p. 220) been compared with the timber structures at Tynemouth and Knockea, but it might also be paralleled by the Glastonbury 'hypogeum' (p. 244) or a newly-found concrete mixer at Northampton. There was a rounded niche at the west end of Building A, and, although nine later burials had cut through the floor around it, underneath them was a stone-filled hole and a handful of bones which could have been from the primary burial. The building had been demolished some time before the end of the Anglo-Saxon period, and a deep pack of clay had levelled up the floor to the surrounding ground surface. This clay had been cut by burials which pre-dated the medieval reconstruction of the site.

Fragments of another concrete floor were discovered in 1969 cut by the return of the medieval south range. To the south of this was another structure (D), of a type hitherto unknown on the site. It was 13 ft (3.9 m) wide externally, and its walls, 2 ft (0.61 m) wide, survived as two foundation courses of rough flat stones bonded with clay. There was no evidence that it might have carried a mortared superstructure, and in appearance it is not unlike the Whitby buildings. The dating of its destruction to the pre-Conquest period depends on the dating of the junction between Walls VI and H. These in their turn are a secondary development of the long Building B.

Building B has now been traced to a point 105 ft (32.0 m) south of the south wall of the modern nave. (The modern wall overlies the south wall of the Anglo-Saxon church.) It seems reasonable to assume that the gallery joined the church as its northern terminus, although it petered out in a modern sewer trench and it has not been possible to investigate the area immediately adjacent to the church. The walls of the structure are at their maximum 2 ft 4.5 ins (0.72 m) high and set in very shallow foundation trenches; they could thus easily have been obliterated in the rebuilding of the church. The structure measures 11 ft (3.35 m) externally. The walls are constructed of limestone blocks, set upright and inclined, and clay bonded for the first two courses. Above these courses they are set in a distinctive creamy mortar, which has been poured over them in a form of concrete construction. This wall construction is identical to that of the west wall of the nave and the porch (as observed in the 1966 church reconstructions). The building seems to have had some sort of mortared floor laid on the natural clay, faint traces of which appear inside the walls. Thin slabs of mortar with a fine red brick facing were found in the destruction level of this building, and they, like the brick-faced mortar from Building D at Jarrow (p. 239), appears too fragile for flooring and could have been an external facing for the walls.[95] Débris from this building indicates that it was roofed with thin limestone slates and had lead flashing, and from the notable concentration of window glass alongside its walls its windows were glazed.[96] In its primary phase this building could be envisaged as a one-storey corridor joining the church to a range of buildings, as yet undiscovered, further south. No traces have been found of another corridor to the east, similar to the early cloister of the St Riquier type, but it could have served the same function as a cloister walk: for reading, writing and meditation.[97] At some stage, however, the gallery underwent major modifications when Walls H and VI were built. Both certainly seem to have continued in use as part of the medieval monastery, and H survived into the early modern period. However, in their primary phase both were constructed of limestone blocks set in the same fashion and with similar mortar, but the walls were wider and had deeper foundations. Wall H was indisputably bonded with B in its first phase, although in a later phase B had been demolished and H, instead of being the north wall of a building, had become the south wall, and a new cross wall had been inserted instead of the passage B. In the first phase of the use of H there had been a small external sunken structure in the angle between it and V1. This structure measured 8 ft by 10 ft (2.44 m by 3.05 m) externally, and was lined with well-shaped ashlar blocks. This little structure, which might have been an external strong room or prison, had been demolished and filled with clean rubble, possibly when the Norman south range was built, because in some charred post-holes set in the rubble were sherds of shelly Saxo-Norman pottery. The pre-Conquest sequence therefore seems to be that a two-storey structure was added to corridor B in the pre-Conquest period, thus enclosing some of the open ground with its paths to the east. More excavation will no doubt determine the extent of this 'regularization' of the monastic layout, but it is clear that only part of the structure survived to be utilized in the Norman buildings. The corridor or gallery B had already fallen into disrepair by then and was demolished in the Norman reconstruction. There is some evidence for rebuilding elsewhere on the site in the late Saxon period,[98] possibly at the same time that the late Anglo-Saxon tower was added. Certainly the site continued in use as a burial-ground. There is, however, no coin evidence later than the ninth century, and the sherds of Saxo-Norman pottery which have been found in destruction deposits could be pre- or post-Conquest.

The importance of this site is that it has produced buildings regularly aligned on the church, in which the quality of construction is reminiscent of Roman work. The painted plaster, decorative stone-carving, and coloured window-glass associated with them, all indicate the re-introduction of an advanced stone technology into the area. However, the dominating position of the cemetery with its shrines, the irregularly placed stone buildings such as D, as well as the motifs on the decorative stone carving, provide a link between insular and continental traditions.

JARROW

Excavation has been mainly concentrated in the Department of the Environment guardianship area to the south of the Anglo-Saxon and modern church lines, although there has been a limited exploration of the interior of the church and the modern graveyard to the north (see fig. 5.11). Trial excavations in 1963, directed by myself, have been followed by excavations in 1965–7, 1969–71 and 1973. In this period the whole area of the medieval court has been explored and a considerable section of the ground between the medieval buildings and the stream to the south.

Roman coins, inscriptions and pottery have been gathered from the immediate environs of the site in the past,[99] and sherds of pottery have appeared in stratified and unstratified contexts in the recent excavations (see p. 239). Nevertheless, the persistent tradition of Roman buildings to the north of the church has not been substantiated by recent excavation. In 1973 Christopher Morris's rescue excavations to the north-east (see fig. 5.11) failed to reveal any Roman structures or finds. Similarly Radford's excavations

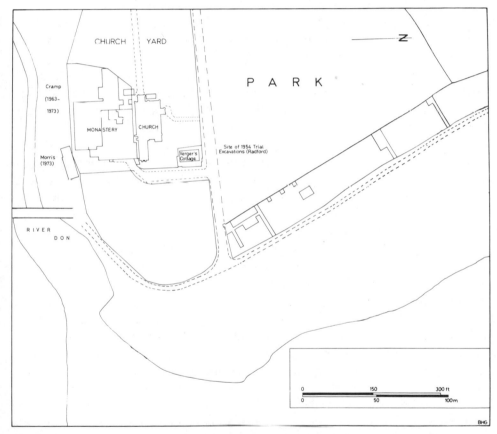

Figure 5.11   Jarrow. Location plan of excavated sites (C. D. Morris and R. Cramp)

nearer the church failed to reveal anything Roman – and indeed any early stratification on the site.[100] Radford's excavations did, however, reveal cobbled foundations about 13 ft wide, which he interpreted as the monastic *vallum*. This *vallum*, if projected south, would come very near to the east end of the Saxon church, but no return has been found in excavations further south. This feature should be re-examined by further excavation since, other than the doubtful Whitby example, this is the only example of a feature attested by abundant literary evidence. The two churches of the Saxon period[101] stood in the midst of the monastic complex if the traditions communicated to Leland is correct, namely that Bede's cell was on the north side of the church.

Limited excavation within the modern nave of St Paul's church, during the re-laying of the floor in 1973, established the internal width of the nave of the major Saxon church as 18 ft (5.48 m), and a length of 68 ft (20.73 m) from what appears to be the west front to the point where the nave narrowed into a square-ended chancel (see fig. 5.14). The walls had been robbed to a foundation level of clay-bonded cobbles of the same type as those found on Building A (see below), while the laying of the Victorian floor had completely demolished earlier floor levels.

To the south and west of the two Anglo-Saxon churches and to the north of the range of stone buildings A and B was a burial-ground in which the bodies appear to be aligned on the churches. Their pre-Conquest character is supported by the clean fill of their graves and the fact that in places they are cut by the foundations of the Norman wall trenches and what could be late Anglo-Saxon timber buildings to the east of B. A small group of burials in the area underlying the Norman east range were on a different alignment, and three of them contained single beads of sixth- or seventh-century type. It is possible that there was an early lay cemetery on the site, which might explain the eccentric relationship of the east end of the Anglo-Saxon chancel and the east end of B. The burials here, however, were merely shadows, it is thus impossible to establish their sex or to attempt a carbon-14 dating. About 52 ft (15.85 m) from the south wall of the eastern Anglo-Saxon church are two stone buildings roughly on the same alignment and separated by a flagged path 3 ft 6 in (1.16 m) wide. It is unfortunate that because of the medieval wall trenches and the standing post-Dissolution buildings it was not possible to establish a clear stratigraphic relationship between the two. Both had the same constructional characteristics and, where they survived, the same mortar type.

Building A, which measured 91 ft 6 ins by 26 ft (27.89 m by 7.93 m) externally, had originally been divided by a partition wall forming a small room at the west end and a larger one at the east. Both rooms had been floored with brick-faced concrete of the Roman *opus signinum* type which had been laid on a bed of stone chippings. The floor was noticeably more worn in the western room. In the centre of the eastern room was an octagonal stone base of red sandstone surrounded by fragments of a shaft carved with heavy plant scrolls and interlace. I originally interpreted this as a column base for subdividing the room,[102] but subsequent reconstruction of the fragments leads me to think that this was a piece about 1.5 m (c. 5 ft) high and that it may have been a stone lectern such as is found in many Middle Eastern monastic refectories.[103]

At some stage during the life of the building the dividing wall was removed, and a large stone-capped drain inserted across the room and the annexe to the south. The capping was then covered by a spread of clay and tile chippings. (In the 1973 excavation a small hut to the south was discovered in which a pile of Roman *tegulae*, *imbices*, and box tile, together with their chippings, were piled on the floor.) The annexe, which has not been fully excavated, had a partially paved floor at a lower level than that of the main room and dished pebble-lined settings for what have been interpreted as areas for standing large butts or storage vessels. It is assumed that the annexe was added after the demolition of the party wall in A, although it is not possible to be certain of this since the junction was at foundation level only. The building had been surrounded by a shallow eaves-drip drain on the north, west and east sides and was roofed with stone slates and lead flashing. The windows had been glazed with coloured glass on the north side and plain on the south. The structure had been faced internally with a creamy plaster, which was still *in situ* on its east wall, and there were indications that its eastern section may have had some sculptural decoration. It seems likely that this building was a refectory, and that the

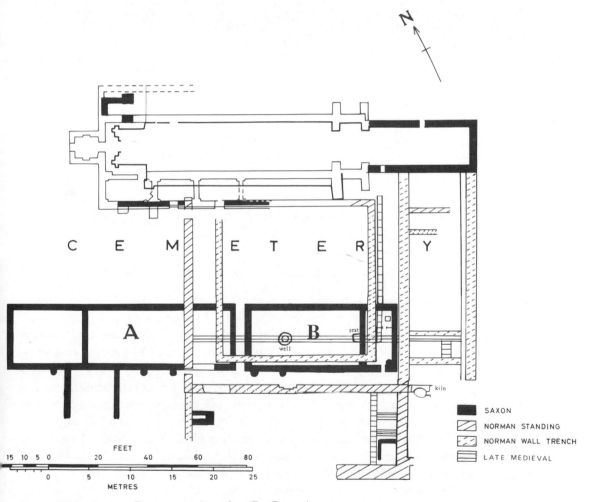

Figure 5.12 Jarrow. Reconstruction plan (R. Cramp)

southern annexe was a servery or storeroom. The building had clearly been destroyed by fire, and the burnt roof-timbers had remained on the floor at the east end. At the west end, however, the clean floor and a scatter of Saxo-Norman pottery indicated a later occupation.

Building B (fig. 5.13) measured 60 ft by 26 ft (8.29 m by 7.93 m) externally and had been subdivided into three rooms. The largest measured 43 ft by 21 ft (14.11 m by 6.40 m) internally. It had the setting for a seat in the middle of its east wall, and a small water hole, 4 ft 6 ins (1.38 m) deep, at its west end. The south and east walls stood two or three

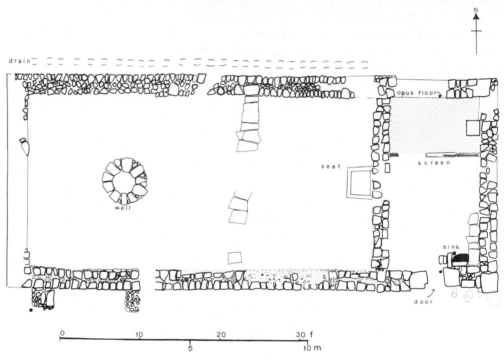

Figure 5.13   Jarrow. Building B (R. Cramp)

courses above the foundation level; it had a thick creamy plaster internally and a plaster skin externally. The eastern section of the building consisted of two rooms measuring 11 ft by 7 ft (3.35 m by 2.13 m) and 14 ft by 11 ft (4.27 m by 3.35 m) internally. They were divided by a grooved stone which probably held a wooden screen. The northernmost had an *opus signinum* floor and, inset into this, a centrally placed stone, perhaps an altar. The southern room, which was entered from a door in the south wall, had a partially paved floor and a sink, or wash-place, in the corner. Fragments of plain and coloured glass were found along the south and east walls. It was clear that building B had burnt down; the floor area of the large room had been disturbed in the medieval period, but there was a large quantity of burnt wood and melted lead in the levels above, and the internal wall plaster was blackened. Finds in this room included a stylus, a stick pin with ring and dot head, and a small whetstone. The floors of the smaller rooms, which had been protected from later disturbances by the walk of the medieval cloister, were thickly covered with ash. It would appear that this building could fulfil, in a later Benedictine monastery, the functions of the east range – the large room serving as a place for assembly and writing and the private suite perhaps used by the abbot or a senior monk. We have, therefore, a type of 'cell' composed of oratory and living room, like that of St Cuthbert on Farne, combined with a public room for communal use. This building is interestingly comparable with the large secular halls of the period.[104]

The solid Roman-looking stone buildings on the upper terrace at Jarrow were like the timber 'halls' of the secular world supplemented by small huts of post or stake construction, the floor platforms of which were cut into the slope between A and B and the stream to the south. One such hut floor excavated in 1963[105] yielded evidence of glass-working in the shape of a millefiori rod and glass slag, as well as a coin of Eanbald 796–830. In 1973 a line of wattle huts was found further south. These also provided evidence for glass working in the form of a millefiori rod and a millefiori bead.

From the 1971 excavations it was clear that the area between the church and the river had been terraced. On the upper slope, Buildings A and B had been buttressed against the slope, and below them was a terrace (part of which was excavated in 1963) on which there was at least one wooden hut and signs of cultivation. This terrace had been supported by a clay and stone bank, drained by stone-filled channels. One sherd of Samian ware was discovered in the channels.

In the eastern section of the site a stone-built structure of some pretensions (Building D) had been cut into the natural clay slope in a form of scooped construction. An area of this building 37 ft by 14 ft (11.28 m by 4.27 m) was contained in the excavation. The north wall, which had collapsed both inside and outside the building, had been constructed from well-shaped small ashlar blocks, of the same type as in B and the existing Anglo-Saxon church, with brick-tempered bonding mortar and painted plaster in the interior. The wall had been set in massive Roman footings revetted into the natural slope of the ground. One of the walling stones was inscribed with the word HELMGYT, apparently a proper name. The flooring of the interior of the building appears to have been divided into two areas, although no sign of a partition wall survived. In the eastern portion of the building a stone bench with a runnel in front ran alongside the north wall, and, where the bench and runnel ended, walkways of heavy flags ran from north to south and from north-east to south-west. This type of partial paving was also discovered in B. The eastern section of the building had a clay floor and appeared to have been reshaped when a large hearth area was constructed. Sherds of shell-tempered pottery were associated with the fill over the hearth.

A considerable quantity of animal bones was recovered from Building D and, during its last phase of occupation (dated by coins of Eanred and Redwulf to the first half of the ninth century), the area seems to have been used for glass-working. Two millefiori rods, a crucible and glass waste, a bone die and several small bronze tools testify to this work.

Other finds from the occupation level of the building include part of a bronze strap-end with ninth-century 'Trewhiddle type' ornament, a stone mortar, Anglo-Saxon coarse pottery and glazed imported pottery. A great deal of coloured and striped window glass – about 900 fragments – was discovered on the floor of the building and, underneath the wall collapse on the exterior, many complete quarries survive in varied shapes. In the interior many had been fused together by heat and it seems possible that there had been an attempt to melt and re-use them after the period of the main occupation of the building. The primary function of Building D can hardly have been a workshop, since the glass windows and the painted and plastered wall would have been quite unsuitable. It seems possible from its position near the river walls which were discovered in Christopher

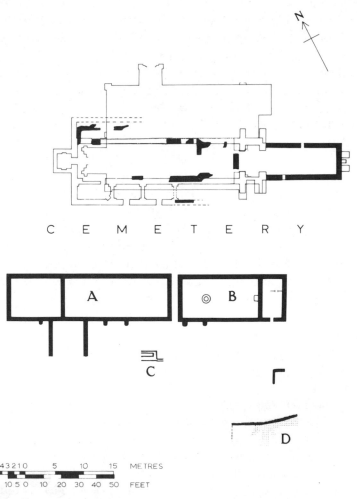

Figure 5.14   Jarrow. Excavated stone buildings, 1973 (R. Cramp)

Morris's excavations (fig. 5.11) that it was originally a guest house for visiting laity. That such houses existed seems feasible in the light of Bede's statement about Lindisfarne (see p. 205). It is possible that it declined in status as a building after the early importance of the site and became a workshop in the ninth century.

Wearmouth and Jarrow founded within ten years of each other under the same direction illustrate well the dangers of trying to find 'type' sites for these early monasteries. So far there is nothing to link the two sites in layout save the position of the cemetery area to the south of the churches, and some constructional characteristics of the buildings. Thus, though the rubble walls of Wearmouth are changed to coursed stone at Jarrow, the mortar-types, roofing materials and glass types are the same. The quality of these buildings well illustrates the Roman manner for which their masons were famous.

The 1973 excavations at Jarrow have demonstrated the infilling of the large stone buildings with flimsy wattle huts or shelters which are not shown on the plan, but on both sites the excavations are incomplete and there are notable gaps. To date there is no evidence for an enclosure, or for the domestic buildings which must have serviced the large communal structures. The monks clearly had few personal possessions,[106] but the lack of kitchens, metalworking shops, or even evidence for water supply and distribution is notable. This is in marked contrast to the bath-houses and sweat-houses remarked on Irish sites like Inismurray.[107] The one small water storage pit in B is hardly comparable even with the line of little wells at Whitby.

Nevertheless these sites have shown the inventive way in which their inmates combined continental and insular traditions of layout and building construction, and further excavation could alter the present incomplete picture.

None of the sites which might have provided a picture of the regular layout of a reformed monastery of the tenth century or later has been fully excavated. However, enough work has been done on some of the major centres of the reform movement to show that massive changes of layout were effected.

GLASTONBURY

Glastonbury is a monastic foundation of uncertain date, but it certainly existed by the mid-seventh century, and most probably by *c*. 600. Seemingly never abandoned as a site, it was reformed in the tenth century.

Of all the monasteries of the pre-Conquest period, the literary evidence is the most copious, if largely suspect. Even the first critical historian, who examined the evidence in the twelfth century, found it impossible to disentangle the confused mass of antiquity. If one leaves aside the claims that the primary foundation is the result of an apostolic mission, or even that it was founded by St Patrick, it was certainly believed in the pre-Conquest period that the original monastery was a foundation of the Irish Church. William of Malmesbury does, however, suggest[108] that the Irish connection, and the burial there of the Irish Prince Indracht with his companions, need not have been earlier than the seventh century.[109]

Finally in support of the pre-Saxon phase of occupation of the site William declares that in 601 a king of Dumnonia granted land, called *Yneswitrin*, to the old church at the request of Abbot Worgret. The existence of a charter as early as 601 is doubtful, and if the name *Yneswitrin* means Glastonbury (as the monks claimed) then it makes nonsense to give it to an existing community.[110] However, we do not know where in the area of the 'isle' the earliest foundations were and Rahtz's work on Glastonbury Tor has enlarged the possibilities.[111]

Nevertheless it seems clear that there was some monastic foundation at Glastonbury when it came into English hands during the reign of Cenwalh, and the first land grant is dated 670, when the king gave two hides at Meare to the Anglo-Saxon bishop Beorhtwald. Beorhtwald found difficulties in maintaining some of his outlying properties in the face of British militancy and abandoned the house to Helmgisl, who was appointed in 678 on the understanding that future abbots should be elected according to the Benedictine rule.[112] After the division of the Wessex see in 705, in which the monasteries in the newly conquered British territories obtained a bishop of their own to support their interests, Aldhelm of Sherborne persuaded King Ine to build a stone church at Glastonbury.[113]

Royal donations to the community continued to be made until Æthelwulf's grant of 857 and at the time of the Viking invasions it must have been one of the richest houses in southern England.

Although there is a cessation of royal grants between 857 and 922 other benefactions from laymen and bishops imply that a community existed into the late ninth century. A postscript to the Anglo-Saxon translation of the *Rule* says that before 954 'there was but a scant number of monks in a few places in so great a kingdom living by right rule, that was not more than in one place called Glastonbury'.[114] Dunstan, who was born near Glastonbury *c.* 909, had received some sort of education there, so if the monastic buildings had fallen into decay the library and school survived, although later records suggest they were maintained by visiting Irish monks. It is clear, however, that the institution declined and in the ninth century was possibly administered by a lay abbot under royal jurisdiction at the time when Edmund appointed Dunstan as abbot, *c.* 940.[115]

In the years from *c.* 943 to 956 Dunstan restored Glastonbury to something approaching a recognizable Benedictine community. According to his biographer he enlarged Ine's stone church, lengthened it considerably and, to make its width square with its length, added aisles and porticus.[116] He enclosed the ancient cemetery, while the area within was raised into a mound to form a pleasant meadow removed from the noise of the passersby, so that it might truly be said of the bodies of the saints lying within 'they repose in peace'. He is credited also with measuring out cloisters and noble buildings.[117]

Dunstan's replanning of the monastery seems from the documentation to have been the last major reconstruction before the Conquest, and it provided a model for the new foundations which sprang up after 957. Glastonbury remained until the Conquest one of the best-endowed and most influential houses in England.

In the excavations which, under a series of directors, have taken place in the site from 1908 to 1962 much of the area of the post-Conquest churches and monastic buildings has been examined, but no full compilation has yet been made of the vestiges of the pre-Conquest structures which have emerged.

The first two reports by Bligh Bond concentrated on determining the plans of the abbey, St Mary's church and the Edgar Chapel. The first reports of early monastic buildings appeared in the third report.[118] A shaft was sunk in the cloister garth and virgin clay was found 8 ft below the grass. On this level a terracotta slab was found and two small fragments 'of ware having a crystalline glaze of brilliant blue-green hue'. The tile was considered Roman and the pottery Egyptian or Syrian. Although older footings are mentioned in the fourth report and although St Dunstan's Chapel was discovered in 1911 and reported on in 1914, it was not until 1913–14 that evidence for an early cemetery was found in the form of a stone cross head from the excavation of 'the extreme south-west corner of the nave'.[119] In the eighth report[120] a rather confused account is given of a structure 'south of the south east angle of the Lady Chapel, as nearly as could be computed mid-way between there and the guest-house block'. The remains were at considerable depth and the footings were of clay-bonded boulders. A post-Conquest structure was attached to this building. In the tenth report of the excavations in 1926, the excavators considered they had found the base of the more westerly of the famous 'pyramids'.[121] In 1927 the new director, Fyfe, discovered the plaster floor of Ine's church, 6 ft $\frac{1}{32}$ ins below the nineteenth-century floor.[122] In the next report, Peers, Clapham and Horne describe this floor in more detail, as 'a thick layer of plaster bedded on small pieces of tufa and lias and rendered with a thin facing of lime mortar containing powdered brick'.[123]

Attempts to locate the Anglo-Saxon cloister by digging trenches 6 ft wide to a depth of 5–7 ft in 1930–31 failed, but in 1934 the deep level of redistributed clay elucidated in Radford's later excavations was noted; so also was the fact that it contained Roman pottery of the first to second centuries and a Henry VIII half groat. These excavations were followed up by Radford in 1951–62. In 1951–4 exploration below the west wall of the thirteenth-century cloister produced evidence of small post-holes in two lines running east–west. They were associated with a roughly trodden floor lying a few inches above the natural surface; 'the pottery recovered from this level included one fragment of second-century terra sigillata, one of native ware of the first century AD and a quantity of sub-Roman fragments'.

These post-holes were considered by Radford to belong to a small chapel within the ancient cemetery of the monastery.[124] In addition the south side of the cemetery was located about 60 ft south of the thirteenth-century church. The earlier burials were in slab coffins, 7 ft 8 ins below the present ground surface. The later, in wooden coffins, lay 3–4 ft higher. The south wall of the cemetery was attached to the chapel of St Michael. To the east of this chapel, south of the cemetery enclosure and stretching south for more than 150 ft, was a block 22 ft wide, robbed in foundation level.[125] These buildings were pre-twelfth century and considered by Radford to be part of Dunstan's cloister.

In 1955 a trial trench was dug from east to west across the medieval cloister. In the west cloister wall traces of more timber buildings were discovered and an early grave appeared, 'some 50 ft east of the cloister wall', proving that the early cemetery extended at least so far in that direction. The section also disclosed the robbed foundation trench of the east wall of the cemetery, 4 ft east of the cloister and approximately in line with the east wall of the Anglo-Saxon church.

The eastern end of the trial trench revealed a glass furnace which appeared as an oval hollow 4 ft by 3 ft, and fragments of the clay walls of the furnace, crucibles, glass vessels, beads and window glass were associated with it.[126] This lay below a twelfth-century level.

This area was fully explored in 1956 and in 1957 a second furnace came to light which was overlaid by a pre-Conquest building. Traces of the domed superstructure were found and three successive floor levels noted: 'The stratigraphy shows that the furnaces were in use at a time when the early bank had become much spread, and that they had ceased to function when a building was erected in the centre of the later cloister garth.' This building was ruined before 1140. In 1956 a well, overlaid by a ditch, was discovered in a trench in the north transept. 'As stone lined walls are unknown in the earlier Saxon period the present example must be Romano–British. This dating is confirmed by two sherds found lying at the bottom of the ditch below the wall.'

The ditch itself and its associated bank was further investigated in 1957 at a point where it ran through the chapter house. The length obtained was at least 200 ft north–south; it was 15 ft wide with steep sides and a V-shaped bottom, dug about 7 ft 6 ins into the old ground surface, and had almost silted up by the twelfth century. The bank lay west of the ditch, 20 ft wide at the base, and although only 2 ft survived as a maximum height, the excavator estimated it could have stood 8 ft 10 ins high, thus providing a massive *vallum monasterii*.

In 1959 a trench cut from east to west across the dorter range south of the refectory brought to light a heavily burnt floor, superficially resembling those of the glass furnaces. Outside the west wall of the same range was an area of rough stone settings which also showed evidence of burning. Both structures had been abandoned and, long before the early twelfth century, an east range was erected. A few fragments of Anglo-Saxon pottery and a bun-shaped ingot of bronze were associated with the area, implying Anglo-Saxon industrial activity.

In 1962 a further investigation was made of the ancient cemetery in an attempt to discover its stratification. A trench 4 ft wide and 60 ft long was cut south from the south side of the lady chapel and disclosed, about 50 ft from the wall, a plaster floor 6 or 7 ins thick and originally enclosed by a thin wall. 'The plaster lay directly on the clay with its surface about one foot below the original surface of the ground.' The floor was covered by the re-deposited clay associated with Dunstan's reconstruction. The excavator concluded that the structure was a hypogeum.[127] This structure could bear some resemblance to Building A at Monkwearmouth.

In default of a published plan which shows all the pre-Conquest features so far identified on this important site it is difficult to say anything conclusive. The site has provided analogous evidence of an early burial-ground, together with associated wattle structures, as well as the most convincing *vallum* enclosure of any Anglo-Saxon monastery. The evidence for glass- and metal-working areas is also unique and clearly illustrates the monastery's importance at the time of the tenth-century reform.

The archaeological evidence in many ways complements the literary. The early cemetery, with its cist graves surrounding a wattle church, links with the traditions of the sub-Roman insular church.[128] The great ditch and bank, which has been investigated at two points, could be secondary to the early cemetery, but this also is best paralleled in the sphere of influence of the Celtic Church.[129] It seems clear that there were modifications in the original foci among the important graves and their monuments in the period between the unknown foundation date and Dunstan's reforms. No really firm evidence exists for the dimensions and layout of the old wattle church. Its position is assumed to be on the same site as the twelfth-century lady chapel, and it is also assumed that it was linked to King Ine's stone church of St Peter and St Paul by a paved passage.[130] Ine's church has been revealed to have a nave about 42 ft long, and lateral side chambers. Its *opus signinum* floor and painted plaster walls compare with the Kentish churches of the seventh and eighth centuries, and with Wearmouth and Jarrow. A hypogeum or crypt to the east of the church, which was later covered by Dunstan's tower, could be of this or a slightly later phase. Also of eighth-century date could be the stone crosses in the old cemetery, the confusing documentation of which has been extensively considered by Taylor[131] and Clapham.[132] The historical personages whose names are inscribed on these crosses centre around AD 700. Their location, despite the claim of the 1926 excavators, is still uncertain. The plaster floor, discovered by Radford in 1962 and interpreted by him as a hypogeum near to which one of the stone pyramids could have stood, might also be of this phase.

The excavations have perhaps best illustrated the extent of the replanning of the monastery under Dunstan. This is to be seen in the major shaping and enlargement of the church, which is outside the scope of this paper, but which is important, not only as a prefiguring of the better-recorded reshaping of the Old Minster,[133] but also because of the consequential replanning of the domestic offices of the monastery. The cemetery with its ancient burials and monuments was cut off from the main activities of the monastery by the wall Radford discovered running from just beyond Dunstan's extensions to the earlier church line. The south wall was established by Radford in 1951–4, some 60 ft from the south wall of the medieval church. The western limit of the enclosure is plausibly indicated by the walls running north and south from the chapel of St John, which seems to be of Dunstan's building. This chapel, which could have been of the gate-house type, would have then provided an entrance to the church and cemetery complex. What is not clear is how the monastic buildings, some of which Radford claimed to find running from the south-east corner of the enclosed cemetery, were linked with the churches. One can see that, if the cemetery had paths across it—as at Monkwearmouth (see p. 231)—the dead there would be at peace. One can also see how the monastic buildings could have been cut off from the laity who would presumably have visited the ancient shrines. What is less easy to see is why the thick deposit of clay was laid over the ancient cemetery, unless there were a removal of an ancient relic such as might have reposed in the plaster-floored structure discovered in 1962 (itself obliterated by the clay). This would suggest a planned refocusing of the pilgrimage centre of the monastery, in which the ancient centre was obliterated by the clay which must have been excavated as part of extensive building works elsewhere. The extent of the tenth-century refurbishing of Glastonbury is well attested by the discovery (unique in the Anglo-Saxon archaeology of monasteries) of the bronze-working hearths and glass furnaces. However, until the excavations are fully published, and indeed complemented by further work, the appearance of this primary reforming centre is still unclear.

WINCHESTER

The Old Minster at Winchester was an episcopal and monastic site of the seventh to ninth centuries, enclosed by a wall in 852–62. It was redesigned as a complex monastic enclave with the New Minster and the Nuns' Minster between the reigns of King Alfred (871–899) and Edward the Elder. The monastic buildings seem to have been extensively renovated and redesigned between 965 and 995 when Æthelwold restored the monastery and 'built all these dwellings with firm walls and new roofs'.[134]

The building of the New Minster at Winchester was initiated by King Alfred just before his death. He is said to have bought land for a chapel, which seems to have been of a temporary nature, and a dormitory (described also as a *monasterium*). His son Edward the Elder completed the work, and 'many workmen and artificers having been gathered, the foundations were laid, the building was begun and proceeded with such enthusiasm that, marvellous as it is to record and difficult as it may seem, the work was finished in two years'.[135]

In 903 the monastery was dedicated to the Trinity, St Mary and St Peter and St Paul, and was called the New Minster to distinguish it from the earlier establishment. The site was carved out of the holdings of the Old Minster. The area contained the temporary church and stone dormitory of King Alfred's *monasterium*, a strip to the south of the church and dormitory and an area 'on the west of the monastery'.[136]

The two monasteries, the New Minster to the north of the Old, were inconveniently close together and in the reign of Edgar (959–73) there was an attempt to create a single monastic enclosure to include not only the old and New Minsters, with enough space in between the monasteries to prevent strife, but also a nunnery (the Nuns' Minster founded by Queen Ælswytha). This female foundation was apparently to the east of the New Minster.[137]

In the complex excavations of the Old Minster and part of the New Minster and its surrounding buildings, undertaken by Martin Biddle between 1961 and 1970, evidence has emerged for the layout of some of the claustral buildings of the monastery.

The monastic complex of the Old Minster probably lay to the south in an area impossible to investigate, and the principal cloister of the New Minster lay to the west of the church. However, in an area to the east of the New Minster a group of important buildings has been revealed which, as a result of the 1970 excavations, can almost certainly be claimed as part of the pre-Conquest monastery.

Part of this complex, Building E, was discovered by Dean Kitchen in 1886, but was not fully excavated until 1970. The more northerly groups A–D were excavated in 1962–3. The final analysis of the Winchester site is not yet complete, but I am grateful to Martin and Birthe Biddle for allowing me to use their interim conclusions.[138]

Building E, the furthest south of this group so far excavated, is now shown to be a structure with seven phases of structural development. The first phase seems to be a north wall traced for 6.5 m near the south-west corner of the fully developed building. It is interpreted by the excavators as a boundary wall and is clearly of post-Roman date. It lies at an angle to the underlying Roman street but is on the same alignment as all subsequent Saxon structures on the site.

In Phase B a small rectangular building was constructed outside the earlier wall and on the same alignment. This building which subsequently became the core of the whole south-west part of Building E lay with its longer axis north–south and measured 13 m by 9 m wide. Its foundations were made by large uncoursed unsharpened flints set in a puddled matrix of chalk and clay including many fragments of building stone, Roman tiles and a distinctive brick-filled pink plaster of Anglo-Saxon type. There was a 'very long series' of floor levels with many small pits and post-holes. The pottery from these layers was not later than the tenth century.[139]

In Phase C a wall of different construction and at a higher level was built south from the south-east corner of the earlier building. It is presumed by the excavators to be a replacement of the original boundary wall.

In Phase D extensive rebuilding took place in the area, a range 34 m by 9 m being added to the east side of the Phase B building. The excavated structures appear to have formed the south range and the southern parts of the east and west ranges of a courtyard complex. The foundations of this phase were very deep, and the interior of the range was divided by at least one original cross wall.

Biddle postulates that this phase could represent a pre-Conquest claustral arrangement, 'but presumably not the principal cloister which seems at this time to have lain further west in the area burnt down in 1066'. He suggests that this could be the infirmary block of the New Minster, reconstructed after 1066 to serve the needs of the entire community.[139] That this was an infirmary cloister like that shown on the ninth-century St Gall plan is only supposition. It is, however, vitally important since Winchester has provided the only evidence of a complex Anglo-Saxon claustral layout excavated under modern scientific conditions. Canterbury, which might have provided a much more complete layout of the major cloister, was unfortunately not excavated under scientific conditions.

ST AUGUSTINE'S, CANTERBURY

The monastery of St Augustine was attached to an episcopal centre outside the wall of the important Roman town of Canterbury, and was founded in 598.[140] Augustine also 'founded a monastery not far from the city to the east, in which Æthelberht, encouraged by him built from its foundations the church of the Apostles St Peter and St Paul and adorned it with various gifts so that the bodies of Augustine himself and all the bishops of Canterbury and the kings of Kent might be placed in it'.

This church, consecrated in 613, was the westernmost of a group of three on the same east–west axis. (A multiplicity of small churches seems to be typical of monasteries of the seventh century in Gaul and England.) The monastery flourished throughout the pre-Conquest period and in fact does not seem to have ceased to function up to the time of Dunstan's reforms in 978. When the church was enlarged, it is possible that the monastic buildings were also replanned and enlarged.

The excavation record of this site is an unhappy one in view of the primary importance of the site in English ecclesiastical history. Most effort has been concentrated on the churches (fig. 4.6) and is not discussed here.[141]

Excavation, or rather exploration, of the area of the cloister to the north of the church of St Peter and St Paul produced some evidence of pre-Conquest structures. These were published in a composite plan,[142] which does not in several respects agree with the commentary on it by Peers and Clapham[143] or the current Department of the Environment Guide. All commentators agree that the earliest structure is a building lying at an angle to the later cloisters. Its dimensions have been given as 30 ft by 18 ft in the *Guide*, 28 ft by 17 ft by Clapham, and 38 ft by 22 ft 6 ins by Potts. It has been compared with the rectangular buildings at Whitby, although there is no indisputable evidence that it is a monastic building at all. There is no doubt that there was a burial-ground between the church and the building, but before the Norman rebuilding there appear to have been two developed claustral plans covering an area about 68 ft square.

Potts felt that the earlier cloister was as early as eighth century, but Clapham was inclined to date the first regular planning to the period of St Dunstan's reform and the later to the mid-eleventh century, when the church was extensively replanned. He notes that the former definitely took into account the enlargement of the north porticus of St Peter and St Paul and the second 'had been planned in connection with a series of steps forming an approach to Wulfric's Octagon of *c.* 1050'. This phase of regular planning produced a cloister of 42 ft east–west and rather less north–south, although the exact time is not determinable. 'The square seems to have had alleys on all four sides, that on the S. barely 11 ft wide and that on the W. rather wider. The W. wall of the E. alley was probably overlaid by the corresponding wall of the later layout.' The cloister was flanked on all but the south side by narrow ranges which were subdivided into irregular rooms. Clapham's description of their dimensions does not fit Pott's plan and it seems impossible without re-excavation to reach a decision as to who was correct. There is no reason why at an important site such as Canterbury the regular claustral plan should not have been adopted by the late eighth or early ninth centuries, as on the Continent.[144] However, since Dunstan formed a new cloister at Glastonbury (see p. 245) it is possible he also formed one here.

The limits of inference

It is clear that the excavation of Anglo-Saxon monastic sites have been so incomplete that little can be said in the form of general summary. Perhaps the most useful final statement is to outline the limits of inference.

Firstly, there is the difficulty of identifying such sites, particularly in the early period. The monastic *vallum* does not appear as a prominent feature in the archaeological record so far, and the distinctive layout of church and cloister with regularly aligned buildings, although it should emerge, has an ambiguous beginning in England. Such obvious characteristics as the presence of church and graveyard as a central focus are less easy to identify in heavily occupied town sites where the early church no longer exists.

Identifying features such as the presence of inscriptions, and evidence for literacy in the form of writing implements and the indication of far-reaching contacts in such artifacts as exotic pottery, may be of more value in the early than the later periods of such settlements.

Similarly stone buildings may in some areas, and particularly in the pre-Viking period, be an indicator of a monastic rather than a secular site.

Having established the location of the site, its ideological nature colours the artifacts which can be expected to be found in a very curious way. One does not find the débris one might expect of a large number of people living in a confined space if, as the literary evidence tells us, the individuals are bound by a vow of poverty and communal existence. The buildings rather than the artifacts indicate the wealth and status of the inmates. The lack of artifacts on some sites adds to the problem of identifying the use of buildings, but the lack of sound dating criteria for Anglo-Saxon pottery as a whole exacerbates the problem. Changes of use of buildings, like the Whitby 'cells' or Building D at Jarrow, must have often occurred, but they are difficult to detect, and the length of time for each type of occupancy is impossible to determine.

However, the greatest problem in the archaeological record at the moment is in the sheer quantity of sites explored and their uneven spread in time and place. Until one of the early Kentish, West Saxon, Mercian or East Anglian houses of the pre-Viking period has been thoroughly explored, the Northumbrian evidence is clearly unbalanced and excavation of at least one of the great reformed houses of Wessex or eastern England would supplement the existing evidence from Winchester and Glastonbury. The study of the archaeology of this type of site has hardly begun. Perhaps, however, the interpretation of any evidence such excavations would provide must depend on an equal concentration on such sites on the Continent.

Although from the evidence so far accumulated the monastic complex is not an implanted model as easily identified as a Roman fort or a later medieval monastic house, this is a type of site dependent on a wider network of influences than the native insular tradition would supply. The resemblances of the major buildings at Jarrow to royal halls in wood such as those at Yeavering might appear in a different light if we could compare them adequately with a plan of Lérins. Likewise, the problems of the Canterbury cloisters might be solved by further excavation of sites like St Riquier or Fleury-sur-Loire.

Notes

1 Knowles (1966) 1.
2 Ryan (1939).
3 *Two Lives*, 96–7.
4 Thomas (1971) 85 and fig. 40; *Two Lives*, 216–17.
5 *HE*, v, 2. Thomas (1971) 83, 85, considers that the word refers to an enclosed cemetery. It seems more likely, however, that the normal interpretation of the word as 'oratory' is correct.
6 Norman and St Joseph (1969) 95–115.
7 *Eddius*, 67.
8 Knowles and St Joseph (1969) 22–3.
9 Although so far not enough research has been done on the association of Roman and early monastic sites, the older antiquaries provide tantalizing notes of possible associations which would repay a programme of detailed research. For example, the site of the monastery of Lyminge would repay further study. Founded by Æthelberg, daughter of Æthelbert, first Christian king of Kent, and widow of Edwin of Northumbria, soon after 633, the site was a royal *vill* and Roman remains have been excavated there. The monastery was supported by rich land grants throughout the eighth and ninth centuries, but lost its autonomy by the tenth century. Fascinating and confusing accounts of the finds from the double monastery are incorporated in Smith and Jenkins (1861) 198, including the discovery by Jenkins of a building 25 ft by 12 ft in the field next to the church of St Mary. This he considered could be a refectory of the early monastery. Jenkins also made the interesting statement that he thought that the male part of the monastery was on the south and east of the church and that the nunnery lay to the west and south-west. Rigold (1968) 35 also cites this as a site worthy of further investigation.
10 *HE*, iv, 13.
11 *HE* v, 12.
12 Æthelwulf, *De Abb.*, ll. 473–86.
13 *Two Lives*, 176–7.
14 *HE*, iii, 26.
15 Æthelwulf, *De Abb.*, l. 27. The reference to metal vessels for the table of the brethren is interesting since the use of large metal vessels rather than pottery in these large communal sites seems reasonable. Fragments of rims of bronze vessels (unpublished) have been found at Wearmouth and Jarrow and Whitby.
16 *HE*, v, 14.
17 Hughes (1966) 136.
18 Eddius, iv, 3.
19 *Two Lives*, 264–5.
20 *HE*, iii, 2.
21 Deanesley (1961) 202. See also Rigold (1968) 27–37 and Bateson (1899) 168–83.
22 *HE*, iv, 7–10.
23 Whitelock (1955) 715.
24 *HE*, iv, 25.
25 Besse (1906) 70.
26 *HE*, iii, 8.
27 Æthelwulf, *De Abb.*, ll. 434–54 and 620–51.
28 Whitelock (1955) 740–43.
29 Emerton (1940).
30 Stevenson (1929) section 30.
31 *Regularis Concordia* (Symons (1953) xxxi). References to a full claustral layout with refectory dormitory and chapter house are also found in descriptions of the reformed house at Abingdon built after 954. See Biddle *et al.* (1968) 45–6.
32 *HE*, iii, 4, and Levison (1940) 28–91.
33 Radford and Donaldson (1957) 38–9.
34 Radford (1950) 85–126 and (1957b). The one feature of the site which can probably be attributed to the age of Ninian are the graves excavated by P. R. Richie: Thomas (1971) 55.
35 Radford and Donaldson (1957) 33.
36 Thomas (1971) 14–15.

37 Thomas (1967) 127–88.

38 Radford (1962) 7.

39 Radford (1939) plan.

40 Ibid., 25.

41 Ibid, 20 and Radford (1962) 14–24, fig. 3.

42 Radford (1962) 9. These points have been further developed by Burrow (1973) 99–103, who produces reasons for doubting whether this is a monastic site.

43 Radford (1956) 59–70 and Thomas (1959) 89–96.

44 The evidence for excavated sites of this date is too sparse to admit of firm judgement as to the significance of imported pottery. See, however, Alcock (1963) 125–37 and Alcock (1971) 201–9. Jarrow also produced sherds of Samian type.

45 *HE*, iii, 19.

46 Charles Green's untimely death in 1972 unfortunately has meant that his summary of earlier work on the site and the report of his own excavations are unpublished, save in *Medieval Archaeology*, iii (1959) 299; v (1960) 319; and vi–vii (1961–2) 311 They are to be published in the future by his daughter, Barbara Green, who has generously given me access to the site plans and allowed me to reproduce the general plan of the site. I have also consulted Green's finds books but have not seen the finds. Anything I have said is therefore subject to revision.

47 Henry (1957) 75–7.

48 Ibid., 88–9.

49 Stenton (1913); Biddle *et al.* (1968) 26–69.

49a Lambeth 42 and BM Cotton, Claudius c. ix.

49b BM Cotton, Vitellius A. xiii.

50 *Chronicon monasterii de Abingdon* (Stevenson (1858), 272f.). It is possible that the monks' cells were attached to the perimeter wall, as in some of the Middle Eastern monasteries.

51 Biddle *et al.* (1968) 35–41.

52 Ibid., 60–67 and fig. 12.

53 Jobey (1967) fig. 1.

54 *HE*, v, 6.

55 Craster (1907) 41–3; *Vita Oswini*, iv, 12–15: Raine (1838).

56 Jobey (1967) 42–9.

57 Cramp (1967b) 99–104.

58 Jobey (1967) 42–3.

59 Ibid., 43.

60 Ibid., 44–5.

61 *HE*, iv, 23.

62 Colgrave and Mynors (1969) 407n.

63 The earliest published account which is anonymous is in *The Gentleman's Magazine* (1833)

218–20. This implies that the inscribed stones were found both under the heads and over the bodies. This account is supported by Gage (1836) 479–82, who adds that a long brass pin or brooch with an oblong head was found, and that vestiges of masonry and foundations were found nearby. Haigh (1875) 367 mentions pins, a bone needle and several pieces of coloured glass as having been found in the 1843 excavations.

64 A lengthy bibliography of commentary on the stones is included in Okasha (1971) 75–6. The most important accounts of the cemetery, however, are to be found in Haigh (1846) 185–96; Baldwin Brown (1903–37) v, 58–101; and Scott (1956) 196–212.

65 *The Gentleman's Magazine*, new ser. x (1838) 536.

66 Ibid., new. ser. xxi (1844) 188.

67 *HE*, iii, 25.

68 Smith (1956) 163 offers a different interpretation. See Whitelock (1955) 640, n. 4. The 'haven of the tribe' would be possible, but in view of the eleven late Roman coins and Roman pottery from the site the 'haven of the watch-tower' from Bede's Latin is apt.

69 No contemporary account exists of this, but it is inferred from the works of later writers.

70 Rahtz (1962) 605–6.

71 *HE*, iii, 24.

72 *HE*, iv, 23.

73 *HE*, iv, 23, and in Gregory's Life, Colgrave (1968) 37–8.

74 Peers and Radford (1943) 41–2, fig. 4. Despite the mention elsewhere in Bede of the maintenance by the Anglo-Saxons of the ancient Christian tradition of elaborate epitaphs, this is the only surviving plaque, and the only other which survives on a cross is from the daughter cell at Hackness.

75 *HE*, iv, 23, and iv, 24.

76 Atkinson (1878) 1.

77 Peers and Radford (1943) 27–88.

78 Clapham (1952) 8.

79 I am grateful to Leslie Webster of the British Museum for so kindly supplying me with copies of this plan and the finds record, the originals of which are deposited in the Department of Medieval and Later Antiquities. I am also grateful to Miss K. Simmons and Miss H. Cayton for their help in sorting through the daily registers in order to build up a picture by areas.

80 Hood (1950) has photographs of the excava-

tions. The originals of these photographs are not available today.

81 Peers and Radford (1943) 27–8.
82 Rahtz (1962) 604–18, figs 1 and 2.
83 *HAA*, 6.
84 *HA*, 5.
85 *HA*, 9 and 15; *HAA*, 25.
86 *HA*, 8. For a fuller account of the history of Wearmouth and Jarrow in the pre-Conquest and post-Conquest periods, see Cramp (1969) 22–9.
87 *HA*, 15; *HAA*, 16.
88 *HA*, 7; *HAA*, 11.
89 *HE*, iii, 26.
90 *HE*, v, 21.
91 Anglo-Saxon Chronicle, E, *sub anno* 794, Whitelock (1955).
92 Cramp (1969) 26–7.
93 Ibid., 29–42 and Cramp (1972) 150–52.
94 Cramp (1969) 31–4.
95 Ibid., 36–7.
96 Glass found on this site has been discussed in a preliminary fashion in Cramp (1970) 327–35 and pl. 54.
97 A single junction building existed linking the palatine chapel and king's hall, at Aachen. At Luxeuil in the ninth century there was a porticus which ran from the church. This a modern commentator describes as a *galerie*, which he compares with St Riquier and Aachen (see Erlande-Brandenburg (1964) 239). It is interesting that Bede in describing the glazing of the major buildings of the monastery by the Gallic workmen mentions the church, the refectories and the porticus, *HA*, 5.
98 Cramp (1969) 38–41.
99 Birley (1961) 157–9.
100 Radford (1954) 205–9.
101 Taylor and Taylor (1965) 343–7.
102 Cramp (1969) 45 and 49.
103 Evelyn White (1933) 244 and pl. 49B.
104 Addyman (1972) 284–5.
105 Cramp (1969) 52, fig. 22.
106 Cramp (1973) 123–4.
107 Wakeman (1893) 39; Lucas (1965) 65–114.
108 William of Malmesbury, *Gesta Pontificum* (Hamilton (1870) 197–8).
109 For a discussion of these, see Slover (1935) 147–160 and Finberg (1964a) 83–94. For the additional tradition of a Welsh connection with Glastonbury, see Bromwich (1961) 217.

110 Finberg (1964a) 83–94.
111 Rahtz (1968) 111–22 and (1970a) 1–81. This site has provided timber buildings of what might be a small monastic cell.
112 Adam of Domerham, *Historia de Rebus Glastoniensis* (Hearne (1727) 49).
113 William of Malmesbury, *Gesta Pontificum* (Hamilton (1870) 196).
114 Knowles (1963) 696, Appendix 2.
115 Robinson (1921) 26–53.
116 William of Malmesbury, *Vita Sancti Dunstani* (Stubbs (1874) 271).
117 Ibid., 271–2.
118 Bond (1910) 75.
119 Bond (1914) 62.
120 Bond (1916) 136 and pl. vii.
121 Bond (1926) 17.
122 Fyfe (1927) 86.
123 Peers *et al.* (1930) 24–9.
124 Radford (1955) 33–4.
125 Radford (1961) 22–4 and fig.
126 Ibid., 69 and 167–8.
127 Radford (1968) 115–16.
128 Thomas (1971) 81–90.
129 Ibid., 29–37.
130 Taylor and Taylor (1965) fig. 110.
131 Ibid., 255–7.
132 Clapham (1930) 61–2.
133 Biddle (1970a) 317–21 and Biddle (1972) 115–17.
134 The first analysis of the documentary evidence was provided by Willis (1845). The research was taken further by Quirk (1957) 43 and Biddle (1974).
135 The *Liber Monasterii de Hyda*, which records the details of the early history of the New Minster, is discussed in Quirk (1961) 17–20; and the topography of the site is provided by the *Liber Vitae*, see Quirk (1961) 49–54.
136 A circuit of these boundaries and later land grants is reconstructed by Quirk (1961) fig. 6.
137 For a discussion of the foundation and impor- see Biddle (1975c).
138 Biddle (1964) 206–11; Biddle (1971a) 48–55, fig. 1; Biddle (1972) 116–23, figs 6 and 8.
1; Biddle (1972) 116–23, figs 6 and 8.
139 Biddle (1972) 122–3.
140 *HE*, i, 33.
141 Taylor and Taylor (1965) 140–42.
142 Potts (1934).
143 Peers and Clapham (1927) 201–18.
144 Reinhardt (1952).

I am grateful to all the excavators who have supplied information about their excavations, and to Miss B. Coatsworth for her aid with the preparation of the text.

6

Craft and industry

David M. Wilson

Knowledge of crafts and industries in Anglo-Saxon England is almost completely dependent on archaeological sources, as only casual references in histories, riddles and homilies and specialized late Anglo-Saxon documents, such as the *Gerefa*, enable the historian to reconstruct any part of this side of Anglo-Saxon life.

It is clear that there was a considerable decline in technical achievement after the Romano-British period. Some crafts – the mason's, for example – were only revived after a number of centuries. But this decline can be overestimated and there is a tendency to dismiss the Anglo-Saxon period in discussions of technological history. In this chapter I shall attempt to outline the evidence for Anglo-Saxon craft and industry in the archaeological record. Such an outline is necessarily sketchy and incomplete, but in some cases a considerable body of evidence is available which redresses the silence of the literary sources.

Carpentry

It seems likely that the most commonly used material in the Anglo-Saxon period was wood, but, because of its nature, little survives to reflect the carpenter's skill. Fine woodwork has occasionally come down to us; the seventh-century oak coffin-reliquary of St Cuthbert,[1] for example (which is chiefly remarkable for its linear carving than for any technical details of carpentry), the lyre and maplewood cups from Sutton Hoo,[2] or the carved applewood and hawthorn flute from the Danish levels at York.[3] The Graveney boat[4] has recently added immeasurably to our knowledge of woodworking of a rather specialized nature. Bowls and platters[5] reveal a knowledge of lathes (presumably a pole-lathe[6]), although no such machine has been found. Coopering, whether by specialists or not, has left little trace, although Gerald Dunning has identified the oak head of a wine barrel from York[7] by comparison with an example from an early Norman pit at Pevensey Castle.[8] A related craft was the making of buckets by means of staves bound with bronze or iron hoops – such objects are of frequent occurrence in graves of the pagan Anglo-Saxon period.[9] Wooden combs and spoons have been recorded at York.[10] The wheelwright and cartwright have left no monuments, although illustrations in late Anglo-Saxon manuscripts[11] and ninth- and tenth-century Scandinavian parallels[12] show contemporary capabilities in this direction. Basketry is considered elsewhere,[13] but other woodland industries – making hurdles or brooms, rakes and other simple tools, handles for iron tools and shafts for spears, and various types of bodging, fletching[14] and bowmaking – have left little or no trace in archaeological terms.

The greatest amount of wood must, however, have been used in the construction of buildings, some of which were made of enormous timbers.[15] The stave method of building known in Scandinavia is found on at least one English site, the church at Greensted, Essex,[16] and certain techniques of the carpenter, the splitting of hardwood and the cutting of a rabbet, are seen in this church. Competent carpenters' work with tree-nailing and half-joints has been observed in the well at Portchester, Hampshire.[17] Wattle work is seen in negative impression in daub,[18] and large timber constructions, like the mill from Tamworth,[19] show fairly sophisticated carpentry.

Examination of coffins shows that they were often clamped or nailed together,[20] although a mortice-and-tenon joint is recorded.[21] We may assume that clamps were also used on buildings, perhaps explaining such phrases as:

> *innan ond utan irenbendum*   (*Beowulf*, l. 774)

or:

> *wæs þæt beorhte tobrocen swiðe*
> *eal inneweard irenbendum fæst*   (*Beowulf*, ll. 997–8)

although Rosemary Cramp was only able to provide a single analogy for these in the small flat pieces of iron found around the Sutton Hoo superstructure.[22] Late eleventh-century oak shingles from Winchester[23] suggest that the Anglo-Saxons could split accurately, and shingling is demonstrated pictorially in the hog-back tombstone series.[24]

The use of clamps referred to above seems to emphasize the reluctance of the carpenter to cut joints. There are, for example, no joints in St Cuthbert's coffin and it is interesting that the only substantial piece of Anglo-Saxon wood-carving in the round to survive – a boxwood casket – is carved out of the solid wood,[25] a feature which is also to be noticed in other house-shaped caskets made in British areas at this period.[26] This may be because of a lack of accurate saws, but saws are known both in this country and abroad.[27] The craftsman certainly knew how to use fine tools for carving (as in the casket referred to) or for construction purposes,[28] but in small objects there seems to have been a tendency to avoid joints.

Carpenters' tools have been considered elsewhere;[29] here I shall merely summarize the evidence. The literary evidence was covered by Brasch in the early years of the century in a now largely forgotten work.[30] The tools come from three main finds, Hurbuck, Durham;[31] Westley Waterless, Cambs.,[32] and Crayke, Yorks.;[33] all of which are dated by associated finds to the ninth or tenth century. We have no similar finds of the pagan period, but tools are occasionally found in graves. Other finds occur in settlement excavation,[34] but again mostly from the later Anglo-Saxon period. A group of tools has been found in the River Thames at London Bridge;[35] this find, however, is not without its controversial side, as the axes found there are often interpreted as the remains of 'one or other of the attacks which, in the days of St Olaf and King Knut, centred round the old timber bridge'.[36] Some of the objects from this find are certainly weapons (the spear-heads, for example), but some of the axes may well have been dropped in the river by workmen repairing or building the bridge (some axes, however, have collars decorated in the Ringerike style and must have been used as battle-axes).

The following carpenters' tools, other than axes (of which many varying forms survive), are found in Anglo-Saxon contexts: hammers, adzes, boring-bits, chisel, gouge, draw-knife, plane, saws and a wedge. Many of these tools would not be exclusive to the carpenter and may well have comprised part of a general agricultural tool-kit. In England we have no parallel to the specialized tool-chest from Mästermyr in Sweden.[37]

The axe was the basic tool of the carpenter, used for felling trees (saws were not used for this purpose until the nineteenth century), for lopping the trunk, and in splitting and dressing the planks. The butt of the axe would be useful as a hammer for driving the wedges by which the trunk was split. In 1927 Wheeler devised a typology of axes of the Viking period;[38] of his six types at least three – III, V and VI – are considered by him to be weapons (he derives them from the *francisca*, a type occasionally found in Anglo-Saxon graves of the pagan period).[39] Type I (fig. 6.1), he saw as a universal cutting axe and Type II, the T-shaped axe (fig. 6.1), is undoubtedly a wood-cutting tool.[40] His Type IV is based on the form of the Mammen axe,[41] which itself is clearly not a tool; on the other hand there seems no reason why such axes, when they were not decorated (as, for example, that illustrated in fig. 6.1), should not be used by the wood-worker. The axe would be equally convenient as a weapon or tool and it might be unwise to distinguish between the two functions. Keller has suggested that axes were not used as weapons until the reign of Knut,[42] but this is perhaps being a little too emphatic, for the *francisca* (from which some of the battle-axes of the late Anglo-Saxon period certainly evolved) cannot only have been used as a throwing axe. Anglo-Saxon battles were elemental and, apart from swords, hand weapons were not very sophisticated; a wood-cutter's axe would be an ideal weapon in much hand-to-hand fighting.

Of the axes which are tools, the T-shaped axe (fig. 6.1) seems to have some chronological significance as it never occurs in pagan Anglo-Saxon graves, although it obviously de-

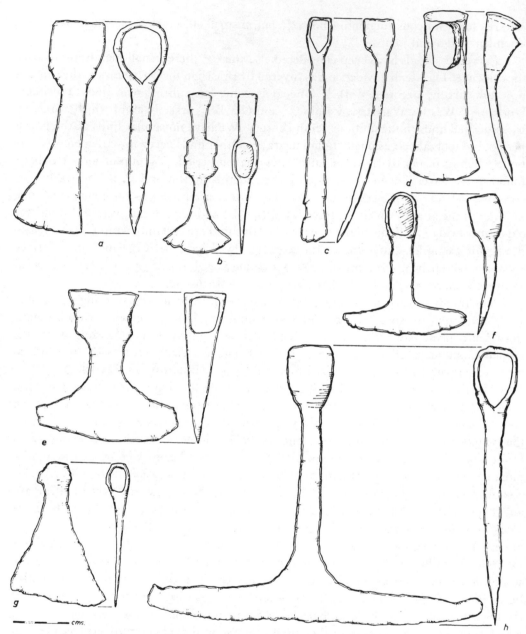

Figure 6.1   Axes and adzes:
a, c, f and g Hurbuck, Durham
b Horton Kirby, Kent
d Thetford, Norfolk
e Sarre, Kent
h Crayke, Yorkshire

rives from necked axes flourishing in that period (like that from the Anglo-Saxon cemetery at Sarre, Kent[43]). It might be suggested that the most exaggerated form of the T-shaped axe appears in the ninth century.

An interesting tool is the axe-hammer like that from Horton Kirby, Kent (fig. 6.1b). Another example occurs at Alfriston, Sussex,[44] and an example from Normandy is quoted by Baldwin Brown as typical of a number of continental specimens.[45] It is perhaps from this type of object that the T-shaped axe develops. An unusual axe-hammer (considered by Bruce-Mitford to be a tool) was found in the Sutton Hoo burial.[46] This has an iron haft and would have been extremely hard on the hands in use – a wooden haft (usually one supposes made then, as now, of ash) absorbs much of the shock of each blow. This extraordinary object might well be a weapon or a ceremonial piece.[47]

Although the axe was obviously used in dressing timber, adzes were also important. The classic type is that from Thetford (fig. 6.1d), which is paralleled throughout Europe from Russia to Portugal.[48] (The Thetford example, incidentally, has a much hammered butt as though it has been used as a wedge for splitting timber.)[48a] Two other English adzes are of less widely spread type; they both come from the Hurbuck hoard. One is T-shaped (fig. 6.1) and is paralleled only in Scandinavia.[49] The other is basically of the same type as that from Thetford but is very narrow and was presumably used for making a groove in the wood. An essential tool in dressing wood was the wedge, and one Anglo-Saxon example is known – from Grave 233 at Sarre, Kent (fig. 6.2f). A series of iron wedges were found with the carpenters' tools in the great find from Mästermyr, Sweden;[50] these would presumably be used, together with wooden wedges, to split timber along the line of strain.

Saws are very badly documented in Anglo-Saxon contexts. Two fragments only are known to me, from Mitchell's Hill, Icklingham, Suffolk (fig. 6.3a), and Thetford (fig. 6.3b). The Thetford example is two-edged and has parallels in Gallo-Roman and Romano-British contexts,[51] and presumably fulfilled a similar function to the modern dowel-saw. The Icklingham saw is without parallel, being quite unlike contemporary frame-saws. It is possible that either or both of these saws could have been used in bone-working.[52]

Only a single plane – equivalent to a small smoothing plane of today – has been found in an Anglo-Saxon context, from a sixth-century grave (no. 26) at Sarre (fig. 6.4); its iron and wedge are lacking. The stock is of antler and is pierced by an oval hole to allow the fingers to grip it. It has a base plate of bronze. In form it is derived from Roman prototypes[53] and has parallels outside the Roman empire in Holland[54] and Jutland.[55] An object of this size would only have been used in fine work.

Draw-knives were also used for smoothing wood and an example survives from Sandtun, Kent (fig. 6.2g). A broken object from Westley Waterless, Cambs., might be a draw-knife;[56] its reconstructed length (28.9 cm) would, however, seem to rule this out.

A single chisel and a gouge are the only representatives of their class to be found in Anglo-Saxon England. The chisel is a small tanged object from Southampton. Together with its tang it is some 15 cm long and about 7 mm broad,[57] and is hardly the kind of

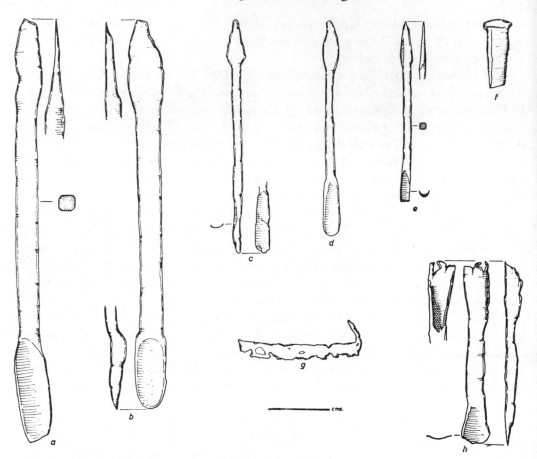

Figure 6.2 Boring-bits, wedge (f), draw-knife (g) and gouge (h):
a Westley Waterless, Cambridgeshire
b Hurbuck, Durham
c Brundall, Norfolk
d and e Thetford, Norfolk
f Sarre, Kent
g Sandtun, Kent
h Crayke, Yorkshire

tool used in rough carpentry. Other so-called chisels (from Sutton Courtenay, Berks., and Crayke, Yorks.) seem too slight for the purpose, although the Crayke hoard has produced a socketed gouge (fig. 6.2h).[58]

A number of boring-bits with spoon-shaped terminals have been found (fig. 6.2).[59] They are of a universal European type and were presumably inserted in a transverse handle, like that which survived in a thirteenth-century context at Mileham, Norfolk.[60] No example of a bow-drill or brace has been recorded.[61] Twist-bits are unknown in Eng-

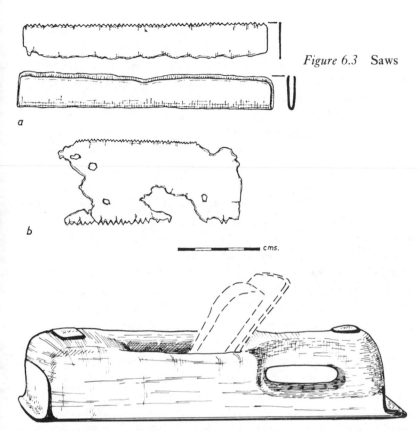

Figure 6.3   Saws

Figure 6.4   Anglo-Saxon plane from Sarre, Kent

land but are recorded in Viking Age contexts in Scandinavia.[62] One must also presume that awls of various sorts were used by carpenters for piercing wood.

Carpenters' hammers are difficult to identify unless they are claw-hammers,[63] and even then they may be farriers' tools; claw hammers are not, however, known in this country. It should be pointed out, however, that the heel of an axe or adze (as fig. 6.1f) would be completely acceptable for driving nails.

It is clear that few carpenters' tools survive from this period; on the other hand it seems probable that the tool-chest – possibly with the exception of the large saw – was quite as sophisticated as that of the carpenter's medieval successor.

Bone and horn working

Workers in bone and horn must have used similar tools to those used by carpenters. Objects made of these two materials were in great demand in the post-Roman period. Some idea of the variety of objects produced in these media can be obtained from the Frisian terps, where Dr Roes has assembled a catalogue of material which includes such diverse objects as combs, dice, cleats, sword-mounts, cheek-pieces of bits, spearheads, wool-combs and mallets.[64] Objects from Anglo-Saxon contexts in horn or bone include bracelets, pottery stamps, pins, needles, dice, combs, gaming pieces, 'draughtsmen', spoons, weaving battens, boxes, pin-beaters, flutes, pendants, a weaving tablet, beads, spindle-whorls, trial pieces for jewellers, a plane, a seal, bodkins, flutes, skates and buckles. To these can be added more luxurious objects of both elephant and walrus ivory, which were certainly made in this country.[65] Bone was also used by artists (the eighth-century whalebone box – the Franks' casket – is, for example, one of the most renowned products of the Anglo-Saxon period).[66]

There is some reason to suppose that bone-working was a specialized craft, at least in the later Anglo-Saxon period, for there is good evidence that it was carried on in towns – a fact which implies specialization – evidence for bone-working occurs at Thetford,[67] York[68] and Southampton.[69] At Dublin[70] and in other towns of north-western Europe, for example Birka,[71] Lund[72] and Sigtuna[73] in Sweden and Wolin in Poland,[74] a specialized bone industry has been recorded. In Lund, for example, reindeer antler was even imported from some distance[75] to be used in the horn industry. Bone-working was reasonably stereotyped; the methods used for manufacturing bone combs at Southampton (pl. 14) are adequately and accurately paralleled, for example, at Dublin. Such objects were clearly made for sale at the markets in the towns where the craftsmen worked.

The tools used by workers in bone and horn have not been recognized; saws, drills and knives seem, with various polishing agents, to be the most-needed tools and there is some evidence of turning bone objects.

Horns were popular in only a slightly modified form as drinking vessels: sometimes, as at Broomfield, Essex,[76] without mounts, sometimes, as at Sutton Hoo or Taplow, with elaborate mounts.[77]

Stone-working

The working of stone for building of some architectural pretension (i.e. other than dry-stone walling in vernacular building) was apparently a late introduction into Anglo-Saxon England, the first stone buildings being churches, presumably those built by the followers of Augustine in the south-east of England. In the north, Eddius records that Ripon and Hexham were rebuilt in stone by Wilfrid in the 670s.[78] Often-quoted passages from Bede's *Historia Abbatum*[79] and from the anonymous life of Ceolfrid[80] tell of Benedict Biscop sending for masons from Gaul to build the church at Jarrow in 674 (see p. 234f.). The implication of these passages seems to be that there were no trained masons in Northumbria until the latter half of the seventh century. The difficulty of dating the churches of the Anglo-Saxon period in England[81] does not, however, allow us to deny the skill of the masons who were eventually trained in the continental techniques both of building and of sculpture. Of the actual technical aids used by the sculptor and mason, nothing survives other than a few drilled holes or chisel marks on sculpture and building stone.

That stone was quarried and carried over fairly long distances has been attested by Jope's work,[82] but from archaeology there is no information concerning techniques of quarrying or of the quarries used – although Romano-British material was re-used from time to time.[83]

That stone was worked at a period before the introduction of Christianity is demonstrated by the presence of quern-stones in pagan graves,[84] but the presence of any masonry building with dressed stone is not attested at this time.

Paint

The use of paint on both wood and stone is well attested in Scandinavia in the Viking Age[85] and it must be assumed that it was used on wood in England – although no definite surviving example of painted wood is known to me. Traces of paint on stone are, however, attested so often that there can be little doubt that the Anglo-Saxons, like their post-Conquest successors, used paint lavishly. Paint is recorded on sculpture, among other places, at Burnsall,[86] Stonegreave and Kirklevington[87] in Yorkshire, at Lancaster,[88] at All-Hallows-by-the-Tower[89] and at St Paul's[90] in London, at Reculver, Kent,[91] and at Deerhurst, Glos.,[92] but many more stones must show traces of pigments, although such embellishment has not been recorded. Paint and whitewash on plaster have been recorded at Monkwearmouth and Jarrow,[93] and at Winchester.[94]

Such paint was obviously very different from that used in the illumination of manuscripts, about which we know a great deal from the studies of Roosen Runge,[95] but the Winchester painting demonstrates that the same *horror vacui* apparent in Anglo-Saxon ornamental metalwork, manuscripts and sculpture was probably given full rein in painting.

The use of iron

Iron was an important element in the material culture of the Anglo-Saxons – probably the most important element after wood. Iron weapons, tools and domestic equipment are found with great frequency in Anglo-Saxon contexts. Little is, however, known about the mining or collecting of raw material in this period. Iron ore – of some quality – is widespread in England; Tylecote says that it has been smelted 'at one time or another in twenty-nine of forty-one English counties', and goes on to say that many of the blank counties may also have produced iron.[96] There are two main sources for iron: water-deposited bog iron (particularly in northern England) and outcrops of carbonate, haematite and limonite ores in various parts of the country.[97] That iron was mined in Anglo-Saxon times is clear from the documents, but whether these mines were simply small pits (like those at West Runton, p. 262f.) or elaborately dug shafts cannot for the moment be determined. We may be sure, however, that open-cast working was carried on at various places.[98]

Smelting is well documented in the late Anglo-Saxon period,[99] but the presence of iron slag on a site is not necessarily indicative of the presence of smelting. One must treat with caution general statements about 'iron smelting',[100] unless they are backed by scientific reports, for the slag could well be derived from a smithy. On this basis, then, we may accept evidence of smelting from the following Anglo-Saxon sites: Southampton,[101] Shakenoak,[102] York,[103] Crayke,[104] West Runton,[105] Stamford[106] and Great Casterton,[107] the three latter belonging to the Anglo-Saxon/Norman overlap period.

The only type of furnace so far documented is a shaft-furnace. Examples have been excavated, or evidence of them found, at Mucking, Essex,[107a] at Stamford, Lincs., at West Runton, Norfolk, and at Wakerley, Northants.[108] The one from Stamford was clay built, the base measured 35 by 25 cm and its slag basin survived. It was associated with a slag heap and two hearths, either for roasting the ore or for the further reduction of impurities in the bloom. It has been dated by archaeomagnetic methods to the eleventh century.[109] It was found on a site in the High Street in the centre of the medieval town and not, as one would expect, on the edge of the town away from the risk of fire. The furnace is dated to the eleventh or twelfth century and probably drew its ore from the outcrops of ironstone which occur on the edge of the town.[110]

The bloomery site at West Runton has been thoroughly investigated by Dr Tylecote.[111] As at Stamford, a shaft-furnace was found together with an outcrop of raw material. The site is loosely dated to the late Anglo-Saxon or early Norman period on the basis of Thetford-ware pottery found in association with the bloomery. At West Runton 'small flattish nodules which consist almost entirely of hydrated iron oxides' are found

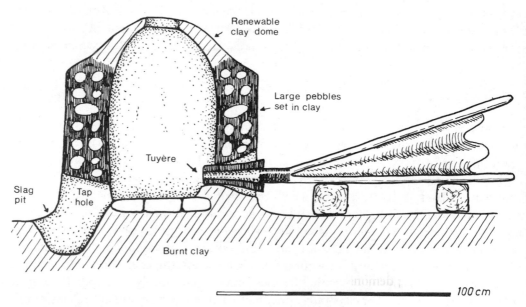

Figure 6.5   West Runton, Norfolk: reconstruction of furnace

in the sands and formed the raw material for the furnace. A series of pits was dug to obtain the ore which occurred in a dark layer of manganiferous iron pan. Tylecote calculates that the excavated pits would each yield about 600 lbs weight of ore yielding on roasting an iron oxide plus manganese oxide content of over 75 per cent. The furnace base of burnt red clay was associated with a roasting hearth and a charcoal pit.[112] The furnace is reconstructed in fig. 6.5.

The unpublished shaft-furnace slag base from Mucking, Essex, is probably to be dated to the early Anglo-Saxon period; indeed they were known in Romano-British contexts[113] and are documented in at least one of the homelands of the Anglo-Saxon invaders.[114] It is usually assumed that the bowl-furnace was more common[115] and that much of the evidence listed below represents this type of smelting.

Few analyses of blooms or slags from Anglo-Saxon sites have been published, but a bloomery cinder from Pit 147 at Southampton produced the following results: silica 44.1 per cent, iron oxide 52.3 per cent, calcium and magnesium oxides 2.0 per cent.[116] The following table is based on figures published by Tylecote[117] and lists analyses of possible Anglo-Saxon slag (of which the samples from Great Casterton, Stamford and West Runton are certainly from bloomeries) – the figures exclude H_2O, CO_2, etc.

	Great Casterton tap slag	West Runton slag	York ninth- to thirteenth-century slag	York post-Roman slag	Stamford red-ore fines
FeO	46.1	58.4	47.9	63.0	–
Fe_2O_3	3.2	–	5.72	5.7	55.8
SiO_2	26.2	25.6	27.4	17.8	25.6
CaO	7.0	1.5	2.6	2.1	1.7
MgO	1.1	0.2	0.54	0.54	–
MnO	0.7	3.1	–	–	–
Al_2O_3	9.5	9.1	3.43	2.05	6.9
P_2O_5	2.3	1.9	2.40	2.00	1.56
TiO_2	0.45	0.2	–	–	–

The smith

The smith is an important figure in heroic literature and assumed an important position in continental folk literature. Weland the Smith was well known to the Anglo-Saxons: he is mentioned in the poem *Deor* and is probably portrayed on the Franks Casket.[118] In certain instances he seems to have had a special place in society, but Loyn points out that there are many exceptions and that his status was not necessarily very exalted.[119] The blacksmith was, however, a ubiquitous member of society; no community could do without him[120] and presumably only the most skilled achieved any real fame. The blacksmith's equipment and smithy are rarely found in Anglo-Saxon contexts.[121] Slag is all that seems to remain of the smith's activity,[122] and no anvil or other major piece of equipment has been found. It is not always wise to use illustrations in manuscripts in interpretation of crafts, but it is clear from, for example, Ælfric's paraphrase of the Penta-teuch (a manuscript of the second quarter of the eleventh century which belonged to St Augustine's monastery, Canterbury[123]), that at this period an illuminator[124] was portray-ing the type of horned anvils found in Scandinavia which are driven into a heavy block of timber (pl. 13). The Scandinavian parallels date from the late Roman Iron Age onwards.[125] An example from Vimose,[126] which must date c. 400, indicates that in at least one area of the original homelands of the Anglo-Saxons this type of anvil was in use. Coghlan, however, quite rightly points out[127] that such small anvils may well be used only for 'fine' work: stone or iron-clad wooden anvils would almost certainly have been used for heavier work (a stone anvil was found in the smithy at Stöng, Iceland, in an eleventh-century context).[128]

Few of the smaller tools of the smith survive, perhaps because the smith re-used the metal: it is interesting, for example, that until the Viking Age there are no major smiths' graves in this country and certainly none to compare with that from Bygland, Norway.[129] However, hammers, cold chisels, tongs, pritchels and a file are known. No sledgehammers or heavy hand hammers have been found, but lighter examples from Thetford and from Soham, Cambs., may well be blacksmiths' tools: they are more or less paralleled on the Continent from Roman times onwards.[130] Swages, fullers and flatters are not recorded, but chisels are known. They would presumably be held with tongs when used as hot chisels.[131] I have not been able to identify the 'drift or chisel' mentioned in the preliminary report on the 1948/9 excavations at Thetford:[132] it is possibly a punch or pritchel (fig. 6.6b); a possible pritchel occurs at Westley Waterless, Cambs.,[133] and another at Paken-ham.[134]

Tongs are known from only two Anglo-Saxon finds, from Grave 115 at Sibertswold, Kent, and from Shakenoak (fig. 6.6a). A file was found at Thetford and is accurately paralleled at Mästermyr in Sweden,[135] and at Héroutvillette in Normandy.[136]

The vast proportion of Anglo-Saxon iron was used for normal day-to-day purposes – the making of nails, the shoeing of horses or the provision of tools. But there were, at the same time, certain specialist smiths at work. Weapon-smiths were presumably the aristocrats of blacksmiths and specialists within this trade are indicated by the use of the term 'sword polisher'.[137] The armourer's position must have been of some importance within heroic society, if only because a man's life could depend on such a craftsman's work. The chief weapons of the Anglo-Saxon period were the spear and shield. Apart from rather ornately decorated specimens of both classes of weapon, most of these could be simply made by a local smith.[138] But weapons like swords or armour of chain-mail, which are much rarer, may have been made by specialist armourers. Only two examples of chain-mail are recorded from Anglo-Saxon England,[139] although if we are to believe the Bayeux Tapestry illustrations it must have been of frequent occurrence at the time of the Norman Conquest. It is hardly worth pursuing the very simple process of manufac-

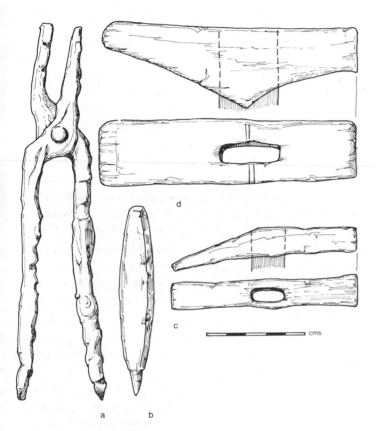

Figure 6.6   Smith's tools:
a tongs from Shakenoak
b pritchel from Thetford
c hammer from Soham, Cambs.
d hammer from Thetford

turing chain-mail, but the work of the sword-smith does require some attention.

Most two-edged Anglo-Saxon swords are pattern-welded. The process is met with in the pagan period and was almost universal by the ninth century; English swords appear in some numbers in Scandinavian graves and in river finds of this period. To a flat iron strip (the centre of the blade) are welded two steel edges, leaving a channel on either face of the sword. Two separate strips – one for each face – are then inlaid in this channel. The strips are made in the following fashion.[140] An iron rod is carburized, piled and drawn down, the process being repeated until there is a laminated rod of iron and steel (the layers of steel being formed by the fusion of the case-hardened surface of the original bars). The bars thus formed are then folded or twisted together and beaten to form the convex-faced central element (fuller) of each face of the weapon. The blade of the sword is then polished. The differing bands of iron and steel from the pattern-welded centre of the blade then appear as light and dark bands which could be emphasized by etching or rust.[141] Such a process – intentional, but not necessary – produced a more or less regular marbled effect on the surface of the weapon and would explain certain descriptive adjectives used in relation to swords in heroic literature, such as *atertanum fah* and *wyrmfah* in *Beowulf*,[142] words which are often, but inaccurately, translated damascened (i.e. etched).[143]

Iron can itself be embellished by various means and at least three techniques are recorded from the Anglo-Saxon period. The first is the tinning of iron by the method known as fusion-plating (equivalent to present-day tin-plate). The technique (which is also applied to bronze) is recorded from prehistoric times onwards but in the Anglo-Saxon period is only recorded on late spurs.[144] Jope has pointed out that this method was used chiefly on spurs in the post-Conquest period and tentatively suggests that there may already, therefore, have been specialist spur-makers in the Anglo-Saxon period. From a male grave, perhaps belonging to the pre-Conquest lay-cemetery at Durham (dated 995-1083), comes an iron spearhead with a faceted socket which has been gilded.[145]

The technique of applying silver, bronze or copper to the surface of iron is reasonably common throughout the Anglo-Saxon period. There are three basic methods: either wires are hammered on to a series of striations cut into the surface of the metal, or a sheet of metal can be hammered over a plate keyed to receive it, or, thirdly, plates can be inlaid into fields already cut in the surface of the iron (the plates being fixed by hammering the edges of the reserved field over the sheet).

This latter is the least commonly used method in ironwork, presumably because of the amount of accurate labour entailed in cutting out the fields, but it is clearly seen, for example, on the late ninth-century Sittingbourne scramasax.[146] The other two methods can be taken together. They occur from the earliest Anglo-Saxon period[147] to the Norman Conquest and beyond.[148] The incised lines can often be clearly seen through the plating; they are accurately cut and in the later Anglo-Saxon period are so regular that they may have been cut with the aid of a wheel in the manner described by the twelfth-century German monk Theophilus.[149] The method was used on the Continent[150] and was particularly popular in Viking Age Scandinavia on weapons, particularly on spearheads, of which occasional examples are found in England.[151]

Finally a word should be said about a practice documented on the Continent, but not so far investigated in England. On many tools and knives a hard steel edge has been welded to the iron body of the object.[152] This technique occurs on Anglo-Saxon swords, but other objects have not yet been investigated for such features.

Metals other than iron and the jeweller's craft

Little is known of the mining or extraction of precious and semi-precious metals. Some metals – particularly gold and silver – were almost certainly imported in the form of coins, plate or ingots, although theoretically they could have been mined in the British Isles.[153]

Other metals were almost certainly extracted from deposits in this country, copper from Shropshire, lead from Derbyshire[154] and tin from Cornwall, for example.[155] But actual evidence for these processes is lacking.

It is further unfortunate that there is a lack of analyses of metal artifacts – the analyses so far published being quite casual identifications of such metals as pewter[156] and copper.[157] Only occasionally has analytical work been done on Anglo-Saxon material, as for instance the work of a group of Oxford scholars on the problems of the changeover from gold to silver for coins and jewellery in the seventh century.[158]

It seems clear from the archaeological evidence that some metals were used more often at certain periods. Thus, while copper alloys were used throughout the Anglo-Saxon period, pewter seems to be more common in the eighth and ninth centuries. Gold was more frequently used for jewellery and for coinage in the late sixth and early seventh centuries, gradually giving way to silver towards the end of the eighth century. The embellishment of metals by means of tinning, gilding and niello seems to have been practised throughout the Anglo-Saxon period, although silver is less frequently gilded in the ninth and tenth centuries. Lead objects are comparatively rare in the pagan Anglo-Saxon period, but some fairly large lead vessels are known from the later period.[159] Lead was also used for glazing and roof flashings at Wearmouth and Jarrow (see pp. 233, 237) – two excavated seventh-century Northumbrian monasteries.[160] None of these factors, however, would have much effect on the method of manufacture, although they might be conditioned by the availability of the raw materials.

Traces of metalworking have been found at a number of sites, but only at Cheddar is there any published trace of a significant amount of bronze slag which could have been produced as the result of a refining process.[161] A bronze furnace has been recorded at York,[162] but the evidence is rather dubious. It is further possible that some smelting of copper was carried on at Thetford, although the dating is uncertain.[163]

Crucibles, presumably most of them used for melting bronze, have been found at a number of Anglo-Saxon settlement sites. Unremarkable objects, they are made of thick clay, have a round base and are rarely more than 8 cm high. Examples have been recorded among other sites at Jarrow (p. 241), Southampton,[164] Cheddar,[165] Sarre, Kent,[166] Sutton Courtenay,[167] Thetford,[168] Glastonbury[169] and Oxford.[170] 'Bronze drippings' and slag are often found associated with such crucibles, but half-fabricated objects are rarely found, although Addyman has recorded a fragment of a pin or decorative rivet-head in association with 'bronze drippings' at Southampton.[171] At Southampton there is an unfinished bronze strap-end of the ninth century,[172] but the only major English find which shows a series of objects (again strap-ends) in various stages of manufacture comes from a ninth-century hoard – presumably a jeweller's hoard – from Sevington, Wilts.[173] This provides an interesting series of artifacts ranging from the first roughly cut ingot to the fully finished strap-end. Although many bronze objects must have been made out of ingots and sheet metal, complicated objects were usually cast by the lost-wax process *(cire perdue)*. Moulds are rarely found, partly because they are extremely friable. New finds from Mucking, Kent, can however be understood in relation to finds from Dunadd[174] and the Mote of Mark[175] in Scotland and Helgö in Sweden; [176] new English finds will surely be forthcoming.[177] Half of a bi-valve mould for casting rings was recorded at Southampton,[178] but it is alleged (on grounds that are not altogether clear) that this object (of marl) could not have withstood the heat of bronze casting. Stone moulds are, however, known (mostly moulds for ingots[179] which may have been used by the Scandinavian invaders, for the objects produced would often be like the silver ingots found in the hoards of the Viking Age).[180] A lead ingot was, however, found at Southampton with other traces of lead-working.[181]

Graves of jewellers, while not exactly common, are familiar on the Continent,[182] but from pagan Anglo-Saxon contexts only a few metalworkers' graves are known. Grave 1 from Barton-on-Humber, Lincs., included a die for impressing a thin sheet of metal with Style II ornament.[183] This seventh-century grave also includes scales and weights which might also have been used by a jeweller. Other dies are known from England – from Salmonby, Lincs.,[184] two from Suffolk[185] and an example in the British Museum, said to be from Salisbury – all of seventh-century date.[186] That the *Pressblech* technique was known earlier is demonstrated by many objects, particularly the applied brooches,[187] while eighth-century *Pressblech* is also well documented.[188]

Metalworkers' tools are rarely found. Collet hammers have been found in Anglo-Saxon contexts at a mixed cemetery at Soham, Cambs.,[189] and in a late Anglo-Saxon hoard of tools at Westley Waterless, Cambs.[190] Despite the lack of jewellers' tools it is possible to reconstruct many of the techniques used in the production of metal objects. The casting of objects has already been considered, and examination of brooches, for example, under low-powered magnification shows that after casting the ornament of an object would often be finished with a sharp tool.[191] An unfinished (and unpublished) saucer-brooch from Cassington, Oxon., shows that lugs and catch plate for the pin were often brazed on. The surface might be marked with punch marks, or decorated in different ways by an inlay of another metal of contrasting colour, or niello; by enamelling (either champlevé or cloisonné); by the application of cloisons filled with stones, paste, bone or glass; by the use of filigree wire of various forms; by granulation; or by a combination of a number of such methods. Metal surfaces were also gilded and occasionally covered with a white metal coating.

Some of these techniques have received considerable attention. Niello, for example, has been examined by Moss,[192] who has demonstrated that pre-eleventh-century niello consists of a single sulphide – usually silver sulphide – inlaid as a powder and gently burnished under a low heat (less than 835°C). After the eleventh century niello consisted of mixed sulphides of silver and copper which could be applied in a molten form.

The white inlay in Kentish jewelled brooches has also been examined and shown to consist of a variety of materials.[193] Further examination of these seventh-century brooches in a European context by Arrhenius[194] has produced some interesting suggestions regarding their methods of manufacture. This investigation suggests that the garnets, which form the most common inlay in this jewellery, were first split and then cut and shaped (with a wheel or by flaking) into a limited group of forms – perhaps sometimes in a central lapidary.[195] By an analysis of the cement used in the make-up of this jewellery Arrhenius has managed to group some of the material together, but the English material needs further study.

Semi-precious stones other than garnet are not usually found in jewellery, but quartz and amethyst occur occasionally. Glass of various colours (including millefiori) also occurs in jewellery and the evidence seems to show that lapis lazuli does not occur, but that the material so often thus labelled is opaque glass.

Sheet-metal objects are of frequent occurrence, many of them bowls which must have been raised by hand. Evidence for the spinning of bowls, although technically possible, is contested,[196] but results of examination of the techniques of manufacture of such vessels have not been published.

Another specialist type of metalwork was bell-casting. St Dunstan is known to have made bells in his youth, but traces of bell-casting are rare. A datable pit is recorded at Winchester[197] and was presumably used for the casting of the bells of the Old Minster between 971 and 980.

Glass

Glass was used for two main purposes, as table-ware[198] and for glazing windows.[199] In other forms it was also used for making beads and (more rarely) in enamelling. Glass-making in England is documented by, for example, Bede,[200] but in only one place – at Glastonbury, Somerset – has evidence been found of actual structures associated with the manufacture of glass. Beneath the medieval cloister (p. 244) Radford found evidence of at least two, if not three, ovens, the uses of which were not clearly established; one may have been a firing furnace, another an annealing oven. Many fragments of pots with glass adhering to them, together with tiny pieces of window- and vessel-glass of various colours, were found, as well as a piece of mosaic cane from which inlay sections could be cut.[201] On the basis of typology it is, however, probable that glass vessels were manufactured in Kent in the seventh century; for, although much of the glass found in Anglo-Saxon contexts was undoubtedly imported from France and the Rhineland, such vessels as bag-beakers and squat-jars[202] are more commonly found here than on the Continent.

The 450 fragments of glass – mostly window-glass – found in excavations at the monasteries of Wearmouth and Jarrow further demonstrate that Benedict Biscop's importation of glaziers from Gaul (as recorded by Bede) did indeed take place. The glass[203] is a soda-lime glass and is cylinder blown. The coloured glass is usually between 2 and 3 mm thick and the plain glass is somewhat thinner. The colours so far found are pale blue, dark blue, blue-green, emerald green, olive green, amber, yellow-brown, red and blue or a blue-green streaked. Some of the glass is trailed. An interesting fragment from Jarrow may demonstrate the high technical competence of the craftsmen, for in reflected light it appears as an opaque greenish-blue and in transmitted light it appears as amber.[204] The window quarries are most commonly triangular, being cut from rectangles of as much as 82 by 52 mm. Many are grozed on two or even three sides. (Similar glass has been found at another Northumbrian site, Escomb.)[205] The quarries were mounted in lead cames of H-shaped section and lead cut-outs were sometimes superimposed on the glass. There is no evidence of the painting of window-glass at any of these sites.[206] There seems no reason to doubt that glass was manufactured in the area, indeed wasters and stringers have been found at Wearmouth.[207] There is unpublished window-glass from Hamwih, Thetford and Old Windsor, and possible evidence for its presence at Tamworth.

The soda-lime glass of Wearmouth and Jarrow continued in use in north-west Europe from the Roman period until the ninth or tenth century, when potash glass was introduced.[208] The lack of any great quantity of late Anglo-Saxon glass makes it impossible to project this technological change into the English area, but it is becoming increasingly obvious that Anglo-Saxon glass-makers kept abreast of their continental contemporaries.

Despite the enormous number of glass beads discovered in Anglo-Saxon graves, little is known about the bead-making industry. A few beads were found at Wearmouth, where there is a strong probability of glass manufacture, but the only place where it has been suggested that there was such an industry is York,[209] where glass slag, glass 'drops' and unperforated or imperfectly finished beads were found on the Clifford Street site.[210]. It is interesting in this context that they were associated with an amber bead industry and it would seem likely that bead-making was completely separate from the glass industry.

Closely related to the bead industry was the manufacture of studs and enamels for use in jewellery.

The textile industry

The importance of the woollen industry in the English economy of the post-Conquest period has been dealt with in considerable detail by historians and the assumption is made that the industry was also important in the pre-Conquest period. Perhaps too much has been made of such casual references as occur, for example, in the correspondence of Offa and Charlemagne; but the evidence for the industry, while slim, stands up to critical examination.[211] The most important recent potential in this field is provided by place-names, where the pattern of settlement on the Lincolnshire wolds may well reflect a development of sheep-farming at the time of the Scandinavian occupation.[212] Such a study is, however, still incomplete.

Although articles of clothing are never recovered in their entirety, many fragments of woollen cloth have been recorded in Anglo-Saxon contexts.[213] Minute fragments found in graves add to our knowledge of cloth – not only is wool known but also linen and silk; the latter, however, was imported, either as thread[214] or cloth.

The processes of preparation of cloth are adequately described elsewhere.[215] Here we need only consider the actual traces of these processes in the archaeological record of the Anglo-Saxon period. Although wool is the commonest material found in this country, linen is also documented, the implements used in the production of linen being similar to those used in the production of wool cloth, save only that a flax hammer[216] is used at an early stage of the process to separate the fibres of the plant from the woody core[217] and a heckle is used instead of a wool-comb.

No special tools are used to obtain the wool – save perhaps shears (which are common) – but the wool has to be carded; fragments of wool-combs (and heckles for carding linen) for this purpose are known from Sutton Courtenay, Berks.,[218] Shakenoak[219] and Harrold, Beds.[220] These are, however, fragmentary; but adequate parallels are provided in Norway and the Scandinavian areas of Britain.[221] Once cleaned and carded, the wool was spun – the spindle whorl is a ubiquitous element in Anglo-Saxon contexts (made of pottery, bone, lead, chalk, stone and even glass). The spindle itself is, however, rarely (if ever) found; the best-known example, from Sutton Courtenay, Berks., may in fact be made up of two separate objects.[222] The distaff being of wood has not survived, and we are unfortunate in that we have neither swift nor reel to parallel those found in the ninth-century Oseberg grave in Norway.[223]

The most important piece of domestic equipment in the Anglo-Saxon house may well have been the loom. Indeed the presence of looms in many *Grubenhaüser* has, in my opinion inaccurately, led to the description of these structures as weaving huts; but as the loom would be a normal piece of equipment in practically every household, there seems no reason to fall in with this suggestion.[224] Looms are represented in Anglo-Saxon contexts by the loom-weights; they are common in the later Anglo-Saxon period and are unknown after the Conquest. Two types of loom-weight from warp-weighted looms have been identified by Hurst,[225] and seem to have some chronological significance. Until the seventh century loom-weights seem to have had an annular form, but later they are 'bun-shaped'. Unfired loom-weights[226] are also recorded, as are lead examples.[227] Both in this country and abroad[228] sites have produced rows of loom-weights – burnt *in situ*. But, from the example found at Pakenham, Suffolk (pl. 15),[229] it is impossible to say whether the rows, which are more than 2 m long, actually represent a collapsed loom; at this length it is unlikely. The suggestion that there were two looms in one house at Upton, Northants.,[230] is not really borne out by the plan of the site.[231] The loom-weights at the east end seem to have been stacked neatly, while those at the west end seem to have been on a loom. The suggested post-holes for the frame of a loom in the floor of a house at Bourton-on-the-Water, Glos.,[232] cannot certainly be thus identified. The lack of loom-weights towards the end of the Anglo-Saxon period suggests, however, that a beam-tensioned loom may have been used.[233] Towards the end of the Anglo-Saxon period there is some evidence from the Continent that the horizontal loom was beginning to be introduced. Perhaps this new machine was also being used at this time in England, which would explain the lack of loom-weights.[234]

The equipment of the loom is represented by only two tools, the weaving baton and the pin-beater – the latter is a small polished piece of bone about 12 cm long with a central swelling and pointed ends.[235] This implement is used for beating down individual threads in the weft of the cloth. Weaving batons (sometimes described as 'weaving swords') occasionally turn up in Anglo-Saxon graves. Those found are of iron with traces of a wooden grip and have an extension at the tip in the form of a tang-like protuberance.[236] Bone examples are found in Scandinavia, and one possible bone example (with an inscription) is known from an Anglo-Saxon context at Wallingford.[237] Mrs Hawkes has pointed out that iron weaving batons are comparatively rare both in England and on the Continent and suggests that they may have been 'a symbol of the rank and social status of their owner'.[238] She further follows a suggestion of Miss Crowfoot that the majority of such objects would have been made of wood. Heddle-bars have not been identified.[239]

The cloth, having been cut from the loom, would then be fulled, but fulling pits and mills have not been identified, although Miss Evison has suggested that a wooden bucket from Harrold, Beds., might have been used for this purpose.[240] Fulling was not, however, universal, as is demonstrated by the textiles from the Birka graves (some of which may have been imported from western Europe).[241]

Dyeing took place either in the skein or in the cloth, and although there are frequent mentions of imported dyed cloth in the literature only rarely are traces of colour seen on surviving pieces of cloth.[242] The gold braids at Taplow were woven on a woollen base which is now dark brown,[243] but too often it is difficult to tell whether the cloth is dyed or merely stained by the earth or by contact with material in the grave.[244] Some are certainly not dyed.[245] Linen[246] is well attested in Anglo-Saxon literature from the seventh century onwards, flax seed[247] occurs at an earlier period and linen itself is found in Anglo-Saxon contexts.[248] Linen would have to be smoothed, and two glass linen-smoothers are recorded from Thetford,[249] while Addyman has suggested that objects of polished stone from Southampton may have been used for a similar purpose.[250]

Among the cloth recognized from this period are a fairly large number of braids, usually used as borders for garments but occasionally as hair bands. Some of these latter have gold threads woven into them and have been identified as *vittae*[251] (brocaded bands worn by aristocratic ladies round the head) or as girdles. All these bands[252] have been tablet woven,[253] but to my knowledge only a single tablet has been recorded in an Anglo-Saxon context, from Kingston Down, Kent, Grave 299; it is of bone, and is square and with a hole in each corner.[254] Finds from contemporary sources elsewhere in Europe and the British Isles are more informative.[255]

Although in most cases our knowledge of the cloth – both linen and woollen – woven by the Anglo-Saxon depends on a few scraps adhering to metal in graves or even to impressions of cloth on corroded metal, we have a fairly good general idea of the capabilities of the weaver of the Anglo-Saxon period, but as with so many craft and industrial processes we cannot generalize in chronological terms. Tabby (or plain) weave is universal, and many varieties of twill[256] are also recorded, particularly broken diamond twill. Anglo-Saxon braids, both tablet-woven and woven on a braid-loom, show a great variety of patterns.[257]

Plates

a Bronze buckle and belt mount (part of a set)
[fr]om Mucking, Essex; b Silver parcel-gilt quoit-
[b]rooch from Sarre, Kent; c Silver-gilt square-
[h]eaded brooch from Chessel Down, Isle of Wight;
[d] Silver-gilt sword-pommel from Crundale Down,
[K]ent. All scale 1:1.

c

11 Vine-scroll ornament on a cross-shaft from Easby, Cumberland.

III a Gable end of ivory casket from
Gandersheim, Germany; b Fragment of
sculpture from Levisham, Yorkshire.

a

b

a

b

IV a Scramasax with inlaid runic alphabet from the
River Thames; b The prophet Daniel from the stole of
St Cuthbert.

v   Sword-hilt from a grave at Coombe, Kent.

VI Sword-hilt from the River Witham, near Lincoln.

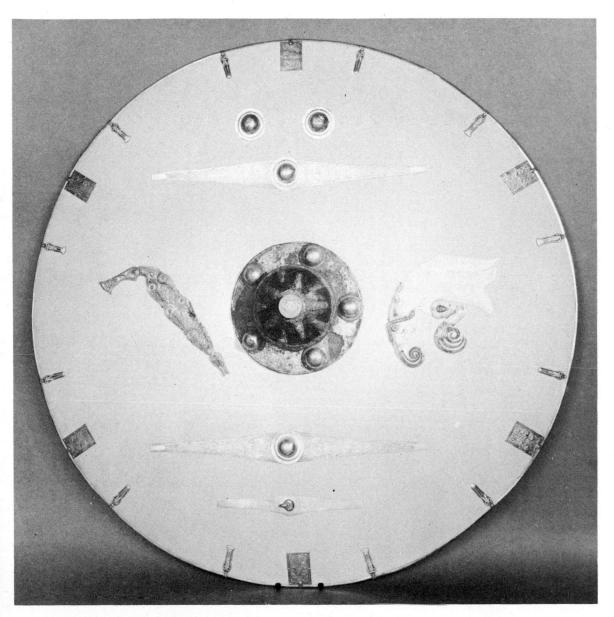

VII   Shield from the Sutton Hoo ship-burial.

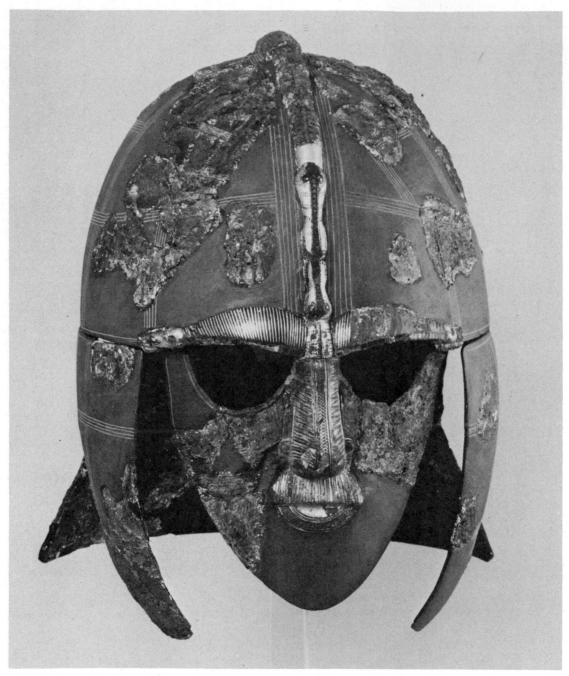

VIII Helmet from the Sutton Hoo ship-burial.

IX   Aerial view of the excavations at Chalton, Hampshire.

x–xi Below, reconstruction of the episcopal complex at North Elmham, Norfolk. Right, reconstruction of the tenth-century royal manor at Cheddar, Somerset.

a

XII a The mill at Tamworth under excavation; b Detail of the Bayeux tapestry, showing houses.

XIII Detail from the Caedmon manuscript (Bodleian Library, Oxford MS Junius II), showing an eleventh-century smithy.

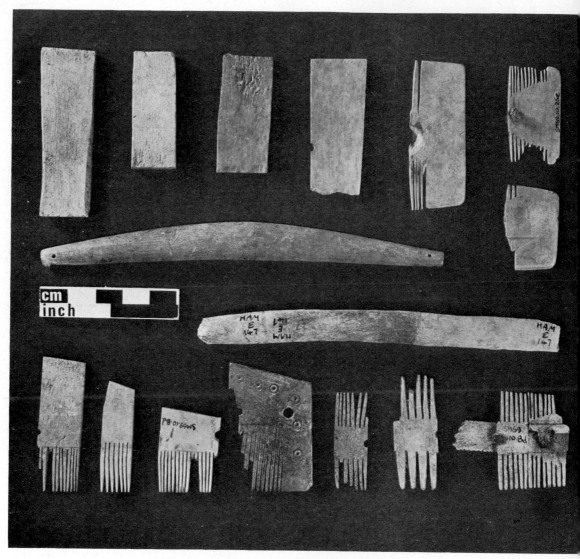

XIV Bone comb-making. The fragments above would be used in making single-sided combs. From Southampton.

xv Two rows of loom-weights found *in situ* during excavations at Grimstone End, Pakenham, Suffolk.

XVI   Hog-backed tombstones from Brompton, Yorkshire.

a West end of church at Bradwell, Essex; b Tower of
ch at Deerhurst, Gloucestershire.

b

a

XVIII   a Church at Barton-on-Humber, Lincolnshire; b Apse of church at Wing, Buckinghamshire.

b

XIX a Interior of Great Paxton church,
Hampshire; b Tower arch of St Benet's church,
Cambridge.

b

a

xx a Great arch at Stow church, Lincolnshire; b
Detail of north corner of south transept at Hadstock
church, Essex.

b

XXI a Blind arcading at Bradford-on-Avon,
Wiltshire; b Capital of tower arch, Barnack,
Northamptonshire; c Capital from Deerhurst,
Gloucestershire; d Great arch of Wittering
church, Northamptonshire.

b

d

c

A kind of shaggy cloth, known in Old Icelandic as *rǫgg*,[258] is also recorded in a seventh-century English context at Sutton Hoo.[259]

English medieval embroidery was justly famous[260] and we are fortunate in having a few groups of embroidery which are of Anglo-Saxon manufacture. A *casula* of St Harlinde and St Relinde at Maeseyck in Belgium is made up of a number of textiles of which some are Anglo-Saxon embroideries executed in southern England in the late eighth or early ninth century.[261] The ornament is made up of a series of roundels containing birds and animals, and two strips of arcading enclosing and incorporating interlace and inhabited scroll-work. Some more or less contemporary embroideries have been identified as English by Hougen in the great Viking Age ship-burial at Oseberg in Norway, but the detailed arguments concerning this have not yet been published.

The best-known group of English embroidery is provided by the stole (pl. 4b) and maniple made (presumably at Winchester) between 909 and 916 under the patronage of Bishop Frithestan and Queen Æflæd and later placed in the coffin reliquary of St Cuthbert.[262] These embroideries were carried out in silk embroidery thread, a red couching thread and a gold thread with a silk core on a silk base with stem stitch and split stitch. Many different colours were used but much has now faded. A fragment of embroidery from St Ambrogia in Milan is executed in the same technique and may have been made in England.[263]

The inventory of a weaver at the end of the eleventh century is described in *Gerefa*,[264] and a knowledge of archaeological material enables us to understand the terms used.[265]

flexlinan	linen	*timplean*	carding tool or heckle
spinle	spindle	*wifte*	warp thread
reol	reel	*wefle*	weft thread
gearnwindan	yarn-winder	*wulcamb*	wool-comb
stodlan	weaving baton or pin-beater	*ciþ*	? a reed or weaving baton
		amb	weaving baton
lorgas	beam of loom (glossed *colus, webbeam, liciatorium*)	*cranesteaf*	swift or reel
		sceaðele	shuttle
presse	clothes-press (glossed *pannicipium* and *vestiplicium*)	*seamsticcan*	? a pin used in sewing a seam
		scearra	shears
pihten	weaver's comb (glossed *pecten*)	*nædle*	needle
		slic	a (flax) hammer

The making up of cloth is ill documented. Needles and thread are frequently found together in late Anglo-Saxon contexts in cylindrical work-boxes of bronze, which usually date from the late pagan period – the sixth/seventh centuries[266] (at a slightly earlier stage small needle-cases are found without the thread);[267] these boxes are usually hung from a woman's chatelaine.[268] Needles of iron,[269] bone[270] and bronze[271] are known from the pagan period, but (due to the lack of grave-goods) needles of the later Anglo-Saxon period are rarely found.[272] Shears for cutting cloth are ubiquitous in Anglo-Saxon graves[273] and are also found in later contexts;[274] but scissors have not been recorded,[275] although found in a tenth-century Viking Age context in Sweden,[276] which indicates their presence in northern Europe at this time.

Nap shears, known in both Roman[277] and post-Conquest contexts,[278] are not known.

Leather

The dressing and use of leather must have been of some importance in the Anglo-Saxon period. Leather was used for a variety of purposes; it chiefly survives in the form of shoes (fig. 6.7) and scabbards,[279] but its use for other purposes is occasionally recorded, on bookbindings,[280] on a shield from Sutton Hoo,[281] as a cup at Benty Grange, Derbyshire,[282] or as a belt at Bekesbourne, Kent.[283] But the vast number of buckles found in Anglo-Saxon contexts cannot all have been attached to braids and we must presume that leather was an important medium for belts and also for clothes,[284] armour, riding equipment and household utensils.

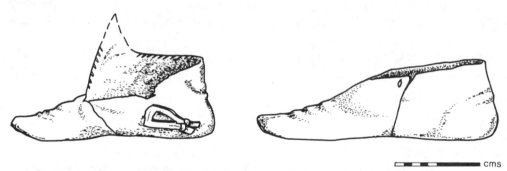

Figure 6.7   Shoes from Anglo-Danish levels at York

At York, however, traces of a considerable leather industry have been recovered;[285] manufactured objects include shoes, laces, belts, garments, bags, sheaths and gloves. More important were the tan pits of Danish date discovered under High Ousegate in 1902. The timber-framed building stood with its gable on High Ousegate and was supported on piles. It measured approximately 28 by 5 m, with a metre-wide aisle or gallery on either side. A number of transverse beams survived which were rebated to take upright boards which stood in some places up to a metre in height. The divisions passed over the pits and Radley suggests that they may have been part of a system of racks for hanging skins. The pits, which are big enough to take whole hides without folding, are symmetrical with the sill-beams. Another building of similar construction was discovered to the east of the tan pits. The leather, all bovine, was tanned with oak bark, but the splitting of the skins was not altogether skilful. Carboniferous limestone found on adjacent sites may represent the lime used in the slaking process.

A specialized aspect of the leather industry was the manufacture of vellum, usually from calf-skins. Other than surviving manuscripts[286] we have no archaeological trace of this material, although it has been suggested (not very convincingly) that a tool found at Whitby Abbey was used to produce the suède-like surface so characteristic of insular vellum.[287] The marks of such a tool have been noted in the Linisfarne Gospels.[288]

The dyeing of leather is shown in bookbindings,[289] the three or four[290] surviving English examples having a cherry red or crimson colour. Another dye is recognized on vellum – purple, a colour which occurs in the Codex Amiatinus and in the late eighth and early ninth centuries on manuscripts of the Canterbury school.[291]

It would be interesting to know whether the leather industry was largely confined to the towns, as it was in the later middle ages. Finds from eleventh- and twelfth-century contexts in Dublin[292] suggest that only a short time after the Anglo-Saxon period there was a specialized industry here. Certainly in the later middle ages English towns had their leather-curing and leather-working quarters – as witness Tanner Lane in York.

Weaving and spinning other than cloth

Before turning from the cloth industry a short note on applied techniques of weaving and spinning is necessary.

The use of baskets in Anglo-Saxon England is hardly attested, although wattle walls and hurdles are evidenced in innumerable ways.[293] Baskets certainly existed, although I know of but one rather doubtful occurrence in an Anglo-Saxon grave – at Hurdlow, Derbyshire[294] – where Bateman claimed that hazel sticks found in a seventh-century grave were the remains of a basket. The use of basketry as shuttering in plastering a circular church window of the eleventh century is demonstrated at Hales, Norfolk,[295] but whether this is the original plaster-work is impossible to say.

Twine, string and rope are a type of spinning rarely encountered in Anglo-Saxon contexts. Fortunately we have finds of both string[296] and rope[297] in the archaeological record, but how far either of these was the product of a craft or of a domestic industry we cannot tell.

Although the Anglo-Saxons had nets no fragment of a net or netting-tool has been recognized.[298]

Milling

It is frequently said that mills increased in number towards the end of the Anglo-Saxon period,[299] but the evidence for this rests on an argument *ex silentio*, based on the large number of mills recorded in Domesday Book as compared with the lack of earlier references. There is no doubt that mills were common in England at the time of the Conquest: of the 9,250 manors recorded, 3,463 had 5,624 mills.[300] There is, however, no reason to suppose that the mill was necessarily a late introduction into England.

Hand-grinding by means of rotary querns was certainly carried on in the pagan Anglo-Saxon period, as evidenced both in graves[301] and on settlement sites,[302] and this practice probably persisted throughout the period.

Mills have survived at two sites. They are both watermills (there is no evidence for windmills before the twelfth century). The earliest of these was found in 1971 at Tamworth (pl. 12a) and is a two-period structure, the remains of a slighter mill underlying more substantial remains which have been dated by the carbon-14 method to the eighth century (four determinations A.D. 755 ± 90, 730 ± 100, 788 ± 100, 710 ± 110).[303] This latter structure consists of two rectangular 'boxes' at different levels, separated from each other by a gap. They are walled with horizontal oak timbers. The upper structure, which was packed round by tons of yellow clay, apparently acted as a mill-pool (fed by a leat from the river), from which water was led by means of an outfall trough (of which one slot survives) to a lower structure with a plank floor, which has been interpreted as the under-croft of a mill (for reconstruction, see fig. 2.19). It seems likely that the mill was powered by a horizontal overshot wheel of the type known from the Atlantic Isles;[304] the power from this wheel would be transmitted by an upright shaft to a rotary quern on an upper floor and an overflow channel could control the supply of water to the wheel. Fragments of some twenty millstones were found, mostly of the local millstone grit but some of Mayen-Niedermendig lava.[305] The stones were between 60 and 70 cm in diameter and the upper stones bear slots for the power drive. The lower stones were apparently bedded in clay which had been baked when the mill burnt down.

This mill is paralleled at only one place in Anglo-Saxon England,[306] at Old Windsor, Berks., but the earliest of the series of the mills at this royal manor (as yet unpublished) was apparently much more elaborate.[307] This ninth-century mill had three vertical wheels[308] working in parallel and powered by water in a great leat dug across a loop in the Thames. The leat was some 1,100 m in length, over 6 m wide and nearly 4 m deep at its maximum. The site appears to have been devastated in the Viking period and a mill of the type discovered at Tamworth with a horizontal wheel was constructed, fed by a narrower leat than that used originally. This small leat was re-dug several times before being abandoned in the early eleventh century.

There is no indication from archaeological sources of a specialist millwright, but the large number of mills in Anglo-Saxon England might suggest their presence.

Notes

1 Battiscombe (1956) 202–307.
2 Bruce-Mitford (1972) fig. 11.
3 Richardson (1959) fig. 19.
4 *Antiquity* xlv, 89–96.
5 E.g. Radley (1971) fig. 11, no. 14; Richardson (1959) fig. 20.
6 A convenient simple drawing of a pole lathe may be seen in Hodges (1964) fig. 24.
7 Richardson (1959) 86.
8 Dunning (1958) figs 4 and 5.
9 E.g. Baldwin Brown (1903–37) iv, pl. cxii.
10 Radley (1971) 52.
11 E.g. Kendrick (1949) pl. xix, 1; Stenton (1957) pl. 41.
12 Brøgger and Shetelig (1928) 3ff. and Roesdahl and Nordqvist (1971) figs 7–12.

13 See p. 275.
14 Arrow shafts are recorded at Chessel Down, Hillier (n.d.) 37.
15. E.g. the great hall at Yeavering, cf. p. 65.
16 Taylor and Taylor (1965) 262–4.
17 *Current Archaeology* (1972) 192.
18 Addyman (1965) fig. 10.
19 See p. 93.
20 Cf e.g. Holywell Row, Grave 11, Lethbridge (1931) 4.
21 Alveston, see Wilson and Moorhouse (1971) 134.
22 Cramp (1957) 72.
23 Biddle and Quirk (1962) 192–3.
24 Schmidt (1970).
25 Nelson (1937).
26 E.g. the Copenhagen shrine, Shetelig (1940) v, fig. 89.
27 See below, p. 257.
28 The cutting and boring of boards used in bookbinding, cf. Wilson (1961) fig. 4.
29 Wilson (1968). Full bibliographical references for each tool are cited there.
30 Brasch (1910).
31 *Victoria History of the County of Durham*, i, 214. Dated on the basis of a Type L sword found with it.
32 *Report of the Cambridgeshire Antiquarian Society*, 1879, xv. Dated by means of an ornamented lead cistern.
33 Sheppard (1939).
34 E.g. at Thetford; Knocker and Hughes (1950).
35 Wheeler (1927) 18ff.
36 Concerning this fluid, see p. 403.
37 Arbman (1961) pls 2–5.
38 Wheeler (1927) 23–5.
39 An example was found, for example, at Howletts. It should be pointed out, however, that the 'bearded' axe (Wheeler's Type III) is not unlike a modern turner's hammer, cf. Arnold (1968) 132.
40 For the latter cf. the Bayeux Tapestry, Stenton (1957) pl. 38; and the Caedmon Manuscript, Gollancz (1927) 54, 63, 82 and 87.
41 Wilson and Klindt-Jensen (1966) pl. lii.
42 Keller (1906) 61.
43 Wilson (1968) fig. 1e.
44 Griffith and Salzmann (1914) pl. xix, 1.
45 Baldwin Brown (1903–37) iii, 232–3.
46 Bruce-Mitford (1972) fig. 14.
47 But compare the Smith's hammer from Vendel, Sweden, Grave 1; Ohlhaver (1939) fig. 54.
48 Parallels cited Wilson (1968) 143.

48a For this practice in later medieval times, cf. Van de Walle (1969) pl. xxiii *b*.
49 Petersen (1951) fig. 120 and Arbman (1961) pl. 2.
50 Arbman (1961) pl. 3.
51 E.g. Champion (1916) pl. iv, 29050; Curle (1911) pl. lxviii; Goodman (1964) 122.
52 See p. 000.
53 Cf. Greber (1956) 92 and fig. 37 and Goodman (1964) figs 44, 45, 48 and 51.
54 Roes (1963) pl. xi.
55 Engelhardt (1869) fig. 31 and pls 18 and 27.
56 Cambridge University Museum of Archaeology and Ethnology, unpublished.
57 Addyman and Hill (1969) fig. 24, 12.
58 Gouges with a socket recorded from the Vimose find in Fyn, Denmark, Engelhardt (1869) pl. 15, 18 and 21. This find dates from *c*. A.D. 400.
59 Listed Wilson (1968) 146; another possible example was recorded from Garton Slack (in a pagan grave), Mortimer (1905) fig. 646.
60 Norwich, Castle Museum, unpublished.
61 But bow-drills were almost certainly used in bead-making. Cf. also Stenton (1957) pl. vii.
62 Petersen (1951) fig. 124. A possible Anglo-Saxon example is recorded at Shakenoak, Brodribb *et al.* (1972) fig. 194. An example from an early medieval central European context is illustrated by Pleiner (1962) fig. 34.
63 Kolchin (1953) fig. 95.
64 Roes (1963).
65 Evidence of ivory-working is seen at York, Radley (1971) 52.
66 British Museum, *Guide to Anglo-Saxon and Foreign Teutonic Antiquities*, London (1923) pl. viii.
67 Knocker and Hughes (1950) 44.
68 Radley (1971) 51–2.
69 Addyman and Hill (1969) 75–7.
70 O'Riordáin (1971) 73.
71 Arbman (1939) 125ff.
72 Blomqvist and Mårtensson (1963) 171ff.
73 Material in Sigtuna Museum.
74 Müller-Using (1953).
75 Bergqvist and Lepiskaar (1957) 26.
76 *VCH, Essex*, i, 322.
77 Bruce-Mitford (1972) 33f.
78 Colgrave (1927) 47.
79 Plummer (1896) 368.
80 Translated in Whitelock (1955) 699.
81 See p. 153–6.
82 Jope (1956).

83 E.g. at Escomb, Durham: Taylor and Taylor (1965) i, 236.
84 Wilson and Hurst (1960) 137.
85 E.g. Wilson and Klindt-Jensen (1966) frontis-piece; Jansson (1962) 149–52.
86 Collingwood (1915) 289.
87 Collingwood (1907) 269.
88 Collingwood (1915) 289.
89 Okasha (1971) 99.
90 Wilson and Klindt-Jensen (1966) 135–6. Cf. Wilson in *Skalk*, 1975.
91 Peers (1927) 251–3.
92 Talbot-Rice (1952) 107.
93 Cramp (1969) 34, 36, 49.
94 Biddle (1967) pl. xxiii.
95 Cf. Kendrick *et al.* (1960) 263ff. and Roosen Runge (1967).
96 Tylecote (1962) 175.
97 These are listed ibid., 178.
98 E.g. Charter of Oswin (C.S., 73), '*unum aratrum in quo mina ferri haberi cognoscitur, quod pertine-bat ad cortem quae appellatur Liminge*', discussed by Schubert (1957) 71.
99 The best account of the process is that of Hodges (1964) 82–3.
100 Schubert (1957) 72f. and 80 discusses certain dues of iron in the late Anglo-Saxon period, and Tylecote (1962) 271 lists bloomsmithies mentioned in Domesday; Loyn (1962) 101f. mentions several other documentary sources.
101 Addyman (1969) 62f.
102 Brodribb *et al.* (1972) 117.
103 Radley (1971) 48.
104 Schubert (1957) 75.
105 Tylecote (1967).
106 Wilson and Hurst (1964) 236, 294.
107 Tylecote (1962) 265.
107a Tylecote (1973) fig. 5.
108 This latter has been only recently excavated: a short report appears in Wilson and Moorhouse (1971) 132.
109 Tylecote (1967) 193.
110 Wilson and Hurst (1964) 294.
111 Tylecote (1967).
112 It is not without interest that we have here one of the few recorded analyses of the wood from which charcoal was made in the Anglo-Saxon period: 78.3 per cent was oak, which as Tyle-cote states has always been the preferred wood for smelting in this country: ibid., 195, 213.
113 Schubert (1957) 52.
114 Denmark, cf. Thomsen (1963) and (1964).
115 As in British non-Anglo-Saxon areas, sum-marized by Tylecote (1962) 260–65.
116 Addyman (1969) 65.
117 Tylecote (1962) 262 and (1967) 193, 213.
118 British Museum, *Guide to Anglo-Saxon and Foreign Teutonic Antiquities*, London (1928) pl. viii.
119 Loyn (1962) 103f.
120 Even monasteries had their smiths. Bede records a drunken monk who was tolerated because of his craftsmanship as a smith (*HE*, v, 14), and Æthewulf tells of a monk, Cwicwine, a smith who lived a saintly life: Campbell (1967) 25.
121 Pleiner (1962) fig. 28 illustrates smithies from Germany and Russia. That from Belaja Veza in Russia is a *Grubenhaus* with a hearth and mouth of the bellows and the wooden base for the anvil. Another smithy is illustrated by Stenberger (1943) 92ff. from Stöng, Iceland. A possible 'smithy' was found during the excavations at Whitby Abbey, Yorkshire (Peers and Radford (1943) 31 and pl. xix), but this building, as was recognized by the authors, cannot definitely be identified as such (see p. 228).
122 Cf. the short notices for Witton, Norfolk, *Medieval Archaeology*, ix, 173; Bristol, ibid., xiv, 156; Botesdale, Suffolk, ibid., x, 174.
123 Wormald (1952) 67.
124 Schubert (1957) pl. vii.
125 Petersen (1951) 91–4.
126 Engelhardt (1869) pl. 18, 1.
127 Coghlan (1956) 122.
128 Stenberger (1943) fig. 51.
129 Blindheim (1962). It is, however, interesting to see that there is an almost equally rich grave in a non-Scandinavian context. At Héroutvil-lette (Calvados), Normandy, one of the few new gravefields of the Merovingian period to be published, Grave 10 produced a wide variety of smiths' and jewellers' tools together with one or two carpenters' tools: Decaens (1971) 12–17 and figs 18–21.
130 Ohlhaver (1939) figs 14–21.
131 Chisels with shaft holes, like modern cold setts, are, however, known in an early medieval con-text in eastern Europe: Pleiner (1962) fig. 26.6.
132 Knocker and Hughes (1950) 45.
133 University Museum of Archaeology and Ethno-logy, Cambridge, unpublished.
134 Brown *et al.* (1957) fig. 28f.
135 Arbman (1961) pl. 3.
136 Decaens (1971) fig. 21.

137 Laws of Alfred, 19–23.
138 For general account of Anglo-Saxon weapons, see Wilson (1971) 108–26.
139 From Sutton Hoo, Bruce-Mitford (1972), and Benty Grange, Derbyshire, Bateman (1861) 30. Both are of seventh-century date.
140 The method described by Anstee and Biek (1961) has to be modified in view of recent research by Thålin and Modin, as yet unpublished.
141 Much of this description is based on that of Hodges (1964) 87f.
142 Cf. Davidson (1962) 129ff.
143 Some good photographs and figures of pattern-welded blades occur in Salin (1957) pls. VI, VII and fig. 23, although his technical description must be reconsidered in the light of Anstee and Biek (1961) and the as yet unpublished work of Thålin and Modin.
144 Jope (1956).
145 Kendrick (1938) 242 and pl. 1v, 26.
146 Wilson (1964) pl. xxx, 80.
147 Evison (1955).
148 E.g. Wilson (1964) pl. xxl, 35.
149 Dodwell (1961) 160ff.
150 Cf. Holmqvist (1951).
151 E.g. Shetelig (1940) iv, fig. 49.
152 Cf. e.g. Pleiner (1962) fig. 22; Salin (1957) pl. iv; Arrhenius (1974).
153 E.g. gold from Dolaucothi, Carmarthenshire, where there were early mines: cf. Lewis and Jones (1969).
154 Domesday evidence summarized by Tylecote (1962) 93.
155 The Trewhiddle hoard (dated 872/5) was found in an abandoned tin-stream in Cornwall (Wilson and Blunt (1961) 75), but whether this was an Anglo-Saxon working site is not clear.
156 E.g. Wilson (1964) 155.
157 E.g. ibid., 153.
158 Hawkes et al. (1966).
159 E.g. at Westley Waterless, Cambs., Fox (1948).
160 Cramp (1969) 50; Cramp (1970) pl. livf; see below, p. 229f.
161 Rahtz (1962–3) 66.
162 Benson (1903) 64.
163 Knocker (1967) 123.
164 Addyman and Hill (1969) fig. 25.
165 Rahtz (1962–3) 66.
166 Maidstone Museum.
167 Leeds (1923) pl. xxviii.
168 Knocker (1967) fig. 12 and Knocker and Hughes (1950) 45.
169 Wilson and Hurst (1966) 174.
170 Jope (1952–3) fig. 37.
171 Addyman and Hill (1969) 68.
172 Ibid., 70.
173 Wilson (1964) pl. xxx, 72–8.
174 Craw (1929–30) fig. 7.
175 Curle (1913–14) figs 11–16.
176 Holmqvist (1972) passim.
177 A mould for a dagger pommel has recently been found at Hereford but I have not seen it.
178 Addyman and Hill (1969) fig. 25, 5.
179 From Whitby Abbey, Foote and Wilson (1970) pl. ib; Oxford, Jope (1958) fig. 22; Thetford, Knocker and Hughes (1950) 45.
180 E.g. Shetelig (1954) figs 85 and 86.
181 Addyman and Hill (1969) 71.
182 E.g. Salin (1957) figs 88 and 89; Werner (1970); Decaens (1971) fig. 18; Dreihaus (1972) 389–404.
183 Capelle and Vierck (1971) fig. 12, 1.
184 Ibid., fig. 9, 1.
185 Ibid., figs 10, 1, and 14, 1.
186 Ibid., fig. 8, 6.
187 Leeds (1912) pl. xxvii.
188 Listed by Wilson (1961) 211f.
189 Cambridge University Museum of Archaeology and Ethnology.
190 Ibid.
191 For a discussion of the functions of such tools in archaeological contexts, cf. Lowery et al. (1971).
192 Moss (1953).
193 Evison (1951).
194 Arrhenius (1971).
195 Cf. ibid., fig. 100.
196 Cf. Tylecote (1962) 151–2.
197 Biddle (1965) 255.
198 Harden (1956) is the standard work on this subject; cf. also Harden (1971) 87–93.
199 Harden (1961) 52ff. and Cramp (1970).
200 Historia Abbatum, v; cf. also Whitelock (1955) 766 (letter of Cuthbert of Wearmouth to Lul).
201 This site has not yet been published and this information is taken from Harden (1971) 87, where a picture of fragments of pots with glass adhering to them is published (pl. vii c). I must acknowledge my gratitude to Dr Harden for allowing me to read the proofs of this article before its publication.
202 Harden (1956) fig. 25.
203 Cramp (1970).
204 Cf. the Lycurgus cup in the British Museum: Harden and Toynbee (1959).

205 Pocock and Wheeler (1971) 26–8.
206 Painted window-glass from Europe is quoted by Cramp (1970) 329.
207 Cramp (1971) 329.
208 References to the technology of north-western European glass will be found in Harden (1971).
209 Waterman (1959) 95.
210 Further evidence of bead-making is provided by Radley (1971).
211 Loyn (1962) 85–6 discusses the trade in a sober and convincing fashion.
212 Cf. Cameron (1965) map 7.
213 An unpublished MA thesis of Birmingham University summarizes the evidence for Anglo-Saxon costume, Cook (1974).
214 Silk thread was used by English embroiderers; cf. e.g. Battiscombe (1956) 377.
215 Cf. e.g. Hodges (1964) 123–47.
216 As at Oseberg, Norway; Brøgger and Shetelig (1928) figs 111–12.
217 Flax-retting trenches have been found in late Anglo-Saxon levels at Oxford; *Current Archaeology*, iii (1972) 320.
218 Leeds (1923) 182. I am doubtful about this identification.
219 Brodribb *et al.* (1972) fig. 51.
220 Eagles and Evison (1970) 42 (thirty-nine teeth were found here).
221 E.g. Petersen (1951) 219ff.
222 Leeds (1947) pl. xxii *a* (d), but see 85. Similar claims have been made for two objects – both bone brooches – from Wingham, Kent, and Little Wilbraham, Cambs. See Akerman (1855) pl. 36 and Neville (1852) pl. 23.
223 Brøgger and Shetelig (1928) figs 121–2.
224 Made most forcefully recently by West (1969a) and Stjernqvist (1967).
225 Hurst (1959) 23–5.
226 E.g. Barton (1962) 68.
227 E.g. Wilson and Moorhouse (1971) 155; Barton (1962) fig. 17.
228 Klindt-Jensen (1957) fig. 2 illustrates an example from Sorte Muld, Denmark.
229 Brown *et al.* (1957) 198–9.
230 Jackson *et al.* (1969) 214.
231 Ibid., fig. 4.
232 Dunning (1932).
233 Such an object is recorded from the Viking Age grave at Oseberg, Norway: Brøgger and Shetelig (1928) pl. xiv.
234 Cf. the loom from Gdánsk; Herrmann (1971) fig. 69. Cf. also Hoffman (1964) 258ff.

235 Wooden pin-beaters were also probably used – they occur e.g. at Hedeby: Schietzel (1970) fig. 8, 4.
236 Conveniently listed by Chadwick (1958) 30–5, where there is a thorough discussion of them.
237 Okasha (1971) no. 118.
238 Chadwick (1958) 35.
239 The term 'heddle-stick' used by Leeds (1947) 88 refers to pin-beaters.
240 Eagles and Evison (1970) 42.
241 Geijer (1938).
242 A wool 'stained or dyed yellow' of the pagan period was recorded by Crowfoot (1952) 190. A number of colours are recorded in the Soumak braid in St Cuthbert's coffin: Battiscombe (1956) 458.
243 Crowfoot and Hawkes (1967) 66.
244 E.g. Crowfoot (1950) 29.
245 E.g. ibid., 30; Davidson and Webster (1967) 38.
246 Bede, *HE*, iii, 10, and iv, 19.
247 Jessen and Helbaek (1944) 62.
248 Crowfoot (1950) 28, 30. Chadwick (1958) 36–7.
249 Knocker and Hughes (1950) 45.
250 Addyman (1969) 74.
251 Crowfoot and Hawkes (1967). Silver-gilt thread occurs on the braids in St Cuthbert's coffin. Cf. Battiscombe (1956) 435.
252 Those identified so far are listed Crowfoot and Hawkes (1967) 43n. and 66–72. Cf. tenth-century braids from Denmark: Hald (1950) 455f.
253 An Anglo-Saxon tablet-weaving pattern is described by Crowfoot (1950) 29.
254 Faussett (1856) 93.
255 Cf. e.g. Oseberg, Norway: Brøgger and Shetelig (1928) 180.
256 Cf. e.g. reports by Mrs and Miss Crowfoot; Whitby (pre-875?) and Sutton Hoo (early seventh century), in Peers and Radford (1943) 86–8; Barrington (pagan Anglo-Saxon) and Mildenhall (sixth or seventh century) in Crowfoot (1950); Finglesham (early sixth century) in Chadwick (1958) 36–7; Coombe, Kent (sixth century) in Davidson and Webster (1967) 37–9; and by Henshall, Blewburton Hill, Berks. (sixth century), in Collins and Collins (1959) 69.
257 Cf. Crowfoot (1952); Crowfoot in Battiscombe (1956) 433–63; Hoffman (1964) 185; Crowfoot and Hawkes (1967).
258 Guðjónsson (1962).
259 Crowfoot (1948–9) mentions this in her discussion of a fragment from a Scandinavian context in Eigg. Another British Viking Age find is

published by Crowfoot in Bersu and Wilson (1966) 81–3.

260 Cf. Christie (1938) 1f. and 31f. for literary references to Anglo-Saxon embroidery.

261 Calberg (1951) 19–26.

262 Battiscombe (1956) 375ff.

263 Ibid., 391–4.

264 Liebermann (1903) i, 455.

265 Translations which have helped me considerably occur in Loyn (1962) 113; Liebermann (1903) 455.

266 A classic case is Grave 6n at Painsthorpe Wold, Yorks. (Mortimer (1905) 117), which included a work-box containing thread and an iron needle.

267 E.g. Finglesham, Kent; Chadwick (1958) fig. 5u.

268 E.g. Burwell, Cambs.: Lethbridge (1931) fig. 26.

269 E.g. Brodribb *et al.* (1972) fig. 52.

270 E.g. ibid., fig. 64.

271 E.g. Evison (1956) fig. 18.

272 But cf. Peers and Radford (1943) 68.

273 Cf. Baldwin Brown (1903–37) iv, 391f.

274 E.g. Peers and Radford (1943) fig. 18, 1. An example from Thetford (Knocker and Hughes (1950) 44) is said to have had traces of a wooden case.

275 An example, Mortimer (1905), fig. 837, is undoubtedly an intrusion in the grave.

276 Arbman (1940) pl. 176, 2.

277 Neville (1856) pl. 3, 30.

278 Carus-Wilson (1957).

279 E.g. Wilson (1971); Bateman (1861) 69.

280 E.g. Wilson (1961); Brown (1969) 45f.

281 Bruce-Mitford (1972) 26.

282 Bateman (1861) 29.

283 Faussett (1856) 152.

284 Lethbridge (1931) 80 suggests that some garments were bound at the cuffs with leather, quoting Thomas (1887) 5, a not altogether convincing source.

285 Radley (1971) 50–1, partly based on Benson (1903). The present excavations in York are yielding further traces of leather-working including tanning; cf. *Interim, Bulletin of the York Archaeological Trust*, i, no. 1, 38ff.

286 For discussion of this evidence cf. Kendrick *et al.* (1960) 61.

287 Peers and Radford (1943) 68 and fig. 18, 4.

288 Kendrick *et al.* (1960) 61.

289 Lowe (1959) 33; Wilson (1961) 205, 215; Brown (1969) 45.

290 The three definite Anglo-Saxon examples are *Codex Bonifat, I* at Fulda, the *Stonyhurst Gospel Book* and *MS Theol. Fol. 21* at Kassel. The binding of the *Cadmug Gospel Book* is, however, almost certainly English; Regemorter (1949) 45–51.

291 Cf. e.g. Bruce-Mitford (1969) pl. A.

292 Ó Ríordáin (1971) 75.

293 E.g. p. 89.

294 Bateman (1861) 54.

295 Taylor and Taylor (1965) fig. 483.

296 Wilson and Hurst (1965) 176, and from Banstead Down, Surrey (unpublished).

297 Evans and Fenwick (1971) 90–91 and pl. xx b.

298 An object from Bidford-on-Avon, Warwickshire, is alleged without foundation to be a netting needle: Leeds (1923) pl. xvi a.

299 E.g. by Finberg (1972) 498.

300 Figures quoted from Syson (1965) 33 and 157–9.

301 E.g. Wilson and Hurst (1960) 137.

302 E.g. Addyman (1964) 59.

303 *Current Archaeology*, iii (1971) 165-8. The account that follows is based on this publication and on personal observation.

304 Cf. The 'click mill' in Orkney: Cruden (1949).

305 Fig. 2.19.

306 An eleventh-century mill from Lund, Sweden, is chronologically the nearest parallel: Thun (1962–3).

307 Wilson and Hurst (1958) 158–9. The excavation was conducted by B. Hope-Taylor in 1957.

308 For reconstructions of the wheel, see Syson (1965) pl. 9.

7

The pottery

J. G. Hurst

Summary

During the last years of the Roman occupation increasing numbers of Anglo-Saxons settled in Britain as mercenaries to help defend it against invaders. Romano-British potters supplied special Romano-Saxon pottery for this market – good-quality industrial wares decorated in the Anglo-Saxon manner. At the same time the settlers brought with them the typical, rough hand-made wares to which they were accustomed in their homeland. With the collapse of Roman Britain in the fifth century the art of throwing pottery on a fast wheel and production on an industrial scale in kilns was lost. For some two hundred years only coarse handmade wares were produced, made locally and fired in simple clamp kilns. Most of the domestic wares were undecorated and simply shaped, but there was a development of funerary pottery from linear to bossed and stamped decoration with increasing specialization of craftsmen potters.

In the second quarter of the seventh century pottery made on a slow wheel was introduced into East Anglia and Northumbria – centred at first on Suffolk and Durham, but later spreading into Norfolk and Yorkshire. Over the next two hundred years this changed little in form and failed to spread outside these two areas. Over the rest of England handmade wares continued to be produced, little changed from the earlier period except that less pottery survives because of the lack of settlement sites and the cessation of the deposition of pots with burials. There were limited imports of pottery from Mayen and Badorf, in the Rhineland, but large quantities of French pottery came to the important trading centre of Hamwih on the south coast.

In the generation before the Scandinavian invasions good-quality wheel-thrown pottery, mass-produced in developed kilns, was made at Ipswich (then a thriving trading centre) and in north Yorkshire and Durham. By A.D. 900 wheel-thrown pottery had spread over a large part of eastern England. With the increased trade following the Scandinavian settlement, the formation of new towns, and the prosperity following the reconquest of the Danelaw, wheel-thrown industrial pottery had by 950 supplanted the rough handmade wares in over thirty centres. Only in north-west England and, surprisingly, the major part of Wessex south of the Thames was it not being produced. There were four groups of wheel-thrown pottery in Somerset and Hampshire; but even in London and Kent (the nearest English county to continental influence) rough, handmade pottery continued in use until the time of the Norman Conquest and beyond. Throughout the middle and late Anglo-Saxon periods there was close contact with the Continent, and pottery was imported from the whole area between the Loire in the west and the Rhine in the east. There was no real shift from Rhenish to Normandy imports in the eleventh century as French pottery had always been coming in.

In the early eleventh century there was a resurgence of handmade pottery with the introduction in southern England of large medieval-type cooking-pots with rims trued-up on a slow wheel but still fired in clamps. This developed simultaneously with the good-quality wheel-thrown wares forming an early medieval overlap until about the middle of the twelfth century, when the pottery industry collapsed and the Anglo-Saxon shapes and wheel-thrown pottery went out of production almost everywhere. Only at Stamford and York did the industry continue and it was from these two centres, ultimately with a move from Stamford to Nottingham, that good-quality industrial pottery was again re-established in the middle of the thirteenth century. Meanwhile in the rest of the country a widespread rural industry was developed, but pottery seems to have still been made mainly in clamps until the thirteenth century.

A. Early Saxon (350–650)

I *Wheel-thrown*
Romano-Saxon

II *Handmade*
Pre-Invasion
Domestic
Funerary

B. Middle Saxon (650–850)

I *Made on a slow wheel*
Ipswich-type ware
Whitby-type ware
Oxidized gritty ware

Reduced gritty ware
Early Otley-type ware

II *Handmade*
Maxey-type ware
Other wares

III *Imports*
Mayen
Badorf
Tating
French wares
Brown black burnished ware

C. Saxo-Norman (850–1150)

I *Wheel-thrown*

East Anglia   Thetford-type ware
    Ipswich–Thetford ware
    Norwich–Thetford ware
    Thetford ware
    Langhale–Thetford ware
    Grimston–Thetford ware
St Neots-type ware

Lincolnshire   Stamford ware
Stamford-type ware
    Decorated Stamford ware
    Northern Stamford ware
    Developed Stamford ware
Torksey ware
    Torksey-type ware
Lincoln-type ware G
Lincoln shelly ware
Shelly ware
Thetford-type ware
Splashed ware

North-east   York-type ware
Shelly ware
Stamford-type ware
Northern Stamford ware

Torksey-type ware
Fine Whitby-type ware
Northern Thetford-type ware
Late Otley-type ware
Splashed ware

Midlands
Leicester ware
Northampton ware
Nottingham splashed ware
Derby-type ware
Chester-type ware

South
Winchester-type ware
Portchester-type ware
Michelmersh ware
Cheddar-type ware

II *Handmade*

III *Imports*
Pingsdorf-type ware
Beauvais red-painted ware

IV *Early medieval overlap*

Terminology

Classification and terminology is a difficult problem beset with many pitfalls. The general headings Middle Saxon (650–850) and Saxo-Norman (850–1150) have long been in accepted use since they were first defined.[1] For the earlier period it is suggested that Early Saxon (350–650) is preferable to the more usual Pagan Anglo-Saxon. Within these three period divisions the pottery has been divided technologically into wheel-thrown, made on a slow wheel or handmade, with separate sections on imports. In the early Saxon period the pottery has been divided into domestic and funerary. Too little work has been done as yet to define local groups but some of the early pre-Invasion wares may be differentiated. In general, descriptive or sites names are preferable to letters and numbers since everyone can remember what Stamford-type ware is, but if it was called C.I.3 it would be much more confusing.

In the middle Saxon period the term Ipswich ware has been long established,[2] but the wider range of Northumbrian wares are only now being recognized and it is perhaps premature to suggest too rigid a classification, especially as no northern kiln sites have yet been located. This immediately raises the basic problem of the wares which have been named after kiln sites (such as Ipswich) and those which have been named after the type site where the ware was first recognized or appears in large quantities (Whitby). It is suggested that to make this distinction clear the term 'Ipswich ware' should only be applied to material from Ipswich itself, which may reasonably be assumed to come from kilns in the town, while 'Whitby ware' should be called 'Whitby-type ware' until such time as the kilns where it was found are located. This follows the precedent for calling red-painted imported wares 'Pingsdorf-type ware' now it is realized that they may come from many centres other than Pingsdorf itself.[3]

In the Saxo-Norman period the problem becomes more complex now that the three original wares have multiplied to over thirty. For East Anglia it is proposed that the pottery should be divided into three: (1) 'Thetford-type ware', (2) 'St Neots-type ware' and (3) 'Stamford-type ware', based on the three distinctive methods of manufacture: (a) reduced sandy, (b) shelly, and (c) oxidized sandy or fine almost untempered ware. Within these groups the products of individual kilns may be identified (as Norwich-Thetford ware[4]), but on most domestic sites where the kiln source cannot be readily determined the general term 'Thetford-type ware' should be used.

For the rest of Lincolnshire, although Torksey and Lincoln-type wares are similar technologically to Thetford-type ware, it is suggested that they should be separated (rather than be called Thetford-Torksey ware). It was originally thought that the Lincolnshire and northern wares were offshoots from Thetford but, as it now seems likely that they had separate origins, it is important not to use a terminology which may make the acceptance of this more difficult. The oxidized fabrics may be termed 'Stamford-type ware', as any kilns further north are part of the same series using the same geological deposits. It is suggested that the shelly fabrics should not be called St Neots-type ware but simply 'shelly ware', for it is now clear that the Lincolnshire shelly wares developed out of local Maxey-type wares and are not influenced from the St Neots area.

The situation in the north-east is more complex, for besides the obvious local fabrics ('York-type ware') most of the others are visually identical with many of the southern wares. It is therefore proposed that until kiln sites can be located they should be called 'Thetford-type ware', 'Torksey-type ware', and so on, but that the shelly fabrics should have a general descriptive name for the time being, especially as the distribution is still uncertain and the numbers of sherds small because of the few Saxo-Norman sites excavated in the area.[5]

In the midlands, Leicester ware and Northampton ware have similarities with both Thetford and Torksey, but it would be safer not to link the terminology with either but to keep it separate. The oxidized Nottingham splashed, Derby-type and Chester-type wares are again a distinct group, the latter having possible southern, rather than eastern, affinities. For the south, the four wheel-thrown fabrics (occurring in an area dominated by handmade wares) should be separated under general headings until their relationships and places of origin are more firmly established. This revised terminology is more complicated and cumbersome than that previously used, but it is important to differentiate the definite kiln material from the general groups the sources of which are not yet located.

Developments since 1959

A large amount of new information on Anglo-Saxon pottery has come to light since 1959 when the last general synthesis on this subject was attempted.[6] This is because of the great amount of work carried out in all areas of the country, where previously very little had been done, and also by increased activity in France. In 1959 the English picture was biased because during the previous ten years my own fieldwork and research had been concentrated in East Anglia, while Jope in Oxford, and fieldworkers and museums in Norfolk and Suffolk, together with earlier workers in Cambridge (notably McKenny Hughes), had collected large groups of middle and late Saxon pottery which was available for study. It was not so much that I ignored other areas but that the material was not available in sufficient quantities in other parts of England to draw significant conclusions. The first distribution map, published in 1955 by Hodges, Jope and myself,[7] purported to show the distribution of late Saxon pottery in England (fig. 7.1A). We now know how misleading this was since what it really showed was research carried out on late Saxon pottery from the centres at Cambridge and Oxford. By 1959 further discoveries had already shown the inadequacy of the concept of good-quality pottery made mainly in East Anglia with offshoots to other areas, but opinions had become firmly fixed and Dunning's map (fig. 7.1B) shows how he tried to break out of the straitjacket, but without really casting off the current dogma.[8]

For the early Saxon period a similar restraint was imposed by the idea that all Anglo-Saxon pottery must date after the *adventus Saxonum* of 450. It took a long time to change this concept and for it to be realized that there could be earlier pottery brought in by Anglo-Saxon mercenaries as early as 400, and possibly even in the late fourth century.

Abroad similar problems were caused by the complete lack of work on pottery in France which, as in many other periods, has completely distorted the picture. As with the work from Cambridge and Oxford in this country, the intensive work carried out by the Landesmuseum in Bonn, over a period of more than fifty years, had so firmly established information on the Rhenish pottery centres that this was taken for granted as the main area of development[9] and even in 1958, when our German colleagues kept telling us that the pottery from Hamwih, for example, was not from the Rhineland, there was reluctance to accept the obvious answer that it was made in, and came from, France. However, the remarkable work carried out in France during the past few years has transformed the picture so that we can now see the contributions and influence from both France and Germany in a much clearer light without the previous bias (fig. 7.1E and F).

These fundamental changes in our concept of Anglo-Saxon pottery which have emerged during the past ten years, and have been very much speeded up during the last five years, have very important implications for the future study not only of Anglo-Saxon

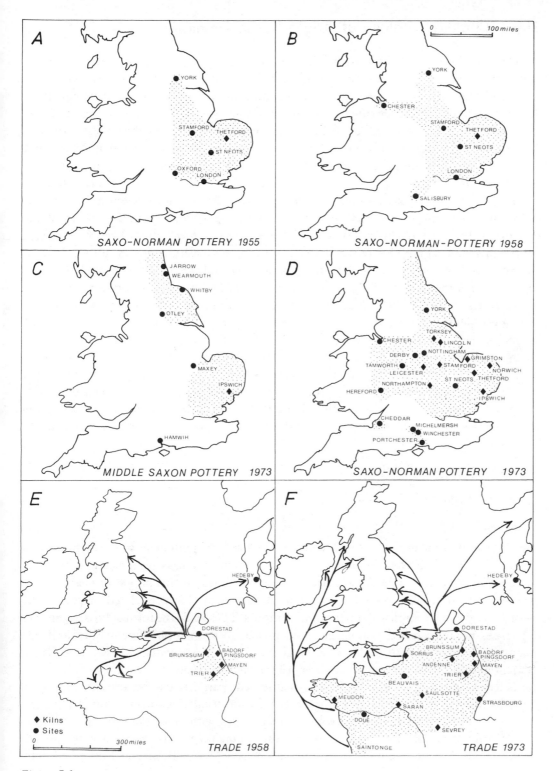

A   SAXO-NORMAN POTTERY 1955

YORK
STAMFORD   THETFORD
ST NEOTS
OXFORD   LONDON

B   SAXO-NORMAN-POTTERY 1958

0   100 miles

YORK
CHESTER
STAMFORD   THETFORD
ST NEOTS
LONDON
SALISBURY

C   MIDDLE SAXON POTTERY 1973

JARROW
WEARMOUTH
WHITBY
OTLEY
MAXEY
IPSWICH
HAMWIH

D   SAXO-NORMAN POTTERY   1973

YORK
TORKSEY
CHESTER   LINCOLN
DERBY   NOTTINGHAM
GRIMSTON
TAMWORTH   STAMFORD   NORWICH
LEICESTER   THETFORD
NORTHAMPTON   ST NEOTS
HEREFORD   IPSWICH
CHEDDAR   MICHELMERSH
WINCHESTER
PORTCHESTER

E   TRADE 1958

HEDEBY
DORESTAD
BADORF
BRUNSSUM   PINGSDORF
MAYEN
TRIER

◆ Kilns
● Sites

0   300 miles

F   TRADE 1973

HEDEBY
DORESTAD
BRUNSSUM
SORRUS   BADORF
PINGSDORF
ANDENNE   MAYEN
TRIER
BEAUVAIS
SAULSOTTE
MEUDON   STRASBOURG
SARAN
DOUE   SEVREY
SAINTONGE

Figure 7.1

pottery but also of other subjects. It shows first of all the dangers of constructing distribution maps on insufficient information which can lead to misleading conclusions. Once these are published they become accepted and subsequent workers try to fit their new finds into this pattern which then quickly becomes a straitjacket. Fig. 7.1 shows simplified versions of some of these misleading maps and a general attempt to state the present situation, but it must be stressed most strongly that the subject is now moving so fast that this account is only an interim statement of the Anglo-Saxon pottery situations as it appears in 1973.

We must not become too firmly set in new dogmas concerning the dual nature of the re-introduction of good-quality pottery into East Anglia and Northumbria with the subsequent expansion of wheel-thrown pottery to the whole of England north of the Thames with certain outliers in Wessex. Likewise, we must not expect France to provide all the answers. There clearly was contact with the Rhineland, though not so much as has previously been supposed. Various options must be kept open for, if work increases at the current rate, the general picture may be much modified again during the next five to ten years. Another disturbing aspect of these changes is the extent to which earlier work becomes out of date. My attempted corpus of Saxo-Norman pottery in East Anglia,[10] although still valuable as a corpus of material for reference, is now very misleading in its general comments, as is much of the material published in the 1959 Symposium.[11] It is often difficult to change outdated theories proposed and hardened in print by other scholars but, if the original basic theory was proposed by oneself, it is easier to start to erect a new edifice: at the same time I hope that the numerous inaccuracies, which will doubtless be found in it by future research, will not become too firmly entrenched.

A. Early Saxon (350–650)

I. WHEEL-THROWN

Romano-Saxon (fig. 7.2)

With the end of the Roman period, and the Anglo-Saxon settlement in the fifth century, there was a complete break in pottery forms. Wheel-thrown mass-produced Roman wares were replaced by rough handmade Anglo-Saxon pots. But at this period of change there was an overlap in the production of normal late Roman commercial red or grey wares with the addition of Anglo-Saxon decorative motifs. These take the form of bosses, dimples and free linear ornament. Stamps are not unusual on Roman pottery but the motifs are alien to the main Roman tradition in England. Myres has divided this Romano-Saxon pottery into nine main types:[12] A. Jars ornamented with one or two lines of shoulder- or belly-bosses; B. Wide-bellied jars ornamented with circular bosses and groups of (usually three) finger-tips; C. Bowls ornamented with circular bosses and groups of finger-tips; D. Tall beakers ornamented with circular bosses with or without groups of finger-tips; E. Bowls ornamented with negative bosses in the form of large circular depressions with various designs in the panels; F. Vessels ornamented with diagonal lines and dots;

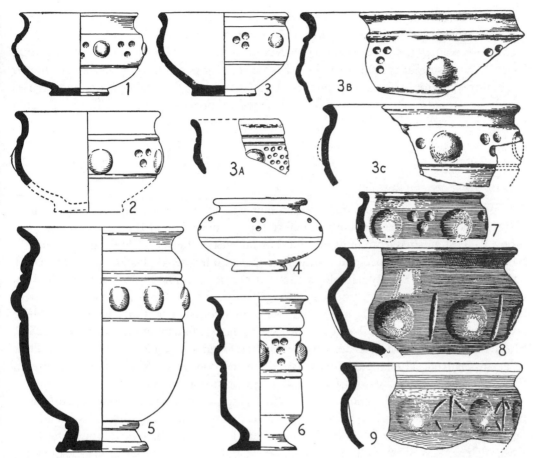

Figure 7.2 Romano-Saxon wheel-thrown wares (scale $\frac{1}{4}$) in Dunning *et al.* (1959) fig. 1:
1. and 6. Colchester, Essex; 2. Verulamium, Herts.; 3. Sittingbourne, Kent; 3a. Brundall,
Norfolk; 3b. West Acre, Norfolk; 3c. Clipsham, Rutland; 4. Richborough, Kent; 5.
Lakenheath, Suffolk; 7. and 8. Caister-by-Yarmouth, Norfolk; 9. Burgh Castle, Suffolk

G. Vessels ornamented with continuous diagonal lines; H. Miscellaneous other types;
I. Vessels with stamped decoration overlying small bosses.

All these types of decoration are closely paralleled on Anglo-Saxon pottery. Romano-
Saxon pottery is found as early as the end of the third century but becomes more common
from the middle of the fourth century onwards. It is found over a wide area of eastern
England and is now recognized from Lincolnshire and Yorkshire as well as in East
Anglia.[13] The distribution for Essex[14] has recently been impressively extended,[15] and
it is likely that similar intensive study of collections of Roman pottery would bring to
light many more examples in other areas. There is little doubt from the distribution in
Saxon shore forts, and near important towns and other Roman centres, that we have here

a class of pottery made by Romano-British potters to meet the tastes of Anglo-Saxon mercenaries brought in during the fourth and early fifth centuries. The recent discovery of Romano-Saxon pottery associated with Saxon pottery in Huts 8 and 9 at Mucking, Essex,[16] adds support to this theory. It has been suggested that these decorative motifs were simply a general fashion of the time, but the evidence for Anglo-Saxon mercenaries is now so strong[17] that the plausibility of Myres' original conception of Romano-Saxon pottery increases with time.

II. HANDMADE

Pre-Invasion pottery (fig. 7.3)

The presence in England of Anglo-Saxon mercenaries in the second half of the fourth and the first half of the fifth century, before the accepted date of the *adventus Saxonum*, is now well established from finds of typical metalwork of the period,[18] from the Romano-Saxon pottery just described and by finds of rough handmade Anglo-Saxon pottery whose parallels abroad are clearly datable to *c.* 400 if not before. The most characteristic form of this type is the faceted carinated bowl, which may have the lower part constricted, be on a pedestal (fig. 7.3, 1), or be shallower with a rounded bottom (fig. 7.3, 2). These are typical of the area on both sides of the Elbe in the late fourth and early fifth century.[19] Sherds from Feddersen Wierde, which was abandoned about 450, are remarkably close to examples from Mucking, Essex, where carinated bowls have been found in many of the huts (some associated with Dorchester-type bronze attachments).

So far this pottery is mainly concentrated in the Thames valley,[20] and Mucking must be regarded as a classic case of a site for Anglo-Saxon mercenaries in view of its remarkable position overlooking the Thames. Carinated bowls are beginning to be found on other sites, such as West Stow, Suffolk,[21] Colchester[22] and Heybridge, Essex,[23] suggesting that many more village sites may have started in the years before 450 than was previously recognized. This dating depends on these distinctive sherds since the main bulk of the rough handmade wares could be of almost any date and none of it distinctive enough to be dated early rather than late fifth century.[24] With all these sites one would expect more evidence from London itself, but the recent find there of a B1 imported Mediterranean amphora[25] suggests that the evidence may be found in levels above Roman buildings.

Domestic

The rough handmade pottery found on Anglo-Saxon domestic sites presents a serious problem. The typical small globular cooking-pots are so simple that they are unlikely to have developed much in form over the centuries. Although material has been collected or excavated from over eighty-nine early village sites,[26] much of it is too fragmentary or unstratified – a factor which makes adequate study difficult. Leeds, at Sutton Courtenay, Berks.,[27] pioneered the large-scale excavations which in recent years at Mucking, Essex, and West Stow, Suffolk, have produced a great mass of material, a lot of it associated

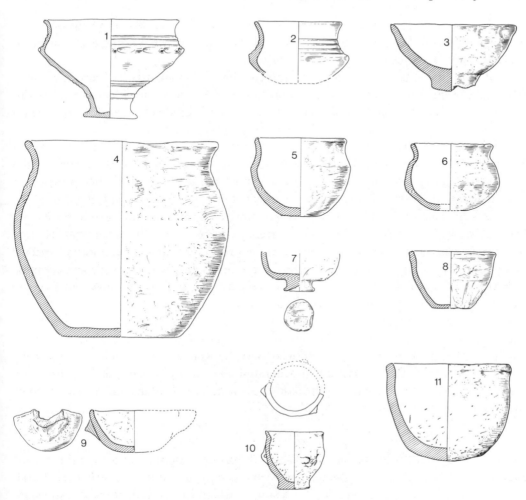

Figure 7.3 Early Saxon handmade pottery (scale $\frac{1}{4}$):
1. Mitcham, Surrey; 2.–11. from Mucking, Essex; 2. Hut 19; 3. Hut 42; 4. Pit 10; 5. Hut 11; 6. Hut 32; 7. Hut 5; 8. Hut 19; 9. Hut 1; 10. Hut 69; 11. Hut 85

with huts or other features. Analysis by West of 12,000 sherds from West Stow[28] has shown how difficult it is to place the coarse wares in any sequence, indeed the same standard shapes seem to last unchanged from the fifth to the seventh centuries. The wares are fine-grained with few grits and are fired quite hard in comparison to the decorated funerary wares. The colours range from brown to grey and black, as is usual for pottery made in clamp kilns, as much Anglo-Saxon handmade pottery must have been despite the apparent finding of pottery kilns at Cassington, Oxon.[29] (fig. 7.32, 1). Many of the sherds show evidence of being coiled. Sixty-five per cent of the coarse wares have smoothed surfaces and 25 per cent are burnished showing that, although coarse, considerable trouble was taken in their manufacture. At Mucking, Margaret Jones has similar problems of dating the coarse wares unless associated with other datable objects (such as the early carinated bowls).[30] Fig. 7.3 shows typical vessels from a number of huts.

At both sites there are also grass-tempered fabrics, though at West Stow this is only 2 per cent of the whole. Grass-tempered pottery is one of the hallmarks of early Anglo-Saxon domestic pottery and is found widely over much of England in varying proportions to other wares. It certainly starts by the early fifth century and might be regarded as typically Anglo-Saxon if it were not for the fact that it also occurs in fifth-century levels at Wroxeter, Salop., in a context well before the Anglo-Saxons arrived. But a similar find at Barnsley, Glos., associated with a Germanic buckle may suggest the early presence of mercenaries in the west midlands.[31] At the moment little more can be said: the wide range in shapes, from small cooking-pots to large storage vessels and other exotic forms, are best illustrated by Leeds in his Sutton Courtenay reports. It is to be hoped that, as more material becomes available from large excavations in different parts of the country, regional and period types will begin to emerge, but at the moment it is hard to see any coherent pattern. Studies now in progress by Freda Berisford in the Thames valley and Everson in Lincolnshire may give us some of the answers.

The Anglo-Saxon settlers used handmade pottery because this was the pottery which was made and used in their homelands – areas far removed from Roman industrial influences. It is not so clear why they did not take over the Roman pottery industry, especially now we know there was at least a two-generation overlap in the early fifth century, but this must be due to the complete breakdown of Roman urban and industrial economy which made mass-production impossible.

Funerary (figs. 7.4–7.6)

The main purpose of this chapter is to discuss the ordinary domestic wares of the Anglo-Saxon period. This is a subject which has been much neglected for the early period and, as discussed in the previous section, it is a subject which badly needs more work despite the difficulties involved. Thirty years ago the situation was the same with the funerary wares and it was thought they were too diffuse a group to classify. We owe a great debt therefore to Myres for his intensive work on these wares, for the fact that he has now nearly completed his corpus of funerary vessels and because we already have a most useful summary of the position.[32] As the sequence is fully set out there I do not propose to repeat his full arguments, only to summarize briefly some of the main forms, types of decoration and evidence for dating. Since the 1930s, when Myres started his work, the material from cremation cemeteries has doubled; this factor has had the virtue of supplying more comparative material but also the effect of slowing down the preparation of his corpus. The position abroad has also changed with the publication since the war of many of the major early groups of pottery. Excavations at Loveden, Lincs., and Spong Hill, Norfolk, in 1972/3, have added over 1,500 additional urns to the total.

Funerary pottery gives a very biased view of the wares available in the Anglo-Saxon period. Far more trouble was taken by the potters in making these vessels than the coarse vessels mainly made for domestic purposes. The funerary pottery falls into two main groups, (*a*) cremation urns and (*b*) small accessory vessels which often accompany inhumation burials. The latter are the easiest to date as they are often associated with datable objects in the graves; but the cremation urns present many more problems. Firstly, most of the several thousand extant urns were not excavated under modern conditions, so that their associations and relations with other pots are not known and, secondly, as a consequence of the cremation fire, objects are often much contorted and are consequently more difficult to date. Although it may overwhelm us with a great mass of material we urgently need a series of complete excavations of cremation cemeteries under modern conditions. This policy was introduced in 1972 with the commencement of excavations by the Department of the Environment at Loveden Hill, Lincs., and Spong Hill, near North Elmham, Norfolk. It is hoped that work here will throw light on the many problems of dating; although with such small holes dug to bury the pots, unless they are set very close, it is hard to determine the relationship between adjacent burials.

Myres has divided the forms of the vessels into nine main types (fig. 7.4):[33] (1) plain biconical urns; (2) plain hollow-necked urns; (3) plain sub-biconical urns; (4) plain shouldered urns; (5) plain bowls; (6) plain accessory vessels; (7) plain globular urns with upright rims; (8) plain globular urns with everted rims; (9) plain vessels with tall narrow necks. He then divides the plain domestic accessory wares, or pots used for poor burials, into three types: (I) small crude accessories, (II) wide-mouthed cook-pots, (III) cook-pots with lugs. This is bound to be an arbitrary series of divisions since, with hand-made pottery, there are so many possible variations that all the types merge into each other. Still a classification must form the basis of any study and Myres' series is most useful.

Myres divides the ornament into linear, boss and stamp designs,[34] which may also be placed in a chronological sequence with a preference for simple linear patterns in the earliest period. This may be horizontal (fig. 7.5, 1–2), biconical (fig. 7.5, 3) or curvilinear (fig. 7.5, 4). Later in the fifth century boss ornament becomes more exuberant, culminating in the highly decorated *Buckelurnen* (fig. 7.6, 1). In the sixth century bosses tend to drop in popularity and there is increasing use of stamps used in conjunction with bosses and lines forming rectangular (fig. 7.6, 2) or triangular (fig. 7.6, 1) patterns, but by the later sixth century bosses gradually disappear. Stamped linear designs are followed by a break-up in regular patterns, but stamps never fully go out of use as they survive in East Anglia in the stamped Ipswich-ware pitchers, which retain stamped ornament in zones (fig. 7.8, 2),[35] and in Wessex where there seems to be continuity right through to the early medieval stamped wares.[36]

The many variations in these forms and their decoration has been fully discussed by Myres.[37] He demonstrates the difficulties of closely dating the pots and the dangers of trying to put them into a typological sequence. Attempts to bring out the differences between Anglian linear and Saxon stamped pottery all go to confirm that most of the settlers coming over were already ethnically mixed before they came.[38] One of the most

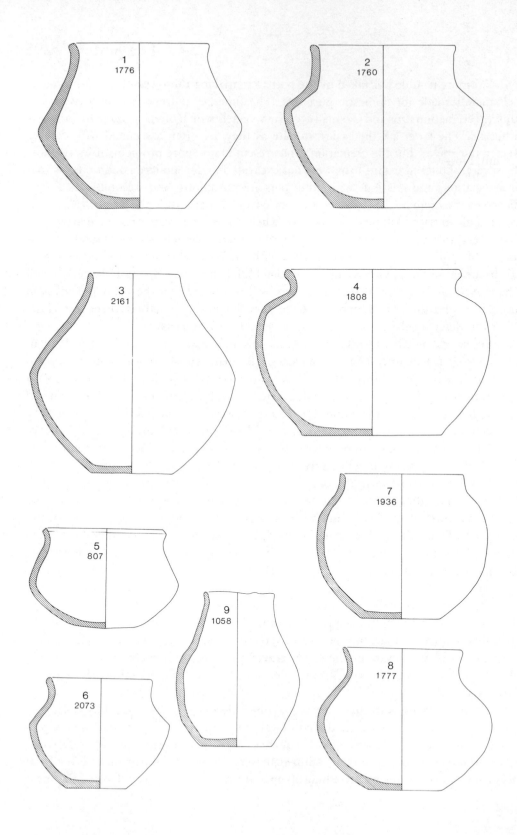

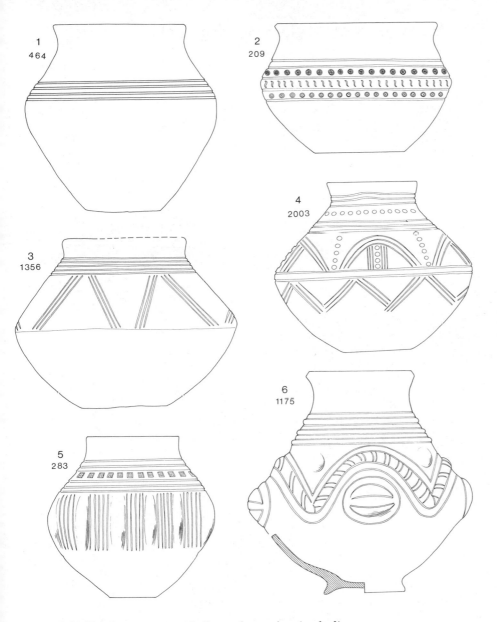

Figure 7.5 Funerary wares with linear decoration (scale ¼):
1. Leicester; 2. Girton, Cambridge; 3. Loveden Hill, Lincs.; 4. Sandon, Yorks.; 5. St John's, Cambridge; 6. Sandy, Beds.

Figure 7.4 (opposite) Plain handmade wares from burials (scale ¼):
1., 2., 4. and 8. Caistor by Norwich; 3. Illington, Norfolk; 5. Milton, Northants; 6. Barrington, Cambs.; 7. Markshall, Norfolk; 9. Barrow, Rutland.

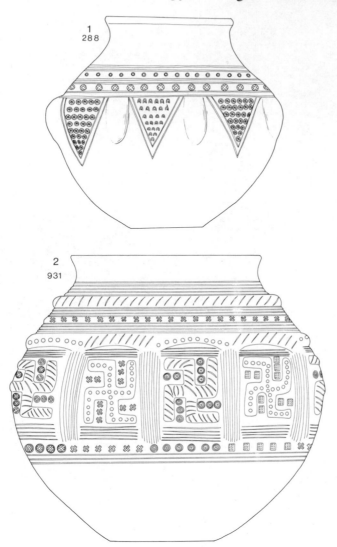

Figure 7.6 Funerary wares with bossed and stamped decoration (scale ¼):
1. St John's, Cambridge; 2. Lackford, Suffolk

important points to emerge from this study of over four thousand urns is the evidence
it gives for types of manufacture. There are considerable differences between the coarse
domestic pottery and the finer funerary wares. The domestic wares were almost certainly
made locally in each village, possibly by each family, and fired in clamp kilns. The
decorated funerary wares, however, have more the appearance of being specially made
at least in one centre in each village in the early stages, with possible specialization by
the sixth century as workshops emerge which serve a much wider area. The Illington/

Lackford potter (fig. 7.6, 2) is the best example of this,[39] his wares being found on many East Anglian sites. Myres has also demonstrated that the designs are by no means solely decorative and may in many cases have had magical or religious significance. There are also other aspects of the pots which have been much neglected but the evidence of grain[40] and textile[41] impressions is one which could be followed up on all types of Anglo-Saxon pottery. There is far too much concentration on typological studies of form and decoration without taking into account the many other things that pottery can tell us about the Saxon economy. There are quite a few Frankish imported pots, especially in Kent, but the evidence for these has never been fully collected. There are many problems as typified by the Kentish and similar bottles.[42]

B. Middle Saxon 650–850

I. MADE ON A SLOW WHEEL

Ipswich ware (figs 7.7 and 7.8)

Ipswich ware was first identified in 1957 as a result of important finds both of pottery and kilns at Ipswich, Suffolk.[43] Four different fabrics may be distinguished:[44] (*a*) hard well-fired sandy grey with a smoothed or burnished surface, (*b*) the same but without the smoothed surface, (*c*) similar but with the addition of some larger grits giving a surface rough to the touch and (*d*) a hard well-fired grey gritty ware, in which the contraction of the clay has caused many of the grits to stick out giving a harsh pimply surface.

Ipswich ware was made on a slow wheel. Since I distinguished between middle Saxon pottery made on a slow wheel and Saxo-Norman pottery thrown on a fast wheel there has been some confusion mainly due to my own loose terminology – as when, for example, I talked of Ipswich ware being thrown on a slow wheel.[45] Saxo-Norman pottery is thrown on a fast wheel in the normal manner, but it is suggested that Ipswich ware was made or turned on a tournet or turntable which was revolved by hand without any mechanical aids;[46] there would thus be insufficient momentum to produce the regular thin profile of a pot thrown on a fast wheel, and the pot was in fact gradually built up, causing the characteristic thick sides to the vessels. There is clear evidence of turning from the presence of girth grooves, but the unevenness of these would be impossible if the pot was thrown on a fast wheel. Nevertheless many of the vessels were very competently made, and technically they stand midway between the early Saxon handmade wares and the later Saxon wheel-thrown wares.

The second important point about the manufacture of Ipswich ware is the fact that it was very well fired to a high temperature in a proper kiln, where both the temperature and the air flow was controlled to give in most cases a uniform reduced grey fabric. Some sherds are underfired or brown, but these are small in number and may be regarded as mistakes rather than intentional variations. This evidence from the pottery itself is confirmed by the finding of two kilns, and many areas of wasters, in the Carr Street/Cox

Lane area of Ipswich in 1935[47] and 1961.[48] It is most unfortunate that in neither case was it possible to recover an adequate plan of the shape of the kiln, but sufficient remained to show that they were well built of clay and were possibly simple single-flue kilns without the more sophisticated raised oven floors of the later Saxon examples (fig. 7.32, 2).

The basic form of Ipswich ware is a small squat cooking-pot with a diameter of between 10 and 15 cm and a height of 12.5–18 cm. There are three basic rim forms, with various subdivisions:[49] (I) simple upright or everted; (II) with an internal hollow; (III)

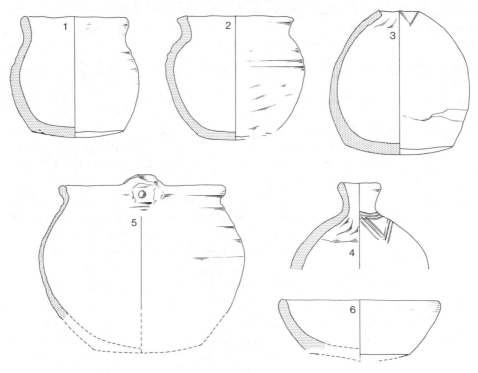

Figure 7.7   Middle Saxon Ipswich ware (scale ¼) from Ipswich

with an external or internal beading. Most of the bases are sagging and commonly have extensive knife trimming near the base, both traits now continuing throughout the rest of the Anglo-Saxon period. Few large groups have been published from associated contexts, but in those from Cox Lane, Ipswich, West has shown[50] that 83 per cent of the pottery was cooking-pots with no other form accounting for more than 5 per cent. Seventy-five per cent of these cooking-pots fell within the diameter range of 11–17 cm with the rest between 10 and 20 cm. Only 30 per cent of the fabrics were pimply, but this is more common on some other sites. Of the cooking-pot rim forms 50 per cent were group I and 25 per cent each of II and III.

Other forms include various types and size of bowl, some of which have upright pierced lugs (fig. 7.7, 5). These lugs are a typical feature of middle Saxon pottery both in Ipswich ware and elsewhere.[51] Rarer forms include bottles and lamps. The second most important type is the lugged pitcher. These form a series of baggy globular pitchers with an applied D- or O-spout and a small strap handle placed opposite the spout. Laterally between these are placed peaked lugs pierced for suspension. On the shoulder is a decoration of stamps in bands or pendant triangles, often defined by incised lines (fig. 7.8, 2), a feature derived from decorated funerary pottery.

The dating of Ipswich ware presents a difficult problem. Like many of the other groups, it is either unassociated or found in contexts without any firm absolute dating. No single site is conclusive, but taking a whole series of finds into account a date between 625 and 650 may be suggested for the start of Ipswich ware at Ipswich and other coastal sites;[52] how quickly it then spread to other parts of East Anglia is more difficult to determine. The earliest stratified examples of Ipswich ware were found in 1938 in Mound 2 at Sutton Hoo, Suffolk, in the sand filling of the pit round the ship-burial.[53] The bottle in the main ship-burial is now also shown to be made on a slow wheel, so this may possibly be an early example of Ipswich ware.[54] Excavations at the monastery at Burgh Castle, Suffolk, founded c. 635 (see pp. 212ff.), have produced Ipswich ware, but with no hand-made pottery.

The settlement site of West Stow which does not seem to have been abandoned later than the middle of the seventh century contained sherds of Ipswich-type ware in its upper levels.[55]

From 650 onwards finds are more common, as at Bradwell, Essex (after c. 654), and Framlingham, Suffolk, with an open-work bronze disc.[56] By the eighth century there are several sites dated by *sceattas*. It therefore seems certain that Ipswich ware starts by 650 and, with the recent earlier suggested dating for Sutton Hoo, a date in the second quarter of the seventh century is becoming more likely.[57] The only reason to doubt this date is the lack of Ipswich ware from cemetery sites. There are no burials known either in or associated with Ipswich ware, but there are two cemetery sites where Ipswich ware was found in a loose association – at Markshall, Norfolk,[58] and at Hall Hill, West Keal, Lincs.[59] This need not mean that Ipswich ware was later in date, for it is clearly primarily domestic in function and there is no reason to expect it to be associated with graves, indeed its introduction may be associated with the conversion. The end date is also a problem, and will be discussed in relation to the starting date for Thetford ware (see below, p. 318).

The distribution of Ipswich-ware cooking-pots is mainly a coastal and riverine one in Suffolk and Norfolk, round to the Wash and up the rivers which feed it. But as most finds are unassociated it is hard to tell how quickly the ware spread from its original centre at the trading port of Ipswich. Finds in Ipswich itself are prolific and almost anywhere where ground is disturbed in the medieval town pits containing large quantities of Ipswich ware are found. The distribution covers and extends beyond the whole of the area enclosed by the medieval defences,[60] except for the southern low-lying part of the town,

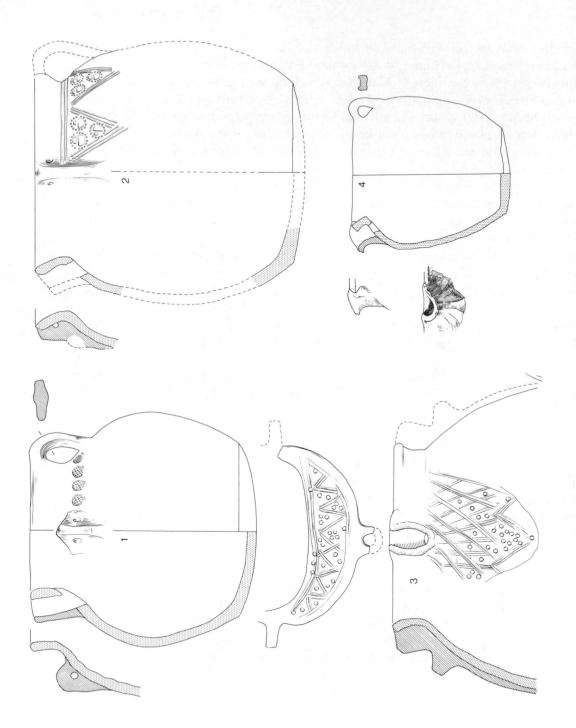

Figure 7.8 Middle Saxon Ipswich-type ware pitchers (scale ¼):
1. Richborough, Kent; 2. and 4. Ipswich; 3. Wakerley, Essex

where recent evidence for extensive post-medieval build-up may explain why recent building development has not produced signs of early settlement. In Ipswich the pottery and other finds range in time from 650, or earlier, up to *c*. 850; but there can be little doubt that in the eighth and early ninth centuries Ipswich was a large and important trading centre, serving the east coast in the way that Hamwih served the south. It is strange that there is no documentary hint of the intense activity shown by the archaeological evidence before *c*. 950.[61] There is little doubt, from the archaeological evidence, that already in the middle Anglo-Saxon period East Anglia was as prosperous and as densely populated as it was, according to Domesday, in the later Saxon period.

The distribution of Ipswich ware has been recently extended by the finding of large quantities by Wade at the settlement site of Bonhunt near Newport, Essex.[62] Besides Castor, Northants., where recent excavations by Wild[63] have produced many sherds from a possible monastic site, there are stray finds from both Brixworth and Thrapston also in Northamptonshire. With these exceptions, however, there is no hint of expansion of Ipswich-ware cooking-pots outside its main East Anglian centres. That both Castor and Brixworth were monastic sites may have some connection with the distribution into the midlands on special sites. It is puzzling that the eighth-century expansion of Mercia eastwards did not lead to Ipswich-type ware spreading further westwards. The stamped lugged pitchers, however, have a much wider distribution, although still basically an eastern coastal one, from Kent through East Anglia, and Lincolnshire,[64] to several finds in Yorkshire.[65]

In 1957[66] the origins of Ipswich ware seemed simple and clear. Here was a pottery which had cooking-pots basically the same as the earlier handmade examples. They differed in that they were turned on a slow wheel and were fired in proper kilns. These features suggested an influx of potters from the Continent. In 1959, however, I modified my views to suggest it was merely the idea which had been brought over, as imported potters would have surely brought the fast wheel with them.[67] The source seemed clearly to be the Rhineland with the apparent Rhenish traits of sagging base, knife trimming and spouted pitchers. In addition the peaked lugs provided a useful link with the elusive Frisian merchants.[68] One therefore saw a picture of renewed contact with the Continent, resulting in a revival of the pottery industry in East Anglia between 650 and 850, with a great break-out into the rest of eastern England in the ninth century where there was almost certainly an influx of actual potters, bringing in the fast wheel and more sophisticated techniques. In the last few years, however, the picture has been much modified by important finds in the north.

Northern groups (fig. 7.9)

In 1943, when Dunning published his account of the pottery from the Anglo-Saxon monastery of Whitby,[69] late Saxon wheel-thrown pottery was known in East Anglia but it was not envisaged that any of the wheel-thrown pottery found in Yorkshire contexts of the seventh to ninth centuries could be local. It was therefore natural to identify them as imports from the Rhineland and no one doubted this interpretation which I accepted in 1959.[70] In this same year Rosemary Cramp started excavating at Monkwearmouth and in 1963 she started at Jarrow; both excavations continue.[71] These two sites have a similar date range to Whitby (mid seventh to mid ninth centuries, with a gap till after the Norman Conquest) and we were hopeful of finding stratified middle Saxon pottery. Unfortunately, even after several years' excavation at each of these monastic sites, very little stratified Anglo-Saxon pottery has been found. No rich deposits associated with the kitchens have been located at either site. Each year I examined the pottery and had to report that none of the pottery found seemed to date from the period of the monasteries. By the mid-1960s it was apparent that something was wrong: the finding of a small number of sherds not only firmly stratified in Saxon levels, but associated with Saxon glass, led to a complete re-thinking of what middle Saxon pottery in Northumbria might be like.

First, a reassessment of the pottery from Whitby showed that the Roman sherds, handmade Anglo-Saxon sherds and most of the so-called imported sherds, were made of the same identical sandy micaceous grey fabric. This same fabric was also present in stratified middle Saxon levels at Jarrow and Monkwearmouth. Some of these vessels were made on a slow wheel,[72] but others were thrown on a fast wheel.[73] At a meeting in November 1968[74] a provisional terminology was agreed for the Saxon wares of the north and it was proposed that this sandy micaceous fabric should be called Whitby-type ware. At Whitby itself this was the only middle Saxon fabric present, except for the hand-made sherds (fig. 7.11, 2–5). At Jarrow and Monkwearmouth, however, there were hardly any handmade sherds (fig. 7.11, 1), but there were two groups of pottery which were almost identical to the pimply and sandy Ipswich wares. These were therefore termed 'pimply Ipswich-type ware' and 'sandy Ipswich-type ware', although it was recognized that they were not necessarily imports from East Anglia but were more likely to be of local manufacture somewhere in the north. In addition there was a sixth middle Saxon fabric, a second type thrown on a fast wheel – very much like Thetford ware, being hard, sandy and grey. This local wheel-thrown ware should now be termed 'reduced gritty ware'. Since this interim account was written a further fabric may also be placed in the middle Saxon period at Jarrow and Monkwearmouth: a hard gritty, oxidized, buff fabric (very similar to the later medieval wares). There are, however, several stratified sherds in early contexts and one rim with a typical middle Saxon shape. Thus, in the seventh- to ninth-century levels at Jarrow and Monkwearmouth there are seven different fabrics, only one of which is handmade. Furthermore, two of them, fine Whitby-type ware and the reduced gritty ware, were thrown on a fast wheel. The full date range of the pottery is not known, but assuming that both sites were abandoned by 875[75] this must mean that full wheel-thrown pottery was in use, and being made in Northumbria, by the middle of the ninth century. This could have important implications for the starting date of other late Saxon groups of pottery in eastern England (see p. 318).

Of far greater importance is the fact that these finds imply two quite separate introductions of pottery made on a slow wheel, one into East Anglia (apparently based on trade contacts and the growth of Ipswich) and the other in Northumbria (apparently linked with monastic sites). It is tempting to associate this with the finding of early Ipswich ware of the seventh century at the monasteries of Burgh Castle and Bradwell (noting also the monastic link at Castor and Brixworth), but a word of caution must be given. Whitby, Hartlepool, Jarrow and Monkwearmouth are the only four sites so far where this pottery has been fully identified. Ipswich-type sherds comparable to those from Jarrow have been recently identified at Newcastle.[76] As more work is done these may well be recognized from all types of site in the north. Already the discovery of pottery made on a slow wheel in an early context at the deserted village of West Whelpington, Northumberland,[77] points the direction for future research.

There is only a handful of middle Saxon pottery from York made on a slow wheel, so far identified, though these are all Ipswich-type ware.[78] Otherwise, outside York, there are only two other sites besides Whitby. From the Archbishop of York's manor at Otley, Jean le Patourel has identified sherds of cooking pots similar to Ipswich ware in a pimply grey fabric, which has been called 'Otley-type ware',[79] while from Wharram Percy, in the East Riding, there are Ipswich-type ware and Whitby-type ware sherds.

Thus in Northumbria a complex picture emerges of many different middle Saxon pottery groups, based either on Ipswich ware or the Whitby types. The situation is as it was in East Anglia twenty years ago and it may well be another twenty years before we understand the picture in the north as fully as we do that in East Anglia now. There is an urgent need for the excavation of more early settlement sites and for the re-examination of previously excavated pottery. The material from Lindisfarne must be re-examined and we badly need information on the sequence from Bamburgh.

Whitby-type ware is a fairly soft sandy fabric with many micaceous inclusions, usually fired to a dark grey or black. It is made on a slow wheel with the thick walls usual for this type of manufacture. It seems to have been fired in a proper kiln but was not fired to a very high temperature; but as no middle Saxon kilns are known outside Ipswich we are groping in the dark. Most of the sherds are too fragmentary to define the basic forms and only at Whitby is it possible to see the typical, small, squat cooking-pot closely comparable with the Ipswich examples (fig. 7.9, 1), with simple everted short rims and a sharp angle at the shoulder. Most of the sherds may come from similar globular vessels, though some of them are larger. Decoration may take the form of incised lines, waves or rouletting. It has so far been found only at the monastic sites of Whitby, Jarrow and Monkwearmouth in contexts between 650 and 850.

Ipswich-type ware is found in Northumbria in two fabrics, pimply and sandy. This is partly a matter of the degree of firing – the pimply ware fired to a higher temperature and the sandy ware less highly fired – but the pimply ware does also have more grit inclusions. No complete profiles are known, but the rims are similar to the typical Ipswich-type cooking-pots, though they tend to be on the large size, from 6 to 8 in in diameter. There is considerable variation in rim form, from simple vertical or slightly flared necks, to quite complex moulding and thumbing on the outsides. It has so far only been recognized from the monastic sites of Jarrow and Monkwearmouth and from under the castle at Newcastle (fig. 7.9, 2–3).

The other three types of middle Saxon pottery from Northumbria made on a slow wheel are not as yet sufficiently numerous, or well defined, to describe in detail. They are (1) at Jarrow, Monkwearmouth and Hartlepool a hard well-fired oxidized gritty ware, (2) a reduced gritty ware, and, at West Whelpington, a globular cooking-pot with typical uneven Ipswich-type girth grooves, a feature which does not seem to occur on the Whitby-type vessels, and (3) early Otley type ware, from Otley only, a hard well-fired pimply

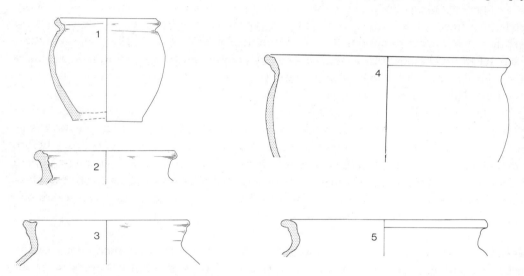

Figure 7.9 Middle Saxon northern wares (scale ¼):
1. Whitby ware, Whitby; 2. Ipswich ware, Jarrow; 3. Ipswich ware, Newcastle; 4. and 5. Otley-type ware, Otley

grey fabric (fig. 7.9, 4–5). The rim form (fig. 7.9, 5) with its developed moulded rim is closely comparable with the Jarrow, Monkwearmouth and Newcastle shapes (fig. 7.9, 2–3).

Too little is as yet known of these five recently recognized fabrics to say much about the origins or the date range within the period 650–850. At Whitby there were about equal amounts (only a sample was kept and it may consequently not be typical) of handmade and pottery made on a slow wheel. As the material was not stratified it is not possible to tell if the two types were contemporary or succeeded each other. At Jarrow and Monkwearmouth, on the other hand, almost all the pottery from stratified Anglo-Saxon levels was made on a slow wheel, but all these levels may be late in the history of the monasteries, especially as much of the Ipswich-type ware in particular seems quite developed in form.

The origin of these northern groups is at present hard to determine. Clearly there are close parallels with East Anglian Ipswich ware, but it could be argued that this is coincidence. Most of the forms, especially of the cooking-pots, are basic handmade Anglo-Saxon shapes, which derive their form from the use of the slow wheel and from firing to a high temperature in a proper kiln. It is, therefore, equally possible to argue for links between East Anglia and Northumbria or to suggest separate contacts across the North Sea. Only when we have a larger corpus of material and some firm early dating will it be possible to draw sound conclusions. But either way the old simple picture of primary developments in East Anglia has to be modified considerably. The presence of these early wheel-made wares in Northumbria makes it even more surprising that Kent – the nearest part of England to the Continent and an area which apparently was in very close contact with the Frankish areas in the early Anglo-Saxon period – did not produce wheel-made pottery in the middle Saxon period.[80] All the examples found may be regarded as imports,[81] and they do not seem to have had any effect at all on local pottery manufacture, which remained rough and handmade until the Norman Conquest.

II. HANDMADE

Maxey-type ware (fig. 7.10)

When I made my last survey of middle Saxon pottery in 1959 the distribution map showed a complete blank for Lincolnshire,[82] since no pottery from that county could be assigned to this period. Since then, mainly due to fieldwork by Rex and Eleanor Russell in the north and Hilary Healey in the south of the county, the picture is filling out and it is possible to assign a major group of pottery to the period 650–850. The recognition of middle Saxon pottery made on a slow wheel over a great deal of Northumbria might imply that similar wares would appear in Lincolnshire, to make a solid belt of good-quality pottery along the eastern seaboard. In fact there seems to be a genuine discontinuity between the Welland and the Humber, in which area only handmade pottery was made until the ninth century.

The first evidence for this came in 1960 with Addyman's excavation at Maxey, then in Northamptonshire.[83] This site produced three groups of handmade pottery one of which (Group III) is most distinctive – its rough shelly fabric clearly coil-built (fig. 7.10, 1) into a series of medium sized flat-bottomed bucket- or barrel-shaped pots with flat or slightly frilled rims. These are very reminiscent of Iron Age forms, but the site was Anglo-Saxon, as was shown by other associated finds. This was most satisfactorily confirmed by a thermoluminescent dating of the pottery to 780 and 830 with a standard deviation of ± 15 per cent.[84] The similarity of Anglo-Saxon and Iron Age handmade pottery has been a problem for many years, and on several occasions Anglo-Saxon pottery has been published as Iron Age.[85] There is little doubt that this difficulty, as well as lack of excavation and fieldwork in many areas, resulted in the apparent dearth of Anglo-Saxon domestic sites, a dearth which has been corrected over recent years. But at some sites, if there is sufficient material, it is possible to distinguish even small sherds between the two periods.[86]

Excavations at Normanby-le-Wold, Lincs., in 1968 and 1969 produced large quantities of this shelly fabric, with many of the same shapes: in particular a series of upright pierced lugs (fig. 7.10, 3).[87] Fieldwork has since produced similar wares from ten sites scattered over most of Lincolnshire,[88] and since 1970 still more sites have been located.

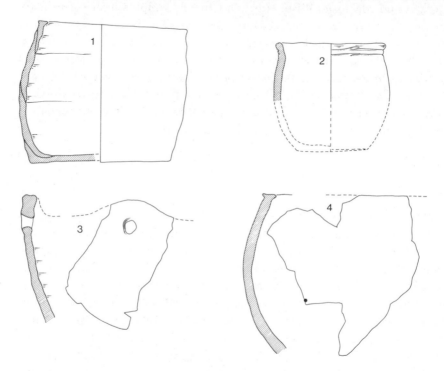

Figure 7.10   Middle Saxon Maxey-type ware (scale $\frac{1}{4}$):
1. Maxey, Northants.; 2., 3. and 4. Normanby-le-Wold, Lincs.

It can now be regarded as the type pottery of the middle Saxon period in Lincolnshire. Surprise has been expressed that there is no Ipswich ware at Maxey, while there are large quantities at Castor only seven miles away.[89] We have, however, seen (p. 303) that there may be special reasons for Ipswich ware and Frankish imports at the Castor monastic site, especially as it is so cut off from the main Ipswich distribution.

The Maxey pottery provided important evidence for methods of manufacture, and Addyman has demonstrated that coils were added to a flat basal pad. The outer surfaces had been carefully finished while still in a wet state, to hide the coarse shell filling which seems to have been fresh and not fossil.[90]

Other handmade middle Saxon pottery (fig. 7.11)

In 1959, except for the Ipswich-ware sites in East Anglia, less than a dozen sites were known from the whole country from which handmade middle Saxon pottery could be identified.[91] This was partly because of a lack of excavated or collected material, but also because of the confusion between Iron Age and Anglo-Saxon pottery. Now, besides the great increase of sites found in Lincolnshire, middle Saxon pottery has been identified in most areas and more is coming to light all the time; though it is still, in many areas, not possible to date it accurately.

In the London area excavations at Northolt, Middx., have shown that in the eighth and ninth centuries there were four basic fabrics:[92] *(a)* grass-tempered; *(b)* sandy; *(c)* rough gritty with large protruding grits; and *(d)* shelly. The sherds are too fragmentary to determine many basic shapes, but similar assemblages have been found at the Treasury site in Whitehall[93] and several other sites in the region (fig. 7.11, 6). In the south the best site is Hamwih (Southampton), where recent excavations have greatly increased the amount of stratified material (fig. 7.11, 9). Much work remains to be done here, but interim reports[94] show the range of coarse local wares. Surprisingly, grass-tempered wares hardly seem to be present: most of the vessels have the coarse gritty fabrics which are common along much of the south coast. The small cooking-pots with their simple rims and tall shape are also typical of the region. Petrological examination has demonstrated that the pottery was made in at least four different places.[95] At Portchester, Cunliffe has demonstrated that similar gritty forms appeared in the late eighth century (fig. 7.11, 10), apparently replacing the grass-tempered fabrics which had first appeared in the fifth century.[96] There is little evidence for grass-tempered wares in the late Saxon period, but the evidence from Old Windsor, where apparently it was still in use until the eleventh century,[97] remains an anomaly. The continuity of stamped decoration has also been demonstrated on local wares in Wessex, stimulated by French imports into Hamwih.[98]

In East Anglia it cannot be assumed that all middle Saxon pottery was wheel-made. Even on the coast itself there are handmade pots very similar to Ipswich ware (fig. 7.11, 7–8),[99] but whether they are contemporary with the Ipswich ware, or earlier, is obscure. In central Norfolk it may be suggested that in the eighth century handmade fabrics were still being made, but there was little pottery of any kind in the earliest levels at North Elmham, despite the strong evidence for intensive occupation.[100] The distinctive shelly types of Lincolnshire pottery have already been discussed.

In Northumbria pottery was mainly made on a slow wheel, but at Whitby there is as much handmade pottery.[101] This is all either sandy or gritty, and the shapes vary from small cooking-pots to bowls and conical cups (fig. 7.11, 2–5). As the pottery is unstratified it can only be dated between 650 and 850, but it is suggested that the more developed pots with carinated shoulders might be late.[102] Grass-tempered fabrics are known from several sites in the north, for example at Wharram Percy, but it is not certain how late they last. We therefore have a very limited picture of middle Saxon handmade wares in

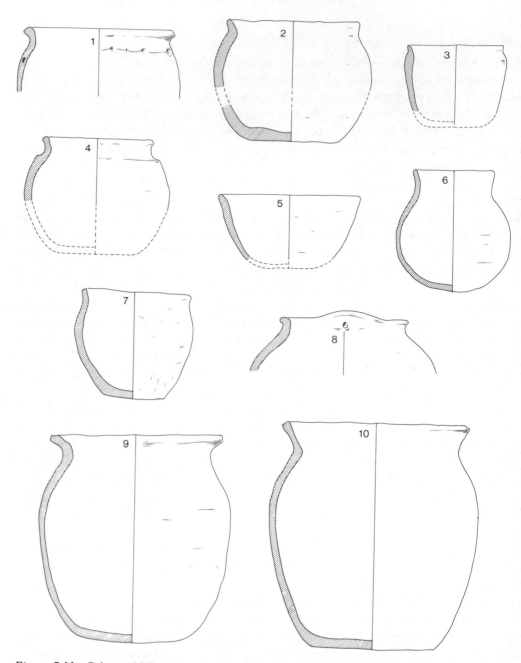

Figure 7.11 Other middle Saxon handmade wares (scale $\frac{1}{4}$):
1. Jarrow; 2.–5. Whitby; 6. Savoy, London; 7. and 8. Broomeswell, Suffolk; 9. Southampton; 10. Portchester

different parts of the country. Much of the rest of the material is too limited to be of much value,[103] but as more pottery of this period is recovered the picture will gradually build up. There has already been a great change since 1959, and material from any stratified sites may give a sequence in different areas (as did recent finds from Kirby Bellars, Leic.).[104]

III. IMPORTS (fig. 7.12)

The traditional picture of contact with the Continent shows good-quality industrial pottery being produced in the Rhineland at Mayen and Trier, with the centre of production gradually moving down the Rhine to Badorf in the eighth century.[105] But actual imports from this area in the middle Saxon period are rare. There are a few possible Mayen sherds from Whitby (fig. 7.12, 1)[106] but not so many as had been previously thought (see p. 304). Even these are now doubtful as a result of recent thin-sectioning.[107] Finds of Badorf ware (fig. 7.30, 1) are also not very numerous,[108] so from the pottery we have a picture of very spasmodic contact with the Rhineland in the eighth and early ninth centuries and certainly no evidence for extensive trade. Tating ware, with its applied tin-foil decoration, is also only found in small quantities on a few sites.[109]

I have suggested above that it is unlikely that actual potters came over from the Continent to establish the Ipswich and Whitby pottery industries. The cooking-pots could well have developed from local forms and are not closely comparable in shape with Rhenish forms.[110] The only firm link is the spouted pitcher, but this has a wide distribution over north-west Europe at this time and (with many examples imported) could well have been copied over here.

The situation at Hamwih is quite different from that in eastern England. Here the rough local wares continue throughout the period, but imported pottery is so common as to account for as much as half the material from some deposits, and 10 per cent of the whole assemblage. A great deal of work is required on this pottery, which has received preliminary study by Dunning[111] and Addyman from more recent excavations.[112] This is now at last in progress with an intensive study including petrological examination by Hodges. There is a range of buff and grey wares in a wide variety of cooking-pots (fig. 7.12, 2) and spouted pitchers, very similar in general form to the English groups. Various types of bowl similar to Roman mortaria (fig. 7.12, 3) are also found. Most of this is unlike the Rhenish material and clearly comes straight across the Channel from northern France. This is confirmed by the preliminary results of petrological examination which show an absence of typical Rhenish inclusions.[113] Unfortunately little work has been done on the French pottery, and this has served to emphasize the Rhenish material, which has been thoroughly studied. This has distorted the picture of survivals of Roman industry which must have existed in much of north-east France, with the Rhineland standing at its limits. The recent important excavations of a kiln site at Saran, near Orleans, by Chapelot,[114] produced wares and shapes very similar (fig. 7.13) to those found at Hamwih, suggesting a major pottery industry in the centre of the Merovingian kingdom responsible for much of this material imported into England. This only seems to come in large quantities to Hamwih and was not imported further inland. In addition it had very little effect on the local pottery which continued to be handmade and rough. This suggests that a lot of the pottery was actually imported and used by foreign merchants (as seems to have been the case at Dorestad) rather than traded to England for general sale and use. This is confirmed by the high proportion of table wares as opposed to storage vessels.

North French imports, in the form of spouted pitchers in a characteristic brown fabric with burnished black surfaces, are found in single examples along the south coast at Sandtun, Kent, up the east coast to Ipswich, Caister-on-Sea,[115] and North Elmham,[116]

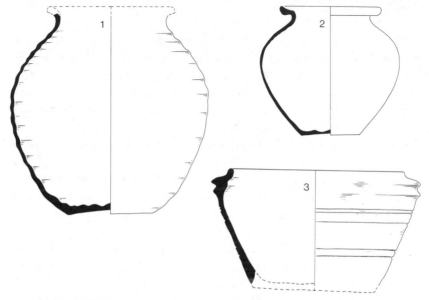

Figure 7.12   Middle Saxon imported wares (scale $\frac{1}{4}$):
1. Rhineland ware, Whitby; 2. and 3. French ware, Southampton

Norfolk, and up the Welland valley from the Wash to the monastic site of Castor, Northants.,[117] and at Bonhunt in north-west Essex, where there is also a considerable range of other French-type imported pottery.[118] Instead of the previously accepted picture of intense contact with the Rhineland and only slight contact with France it would be much more correct to envisage a general contact with the whole area of north-east France, where there must be many other kilns like Saran, extending as far as the Rhineland, the wares from which are only one part of the whole continuum of good-quality industrial pottery in Merovingian times between the Loire and the Rhine. An examination of the material from recent excavations, like Bonhunt, suggests that there may be a far greater number of imported sherds, mainly from French or Belgian sources, than has previously been recognized. Previously only the typical Rhenish oxidized Badorf-type wares were looked for and many reduced wares have not been recognized.

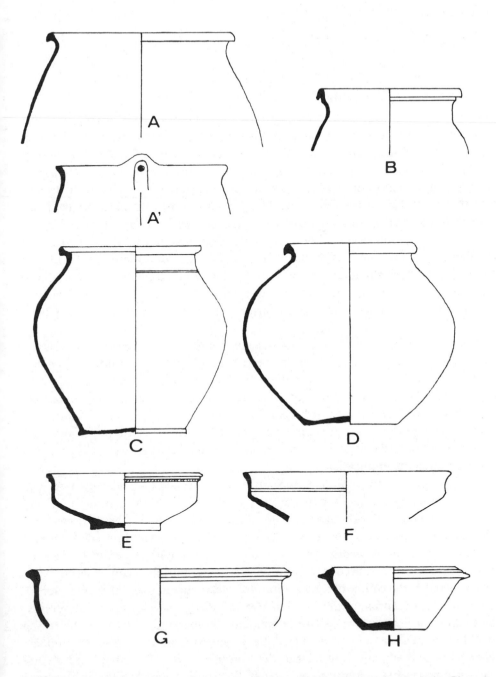

Figure 7.13 Ninth-century pottery from the Saran kiln, France (scale $\frac{1}{4}$) in Chapelot (1970) fig. 21

C. Saxo-Norman (850–1150)

I. WHEEL-THROWN

East Anglia

Thetford-type ware (figs 7.14–7.16)

Thetford-type ware is a hard well-fired grey sandy fabric and has a wide distribution over most of Norfolk and Suffolk.[119] It is wheel-thrown and fired in fully developed kilns (fig. 7.32, 5–6). In pre-Conquest times it seems to have been only made in towns (Ipswich, Norwich and Thetford), but in its later period it was also made at country sites (Langhale and Grimston). The most common form is a well-made cooking-pot of similar small shape and size to the middle Saxon Ipswich ware. The process of throwing on the wheel tends to raise the vessel to a taller and narrower form. The cooking-pots are thin-walled and globular, with either simple everted hollowed or rounded rims (fig. 7.14, 1–4); bases can be either sagging or flat and decoration takes the form of bands of rouletting (usually diamond notched) round the shoulder. Other forms include spouted pitchers, bowls, spiked and pedestal lamps, crucibles, barrel and globular costrels (fig. 7.15), and large storage vessels with multiple handles and applied strips (fig. 7.16), copied from relief-band amphorae.

The exact date range of all the Saxo-Norman wares is uncertain as there are few stratified sites which are absolutely dated in the crucial periods of the ninth and twelfth centuries. It is clear that for all the wares the main *floruit* was in the tenth and eleventh centuries, but we know less about their presence in ninth-century contexts or about the extent of their survival into the twelfth century. Likewise it has proved difficult, with a few certain exceptions, to distinguish a development in form or rim type; in the main the forms remained remarkably stable throughout the three hundred years they were in use. This has important implications.

I have suggested that the middle Saxon wares made on a slow wheel came into East Anglia and Northumbria as a result of increasing contact with the Continent in the second quarter of the seventh century, both as a result of trade and through Christian contacts. Pottery production remained remarkably constant for a further two hundred years with very few changes or improvements. Then at some point in the ninth century excellent-quality wheel-thrown pottery, fired in fully developed single-flue kilns with pedestals, suddenly appeared and in the course of the next hundred years spread over the whole country with the remarkable exception of the London area and Kent, as well as parts of Wessex, Devon and Cornwall, Lancashire, Westmorland and Cumberland. What was the reason for this sudden appearance of good-quality pottery, and why did it have so little impact on south-east England which was nearest to the Continent? We know that good-quality wheel-thrown pottery was being used at Jarrow, Wearmouth and Whitby in the third quarter of the ninth century before the Scandinavian invasions. From Ipswich we have reasonable evidence for the changeover from Ipswich ware to Thetford-type ware about

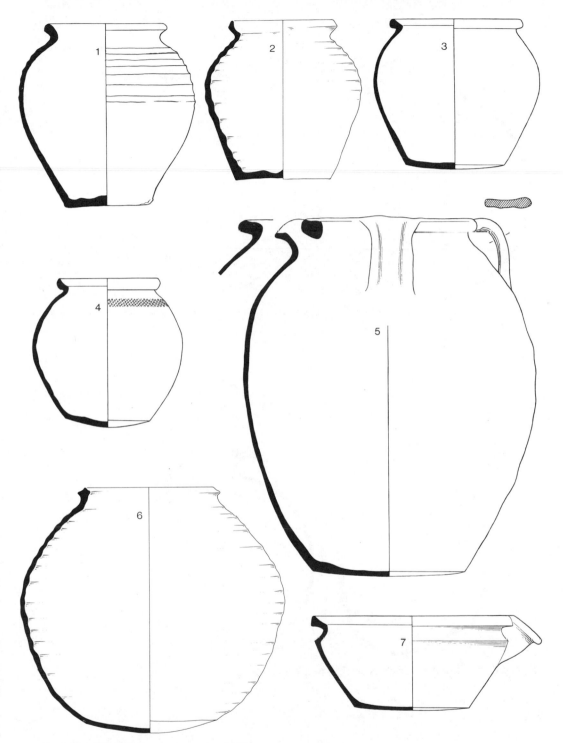

Figure 7.14   Thetford-type ware (scale ¼):
1. Carr Street, Ipswich; 2. and 6. Pottergate, Norwich; 3.–5. and 7. Thetford

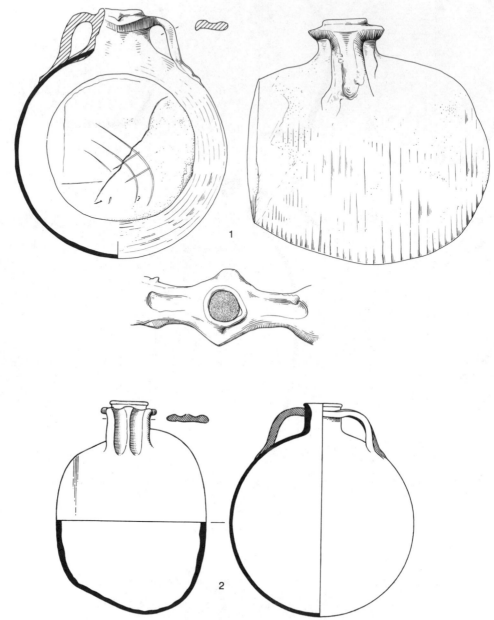

Figure 7.15 Thetford costrels from Thetford (scale ¼)

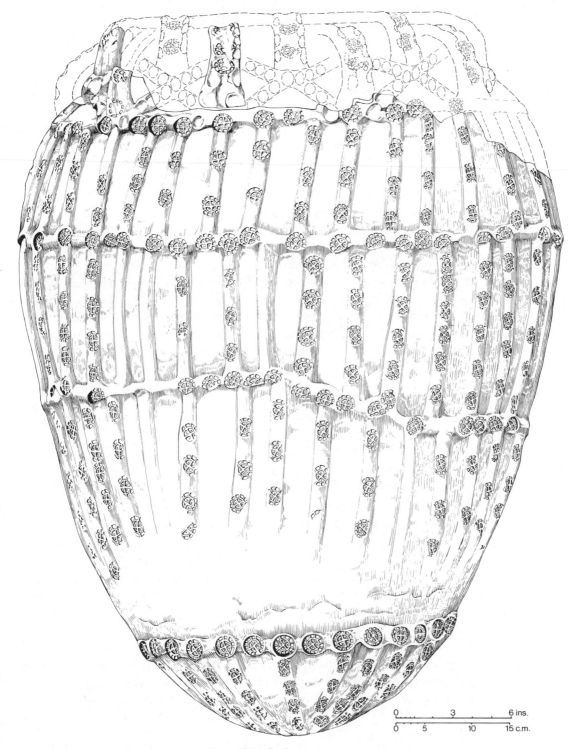

0   3   6 ins.
0   5   10   15 c.m.

Figure 7.16 Thetford storage jar from Thetford

the same time, although the dating evidence is not so certain as in the northern monasteries (where there is a clear break $c.$ 875). It is possible that St Neots-type ware and Stamford ware were also introduced before the Scandinavian invasions, but the evidence is ambiguous as it is not possible to distinguish between some deposits of 850–75 or 875–900. In any case it can be established that some of the Saxo-Norman wares were introduced before the Scandinavian raids and settlement. The sudden surge and spread of the Saxo-Norman wheel-thrown wares seems to have occurred during the last quarter of the ninth and the first quarter of the tenth century so that by this time most of the other twenty Saxo-Norman wares were established. This sudden spread seems to be linked with the Scandinavians and their trading activities, though it goes beyond the confines of the Danelaw and gathers even more momentum after the reconquest of the Danelaw, to which is dated ($c.$ 925) the pot with the Morley St Peter coin hoard.[120]

I have changed my ground in thinking that actual potters came to England to establish middle Saxon pottery made on a slow wheel, and it may also be necessary to change the idea that potters came to establish the Saxo-Norman pottery industry. The processes of change are very imperfectly understood, but there are now so many groups of Saxo-Norman pottery (with new ones being identified each year) that it is harder to imagine groups of immigrant potters coming over to set up the industry. All that is really required is the knowledge of the potters' wheel and an improvement in kiln techniques. Both of these are ideas which could be brought over by a single person and then, if the time was ripe (such as the sudden changes brought about by the Scandinavian invasion and settlement), these new ideas could spread rapidly. Again the new evidence from Northumbria has been important, for fine Whitby-type ware is almost identical to Whitby-type ware, but made on a fast wheel. It has been suggested that Thetford-type cooking-pots are based on Rhenish shapes, but in fact they are very unlike the cooking-pots of the Rhineland and are simply the small rough pagan Saxon cooking-pots that would naturally develop with the use of first the slow wheel, then the fast wheel.

The continuity of form of the Saxo-Norman wares from $c.$ 850 to 1150 shows a remarkable conservatism. In the medieval period we are realizing that most pottery types have a long life, but even so these never remain so stable over such a long period. I originally thought that this was due to the immigrant potter families imposing a monopoly and not being willing to change. This was the reason why when in the eleventh century 'early medieval pottery' (i.e. that made between 1000 and 1150) appeared simultaneously with the Saxo-Norman wares, there was very little overlap until fashion dictated the replacement of such fine well-made Saxo-Norman wares by the rough semi-handmade early medieval wares. We must look for other reasons for the twelfth-century collapse of the Saxo-Norman pottery industry over so much of England, but one reason may have been the presence of a larger number of kilns in the countryside and of less in the towns.

Ipswich-Thetford ware

Thetford-type ware was first made at Ipswich, where there was already a two-hundred-year tradition of pottery-production on an industrial scale. West's excavations in Cox Lane produced many pits in which Ipswich ware, Thetford ware and other types of pottery were mixed together at the period of the changeover from middle Saxon to late Saxon pottery.[121] There is no absolute dating, but it is clear that the change took place about the middle of the ninth century, when Badorf ware was still being imported and before Pingsdorf ware appeared. The exact date of the start of Pingsdorf potteries is at present under review,[122] but there is every reason to think that the changeover to wheel-thrown pottery in this country took place just before the Scandinavians arrived, and certainly before the period of Scandinavian settlement.

The first Ipswich kilns (found in 1928[123] in Carr Street) were not satisfactorily investigated, but two others (fig. 7.32, 2) were found nearby in Cox Lane in 1961.[124] I tried to place these in a typological sequence[125] together with the material from other features, but this hypothesis still has to be tested by stratified excavation in the town. The early cooking-pots seem to have had girth grooves, hollowed everted rims and rouletted bands, while the later pots had plain bodies with simple everted rolled rims. All the bases were flat, and most show traces of the wire with which they were cut from the wheel; a few sagging bases appear towards the end of the sequence. Magnetic dating suggested that the early Kiln IV might be of early tenth century date while Kiln I might be of late tenth-century date, with the later finds of eleventh-century date.

Norwich-Thetford ware

Thetford-type ware wasters were first found in Pottergate in the last century (fig. 7.14, 2),[126] but it was not until development in this area in 1963 that a further large group of wasters was excavated by the Norwich Museum.[127] Most of the pots made at the Ipswich kilns were cooking-pots, but at Norwich there was a much wider range, including bowls, cressets and storage vessels. The cooking-pots mainly had flat bases, hollowed everted rims and some rouletting – features which might suggest a tenth-century date. The kilns themselves have not yet been located, but may be just outside the *burh*, between it and the trading centre at Westwick.[128]

Thetford ware

The first kilns (fig. 7.32, 5) were found by Knocker in 1948,[129] others were found by Davison (fig. 7.32, 6) in 1964 and 1966.[130] Large quantities of Thetford-type ware were found in the extensive excavations carried out by both Knocker and Davison. A detailed survey of this material has not been published, but the constant digging over of the ground, leading to the incorporation of large quantities of earlier material in every new pit, has very much confused the attempts to work out a sequence of pottery types. Knocker had two main dating points, *(a)* that rouletted cooking-pots were early (as has been suggested at Ipswich), and *(b)* that sagging bases were early and flat bases late.[131] This is in marked contrast to Ipswich and Norwich where the flat bases are early. At Thetford as many as 80 per cent of the tenth-century cooking-pots had sagging bases while in the eleventh century

50 per cent were flat. There was never a complete change. This is of considerable interest as these sagging bases are more closely linked westwards with the nearby St Neots and Stamford groups than with the pottery from the kilns at Norwich and Ipswich.

Langhale-Thetford ware (fig. 7.17, 1–6)

All late Saxon kilns so far found in East Anglia have been in towns and it seems that most tenth- and eleventh-century wares were made in towns, but two Thetford-type ware kilns have been found in the country – at Grimston and at Langhale. The last named kiln (fig. 7.32, 8) was excavated by Wade in 1970,[132] and was very similar to those found at Thetford. The products included squat cooking-pots with everted rims, flat bases (showing wire removal marks from the wheel); spouted pitchers with thumbed neck bands; 'ginger jars' and straight-sided bowls with hammer-headed rims. Decoration takes the unusual form of incised waves. The date is uncertain, but to judge from some of the developed forms it probably should be placed in the eleventh or twelfth century.

Grimston-Thetford ware (fig. 7.17, 7–11)

At Grimston a simple single-flue kiln was found in 1963 (fig. 7.32, 4) and further excavation in 1964 produced quantities of pottery but no more kilns.[133] Grimston ware has a light to dark grey core, often with reddish-brown to grey surfaces. It is coarse and sandy with some large grits. The cooking-pots are of normal shape but are on the large size, 15–20 cm in diameter. There are shallow and deep bowls with out-turned rims, a few lids and costrels, spouted pitchers (in a finer ware) and ornate storage vessels (in a coarse ware). There is no absolute dating, but from the forms, including the large cooking-pots and the complex storage vessels, a date in the second half of the eleventh or the first half of the twelfth century may be suggested. Analysis of the material shows a remarkably high proportion of bowls over all other types.[134] The term Grimston-Thetford ware has been used, but there are many links and parallels with Torksey (as for example in the bowls with their out-turned flanges, compare fig. 7.17, 7–9, with fig. 7.21, 2–3) so that there must be close links north-westwards as well as eastwards.

St Neots-type ware (fig. 7.18)

Sandy Thetford-type wares hardly penetrate west of the Wash, except for the export of spouted pitchers and storage vessels. In this area, centred on Cambridgeshire, Huntingdonshire and Bedfordshire, shelly wares predominate. St Neots-type ware is a fairly rough fabric tempered with crushed shell. It is low-fired, usually with a black core and oxidized surfaces which vary in colour between brown, red and purple.[135] These frequent colour variations suggest uneven firing in a clamp or primitive kiln lacking complete air control. No kiln sites have been found, indicating that it was perhaps produced on a local scale unlike the highly organized Thetford-ware industry. This was the first Saxo-Norman ware to be recognized when Tebbutt excavated at St Neots between 1929 and 1932.[136]

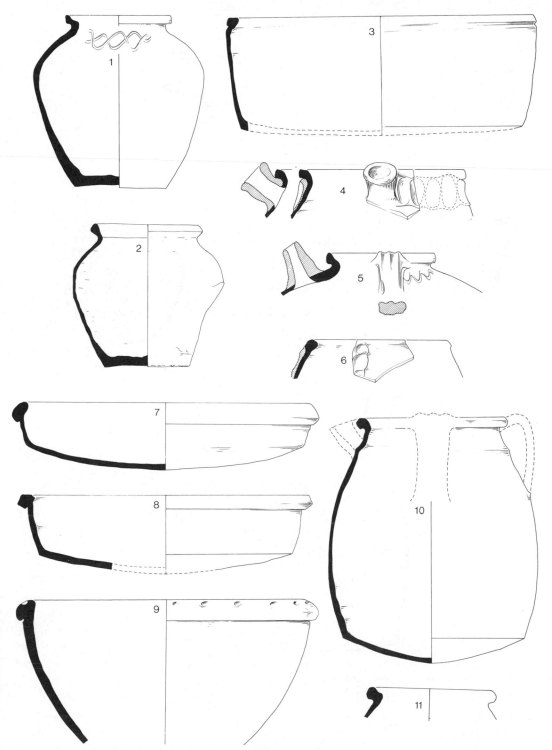

Figure 7.17 Langhale- and Grimston-Thetford wares (scale ¼):
1.–6. Langhale; 7.–11. Grimston

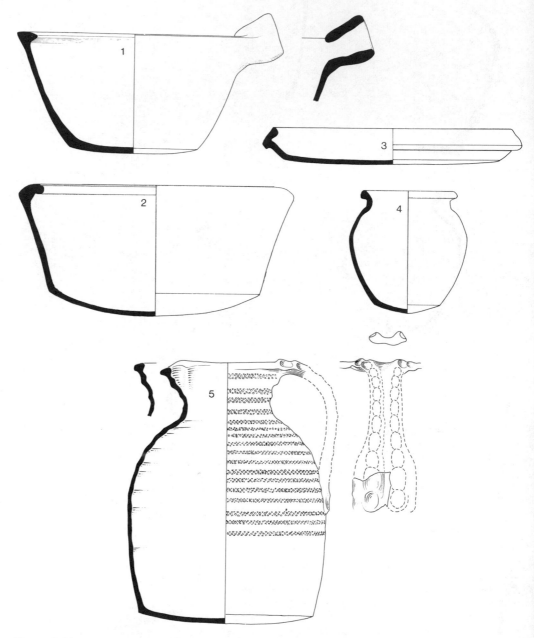

Figure 7.18 St Neots-type ware (scale ¼):
1. and 2. Bedford; 3. and 4. St Neots; 5. Ely

In recent years more important evidence has been obtained by Addyman from excavations both at St Neots and at other late Saxon settlement sites in the area.[137]

The forms are similar to those of Thetford ware, with wheel-thrown small cooking-pots, almost always, however, with sagging bases. The bowls are distinctive, with inturned or hammer-headed flanges. Lamps and storage vessels occur late in the series, but there are no spouted pitchers. Presumably the ware was too friable to be an efficient liquid container, for which purpose the St Neots area had to import either Stamford or Thetford ware pitchers.

Again there is no absolute dating and no site in the main area is datable before 900; it was, however, exported to Thetford to appear in late ninth-century levels. The earliest dated examples come from early tenth-century levels in Cambridge,[138] and it was clearly in full production during the tenth century.

There is no clear end date to St Neots-type ware for, unlike Thetford-type ware which was replaced by a quite different product, it gradually merged into medieval shapes and rougher sandy fabrics during the twelfth century. This is the developed St Neots-type ware and a large part of the original published material belongs to this later type of the twelfth century onwards.[139] St Neots-type ware must be seen as part of a belt of shelly wares extending up into Lincolnshire, Yorkshire and Durham. The basic fabric seems to have developed out of Maxey-type wares, with the addition of the new wheel-thrown shapes. But, although the centre was further south, shelly St Neots-type wares are found in Saxo-Norman contexts throughout Lincolnshire, but never in as large a proportion as the various other local wares. These shelly wares are found throughout most of the medieval period; it is, therefore, difficult to date it from sherds alone. The distinctive early small cooking-pots and the bowls are usually easy to recognize, so also is the soft soapy feel of the earlier examples, since in later periods there was an increased tempering of sand.

Lincolnshire

Stamford-type ware (figs 7.19 and 7.20)

The best-known Stamford-type ware is the very fine, almost untempered, off-white fabric which was used for the glazed spouted pitchers and bowls. This was traded widely over most of England, but in the Stamford area itself there is the more typical coarse ware, a sandy off-white or pinkish fabric, from which cooking-pots were made.[140] The fabric contains fossils from the estuarine clays which are found in Stamford and which stretch through central Lincolnshire.[141] Stamford ware is finely potted on a fast wheel and fired in a developed single-flue kiln, an example of which was found in 1968 by Christine Mahany in Wharf Road, Stamford (fig. 7.32, 7). Typically few of the products of this kiln, mainly unglazed coarse wares, have been found in excavations in the town or elsewhere.[142]

Stamford cooking-pots have the normal Saxo-Norman form: the bowls are usually deep, with everted flanges often thumbed on top and with applied vertical thumbed strips;

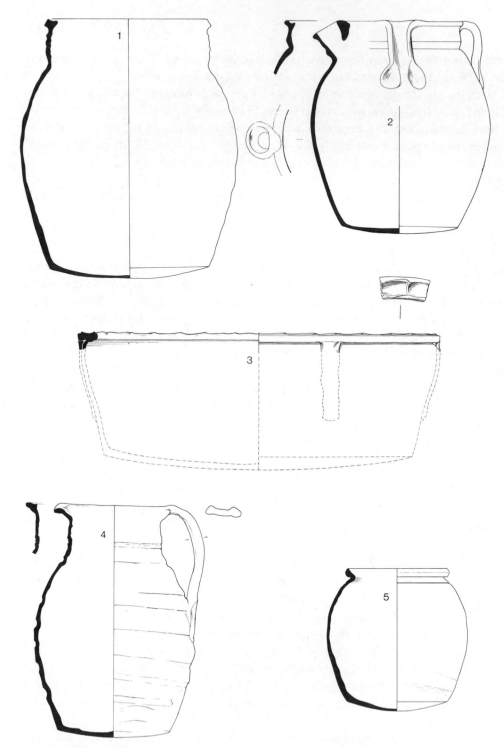

Figure 7.19 Stamford-type ware (scale ¼):
1. Leicester; 2. and 3. Cambridge; 4. Broad Street, Leicester; 5. Normanton, Lincs.

other forms include cressets, crucibles and ring vases. The most distinctive type is the spouted pitcher, typical of other groups but in this case usually glazed. The glazes on Stamford ware appear pale green, pale yellow or orange, depending on the fabric.

There is still no early dating of Stamford ware in its area of manufacture. A sequence of stratified levels in Stamford itself from the recent excavations by Christine Mahany provides no absolute dating. Again, therefore, its starting date in the ninth century depends on evidence from Thetford, where it was imported by 900. At the other end of the time scale, jugs appear during the later eleventh century – the first reappearance in England

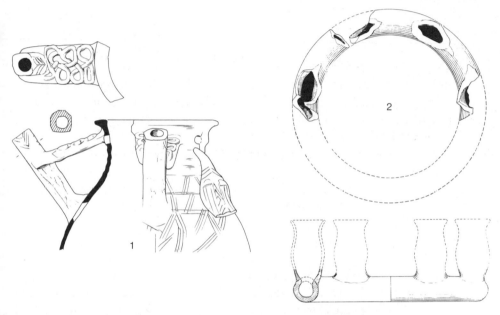

Figure 7.20   Less usual Stamford-type wave forms (scale $\frac{1}{4}$):
1. London; 2. Glaston, Rutland

of the proper jug with a lip and long handle since Roman times. Stamford-type ware is found on many castle sites of the late eleventh and early twelfth centuries, but by the time of the Anarchy, developed Stamford ware, with a mottled green glaze, was coming in. Recent excavation however, at Lyveden, Northants., suggests that the ordinary Stamford ware continued parallel with the developed ware at least through the rest of the twelfth century.[143] This is important as it shows that there was no break in the pottery industry at Stamford and that fine wares continued to be made until evidence of the industry suddenly disappears in the middle of the thirteenth century. But before it does disappear, we have hints of the later highly decorated medieval pottery, such as the fine top of a tubular spouted jug from London with applied birds (fig. 7.20, 1). It is therefore possible that it was out of the Stamford industry (with a move to Nottingham) that the full recovery of medieval pottery after the partial collapse in the eleventh and twelfth centuries was achieved.

Stamford-type ware has the widest distribution of any of the Saxo-Norman wares, since the glazed spouted pitchers and jugs were much sought after and are found in at least small quantities in almost every county of England with examples as far away as Hen Domen, Montgomeryshire,[144] and Dublin.[145] The main centre for Stamford ware, and the area where the coarse cooking-pots are found, is in a limited area round Stamford itself. Published distribution maps[146] are misleading as they do not differentiate large groups from single finds.

Decorated Stamford ware

There are two other varieties of Stamford-type ware: first, a distinctive type with complex applied strip decoration of which large quantities have been found by Hebditch in Leicester.[147] This has not been found in Stamford itself, which might suggest another kiln source (but judging from the fact that none of the Wharf Road kiln products is found elsewhere this does not necessarily follow). This type seems to be late in date, but the full range has not yet been published.

Northern Stamford ware is the second variant. This is a coarser variety of Stamford ware and is found in Lincolnshire and south Yorkshire, where the fine Stamford-type wares are also found. This often contains some sand tempering but is best recognized by the tendency for the core to be slightly reduced, giving the whole fabric and the glaze a dark tone.[148] It is thought that there might be a kiln for this type somewhere in Lincolnshire, or even south Yorkshire where the belt of estuarine clays extends.

The origins of glaze have recently been fully discussed,[149] so it is sufficient to say here that until the exact starting date of glazed Stamford ware is determined this argument cannot be resolved. It seems, however, that Stamford ware is much earlier than Andenne ware and other glazed wares in the Low Countries and that, if there are links with northern Europe, these are more likely to be with France, though the idea of glazing may have come direct from the Mediterranean.

Torksey-type ware (fig. 7.21, 1–3)

Seven kilns have been found at Torksey over the past twenty years. The characteristic fabric (as found in Kiln 1) is sandy, but rougher than Thetford-type ware because of the addition of quartz fragments, and is usually fired with black outer surfaces and a partly oxidized reddish-brown core or margins.[150]

Other kilns produced a more usual grey fabric. Kiln 1 was a fully developed pedestal kiln (fig. 7.32, 10), but Kiln 2 was of simple construction (fig. 7.32, 3). The products from all the kilns include a full range of cooking-pots, bowls with a characteristic down-turned outer-thumbed flange, cressets, ring vases, storage vessels and a few spouted pitchers. It is hard to put the seven kilns in sequence. Magnetic dating suggests an early eleventh-century date for Kiln 1, and Barley has suggested that Kiln 2 may be of late tenth-century date, on the evidence of rouletting and bases. Unfortunately this is a circular argument in view of the differing sequences at Thetford, Norwich and Ipswich. My own suggested typology at Ipswich[151] was based on very slender evidence, so it would be unwise to try and place the seven Torksey kilns in sequence.

There is as yet no evidence for a date earlier than the mid to late tenth century for Torksey ware, but on general grounds (if one accepts the spread of late Saxon wares by

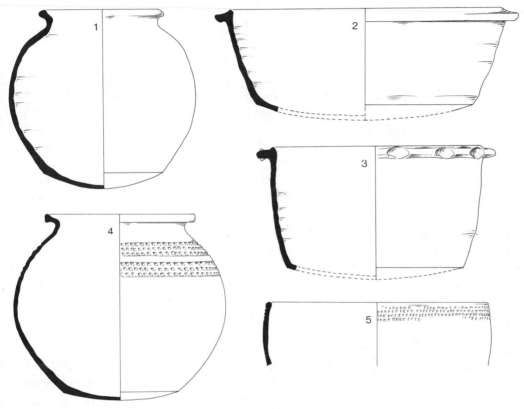

Figure 7.21   Torksey and Lincoln-type wares (scale ¼):
1.–3. Torksey; 4.–5. Lincoln

the Scandinavians) a starting date at least in the early tenth century, if not earlier, might be suggested. The products from Kiln 1, or a similar kiln, were certainly still in use in the late eleventh and early twelfth centuries, so an end date in general terms of *c.* 1150, as with the other types, seems probable.

Torksey ware, particularly the distinctive Kiln 1 fabric, has a wide distribution over Lincolnshire, up the Trent to Nottinghamshire and north down the Trent, to the Humber and into Yorkshire, for distances of more than thirty miles overland.[152] This distribution may suggest an origin from Northumbria up the Trent rather than influence from Thetford.

Lincoln-type ware G (fig. 7.21, 4–5)
Amongst the pottery excavated from Flaxengate, Lincoln, in 1948, was a large group of pottery unlike any of the other late Saxon fabrics.[153] This was a hard, sandy fabric, similar to Thetford-type ware but fired to a higher temperature giving it a metallic finish; its colouring varied from dark grey to orange. The finds included a second or possible waster, suggesting the kiln was not far away, and many of the sherds seemed overfired. The forms are globular cooking-pots and straight-sided bowls, but the rouletting is coarse. Coppack, in a study of the Flaxengate material, assigns this (fabric G) to the eleventh century so here again we have no evidence for early dating. So far this fabric has not been identified outside Lincoln itself, but the storage vessel from the technical college[154] is possibly in the same ware, and other recent finds from the city may be of this fabric. It is hoped that current recent finds from the city may be of this fabric. It is hoped that current excavations in Flaxengate on stratified Saxo-Norman levels[155] will enable a sequence of fabrics and types to be worked out.

Shelly ware
Shelly fabric in the St Neots tradition is common over most of Lincolnshire. In view of its likely independent development from the shelly middle Saxon Maxey-type wares, and the fact that a kiln source has now at last been found in recent excavations in Lincoln,[156] it is preferable to use the term shelly ware rather than St Neots-type ware. On most sites where St Neots shelly pottery is found, Stamford and Torksey-type wares are found in similar quantities, but this is mainly unstratified material. Recent excavations at Goltho, where for the first time in central Lincolnshire stratified levels of the tenth and eleventh centuries are being found, suggest that shelly wares predominated in central and northern Lincolnshire, with the Stamford and Torksey-type wares as imports.[157]

Thetford-type ware
In addition to the obvious Torksey-type wares and the Lincoln-type ware G, there is a wide distribution of grey sandy fabrics in Lincolnshire which cannot be assigned to production centres. Until these are located (perhaps at sites like Caistor), they should be termed Thetford-type ware as long as it is clear this does not necessarily mean that they are traded from Norfolk.

Splashed ware
This is now being identified from Lincoln and other sites to an extent such as to suggest it may have been made there as well as at Nottingham. The dating is still uncertain and there is so far no proof of it earlier than the eleventh century.

North-east
York-type ware (fig. 7.22, 1–3)
York-type ware is a very hard fabric with much grit included which gives a pimply appearance. The firing is uneven, often with marked contrasts and a very wide colour range

(though light colours are rare); some vessels are oxidized. It was well made on a fast wheel and fired to a high temperature in a developed kiln, but the colour variations suggest a failure to control the air intake. No kiln sites have been found. The forms are similar to other types, with the typical small cooking-pots with sagging bases and bowls with everted, rouletted flanges. No storage vessels have yet been identified. There is only one example so far recognized of a spouted pitcher.[158]

York-type ware was first identified at Hungate, York, where it was termed fabric A.[159] Further finds were then made at other sites in York and the term York-type ware was introduced.[160] But only 21 per cent of the Saxo-Norman sherds in York are York-type.[161] At Hungate, York-type ware was found in tenth-century levels, but we do not

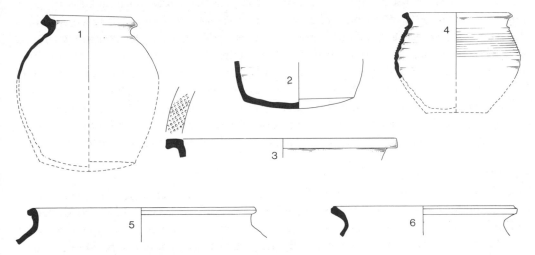

Figure 7.22   York-, fine Whitby- and Otley-type wares (scale $\frac{1}{4}$):
1.–3. York-type ware, 1. and 2. from Hungate, York, 3. from Jarrow; 4. fine Whitby-type ware from Whitby; 5. and 6. Otley-type ware from Otley

know when it first appeared. Recent excavations at Lloyds Bank, York, suggest on this site that York-type ware is late.[162] York-type ware has now been found on other sites in Yorkshire both in the West and East Ridings. Excavations at Pontefract produced important evidence for the latest date of York-type ware,[163] since it was found in the earliest levels of the priory in the late eleventh and early twelfth centuries, but not at Kirkstall Abbey, founded in the middle of the twelfth century. This fits in with the general date throughout the country for the end of Saxo-Norman pottery and its replacement by medieval types *c.* 1150.

At York, however, as at Stamford, there was no break or collapse in the pottery industry and pottery continued to be made on an industrial scale. York-type ware developed directly into northern pimply ware during the twelfth century, with very little variation in fabric save for a change into larger medieval shapes and the development of squared rims. At York,[164] and other sites in Yorkshire,[165] other Saxo-Norman fabrics have been found, but we do not know when they were introduced. Shelly wares have a wide distribution over southern Yorkshire, but represent only 4 per cent of Saxo-Norman wares in York. There is little doubt that most of these were made locally, as in Lincolnshire, rather than imported from the St Neots area (where in any case there is no evidence for mass-production). Stamford ware and Torksey ware, on the other hand, were genuinely traded, presumably up the Trent to the Humber, but were then distributed quite far inland, as for example to Wharram Percy on the Wolds. It is not clear whether northern Stamford ware was made in Lincolnshire, Yorkshire or both. Seventeen per cent of the Saxo-Norman sherds in York are Stamford-type ware. The origin of northern Thetford-type ware is unknown, possible sources include Lincoln itself, north Lincolnshire or kilns in south Yorkshire. Jean le Patourel has recently shown that 48 per cent of the Saxo-Norman sherds in York are either Torksey or northern Thetford-type ware,[166] which may suggest a local source of manufacture (at least for the Thetford-type ware), so the term northern Thetford-type ware is suggested. As there is better evidence for an early appearance of late Saxon wares in York, it is likely that this was started by separate influences from those in East Anglia, especially as there is no early evidence from Lincolnshire, which seems to have been a pottery backwater in the middle Saxon period. The trading to Yorkshire of Stamford and Torksey wares was possibly a result of Scandinavian influence.

Fine Whitby-type ware (fig. 7.22, 4)
Fine Whitby-type ware has a sandy fabric with micaceous inclusions. It is exactly the same as middle Saxon Whitby-type ware but is thrown on a fast wheel and therefore is thinner and better made. No kiln sites are yet known in the north, but this type must have been kiln-fired. The fabric is usually grey or black, but not very highly fired as it is still sandy to the touch. The only form so far known is a squat cooking-pot with simple, squared, everted rim and an apparently flat base, in contrast to the sagging base of York-type ware.

To the north fine Whitby-type ware has so far only been found on the three monastic sites of Jarrow, Monkwearmouth[167] and Whitby,[168] and the possible monastic site at Hartlepool. At the two former sites there are only small sherds and only at Whitby do larger sherds make some reconstruction of profiles possible. All three sites were abandoned after the Scandinavian plunder in the third quarter of the ninth century, so while at Whitby where the sherds are unstratified the fine Whitby-type ware could date from the reoccupation of the eleventh century, the stratified sherds from Jarrow and Monkwearmouth must date before 875.[169] Thus in Northumbria late Saxon wheel-thrown wares were in production before the Scandinavians arrived to settle, and support the thesis that the same was true at least at Ipswich; although the main spread of Saxo-Norman wares seems to have taken place in the last quarter of the ninth and the first part of the tenth century, as a result of Scandinavian trade contacts.

A new fabric recently identified[170] (particularly at Wharram Percy, in the East Riding) is a fine light or dark grey sandy micaceous ware with black outer surface, very similar to fine Whitby ware. It may be that this will prove to be the locally produced Saxo-Norman wheel-thrown fabric in the East Riding, but evidence is required from other sites. (Other finds from Wharram Percy include all the other fabrics found in York – northern Thetford-type ware, shelly ware, Stamford-type ware, Torksey-type ware and York-type ware.) Meanwhile it should be classed with the Whitby and other northern micaceous wares as fine Whitby-type ware.

Late Otley-type ware

The archbishop's manor at Otley[171] also contained five Saxo-Norman rims of both large and small cooking-pots made on a fast wheel in a fabric clearly derived from early Otley-type ware (fig. 7.22, 5–6).

Also at Jarrow and Monkwearmouth, but presumably datable to the reoccupation in the later eleventh century, were sherds of York-type ware, northern Stamford ware, and shelly ware and northern Thetford-type ware.[172] The Stamford-type ware is almost certainly imported, as probably is the York-type ware, which is so similar to the York material. We do not know whether the northern Thetford-type ware was made at local centres.

Splashed ware is now being identified in York but so far not in contexts earlier than the eleventh century.

All late Saxon kilns in East Anglia and the midlands seem to have been in towns and, as we have seen (p. 320), it is not until the later eleventh century that rural pottery industries develop. This presents a problem so far as the fine Whitby-type ware is concerned, for there were no towns north of York at this period. It may be that the industry was connected with the monasteries, but far more excavation is required as the monastic concentration may be coincidental. The isolated Wolds village of Wharram Percy has examples of all the main groups of middle and late Saxon pottery so one might expect most domestic sites in northern Northumbria to produce a similar material; so far, however, such sites have not been located, save for hints at West Whelpington.[173] There is a similar problem in Wessex (p. 338).

Midlands

Leicester ware (fig. 7.23, 1)

In 1964 the stoke-pit of a kiln containing wasters was found by Hebditch in Southgate Street, Leicester.[174] The fabric is hard, sandy and grey, with a number of quartz inclusions which give it a surface harsh to the touch. Unfortunately the rest of the kiln could not be excavated, but we have here another type of well-made wheel-thrown pottery fired in a developed kiln. The cooking-pots are of the usual shape but have a rather more sagging profile than usual. The rims are either simply everted or have distinctive external mouldings. The only other finds are strap handles from pitchers or storage vessels and a hand-made dish which may not be typical. The bases are flat, being similar to Kiln II at Torksey,[175] and there is knife-trimming and wire marks of removal from the wheel. The closest comparable fabric, however, is Lincoln-type ware G.

There is no dating evidence for this kiln and Leicester ware does not seem to have been found in excavated deposits in Leicester. But the fabric and shapes are so similar to Roman wares that it is possible that it has not been recognized: it does not seem to appear in any quantity in twelfth-century groups, so in general terms this ware should date to the tenth and eleventh centuries.

Northampton ware (fig. 7.23, 2–3)

In 1971 a number of wasters were found by Williams at the junction of St Mary's Street and Horsemarket, Northampton.[176] This comprised a wide range of hard fired fabrics in a sandy ware, varying in colour from grey to brown; the forms are mainly the usual types of cooking-pots. As in Leicester this pottery does not seem to be known from other sites in the town or in the county. Some of the cooking-pots are, however, very much like coarse Stamford ware or the so-called variations of Thetford ware. It may well be, therefore, that some of these isolated examples come from Northampton.[177]

Nottingham splashed ware

In 1957 and 1961 excavations of the Saxon ditch in Bridlesmith Gate, Nottingham,[178] produced quantities of a distinctive brown sandy ware, often with splashes of glaze dusted on. These included typical late Saxon cooking-pot forms. It was not clear whether this pottery was found in the ditch supposedly filled in soon after the Conquest when the town was extended, or in pits dug into the ditch. Recent excavations by Young have not fully clarified the early date for splashed ware, and for the moment, therefore, there is no firm evidence for it being earlier than the eleventh century; but the large quantities of pottery now being excavated in Nottingham may produce some answers. That this was not simply a Nottingham phenomenon is shown by recent finds from Lincoln and York, but again in eleventh-century contexts at the earliest.

Derby-type ware (fig. 7.23, 5–7)

Kilns, or distinctive Saxo-Norman wares, have been found at four of the five Scandinavian burhs, Stamford, Lincoln, Leicester and Nottingham. One would therefore expect kilns in Derby. Unfortunately no excavation has been carried out in the Scandinavian town, the limits of which are not even known. Excavation at the village of Barton Blount, a few miles to the west, have produced a sandy brown ware with typical Saxo-Norman shaped cooking-pots,[179] which may have been made in Derby.

Chester-type ware (fig. 7.23, 4)

The first hint that good-quality, industrially produced late Saxon pottery was not only made in eastern England came in 1950 with the finding in the Chester hoard of a typical late Saxon type of cooking-pot.[180] The hoard dated the pot to *c*. 970. The pot is of a hard, sandy brown fabric, the rim distinctive with an upright neck and out-turned flange; the latter feature is in marked contrast to all the previous groups with their simple rounded everted or hollowed rims. There is rouletting on the neck and the base sags (fig. 7.23, 4). Other examples of Chester-type ware were soon recognized in Chester,[181] all having

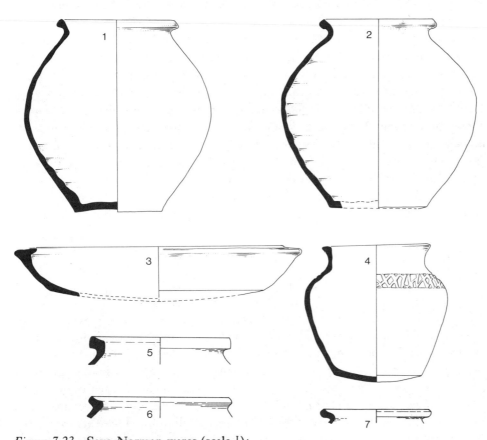

Figure 7.23   Saxo-Norman wares (scale $\frac{1}{4}$):
1. Leicester ware (Southgate Street); 2. and 3. Northampton ware; 4. Chester-type ware; 5.– 7. Derby-type ware (Barton Blount)

the characteristic oxidization, flanged rim and often with rouletting on the shoulder. During the early 1960s it was thought that Chester-type ware was an out-lier from the main eastern groups.[182] In 1967, however, excavations in Hereford[183] produced Chester-type ware associated with the Saxon defences. In 1968 further excavations brought to light large quantities of stratified Chester-type ware between periods 5 and 6.[184] It is assumed that these sherds lie over the defences constructed by Æthelflæd in 913–15 and under the rebuilding in the early eleventh century, which included the addition of a stone wall.[185]

There is similar, but less certain, Æthelflædan evidence from Chester.[186] This gives a date for Chester-type ware in the tenth century, at the same time as most of the eastern groups, and indeed earlier than many of them. The Chester hoard confirms this date.

Other sherds of Chester-type ware have been found at Tamworth, but not in stratified contexts.[187] It was by no means confined to towns, as is shown by finds at Ellesmere Port, north of Chester,[188] and at Barton Blount, Derbyshire.[189] We have, therefore, a very wide distribution from Chester to Hereford, covering most of Mercia, with a uniform late Saxon oxidized fabric. It may be assumed that most tenth- and eleventh-century occupation sites in the west midlands will contain sherds of Chester-type ware; the lack of wheel-thrown pottery in Mercia is thus more apparent than real. Previously the boundary of these good-quality wares was thought to coincide broadly with the boundary of the Danelaw,[190] but this theory is no longer tenable. The two groups described below – Winchester-type ware and Portchester-type ware – likewise break out of the Danish strait-jacket and raise the problem of just how much the Scandinavians had to do with the spread of late Saxon wheel-thrown pottery. The final spreading period may possibly date to the second quarter of the tenth century (after the reconquest of the Danelaw). The ensuing increased trade and growth of towns would greatly have enhanced the prospects of these industrialized potteries by providing ready and increasing markets in distant parts.

South

Winchester-type ware (figs 7.24 and 7.25)
From 1961 onwards excavations by Biddle in Winchester have produced increasing quantities of a hard, well-fired, sandy brown fabric glazed with a yellowish red to green or a dark olive-green, mottled with orange.[191] The colour changes are due to varying firing conditions in the kiln and a 3–4 per cent iron content. There are still very few complete profiles, but the main bulk of finds (82 per cent) comes from various types of spouted pitchers, often with a simple rounded, everted rim. A particular feature is the number of decorated examples with applied notched strips, applied strips with circle, and cross stamps. The strips often form scroll patterns and are flanked by incised dimples. There are other patterns of incised triangular zones and waves, as well as stamps and different types of rouletting[192] (simple square, rectangular, trellis or complex).

Other forms are poorly represented, but there are cups, bowls, globular bottles (imitating leather),[193] small gourd-like pots and sprinklers, lids, handled jars, tall narrow jugs and tripod pitchers. The full date range is still being worked out, but the main *floruit* was in the eleventh century. It is not clear how far back into the tenth century it extends, but it had largely gone out of use soon after 1100, when it was replaced by tripod pitchers in rougher fabrics. Winchester-type ware has now been found in a wide belt across southern England from Gloucester, Bristol and Bath and eastwards to London. In Wessex, sherds are found at Southampton, Portchester and Bishops Waltham. The kiln source is not known.

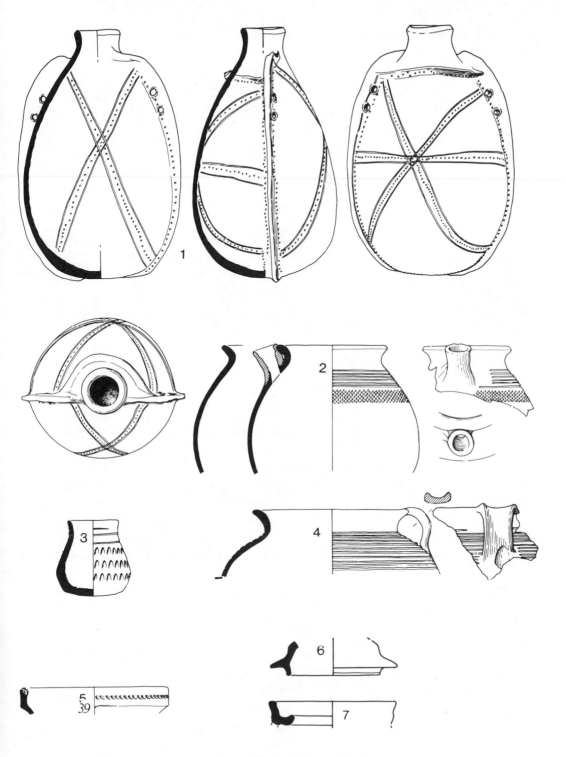

Figure 7.24 Winchester-type ware (forms) (scale ¼) from Winchester

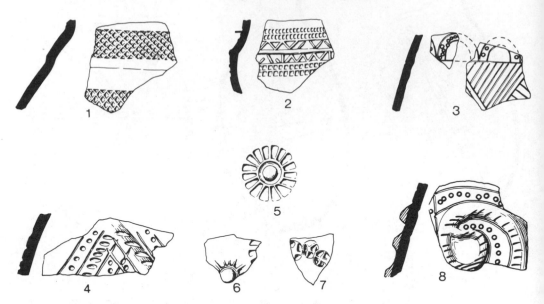

Figure 7.25   Winchester-type ware (motifs) (scale ½) from Winchester

Portchester-type ware (fig. 7.26)

Excavations at Portchester by Cunliffe have produced another group of wheel-thrown pottery in tenth-century levels.[194] This is a hard sandy fabric, tempered with finely crushed flint grit and fired to a reddish or brown surface. The cooking-pots are unusual as they are wide, squat, medieval forms, quite unlike any of the other typical Saxo-Norman groups; the rims are everted with various forms of moulding, the body is covered with girth grooves and the bases are sagging, some decorated with a coarse roulette. The other main form is a shallow dish with either a simple or complex rim.

The distribution is centred on Portchester and seems to extend westwards as far as the River Meon (it is not found at Southampton) and eastwards as far as Bishops Waltham.

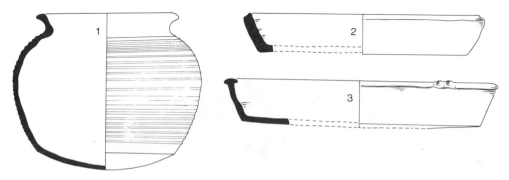

Figure 7.26   Portchester-type ware (scale ¼) from Portchester

Only a few sherds have been found in Chichester and hardly any as far north as Winchester. The kiln source is not known.

Michelmersh ware (fig. 7.27)

The third Wessex type of wheel-thrown pottery was made at Michelmersh in the New Forest,[195] west of Winchester between Stockbridge and Romsey; the actual kiln site has recently been located on high ground overlooking the Test valley. It comprises a single flue kiln with a raised floor (fig. 7.32, 9) which produced smooth buff, reddish-brown, sandy and grey to black fabrics. The forms include pitchers with spouts applied at the shoulder, complex mouldings to the rim and cordons on the shoulder; decoration is either rouletting or applied curvilinear stamped strips. Forms include cooking-pots with everted rims, upright and sloping dishes, and all the bases are sagging. Examples have been found

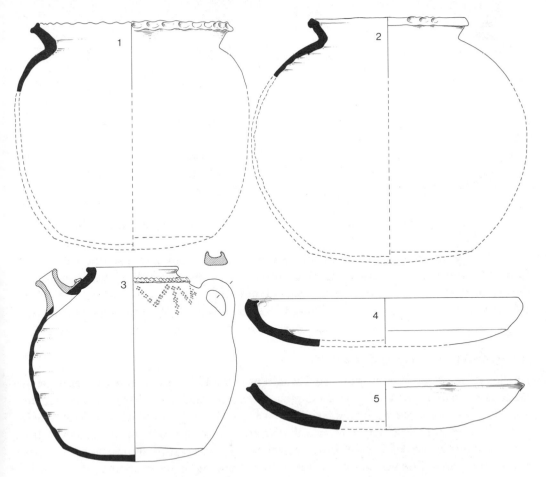

Figure 7.27   Michelmersh ware (scale ¼) from Michelmersh

at Hamwih and Portchester in tenth- and eleventh-century contexts but the full distribution has not yet been determined. Here in Wessex, therefore, we have a rural kiln in contrast to the urban kilns of eastern England.

Cheddar-type ware (fig. 7.28)
The fourth wheel-thrown group in the south was made in Somerset and is best known and dated from excavations by Rahtz at Cheddar.[196] It comprises three types: E is a thick red-buff to dark grey fabric, with a black or dark grey burnished pitted surface. It is wheel-thrown and tempered with quartz, but most of the grits have burnt out to give a corky appearance; it was associated at Cheddar with a coin of *c*. 945. EE is a harder fired fabric with more grits giving a pimply surface, which develops in the later tenth century; B is a black or dark grey thick coarse fabric, slightly soapy, with limestone grits (fig. 7.28).

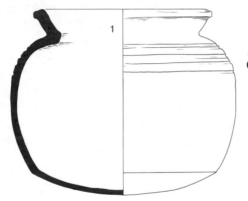

Figure 7.28   Cheddar-type ware (scale $\frac{1}{4}$) from Cheddar

Cooking-pots are globular with a thickened rim, horizontal grooves on the shoulder and a sagging base.

These four groups of wheel-thrown wares, widely spaced across southern England, show how the Saxo-Norman wheel-thrown influences spread south of the main area to the north of the Thames. Handmade wares continued as the main product in all these areas, as they had at Hamwih in the middle Saxon period. How this was possible in view of the close contacts with France is a problem to which no answer may yet be given.

II. HANDMADE POTTERY (fig. 7.29)

In 1959 it was thought that future work would produce a large number of groups of handmade late Saxon pottery in those areas outside eastern England, where the good-quality wheel-thrown wares were not being made.[197] In fact, the widespread discoveries of wheel-thrown wares in general terms leave only the area south of the Thames, and even here there are four groups of Saxo-Norman wheel-thrown wares superimposed on the coarse handmade wares. The best pottery sequence was found at Portchester where Cunliffe has demonstrated one of the most complete culture sequences of any Anglo-Saxon site in the country.[198] Here the middle Saxon handmade, narrow, tall cooking-pots made in a gritty fabric continue until the tenth and eleventh centuries when they were replaced by Portchester wheel-thrown ware and the early medieval cooking-pots in large squat medieval shapes. The same sequence and change is seen in the later levels at Hamwih and the earliest levels in the newly founded Southampton. The pattern is widespread along the south coast and may also be seen at Winchester, Chichester (fig. 7.29, 1),[199] Medmerry,[200] and other sites as far as Kent.[201]

To the west, these late Saxon gritty wares are found west of the New Forest at Milton.[202] But beyond this point little is known about late Saxon pottery until one comes to Somerset and the excavations by Philip Rahtz at Cheddar.[203] In this area the

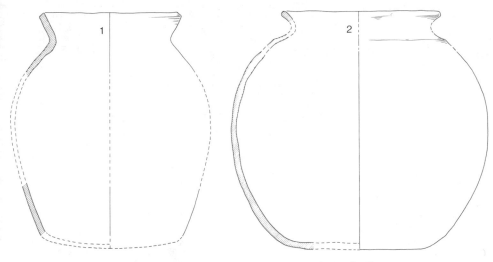

Figure 7.29 Late Saxon handmade wares from the south (scale $\frac{1}{4}$):
1. Chichester; 2. Hatton Rock, Warks.

middle Saxon period seems to have been largely aceramic, as is shown by levels at Beckery, Pagans Hill, Glastonbury Tor, Glastonbury Abbey and Cheddar palace itself (where the first pottery does not appear until between 850 and 930). This dearth of pottery was not because of lack of occupation, as is shown by the many thousands of animal bones, four coins and various other objects. The Cheddar sherds include gritty and grass-tempered fabrics, which must be dated later than the comparative material in Wessex. By the middle of the tenth century better-quality wheel-thrown pottery (see p. 338) was being made, while in the eleventh century the pottery seems to degenerate again. At both Bristol and Gloucester small, rough cooking-pots have been identified in recent excavations; these should be tenth or eleventh century in date, but there is no absolute dating. The distribution is limited northwards by the spread of Chester-type ware and the other Saxo-Norman wheel-thrown groups.

III. IMPORTS (fig. 7.30)

In the late Saxon period the general picture built up over the past twenty years has again emphasized the contacts with the Rhineland – mainly centred on the shift of the main pottery industry from Badorf to Pingsdorf,[204] and the setting up of secondary centres at Brunssum.[205] For this period the number of Rhenish imports is much increased as eighteen sites are now known which have produced Pingsdorf-type ware and only nine sites producing imports of Badorf ware.[206] It has recently been shown that there is considerable

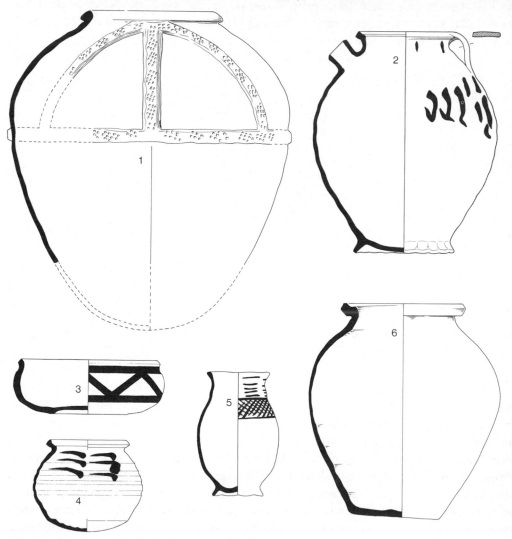

Figure 7.30   Late Saxon imported ware (scale ¼):
1. Badorf, Rhineland; 2., 4. and 5. Pingsdorf, Rhineland; 3. Beauvais, France; 6. Northern France

doubt as to whether Pingsdorf ware, with its characteristic decoration of red slip, was made before 900.[207] All the early red-painted wares, however, such as the Zelzate costrel, dated by coins to 870–80,[208] have straight painted lines rather than the comma-type early Pingsdorf decoration (fig. 7.30, 4). Recent work at Hamwih has produced similar red-painted sherds in late eighth- and early ninth-century contexts.[209] The Cricklade bowl (fig. 7.30, 3), associated with the early eleventh-century *burh* wall, is not only not a Rhenish shape but also has this straight-line decoration.[210] The situation is, however, confused by the Pingsdorf return to straight-line decoration in the twelfth century (fig. 7.30, 5).

The origin of this pottery must again be sought in France, where recent work at Beauvais by Chami and Leman has produced important evidence for early red-painted wares of just this type.[211] Here there are good stratified levels but no absolute dating before the tenth century, depending on the much-debated date of the *Basse Œuvre*. There is no doubt that this pottery goes back into the ninth century and the evidence from Hamwih suggests further that red-painted pottery was being made in France before 800, a good hundred years before Pingsdorf ware started.

The same changes in our ideas on glaze have recently become necessary as a result of the realization that the glazed wares of the Low Countries have been dated too early by a circular argument with Stamford ware.[212] While excavations by de Bouard at Doué La Fontaine, Maine et Loire, have demonstrated that glazed pottery was in full production in Anjou at least by 900.[213] At Beauvais, Leman also has early painted sherds with spots of glaze, showing that they were fired in the same kilns at the same time. So here again we see the primacy of France in the introduction of new pottery techniques: indeed as far as glaze is concerned the Rhineland was always peripheral, as glaze was never used there between Roman and late medieval times. Whatever the real origins of red paint and glaze, and however they came up from the Mediterranean (and this is hotly debated by continental scholars),[214] there is no doubt that central and northern France was much more at the centre of pottery developments than was the Rhineland, which was in many ways just as peripheral as England and the Low Countries.

The accepted pattern of intense Rhenish influence in the Anglo-Saxon period, replaced by contact with Normandy after 1066, must be modified into a much more general picture of influences and imports coming from the whole area of northern France and the Rhineland. With the import of E ware up the west coast from western France in the middle Saxon period[215] and the large quantities of Normandy pottery imported into Dublin in the eleventh century,[216] one must consider the whole as a linked pattern of influences and trade from western France to the Rhineland. A map recently published by Hill[217] shows in a most striking way how many more contacts there were with France than with the Rhineland in this period. The primacy of the Rhineland has held sway too long, but the French themselves have been much to blame for this bias as they have done little significant work on their pottery. That this has been changed so fundamentally in the past five years by the work of a handful of people shows that in another ten years the whole picture may fill out and we should be able to understand these events very much more clearly. The recent discovery of a kiln site at Sorrus,[218] near to the trading centre of Quentovic and producing reduced wares of a type known from a number of sites along the south English coast[219] (fig. 7.30, 6), is a further breakthrough in our knowledge of these wares.

There are many puzzling features. If we accept these French contacts why was it in southern England (in the area opposite France) that handmade wares continue, with few exceptions, through the Anglo-Saxon period? What is the link between the Anjou glazed wares, Winchester ware and Stamford ware? The flanged rims of the Chester-type ware are characteristically French and are closely paralleled at Beauvais. In addition, at Hereford the tenth-century levels containing Chester-type ware also included a number of French imports. Why were these influences felt so much more strongly in Mercia than Wessex? Only time and more intensive work both in England and France will answer these problems and many others which have been raised by recent work. The other fundamental question which has barely been tackled is to what extent pottery was traded as pottery, or traded as containers. The actual trading centres themselves where alien merchants lived is a different problem. There is little doubt that most of the imports were connected with the wine trade. The amphorae were containers, but the pitchers and beakers were a by-product, possibly being sold with the wine so that at table Rhenish wine might be served in Pingsdorf spouted pitchers (fig. 7.30, 2) and drunk out of Pingsdorf beakers (fig. 7.30, 5).

IV. EARLY MEDIEVAL OVERLAP (fig. 7.31)

From the dating evidence presented for over thirty groups of Saxo-Norman pottery now identified, although it is difficult to substantiate each individual case, it seems likely that these good-quality wheel-thrown, industrially produced wares suddenly went out of production in the middle of the twelfth century and were replaced by rougher, semi-handmade wares, often only fired in clamp kilns. The early medieval wares had developed c. A.D. 1000 out of a series of late Saxon handmade local groups. It was at this time that the large, wide, squat medieval cooking-pot came into common use. For over a century these two quite different wares appear to have coexisted side by side with very little effect on each other. Of all the wheel-thrown wares only Portchester-type ware and Cheddar-type ware took over these new shapes. Other potteries continued making the tall, narrow Saxon type of cooking-pot and were hardly affected by the new developments. This is hardly surprising in view of the poor quality of the new wares, which must have been very porous and impractical. It is surprising, however, that the pottery industry should almost completely collapse in the twelfth century. That the collapse was not altogether complete is shown at York and Stamford, where good-quality industrially produced wares continued with Saxo-Norman fabrics. Over most of the country, however, there was a steady decline in pottery manufacture, which did not pick up again until the revival of the industry in the second half of the thirteenth century. This was not simply a technological factor since there was also a fundamental change in shapes, from the small individual

Saxon cooking-pots and spouted pitchers which had been in use throughout the whole period to the larger medieval type of cooking-pot and the jug (almost unknown since Roman times). This must presuppose a major change in cooking habits from the individual preparation of small quantities of food to the mass cooking of stews for the whole family. The uses to which pots were put is a much neglected study.

These early medieval wares were first discussed in general by Dunning.[220] I expanded the discussion dealing with wares in East Anglia,[221] the London area[222] and Wessex.[223] But the first major study of a group of early medieval pottery was the discussion by Jope of the material from Oxford, sealed underneath the castle mound before 1070.[224] In East Anglia, the London area and Wessex, there are various similar types of pottery – all basically of a hard thin sandy fabric, the cooking-pots being globular with sagging bases. They were built by hand with the addition of a simple everted rim, which was separately applied; the whole was trued up on a slow wheel. The characteristic sloping marks of this joining operation is one of the distinctive features of early medieval wares (fig. 7.31). At Oxford

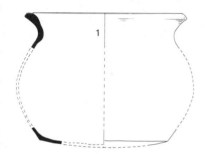

Figure 7.31   Early medieval ware made on a slow wheel (scale $\frac{1}{4}$) from Norwich

there are a few (about 5 per cent) sandy wares, but the main bulk are of a much coarser and thicker fabric. Dating, as with the Saxo-Norman wares, is a problem, but there is no doubt that all these wares were in use well before the Conquest and a date of about 1000 (but not necessarily in all areas) seems likely. This demonstrates very clearly that the Norman Conquest had no impact at all on pottery manufacture in England. The fundamental changes from Saxon to medieval pottery were already well advanced in the early eleventh century and were very much a local Anglo-Saxon development. The end of Saxo-Norman pottery occurred a century after the Conquest and can hardly be attributed to the Normans. The only Norman influence is a single group of pottery with collared rims in the French style from Castle Neroche, Somerset.[225] Finally the supposed Norman swing in trade from the emphasis on the Rhineland to Normandy[226] can no longer be sustained.

Kilns

Fig. 7.32 shows the range of different types of kiln found in the Anglo-Saxon period. These are all of the same basic form with a single flue, though the ovens may be round

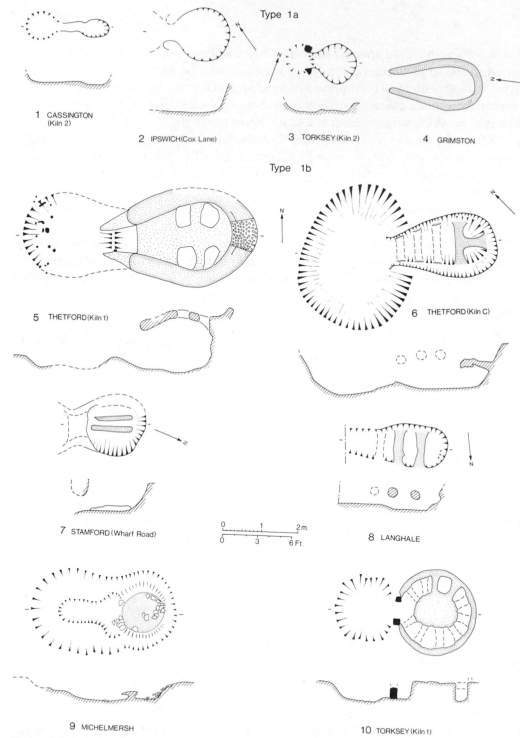

Figure 7.32 Anglo-Saxon kiln plans and sections:
1. Cassington; 2. kiln 4, Ipswich; 3. kiln 2, Torksey; 4. Grimston; 5. kiln 1, Thetford; 6. Thetford; 7. Stamford; 8. Langhale; 9. Michelmersh; 10. kiln 1, Torksey

or oval and there may or may not be internal structures. Musty has divided kilns into four types[227] and all these fall into his Type 1. There are no double-flued kilns (Type 2) or multi-flue kilns (Type 3) in the Anglo-Saxon period. His Type 4 is rectangular and linked with tile kilns. A single example of this type has recently been found at Silver Street, Lincoln, producing shelly wares.[228] All the known continental kilns of the period in the Rhineland are single-flue Type 1, but the kiln complex at Saran[229] includes a rectangular example as well as the more usual round examples.

The evidence for kilns in the early Saxon period is very difficult to assess. From examination of the pottery most of it was made in clamps where there was poor air and temperature control. The only possible kiln is that at Cassington (fine 7.32, 1).[230] In the middle Saxon period we unfortunately only have poor evidence from Ipswich,[231] but it is assumed that they were simple Type 1 kilns, though they must have been efficient to produce the highly fired uniformly reduced Ipswich-type wares.

In the Saxo-Norman period both forms of Type 1 kiln are known. In A there is no internal structure (fig. 7.32, 1–4) while in B there is a raised oven floor (fig. 7.32, 5–10). There is no apparent development and the kilns vary considerably in size as can be seen from fig. 7.32 where they are all drawn on the same scale. There is no set pattern for alignment to take advantage of prevailing wind, and recent kiln experiments have shown that this is not necessary. In the Type 1A kilns the oven pit is on the same level as the stoking pit. The two pits are joined by the stokepit arch or flue and the whole kiln is dug into the ground. They can be round as at Ipswich (fig. 7.32, 2) or oval as at Grimston (fig. 7.32, 4).[232] Torksey kiln was round and very small (fig. 7.32, 3).[233] Type 1B kilns are the most common. In these the oven floor is raised. This may spring from the oven walls in the form of parallel bars without a central support, as at Thetford[234] and Langhale[235] (fig. 7.32, 5, 6, 8) or be supported on a central pedestal with radiating supports as at Torksey kiln 1 (fig. 7.32, 10).[236] At Stamford there were two parallel pedestals (fig. 7.32, 7).[237]

How these kilns worked is a subject of much debate, but a recent series of experiments has begun to give some of the answers.[238] In the middle and late Saxon periods all the kilns in East Anglia and the Midlands seem to have been in urban centres with rural kilns coming into use in the eleventh century (at Langhale and Grimston, Norfolk). In Northumbria no kilns have so far been located and there is the problem of the lack of urban centres north of York. In Wessex the only kiln so far located is a rural one at Michelmersh. There is no documentary evidence for Anglo-Saxon kilns to help us. At the time of Domesday we simply have, possibly by chance, the three well-known references to potters at Bladon, Oxon., Hasfield, Glos. and Westbury, Wilts. Le Patourel[239] has shown that these entries suggest several potters with a sizeable industry in progress. It is therefore remarkable that this is an area where there is no evidence for large-scale production of wheel-thrown pottery and a local handmade production would be expected. Place-name evidence, such as Potterton, Yorks. WR, which is so-called in Domesday, provides further hints for rural kilns, but the second half of the eleventh century is just the time that rural pottery industries seem to be established so this does not necessarily prove the position in the ninth or tenth century. This is an important subject which requires further consideration as more kilns are discovered, especially in areas outside East Anglia.[240]

Notes

1 Hurst (1955–7).
2 Hurst and West (1956).
3 Hurst (1969).
4 I am indebted to K. Wade for this suggestion: Wade (1972).
5 H. E. J. le Patourel is working on a classification and typology based on finds from Yorkshire.
6 Dunning *et al.* (1959).
7 Hurst (1955) 45, fig. 1.
8 Dunning *et al.* (1959) 70, fig. 39.
9 Dunning (1956) 220, fig. 48.
10 Hurst (1955), (1956) and (1957).
11 Dunning *et al.* (1959).
12 Myres (1956).
13 Myres (1969) 66–7.
14 Myres (1956) 36, fig. 9.
15 Rodwell (1970).
16 Myres (1968) 223–4.
17 Hawkes and Dunning (1961).
18 Hawkes and Dunning (1961).
19 Myres (1968) 224–5.
20 Myres (1969) 77–80.
21 West (1969a) 11–13, fig. 9, nos 1–5.
22 Information P. Crummy.
23 Information P. Drury.
24 Jones (1969) 147.
25 Cook (1969).
26 Hurst in Beresford and Hurst (1971) 147.
27 Leeds (1923), (1927) and (1947).
28 West (1969a) 11 and (1969b).
29 Arthur and Jope (1962–3).
30 Jones *et al.* (1969) 147.
31 Wilson (1970) 293.
32 Myres (1969).
33 Ibid., 25–9 and figs. 1–12.
34 Ibid., 29–61 and figs 13–51.
35 Hurst and West (1956) 41, fig. 5, and Dunning *et al.* (1959) 22, fig. 5.
36 Dunning *et al.* (1959) 35, fig. 11, and Cunliffe (1974).
37 Myres (1969).
38 Myres (1970).
39 Myres (1969) 132–6.
40 Hope-Taylor (1949).
41 Pearce (1966).
42 Evison (1974).
43 Hurst and West (1956).
44 Hurst in Dunning *et al.* (1959) 14.
45 Hurst and West (1957) 29.
46 West (1963) 246–7.
47 Hurst and West (1957) 32.
48 Smedley and Owles (1963).
49 West (1963) 248.
50 West (1963) 246–8.
51 Hurst in Dunning *et al.* (1959) 17.
52 Hurst (1965) 216–17 and Hurst in Dunning *et al.* (1959) 16.
53 Green (1963) 27–9.
54 Information R. L. S. Bruce-Mitford.
55 Knocker (1956) 78–9.
56 West (1969b) 18.
57 Bruce-Mitford (1968) 47–51.
58 Hurst in Myres and Green (1973) 240–42.
59 Information J. B. Whitwell: a knife-trimmed base in the Lincoln Museum.
60 West (1963) 235, fig. 31.
61 West (1963) 236.
62 Excavations 1971–2 by K. Wade.
63 Information J. P. Wild.
64 Addyman and Whitwell (1970).
65 Hurst in Richardson (1959) 76 and Stead (1959) 426.
66 Hurst and West (1957) 30.
67 Hurst in Dunning *et al.* (1959) 28.
68 Dunning in Hurst and West (1957) 40.
69 Dunning in Peers and Radford (1943) 75–82.
70 Hurst in Dunning *et al.* (1959) 26–7.
71 Cramp (1969).
72 Dunning in Peers and Radford (1943) 81, fig. 26, nos 24–6, 29 and 31.
73 Ibid., 81, fig. 26, nos 27–8 and 30.
74 Hurst in Cramp (1969) 60, n. 75.
75 Cramp (1969) 24–5.
76 Harbottle (1966) 119, no. 102.
77 Jarrett (1970) 267–8, no. 81.
78 Le Patourel (1972).
79 Le Patourel (1973).

80 Frere (1970) 108–9.
81 Hurst in Dunning *et al.* (1959) 19–21.
82 Hurst in Dunning *et al.* (1959) 30, fig. 8.
83 Addyman (1964).
84 Addyman and Whitwell (1970) 100.
85 Clarke (1937); for reassessment, see Clarke (1957) 407.
86 Jones (1969) 149.
87 Addyman and Whitwell (1970) 96–8, fig. 2, nos 1–13.
88 Ibid., 97, fig. 1.
89 Addyman (1964) 49.
90 Ibid., 50–51.
91 Hurst in Dunning *et al.* (1959) 30, fig. 8.
92 Hurst (1961) 255–6.
93 Information H. M. J. Green.
94 Addyman and Hill (1969) 91–3.
95 Information R. Hodges.
96 Cunliffe (1970) 72–3.
97 Hurst in Dunning *et al.* (1959), 21.
98 Cunliffe (1974).
99 Hurst and West (1956) 37–9.
100 Wade in Wade-Martins (1970) 71–4.
101 Dunning in Peers and Radford (1943) 76–9.
102 Hurst in Dunning *et al.* (1959) 26.
103 Ibid., 19–28.
104 Hurst (1967–8).
105 Dunning (1956).
106 Dunning in Peers and Radford (1943) 80–82.
107 Information M. Fulford.
108 Dunning *et al.* (1959) 52–4.
109 Ibid. 52, with the addition of North Elmham, Norfolk, London Treasury site and further finds from Hamwih.
110 Tischler (1952).
111 Dunning *et al.* (1959) 50–52.
112 Addyman and Hill (1969) 91–3.
113 Information R. Hodges.
114 Chapelot (1970).
115 Hurst in Dunning *et al.* (1959) 18 and 21.
116 Information P. Wade-Martins.
117 Information J. P. Wild.
118 Information K. Wade.
119 Hurst (1956).
120 Clarke and Dolley (1958).
121 West (1963).
122 Hurst (1969).
123 Hurst (1956).
124 Smedley and Owles (1963).
125 Hurst in Smedley and Owles (1963) 214–18.
126 Jope (1952) 307–8, fig. 9 nos. 2–3.
127 Wilson and Hurst (1965) 173.
128 Hurst (1963).
129 Knocker and Hughes (1950) 43–4.
130 Davison (1967a) 192–4.
131 Information G. M. Knocker.
132 Wilson and Moorhouse (1971) 129.
133 Clarke (1970).
134 Wade (1972).
135 Hurst (1955).
136 Lethbridge and Tebbutt (1933).
137 Addyman (1965) and (1969).
138 Information J. Alexander.
139 Hurst (1955) 59, fig. 4.
140 Hurst (1957).
141 Swinnerton in Dunning (1956) 230.
142 Wilson and Hurst (1969) 234–5, fig. 70.
143 Information S. Moorhouse.
144 Information P. A. Barker.
145 Information B. Ó Ríordáin.
146 Dunning *et al.* (1959) 49, fig. 17.
147 Hurst (1957) 56, fig. 4, no. 1.
148 Hurst (1957) 39.
149 Hurst (1969).
150 Barley (1964).
151 Hurst in Smedley and Owles (1963).
152 E.g. to Wharram Percy.
153 Coppack (1973).
154 Hurst (1956) 60.
155 Excavations by Christine Colyer for the Lincoln Trust.
156 Excavations by J. Wacher at Silver Street in 1973.
157 Excavations by G. Beresford in 1973 and 1974.
158 Information H. E. J. le Patourel.
159 Richardson (1959) 76.
160 Stead (1959a) 522.
161 Le Patourel (1972). These percentages are based on pre-1972 finds and will need modification following the examination of recent finds from York, Wharram Percy, etc.
162 Information P. V. Addyman.
163 Le Patourel in Bellamy (1962–4) 109–10.
164 Waterman (1959) 99–102 and le Patourel (1972).
165 Le Patourel in Bellamy (1962–4) 109.
166 Le Patourel (1972).
167 Hurst in Cramp (1969) 59–66.
168 Dunning in Peers and Radford (1943) 80–82.
169 Cramp (1969) 24–5.
170 Le Patourel (1972).
171 Le Patourel (1973).
172 Hurst in Cramp (1969) 59–66.
173 Jarrett (1970) 267–8, no. 81.
174 Hebditch (1967–8).
175 Barley (1964) 178, fig. 7, no. 5.

176 Information J. H. Williams.
177 Addyman (1969) 80–82, no 26.
178 Wildgoose (1961), but the splashed ware was not published.
179 Beresford (1974).
180 Webster *et al.* (1953).
181 Petch and Thompson (1959) 59–60.
182 Dunning *et al.* (1959) 70, fig. 39.
183 Noble and Shoesmith (1967) 61–3.
184 Rahtz (1968) 244.
185 Excavations at Mill Street, Hereford, in 1972, have produced good evidence for the stone wall which replaced the Æthelflædan timber defences.
186 Thompson (1969) 11–12.
187 Gould (1967–8) 26, fig. 6, no. 1.
188 Wilson and Hurst (1967) 301.
189 Beresford (1974).
190 Dunning *et al.* (1959) 70, fig. 39.
191 Hurst (1962b), and Hurst in Cunliffe (1964) 124–5.
192 Biddle (1974).
193 Biddle (1964) 195.
194 Cunliffe (1970) 75–80.
195 Addyman *et al.* (1972b).
196 Rahtz (1974).
197 Dunning *et al.* (1959) 70, fig. 39.
198 Cunliffe (1970).
199 Dunning and Wilson (1953).
200 White (1934).
201 Dunning *et al.* (1959) 31–4.
202 Hurst and Hurst (1967) 59–61.
203 Rahtz (1974).
204 Dunning (1956).
205 Dunning *et al.* (1959) 55–6 and 59, fig. 30.
206 Hurst *et al.* (1968).
207 Lobbedey in Hurst (1969) 121–8.
208 Verhaeghe in Hurst (1969) 106–8 and pl. xiia.
209 Addyman and Hill (1969) 91–3.
210 Dunning *et al.* (1959) 65, fig. 36, no. 6, and Radford (1972).
211 De Bouard in Hurst (1969) 113–14.
212 Van Altena in Hurst (1969) 129–32, and Braat (1971).
213 De Bouard in Hurst (1969) 115–18.
214 Hurst (1969).
215 Peacock and Thomas (1967).
216 Information B. Ó Ríordáin.
217 Hassall and Hill (1970) 190.
218 Information J. Chapelot.
219 Dunning in Cunliffe (1964) 125–6.
220 Dunning *et al.* (1959) 44–8.
221 Hurst (1963) 155–7.
222 Hurst (1961) 259–61.
223 Hurst (1962b) 189, and Hurst in Cunliffe (1964) 123.
224 Jope (1952–3).
225 Information B. K. Davison.
226 Dunning *et al.* (1959) 72, fig. 40.
227 Musty (1974).
228 Information J. S. Wacher.
229 Chapelot (1973).
230 Arthur and Jope (1962–3).
231 Smedley and Owles (1963).
232 Information J. Nicholls.
233 Barley (1964).
234 Davison (1967) and information the late G. M. Knocker.
235 Information K. Wade.
236 Barley (1964).
237 Wilson and Hurst (1969) 234–5.
238 Musty (1974).
239 Le Patourel (1968). The dating of kilns presents serious problems since the finds usually comprise large quantities of pottery not associated with datable objects or stratigraphically associated with other levels. Magnetic dating has enabled many of the kilns found to be put in a provisional sequence, but absolute dates are harder to assign and the chronology is floating at the moment, awaiting more refined techniques, possibly from thermoluminescent dating. Hurst (1962a), Hurst (1963a) and Hurst (1966).
240 This chapter was written in 1972 and final amendments made in 1973.

8

The coins

Michael Dolley

Introduction

For the Anglo-Saxon archaeologist properly to understand such coins as come his way it is necessary first that he should have some knowledge of their historical background. Particularly relevant in this connection is the need for comprehension of the comparatively limited periods for which most Anglo-Saxon coins appear to have been current. A *thrymsa*, for example, almost by definition cannot have been struck before 650 and is unlikely to have been lost much later than the end of the third quarter of the seventh century, while Offa's pennies of the 780s and 790s seem to have been demonetized in practice, if not in strict theory, by the 850s at the latest. For a generation after that the lifespan of a West Saxon and Mercian penny can be reckoned in years rather than decades; while tenth-century hoards, so many of them from outside the effective jurisdiction of the English king, give what is perhaps a misleading impression of the domestic longevity of individual issues. After 973, of course, the date when a single coin is likely to have been lost can be established within a matter of years, while after 1035 the bracket is even narrower. There are even instances where the striking and loss of a coin can be assumed to have taken place within a matter of months. It is for this reason, then, that the present chapter begins with a summary outline of the history of coinage in Britain from the arrival of Hengist and Horsa to the death of Harold II. Related is the problem of the very different importance that can attach to geographical provenance in different centuries. For a Southampton penny of Ecgbeorht to occur as a single find north of Oxford would undoubtedly occasion a measure of surprise, but after Eadgar's great reform the new English penny appears to have passed freely from one end of the country to the other so that for a Maldon penny of Æthelræd II to be found at Winchester proves no more remarkable than the discovery of a Canterbury penny of Edward the Confessor in excavations at Chester. Without the historical background, though, the picture of the Anglo-Saxon coinage can be very confusing, and there is the further consideration that the archaeologist's numismatic horizons should not be limited to evaluation of the limited number of coins that he himself is likely to recover from excavations. A proper understanding of the mechanics of the Anglo-Saxon coinage cannot but give the student new insights into the technological, artistic and above all governmental achievement of England in the centuries preceding the Norman Conquest.[1]

The story of the coinage

Early in the fifth century of the Christian era, the provinces of Roman Britain were allowed, by a western empire increasingly preoccupied with the defence of its Rhine and Danube frontiers, the chance to 'go it alone'. In the past this departure of the legions too often has been represented as a cynical abandonment of what had become an imperial liability, but increasingly it now appears that Britain both was deemed, and considered itself to be, a viable proposition, with its own defence a local responsibility by no means beyond its resources. Quasi-independence at least ensured the departure of the imperial tax-agencies, no unimportant consideration when the Roman empire as a whole was experiencing a 'gold–drain' eastwards. This was not merely one painful consequence of an adverse trade balance within the mediterranean area, the western provinces having little to offer the eastern in the way of exports, and the East squandering sorely-needed gold in the purchase of those luxuries from the furthest Orient which both halves of the empire were equally unwilling to forgo. By the time that the last legions had taken ship for Gaul, though, the state of the British economy was parlous. Gold was being hoarded desperately – when it could be obtained – and attempts to supplement it with silver had very largely failed, while the disappearance of central fiscal authority meant that a vast coinage of bronze had become an irrelevance. The gathering crescendo of attacks, Irish, Pictish, Jutish and Anglo-Saxon, was being mounted against a society and an economy which already had effectively relapsed into coinlessness, so that the new kingdoms to be erected by the Germanic invaders would have had no tradition of the use of coin even if there had been, which there was not, any significant survival of the Romano-British population.

It is necessary to state these simple facts so baldly because for too long dark-age British studies have been haunted by the spectre of a sub-Roman coinage, the consequence of a misinterpretation of the archaeological horizons of two principal series, the so-called 'barbarous radiates' and '*minimissimi*'. These now at last are recognized as regional attempts to supplement inadequate supplies from Gaul of the late third- and early fourth-century bronze issues of which they are contemporary imitations.[2] When Roman coins do appear in fifth- and sixth-century pagan graves, the gold pieces (most of them heirlooms apparently acquired by their first barbarian owners while still on the Continent) are often individually mounted as pendants, and the silver coins as necklaces, while the bronze pieces were 'antiques' picked up on already derelict Roman sites and often adapted as weights. It was only at the end of the sixth century, with the gradual growth of stable societies along the eastern and southern coasts of emergent England, that there seems to have been a formalization of regular commerce with the Continent. Thus the pagan Anglo-Saxons were to be schooled in the use of coin by the Franks who a century earlier had accepted Christianity and with it a very substantial degree of Romanization. It is no coincidence that the first English as opposed to British coin hoard, a very minor part of the celebrated Sutton Hoo ship-burial grave-goods, consists of Merovingian gold coins, thirty-seven of the aspirin-sized *tremisses* or *trientes* ('thirds') which had supplanted the *solidus* as the standard gold coin of the sub-Roman West, together with three blanks and a forgery.[3] By now gold had become so precious that it had to be minted into more and smaller coins if there were to be enough to go round, and even within France decentralization of authority only too visible in the new diversity of types and legends was having less obvious repercussions on the fineness of the metal. Increasingly the new coins were being debased by the admixture of silver and copper, and, once committed to this slippery path, weakening central control was in no position to halt let alone reverse the process. By the end of the seventh century Western Europe was on the point of accepting the reality of the situation, and the burgeoning commerce of the North Sea and Baltic areas was conducted with silver and not gold as its principal precious metal. The break with the old gold-based economy of the mediterranean world was complete, granted that there was to be intermittent coinage in gold throughout the Anglo-Saxon period (albeit on a scale that was nominal by any standard).

It was, though, when the pretence of a gold standard still was being maintained that the Anglo-Saxons struck their first coins. These insular *tremisses*, usually known to students today as *thrymsas*, were put out in still reasonably fine gold from several centres in south-east England, most notably London, and there seems also to have been an issue which was as exiguous as it was ephemeral at York.[4] In the pages of Bede the bride of a Northumbrian prince is termed 'a gold coin from Kent', and the vivid metaphor reflects historical reality. In the early Anglo-Saxon period coinage is associated only with those parts of England closest to the Continent, and it is not until the ninth century that we find any effective penetration of money into the English lands west of an arc from the Wash to Southampton Water.[5] The Celtic principalities of Cornwall, Wales and Cumberland and the Gaelic and Pictish kingdoms of Scotland were all effectively coinless, as was Ireland, and a distribution map based on the recorded find spots both of Merovingian *tremisses* and of English *thrymsas* reveals a heavy and significant concentration in the southeastern counties of England. There is one critical hoard, a group of exactly one hundred coins with one forgery discovered in 1828 at Crondall in Hampshire, and it comes, as is so often the case with coin hoards, from the periphery and not the epicentre of the circulation area.[6] The great majority of the coins are Anglo-Saxon, a substantial proportion of them struck at London (which had only recently passed under Mercian control), but some are Merovingian. In each case the ultimate inspiration of the designs is still recognizably Roman, but the crudity of the execution of so many of the pieces makes it only too clear that the classical world is a memory and the new idiom one still to be mastered.

The Crondall hoard presumably was concealed somewhere about the middle of the third quarter of the seventh century, and within a generation the gold standard had been abandoned. Not later than the 690s the *thrymsa*, after a period of dramatic debasement with coins from the same dies struck in pale gold and in virtual silver, was superseded by an overtly silver coin of the same fabric.[7] By numismatists today the coins are usually termed *sceattas*, but there can be little doubt that by their users they were called pennies, and one would like to see 'proto-penny' adopted as a generic name, for these coins which with their dumpy, cast flans are essentially different in their fabric from the penny proper struck on spread discs sheared from hammered sheets of metal. The effective circulation area of the proto-penny continued to be delimited by an arc from the Wash to Southampton Water, and a distribution-map which now has to take into account one major and a number of minor hoards as well as single finds, suggests manufacture and currency concentrated in East Kent, the Medway valley, the lower Thames valley, East Anglia and the immediate hinterland of Hamwih (Southampton). Again, too, there is a flicker of activity north of the Humber, but the rise of Mercia and the emergence of a strong Strathclyde appear to have precluded access to such sources of native silver at Derbyshire, North Wales and Cumberland, and the Northumbrian proto-penny seems never to have become a really viable proposition.[8] Interestingly, though, the rare coins which have survived include pieces which are indubitably archiepiscopal, and it is only in Northumbria at this date that we have legends which explicitly include the names of different kings and prelates.

That the mints of the proto-penny take in London, Canterbury, Rochester, York and Southampton cannot well be doubted, and the list may not be all that much longer even though the identity of the mint or mints in East Anglia remains mysterious. As we have seen, the earliest coins belong to the 690s, and in south-east England they continued to be struck at least as late as the middle of the eighth century, with the West Saxon and the East Anglian mints opening late rather than early within this general bracket. A complicating factor is one extensive series which is found on both sides of the North Sea, and which is certainly Frisian, and the fact that some of the proto-pennies of undoubted English provenance have been found on the Continent must corroborate the view that the so-called *sceatta* had a commercial role. But it remains undoubtedly true that a proportion at least of international trade depended in the last resort on barter, with English wool and woollen stuffs perhaps being exchanged even at this early date for continental silver in bar or ingot form. The designs of the proto-pennies exhibit a rich variety, and the tendency to eschew legends enables the engravers to give full rein to their skills, and, if some of the coins are crude, others exhibit a delicacy and consistency of execution which anticipate the acknowledged mastery displayed on the later coins of Offa of Mercia. Most of the types can be shown ultimately to be derived from Roman models, though in some cases Merovingian intermediaries seem also to be involved; but the whole ethos by now is English and not classical, with a number of the designs harking back to pagan motifs with all the confidence of a neophyte Christianity as convinced of its own acceptance as eclectic in its art. What legends there are seem generally meaningless, though the name of London does appear on a few coins in relatively unblundered form, and more often than not they do not extend beyond a few letters; although in the East Anglian series this tiresome pseudo-epigraphy does sometimes give place to the odd personal name written in the runic alphabet. These names appear to be those of moneyers, that is of private individuals guaranteeing the quality of the coins, rather than those of temporal rulers or of prominent ecclesiastics, and so are of little or no use for dating the issues in question.

In 755 Pippin III, first of the Carolingians, revolutionized the Frankish coinage (which under the last of the Merovingians appears to have been going through the doldrums) by introducing the *denarius*, a silver coin struck no longer on a pellet but on a sheared disc. Overnight the surface area of obverse and reverse alike was more than doubled, and scope given for the engraver to attempt meaningful legends. In south-east England the development must have been noticed, but an apparent recession in the English coinage seems to have delayed for as much as thirty years insular adoption of the new technique. Some rare pennies with the names of the Kentish co-monarchs Heaberht and Ecgberht probably belong somewhere about the end of the third quarter of the century, and it may not have been until after another decade that Offa of Mercia harnessed the Canterbury mint to the striking of the new pennies in unprecedented quantity.[9] From the 780s until the end of the Anglo-Saxon period the intelligibility of the legends was to be paramount, and it is the exceptional coin that does not proclaim the kingship of so-and-so, often with the addition of the name of his people, and add that such-and-such an individual – the moneyer – had made himself responsible for its weight and fineness. Here, incidentally, there was an early divergence from Carolingian models which prefer to give the name of the place where the coin was struck, information which would not become an essential of the English reverse legend for another two centuries. Offa was able to strike at Canterbury by virtue of Mercian overlordship of the whole of England south of the Humber, but his relations with Kent seem never to have been easy, and it is surprising perhaps that the great bulk of his coins should have been struck there and not at London. Two principal issues may be distinguished, the earlier struck on slightly smaller flans and including a very substantial proportion of coins with the royal portrait as well as name, and the later struck on wider and heavier flans but generally of simpler design and eschewing regal iconography.

There can be little doubt that Offa's coins were considered by him a vehicle of propaganda. A few coins from the later 780s replace his name and likeness by his queen's, and for this substitution of Cynethryth's name and title we must go back to the Roman empire to find precedents, though it is a little curious perhaps that we should have no coins of his son Ecgfrith, hallowed king as early as 787 and in 796 his successor for 141 days.

At Canterbury, too, we find coins of the archbishops Jaenberht and Æthelheard but always it is with the Mercian king's name on the other side, and the only coins struck by another authority at this period south of the Humber are the rare pennies of Æthelberht of East Anglia who does not acknowledge Offa's sovereignty and who was decapitated by order of the Mercian king in 794. That there was a mint in East Anglia after this is attested by the existence of a few coins of Offa put out by the same moneyer and three others, and exhibiting identical characteristics; it has been argued that Offa had founded the mint and that it had passed temporarily under Æthelberht's control. Offa's son-in-law Beorhtric established on the West Saxon throne in 786 did strike coins, but it probably was not in Offa's lifetime. It is not even certain that the great Mercian king struck at London, though coins of his have been attributed on the basis of their bearing the name Eadberht followed by a mark of contraction conceivably expandible as *episcopus*, and of their appearing to be contemporaneous with the episcopate of a certain Eadberht at London. The new penny did not penetrate north of the Humber, and what coinage there was consisted still of the so-called *sceattas*, a mark of Northumbrian isolation and decline.

Offa, of course, was an international figure, and it is a curious fact that more of his coins are recorded with continental than with specific insular provenances, though undoubtedly the majority of the 250 or so of his extant coins in fact were found in England. The quality of these pennies was recognized when they were imitated as far away as Lucca in Italy and it seems to have been in furtherance of his negotiations with the papacy for the erection of a metropolitan see of Lichfield that a silver penny now lost was put out with the legend S. PETRVS, and also a gold *dinar* struck on an Islamic model through a Massiliot intermediary. Both pieces were found in Italy, the latter actually at Rome, and it is perhaps a mistake to suppose that eighth-century papal susceptibilities were as tender as those in the heyday of the Crusades. A second gold coin by one of Offa's moneyers seems domestic in character, and significantly omits the name of the king.[10] It was known in the seventeenth century, but vanished only to turn up again early in the 1960s when it was presented to the British Museum.

The death of Offa in 796 was followed by a period of instability. Before Coenwulf restored the position, there were revolts in Kent and East Anglia which resulted in ephemeral coinages of Eadberht Praen at Canterbury and of an unknown Eadwald. Archbishop Æthelheard for a time had to abandon his see, but the dismantling of the Mercian archdiocese at his insistence may have reconciled him to his flock, and by 798 the Canterbury mint was also striking extensively for Coenwulf and for a Mercian nominee Cuthred whose nominally independent kingship appears to have been an effective sop to Kentish separatist aspirations.[11] After 805, however, Æthelheard's successor, Wulfred, omitted from his coins the name of a temporal authority, and with Cuthred's death in 807 the pretence of a secular Kentish coinage lapsed. Coenwulf seems to have accepted the reality of the position, and in the second half of his reign we can for the first time in the penny coinage clearly distinguish mints operating at London and Rochester as well as at an unknown place in East Anglia, while a now independent Wessex under Ecgbeorht had its minor mint at Southampton. Northumbria, victim of Scandinavian plundering, still held aloof, but her poverty is mirrored in the substitution of copper for silver as the metal of her coinage. The coins remain essentially proto-pennies, though known to numismatists today as *stycas*, but their purpose can only have been fiscal, a reminder of the neglected tax-function of the whole of later Anglo-Saxon coinage.[12]

After the death of Coenwulf the new balance was violently disrupted and power shifted south-westwards. Canterbury, Rochester and London passed under West Saxon control and within the space of a decade Mercia knew four kings, Ceolwulf, Beornwulf, Ludica and Wiglaf, before the position stabilized.[13] As part of the final settlement London was restored to Wiglaf, but the East Anglian mint had passed definitively into the hands of an independent monarchy first exemplified in the person of an Æthelstan who maintained close relations with Wessex. In Kent there was one final flicker of autonomy under a certain Baldred who appears to have attempted to profit from the confrontation of Mercia and Wessex, but Ecgbeorht had little difficulty in imposing West Saxon overlordship. When he died in 839 Rochester and Canterbury were for practical purposes West Saxon mints, though Wulfred's successor Ceolnoth maintained a façade of archiepiscopal independence by continuing to strike coins without reference to a temporal authority. Canterbury was still the most important mint in England, and even London lagged far behind. Rochester and Southampton remained minor mints, but the East Anglian mint – or mints – seems to have flourished, while at York the kings and archbishops turned out a spate of copper *stycas* which presumably filled some internal need – to judge from their sheer volume and variety.

Under Ecgbeorht England was already beginning to experience Danish as opposed to Norwegian attacks, and the common peril probably explains the controlled Mercian resurgence under Wiglaf and his successor Berhtwulf. Ecgbeorht himself was succeeded by Æthelwulf who was unable to prevent, although he did contain, Danish onslaughts which destroyed the mint at Southampton, left the palace at Winchester in ashes and massacred many Londoners.[14] Canterbury's exposed position meant that the writing was on the wall where her traditional near monopoly of coining was concerned, and London would be the principal beneficiary. Before that, however, there was a major reform of coinage theory, and experimentation with the concept that all coins struck in a given period should be of identical design, an innovation that should make it possible for there to be a demonetization of older coins not conforming to the new model.[15] It is a mark of the essential strength of English society that the principle largely prevailed over the next generation only to be abandoned when the essential victory of Wessex over the Danes had already been won. Undoubtedly, though, its early wide acceptance was facilitated by the disasters of the late 860s and early 870s. Mercia joined Wessex in a species of numismatic union, while the East Anglian mint, which under Æthelward and now Eadmund had held aloof, was utterly destroyed. When Halfdene withdrew from London in 872 Alfred of Wessex and his brother-in-law Burgred of Mercia were left with what was for practical purposes the only viable mint in England, and even the puppet Ceolwulf who succeeded Burgred had to accept the reality of the situation, and continue issues jointly with the West Saxon king.[16]

In 886 Alfred ended London's 'open city' status by restoring the Roman defences and installing a West Saxon garrison, and the event was duly marked by a coinage of portrait coins with a monogram of London as their reverse type. Over the next few years the Canterbury mint still continued to function, but the Danish attack at 892 meant a quarter of a century of closure. The mint at Rochester had already disappeared, but the 890s did see the opening of mints in Wessex proper, one at the newly laid-out city of Winchester and one at Exeter. In Mercia Alfred's son-in-law Æthelred seems to have had no regal aspirations, and Alfred for his part exhibited constitutional delicacy with his new numismatic titulature ALFRED REX neatly avoiding the issue of the people or peoples over whom he claimed sovereignty. Earlier he had struck at Gloucester, but the prolific 'Mercian' mint during the last decade of the century was anonymous but almost certainly located further to the north, perhaps even at Chester. A feature of these last coinages of Alfred was the simplicity of their types. The portrait disappeared, and the economy of the legends was duly carried over into an exceptional eleemosynary issue of silver sixpences where the reverse legend's stark ELI MO – *(elimosina)* has even been mis-construed as indicative of a Jewish moneyer![17] The practicability of the design is seen, however, in the fact that until 973 the commonest reverse of an English penny would be the name of the moneyer written in two lines and followed by a contraction M–O denoting unambiguously his office.

East of the projection of the line of Watling Street that was to mark the effective limit of Danish settlement, there was in the last decade of the ninth century a quite remarkable recrudescence of coinage. The Danes of East Anglia had begun a strongly continental-influenced coinage of pennies according to the martyred Edmund the status of a saint, while their cousins to the west appear under Guthrum briefly to have obtained access to Alfred's mint at London.[18] Further north there was a large emission of copies of contemporary English pence and halfpence at one or more centres in the area of the Seven Boroughs, while in Northumbria the York mint struck large quantities of coins in the name of a mysterious Cnut and of a Siefred who may or may not be the Sigeferth who had raided down the English Channel in the 890s. More than a random sample of these Viking coinages mixed with English and continental plunder came to light in 1840 at Cuerdale in Lancashire, and this great hoard of more than 7,000 coins and nearly 1,000 ounces of uncoined silver must inevitably dominate and distort our still incomplete picture of the state of the English and Viking coinages of these islands about the year 900.[19] It is already clear, though, that the Danish colonists not only had a taste for coin themselves, but that their commercial instincts were materially affecting the English economy as well as their own. A feature of the first half of the tenth century is the flow into the Viking-controlled parts of these islands of Kufic *dirhams* which had traversed Russia and Scandinavia, and it is in the Cuerdale hoard that they first occur in any quantity.[20]

The reign of Edward the Elder virtually coincided with the first quarter of the tenth century, and witnessed the incorporation in the new English kingdom of Mercia and of the Danish lands south of the Humber. Not surprisingly the autonomous Danelaw coinages come to an end,[21] but unfortunately very few of Edward's coins are mint-signed. The broad picture is clear, however, with a steady increase in the number of mints south and north of the Thames. Early in the reign the coins struck were of two main types, with and without portrait, but later a much more regional pattern becomes discernible with the coins generally struck on slightly broader flans. Except in East Anglia portrait coins become the exception rather than the rule, while in Mercia and the east Midlands the portrait is totally eschewed. In the north-west, though, there is a remarkable series of coins with novel reverse types, churches and church-towers, flowers, birds, the *Manus Dei*, etc, and coin-hoards from as far afield as Rome provide evidence that the policy of strict uniformity of type had had to be abandoned. In Northumbria secular coinage was on a small scale, even after the advent before 920 of a short-lived Hiberno-Norse dynasty in the persons of the cousins Regnald and Sihtric Caoch, and the principal output of the York mint was an overtly-ecclesiastical coinage in the name of St Peter, the patron saint of the province.[22] The picture here is one of relative stagnation, and it is very noticeable that Hiberno-Norse intervention raised rather than lowered standards of design and execution.

Æthelstan's incorporation of York into the English kingdom and successful campaigns against the Cornish, Welsh and Scots could not but have had important consequences for the English coinage, and early in his reign he legislatively enunciated the cardinal principle that there should only be one coinage throughout the kingdom and that the king's. His Grateley enactment for the English south of the Thames reveals his design, which was that all places of any importance should be entitled to a mint, and in fact thirty different mints are known even though he was unable to impose on them the absolute uniformity after which he so clearly hankered. The old regional organization remained intact, and for the next half-century, for example, coins from the Chester area were to be distinguished by the inclusion in their types of at least one rosette of pellets.[23] It proved impractical, too, to insist on a mint-signature, and only a proportion of the coins flaunted the new royal style REX TO BRIT (*rex totius Britanniae*, 'king of the whole of Britain'). Nor was it possible to call in the coins of the previous reign even though enhanced royal control did register considerable success in driving out of circulation the non-English coins whose currency was now specifically banned. Ever since the time of Offa there had existed prejudice at least against foreign specie, but the turmoil of the Danish invasions had weakened resistance to it, and any erosion of the principle over the next century would have undermined the whole theory of the English coinage which was that the amount of silver in an English coin was for the king to decide, a penny passing as such even if the silver in it did not amount to half its face-value.[24]

The relatively short reigns of Eadmund and Eadred were dominated once more by the problems of York where first Hiberno-Norse kings and later a Norwegian prince succeeded in establishing themselves for brief periods. Coins are known from the two Anlafs, cousins, their brothers Regnald Guthfrithsson and Sihtric of the Jewels, and the formidable Eric Bloodaxe. After 954, however, English authority was restored, and English generosity was seen once more to pay off in 957 when for two years England was peacefully partitioned along the Danelaw mearing under the brothers Eadwig and Eadgar, for reasons that are far from clear today. All this time, however, the English coinage went on its settled way, unruffled and largely unchanged. The regional pattern which had emerged under Edward the Elder persisted, with mint-signatures continuing to be the exception, and even after he had become sole king in 959 the great Eadgar was slow to tamper with the essential structure. Probably in 973, however, he instituted a major reform which set the pattern of the English coinage for the next century and a half and more.[25] All coin in circulation had to be demonetized and brought in to be melted down and coined into pence of absolutely uniform type which would then be current only for a fixed number of years. To facilitate this, the number of mints had to be raised very substantially, probably from about forty to about sixty, but the production of dies would have been concentrated at a single centre. The preferred royal style REX ANGLORUM was one with which Alfred and Eadred had briefly toyed, and Eadger himself experimented, and the royal portrait once more became *de rigueur*. Added to the reverse type as an invariable element was an indication of the minting-place and not until the reign of Henry II was there to be any fundamental departure from the principles now enunciated. Periodicity of recoinage was the essential characteristic and one of the strengths of the English coinage throughout the great Danish attacks that were to come, surviving even the Norman Conquest. At first the currency of each issue was six years, but later the period was more than halved.[26]

Eadgar's death in 975 was followed by the minorities of the brief reign of Edward the Martyr and of the early part of that of Æthelræd II. The coins mirror something of the relaxation of royal authority, the production of dies being progressively decentralized until the middle of the 980s when uniformity was once more achieved. England was now suffering a recrudescence of Viking attacks, and sacks such as those of Chester and Southampton left their mark on the coinage of the mints concerned.[27] In 991 the fatal decision was taken to pay *danegeld* and payments over the next thirty years amounting to tens of millions of coins have transformed our knowledge of the English coinage. Large quantities found their way to Scandinavia, and were there, and particularly on the Swedish island of Gotland, consigned to the ground for security in an age without banks.[28] For the first time since the handful of much smaller *Romescot* hoards of the first half of the tenth century the student has a representative cross-section of the English coinage as a whole; this is in marked contrast to the period before Eadgar when too many of our coins derive from atypical finds from Ireland and the Scottish Isles with consequent imbalance in favour of the products of the mint of Chester and its hinterland. It is no coincidence, too, that it is coins of the type current from 991 until 997 which provide the prototypes of the first native coinages properly so-called of Ireland, Norway, Sweden and Denmark, even if at Hedeby and in Skåne there had been earlier attempts resulting in anepigraphic pieces without obvious connection with the German and Kufic coins beside which they circulated.[29]

In 997, after a brief period of experimentation, Æthelræd II struck the first of the Long Cross pennies which for most people typify the later Anglo-Saxon coinage. Initially they weighed twenty-seven grains, but towards the end of the issue the weight was reduced quite appreciably, the lighter pieces possessing a distinctive style which could be deliberate. From the first there seems to have been decentralization of die-cutting, the two centres being identifiable as London and Winchester. The process was one which continued in the Helmet issue introduced in 1003, and is particularly pronounced in the Last Small Cross type which began in 1009 and continued under the pressure of events to be current for eight and perhaps nine years. In the summer of 1009 a phase of innovation, which may reflect Wulfstan's moralizing, had resulted in the Agnus Dei pence of which only a dozen specimens are known today, and which were perhaps too revolutionary with substitution of the Lamb of God for the royal portrait and of the Dove of the Holy Ghost for the cross that had become an integral part of the reverse type. The constant drain of the *danegeld* was now swollen by the recurrent charge of the *heregeld*, and by Æthelræd's last months the weight of the English penny had fallen to a bare fifteen or sixteen grains. Still, however, royal control of the mints was unbroken, and when Eadmund Ironside succeeded his father in 1016 the eight or so die-cutting centres serving sixty-odd mints up and down the country waited for central authority to order the consequential changes which in fact were never made. To this day the numismatist cannot point to a single penny of Eadmund Ironside nor to a single penny of Knut struck at an English mint prior to the introduction of the new Quatrefoil type in 1018.[30]

Knut, then, found the organization of die-cutting regional, and at first seems to have encouraged even greater fragmentation. With his second issue which began in 1024, however, the number of centres was sharply reduced, while the last type of the reign exhibits remarkable uniformity. Two 'hands' can perhaps be recognized, but still it has not been possible satisfactorily to identify them either with London or with Winchester, and it seems possible that both engravers were working at the same centre. As the reign went on, too, the weight of the penny was stabilized, and in the last two issues there is no obvious falling away from a standard of eighteen grains. If anything the last type is the most English-looking of the three, and the picture that the coinage presents is one of a successful if unimaginative return to principles first laid down by Eadgar and maintained with surprising success for the greater part of the reign of Æthelræd II. The English administrative machine was intact, and Knut was wise enough not to destroy a system of efficient coin-production without rival in Europe.

The brief reigns of Harold Harefoot and Harthacnut, however, did bring about one significant change, the substitution of a biennial cycle for the sexennial one which had previously obtained. The restoration of the West Saxon line in the person of Edward the Confessor at first brought no improvement. Indeed, by 1050 the state of the English coinage was critical. The weight of the penny had fallen once more, and without official connivance there was significant debasement with zinc as well as copper.[31] At the root of the evil was the steady drain of silver out of the country, and it cannot well be a coincidence that in 1051 the abolition of the *heregeld* and the dismissal of its recipients was followed in the same year by a significant increase in the weight of the penny.[32] To return to a sexennial cycle proved impossible, but at least the period of currency of each type was raised to three years, while the next decade saw a certain rationalization of minting with new mints being opened and those no longer viable closed. When the crisis of the autumn of 1065 hit the English monarchy, the coinage was in better shape than it had been for years, and particularly successful would appear to have been a dramatic overall reduction in the number of moneyers. Fewer men striking more coins seem to have been more easily controlled, and even if there was a brief grant to York of a die-cutting centre for the north-east, ultimate authority still resided with the king.[33] From the 1050s, too, a complete change comes over the superficial appearance of the coinage, the royal portrait being less formalized and corresponding to German imperial rather than to ancient Roman models. It proved an easy matter for Harold in 1066 to take control of the existing system, and it is perhaps an indication of his awareness that there was an element of controversy in his undisputed succession that almost at once new dies were sent down from London. The existing coins of Edward the Confessor seem not to have been demonetized, but they began to be supplemented by others with the name of Harold and with a reverse type consisting of the word PAX displayed in a label across the field. As it happens, the first issue of Edward the Confessor had had the letters PACX disposed in the four quarters of the reverse, and the import of the new coins was clearly that Harold was Edward's rightful successor, with a claim on the same chauvinist English loyalties which had rallied in 1042 around the representative of a non-alien line. Nine months later Hastings was to end the dream, but the coin-hoards from the later 1060s show how William in his turn was to inherit a highly sophisticated and efficient system of coinage which needed only a royal directive to continue to function under its own momentum. Within months at most of William's landing, new dies were being distributed to each and every mint up and down the country, so that when in the autumn of 1069 the triennial recoinage fell due, the coins demonetized, although constituting one issue, were of three types. Some obverses bore the name of Edward the Confessor, others of Harold, and others of William, but all the coins seem to have possessed the same validity. The obverses of new coins which replaced them bore of course only one name, that of William, but the men who put out King William's money were essentially the same as those who had been operating the mints on the day that King Edward had been alive and dead. It is 1154 and not 1066 that marks the one fundamental divide which occurs in the English coinage between Eadgar's reform of 973 and Edward I's of 1279, and even then there was to be no break in the continuity of personnel. What still is not fully understood by the great majority of students is just how different was the English coinage-system from those which obtained elsewhere. Its particular strength lay in its very English blend of conservatism and adaptability.

The mechanics of coin-production

The equipment of an Anglo-Saxon mint must have been relatively simple. The only item that might not have been readily transportable by pack-horse would have been a furnace capable of reducing to its molten state bar-gold and silver and obsolete coin. Smelting of ore and even the refining of large quantities of sub-standard silver were not operations likely to have been carried out at the run of mints. We do well to remember that the bulk of the gold and silver struck derived from coins removed from circulation, and provided only that moneyers were careful to weed out from the money they changed any forgeries and continental coins struck to other standards, there would be no need to carry out more than the random assay. The other major sources of bullion would have been ingots of sycee type sent down by the central authority, and here the purity would have been the responsibility of others. Recently some long overdue work has been undertaken to determine the fineness of the Anglo-Saxon penny, and already it can be said that a standard approximating to 925 fine ('sterling') was one well within the capacity of an Anglo-Saxon craftsman to achieve, and that it was rare for a standard comfortably in excess of 800 fine not to be maintained over the country as a whole.[34] Normally, then, no very elaborate metallurgical processes were carried out away from London and/or the mints, and it is perhaps unreasonable to expect the site of an Anglo-Saxon mint – and one has still to be excavated – to produce more than the odd crucible or spatter of coagulated dross. Indeed it might be a very difficult matter for an archaeologist to distinguish the débris of such an atelier from that of the workshop of a silversmith or jeweller.

The remaining equipment of the mint can be inferred from the fairly simple techniques that seem to have been involved in the conversion of the molten metal into coin. In the early period the flans seem to have been obtained by pouring measured droplets into clay-moulds and hammering the cold pellets individually on an anvil. After the introduction of the penny it would appear that as a first stage cakes of silver were weighed out and hammered into circular plates, and this would have entailed the use of simple balances, probably of bronze, and of iron hammers and iron rims on a slab of stone or iron.[35] There is much to commend the view that to produce, say, sixty-four pennies a cake with the weight of ninety-six was beaten out, and the square contained by the resulting circle sheared into eight strips each of which in turn was cut up into eight squares with a side equal to the diameter of the intended coin. Each square was then placed between a pair of tempered iron dies, the lower set in a block of wood, and the upper held in the left hand of a workman who struck it a heavy blow with a large-headed, short-hafted hammer. One blow would have been sufficient to transfer the impression of the two-die faces simultaneously to the blank which would then be passed to another workman who stamped out the round with a circular punch not unlike a pastry-cutter. The upshot of the whole operation would be a pile of sixty-four silver pennies of uniform size and weight, and a heap of 260 pieces of scissel, four large and the rest quite small, which could be checked for weight against half the pennies and then returned to the crucible. Some hammers, then, a pair of shears, some iron rings, a balance with its pans and a special weight, a circular punch, the dies and very little else would be all the archaeological detritus of a minor mint subjected to the cataclasm of a sack at the hands of the Vikings, and only the dies would be implements of a kind peculiar to moneying. Only the dies, too, would have been the object of special security, and so might well not be in the moneyer's workshop at the time of the sacking, and alternatively if present they would be very likely to be snatched up by the raiders along with any silver in process of being coined. A single mint-weight may have survived, a square block of lead from London with the imprint of an early Alfredian die, but no Anglo-Saxon coin-die is known, and it is unlikely in fact that any will be discovered. Mint-security demanded rigid control, and the moneyer would have a vested interest in seeing that a reverse die with his name did not fall into other hands. At each recoinage all available dies would be returned to the appropriate centre, and there reworked and re-engraved.

The production of dies was a craft not normally conducted inside a mint. Recent experiments have shown that they could be produced very rapidly, with one craftsman engraving several dozen in the course of a day. The spiked trussel or lower die appears on later analogies to have been shouldered to prevent it being driven into the block of timber in which it was set, and tapered to a square section of which the side was little longer than the diameter of the coin to be struck. A circle was inscribed on the face with a compass and incised with overlapping strokes of a punch and the portrait or other obverse type put in with a handful of punches of a few geometric shapes. A second concentric circle would be scribed and deepened, and similar punches used to put in the lettering, the engraver having to remember to work in reverse so that the inscription would not be retrograde when transferred to the coin, and building up each letter from three or four basic elements. When the die was complete, it would be case-hardened by being brought to red-heat and plunged into a tub of water. The reverse die or pile, a simple bar of metal of the same section as the face of the trussel, would be engraved and tempered in the same way, and the two dies kept in alignment during striking by a loosely-fitting collar. Normal practice, too, appears to have been to supply more reverse dies than obverse, it being the pile that took the shock of the hammer and was more prone to fracture, but there is as yet no evidence to show that there was a later medieval fixed ratio of two piles for each trussel.

As already implied, die-production was normally confined to a few centres, and at the end of the Anglo-Saxon period there appears to have been only one, this being London. It would seem that lists of names of moneyers were sent up from the individual mints, and there is a little evidence that these were dealt with in rotation, peripheral mints being served before those in the more immediate vicinity. The picture given is one of a very considerable degree of administrative sophistication, and at a period of recoinage literally thousands of dies would have had to be engraved in a matter of weeks rather than months. The close resemblance of surviving seal-matrices and seals to coin-types must suggest very strongly that between coinages the die-engravers undertook both official and private commissions for signets, and clearly it would have been undesirable for too many in the community to have been masters of a skill which misapplied could result in forgery. Generally, though, counterfeiting does not appear to have been prevalent, though the contingency was provided for by savage penalties in the tenth- and eleventh-century law–codes. It is only in Scandinavia that coins were systematically 'pecked' with oblique blows from a knife-point or minute gouge – apparently to detect locally-produced plated forgeries – and the number of counterfeits which have occurred in English contexts is very small indeed.[36] Fraudulent moneyers appear to have struck their coins light rather than base, and post-Conquest practice suggests that, when detected, more often than not these men of standing were mulcted by very substantial fines rather than physically mutilated, a form of punishment more appropriate to their dishonest servants and to counterfeiters outside the mint as such.

The number of mints in later Anglo-Saxon England was rarely fewer than sixty, and the quota of moneyers at each mint might vary between one, in the case of a few very small mints, and fifty or more in the case of the largest. At the very end of the Anglo-Saxon period an attempt was made to cut back the number of moneyers to a maximum of a dozen with the smaller mints in proportion,[37] but it will be gathered that for the period of close on three centuries spanned by the Anglo-Saxon penny the student of Anglo-Saxon personal names is afforded closely dated and strictly contemporary forms running into thousands. These are only now beginning to be exploited by linguists, and some of the implications of this work are not without significance for the archaeologist. Light is thrown, for example, on the pattern of the ninth-century Danish settlement, while the incidence of names of continental German and of Irish origin affords some clue to the extent of contacts overseas. It is likely, too, that there is some relationship between the size of towns and the number of their moneyers. Langport, for instance, on this telling appears to have been a place of rather more importance under Æthelstan that it was to be under Æthelræd II, while the 1003 sack of Wilton is neatly mirrored in the departure of its moneyers to neighbouring Old Sarum.[38]

Where there was more than one moneyer, overnight custody of the obverse dies was probably reserved to a single royal officer (such as the sheriff or port-reeve) who would have locked them away in a common chest. Each moneyer, though, would have retained possession of his reverse dies, and it was the design appearing on the reverse that in the last century of Anglo-Saxon England appears to have been critical in deciding the issue to which a coin belonged. Mules are known linking two issues, but it is always an old obverse that is pressed into service with a new reverse, and never an old reverse with a new obverse, while a follow-up of the subsequent careers of moneyers who strike these mules suggests that in certain circumstances the practice must have been entirely legal.[39] Presumably the sheriff or port-reeve could authorize the expedient when early in a new coinage there was a dearth of obverse dies. Security and convenience alike would have demanded that coin-production took place in one particular quarter of the town, while some species of building must have been needed for the safe storage at night of bullion and coin along with the obverse dies. It is not necessary to suppose, though, that all the processes of coining were necessarily conducted within its four walls, and many moneyers may well have operated in adjacent but separate *ateliers* during the day. In this connection it should be borne in mind that one important function of the later Anglo-Saxon moneyer was the operation of an exchange. At each periodic demonetization it would be for him to change old money into new at a fixed rate, probably ten new pennies for twelve old, an element of compulsion being introduced by the consideration that after a moratorium only new coin would be legal tender. The 'profit' may seem exorbitant, but out of it the moneyer would have to pay all his expenses as well as certain fees to the Crown, and there could be occasions when the ten new coins paid out might weigh more than the twelve received, though here presumably the deficit would be subsidized by bullion sent from the royal treasury at Winchester. As long as he scanned the proferred old money with care so as to exclude forgeries and continental coins struck almost invariably to a lower standard, the moneyer could consign it to the crucible with an easy mind, and it was almost certainly this at worst sexennial scrutiny at local mints which explains the consistently high standard of the English coinage and its enormous reputation both in Ireland and on the Continent. The face value of an Anglo-Saxon penny was substantially more than its silver content, and it was only when in the course of the eleventh century the weight of the penny had fallen consistently over a number of issues that people were tempted not to bring into the mints the totality of their obsolete coin. The fact that coin-hoards from the reign of Edward the Confessor include an increasing proportion of coins many issues out-of-date may reflect confidence in silver's stability rather than want of trust in a coinage managed as much to the realm's advantage as to royal profit. Once melted down an obsolete penny of Knut could not be distinguished from an obsolescent penny of the current reign, and whatever formal ban there may have been on the exchange of coins from the penultimate and earlier types, it would have been difficult to prevent the practice; the more so when the moneyer had every incentive to prefer coins he knew to be uncontaminated by the zinc which was so prominent an adulterant in the 1040s.[40]

Community of interest, then, bound the moneyer to the Crown, and the population at large had every reason to acquiesce in arrangements which had the great advantage that they worked, and were seen to work, to the end to which they were directed. Manipulation of the weight of the penny meant that there were always enough coins in circulation for every man to obtain what he required to pay his taxes, and an increasing tendency for weight to be manipulated even within an issue meant that ordinary users were not preoccupied with metrology, and took each penny quite literally at its face value. That coin was heavily 'over-valued' as regards its previous metal content ensured that it would not be culled for the crucible, and at the same time speculative export was effectively discouraged. The Crown for its part knew precisely where it stood, and if large sums were siphoned from the country in *danegeld* and *heregeld*, the exact figures were in its possession. Overall losses could be made good by a combination of adjustment of weight of subsequent coins and of diversion to coinage of the bullion reserve constantly accumulating as a result of mining operations which themselves were under strict royal control, and of the trading activities of English merchants buying up silver abroad against exports of commodities. That the Crown made a continuing profit seems not to have been resented when the system gave England a coinage without peer in Western Europe, though it is interesting that at the end of the Anglo-Saxon period there does seem to have been a recrudescence of speculative hoarding, perhaps because of too violent swings of weight, upwards as well as downwards, over the preceding years. It should be borne in mind, though, that the Crown had been faced on that occasion with the special problems following debasement with zinc, and there is no evidence that an Anglo-Saxon successor to Edward the Confessor would not have arrived at the same solution as that adopted by William the Conqueror in the early 1070s, the proclamation of a stable *('steorling')* weight and fineness extending over successive issues, loss to the revenue being made good by the institution of a new tax, the so-called *monetagium*.[41] Not to be overlooked is the fact that the Anglo-Saxon machinery of coin-production was taken over lock-stock-and-barrel by the Normans so that the advice taken early in the 1070s may very well have been tendered by the same person or persons who had been responsible for monetary policy over the whole of the preceding decade.

The ordering of the material and its interpretation

What it is hoped has been achieved by the foregoing is some indication to the non-numismatist of the potentiality of numismatic evidence – and also of its limitations. Anglo-Saxon coins may impinge on the work of an archaeologist in a number of ways. They have an official nature as no other class of artifact, and a durability which puts them in a category apart from more conventional if more extended documents. It is as well perhaps that the non-numismatist should have some understanding of the manner and reliability of their classification. How does the numismatist knew that a coin of a King Edward was struck, say, by Edward the Elder and not by Edward the Martyr? How, too, can he state that a particular coin of the former belongs early rather than late in the reign? The key to the problem lies in the hoards of coins concealed by their anonymous owners and not recovered until modern times. Since the seventeenth century such hoards have been the subject of record and of study, and publication of such as occur in our day is one of the more exacting duties incumbent on all students with any concern for posterity. To take one very simple example, the sequence of the English kings after Alfred is Edward the Elder, Æthelstan, Eadmund, Eadred, Eadwig and Eadgar. If a hoard is discovered, as one at Morley St Peter in Norfolk in 1958, which contains West Saxon coins of Alfred and Æthelstan, but no English coins of Eadmund, Eadred, Eadwig and Eadgar, then the coins of an Edward cannot well be attributed to an Edward other than the son of Alfred and the father of Æthelstan, i.e. Edward the Elder.[42] In the same way, a hoard from Chester discovered in 1914 contained coins of an Edward along with coins of Eadgar and of an Æthelræd.[43] All but a few of the coins were of one type and exhibited remarkable uniformity of workmanship. Purely on commonsense grounds, then, the Edward coins can be given to the short-lived Edward the Martyr, Eadgar's son, and the Æthelræd coins to Æthelræd II (the Unready) who was Edward the Martyr's half-brother and successor.

A massive corpus of such information has been built up over the years by noting which coins occur in which hoards, and there are very few links in the chain which depend in fact on the evidence of only one hoard. The pattern is a cumulative one, and it is not long before the numismatist notices that his Edward the Elder coins virtually never have a Scandinavian provenance, whereas his Edward the Martyr coins come predominantly from hoards concealed in the lands around the Baltic. An extension of the same method can be used to establish the order of types within a reign. In the Morley St Peter hoard, for example, the fact that there were several hundred coins of Edward the Elder and only one of Æthelstan must suggest that the hoard was concealed relatively early in the latter reign, and hence that early coins of Æthelstan will resemble the single coin of that king. In the same way, the relatively few coins of Æthelræd II in the 1914 Chester hoard which are not of the same type as those of Eadgar and of Edward the Martyr may be presumed to belong to the second issue of Æthelræd's reign. A close study of the literally tens of thousands of extant coins of Æthelræd II has established that six types and six only were struck in significant quantity: First Hand (established by the Chester find as the second of the reign), Second Hand, Crux, Long Cross, Helmet and lastly Small Cross; the names are those given by modern students and relate to the more distinctive features. A glance at published hoards is sufficient to establish that there are finds which include Eadgar, Edward the Martyr, First Small Cross – a variety not struck in quantity and presumably ephemeral – First Hand and Second Hand, but not Crux or Long Cross. It is reasonable to suppose, then, that Second Hand is the third type of the reign. When, too, the numismatist remarks a group of hoards which comprise Second Hand and Crux but nothing else, it is reasonable to assume that Crux is the type that followed Second Hand. The process can be continued to the point that one notices that it is the types after Crux which occur in increasing proportion in those hoards which also contain one or more of the issues of Knut, Æthelræd's successor. In other words, the relative order of the different issues of Æthelræd II is, as was claimed earlier, something that can be established just by noting which types occur in which hoards, so that it may come as something of a surprise to know that it is only in the last twenty years that numismatists have reached general agreement on the exact ordering of the types of the English coinage between Eadgar's reform of *c.* 973 and the death of Henry I in 1135. In fact the hoard evidence has always been there, at least since the nineteenth century and where the Anglo-Saxon issues are concerned, but too few students have been prepared to seek it out.

Once the framework of the sequence of the principal issues has been established, other pieces of the puzzle fall fairly easily into place. First there are the so-called 'mules', coins from an obverse die of one issue and the reverse die of another. These usually combine consecutive issues – but not necessarily – and normally the reverse die belongs to the later and the obverse to the earlier. Then there are the coins of abortive issues, types which for one reason or another failed to achieve real permanence. At the end of each issue there appears to have been a certain amount of experimentation, and some of the products found their way into circulation. The best-known example is the rare Agnus Dei type already mentioned (p. 359), but others exist in almost every reign. Often they occur as 'mules', and there is little real difficulty in establishing their place in the sequence. In the case of a substantive issue, too, some dies almost by definition are 'early' and others 'late', and the isolation of these on stylistic and metrological grounds is often feasible. It has been observed, for example, that where a type demonstrably the latest in a find exists, the coins are – or tend to be – heavier than the average for the issue as a whole, while the last element of the obverse legend is rather fuller than is typical for the totality of the coins of the issue in question. For example, most Long Cross pennies have the ethnic ANGLO or ANGL and weigh approximately twenty-five grains (1.4 grammes), but 'early' coins read ANGLORX and tip the scales at a shade over twenty-seven grains (1.75 grammes).[44] In other words, there are quite a number of Anglo-Saxon coins which ought to be capable of being dated within a bracket of months if only it should prove possible to establish for the substantive types an absolute as opposed to a merely relative chronology.

If, for example, it can be shown that the Crux issue of Æthelræd II ran for six years from, say, Michaelmas 991 until Michaelmas 997, a number of consequences ensue which have very important non-numismatic implications. To begin with, there are the rare coins of the so-called Benediction Hand variety which immediately preceded the Crux issue proper. The production of these would be dated to the summer of 991, while English hoards suggest that demonetization of all Hand coins in the winter of 991/2 was efficient and effective. In other words, any archaeological context which is securely dated by the finding of a coin of this variety might well belong to the second half of 991. There are, though, a number of Crux coins where the engraver has not thrown off the Benediction Hand idiom, and which clearly belong not long after the Benediction Hand issue, i.e. would have been struck not much later than the autumn of 991. Their legends may well afford evidence to a linguist of a particular sound-change or alteration in orthographic convention having occurred by 991, but the archaeological implications of a single find may prove rather different. The issue was current from the autumn of 991, but final demonetization probably did not occur until the spring of 998. Since the coin could have been lost at any time within that bracket, a level in an English excavation dependent for its date on a coin of this variety should not be dated more closely than '991–8'. Even so, everything depends on the correctness or otherwise of the dates ascribed to the main issue, and here there has been a certain amount of controversy.

For more than a decade the 'orthodox' view has been that Eadgar's reform occurred in 973, that First Hand was introduced in 979, Second Hand in 985, Crux in 991, and so on.[45] Critics, who have changed their ground and even in at least one case retired from the fray, have criticized the assumption of the sexennial cycle, but only occasionally have they suggested a positive, let alone plausible, alternative. When they have, their proposed chronologies have without exception run into serious difficulties. By definition an imitation cannot precede its prototype, and too little account has been taken of the implications of revisions of the accepted chronology for such related series as the Hiberno-Norse from Dublin and the Norwegian and Swedish. Two successive body-blows were given to one of the more intelligent of alternative chronologies by belated realization of the neglected truths that at Dublin Sihtric Silkbeard, *pace* numismatic textbooks, did not in fact succeed his uncle in 989, while Olafr Tryggvason tarried in England until the spring of 994.[46] The argument that in 973 Anglo-Saxon England could not have got the sexennial cycle right without a period of experimentation conveniently ignored the fact that something very similar had been the subject of sustained experiment a century earlier. While, then, much remains to be done, such work as is in progress seems generally to support the chronological estimates made more than a decade ago, and it seems unlikely that there is any very substantial error in the datings then proposed for the substantive issues of the English kings from Eadgar to Harold II. It is, after all, curious that First and Second Hand coins of Chester can be shown to have been struck on an exiguous scale that accords perfectly with the Viking descent on Wirral in the winter of 979/80;[47] curious, too, that the Salisbury mint opens in Helmet with a complement of Wilton moneyers when Wilton had been sacked and burnt in the summer of 1003;[48] and more curious still that we have only very 'early' Last Small Cross coins of an Oxford sacked and burnt at Christmas 1009.[49] This far from exhausts a whole chapter of coincidences, and it is not sufficient for critics to imagine that they have destroyed the case for the cycle calculated from 973 by blowing on some of the admittedly weaker links in a whole chain of interlocking argument. The case is a cumulative one with coincidence piled upon coincidence, and it is not for the mere numismatist to suppose that it will be pulled down on one narrow front by pressing, say, the metrological position at the expense of all the other factors involved. Ultimately it is the coins that must be fitted to history, and not history to the coins.

It is not, though, simply as artifacts capable of being dated with exceptional precision – both as regards their period of use and their manufacture – that coins are of interest to the archaeologist concerned with the Anglo-Saxon period. Obviously they date contexts in which they occur, and a special case is afforded by grave-deposits and hoards which, as at Sutton Hoo and Cuerdale, often contain other objects for which the numismatic evidence at least provides a satisfying *terminus ante quem*. The pattern of coins' incidence as single-finds may also be significant, chronologically as well as geographically. The excavator of Southampton and of Winchester, for example, cannot and does not ignore the profusion of pre-840 coins from the former site, and the relative paucity of later pieces, nor fail to note the steady build-up of post-890 coins from Winchester which contrasts with an almost total absence of earlier issues. When, too, archaeologist and historian alike are faced with the problem of estimating the degree and extent of continental influences, it is surely relevant that finds of Merovingian coins should be virtually confined to the south-east, and that as late as the eleventh century there is clearly discernible at Winchester a little group of moneyers with continental Germanic (Frisian?) names. In the same way, not just the numismatist will be interested in the occurrence of Hiberno-Norse personal names on coins from Chester and from York.

It is not only in England, though, that the pattern of single-finds and of coin-hoards has attracted the interest of the Anglo-Saxon historian and archaeologist. It is, for example, only quite late in the ninth century that Anglo-Saxon coins begin to occur in Irish contexts in any quantity, and the total absence from that island of the Kentish *thrymsa* and English proto-penny cannot but suggest a paucity of commercial and even cultural contacts between Ireland and south-east England in the pre-Viking period. In the tenth century, too, it is the coinage of north-west England that is found dominating a plethora of hoards from the Irish Sea area, while in the 990s there is a curious and still largely unexplained shift of emphasis with Bristol very soon afterwards replacing Chester as the principal port for Ireland.[50] It is precisely at this juncture, moreover, that there occurs a dramatic regression in the number of Anglo-Saxon pennies found in the Irish Sea area, and this is accompanied by a pronounced contraction in their area of circulation. The Scottish Isles seemingly relapsed into a coinlessness which contrasts markedly with the position which had obtained over the preceding century.[51] From mainland Scotland and from Wales, on the other hand, the number of Anglo-Saxon coins of any period that have come to light in modern times must be considered minimal, a reminder of the fact that Gaelic and Celtic society had no endemic tradition of the use of coin as such. This is not to say that trade and cultural contacts with the Anglo-Saxons were not re-established after the defeat of paganism, but one of the more intriguing aspects of pre-Norman England would be its acceptance of Welsh and Scottish separateness at the same time as what might have been thought much more precarious links with the Continent were a source of continental inspiration and profit.

In Western Europe both the *thrymsa* and the proto-penny appear to have crossed the English Channel in quantity, and numerous examples have come to light the length of the littoral from the Frisian islands to as far west as Brittany. The Offa penny, on the other hand, achieved a much deeper penetration, and there is a fair scatter of findings from the Rhine area with other pieces crossing the Alps and making their way as far south as Rome. In the ninth century, too, the occasional English penny begins to be found in Scandinavia in circumstances which, as at Kaupang and Birka, suggest that trade and not loot may have been the occasion of their export. Generally though, the ninth century Scandinavian visitor to England appears to have been land- rather than silver-hungry, while in the first half of the tenth century our only major non-insular finds of Anglo-Saxon pennies are from Italy. So significant was the English contribution to the papal finances that we even find Anglo-Saxon pennies occurring in a Sicilian context most readily explicable on the hypothesis that Rome was subsidizing with English coin a revolt of the Christian population against their Islamic masters.[52] It is no less remarkable that two at least of the English penny types should have been the subject of imitation of papal coins of the period.

The resumption of Scandinavian attacks on England in the last quarter of the tenth century resulted in a crescendo of the importing of Anglo-Saxon pennies into Scandinavia, and from the beginning of the 990s until well into the 1040s the great majority of English coins available for study today derive from Swedish hoards.[53] More than 50,000 Anglo-Saxon pennies have been discovered on the island of Gotland, and from the mainland finds containing as many as 1,000 English coins are by no means unknown. Only Norway and Denmark are less rich in hoards with Anglo-Saxon pennies, and from Finland, Russia, Poland, the Baltic Republics and North Germany the quantity of English coin turned up by the plough in modern times is such that the major collections in those countries cannot be ignored by serious students of the series. After the middle of the eleventh century there was, of course, a marked falling off in the import of English coins into the area – the latest pennies of Edward the Confessor and those of Harold II are virtually unknown – but there is a curious if limited resumption for a few years in the 1080s which makes the point perfectly that William the Conqueror inherited the strategic preoccupations of his Anglo-Saxon precursors, the threat of an invasion from Denmark being still very real. Even in twelfth-century hoards, however, the great bulk of the English coins continue to be obsolete Anglo-Saxon pieces that had been struck in the heyday of the *danegeld* and the *heregeld*; it is these coins in the names of Æthelræd II and Knut which from the 990s onwards provided the prototypes for official and unofficial coinages put out in quantity at a number of mints associated with the West Baltic area in particular. Fortunately very few of these pieces appear to have trickled back into England, for the series is one of unusual complexity and still awaits authoritative elucidation of most of its mysteries. A measure of the degree of sophistication involved may be thought to be the circumstance that it is only in recent years that students have begun to consider such niceties as whether a particular piece might or might not be a Danish imitation of a Hiberno-Norse copy of an earlier Dublin imitation of an English original,[54] and it will be gathered that it is not unknown for mid-eleventh-century Scandinavian pieces to have as their immediate prototypes Anglo-Saxon coins already obsolete in England for a generation and more.

After all this, Anglo-Saxon numismatics could well be thought an area where a non-specialist treads at his peril, but it is a mark of the extent to which the subject has been neglected that some of the most important contributions have been made by those who would disclaim any particular expertise. Mr Robert Stevenson's brilliant stylistic analysis of the tenth-century pattern of die-production is a case in point.[55] Already at the end of the sixteenth century, though, English antiquaries of the calibre of Speed and Camden were exhibiting a remarkable appreciation of the potentialities of numismatic evidence, and a century later Sir Andrew Fountaine laid the foundations of what was to become a real academic discipline. Beside the great collectors of Anglo-Saxon coins, and here such names as those of Hunter, Rashleigh, Montagu, the elder Carlyon-Britton and Lockett come at once to mind, there has been a continuing tradition of detached scholarship, best exemplified perhaps in men such as Richard Southgate, Taylor Combe, Edward Hawkins, Daniel Haigh, Sir John Evans, Charles Keary, George Brooke and Elmore Jones, which has done much to break down the too often justified prejudice of pure historians. Curiously little has been contributed as yet outside England, and often what has been done has not received due recognition – contemporary reviews of pioneer works such as those of John Lindsay[56] in the nineteenth century and of Carl Axel Nordman[57] in this make sad reading – though the exception that proves the rule is the still standard second edition of Bror Emil Hildebrand's classic work.[58] Perhaps the most exciting prospect as Anglo-Saxon numismatics enter the last quarter of the twentieth century is the progressive realization made possible by the late Sir Frank Stenton's decisive sponsorship of Christopher Blunt's inspired wartime pipe-dream of the *Sylloge of Coins of the British Isles*.[59] No less critical has been the access to the great Scandinavian coin-hoards granted to students from these islands with a generous absence of what could have been understandably chauvinistic *Prioritätsrecht*; if precedence is given here to the name of Nils Ludvig Rasmusson over those of Georg Galster, Jouko Voionmaa and the late Hans Holst it is simply because of the sheer volume of the quite unpublished Swedish material that has been made available in this way.

Notes

1 Generally reliable introductions to the Anglo-Saxon series are provided by Dolley (1964) and Sutherland (1973), and the former may usefully be supplemented by Dolley (1965) and the earlier pages of Dolley (1966b). Very comprehensive listings of the coins occur in Brooke (1950) and North (1963).
2 Kent (1961).
3 Bruce-Mitford (1972) 47–51.
4 For the pre-penny period see especially Grierson (1961b).
5 Dolley and Metcalf (1957).
6 Sutherland (1948).
7 Sutherland (1942); Rigold (1960); Rigold (1966).
8 Lyon (1956); Pagan (1969).
9 Blunt (1961).
10 Blunt and Dolley (1968).
11 Blunt, Lyon and Pagan (1963).
12 Lyon (1958); Pagan (1969).
13 Blunt, Lyon and Pagan (1963).
14 Dolley (1970).
15 Dolley and Skaare (1961).
16 Dolley and Blunt (1961).
17 Dolley (1954b).
18 Blunt (1969).
19 Lyon and Stewart (1961).
20 Wilson (1955).
21 Dolley (1965).
22 Dolley (1957).
23 Stevenson (1951).
24 Petersson (1969).
25 Dolley and Metcalf (1961).
26 Dolley (1973a) reviews and reaffirms the case for the original sexennial cycle.
27 Dolley and Pirie (1964).
28 Rasmusson (1961).
29 Malmer (1966).
30 Dolley (1958a).
31 McKerrell and Stevenson (1972); Forbes and Dalladay (1960).
32 Seaby (1955).
33 Dolley (1971).
34 McKerrell and Stevenson (1972).
35 Sellwood (1962).
36 Dolley (1955).
37 Dolley (1971).
38 Dolley (1954a).
39 Dolley and Elmore Jones (1961).
40 Forbes and Dalladay (1960).
41 Grierson (1961a).
42 Dolley (1958b).
43 Hill (1920).
44 Dolley (1961b).
45 Dolley and Metcalf (1961).
46 Dolley (1973a).
47 Dolley and Pirie (1964).
48 Dolley (1954a).
49 Lyon (1966).
50 Dolley (1960).
51 Dolley (1966a).

52 Dolley (1961a).
53 Rasmusson (1961).
54 Dolley (1973b).
55 Stevenson (1951).
56 Lindsay (1842).
57 Nordman (1921).
58 Hildebrand (1881).
59 Twenty fascicles of this series have appeared over the last fifteen years, and the Anglo-Saxon collections already more or less completely illustrated include those at Cambridge, Glasgow, Copenhagen, Chester, Edinburgh, Oxford, Reading, Bristol, Gloucester, Birmingham, York, and a wide range of museums in the midlands. A beginning has also been made with selected private cabinets.

9

The animal resources

Juliet Clutton-Brock

A major resource for every human economy has been provided by the exploitation of animals. Through phases of hunting, domestication, and intensive husbandry man has progressively refined his command over animal populations and this sequence can be followed from prehistoric to historic times in Britain. During the prehistoric period the record can only be traced from study of the fragments of animal bone yielded by archaeological excavation. There is little or no pictorial or literary evidence to illustrate the progressive use of domestic animals, or the emergence of breeds, until Roman times and even then the references are flimsy. The Saxon period is the earliest phase of British history when man's interdependence with animals can be studied, not only from the bones recovered from food debris on archaeological sites, but also from historical references.

Deductions about animal resources or agricultural practices that may be made from excavated animal remains are often probably quite accurate, but they may also be grossly misleading. Chaplin[1] has described methods that may be used in the interpretation of data obtained from animal remains, taking as one example the material from a Saxon farm in London. But however skilful the treatment of the data, it must still yield results that are to a certain extent speculative, unless there is documentary evidence to substantiate the osteologist's findings.

Unfortunately there are very few archaeological sites where animal bones and written accounts are both available. One such example has been provided by Guilday[2] for a site in North America. In a neat tie-up between bones excavated and documentary evidence Guilday has shown that, at an eighteenth-century British fort, the minimum number of animals calculated from the excavated bones would have supplied the garrison for just one day, whereas the written evidence shows that the fort was garrisoned continuously for eight years (although the numbers of men varied greatly during this time). The major part of the meat ration over the whole period consisted of boned salt pork which left no archaeological record.

This may bear some relevance to Anglo-Saxon sites where pig bones are not usually found in great abundance although it is known that the domestic pig was kept in very great numbers.

So, although the literary references for the Anglo-Saxon period are scant, the information that can be gleaned from them on agricultural and hunting practices is an invaluable supplement to the study of the animal remains. The sources of written information are chiefly to be found in the Anglo-Saxon Chronicle, the early codes of laws, and Saxon charters and wills.

At the close of the Roman period, deciduous forests still dominated the landscape of Britain. Livestock husbandry was ubiquitous but it is likely that wild animals, killed in the chase, still provided a fair proportion of the meat, especially in winter.

Of those large mammals that survived the end of the Ice Age the reindeer, the elk, and the aurochs (*Bos primigenius*) were extinct but there were plenty of other wild animals to be hunted: red deer, roe deer, wild boar, feral cattle, wolf, bear, beaver, otter, fox and hare. Wild cats and the smaller carnivores and rodents were also common, but there were no donkeys, rabbits or rats, and probably only a few fallow deer. The domestic animals were cattle, horses, sheep, goats, pigs, poultry, dogs, cats and bees. Fish was an important food, salmon and eels being often mentioned in the literature.

After the Roman administrative system in Britain had collapsed much farmland was neglected and went out of cultivation. This land reverted first to grassland and scrub and then to woodland. As has been shown at the Anglo-Saxon site of Shakenoak in Oxfordshire this regenerated forest was very different in composition from that of the original post-Pleistocene forests. Oak still remained a dominant species but the alder, elm and lime of the pre-Neolithic period were replaced by ash, birch and many more shrubs, such as hazel and hawthorn.[3]

Shakenoak was probably typical of many Anglo-Saxon settlements in being surrounded by open ground with some arable crops. Beyond this there would be sheep and cattle pasture which merged into scrub and mixed-age woodland, and then into the dense primary forest that had changed little since Roman times but which was increasingly cleared throughout the Anglo-Saxon period. Perhaps the remark in the Anglo-Saxon Chronicle[4] that strange adders were seen in Sussex in the year 776 may be a reflection of the changing environment and the emergence of new heathlands.

The Laws of Ine, 688–94, are the earliest written documents that give information on pastoral life in England during Anglo-Saxon times. Much fascinating detail can be learnt from these laws about the value of stock and the relative values of the food animals. The following examples may be quoted:

55. A ewe with her lamb is worth a shilling until 12 days after Easter.

58. The horn of an ox is valued at tenpence.
59. The horn of a cow (is valued at) twopence; the tail of an ox is valued at a shilling; that of a cow at fivepence; the eye of an ox is valued at fivepence, that of a cow at a shilling.
69. A sheep must go with its fleece until midsummer, or else the fleece is to be paid for at twopence.
70.1. As a food rent from 10 hides; 10 vats of honey, 300 loaves, 12 'ambers' of Welsh ale, 30 of clear ale, 2 full-grown cows or 10 wethers, 10 geese, 20 hens, 10 cheeses, an 'amber' full of butter, 5 salmon, 20 pounds of fodder and 100 eels.

As has been pointed out by Trow-Smith[5] the Laws of the Ine show that the buying and selling of stock was already well-established and that cattle-thieving was a common activity against which there were the most stringent laws. The following passage from a lease of Beddington by Denewolf, Bishop of Winchester, to Edward the Elder (899–924) throws light on the numbers of animals kept on farmland 200 years later than the Laws of Ine:

Then there is 70 hides of that land, and it is now completely stocked, and when my lord first let it to me it was quite without stock, and stripped bare by the heathen men. And I myself then acquired the stock for it which was afterwards available there. And now we very humbly grant it to you. Moreover, my dear lord, the community are now desirous that it be given back to the foundation after your death. Now of the cattle which has survived this severe winter there are 9 full-grown pigs and 50 wethers, besides the sheep and the pigs which the herdsmen have a right to have, 20 of which are full-grown; and there are 110 full-grown sheep, and 7 bondsmen, and 20 flitches; and there was no more corn there than was prepared for the bishop's farm, and there (are) 90 sown acres.

Horses, cattle, sheep, and poultry were kept in enclosed pastures and penned at night, often in a room adjoining the house, where they were safe from the very real danger of being killed by wolves and foxes. The custom of pannage for pigs, however, was quite different. Pigs were allowed to graze free-range in the woods and forests in great numbers and they survived the winters by feeding on acorns and beech-mast.

The economic role of domestic animals

In order to make some assessment of the interaction of animals and man in Anglo-Saxon England, data on the animal remains from five sites have been analysed. Three of these sites are in Norfolk, one is in Kent and one in Cornwall. It would have been more rewarding if sites with a wider distribution throughout Britain could have been chosen. Despite the large numbers of Anglo-Saxon sites that have been excavated, however, there is a lack of detailed information on the animal remains which made this impracticable.

A very short summary is given of the excavation of the sites followed by descriptions of the species of animal identified and some suggestions on their role in the Anglo-Saxon economy.

NORTH ELMHAM, NORFOLK

North Elmham was the site of the bishopric of East Anglia until it was moved to Thetford in 1071. The site was excavated between 1967 and 1972 by P. Wade-Martins and the animal remains have been identified and extensively studied by B. A. Noddle[6]. More than 3,000 animal bones have been identified from one part of three middle Saxon north–south ditches. This part of the excavation has been dated to 650–850.

THETFORD, NORFOLK

Part of the Anglo-Saxon town of Thetford was excavated by the late G. M. Knocker between 1948 and 1952.[7] Very large numbers of mammal and bird bones were reported in detail by Miss J. E. King and the late Miss M. Platt respectively. These reports have not yet been published.

At the end of the Anglo-Saxon period Thetford was a flourishing town with a population of 4,000 at the time of Domesday. The area excavated by Knocker lay in a peripheral position near the town's defences. With the exception of one large house the buildings were small and straggled along narrow cobbled roads. It was an artisans' quarter of the town.[8] The area excavated is believed to date from the ninth to the eleventh centuries.

The animal remains were mostly recovered from refuse pits, of which more than 180 were excavated.

SEDGEFORD, NORFOLK

North Elmham and Thetford were both Anglo-Saxon towns, whereas Sedgeford was probably only a small country hamlet a few miles from the sea. Excavation of the fringe of the settlement and part of the Christian cemetery was carried out by P. A. Jewell in 1958. The animal remains were studied by the author and the full report on the excavation is at press. Pottery that was *in situ* at Sedgeford was predominantly Ipswich ware which dates the site to between 650 and 850.

SANDTUN, KENT

The site of Sandtun lies in Romney Marsh near West Hythe, Kent. The settlement was excavated by G. Ward in 1947, but no report of it has been published. The site was covered with sand and the precise chronology has not been published, but the fairly large number of interesting animal remains were identified by F. C. Fraser. Other Anglo-Saxon finds from Sandtun are mentioned by Wilson.[9]

MAWGAN PORTH, CORNWALL

Mawgan Porth is a small bay on the north coast of Cornwall. In contrast to the other four sites mentioned here, the Anglo-Saxon invasions can have made little impact on this

Cornish settlement which flourished as a small hamlet between the ninth and the eleventh centuries. It was finally abandoned and covered with blown sand as were other Christian sites along this coast in early medieval times.[10]

The animal remains from Mawgan Porth were initially identified by F. C. Fraser, J. E. King, and M. Jope.

These sites all produced skeletal remains of domestic cattle, sheep, pigs and horses in differing proportions as well as carnivore and bird bones. The species of animal are described under separate headings. The numbers of bones of each species from Thetford

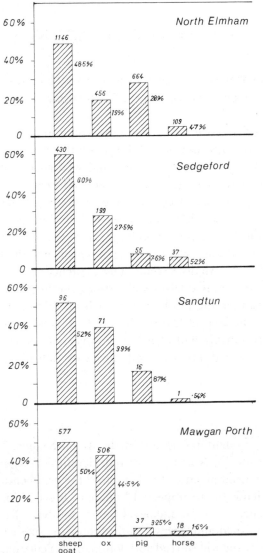

Figure 9.1 Frequency diagrams to show the relative numbers of sheep/goat, ox, pig, and horse bones found on four Anglo-Saxon sites

were not counted. The relative numbers of specimens of sheep/goat, ox, pig and horse from the other four sites are given in fig. 9.1.

The pig

It is possible that during Anglo-Saxon times pigs greatly outnumbered all other domestic animals and were the basic component of the agricultural economy, although their skeletal remains are usually found in lower numbers than those of sheep and cattle. Very large herds of free-ranging pigs must have been a common sight in all woodland areas. The Laws of Ine state that:

> 44. If anyone cuts down a tree under which 30 swine could stand, and it becomes known, he is to pay 60 shillings.

Saxon swine may be pictured as small dark-skinned hairy pigs with relatively long legs, comparable to the unimproved small domestic pigs that are kept today by some Central European peasant communities.

It is possible that the Anglo-Saxon pigs still freely interbred with the wild boars which were living in the forests. Throughout the Anglo-Saxon period, however, the extensive clearing of the forests led to a decline in the numbers of domestic and wild swine, so that by Domesday the ox and sheep had truly replaced the pig as food producers.

The system of allowing huge herds of pigs to roam free-range meant that meat was available in the winter months when other stock was low due to the lack of fodder. It is a little difficult, however, to understand the lack of correspondingly large numbers of pig bones from Anglo-Saxon sites, unless the meat was customarily eaten boned and salted as bacon. Certainly bacon was well-known to the Anglo-Saxons. The existence of very large numbers of swine in the ownership of a few individuals is well-attested in the literature if not by their skeletal remains. For example the ninth-century will of Ealdorman Alfred of Surrey states that 2,000 pigs are to be bequeathed to his wife.[11] The herds of pigs were in the care of swineherds who presumably had little control over individuals but were able to cull whatever number was needed, for pigs are notoriously difficult to control.

Cattle

Wilson, in 1909, asserted that red cattle were brought to England by the Anglo-Saxons.[12] These cattle are represented today by the Lincoln, North Devon and Hereford breeds. Wilson maintained that these red cattle were widespread in England until the eighteenth century when they were replaced in the midlands by the imported Longhorn breed. This may be so but there is no osteological evidence for it. By medieval times, however, distinctive breeds of cattle were certainly established and Trow-Smith quotes the literary evidence for them.[13] Black cattle were by this time widespread and dominant in Scotland,

Wales and Cornwall; polled dun cattle were common in East Anglia, perhaps as a result of imports from Holland and Belgium.

What the osteological evidence does show is that Anglo–Saxon cattle were, on average, little if any larger than Iron Age cattle. The very large numbers of ox bones from Thetford were carefully measured against the bones of a present day Chillingham ox (the unimproved feral breed of white park cattle) which would have had a withers height of approximately 135 cm. It was found that the Thetford cattle bones were, on average, from slightly smaller animals.

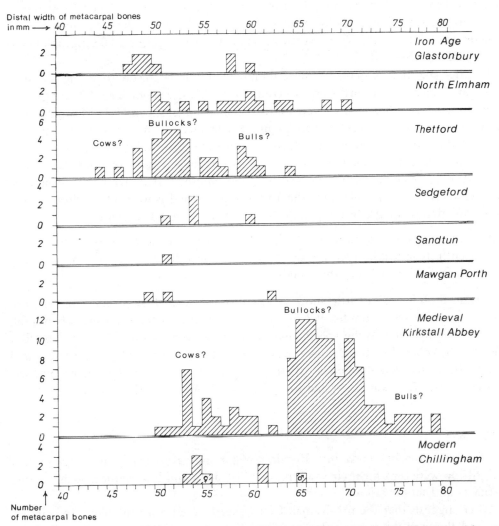

Figure 9.2   Frequency diagram to show the range in distal widths of ox metacarpal bones from Anglo–Saxon sites compared with those from the Iron Age site of Glastonbury, the medieval site of Kirkstall Abbey, and modern Chillingham cattle

The chart (fig. 9.2) supports this result and shows that many of the Anglo-Saxon bovines must have been as small as the present-day diminutive Kerry breed. They were markedly smaller than the cattle from the medieval monastic site of Kirkstall Abbey in Yorkshire. Similar measurements of metacarpal bones from this site[14] are also shown on the chart.

Fig. 9.1 shows that in terms of absolute numbers of bones and teeth, cattle were most-commonly killed at Mawgan Porth and least-commonly at North Elmham. Despite Chaplin's very just criticisms against counts of absolute numbers of bones as opposed to a calculation of the minimum numbers of animals represented, these results probably reflect the true proportions of animals husbanded. It is likely that sheep farming for wool was the major agricultural industry at North Elmham and pannage for 2,000 pigs is quoted for the village in Domesday.

At other sites the ox played a more dominant role in the economy. The numbers of bones excavated at Thetford were not counted, so this site is not included in figs 9.1–9.4, but King has stated that there were more ox remains than sheep.[15] At Mawgan Porth there were more ox remains relative to the number of sheep than at North Elmham and this is probably a true reflection of the farming system, for Cornwall is not sheep-country.

The literary evidence for the view that the ox was the only plough animal in Roman and pre-Roman times has been reviewed by Trow-Smith.[16] It is likely that oxen were used exclusively for ploughing during the Anglo-Saxon period as well. The earliest written evidence for the use of the heavy plough is provided by the Laws of Ine:

> 60. The ceorl who has hired another's yoke (of oxen), if he has enough to pay for it entirely in fodder – let one see that he pays in full; if he has not, he is to pay half in fodder, half in other goods.

Certain limb bones of cattle show a clear distinction in their proportions between the sexes. It can be seen from fig. 9.2 that the distal widths of the metacarpal bones fall into two size ranges for all the specimens except those from North Elmham, Thetford and Kirkstall Abbey. For these sites the size range has a much wider distribution and it may be suggested that the bones with an intermediate width are those from bullocks (castrated bulls). This was suggested for the Kirkstall Abbey cattle by Ryder.[17]

Sheep

Sheep farming probably grew into Britain's major industry during the Anglo-Saxon period. Sheep were kept for their wool, meat, milk, dung and by-products such as bone for artifacts and fat for tallow.

Ryder suggests that the pre-Roman Celtic sheep were brown in colour and similar in size and fleece to the present day primitive Soay sheep.[18] He provides evidence to suggest that the Romans introduced a white breed with a finer fleece.

Ryder's evidence, based on the analysis of wool fibres from textiles, shows that

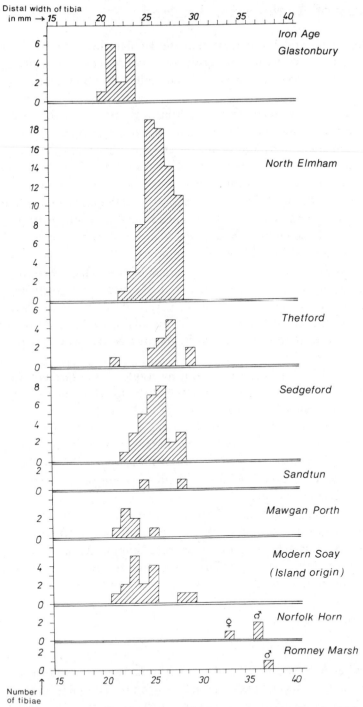

Figure 9.3 Frequency diagram to show the range in distal widths of sheep tibiae from Anglo-Saxon sites compared with those from present day breeds and with those from the Iron Age site of Glastonbury

Anglo-Saxon sheep had fine wool and he suggests that the Roman fine-woolled sheep evolved into the early-improved sheep with a primitive longwool fleece. A present-day example of a sheep with this type of fleece is the white-faced, polled, Romney breed from Kent.

It is of interest, however, that the sheep from Sandtun in Romney Marsh did not bear any resemblance to the present Romney breed, as far as can be deduced from the skeletal remains. The Sandtun sheep were much smaller and were horned.

Comparison of the sheep bones from the five Anglo-Saxon sites described on p. 376 showed that all the sheep were remarkably similar in size and shape of horn core and that they still closely resembled the primitive Soay. At North Elmham, however, four rams' horns were found that were larger and differently shaped from this general pattern.[19] These four horn cores more closely resembled those of the Scottish black face or Norfolk horn sheep which is a semi-improved breed like the Romney.

The majority of Anglo-Saxon sheep were slightly larger than the Iron Age sheep and their skeletal remains are at an interesting stage in the gradual process of improvement. In fig. 9.3 the distal widths of the sheep tibiae from Iron Age Glastonbury are shown for comparison with those from the Anglo-Saxon period. (The possibility that some bones from this sample are of goat rather than sheep cannot be discounted but wherever possible the identifications were checked.)

It is unlikely that selective breeding was carried out by Anglo-Saxon farmers, who would have relied on the large numbers of sheep that they kept for providing enough wool for profitable trading. Measurement of the sheep bones from North Elmham suggests that the majority of sheep on this site were wethers (castrated rams). Wethers produce a heavier fleece than rams or ewes, and large flocks of wethers were kept in the Middle Ages for the production of wool. Noddle has deduced from measurement of the bones that the sheep would have weighed on average 90 lbs. The live weight of a present day Norfolk horn sheep is approximately 110 lbs.

The North Elmham sheep were nearly all fully mature and at least six years old at the time of their death. This is shown by the relatively large number of worn teeth. On the other hand the sheep from Sedgeford, a much poorer community, were mostly immature, and only two out of twenty-six mandibular rams had the third molar fully erupted. Presumably these sheep were bred primarily for meat and were killed when less than four years old.[20]

The goat

Goat horn cores were found at Mawgan Porth and at Thetford. As is well-known it is very difficult to distinguish goat from sheep bones especially when the material is fragmentary. For this reason it is hard to give a true assessment of the proportions of goat to sheep from any one site and the bones are usually described as goat/sheep. It is likely that goats were husbanded in small numbers at most Anglo-Saxon settlements but that their numbers declined as the woodland was cleared, for the goat is a browsing animal that does best in scrubland.

The horse

The remains of horses are found in small numbers on most Anglo-Saxon sites (fig. 9.1). Horses were not kept as food animals but they were eaten if there was an exceptionally bad winter. The horse bones from Sedgeford have exactly the same chopping marks as the ox bones, suggesting that they are the remains of food. Seddon has suggested that at Maxey, Northamptonshire, horses were ridden until they were five years old and were then eaten.[21]

Probably little attention was paid to the selective breeding of horses, although reference is made in the will of Atheling Athelstan (1015) to a white horse, a black stallion and a pied stallion.[22] But these were the property of the nobility and not farm animals.

There is no evidence that horses were used for ploughing during Saxon times; this was the prerogative of the ox. There is no doubt, however, that horses were used as draught animals as well as being the principal means of travel. St Columba is said to have had a white horse which was used to carry the milk pails to and fro between the byre and the monastery.[23] The Laws of Ine may be quoted again for the statement that:

33. The King's Welsh horseman, who can carry his messages, his wirgild is 200 shillings.

The Romans imported horses into Britain which enlarged the size and presumably improved the strength of the native stock. The Anglo-Saxon invaders also brought their horses with them and it is not unusual to find horse bones from Anglo-Saxon sites that came from animals with a withers height of approximately fourteen hands (142 cm). The earlier Celtic ponies whose remains are found on Iron Age sites only stood about twelve hands (122 cm) at the withers (shoulders).

An interesting account of an invasion complete with horses is given in the Anglo-Saxon Chronicle:

892. On this year the great host about which we formerly spoke went again from the east kingdom (the kingdom of the East Franks) westward to Boulogne, and were there provided with ships so that they crossed in one voyage, horses and all, and then came up into the mouth of the Lympne with two hundred and fifty ships. That estuary is in east Kent, at the east end of the great forest which we call Andraed (the Weald). This forest from east to west is a hundred and twenty miles long or longer, and thirty miles broad. The river which we mentioned before flows out from the forest; they pulled their ships upstream as far as the forest, four miles from the entrance to the estuary, and there stormed a fort within the fen.[24]

This description is of some importance because it can be readily seen how horses that survived such skirmishes could wander into the forest and become feral animals, mixing with the already half-wild herds that were rounded up from time to time, much as they are in the New Forest today.

It was during the Anglo-Saxon period that a Chinese invention reached Britain which, it has been argued, had a greater impact on the history of the early middle ages than any other. This was the stirrup. It must be remembered that the Romans did not have stirrups, and a cavalry without stirrups has little power in armed combat, for the horsemen must concentrate on sticking to their chargers. In the ancient world horses were more frequently harnessed to chariots than ridden for warfare.

The earliest reference to the stirrup is in the Chinese literature of A.D. 477.[25] It was brought across Central Asia by nomadic horsemen and reached Germany, via East Prussia and Lithuania, in the early part of the eighth century.

The invention of the stirrup completely changed the method of warfare in Western Europe. For horsemen could now use the principle of mounted shock combat; whilst the horses were at a gallop the men could thrust their pikes and swords at the enemy without hurling themselves off. Armour became increasingly heavy in order to withstand this shock combat and White states that the military equipment for one man cost about the equivalent of twenty oxen or the plough teams of ten peasants.[26] The horses had to be larger to carry the heavily armoured men and consequently more land had to be given over to growing fodder. Only the rich could afford to be cavaliers, and this led to heavy taxes being levied against the peasantry. The result was the emergence of a mounted warrior class and the build-up of the feudal system.

The Anglo-Saxons used the stirrup but did not realize its power. At the Battle of Stamford Bridge Harold Hardrada of Norway said of Harold of England, 'That was a little man but sat firmly in his stirrups.'[27] But when the Anglo-Saxon army reached Hastings the horsemen dismounted and fought in the old way on foot, to their loss. William had the advantage from the beginning of the battle with his mounted cavalry and bowmen. White's concluding remark on this subject may be aptly quoted; 'Antiquity imagined the Centaur; the early Middle Ages made him the master of Europe.'[28]

The cat

The Anglo-Saxons must have been fond of cats for their remains are found with remarkable frequency on nearly all Anglo-Saxon sites.

The Laws of Hywel Dda (Howell the Good), written in about 945 in Wales, have this to say about cats: 'The price of a cat is four pence. Her qualities are to see, to hear, to kill mice, to have her claws whole, to nurse and not devour her kittens. If she be deficient in any one of these qualities, one third of her price must be returned.'[29]

Cat bones were recovered from four of the five sites described in this chapter, the exception being Sedgeford. A skull and nearly complete skeleton of an adult domestic

Table 1: Measurements of the bones of domestic cats from Thetford and Sandtun.

	Thetford mm	Sandtun mm
Condylo-basal length of skull	74.7	75.3
Length of mandible	54	53
Length of scapula		62.1
Length of humerus	82, 95, 88	86.6
Length of radius	76, 93, 85	86.8
Length of ulna	109, 101	101.3
Length of innominate bone		72.6
Length of femur	90, 103	99.4
Length of tibia	97, 113, 103	106.2

cat were found at Sandtun and at Thetford the remains of at least eighteen cats and kittens were identified. Measurements of some of these bones are given in Table 1 and show that these Anglo-Saxon cats were very much smaller than the British wild cat.

The dog

The value of a trained hunting dog was as high in Anglo-Saxon times as it is today. The kinds of dogs to be found in Wales in the tenth century are described by Hywel Dda:

> The value of the King's buck-hound is one pound, when trained; one hundred and twenty pence untrained and sixty pence when a year old; thirty pence when a young cub in the kennel; and fifteen pence from the time of its birth until it opens its eyes.
> The King's greyhound, if trained, is worth one hundred and twenty pence.
> The King's lap dog is worth a pound; the lap dog of a freeman, one hundred and twenty pence; that of a foreigner, four pence; and a common house dog is of the same value as the latter.
> A freeholder's buck-hound is of the same value as the King's greyhound.
> Whatever dog a stranger may possess, its value shall be the same as that of a dung-hill dog, its value is fourpence.
> A shepherd's dog shall go in the morning before the flock, and fetch them home at night.

Probert wrote a footnote that may also be quoted in this context: 'It is singular that animals and birds should be priced not according to their intrinsic value, but according to the rank of those who kept them.'[30]

The remains of dogs are frequently found on Anglo-Saxon sites. When the dogs died or were killed they were thrown into the general rubbish pits along with the food refuse.

Table 2: Measurements of domestic dog skulls from Thetford. The skulls are in the collection of the British Museum (Natural History) and the series is numbered 1969.676. All measurements are in mm.

	204	204	200	194	190	190	181	174	170	170	165			
Condylo-basal length of skull	204	204	200	194 est.	190	190	181	174	170	170	165 est.	–	–	–
Maximum width of maxillary region, across the tooth rows	73.2	77 est.	71.1	65.2	68.8	64.1	60.0	63.3	65.8	67.0	–	60.4	57.9	57.6
Length of upper tooth row	110.3	108.1	106.8	102.9	100.5	104.8	96.5	93.2	98.0	93.7	90 est.	–	86.4	–
Length of lower carnassial tooth	23.3	–	–	–	22.7	22.5	21.0	21.5 est.	–	21.0	20.2	19.6	–	20.5
Depth of mandible under anterior cusp of lower carnassial	26.6	–	–	–	23.6	25.6	24.1	22.0	–	21.1	19.5	21.3	–	19.6

As the dogs' carcases were not butchered it is often possible to retrieve whole skulls and occasionally whole skeletons from these pits.

Thetford produced a fine collection of skulls and some skeletons from the excavated pits. The majority of this material was presented to the British Museum (Natural History) and measurements of the skulls are given in Table 2.

The Thetford dogs were remarkably large animals. All the skulls are of the hound type with relatively long muzzles, and most of them came from dogs that were about the size of a present-day retriever. The bone shows no sign of periodontal disease which is common in the jaws of animals that are fed on an inadequate diet, but in most of the specimens the teeth are very much worn even in those skulls from dogs that were less than two years old at the time of death (ageing based on degree of suture closure). The Thetford dogs were all adult but in only one skull are the sutures so closely fused as to suggest an aged animal.

The size of these dogs makes it unlikely that they were the 'dunghill dogs' of Hywel Dda. It is more likely that they were shepherds' dogs and some were large enough to fall into the category of 'buck-hounds'.

Wild and domestic birds

A large and remarkably varied list of species of birds has been identified from North Elmham by D. Bramwell and from Thetford by M. I. Platt. The species represented are listed below:

North Elmham	*Numbers of individuals*
Ardea cinerea, heron	1
Anser anser, grey lag goose (domestic)	30
Anser cf. *albifrons*, white-fronted goose	1
Anser cf. *fabalis brachyrhynchus*, pink-footed goose	1
Branta cf. *leucopsis*, barnacle goose	1
Branta bernicla, Brent goose	1
Tadorna tadorna, shelduck	1
Anas platyrhynchos, mallard	5
Anas platyrhynchos, domestic mallard	7
Anas crecca, teal	1
Anas penelope, wigeon	1
Accipiter nisus, sparrow hawk	1
Buteo buteo, common buzzard	1
Gallus sp., domestic fowl	*c.* 60
Grus grus, common crane	2
Pluvialis apricaria, golden plover	1
Numenius arquata, curlew	1
Columba palumba or *oenas*, wood pigeon or stock dove	1

Thetford	Numbers of bones
Gallus sp., domestic fowl	86
Anser anser, domestic goose	14
Anser anser, grey lag goose (wild)	6
Aythya ferina, pochard	1
Anas penelope, wigeon	3
Anas platyrhynchos, mallard	3
Spatula clypeata, shoveller	1
Unidentified wild duck	1
Melanitta fusca, velvet scoter	1
Pavo cristatus, peacock	2
Grus grus, common crane	1+1 artifact
Haematopus ostralegus, oystercatcher	1
Numenius arquata, curlew	1
Corvus corax, raven	2
Unidentified small birds	5

Goose bones are commonly found on Anglo-Saxon sites in Norfolk (they were the only bird remains from Sedgeford), and domestic geese are frequently mentioned in the literature, where they are given the same value as domestic fowls.

It is possible that the goose was domesticated from the local wild grey lag goose which nested in Norfolk until about 200 years ago.[31]

Both at North Elmham and at Thetford the majority of the fowl bones were from birds that were a little larger than the present day bantam, but at the former site there were a few longer limb bones that were more like those of a small game fowl. Small fowl bones were also found at Mawgan Porth.

It is likely that the sparrow-hawk bones were from birds that had been used for hawking which was a common sport and method of catching small birds in Anglo-Saxon times. The value of hawks is given in the Laws of Hywel Dda as follows:

A hawk's nest is worth one pound. The young unfledged hawks are worth one hundred and twenty pence; and after they are fledged and become fair, they are worth one pound, if they belong to the King.

The nest of a sparrow hawk is worth twenty four pence; before the young ones are fledged, they are worth twelve pence; and after they are fledged, their value is twenty four pence.

The hawk was presumably the peregrine falcon and was a bird of great value so it is not surprising that only the bones of the less-prized sparrow hawk have been excavated from the commoners' land at North Elmham and Thetford.

It is interesting but not remarkable that the bones of the common crane have been found at these Norfolk sites because this bird is thought to have still bred in Lincolnshire in the eighteenth century.[32] The peacock bones are perhaps more peculiar finds. The peacock was probably introduced into Britain by the Romans[33] and may have survived in small numbers either as a domestic bird or as a small feral population. Confirmation of the correct identification of the two peacock bones, however, would be welcome.

Bees

Honey was an essential ingredient in the diet of the Anglo-Saxons, as it was for everyone else in Europe until the introduction of cane sugar in the middle ages. The Laws of Hywel Dda show the value that was put on a swarm of bees:

> The value of an old swarm of bees, is twenty four pence; that of a virgin swarm is sixteen pence; and that of a second swarm is twelve pence. A swarm, from the virgin swarm, is worth twelve pence, and that from the second swarm is eight pence. If a hive swarm after August, its value is four pence, and it is called a winged swarm. The value of a hive of bees is twenty four pence, and so to the first day of winter.

Fish and shellfish

The Hunting Laws of Cambria[34] throw light on the method of salmon fishing in Wales in the tenth century:

> Salmon is called a common hunt, because when they are taken in a net, or with a fish spear, or in any other manner, if any person whatever come up before they are divided, he is entitled to an equal share of them, with the person who caught them, if it be in common water.

Freshwater and marine fish remains are quite often recovered from inland Anglo-Saxon sites. At Thetford bones and scales of cod *(Gadus callarias)* and plaice *(Pleuronectes platessa)* were identified as well as the scales of a freshwater perch *(Perca fluviatilis)*.

Oysters were as popular with the Anglo-Saxons as they were before and after this period. At Sedgeford (five miles inland) vast numbers of mussel shells were unearthed, as they were at Thetford, where cockle, winkle, whelk and topshell were also identified.

Conclusions

It may be concluded that Anglo-Saxon peasants lived much as farmers on small-holdings in the less accessible rural areas of Britain have lived until quite recent times. The people rode horses, ploughed their land, kept cats and dogs, made bacon, and husbanded cattle, sheep, goats and poultry. Their unimproved farm animals, however, bore little resemblance to present-day breeds and the countryside differed vastly from that around any British farm of the present day. Very large forest areas were close at hand and were inhabited by the wolf and the bear as well as by deer and wild boar.

There was close interaction between man and the wild fauna around him and this is reflected in Anglo-Saxon art and in the literary references to hunting. The animals had a symbolic value of importance to royalty and to the warrior class, as well as being of economic value. In this context a short description is given below of the animals represented at Sutton Hoo.

It is probable that the treasure discovered at Sutton Hoo, Suffolk, will for all time make this ship-burial the most famous relic of Anglo-Saxon times in Britain.

Although no human burial was discovered at Sutton Hoo and there were no animal remains in the ship there are other representations of animals that are of great interest. Perhaps the best known of these is the small bronze stag that until recently was thought to have surmounted the iron standard from the grave. It is now believed that the study should be attached to the top of the ceremonial whetstone or sceptre.[35]

Previously it was thought that this figure (which is no more than four inches high) was complete but that the antlers were unusually shaped. In fact they more closely resembled the antlers of Eld's deer which is found in south-east Asia than they did those of the red deer.

It must be recalled that the excavations at Sutton Hoo were carried out in great haste in 1939 because of the impending war. Thirty years later it was decided to re-excavate the dumps to see if anything of value had been missed. Soon after this an examination of the stag was requested by the British Museum and it was found that a tine was missing, in the position of the bez tine, on each antler, the cause of its misleading appearance. On searching through the tiny metal fragments recovered from the recent re-excavations one of these minute tines was found so it is now possible to restore the figurine more accurately and to ascertain that it does represent a red deer.

A red deer stag that carries twelve points on the antlers is known as a 'royal'. The antlers have brow, bez, trez tines and a terminal cup or crown of three points. In the Sutton Hoo stag this crown is particularly pronounced and it can be speculated that this figurine of a 'royal' stag was of some ritual significance. It would be interesting to know when the term 'royal' was first applied to stags with antlers grown in this way.

Another mammal represented at Sutton Hoo which was of ritual significance is the wild boar. The boar was associated with the god of war and it is believed that soldiers' helmets commonly carried a moulded boar on the crest.

Only two helmets have been discovered in Anglo-Saxon England. One is from Sutton Hoo, and one was found at Benty Grange in Derbyshire. The Sutton Hoo helmet has a gilt boar's head at each outer edge of the eyebrow mouldings. The Benty Grange helmet has a boar standing on the crest.

A passage in *Beowolf* leads to the assumption that helmets were commonly constructed in this manner:

Hnaef, the Danish hero, was prepared for the funeral pile. Bloodstained corselets, iron helmets, with golden boar crests and numbers of dead chieftans were plainly to be seen upon the pyre, for many notable men had fallen in battle.[36]

The boar, like the red deer, was later to be preserved for royalty to hunt. This conservation prevented the wild boar from becoming extinct in Britain until the seventeenth century.

The lyre from Sutton Hoo was found in what remained of a beaver skin bag.[37] It is probable that beavers were rare and much-valued in Britain in Anglo-Saxon times. Hywel Dda states that the price of a beaver's skin in Wales was 120 pence, that of a marten twenty-four pence and that of a wolf, fox, and otter eight pence. As well as the pelt being used beaver meat would have been eaten and parts of the body were much valued as medicines. A few last beavers are said to have survived in Wales until the sixteenth century, having died out in the rest of the country considerably earlier.[38] The remains of a skin cap were also found at Sutton Hoo and it has been confirmed recently at the British Museum (Natural History) that this was made from otter skin.

Finally from Sutton Hoo there is the model of a fish in the hanging bowl. This figurine probably represents a salmon, perhaps the most important fish in the Anglo-Saxon economy, although no remains of salmon from Anglo-Saxon sites are known to the author.

The Hunting Laws of Cambria quoted from Harting (1880) and Probert (1823) states that:

> The best flesh of the chase is that of the stag, the hare, the wild boar, and the bear. Greyhounds were used for the chase; the men rode horseback and carried a horn, and bow and arrows.[39]

In Anglo-Saxon times some animals, particularly the bear and the beaver, were becoming scarce but there were as yet no laws against hunting by commoners. Anyone who wished to go hunting could do so and could claim at least a share of the meat that he killed even if the kill was made on another's land.

This freedom to hunt was ruthlessly denied to the peasantry after the Norman Conquest when William I established the royal forests, thereby ensuring the survival of at least the red and roe deer as wild animals that are still to be found in Britain today, even if he was not so successful with the conservation of the bear and the boar.

The Anglo-Saxon Chronicle may be quoted on what the people thought of William the Conqueror and his game laws:

> He was sunk in greed
> and utterly given up to avarice.
> He set apart a vast deer preserve and imposed laws concerning it.
> Whoever slew a hart or a hind
> Was to be blinded.
> He forbade the killing of boars
> Even as the killing of harts.
> For he loved the stags as dearly
> As though he had been their father.
> Hares, also, he decreed should go unmolested.
> The rich complained and the poor lamented.[40]

Acknowledgements

I would like to express my gratitude to Miss B. A. Noddle for her unstinting help and her willingness to let me quote from her unpublished work on the mammal remains from North Elmham. My thanks are also due to D. Bramwell for allowing me to quote from his unpublished report on the bird remains from North Elmham and to Dr P. Wade-Martins, the excavator of the site.

References

Note: The Laws of Ine and all other references to Saxon charters and wills are quoted from Whitelock (1968), except for the quotations from the Laws of Hywel Dda which are taken from Probert (1823). These quotations were also checked with the translation of the Laws given by Owen (1841). The translation used for the Anglo-Saxon Chronicle is that of Garmonsway (1955) and that of *Beowulf* is by Wright (1960).[41]

Notes

1 Chaplin (1971).
2 Guilday (1970).
3 Brodribb *et al.* (1972).
4 *ASC*, 774C, D, E, F, G, 773A.
5 Trow-Smith (1957) 48.
6 Wade-Martins (1969), (1970), (1971).
7 Knocker (1950), Dunning (1951).
8 Davison (1967a).
9 Wilson (1971) fig. 14.
10 Bruce-Mitford (1956).
11 Whitelock (1955) 496
12 Wilson (1909).
13 Trow-Smith (1957).
14 Based on Ryder (1956).
15 Unpublished information.
16 Trow-Smith (1957).
17 Ryder (1956).
18 Ryder (1969).
19 Noddle (1971).
20 Ageing from Silver (1969).
21 Seddon *et al.* (1964).
22 Whitelock (1955) 550.
23 Trow-Smith (1954).
24 Translation by Garmonsway (1955).
25 White (1962) 15.
26 Ibid., 29.
27 *Heimskringla*, iv, 44.
28 White (1962) 38.
29 Probert (1823) 230.
30 Ibid.
31 Whitlock (1953) 74.
32 Ibid., 28.
33 Zeuner (1963) 456–7.
34 Probert (1823) 367.
35 Bruce-Mitford (1972) fig. 5.
36 Wright (1960) 53.
37 Bruce-Mitford (1972) 28.
38 Harting (1880).
39 Ibid., 17, and Probert (1823) 368.
40 E, *sub anno* 1086.
41 This chapter was submitted to the editor for publication in 1972.

10

The Scandinavians in England

David M. Wilson

The Scandinavian attacks on England can be divided into three phases. Firstly, the period of the raids; secondly, the first settlements in the north of England by Danes and Norwegians; and, thirdly, the political conquest of the whole country in the early eleventh century under the Danes, Sven and Knut. In this chapter I shall attempt to outline the archaeological evidence for the Scandinavian settlement of England; this is little enough, and it is to be emphasized that the archaeological material is to be seen against a fairly well-illuminated background of historical and place-name material. This background must be outlined here so that the picture may be set in proper perspective.[1]

The first recorded event which concerns the Scandinavians in Britain is not in itself a raid but appears almost as a symbolic prologue to the disasters that followed. It occurred in 789 on the south coast[2] and encompassed the murder of a king's reeve, named Beaduheard.[3] It is probable that this was not a raid but a trading mission which got out of hand. If these men were Norwegians, they were people already familiar as traders in England. Shortly afterwards, in 793, came the first recorded raid, the pillaging of the Anglo-Saxon monastery at Lindisfarne – one of the most important monasteries in the country – an attack which was apparently of unusual character in that such a man as Alcuin could write as follows to the king of Northumbria:

> ... never before has such terror appeared in Britain as we have now suffered from a pagan race, nor was it thought that such an inroad from the sea could be made. Behold, the church of St Cuthbert spattered with the blood of the priests of God, despoiled of all its ornaments; a place more venerable than all in Britain is given as a prey to pagan peoples ...[4]

Figure 10.1 Map of Scandinavian graves in England

The raids which followed are not chronicled in any detail in the Anglo-Saxon Chronicle (which largely deals with events in the south of England), but we may assume that, during the period up to 834, a year which appears to be a turning point in the history of the Scandinavians in England, raiders were present on the coasts of northern Britain. From 835 onwards there is hardly a year in which we do not read of attacks on various parts of the country, attacks which culminate in 851 when the Vikings first wintered in England. In 865 the first payment of the *danegeld* is recorded, while in 867 the character of the raids changed completely when Healfdene seized York and put an Anglo-Saxon puppet on the throne of Northumbria. In 876, in the words of the Chronicler, 'Healfdene shared out the land of the Northumbrians, and they proceeded to plough and to support themselves'. Alfred's treaty with Guthrum in 878 finally established the right of the Danes to settle in the north of England and in the Five Boroughs.

Against this bald outline of the historical sources and additional evidence provided by place-names[5] the archaeological material must be considered. The picture that emerges from these sources is that, *c*. 900, an area of eastern England stretching from the Tyne to East Anglia was more or less settled by Danes, who also held central England with their series of fortified towns–known collectively as the Five Boroughs. Western England from Cumberland to Cheshire had been settled by Norwegians,[6] who were largely drawn from the Norse kingdom of Dublin and were ultimately to lose power after the battle of Brunanburh.[7]

Raids

The amount of destruction caused by Scandinavian raids can hardly be adequately assessed from historical records, and archaeology is of little help. A mould from Whitby Abbey was perhaps used in making ingots from melted church plate after the raid of 867,[8] while the smoke-blackened bishop's throne at Norwich may have been burnt during a Scandinavian raid on the cathedral at North Elmham.[9] Similarly, signs of burning at Monkwearmouth and Jarrow may reflect Scandinavian attacks on these monasteries, but as Rosemary Cramp rightly remarks, such burning could also have been carried out by the Scots.[10] There is further a suggestion that some of the buildings of the elaborate water-mill at Old Windsor, Berks., were destroyed in a Scandinavian raid of the late ninth or early tenth century.[11] Such minor indications as these are all that remain of a major series of raids.

Certain archaeological finds of insular origin found in Scandinavian graves are often used to illustrate the raids.[12] Some – but not all – were torn from their original contexts by the Scandinavians, and adapted as brooches or other ornaments for their women.[13] A few of these were originally ecclesiastical objects, mounts from book-covers and shrines for example, which have found their way into pagan Scandinavian graves of the ninth century.[14] But such objects tell us little of the chronology of the Viking raids, and only illuminate the fact of piratical attacks.

Only a single Scandinavian hoard from the period of the raids contains an Anglo-Saxon object (a gold ring found in a mid-ninth-century context at Hon, Haug, Norway)[15] but as very few hoards of ninth-century date have survived in Scandinavia, such negative evidence is of little value.

The fortifications thrown up temporarily by the Danes in the period of the raids have not been recognized archaeologically, although traces have been recorded of an alleged fort of this period at Shoebury.[16] The place-names 'Danes Camp' or 'Danesbury' may reflect nothing more than tradition. Many years ago Hadrian Allcroft drew attention to a group of earthworks in the south of the Danelaw[17] which he identified as Scandinavian, but although his interpretation is possible there is as yet no archaeological proof. Similarly the striking resemblance between the Danish fortifications of the Trelleborg type and that at Warham, Norfolk,[18] seems to be coincidental since the Warham site appears to date from the Romano-British period.[19]

Evidence of settlement

Archaeological evidence for settlement is derived from three main sources. Firstly, there are a number of Scandinavian graves, accompanied in the pagan fashion by grave-goods. Secondly, a number of coin hoards have been uncovered which go a long way to illuminate the story; and, thirdly, many pieces of sculpture have survived which by their decoration show the influence of the Scandinavians on Anglo-Saxon England. I ignore here single finds of archaeological objects of the Scandinavian period found throughout England, as they do no more than confirm the actual presence of the Scandinavians in the country.[20]

The grave-finds (fig. 10.1) are hardly capable of historical interpretation, either as evidence of settlement or as evidence of raids. Only two cemeteries are known (a series of barrow burials at Ingleby, Derbyshire,[21] and a group of burials under the church at Kildale, Yorks.),[22] and only twenty-three other finds remain which can definitely be recognized as graves of Scandinavians. The objects found in the graves cannot easily be dated, and their distribution is to all intents meaningless, although for the most part these grave-finds occur in the area of Britain which was settled by the Vikings. In fact most of the graves recorded from the purely Anglo-Saxon parts of England are questionable.[23]

From the area of the Five Boroughs three burials have been recorded: two from near Nottingham,[24] and a find from Repton in Derbyshire which may be interpreted as a grave. All the other finds occur in the Scandinavian areas of north-east or north-west England. To achieve this total of twenty-three, four single finds from churchyards at Brigham, Cumberland, Repton, Derbyshire, Farndon, Notts., and Rampside, Lancs., have been added; these are generally assumed to be remains of graves. The churchyards of northern England were in continuous use throughout the Anglo-Saxon period, and were presumably used as a matter of course by the Scandinavians[25] – a hypothesis supported by the presence of stone sculpture of Scandinavian taste in village churchyards with English names (see below). The invaders – whether settlers or raiders – of England apparently buried their dead in the churchyards of the newly-conquered country, respecting the strict nature of the existing burial grounds. Although they practised the pagan ritual of their ancestors, they were perfectly willing to let their dead lie in cemeteries hallowed by followers of a different religion. It may be assumed that at this time the religion of the Scandinavian invaders and settlers of England had become formalized and loose. Their religion could admit quite easily to its pantheon a Christian God who would have as much, or perhaps even more, power than the pagan gods. If the Scandinavians did indeed bury their dead in the churchyards, the lack of grave-goods in England is hardly surprising in view of the disturbed nature of the soil in such places.

The grave-finds are difficult to date. I am sceptical in the matter of accurate typological dating in the Viking period, believing, with Almgren,[26] that it is difficult to date any object to a period within a hundred years if there is no documentary source to assist the dating. It is easy to classify the swords found in Scandinavian graves, but it is impossible to assign any date other than 'ninth century' to them. It is consequently impossible to say whether they represent people buried in the period of the raids or in the period of settlement. It seems probable, however, that some of them represent a settled society, as a Christian community would probably not tolerate a pagan burial in their churchyard unless it were under pagan control.

One detail of the distribution map of graves (fig. 10.1) might modify certain normally-held assumptions. There is a concentration of finds in north-west England, an area usually said to have been settled in the early years of the tenth century. Such finds would appear to be more or less physically equivalent to those found in other parts of the country, where they are usually taken to belong to the period of the raids or to the first generation of settlement. This concentration (although by no means a valid statistical sample) would suggest that, during the period of raids and initial settlement in this area, some proportion of the Scandinavians in north-west England were pagan. Although it is possible that they had not been Christian in their Irish homeland (or had been strengthened by a considerable body of pagan Norwegians or Icelanders) it might equally be proposed (although with little confidence) that the Viking conquest of the north-west was a much earlier and more gradual process than it has hitherto been considered.

The hoards

Mr Dolley has recently done a signal service to scholarship by listing and dating all the Anglo-Saxon coin-hoards found in the British Isles.[27] From his list we can draw certain statistical and chronological conclusions of interest. He has recorded fifty-five coin-hoards of the ninth century from the British Isles, forty-six of which come from England, one from Wales, five from Scotland and three from Ireland; and he has been able to date these within a reasonably narrow margin of time. If we plot these hoards graphically,[28] it is possible to demonstrate a significant rise in the deposition in the period between 869 and 878, when the Scandinavians were most active in their settlement in England. In 1956

Mr Lyon argued, coherently if to a certain extent unconvincingly,[29] that the deposition of hoards of the copper styca coinage of Northumbria between 865 and 875 has nothing to do with the Scandinavian settlement or invasions of the north. Even if one accepts his argument it is an interesting fact that, if one discounts the styca coinage and concentrates on the sceatta silver coinage, there is a considerable peak in the graph between 865 and 875, when Scandinavian activity was at its height and when the settlement began.

Although this evidence backs the historical evidence in a tidy fashion, such a convincing demonstration of instability could as easily have been achieved from ordinary historical sources. The hoards provide only a dramatic highlight to an otherwise well-documented account of the condition of England, and particularly northern England, in this period. It may not be without significance that the next peak (be it only a minor one) appears in the 920s when the Anglo-Saxon kingdoms of Wessex and Mercia were trying to straighten out the political situation in the north.

Sculpture and settlement

The most dramatic reflection of the Viking settlement of England is, however, to be seen in the quantity of Viking sculpture in the north of England. The Scandinavian settlers came to a land rich in stone sculpture. In churchyards throughout England there were already a fair number of free-standing sculptured stone memorials, many of which survive fragmentarily to this day. The majority of the surviving fragments of pre-Conquest sculpture in England, however, belong to the period after the Scandinavian settlement.

In their homeland the Scandinavians were quite accustomed to erecting monuments – whether only a wooden post, or a plain stone – over their dead;[30] but, apart from the occasional runic inscription, we have little evidence in Scandinavia (with one important exception) of any stone-carving before the middle of the tenth century. The exception is the series of Gotlandic picture stones which from the early migration period continue in an unbroken tradition to the end of the eleventh century.[31] But Gotland does not seem to have influenced the rest of Scandinavia. In fact, it seems that the tenth-century Jelling stone was the first non-Gotlandic, decorated stone to be erected in Scandinavia. This was a royal monument in the royal necropolis of Denmark. I have suggested elsewhere that this stone was the unique model for many of the succeeding south Scandinavian memorial stones,[32] which appear in increasing numbers towards the end of the tenth century and throughout the eleventh century. I further believe that, before the erection of the Jelling stone between 965 and 985, there was no stone sculpture (other than that from Gotland) in Scandinavia.

The ornament which the Scandinavians found on the crosses in the English churchyards was not inimical to their eyes, and they set about adapting it to their own taste. Some time ago Alan Binns drew attention once again to a group of sculptures confined to a small area along the northern edge of the Vale of Pickering.[33] Here, in an early phase of Scandinavian settlement, sculptors produced stone crosses decorated in a most incompetent fashion. Middleton B, for example, while having all the form of a true Anglo-Saxon cross of the ninth century, is decorated with an animal of late ninth- or early tenth-century date.[34] Although badly executed it does demonstrate in its contour and interlace the true Scandinavian Jelling style, which was already well established on metal objects in the northern lands. Stones like that from Middleton were apparently carved and erected in the period immediately after the primary Scandinavian settlement of England – in the last quarter of the ninth century in other words – and it is interesting to note on two of the Middleton crosses representation of warriors,[35] at least one of whom may lie fully armed in his grave. This surely demonstrates a peculiar mixture of Christianity and paganism which is frequently met with in the Scandinavian area of England. The Scandinavian patron of the stone, as is demonstrated by the cruciform head of the cross, had contact with Christianity, but the pagan idea of accompanied burial was still strong in his mind. We might thus infer that some of the pagan-type graves discussed above could be dated to the period of settlement rather than to the period of the raids.

It is difficult to say whether the first rude crosses were carved by Anglo-Saxons struggling with a new art form or by Scandinavians struggling with a new material. It is clear, however, that the Scandinavian command of stone-carving soon became more competent. The ornament of stones like that from Collingham,[36] demonstrates how Viking art triumphed over the new medium to produce inherently satisfying designs in a mixture of Scandinavian and English styles.

One can trace quite clearly in the art of the north-east the successful blend of two different artistic traditions; a blend which illustrates the congruity of two different artistic traditions, English and Scandinavian. The mixture illustrates the similarity of outlook of two different people, talking closely-related languages, living in the same area, worshipping the same god and having a certain continuity of political and even ecclesiastical organization.

Sculpture and other material shows that the settlers of the much less fertile north-west England came from Ireland, and their origin is reflected in their art. In Ireland much of the ornament of the indigenous high crosses took the form of scenes of a religious character set in panels.[37] This is exactly what is found in the western English Viking settlements. Crosses like those from Dacre[38] and Gosforth,[39] with their similar type of religious scenes, are presumably derived from an Irish prototype. But many crosses have motifs taken directly from Scandinavian sources. Particularly noticeable is the Borre ring-chain or interlace motif, which is seen at its best on the Gosforth cross but which also occurs elsewhere in England,[40] in the Isle of Man[41] and occasionally in Ireland.[42] Much of this sculpture was presumably carved between the end of the ninth century (when the first Scandinavians appeared in the north-west) and 937 when the defeat of the Scandinavians at the Battle of Brunanburh destroyed to a large extent the independence of the Scandinavians. Sculpture, of course, continued to be produced after this, and towards the middle of the tenth century there seems to have been a community of taste between east and west, typified by the Leeds cross.[43]

What conclusions can be drawn from the sculptural evidence? Firstly, the Scandinavian taste in sculpture developed within the first generation of Healfdene's settlement. Crosses like that from Middleton must be dated somewhere in the last quarter of the ninth century. Such a date illuminates slightly the story of the settlement revealed in the documentary sources. Secondly, the large quantity of sculpture executed in Scandinavian taste found in northern England suggests that Scandinavian settlement here was quite heavy. Perhaps it denies Sawyer's low estimate of the number of settlers. Thirdly, if we accept the fact that the church building is the centre of a named settlement, a study of the sculpture demonstrates occasionally that, as at Middleton, the Scandinavians settled in existing villages (for the place-name is of Anglo-Saxon not Scandinavian origin). Rather more rarely (as at Easby) it can be shown that the settlers changed a place-name, for pre-Viking Age sculpture is found in this village which has a name of Scandinavian origin. Fourthly, it is possible to recognize a distinct difference between the earliest sculpture of north-east England and that of the north-west – a difference presumably caused by the different origins of the settlers.

A tantalizing piece of evidence is provided by a small body of sculpture found in the south and west of England executed in modified Scandinavian styles. There are not a great number of such pieces – examples from St Oswald's Priory, Gloucester,[44] Ramsbury, Wiltshire,[45] Bibury, Gloucestershire,[46] and Cardynham, Cornwall,[47] are the best examples – but they indicate tenth-century Scandinavian taste in the south and west of England. Is it possible that there was some special influence behind this artistic phenomenon? There was undoubtedly a Scandinavian presence in the south-west. That this was commercial is indicated by the type of Scandinavian names found along the north coast of the Bristol Channel, many of which are sea-markers.[48] The importance of Dublin in western trade at this period was probably the reason for this distribution – Scandinavian merchants from Ireland presumably fed England with many of the products of the Atlantic trade. These stones may reflect this trade, just as some of the earliest Irish coins – at the end of the tenth century – were modelled on the mints of western England.[49] At a later stage – under Knut – Scandinavian art styles occurred alongside the English Winchester styles and it may be that these also came from the west. It is interesting, for instance, that at some date in the 1020s a Winchester style manuscript was illuminated with competent Ringerike elements, probably at the Gloucestershire abbey of Winchcombe.[50] It would be wise not to place too much reliance on such slender evidence – the evidence of Scandinavian place-names is slight[51] – but there may well have been a prosperous Scandinavian element in the population of the south-west. In the towns of York, Nottingham and Derby antiquities have been discovered which reflect the Danish settlement,[52] but only in York has excavation illuminated the Scandinavian phase of a town's history.[53]

Excavation in Stamford and Nottingham has recently revealed the line of the Danish boroughs' fortifications,[54] but other sites, even Thetford, have produced little of importance for our understanding of the Scandinavians in England. At no site so far excavated has it been possible to recognize either a Scandinavian farm or a village. This may be due partly to the lack of excavation in the Scandinavian areas, but it is also probably due to the fact that the Scandinavian settlers–an adaptable people–adopted the houses and settlements of the indigenous population. In any case there would little to distinguish in ground-plan the house of the Anglo-Saxon and the Scandinavian, and even if there was a distinction the houses would probably have been built by Anglo-Saxon craftsmen for their new overlords, as probably happened in Russia where the Slavs built houses for the incoming merchants.

Some idea of the appearance of the houses of the Scandinavian settlers can be gained from the hog-back tombstones (pl. 16). Current study of these monuments by Holger Schmidt[55] holds out hope for a real measure of enlightenment.

The later Scandinavians

The presence of Scandinavians in England in the wars leading to the conquest of Sven and Knut is documented in the pages of the chroniclers. Contemporary evidence in Scandinavia drawn from the Swedish rune-stones is also important.[56] Archaeology merely underlines the historical record of these wars and of the reign of the Danish kings.

The attack on London c. 1000 by Olaf, and the alleged destruction of London Bridge,[57] has been associated by Wheeler[58] with the find of at least sixteen weapons and tools at the north end of London Bridge. The decoration of the sockets of the spearheads and of at least one of the axes (which is Scandinavian) lends support to this theory, but some of the objects could have been lost by workmen and the weapons might have been thrown into the river as an offering–a factor well-known and so interpreted in relation to many swords of the late Anglo-Saxon period.[59]

By this time the Scandinavians in Denmark and England were nominally Christian and their burials appear to have been unaccompanied. A few sculptured funerary slabs[60] accurately reflect in their ornament the Scandinavian Ringerike style of the early eleventh century, but there is no other evidence of their presence in the funerary practices, which appear now to have been Christian.

Likewise the evidence of the hoards is disappointing. Between 990 and 1017 (the year of Knut's accession) only nine hoards are recorded from England (and four of these are dated to 1002–perhaps part of the £24,000 danegeld paid in that year). The evidence of the hoards found in Scandinavia, however, gives some idea of the wealth that left England. Recent research in Sweden has estimated that some 50,000 English coins have been found in hoards, most of which were minted for Æthelræd or Knut (i.e. between 978 and 1035).[61] In Denmark (including Skåne) the most recent estimate is of 14,833 Anglo-Saxon coins in 114 finds, of which the vast majority are of Æthelred and Knut.[62] Far fewer coins are recorded from Norway but an estimate of between 2,600 and 3,000 may not be far from the truth.[63] This material reflects in a real fashion the recorded payments to the Scandinavian invaders, and the number of coins from Sweden reflects the story hinted at in the Swedish runic inscriptions.[64] It is further interesting that there is little hack-silver in the hoards which can identified as English and few complete English objects.[65] The Scandinavians were obviously being paid in coin.

A remarkable feature of this late Danish period is the presence of a completely Scandinavian artistic taste in England.[66] The Ringerike style, which is the contemporary Scandinavian style, makes its appearance in a number of guises, in sculpture, metalwork and stone. The competence of the craftsmanship and the manner in which it chimes with the Anglo-Saxon Winchester style have been commented upon in the sources cited and need no further discussion here. This taste was to continue as an undercurrent in English style until the end of the century, for Urnes style objects such as the Pitney brooch and Bishop Flambard's Crozier[67] were undoubtedly produced in this country in the last half of the eleventh century. But these Scandinavian styles never became dominant in England and their position perhaps reflects the general status of Scandinavian culture in the last years of Anglo-Saxon England.

Notes

1 This chapter is a much revised version of Wilson (1968a).
2 Anglo-Saxon Chronicle, *sub anno* 789.
3 Cf. Æthelweard: Campbell (1962) 27.
4 After the translation by Whitelock (1955) 776.
5 Most conveniently summarized in Sawyer (1971) 149ff., where there are references to other works. This is, however, a slightly modified version of his original thesis.
6 Cf. e.g. Smith (1967) xxxix ff.
7 For recent summaries of the archaeological evidence for the Scandinavians in Scotland see Wilson (1971a); for the Isle of Man see Wilson (1974); for Ireland see Graham-Campbell in the *Proceedings of the seventh Viking congress* (forthcoming).
8 Foote and Wilson (1970) pl. Ib.
9 Radford (1959) 120.
10 Cramp (1969) 125.
11 Wilson and Hurst (1958) 185.
12 E.g. Bloch (1965) 18.
13 Most conveniently listed in Shetelig (1940) v; see also Bakka (1963) *passim*. Others are listed in Wilson (1964) 99–116 seriatim.
14 E.g. Bakka (1963) fig. 33.
15 Shetelig (1940) v, 17. The date of this hoard is discussed in Wilson and Klindt-Jensen (1966) 92.
16 Allcroft (1908) fig. 115.
17 Ibid., 384–7, recently reconsidered by Dyer (1972).
18 First pointed out by Nørlund (1948) 156f.

19 Gray (1933) apparently supported by evidence from a later trial excavation (unpublished) which produced Romano-British pottery.
20 These are listed in Shetelig (1940) iv, 55–74.
21 Posnansky (1956).
22 Elgee (1930) 220 and fig. 67. Ormside, which produced the well-known Anglo-Saxon bowl (Kendrick, 1938, pl. LX) as well as a furnished Scandinavian burial (Shetelig, 1940, iv, 18f.) may possibility be interpreted as another cemetery.
23 The four burials listed from the non-Scandinavian areas of England by Shetelig (1940) iv, 11–12, prove on further examination to be very questionable as Viking graves. The only example recognizable as a grave – that from Basingstoke – may well be of pagan Anglo-Saxon date as the objects are not of normal Viking type. The Reading and Oxford finds were not associated with skeletons and seem to be casual finds. The Walthamstow deposit may possibly be a grave, but the original records are too vague to throw any light on this. The grave from Saffron Walden – Evison (1969) – is often said to be much later than the settlement period. A closer examination of the ornament of the pendants show elements of ninth-century Scandinavian ornament – particularly features of the early Borre Style – a date which would fit the Anglo-Saxon objects in the grave more easily and the grave must be seen as belonging to the period of the raids or settlement. A grave at Sonning, Berkshire (ibid.), is almost certainly the grave of a Scandinavian, but the

grave from Harrold, Bedfordshire – Eagles and Evison (1970) – is almost certainly not.

24 Possibly a cemetery site.
25 Cf. Wilson (1967) 45f.
26 Almgren (1955) 70–87, cf. Wilson (1959) 112–19.
27 Dolley (1966a) 47–54.
28 As in Wilson (1968a) fig. 2.
29 Lyon (1956).
30 E.g. Andersen (1951) *passim*.
31 Lindqvist (1941).
32 Wilson and Klindt-Jensen (1966) 121f.
33 Binns (1956).
34 Ibid., fig. 4.
35 Wilson (1968a) fig. 3; Lang (1973) does not agree with this interpretation.
36 Wilson and Klindt-Jensen (1966) fig. 48.
37 E.g. Henry (1965) pl. 74.
38 Collingwood (1927) fig. 172.
39 Kendrick (1949) pl. XLIV, 2.
40 Collingwood (1927) fig. 182, 1966.
41 Wilson and Klindt-Jensen (1966) fig. 50.
42 Mahr (1932) pl. 57, 2.
43 Kendrick (1949) pl. xli.
44 Kendrick (1938) pl. lxxxii.
45 Ibid., pl. c.
46 Wilson and Klindt-Jensen (1966) pl. lxviii.
47 Kermode (1907) fig. 29, 6.
48 Richards (1962).
49 Dolley (1966a) 122f.
50 Wormald (1952) 59.
51 E.g. Smith (1965) 44f.
52 Shetelig (1940) iv 77–99, and Waterman (1959).
53 Richardson (1959) and Radley (1971); cf. also the journal *Interim*.
54 Wilson and Moorhouse (1971) 127 and 132.
55 Schmidt (1970). Cf. Schmidt in *Medieval Archaeology*, XVII (1973) 52ff.
56 Jansson (1966).
57 Both Richard Perkins and Peter Foote have pointed out to me that the Old Norse word *bryggjur*, used in the Norse description about this attack, means 'wharves' and that the *Heimskringla* account may be inaccurate.
58 Wheeler (1927) 18–23 and fig. 1.
59 Wilson (1965) 52.
60 E.g. Wilson and Klindt-Jensen (1966) pl. lxv *a*.
61 Malmer (1968) 93.
62 Galster (1964) 24.
63 Holst (1943).
64 Jansson (1966).
65 Cf., however, the English disc-brooch from Stockholm, Bruce-Mitford (1956) 199–201.
66 Cf. Wilson and Klindt-Jensen (1966) 135ff.; Wormald (1952) 40f.; Kendrick (1949).
67 Wilson and Klindt-Jensen (1966) pl. lxiii*e* and fig. 68.

Appendix A

Gazetteer of Anglo-Saxon domestic settlement sites

Philip Rahtz

The gazetteer includes sites which have yielded definite evidence of domestic settlement. Normally this will be evidence of buildings, but in some cases pit, ditch or hearth complexes are included. Such a list cannot be exhaustive or consistent; the urban entries especially are only those which are most obvious. It is not thought however that any important site or building has been omitted. The gazetteer is arranged in alphabetical order so that a particular site can quickly be located. It will serve as a preliminary basis for more thorough regional studies, in which the present data can be amplified, modified and related to soil, topography and other factors. Hurst's numbers are included for rural settlements, as certain detail in his gazetteer is not included here.

Details of sites which are included in the text, or in the drawings reproduced, have not generally been given in the gazetteer, except in outline; and sites with much rather ambiguous detail (Wykeham), or those with much information published in sources which are well-known and easily accessible (Sutton Courtenay) have also been dealt with summarily. National grid references are all derived from the printed or other sources and have not been verified.

Details are mainly restricted to those available at the time of compilation (1972); since this date there have been significant additions to some sites such as Chalton and Wicken Bonhunt, or new discoveries such as the settlement of framed and sunken-featured buildings at Catholme (Staffs.). Preliminary notes on these and other sites will mostly be found in the pages of *Medieval Archaeology* or *Current Archaeology*; those in *MA* 17 (1973) have been added to the gazetteer, but not incorporated in the totals.

Abbreviations of site details

Building type and construction	FB	'framed' building(s)
	SFB	sunken-featured building(s)
	PP	post-in-pit construction
	PH	post-hole(s)
	SH	stake-hole(s)
	SBS	sleeper-beam slot (either to hold beam or, filled, as foundations for it)
	PHT	post-in-trench
	SHT	stake-in-trench
	TT	timber-in-trench (plank etc)
	PAL	palisade ditches
Materials	WD	evidence of wattle and/or daub
Finds	LW	loom-weight(s)
Depth	N	from natural
	S	from present surface (otherwise uncertain or unspecified)

Date (see p. 56)	VE (very early)	c. 400–c. 450
	E (early)	c. 450–c. 650
	M (mid)	c. 650–c. 850
	L (late)	c. 850–c. 1066
	V–XI	fifth to eleventh centuries, etc

Dimensions are in metres to nearest 0.1 m unless specified, either taken from references or measured from drawings, between wall-centres.

Abbreviations of periodicals

Entries arranged: periodical, volume, year, pagination, separated by stops, all in arabic numerals. Other items refer to list of sources, pp. 463, plus pagination.

AER	*Annual Excavation Reports* of the Inspectorate (now Directorate) of Ancient Monuments, Department of the Environment, (formerly Ministry of [Public Buildings and] Works).
AJ	*Antiquaries Journal*
ANL	*Archaeological News Letter*
ANT	*Antiquity*
BAJ	*Berkshire Archaeological Journal*
CA	*Current Archaeology*
CAS	*Congress of Archaeological Societies*

COA	*Cornish Archaeology*
DMVRGAR	*Deserted Medieval Village Research Group Annual Reports*
JLS	*Journal of the London Society*
JRS	*Journal of Roman Studies*
LAASRP	*Lincolnshire Architectural and Archaeological Society Reports and Papers*
LAHS	*Leicestershire Archaeological and Historical Society*
LHA	*Lincolnshire History and Archaeology*
MA	*Medieval Archaeology*
NA	*Norfolk Archaeology*
OSM	Ordnance Survey Map, Britain in the Dark Ages (2nd edn, Chessington, 1966)
Oxon.	*Oxoniensia*
PHFC	*Proceedings of the Hampshire Field Club*
PSIA	*Proceedings of the Suffolk Institute of Archaeology*
PWCFC	*Proceedings of the West Cornwall Field Club*
SAC	*Surrey Archaeological Collections*
TBAS	*Transactions of the Birmingham Archaeological Society*
TLAHS	*Transactions of the Leicestershire Archaeological and Historical Society*
VCH	*Victoria County History*
WAM	*Wiltshire Archaeological Magazine*
WMANS	*West Midlands Archaeological News Sheet* (CBA Group 8)
YAJ	*Yorkshire Archaeological Journal*

Other abbreviations

forth.	forthcoming
inf.	information kindly given by
JGH	J. G. Hurst
PAR	P. A. Rahtz
PVA	P. V. Addyman
NV	reference not verified by present author

Sites mentioned in the text but without detailed entries in gazetteer

Athelney (Somerset)	Laver (1909)
Brebières (France)	Demolon (1972)
Dorestad (Holland)	Van Es (1969) and *pers. comm.*
Ezinge (Germany)	*Germania* 20 (1936) 42
Feddersen Wierde (Germany)	*Germania* 34, 125–41; 275–317; 39, 42–69; 41, 280–317; conveniently summarized in *Current Archaeology* 13 (1969) 56–61; see also Parker (1965)

Tilleda (Germany)   Grimm (1968)
Vallhagar (Gotland)   Anderson (1955), Stenberger (1955), see Parker (1965)
Warendorf (Germany)   Winkelman (1958)
Wijster (Holland)   Van Es (1967)

Sites deleted from other lists (pottery only, or other insufficient evidence of settlement or buildings, or post-1066)

Brandon, Suffolk (OSM)
Caldecote, Norfolk (Hurst 132): probably Iron Age (inf. JGH)
Chilbolton, Hants (OSM)
Eynesbury, Hunts (Hurst, 79): probably Iron Age (inf. JGH)
Kettleby Thorpe, Lincs (Hurst, 110)
Kingston-on-Thames, Surrey (OSM)
Tarring, Sussex (Hurst, 231)

Site name and county	Location or NGR ref.	Evidence	No. of Build-ings	Dimensions in metres	Depth of floor	Date	Hurst No.	Remarks	Sources
Abingdon Berks.	'beyond St Helens church to S' (SU 4997)	SFB	1	c. 2.5 × 1.80	0.5N	VE–E			inf. C. Hi Henders Report by C. Simp Upper Thames Archaeo cal Commit 1971
		?SFB	2	c. 3.2 × 3.1	0.2N	?E			
				c. 2.4 × 2.6	0.2N	?VE			
		PH							
Alveston Warks.	SP 213554	LW				E	234	gravel quarry pre-1939	inf. W. T.
	SP 208548	PAL enclosures, pits, PH small rect. structure	1			E		by cemetery	WMANS 1970. 41 WMANS 1971.21 MA 15. 1971. 134
Ashbocking Suffolk	TM 175551	floors of buildings, hearths, WD walling	2+			L	200	? around central court	PSIA 25. 1949–51. 2 OSM

Name County	Location or NGR ref.	Evidence	No. of Buildings	Dimensions in metres	Depth of floor	Date	Hurst No.	Remarks	Sources
...ton ...rks.	SP 342747	SFB	1	4.0 E–W	0.5N 1.5S	E	235	under DMV	inf. G. G. Wilkins WMANS 5. 1962. 4
...oor ...ncs.	SE 893181 ?	SFB	1			E	104	possibly same site as Normanby (Burton-in-Stather) (Hurst 114)	Myres 1951. 96 Dudley 1949. 224
...n Blount ...rbys.	SK 209346	settlement area with late Saxon pottery under DMV				L	34		MA 13. 1969. 276–7 MA 14. 1970. 198–9
...n-on-...mber ...ncs.	TA 033220	structures				E	105		inf. JGH
...ngs (Little) ...ffolk	TM 228464	?SFB, LW	3			E	201	over urnfield	PSIA 28. 1958–60. 90 OSM
...ord ...ds.	TL 053597	Saxon *burh* PH, SBS with PH, 'one or two substantial buildings'	1–2			M–L			MA 15. 1971. 124
...ord-on-Avon ...rks.	SP 099519	parallel slots, PH at ends, possibly pens; ditch with WD and querns; ditches and PH further W				E		near cemetery	WMANS 14. 1971. 21 MA 16. 1972. 163

Site name and county	Location or NGR ref.	Evidence	No. of Build-ings	Dimensions in metres	Depth of floor	Date	Hurst No.	Remarks	Sources
Bishopstone Sussex	TQ 468007	Hall 1–FB, PH (double), outer PH slope inwards; pot of VI	1	9.1 × 4.9		VE–E	220	fig. 2.15	MA 12. 1968. 1 MA 13. 1969. 2
		Outbuilding B1, FB, PH	1	? 3.0 wide				fig. 2.15	Dup. int. of Bish Rsch. C 1970 an
		? second hall, 14 single, double and treble PH	?1					? as hall 1	Armstron 25–27 a (SFB I
		FB in grave-free area in cemetery, burial across entrance; ? religious, ?lych-gate	1					2 FB in cemetery may be one and same building	Lecture b M. Bel Oxford
		FB, PH, adjacent to cemetery, trape-zoidal, central large PH	1	6.1 × 2.1– 2.7					Inf. M. B MA 16 162
		FB, circular	1	9.1 diam.					
		SFB 1, 2-post, ? secondary hearth in mid-floor, SH	1	3.7 × 2.7	1.0			fig. 2.11	
		SFB II, 2-level floor, ? cellar	1	4.0 × 3.7	0.5– 1.1N			? floored over deeper area, fig. 2.11	
		pits with cow skeletons, PH, gully; trodden floor, ? threshing							
Bishops Waltham Hants.	SU 553175	? episcopal estate FB per. 1, light SBS construction with single partition; ? barn or large ? shed or ? fenced yard with stalls	1			L		no scale on CA plan	Dup. int. May 19 CA 10. S 1968. 274–6 v plan
		FB per. 2, aisled hall with cross passage, screens, ? solar, ? porch, SBS and PH	1						MA 10. 1 249
		pits fence earlier							

Name County	Location or NGR ref.	Evidence	No. of Build-ings	Dimensions in metres	Depth of floor	Date	Hurst No.	Remarks	Sources
...ow Hill ...rks.	SP 290675	pits and PH in rock, up to 1.2 m in diam. circular and square; square PH form two parallel arcs; two pagan graves, one with *seax*; a few possible Saxon sherds				E		at E end of spur over crest looking E; possibly religious structures	inf. W. T. Ford WMANS 14. 1971. 21.
...on-on-the- ...ter ...s.	SP 171221	SFB, entrance on W, hearth and LW in E part, midden in NW, stone seat by S wall, loom PH 1.5 m apart, 13 PH on margin, sloping inwards, LW and whorl	1	6.1 × 3.8	0.9N	E	60	fig. 2.12	Dunning 1932 OSM
...ock ...rthants.	SP 945855	SFB	sev-eral			E	144		inf. JGH OSM
...l	Mary-le-Port St ST 588729	late Saxon town FB, SBS, and PH, ? plank walls, hearth and cess-pit, drain into sunken road	1	5.0 E–W		XI			exc. PAR 1962–3 MA 8. 1964. 264–5
	Castle St at ST 593732	FB under rampart, SBS and PH; slag, oven	2+			pre-1080			MA 14. 1970. 156
...lstairs ...nt	*c.* TR 4168	cemetery penannular PAL ditches round graves sub-rectangular slots round 7 graves; each had slabs of local sandstone on edge to form 'walls' round grave				E		MA NGR ref. is in sea	MA 15. 1971. 126 Hogarth 1973

Site name and county	Location or NGR ref.	Evidence	No. of Build-ings	Dimensions in metres	Depth of floor	Date	Hurst No.	Remarks	Sources
Buckden Hunts.	TL 201680 (JGH)	SFB PH scattered	1	1.9 × 1.4		L	76	TL 202680 on OSM	MA 6–7. 1962–3. OSM
		FB, bow-sided, PH long walls, SBS side walls	1	14.0 × 4.6–5.2		XI	77	fig. 2.16	Tebbutt 1 Hope-Tayl 1962
Bulmer Essex	TL 834384	SFB pit	1	3.7 × 2.7	0.3	E–M	54		Blake 1959
Bunwell, Lincs.	TM 129932	pit or ? SFB ditch, WD	?1	1.3 diam.	1.2	L	130	E in JGH ref.	MA 9. 196 172
Burgh Castle Suffolk	TG 474045	Saxon shore fort, circular huts of WD construction, ?monastic ?cells clay floor-tiles	2+			M (635 +)			AJ 106. 19 66–9 MA 3. 1959 MA 6–7. 1962–3. ANL 7. 19 166 JRS 52. 19 178
Burpham Sussex	TQ 039086	FB, PH, end-to-end, partitions and extension	2			?L		not in fig. 2.16	MA 19. 19 150
Butley (Neutral Farm) Suffolk	TM 379500	SFB, one with hearth, with ox skull on iron spearhead	sev-eral			E	203		PSIA 25. 1 207–8 OSM
Butley (Church site) Suffolk	TM 374500	FB with exterior hearth hearth sites	1	13.7 × 4.6		E	204		PSIA 25. 1 207–8 OSM
Caistor-by-Yarmouth Norfolk	TG 515123	Roman town sub-circular SFB in main street and in spaces of adjacent insula	2+			E–M	131		JRS 42. 19 96–7 JRS 43. 19 122 and f NA 31. 195 407 OSM
		SFB shown in JRS fig. 37, by street, also 'post-Roman cuttings'	2+	c. 5.5 × 5.5					

ame / ounty	Location or NGR ref.	Evidence	No. of Buildings	Dimensions in metres	Depth of floor	Date	Hurst No.	Remarks	Sources
ridge mbs.	TL 445592 etc.	Saxon town hut site, burnt; pits, some wicker-lined; ditches evidence of structures on many sites				L			OSM Alexander 1964 Addyman and Biddle 1965 etc
rbury nt	TR 150575 etc	Roman/Saxon town 6 SFB, parallel with Roman street and 8 m from it, one trapezoid, one square other SFB, floor with row of LW	6 1+	1.8 × 1.7 to c. 4.0 × c. 2.5	0.3– 0.6	E IX		'abodes of settlers of rank and file, or mercenaries'	ANL 3. 1951. 151 ANL 4. 1953. 177–8 ANL 5. 1954. 16 ANL 5. 1954. 134 Hawkes 1958. 67–8 MA 4. 1960. 135 Frere 1966. 91–3 and fig. 19 MA 16. 1972. 126
	TR 149575	4 PH in quadrilateral; floor level 0.6 above Roman	?1						
ngton (olley Pit) xon.	SP 453103	SFB, 10 LW in row, whorls	25+		0.4– 0.6N	E	171		VCH Oxon. I. 359 CAS 1932–3, 28 CAS 1934. 28 Leeds 1936. 21 Oxon. 3. 1938. 165 Oxon. 5. 1940. 3 Oxon. 7. 1942. 61–2 OSM
ington urwell Farm) xon.	SP 444121	20 SFB in two groups; small square, oblong or oval hollows, 2 post; burials, hearths, LW PH, 5 in a row	20 ?1	av. 2.7 × 1.8	0.3 or less N	E	172		Oxon. 23. 1958. 130 MA 2. 1958. 188 MA 4. 1960. 136 Arthur and Jope 1962–3 OSM

Site name and county	Location or NGR ref.	Evidence	No. of Buildings	Dimensions in metres	Depth of floor	Date	Hurst No.	Remarks	Sources
Casthorpe Lincs.	SK 872351	? SFB – dark patches	2+			E	106	=Barrowby	East Midlar Archaeol. Bulletin 3 1960. 8
Castle Rising Norfolk	TF 666246	castle site settlement traces				L			MA 15. 19ᵗ 128
Castor Northants.	TL 125984	SFB	1			M	145	? Nunnery of St Kyneburgha	inf. JGH Addyman 1 22
		?hut over *praetorium*; pits	1			M			MA 16. 1972. 15ᵗ
Catholme Staffs.	SK 203175	FB, PH and PHT SFB	26 2			? E		not in fig. 2.15	inf. S. Losc Bradley (ᵗ Valley Co mittee)
Catterick Yorks.	SF 2498	stone building of V with 'grandiose' entrance	1			VE			JRS 50. 1960. 218 Frere 1966. 96–7
		timber building of V with posts in ground or on stone blocks	1						
	SE 225988	SFB	1	*c.* 4.0 × 2.0		E			MA 17. 1973. 150
Caythorpe Lincs.	SK 940470	? structures, LW, graves				E	107		Philipps 19. 146–7, 16 OSM
Chadwell St Mary Essex	TQ 657779	SFB	1			E	55		inf. JGH

ame unty	Location or NGR ref.	Evidence	No. of Build-ings	Dimensions in metres	Depth of floor	Date	Hurst No.	Remarks	Sources
on ts.	SU 734145	downland village PHT construction succeeding separate PH				E	68	sherds over 5 hectares and lynchets of field system	MA 15. 125 Addyman *et al.* 1972 Addyman *et al.* 1973
		2 FB, end-to-end, both 3 doors, 2 in mid side walls, one in end wall; both have internal partition cutting off ⅓ of building; paired posts fences	1 1	11.50 × 6.25 11.0 × 6.25				fig. 2.15	since 1972 CA 37. 1973. 55–61
								pl. 9	
		other FB smaller many other buildings in 1973 including SFB (one only, with total of 33 FB now recorded)	2+					not included in totals	
dar merset	ST 457531	palace complex IX–XI per. 1: FB including Long Hall and 5 lesser buildings of PHT, PH, SH construction	6			pre- *c.* 930		see figs 2.7, 2.8, 2.16 and 2.20 for details	Rahtz 1962–3 Colvin 1963. 4–6, 47, 907–09 and figs. 2, 67
		per. 2: FB including West Hall 1, latrine building, fowl-house; of PP, PH, SH, construction with SFB elements in fowlhouse	3			*c.* 930 –1000		pl. 11	Rahtz 1964 Rahtz forth-coming
		per. 3: FB, West Hall II; iron-working building with stone footings and PH ditches, pits, boundary fences, ? flagstaff etc	2			XI			

Site name and county	Location or NGR ref.	Evidence	No. of Build-ings	Dimensions in metres	Depth of floor	Date	Hurst No.	Remarks	Sources
Chichester Sussex	SU 8704	town WD, LW, 'loom-pit'; occ. material on streets				L			ANL 2. 19 149 CBA Calen summari
Clopton Cambs.	TL 302488	structures and ditches				M–L	20	under DMV	Alexander
Collingham Notts.	SK 8154	LW, pits							MA 13. 19 236
Congham Norfolk	TF 718233	huts; dark soil etc round fired-clay hearth; covered by 50 kg of daub; 5 ridge PH down centre	1	5.5 × 4.0		M			MA 16. 19 157
Colchester Essex	TL 997251	SFB, planking slots for benches	1			E		Roman town; not in fig. 2.10	MA 17. 19
		SFB, 2-post	1	2.8 long		E			140
Crossgates (Seamer) Yorks.	TA 032832	20 hearths over 0.1 hectares; some within hut-floors				E	277	OSM Seamer	Rutter and Duke 19
		? SFB	1	2.2 × 1.1					YAJ 41. 1 10, 17, 562
		SFB	1	2.4 × 4.3	0.6S				OSM
		SFB, pear-shaped, higher ledge on N side; hearth quern, pot-boilers	1	4.3 × 3.0	0.3– 0.4N			fig. 2.11	
Darenth (Roman Villa) Kent	TQ 563707	FB, substantial timber-framed SFB, recut	1 2			E E		not illust.	MA 17. 19 145
Dartford Kent	TQ 546746	?SFB	1		1.0	E	92		Tester 195
Doncaster Yorks.	SE 5803	town floor and hearth of sandstone roof slabs				E			MA 15. 19 135
		ditch				L			inf. P. Bucklan

...me nty	Location or NGR ref.	Evidence	No. of Build-ings	Dimensions in metres	Depth of floor	Date	Hurst No.	Remarks	Sources
...ster-on- ...nes ...	SU 575945	Roman town							
		small building of unmortared stone footings for ? half-timbered upper structure; later than Honorius coin; housing for military?	1			?V		stone is innovation in Dorchester in V	Frere 1962 Frere 1966. 93–4 OSM
		SFB, with extension leading to steps up to Roman street, forest of PH outside, hearth and fuel-box, stakes in floor for ?benches, ?lockers, ?bedding	1	3×3.5	0.7N	VI		fig. 2.11	
		part of rectilinear building of PHT construction, PH at 0.9 m intervals, internal partitions	1			?IX			
		PHT, posts of 0.85 scantling SFB (1973 ref.)	1			?IX			
		Flint and clay-walled buildings of three phases (1973 ref.)	2			E E–L			MA 17. 1973. 148
	TR 318414	buildings with footings of flint and pebble	2+			L		inside Saxon Shore Fort	MA 15. 1971. 126
		buildings of WD metalled road 15 LW in ruins of terrace buildings	2+						

Site name and county	Location or NGR ref.	Evidence	No. of Build-ings	Dimensions in metres	Depth of floor	Date	Hurst No.	Remarks	Sources
Dunbar (Doon Hill) E. Lothian	NT 680792	? thane's palace succeeding 'British' one, with PP construction				VII			MA 10. 176–7 Lecture B. Hop Tayl to Soc Antiq.
		FB, hall, 88×40 units of 'Dunbar foot' of 10.0 ins.; TT construction, cf. Yeavering of c. 635; double partition, threshold and annexe PAL octagonal enclosure between half-treetrunks in trench	1	22.3 × 10.1					OSM
Dunstable Beds.	TL 003235	SFB SFB also on this ridge c. 10	2			E E			MA 16. 1972.
Eaton Socon Hunts (formerly Beds.)	TL 173588	FB, hall PH and WD; 1 divided internally 1:2; entrances mid long sides; squared timber impressions seen in WD; no hearth (?brazier); little pairing, poor alignment building under castle bank, hearth of cobbles and chalk set in clay see 1973 ref.	1	11.6 × 5.5 plus annexe 3.5 × 3.5		L L V–VII	78		Addyma MA 17. 1973.
Elmswell Yorks.	TA 000576	pits, floors, domestic objects				E	259		Congre Congre OSM
Ely-Trinity Cambs.	TL 568801	SFB	1			L or post 1066			MA 4. 1960. inf. JG

ne nty	Location or NGR ref.	Evidence	No. of Build- ings	Dimensions in metres	Depth of floor	Date	Hurst No.	Remarks	Sources
ham nd	SK 944077 SK 942080	SFB under cemetery SFB, 2-post	1 1	4.0 × 3.30		E	185		MA 12. 1968. 160 MA 17. 1973. 149
th .	SU 746054	SFB	1			L	69	dug 1957	inf. JGH
n		stone walls	2			VE			CA 39. 1973. 102–10
n land St) 	SP 436098	SFB	2+			E	174	see also New Wintles	Oxon. 3. 1938. 167 OSM
n .	SP 430108	FB SFB 4-post structure well	1 1	10.6 × 4.6				1973 ref. only	MA 17. 1973. 148
n rove Pit) y	SU 842466	SFB with LW	1	4.0 × 5.0	0.6	E	215	SU 840460 on OSM	SAC 36. 1925. 123 Morris 1959. 140 Oakley et al. 1939. 255–9 OSM
ham	SP 990578	pit in shallow depression, ?SFB depression 10 m from pit PHS and shallow pits	1	3.7 long	1.0	E L	1		Jope 1951 OSM
? .	SO 996464	FB, PH construction, store bread-oven in SFB, circular, with hearth recess to W, access by flight of wood steps through wall of WD LW, lava quern	1 1	6.0 × 2.0 2.0 diam.	 c. 1.0	M–L	256	C14 date in mid IX; ?episcopal palace or ?monastic settlement fig. 2.16	Peacock 1967 MA 12. 1968. 162
horpe	c. TL 834 385	timber structures, possibly huts above level of IV	2+						MA 3. 1959. 282, 285

Site name and county	Location or NGR ref.	Evidence	No. of Build- ings	Dimensions in metres	Depth of floor	Date	Hurst No.	Remarks	Sources
Gloucester Glos.	Bell Hotel and Tele- phone exchange site SO 8317	pits, PH, in lowest of three layers separated from Roman by sterile loam				L			CA 26. 77–83 (inf. H Hurst 19 esp. 5
		substantial parts of large houses of WD in middle layer, preserved wattle	2						
		late pot in top layer sunken building, cellar, ?stone wattle fences and clay floors	1						
Goltho Lincs.	TF 116774	houses, PH, walls of clay and straw?	2			L		fig. 2.17 lettering of buildings not as pub. ref.	DMVR(18. 19 inf. G. Beres
		house A	1	?9.0 × 4.5					
		house B	1	9.0 × 4.5					
		houses C, E, F defined by floor spreads, eaves trenches and floor wear, no wall traces, studs on ground?							
Grantchester Cambs.	Fiddlers Close	SFB, 2-post, living floor on air space, whorl	1	3.1 × 1.75	0.14N	V			inf. J. Alexa
	TL 4351	hollow-way, banks and ditches				M–L			MA 16. 148

e ty	Location or NGR ref.	Evidence	No. of Build-ings	Dimensions in metres	Depth of floor	Date	Hurst No.	Remarks	Sources
unmow	TL 626219	SFB, floor at subsoil level of gravel and stone	1	c. 6.0×9.0	0.2–0.3S	E			Dup. Int. Rep. by P. Drury 1971
		FB, central rectangular structure of two bays; walls SBS, roof on posts in PH, 0.75–1.00 inside walls; lean-to structure on W side, semi-circular in plan with inclined rafters – possibly another on E side; underfloor space, parabolic in section, constricted at edge to make platform for walls; floor supported on post on long axis, on flint pad; ramp access at E end. See 1973 ref. for further information	1	19.0×2.7 floor 2 m. wide	 1.50	E		Over Roman gravel-pit; early Saxon pottery also in filling of sunken floor of late Roman shrine depth is headroom	MA 16. 1972. 152f. MA 17. 1973. 140
ne End k	TL 935690	SFB, whorls	1	5.0 wide	0.5	E	205	Pakenham on OSM (TL 936693)	Brown et al. 1957, 197–207
		SFB, whorls	1	3.0 wide	0.5				PSIA 27. 1957. 178–85
		?FB, circular, delimited by rows of stones; weaving implement 2 sets of LW in rows or groups strung on sticks before firing Iron-working hearths, slag clamp kiln, clay floors burials	1	4.0 diam.					PSIA 30. 1964. 116–23 PSIA 30. 1965. 188–97 MA 9. 1965. 174–5 MA 10. 1966. 174 OSM
all	SW 585416	4 buildings including 1 of stone	4			E–L	25	?Saxon	ANL 6. 1958. 131–8 Thomas 1958 other refs. in Beresford and Hurst 1971

Site name and county	Location or NGR ref.	Evidence	No. of Build-ings	Dimensions in metres	Depth of floor	Date	Hurst No.	Remarks	Sources
Haddenham Cambs.	TL 469755	timber outbuildings, WD	2			L or post 1066			MA 14. 1970.
Ham Surrey	TQ 169715	SFB, LW	1				216		SAC 52. 1952. Morris 1 143
Hanwell Middlesex	TQ 153800	settlement, LW				E	127		Wheeler 136–9
Harrold Beds.	SP 954572	SFB ?SFB, spread of rubbish, cemetery between two	1 ?1	3.0 × 2.0		E–M	2		Eagles a Evisor OSM
Harston Leics.	SK 850314	SFB, weaver's hut ? weaving tool, whorl ?SFB, pit or trench, LW, ? cellar	1 1	4.0 × 2.0 2.0 × 1.0	0.7N 0.7N	E	100		Dunning OSM
Hatton Rock Warks.	SP 237577	?palace complex (air-photo) FB and SFB ? TT construction SFB sectioned in pipe-trench	16+	see fig. 2.17 and text				fig. 2.17 C14 date in IX	Rahtz 1 Hirst an Rahtz
Hellesvean Cornwall	SW 506400	building	1			L	26A		Guthrie Thomas Guthrie 60 Barton
Hemingford Grey Hunts.	TL 302690	SFB	1			E	81		Coote 1 OSM
Hemsby Norfolk	TG 494171	12 LW at depth of 1.5 m	?1		?1.5	E	135		MA 8. 237 OSM

Name County	Location or NGR ref.	Evidence	No. of Build-ings	Dimensions in metres	Depth of floor	Date	Hurst No.	Remarks	Sources
...men ...tgomery	SO 214981	FB under castle rampart, PH construction, paired and central PH stormwater gully	1	7.0 × 5.0		E–M		? Saxon	WMANS 13. 1970. 42 MA 14. 1970. 165 MA 15. 1971. 137 Barker 1971b. 65
...rd ...fords.	SO 508404	Saxon town structural features under rampart of ?1055; corn-drying ovens burnt timber building with SBS and PH metalworking furnaces pits	2 1			?M L L L		C14 date in VIII	1968 excavation by I. M. Gray and PAR CA 9. 1968. 242–46 MA 13. 1969. 233
...dge ...	TL 850082	SFB, see 1973 ref. for details	5			E		not illust.	MA 17. 1973. 140
...on ...s.	TL 287717	SFB	1			E	82		Coote 1952. 71 OSM
...Tor ...n	SX 745789	10 phases of buildings before XIII turf walls faced with wattles in SH also PH long-houses with opposed entrances and cross-passages towards lower end; hearths and hard outlines of floors small U-shaped foundation trenches SFB sub-rectangular SFB	10+ sev-eral 1 1	see fig. 2.14 3.4 × 2.1 3.6 × ?		L	38	cf. Hutholes and Lydford fig. 2.14	MA 6–7. 1962–63. 341–3. fig. 102 MA 8. 1964. 282–5. fig. 91 MA 9. 1965. 210–11 MA 10. 1966. 210. fig. 86
...es ...n	SX 702758	7 phases turf wall long-houses as Hound Tor; central row of posts supported roof; hearths	7			L or post-1066	40		MA 9. 1965. 212 MA 10. 1966. 210

Site name and county	Location or NGR ref.	Evidence	No. of Build-ings	Dimensions in metres	Depth of floor	Date	Hurst No.	Remarks	Sources
Ipsley Worcs.	SP 067666	building, rectangular, internal divisions; cattle pen PH and gullies with PH in bases at 45° to Roman road *francisca* of V associated or just above ? building or droves	1 ?1	8.2 × 5.5		Late IV– ?V			WMANS 1969. inf. P. F
Ipswich Suffolk	TM 1745	Saxon town areas of PH, SBS, pits				M–L			MA 3. 1 299 West 19(
Kemp Howe Yorks.	SE 962662	oval SFB, central hearth, close to burials	1			E	264		MA 13. 241
Keston (Lower Warbank Field) Kent	TQ 415633	SFB, ? weaving, 2-post and 1 extra PH, 29 SH in floor, arc of PH outside, lead LW, weaving needle FB in 1973 ref.	1 1	4.0 × 3.6	0.2– 0.4N	VI		not illust.	Philp 19 MA 15. 127. f MA 17. 145
Kirby Bellars Leics.	SK 718183	trench with burnt soil and ditch				L	101		TLHAS 1966– 72 Hurst 19
Langhale (Kirstead) Norfolk	TM 302969	scatter of pot marks site of village 1 km. from pot kiln				L			DMVR(18. 19 20 MA 15. 129
Latimer Bucks.	SU 998986	buildings in Roman villa complex FB cruck-building, SBS, PH, door at ?N end FB, PH, 6 or 8 post ?granary other buildings indicated by floor areas	 1 1 3	 15.2 × 3.4 5.8 × 3.4 10.5 × 4.5 9.0 × 4.0 9.5 × 2.0		?V	14	*cf.* Wijster fig. 2.2 fig. 2.2 fig. 2.2	MA 11. 263 Branigan Branigan espec.

e/ty	Location or NGR ref.	Evidence	No. of Buildings	Dimensions in metres	Depth of floor	Date	Hurst No.	Remarks	Sources
xton	TL 192624	enclosures, one circular, PAL trenches, droveway, field boundaries, ?FB, pits (stores and latrines), wells (wood-lined), querns, ovens PVA: individual farm units with ancillary buildings and home-fields and droveways leading to village centre				L	85	fig. 2.4	MA 6–7. 1962–63. 308 MA 8. 1964. 234–6 Addyman 1969
	Cannon St (Financial Times)	Saxon town							
		SFB, boarded cellar, massive D-shaped PH against walls	1	3.6 × ?2.7		?L		fig. 2.10	Grimes 1956 MA 4. 1960. 136
		SFB, SBS with massive PH at c. 1 m intervals along it; planked floors and wall-lining on W and N sides; entrance mid S side; wood sill or doorway and ? porch	1	9.8 × 5.2	1.8 but wall height 3.0 in all	?L		fig. 2.11	Grimes 1968, espec. 153–60 and figs. 34 and 35
	Bucklers-bury	SFB, 2 plank floors one above the other	1	2.4 or less wide	1.0	?L			Grimes 1968. 158
	Addle St	SFB, part, cf. Cannon St, SW angle and part of 2 sides, PH	1		1.5	L			Grimes 1968. 158
	Other sites	SFB, ? cellar, heavy floorboarding in fill	1	3.0 square	1.6+	L			
		pits and stone wall				L			Marsden 1967

Site name and county	Location or NGR ref.	Evidence	No. of Build-ings	Dimensions in metres	Depth of floor	Date	Hurst No.	Remarks	Sources
London (cont.)	TQ 300799 Whitehall (Treasury site)	FB? weaving, basin dug out of gravel, lined with bracken and other organic; on this, raft of planks and poles for clay floor; planks up to 2.1 long, bays defined by 22 cm posts along wall face, SBS for plank walls, porch at E end, own door in front of main entrance; stone ? roof weights, LW, thread pickers, whorl, Badorf ware lava querns, in 0.3 depth of floor dirt	1	6.4+ long 7.9 wide 5.5 length of bay		IX			Green 1 MA 6–7 63. 30 MA 8. 1 236 JLS 367 48–50
	Savoy	SFB, oval, LW and loom PH, hearth	1	6.1 long		E			Wheeler 139
	West-minster Hall	arrangement of but-tresses and inward curvature of stone medieval hall suggests built round pre-Conquest hall of bow-sided plan of timber construc-tion	1	c. 75.0 × 21.15–22				fig. 2.8 length uncertain – discrepancy in Colvin text and figure	Colvin 1 and fig
Loveden Lincs.	SK 908458	rectangular stone foundation in cemetery	1			E			inf. JGH cemetery in MA
Lydford Devon	SX 510847	Saxon *burh* SFB FB, 'substantial', PH. PHT FB with turf walls and hurdling as Hound Tor etc property boundaries, SH, ditches	1 2+ 2+	10.65 × 4.0		L			MA 10. 168–9 MA 11. 263 MA 12. 155 Addyma Saund forth. inf. PVA

me unty	Location or NGR ref.	Evidence	No. of Build- ings	Dimensions in metres	Depth of floor	Date	Hurst No.	Remarks	Sources

n
x
	TL 851070	timber structures
		  fronting street
		  hall, ? aisles,
		  beams and studs
				11.0 × 6.0		L		not illust.	MA 17. 1973.
									  148

m (ls Farm) s.	SE 910034	pot and slag				E	113		Dudley 1949. 234 Myres 1951. 98

an Porth
nwall
	SW 852673	hamlet or small
		  village, buildings
		  round yard
		  including long-
		  houses, opposed
		  doors
		walls 2.1 high max.,
		  0.6 wide pointed
		  with yellow clay
		slab-lined recesses or
		  cupboards, box beds
		PH for timbers of
		  slate roofs
		illustrated building
		  had centre PH and
		  partition; doors in
		  side and end walls
			c. 10	10.0 × 4.6		L	28	fig. 2.4
								
								fig. 2.14
									Bruce-Mitford
									  1956

Site name and county	Location or NGR ref.	Evidence	No. of Build-ings	Dimensions in metres	Depth of floor	Date	Hurst No.	Remarks	Sources
Maxey Northants.	TF 124081	village or estate, many buildings over area of *c* 0.75 hectare; around space ? PH concentrations, ? racks				E–M	150	fig. 2.4	Addyman OSM
		SFB, atypical	5+						
		SFB or cellars	2						
		FB or PH, PHT, and SBS construction							
		FB 'A': 3-bay, ?buttresses, ? plank walls, 3.0 entrance marked by triple PH	1	14.6×6.1+					
		FB 'B': central SBS in 2.1–3.4 lengths	1	15.2×6.1					
		FB 'C': massive PH	1	6.1 wide					
		FB 'D': PH, PHT, porch, ? hearth	1	9.7×4.9					
		FB 'E, F': 4 parallel lines of PH	? 2						
		querns etc. 55 pits, gravel-holes, clay storage, covered cellars, fire pits, latrines, soak-aways, flagstaff hole							
Medmerry Sussex	SZ 837937	settlement in eroded cliff				L	228	OSM Selsey	White 193 OSM
		? SFB	sev-eral						
		clay floors, shell middens FB with WD and ? board construction LW and WD querns							
Messingham (Greetwell Farm) Lincs.	SE 930040	pot and slag, ? hut site	?1			E	112		Dudley 19 143 and Myres 195 OSM (Ma Warren)

ne nty	Location or NGR ref.	Evidence	No. of Build- ings	Dimensions in metres	Depth of floor	Date	Hurst No.	Remarks	Sources
d n) humberland	NT 941339	palace complex on air photograph halls, ?ditches etc.	sev- eral					3 km from Yeavering	Knowles and St Joseph 1952, 270 Colvin 1963 OSM
s.	SZ 238941	PAL enclosure and ditches,				L or post- 1066	70	under moated site	Hurst and Hurst 1967, esp. 52–5
		yard or building, PH and SBS	?1	5.2 × 4.9					
		another building PH, SBS	1						
		SFB	1	3.7 × 1.8	0.3				
ng (Linford rry) x	TQ 672803 (close to Orsett Quarry)	FB of PH; door at centre of E end, with 1.8 m gap, central hearth, charcoal in SE corner; living house	1	7.3 + × 4.6		VE–E	56	figs 2.3 and 2.15	Barton 1962 OSM
		SFB oval with centre PH and open hearth to W	1	4.3 × 3.7				SFB may be part of larger building	
		SFB and ? FB, weaving, PH, SH, S side integrated with PAL; querns, 20 LW	1	4.3 × 3.0					
		SFB, 30° batter, PH round edge, 2-post, thick charcoal in centre, raised entrance to S	1	3.7 × 3.0	0.9			fig. 2.11	
		SFB, 2-post, flat floor, 2LW and whorl	1	3.0 × 2.4	0.9				
		?threshing-floor, 3.0 diam., thick clay, PH E end							
		?food store pit							

Site name and county	Location or NGR ref.	Evidence	No. of Build-ings	Dimensions in metres	Depth of floor	Date	Hurst No.	Remarks	Sources
Mucking (Orsett Quarry) Essex	TQ 673803	103 SFB dug up to end of 1971; *c.* 50 more visible in air photo over 1 km. 3 more in 1973 ref.	103			VE–E	56A	?mercenaries guarding London	ANT 38. 217 an(37 MA 11. 264–5
		SFB smaller type, 2-post		av. 3.7 × 3.0	0.3–0.4N				Jones *et a* 1968
		SFB larger type, 2-post plus PH or SH at corners and along edges		av. 6.1 × 4.3	0.6–0.9N				MA 13. 1 231–2 Jones 196
		long axes along slope							MA 14. 1 155–6
		LW (140 in one SFB)							MA 15. 1 124
		flat clay cooking slabs							MA 16. 1 153
		ditches 100 m+ long							inf. M. U Jones
		slag in one SFB							MA 17. 142
		PH building, close-set posts	1	*c.* 7.0 N–S				E–W not yet excavated	
New Wintles (Eynsham) Oxon.	SP 432108	settlement of *c.* 3 hectares				E	175	fig. 2.3 fig. 2.17	MA. 13. 237–8
		FB, PH ?yard ?house or with internal division, 122	1	12.0 × 6.0					Hawkes a Gray 1
		FB, PH ?house, square with central post, 130	1	5.0 × 5.0				fig. 2.17	MA 15. 133 inf. I. M
		FB, PH, ?house, no fourth wall, possibly fence, 255	1	4.5 × 6.0				fig. 2.17	inf. N. C
		?pens, SBS, partitions	2+	width 4.5				fig. 2.17	
		11 SFB, all 2-post; SHS round perimeters; LW in 3, slots in floors	11	3.5–5.5 × 2.5–4.0	0.3–0.6			fig. 2.3	
		6 SFB (1971) (field to E), 15 LW in pit	6	similar to above					
		13 pits							
		trackways, ?enclosures							
Normanby (Burton-on-Stather) Lincs.	SE 896165	LW and domestic finds				E	114		Dudley 233 OSM

e ty	Location or NGR ref.	Evidence	No. of Build-ings	Dimensions in metres	Depth of floor	Date	Hurst No.	Remarks	Sources
y-le-	TF 126941	stone ?alignments and rubble path ? leading to spring LW and thread-picker				M	115		MA 12. 1968. 159
									LHA 3. 1968. 19–39
									MA 13. 1969. 234
									MA 14. 1970. 161
mham k	TF 987215	episcopal estate of 4 periods buildings of PHT, PH, SBS, PP construction with suggested sequence VII–XII 1. PHT and SBS 2. separate PH and interrupted SBS 3. continuous SBS 4. PP and bow-sided	46			M–L		fig. 2.6 pl. 10 reconstruction drawing in ILN	CA 6. 1968. 148–152 Wade-Martins 1969 CA 19. 1970. 226–231 Wade-Martins 1970 Illust. London News. 25 July 1970 Wade-Martins 1972 and pers. comm. CA 36. 1973. 22–8
esex	TQ 133841	buildings under moated site PH and cesspit				M	128		Hurst 1961 MA 6–7, 1962–63. 309–10
		FB of PH and SBS, with entrance NE side, gravel floor, hearth opposite entrance	1	4.6 × 5.2–5.8		M–L			Addyman 1964. 42 MA 8. 1964. 272
		pebbled yard and 3 FB of PH and SBS	3			L			MA 9. 1965. 213–14 MA 11. 1967. 298 MA 12. 1968. 201 and fig. 55 OSM

Site name and county	Location or NGR ref.	Evidence	No. of Build-ings	Dimensions in metres	Depth of floor	Date	Hurst No.	Remarks	Sources
Norwich Norfolk	TG 2309	town buildings FB 4 rooms, ? merchant's house or warehouse, of SBS and PH construction	1			L			NA 31. 409–1
		room I		1.8 × 1.8					Hurst 1
		room II		2.1 wide					esp. 1 2c and
		room III		2.4+ one dimension					MA 8. 1 267
		other lesser SBS and PH, clay and chalk floors							MA 9. 1 173
Nottingham	at SK 574396 etc	town with pre-1086 occupation ? pre-*burh* ditch				L			MA 14. 183
		? SFB cutting this ditch	?1			L			MA 15. 132
Oakley (Little) Essex	TM 222292	2 pits and hearth				E	57		Colches Archa Bull. 43–5
Old Erringham Sussex	TQ 204075	SFB, weaving-hut; PH in gable end and 3 other ridge PH; hollow trench to entrance in NW corner; 75 LW in 2 groups in lines on sunken floor, ?2 looms, looms sloping?, chalk and flints for ? rafters on S side	1	4.9 × 3.4	0.3N	M–L	223	reconstruction in open-air museum at Singleton, Chichester	MA 9. 175 MA 10. 149–5 OSM CA 21. 287
								Old Shoreham on OSM fig. 2.12	Armstro 1971. and f

e ty	Location or NGR ref.	Evidence	No. of Build-ings	Dimensions in metres	Depth of floor	Date	Hurst No.	Remarks	Sources
ndsor	SU 991746	palace estate rectilinear houses, side-walls or SBS, end walls on ?transverse beams on longitudinal timbers	2+			M–L	9		BAJ 55. 1956–7. 86 MA 2. 1958. 183–5 MA 3. 1959. 288–90
		early huts ?SFB	2+						Hope-Taylor 1962 OSM
		building on E bank of mill-leat, WD, plaster, flint, chalk, sarsen, Roman tile	1						
		building associated with mill?, ? glazed windows and tiled roof	1					possibly same as above	
		mill of IX, 3 parallel vertical wheels, leat off Thames 3.7 deep								
		mill of XI, horizontal type								
		'huge' ditch of VII–VIII								
gueville ts.	TL 170965	SFB	2+			E	83		inf JGH OSM
rville ts.	TL 157963	SFB	2+				134		inf JGH OSM
nby s.	TF 063388	FB	1					not illust.	inf. B. Simmons (1974)
s.	SE 201457	PH and SH under episcopal palace				L			MA 13. 1969. 274 MA 14. 1970. 173
orpe s.	SE 820515	FB, PH and slots	1			L	266		inf. JGH

Site name and county	Location or NGR ref.	Evidence	No. of Buildings	Dimensions in metres	Depth of floor	Date	Hurst No.	Remarks	Sources
Oxford Oxon.	SP 4509	town buildings of timber and WD, many cellars – square (?latrines) (clay linings or shallow extensions) – 2 m into natural·	several			L			Jope 195 Jope 195 Oxon. 2: 19ff. MA 4. 1 136 MA 6–7. 63. 31
		pits, walls, PH, roads							Benson a Cook fig. 4
		FB in Queen St							CA 24. 22–7 inf. PVA
	SP 511061	SFB	1			L			MA 17. 148
Pagham Sussex	SZ 8998	cobbled floor, stumps of row of stakes embedded in it at irregular intervals	?1			?L			Collins a Flemi 1958.
Peterborough Hunts.	TL 189974	7 SFB, circular, square, and trapezoid, cooking-pit, PH WD querns ditches	7	1.5–3.0 long, 1.5 av. diam.		E	153		Kendric Hawk 323–4 OSM
Petersfinger Wilts.		hut	1			E			inf. PVA

...ne ...nty	Location or NGR ref.	Evidence	No. of Build-ings	Dimensions in metres	Depth of floor	Date	Hurst No.	Remarks	Sources
...ster ...s.	SU 625046	(occupation in Roman fort)							Cunliffe 1966. 43–7
		SFB	1	3.4×2.7+	0.45	E			Cunliffe 1967
					N				
		SFB, 2-post, sub-rectangular, entrance to road – related to roads in spaces between buildings of IV? (PVA)	1	4.9×4.3					CA 4. 1967. 100–104 MA 12. 1968. 157 MA 13. 1969. 232
		FB, vertical timbers in PH	1	6.7×4.9		M		fig. 2.16	Cunliffe 1969
		well, large adzed planks, cross-strutted with frames pegged together							Cunliffe lecture Oxford 1970 Cunliffe 1970
		cess-pit, rubbish pit and ?boundary ditches							MA 14. 1970. 157 MA 15. 1971. 125
		(occupation in *burh*)				L		fig. 2.5	MA 16. 1972. 154
		1. FB, PHT, internal divisions; outer wall buttressed by inward sloping PH; hearth and ?stair	1	14.0×7.0					CA 30. 1972. 189–94 (plan in latter more up-to-date than fig. 2.5) Cunliffe 1972
		2. square stone ?tower ?church, 2-period, 4 PHS in later, ext. plaster; FB below	1	6.5×6.5					MA 17. 1973. 143
		3. FB, aisled hall, PH, S.BS, arcade in PP; another similar below	1	12.8×8.2					
		4. FB, PH, no doors	1	9.7×6.1					
		5. FB, PHS	1	*c.* 8.0×5.0					
		gate of fort rebuilt with dressed stone and clay							

Site name and county	Location or NGR ref.	Evidence	No. of Buildings	Dimensions in metres	Depth of floor	Date	Hurst No.	Remarks	Sources
Postwick Norfolk	TG 300074	SFB, ?hearth, secondary stone floor, whorls and LW	1	4.0×2.0	0.3 N	E	138	originally Iron Age, re-interpreted	Clarke 19... NA 31. 1... 407 OSM
Puddlehill Beds.	TI 004234	FB/SFB, PH, SBS or rain gulleys and PHT, mound over all 0.3 high, ?turf roof, ashes in SFB	1			E	3	OSM ref. TL 006235 (Houghton Regis) fig. 2.13	Matthews 1962. 9... 53, fig. 1... OSM?
		SFB part		5.5×?2.5	0.3 N				
		FB including SFB		max. 13.0×? 4.0–?7.0					
Radley Berks.	SU 513982	SFB (1928)	2+			E	4		Leeds 19... 21 OSM
		SFB (1965)	2			E	4A		
Rendlesham Suffolk	TM 340510	burnt earth hollows, ?kilns				L	206		PSIA 25 1949–... 308
Rickinghall Inferior Suffolk	TM 040760	SFB	several			E	207	TM 043760 in MA 14	PSIA 30 1964... MA 14. 1970.
Rickinghall Superior Suffolk	TM 042788	SFB	2+			E	208	another OSM ref. TM 044756 (Rickinghall Superior)	inf. JGH... OSM (R... ingha...
	TM 038743	structures				E	209		inf. JGH
Rivenhall Essex	TL 828178	pot in west wing of Roman villa Roman aisled barn re-used shallow well ?SFB	1	48.0×16.0 1.5 deep		V		Saxon pot under fallen Roman roofing	MA 16. 1972. CA 30. 1... 184–5 CA 36. 1... 14–18

me nty	Location or NGR ref.	Evidence	No. of Build-ings	Dimensions in metres	Depth of floor	Date	Hurst No.	Remarks	Sources
ans ulamium) s.	TL 1707	Roman town corn-drying furnace				late IV–V			JRS 50. 1960. 227 Frere 1966. 97–8
		building with buttresses (hall or barn) cut by water-pipe	1						
ts ts.	TL 186602	SFB, sub-rectangular, one area only fire holes, LW (lead) querns	8	c. 1.8×1.5, up to c. 3.0×2.0		L	86	table of measure-ments in L and T 1933	Lethbridge and Tebbutt 1933 ANL 7. 1961. 117
		FB, SBS and PH construction	1					8 hectare site	MA 6–7. 1962–3. 308, fig. 96
		FB bow-sided	1	18.0+ long					
		FB, SBS walls, inside these parallel slots, ? joists, at intervals of c. 1 m; PH at corners	1	12.0×6.0				fig. 2.16	MA 8. 1964. 236 Addyman 1972a
		ditched or fenced areas with access ways							OSM
by s.	TF 332731	hut floor of compacted earth, low bank of sand-stone rubble may be dwarf walls	1	4.0×2.5		E	118	OSM ref. TF 330734	LAASRP. 6. 1955. 10–11 LAASRP. 8. 1959–60. 20–22
		other huts	2+						MA 3. 1959. 297
		LW, whorls							OSM
by 1971 s.	TF 317735	SFB, 2-post, LW 6 other SFB visible as soil-marks	1	4.0×3.25	0.4N	E			1971 find: inf. P. Everson MA 17. 1973. 146
n	TR 120340	occupation layers in mound				M–L	95	OSM West Hythe	MA 3. 1959. 21 OSM

Site name and county	Location or NGR ref.	Evidence	No. of Build-ings	Dimensions in metres	Depth of floor	Date	Hurst No	Remarks	Sources
Sedgeford Norfolk	TF 711363	circular hut	1			M	139		NA 31. 1 407
		FB, SBS and WD lines in trench, flint floor, entrance in side 2.0 m wide, large door PH, burials nearby	1	c. 15.0 × 6.0		L	139A	K. Wade suggests pot late, not mid as previously	MA 3. 19 298 Addyman 42 OSM
Sewerby Yorks.	TA 205691	?circular trench in cemetery, no grave inside, ?shrine	?1	c. 6.0 diam.		E			excavatio PAR 1 MA 4. 1 137
Shakenoak Oxon.	SP 373138	finds of V–VII on villa site, esp. in Roman ditch fill				VE– E	181		MA 11. 268 Brodribb 1968, 1 and 19 (main
		iron-working, LW etc							MA 14. 162
Shepperton Middlesex	TQ 070676	circular multiple PH building, hearth and pits lined with 'burnt' humus	1	6.0 diam.		E			MA 12. 159 inf. R. A Canha
Snettisham Norfolk	TF 692332	WD, LW, whorls, slag					140		NA 31. 407 OSM

me nty	Location or NGR ref.	Evidence	No. of Build-ings	Dimensions in metres	Depth of floor	Date	Hurst No.	Remarks	Sources
mpton ih) s.	SU 434133 etc	Saxon town of 30+ hectares				M–L			ANL 2. 1949. 13–14
		huts	2+	up to 7.0× 4.0					ANL 2. 1950. 142
		SFB, WD in fill	1	4.0×2.4					MA 3. 1959. 310, fig. 103
		SFB, WD in fill	1	3.7×1.8					Addyman and Hill 1968 and 1969
		substantial buildings in PH, PHT, SBS construction	2+						MA 13. 1969. 232.
		FB, PH and SBS stake-constructed booths and fences 2-cell timber structure, possibly church hearths, wells pits (hundreds), with burning, WD, kiln debris, slag latrines in small timber buildings	1	17.0+ long					MA 14. 1970. 157 inf. PVA
mpton ts.	Bargate St	late Saxon town small sub-rectangular hut, individual PH				L		associated pot now probably pre-1066	MA 3. 1959. 310–11, fig. 103
Cadbury erset	ST 620250	timber buildings of burh in hillfort				L			inf. L. Alcock and C. Musson ANT 46. 1972. 29–38 with refs.
e ts.	TL 1863	under moated site, ?court with tiled buildings around, ?bricks ?SFB or ?cellar or ?pit latrine pit with PH and chute red tile ?standing for barrel burnt red clay floor (?threshing)		2.0×1.0	2 m deep	L			Lethbridge and Tebbutt 1936–37. 158–163

Site name and county	Location or NGR ref.	Evidence	No. of Build-ings	Dimensions in metres	Depth of floor	Date	Hurst No.	Remarks	Sources
Southwell Notts.	SK 7053	occupation on site of Roman villa bases of 7 PH in mosaic – ?hut dug from higher level				L			Daniels 1 31
Spelsbury Oxon.	SP 339213	SFB, 2 post, whorl	1	3.9×2.4		E	178	Dean	Oxon. 3. 168 OSM
Stamford Lincs.	TF 032072 etc	traces of timber structures, linear slots and PH may be part of defences rather than buildings pits incl. latrine, industrial features, quarries				L			MA 11. 1 267 CA 10. 1 266–70 MA 13. 1 234 MA 15. 1 127
Standlake Oxon.	SP 385045	SFB, sub-circular	many	one was c. 3.7 long	0.15+	E	179		Stone 18 71, 92– VCH Ox 363 OSM
		?SFB				E	179A		Oxon. 8– 1953–4
Stanton Harcourt Oxon.	SP 403055	SFB	sev-eral			E	180		Stone 18 215–16
	Beard Mill	?SFB	2+			E	180A		Oxon. 7. 104
Staxton Yorks.	TA 024794	habitation site, structures				E	270	OSM has Willerby	Brewster 220 OSM inf. JGH
Stevenage New Town Herts.	Broad-water Crescent TL 2424	hut-site	1+			V			MA 8. 19 234 MA 10. 1 223 Frere 196
Steyning Sussex	TQ 214051	ditches, gullies, pits, PH, cobbled area of flint				L or post-1066			MA 12. 1 162 MA 13. 1 267

me nty	Location or NGR ref.	Evidence	No. of Build-ings	Dimensions in metres	Depth of floor	Date	Hurst No.	Remarks	Sources
m bs.	TL 532726	hut site	1			L or post 1066			MA 4. 1960. 134
n-on-Fosse ks.	SP 218383	sunken and surface features associated with cemetery pits				E	236		MA 13. 1969. 241
									MA 14. 1970. 163
		trapezoidal ditch enclosure							MA 15. 1971. 134 inf. W. T. Ford
ve thants.	SP 557453	hall, under that of Norman ringwork, 5 square bays and open cobbled porch, service end, screens passage, central hearth, benches	1	24.4 long × c. 6.1 wide		XI		fig. 2.5	MA 6–7. 1962–63. 333 and fig. 100 MA 8. 1964. 237
		L or T-shaped chamber block, ?oversailing hall, stone footings						fig. 2.5	Davison 1967a Davison 1968
		timber kitchen	1	5.5 × 3.0				fig. 2.5	CA 12. 1969. 19–22
		stone building	1	10.7 × 9.1 × 2.1 surviving height				fig. 2.5 (not now thought to be tower)	MA 13. 1969. 236
		SBS and PH construction							MA 17. 1973. 147
n Courtenay ks.	SU 489940	SFB, of various types	31	3.0 × 2.4 to 5.5 × 5.5	0.5 to 1.0+	E		fig. 2.3; mainly on 2 sides of area of c. 10 hectares	Leeds 1923, 1927 and 1947
		FB, PH, stone pavement, pits and burials						figs 2.10 and 2.11	Radford 1957. 28–30 OSM

Site name and county	Location or NGR ref.	Evidence	No. of Build-ings	Dimensions in metres	Depth of floor	Date	Hurst No.	Remarks	Sources
Tamworth Staffs.	SK 207041	PH and PP	1+			M–L			CA 9. 19
	SK 208041	FB corner – 2 rows of closely-spaced PH	1+			M–L			MA 14, 185 MA 15. 133
	Bole-bridge St	watermill with preserved timber frames and mill pool, C14 dates in VIII	1			M		figs 2.18 and 2.19 pl. 12a	mill exca by PA K. Sh 1971
		wood and stone streets, and PH				L			CA 29. 1 164–68
		building material, including stone, timber, painted plaster and Roman tile, in ditch						excavated 1968 by Young	MA 16. 161
Telscombe Sussex	TQ 405033	?SFB, LW and hearth	1			L	232		Holden MA 9. 1 175
Thakeham Sussex	TQ 104174	SFB and slag	1	8.5 wide at top, 4.0 wide at base	1.4N	L	233		AJ 14. 19 425–6
Therfield Herts.	TL 335373	under castle earthwork, 3 slots in echelon, pit, ditch, gully, querns, clay				L			Biddle 19

ne nty	Location or NGR ref.	Evidence	No. of Build-ings	Dimensions in metres	Depth of floor	Date	Hurst No.	Remarks	Sources
rd olk	area dug by Knocker and Hughes 1947–58 TL 8384	Saxon town, 'artisans' quarter' with streets,				L			Dunning 1949 Knocker and Hughes 1950 NA 31. 1957. 408
		5 huts in single dug-out area with hearths	5	av. 3.7–4.3	0.4–0.6				
		clay floor with 16 big PH	1	4.9 × 3.7					
		FB – 3 rooms	1	10.7 × 4.6					
		FB with PH along W edge and in centre (later with wicker walls, on SFB)	1	13.7 × 7.6					
		FB, bow-sided building, with burnt clay floor, central hearth, cross walls, 5 compartments	1	15.2 × 4.6					
		FB with PH, oval depression	1	7.6 × 6.1					
		FB, broken clay floor, ?potter's workshop	1						
		SFB, FB, lowest course of posts in double skin of oak planking, spaces packed with sand; wood floor		5.5 × 4.6					
	area dug by Davison 1964–6	Saxon town, area with streets						fig. 2.4	Davison 1967
		SFB, 2-post, one with corner step entry, one with door in mid long side, one heated, one with item of equipment fastened to floor	4	3.4–6.1 long 2.9–4.1 wide	0.6N	E			
		FB, units 'B', 'C', 'D', cumulative PH	3	41.2 × 5.4		L		fig. 2.9 for rest	
		FB 'E', paired PH and SBS, stair	1	21.3 × 5.4		L			
		FB 'F' PH outbuilding	1	5.4 × 4.8					
		FB, 'G' aisled hall PH	1	33.4 × 9.5		L			

Site name and county	Location or NGR ref.	Evidence	No. of Buildings	Dimensions in metres	Depth of floor	Date	Hurst No.	Remarks	Sources
Thetford (cont.)		FB, 'K', 'H', small detached properties, PH flanking roadways	2	see fig. 2.9		L			
		SFB, 'L' framed on uprights set in SBS embedded in cobbled floor of cellar	1	5.7×3.3		L			
		SFB, 'J' mortared floor of cellar laid against SBS at sides, and PH at ends; struts raking inwards at 45° for floor above, entry by ramp at E	1	6.0×3.6		L			
Thurgarton Notts.	SK 693489	ash layers and wall footings near religious site				L	167 167A		Hodges 1 Gatherco Wailes
Torksey Lincs.	SK 836785	FB, ?potter's house, SBS, cooking hollow outside, and path	1	c. 5+×?1.5		L			MA 6–7. 63. 329 Barley 19 184, fig MA 12. 1 159
Tresmorn Cornwall	SX 161977	turf-walled houses of ?hamlet				mid X to late XI		among shrunken village site between 2 med. farmsteads; later periods of cob and finally – stone see fig. 2.14	MA 9. 19 210 MA 10. 1 209 MA 11. 1 305–6,
		house A, SH, SHT, entrance N wall, 2 hearths	1	4.3+×3.0					
		houses B, C, D, SH, 3 superimposed, latest 2-rooms, hearth in one	3	c. 8.5×3.0					
		house E, SH, byre with central door and living room with hearth	1	7.6+×3.0					MA. 12 1 199 inf. G. Beresfo 1972 Beresford
		houses F, G, SH, 2 superimposed	2						
		house F		4.9×2.4					
		house G – 2 rooms		6.9×2.7					
		house H, SH, living room and hearth and byre	1	7.6×3.0				+see fig. 2.14	

me unty	Location or NGR ref.	Evidence	No. of Build- ings	Dimensions in metres	Depth of floor	Date	Hurst No.	Remarks	Sources
ld wall	SX 124903	?SFB, depression, PH round edge	?1	2.4 × 1.8		L & post 1066	31		MA 8. 1964. 282
		?SFB, depression, PH near	?1	2.7 × 2.1					Dudley and Minter 1966, esp. 36–43
		8 phases of ?turf- walled SH and SHT, some of latter with slate edging							
		phase 9, SH	1	11.3 × 3.4					
		phase 11, SH	1	14.3 × 3.4					
		phase 11, tripartite rect. house, SH and	1	12.8 × 3.4				fig. 2.14 combines 11 and 12	
		SHT, + byre, door 1.8 wide, marked by SBS in main walls		4.9 × 3.4					
		phase 12, bi-partite long-house SH, with gaps for entrances in long walls	1	20.1 × 4.0					
		shallow gully in phase 12 suggests width of turf wall to be 1.5 m							
		phase 13, stone facing replaces inner and possibly outer hurdling, with slate roofs							
Nervet ks.	SU 617690	SFB, oval, SH around	1	3.0 long	0.27 N	E	8		BAJ 60. 1962. 114–19 OSM
(Blockley) s.	SP 152344	features under DMV PH, stone-packed, gully				L	67 67A		Rahtz 1969 MA 13. 1969. 232

Site name and county	Location or NGR ref.	Evidence	No. of Build-ings	Dimensions in metres	Depth of floor	Date	Hurst No.	Remarks	Sources
Upton Northants.	SP 714602	large SFB, weaving building SBS, PH, SH, burnt timbers, H-structure centrally; WD walls non-loadbearing; daub with timber impressions; timber ?fittings and ?furniture; 2-post ?loom emplacement, or were looms against end walls? ?box-bed, ?shelving, ?benches, ?racks for storing LW; 60+ LW in rows, threaded on sticks	1	9.1×5.5	up to 0.9	E (late VI– early VII)	156	fig. 2.12	MA 10. 1 172 Jackson e 1969
Wallingford Oxon.	SU 608898	Saxon *burh* SFB with bake-oven, curving gully				L			Brooks 19 MA 11. 1 262–3 inf. N. P. Brooks
Waltham Abbey ?Essex	TL 381007	structure under abbey				L after 850		?Danish	MA 14. 1 166
		divided long-house or hall, entrance W end, SBS construction (beam on filled trench), ?turf and WD walls, PH for ?wainscoting, cross-wall central with its entrance pre-building gullies and ditch pond LW	1	15.24+ × 7.62 (not more than 30.4 long)				fig. 2.16	MA 15. 1 125 MA 16, 1 153 London Archae I (11) 243–8.
Warwick Warks.	SP 279648	Saxon town traces of timber buildings, pits				L			MA 11. 1 294 MA 12. 1 185 inf. S. Ta and M.

me unty	*Location or NGR ref.*	*Evidence*	*No. of Build-ings*	*Dimensions in metres*	*Depth of floor*	*Date*	*Hurst No.*	*Remarks*	*Sources*
beach bs.	TL 489656	SFB trapezoid, WD, whorl, midden on floor, dog buried in floor	1	1.8×3.0× 2.7	0.7	E	21	fig. 2.11	Lethbridge 1927
		SFB, LW and whorl	1	1.8 diam.	0.9				Lethbridge and Tebbutt 1933. 133 and Table I
		SFB	1	3.0×2.4	0.6				OSM
Newton ts.	TL 108969	PAL trench or corner of building central packing of clay between timber revetments, keyed into sleeper beam ditch				L	89		Green 1962–3. 70–71 MA 3. 1959. 296–7
sfield olk	TM 006741	structures				E	211		inf. JGH OSM
	TM 005731	structures				E	212		inf. JGH
ens Ambo ex	TL 510365	2 SBS and 2 PH	?1			L	59		MA 3. 1959. 295–6
ury ts.	ST 873503	settlement site					251		WAM 59. 1964. 187–8 WAM 60. 1965. 136 WAM 61. 1966. 31–7

Site name and county	Location or NGR ref.	Evidence	No. of Buildings	Dimensions in metres	Depth of floor	Date	Hurst No.	Remarks	Sources
West Stow Suffolk	TL 797714	2.5 hectares of settlement on knoll				VE– E	210 210A	fig. 2.3	MA 2. 19. 189–90
		3 halls PH	3	8.2 × 4.3 10.0 × 4.6 6.4 long				fig. 2.8	MA 3. 19. 300
		42 SFB (to end of 1970)	42					fig. 2.10	MA 4. 19. 137
		22 pits							MA 5. 19. 311
		4 hollows		9.0–24.0 long					MA 10. 1 174
		6 hearths – fired clay on flint bed circular ditch – raw clay within SFB 6-post type succeeded by 2-post type							MA 11. 1 269–70 CA 1. 196 17 West 1969 West 196 (ROB) MA 14. 1 163 MA 15. 1 134 MA 16. 1 162 MA 17. 1 149–50 OSM CA 40. 19 151–8
West Whelpington Northumberland	NY 974837	under DMV rock-cut drain and PH				?E	162		DMVRGA 17. 1969 MA 14. 19 162
Wharram Percy Yorks.	SE 858642	under DMV settlement features, bank, ditch				L	274		MA 14. 19 fig. 69 a others ir and DMVRG
Wicken Bonhunt Essex	TL 511335	hut-sites FB these included in 27 buildings described in 1973 ref. with PH and PHT construction	2+ 1+	5.5 square to 19.0 × 6.0		L M	53	Bonhunt in Hurst	DMVRGA 16. 1968 MA 12. 19 201 MA 17. 19 143

ame / unty	Location or NGR ref.	Evidence	No. of Build-ings	Dimensions in metres	Depth of floor	Date	Hurst No.	Remarks	Sources
ord uchamp ex	TQ 762937	hearth				L			MA 14. 1970. 156
gton bys.	SK 287277	SFB, 3 PH, LW; occ. layer and secondary layer with ?turves	1		0.18–0.20N	E			Ann. Rep. Trent Valley Archaeol. Res. Gp. 1971
		SFB, 2-post, LW	1	4.3 × 4.0	0.65N				
		SFB, 2-post, ?turf in fill, lined sides	1	5.0 × 4.0	0.55N				
ughton cs.	SK 933925	SFB, 'rough hut floor', ?wood traces				E	125		Philipps 1934. 154 Dudley 1949. 232 Myres 1951 88–89 OSM
hester nts.	Brook St. etc. SU 4830	Saxon town timber and stone buildings				VE–L		see ch. 3	
n folk	TG 337322 (Hurst)	SFB, sub-rect., slag and WD in fill, hearth internal	1	4.3 × 3.7		E	142	(TG 316319 in MA 8)	MA 6–7. 1962–63. 309 MA 8. 1964. 237
		SFB, 6-PH, clay in fill	1	4.9 × 3.0					
		iron-working and other hearths							MA 9. 1965. 173
	TG 366320 (OSM)	SFB, central stone hearth, beach-stone perforated, flint, ?LW, line 0.6 long	1	c. 5.5 × 3.7			142		OSM MA 6–7. 1962–63. 309
		SFB, sub-rect, external hearth slag and WD in fill	1	3.7 × 3.0					
		SFB not dug	2						
lston nts.	TL 182973	SFB	2+			E	91	OSM has TL 180975	inf. JGH OSM
sthorpe cs.	SK 848335	'hundreds' of rubbish pits over area 150 m long; some 2.7 × 1.8 × 1.8 deep, ends semicircular, LW and WD 'very extensive village'				E	126		LAASRP 18. 1885. 132–4 Philipps 1934. 147 and 187 LAASRP 6. 1955–6. 11 OSM

Site name and county	Location or NGR ref.	Evidence	No. of Build-ings	Dimensions in metres	Depth of floor	Date	Hurst No.	Remarks	Sources
Worlington (West Row) Suffolk	TL 673742	SFB, 2 whorls	1	3.6 × 2.4	0.6	E	213		Lethbridge Tebbutt OSM
Wootton, Hordley Oxon.	SP 445187	SFB, Roman and Saxon sherds	1	3.0 × 2.0		E		not illust.	MA 17. 1 148
Wootton Wowen Warks.	SP 152632	SFB, PH, ?PHT, in churchyard	1+			?L		not illust.	WMANS 1974. 6
Wroxeter (Viroconium) Salop.	SJ 5709	building with stone, tile, PH and SBS elements; rough tile/stone floors	2+	3.4+ × 0.6–1.0		late RB or VE		fig. 2.2	Frere 196 94–5 Barker 19 228–33 CA 14. 19 82–6 CA 25. 19 45–9 Barker 19 CA 39 19 111–16
Wykeham Yorks.	SE 966837	settlement over c. 2 hectares irregularly laid floors of stone slabs, pebble entrance paths, stone settings for roof-supports, PH, hearths, querns, LW sunken floors, ?SFB but not typical type A – small, deeply concave profile, circular, vertical walls supporting roof, entrance ramps, cf. local Roman huts type B – shallow concave, pebbled entrances; roof supported by posts on internal stone settings or pads; one may include paved byre c. 12.2 m long; LW only in type B type C – sunken floor, flat-based, oval plan	c. 24	c. 3.0 diam. c. 7.6–8.5 diam.	c. 0.6	E	284		Moore 19 Gelling 19 93 (nam OSM

...me ...nty	Location or NGR ref.	Evidence	No. of Build-ings	Dimensions in metres	Depth of floor	Date	Hurst No.	Remarks	Sources
...ing ...folk	TF 692207	huts defined by SH, sometimes in 2 concentric circles 2–3 cm apart; hearth in centre of some trackway	several	2–2.5 diam.		L	143	?charcoal-burners' huts	MA 8. 1964. 286 inf. K. Wade to JGH
...ring ...thumberland	NT 925305	palace site 7 halls ('A' range): A1 3 phases TT ?aisled hall	7			VII		fig. 2.7	Knowles and St Joseph 1952. 270
		A2 ?aisled hall, TT, annexes, posts in PAL construction, alternate deeper and shallower A3 2 phases TT							The Listener 1439. vol. 61 649
									MA 1. 1957. 148–9
		A4 (temp. Edwin) aisled hall TT, trenches c. 2.4 m deep, external posts in PP are buttresses						fig. 2.8	Hope-Taylor 1961 Colvin 1963, 2–6 and fig. 1.
		A5 A6 PH A7 PH		8.3 × 5.8					
		inner edge of Fort ('B'): hall-like, with annexes, focus of burials	1						
		4 minor buildings ('C' range): in echelon from 'A' range, C3, all 4 sides flanked by double rows of external PH	4						fig. 2.7	
		6 minor buildings ('D' range): D2b temple, later church, D3 SFB, wood-lined and clay floor	6							
		'grandstand' 7.6 m high at back platform for man to stand, screened behind by semi-circular WD walls and flanked by WD screens	1						fig. 2.7	

Site name and county	Location or NGR ref.	Evidence	No. of Build-ings	Dimensions in metres	Depth of floor	Date	Hurst No.	Remarks	Sources
Yelford Oxon.	SP 360040	SFB, whorl etc.	1	3.7 square	0.45	E	183		Stone 185: 214–15 Leeds 192 189–90 VCH Oxo 363 OSM
York Yorks.	SE 6052	row of small buildings solidly built in Roman manner, over furnaces of hypocaust of late IV; overlaid by later cemetery	2+			?V			Cramp 19
		stone buildings				VII– VIII			
		stone buildings over fortress ditch				pre- Dan- ish			
		two similar buildings 12 m apart				IX– X			
		burnt stone building with coin of IX				?IX			
		wooden building, bone and antler working				M			MA 16. 1 16
		SBS building, doorway 1.25 m wide, clay and mortar floors	1			L			Stead 195 MA 2. 19 200
		PH, gully and slot in Roman floor, ?fence or ?wall, associated with fish-processing	1						MA 6–7. 63. 312
		building in top of Roman rampart SH and WD fence, gravel floor with WD	1						Ann. Rep Yorks. Soc. 19 41–60 Cramp 19 MA 14. 1 164
		wicker-lined pit							Radley 19 CA 37. 19 45–52 MA 17. 1 151

Appendix B

Analysis of the finds register and location plan of Whitby Abbey

Rosemary J. Cramp

Since no site notebooks or foreman's reports have survived from Whitby, the finds register which records the finds numbers from 1–1136, with date and some location, has proved of great value. In some cases it enables one to locate finds in relation to structures, in others to determine foci of evidence, and finally it provides some idea of the progress and conduct of the excavation.

The first finds from the site were recorded as 'Between November 8th and 11th, 1920' and the last finds on 'May 30th, 1928'. However, the excavators did not begin to dig systematically, recording within measured areas, until December 1924. A plan to the scale of 41.66 ft. to the inch (126/132A) survives which divides the area north of the present abbey into thirty-nine sections of 40 ft squares. These areas are here called sections because it is difficult to see how they worked as grids. The sectional plan (fig. 5.8) is dated April 1920. Since this is seven months before any excavation began it is somewhat surprising to find a large irregular area in the centre about 170 ft. by 205 ft. which is marked 'area excavated and measured'. It will be seen from the account below that many of the sections (for example 13–23 and 25–33) which are laid out on this plan were never excavated, but it is difficult to escape the conclusion that something is wrong with the date of the squared plan when one sees how much had apparently been excavated before the system of squares was laid out around the 'hole' in the middle.

Until the finds were recorded in gridded areas or sections, it is almost impossible to determine the location of individual finds in this large northern section. There were apparent specific trenches, since the list of finds refers to 'North Area, W. Trench; N. Area E. Trench', but very few of the recorded finds are related to these trenches; for example, all that came out of the middle trench was a 'coin in three pieces'. The majority of the significant finds came from unidentifiable areas such as:

(a) 'North side opposite Chancel'
(b) 'North area in line with Chancel'
(c) 'North area N. of Chancel'
(d) 'North side of Chancel'
(e) 'N. side N. Transept'.

Presumably some of these loosely defined terms could refer to the same areas but there is some ambiguity about the location of particular areas. For instance many finds came from an area described 'North Boundary Wall'. This could refer to the Anglo-Saxon boundary wall discovered by the excavation, referred to on the report (p. 29) as a 'boundary' (this is referred to on fig. 5.7 as Road, Wall, or Bank) or the boundary of the present abbey grounds. The latter seems more likely since the *vallum*/boundary lies to the north-east of the site; but it is puzzling to find that the plan of the excavation, published with the 1943 report, shows hardly any excavation by the modern north boundary wall. In addition the report notes that digging first began in the 'western range', south of the existing church; but no finds are recorded from that area.

According to the finds record work began around the north wall of the nave in November 1920 and finds were measured in depth 'below turf' and located vaguely 'nave near west end', 'North side of abbey'. Until August 1923 work seems to have consisted in excavating or clearing out the Abbey Church and its immediate surroundings, but in September 1923 a 'North area opposite North transept', which is divided into three trenches, seems to have been opened and after that time major finds are sent to Mr Peers as well as to Mr Heasom, and we may presume that the excavation of the monastic buildings proper had begun.

The area first examined is that shown on the sectioned plan (fig. 5.8) as 'area excavated and measured'. Here, although very interesting finds emerged, it is impossible, as already noted, to relate them to structures shown on the published plan. No depths are provided for the finds but perhaps the vigilance was tightened up a little for in December 1923 a new column appears in the finds list – 'Reward'. Metalwork and in particular coins were the most highly rewarded, the pinnacle of reward being 2s 6d, but Anglo-Saxon coins rarely dropped below 1s. The phenomenal number of coins recovered for this site is perhaps directly related to this system. 'Rewards' ceased for four months in 1924 but afterwards returned in a more intermittent fashion.

However in November 1924 excavation began in a more orderly way. A datum was fixed (top step of the north door of the Abbey) and sections 1–4 were opened. The taking off of the 'top level' took from 21 November to 4 December but after that stripping did not proceed at the same rate. For example on 3 December section 1 was at a 'low level' while section 3 was still at a middle level and did not reach a 'low level' until 9 December. Just before or after Christmas 1924 (the records do not make this clear) sections 38 and 39 were opened and then, early in 1925, 34–7. In February 1925 sections 8.7.6 were opened and worked until 30 November 1925. Section 12 was never completed, although the published plan shows it may have been begun. The other sections, 13–23 to the north, were not touched. Effectively, then, excavation was completed by the end of 1925 although many objects were discovered (in 1926) in the three to four months of filling.

It has seemed worthwhile to recover what one can of the progress and recording of this excavation, although the record is dispiriting. The whole of the central area of the site (in which buildings E, J, A, B, N, O, K and H appear) is irrecoverable as far as the location of finds is concerned.

The area between the west wall of the present north transept and the west wall of the nave (sections 1–4) produced evidence that this area had been used as a burial ground at the time the monastery was still in use. The finds record also possibly shows changes of use in the Anglo-Saxon period.

In section 1 there was abundant evidence for medieval disturbance in that more than 160 sherds of medieval pottery were found, perhaps indicating the occupation of the medieval building marked on the composite plan. There was also at least one medieval grave. However there were also four Anglo-Saxon coins, one of Æthelræd at a high level and one said specifically to be at a low level. There were also four portions of Anglo-Saxon crosses, one with an 'incised border'; but the lowest finds of all recorded for that area are three pieces of pottery 'below the Saxon paving'. Are we to see the Building D as overlying an earlier occupation level and possibly inserted into the graveyard area?

Section 2, which is shown as devoid of buildings, produced clear evidence that it was the focus of important Anglo-Saxon burials. Other than fifteen pieces of 'black pottery', and a pin and sceatta (both of which could have been in graves), finds from this section were all of stone. They were a baluster shaft; four cross heads and a shaft; an Anglo-Saxon headstone; a cross inscribed Rht; another inscribed h I C (? no 11);[1] a long inscription (? the epitaph of Ælflæd);[2] another 'long inscription' (? epitaph of Cyneburg);[3] a portion of a runic inscription; and a 'cross shaft incised with beasts'.[4]

In the area to the West (section 3) which appears equally full of burials, the 'low level' provided 'a small portion of an Anglo-Saxon cross, but otherwise a silver coin, a bone pin and a stylus'.

Area 4, where the excavators have recorded few features, likewise produced Anglo-Saxon burial evidence: an inscribed stone and the shaft of an incised cross on the higher level; from the low level 'a portion of an Anglo-Saxon coffin slab'; a 'deeply incised portion of a cross'; two other cross fragments; three pins; three rings; a bronze circular ornament (? possibly associated with burials); a bone implement or pin; comb fragments; twelve Anglo-Saxon and one Roman coin; a 'pierced circular object, below paving'; an Anglo-Saxon millstone; and a loom-weight. If we could assume that the coins were associated with burials then only the millstone and loom-weight imply a domestic occupation in this area.

Section 5, which encloses the square building F, indicates the limit of the demonstrably Anglo-Saxon burials with one 'portion of an Anglo-Saxon grave cover'. Otherwise the middle level produced tweezers, bronze fragments, hand shears, needles, three styli (one in a well) and a 'silver coin Edward'. The lowest level showed equally domestic occupation: four coins: Eanred and Edilred; a stylus and a small pointed instrument (? a dry point); three pins; one needle; one bronze and one silver ornament; and a pudding stone quern. The mixed activity implied by these vestiges hardly gives a clue to the function of building F.

A very similar spread of material is found immediately to the west in section 6. The upper levels here have been much disturbed in the medieval period, but the 'low level' produced nine coins including one sceatta, and coins of Eanred, Eanbald and Edilred, fifteen pins, a ring, part of a bronze vessel, three fragments of glass vessels, a spindle whorl, a stylus and a key. The occupation spread supports Rahtz's conjectural building M, which he has disinterred from the welter of medieval graves in this area.

Section 7 includes the two roomed building G1, G2, postulated as a smithy by the excavators. Unfortunately the finds register does not associate the finds with the individual rooms. The middle level (which was apparently dug through in two days) produced one stylus, thirty-six pieces of pottery, a small bronze ornament and a pin. (One would like to know whether the portion of a book clasp and piece of a book hinge which were reclaimed from the area tip five months later also came from this hastily dug layer!) The 'low level' produced four coins (one of Edilred) and two half coins; eleven pins, two buckles, one pair of tweezers, various fragments of bronze, eighteen loom-weights, a circular lead weight marked Eanred, a stylus, a 'Saxon cresset stone', and rather surprisingly two broken Anglo-Saxon grave-covers. This spread of female debris hardly seems to imply that this building was a smithy. If there is a concentration of any activity it is weaving.

The area immediately to the west of this, section 8, has a thinner spread of finds, although the middle level produced seventy-one 'pieces of pottery'. The low level produced eleven pins, five coins: Edilred, Ædilræd, a ring, a pierced circular object and a pin.

It is the area immediately to the north of G (section 11) which provides links with the specific activities noted in G. Perhaps indeed it was all part of the same building complex. In section 11 the low level produced two styli, a bronze instrument, and part of a 'book-clasp', nine pins 'two broken' (below paving), three coins, a spindle whorl, fragments of glass vessels and bronze and a portion of an incised Anglo-Saxon Cross.

Section 10 produced almost as many objects from the infill as from the excavation proper. However here the finds are less industrial: two broken styli, a 'Saxon stone used as a mould', three large-headed pins, two pins (below paving), a ring, a pectoral cross, bronze fragments and eight styccas.

There is little evidence for changing activity as one goes further east to section 9, but since Building L is cut by the arbitrary sectioning it is possible that the finds in both sections were associated with this building. The low level produced one portion of a 'book clasp', two ornamental spindle whorls, one bronze and one bone instrument, a bone pin, a pair of tweezers, a chain, one corroded coin, a sceatta and a stycca of Eanred, and one piece of Samian ware.

The eastern area

The most easterly sections of the site (34–9) present certain problems. The report indicates that this area is outside the Anglo-Saxon boundary and that the occupation there was medieval. Section 37 yields nothing but undated pottery (sixty-nine pieces at a 'low level') but thirty-six provided two Anglo-Saxon coins, 'a piece of large rim of early pottery', and a bronze object. Section 35 yielded two sceattas, one other Anglo-Saxon coin, a coin of 'Eadwin', and an Anglo-Saxon cross head and shaft (from the well), in addition to anonymous bronze fragments and a pin. Section 39 to the north provided two more Anglo-Saxon coins, two portions of 'book clasps', portions of a bronze vessel, a bronze instrument, a rectangular headed pin, a spindle whorl and a bone 'handle'. Section 34 produced five Anglo-Saxon coins, two pins, four bronze objects, a silver ring, a piece of incised jet, reindeer horn, one small loom-weight and half a large loom-weight. Under the paving was found a piece of pottery and a whale's vertebrae.

To the north (in 38) were seven Anglo-Saxon coins, a pair of tweezers with a twisted handle, a bronze handle, a jet ornament, two loom-weights and ninety-nine pieces of pottery. In fact this area (34–8) has a very similar spread of artifacts to the other working buildings inside the presumed *vallum*.

Notes

1 Peers and Radford (1943) ?no. 11, fig. 6.
2 Peers and Radford (1943) fig. 4.
3 Peers and Radford (1943) fig. 5.
4 Peers and Radford (1943). pl. XXII.

I am grateful to all the excavators who have supplied information about their excavations, and to Miss B. Coatsworth for her aid with the preparation of the text.

Appendix C

The building plan of the Anglo–Saxon monastery of Whitby Abbey

Philip Rahtz

The title of the plan is 'Whitby Abbey:[1] foundations of early monastery, shown in red'. The portions shaded red are the walls of seven buildings which could be clearly distinguished among the more fragmentary foundations surrounding them, and are so described (and tentatively identified) in the text. The walls of the red-shaded buildings and all the other stones and foundations were carefully drawn, stone by stone, in a manner which is standard practice in modern excavations, but less usual in 1925. The drawings were done, so Mr R. Gilyard-Beer informs me, by a professional surveyor who had little knowledge of the archaeological implications, and who nevertheless produced what is retrospectively a most useful and objective record of the stones uncovered by the excavators, complete with spot levels. The authors of the report were, not surprisingly, reluctant to attempt interpretation of all the stones uncovered, and contented themselves with reproducing the 1924–5 plan, which includes remains of all periods, and shading the recognizable buildings in red. This in itself was no more than legitimate interpretation, since it can clearly be seen that the red areas are only selected from many others, and that the 'red' buildings are not isolated from each other, but are 'rooms' in larger ranges. Misinterpretation only began when the 'red' buildings were reproduced by themselves, without the rest of the plan. They then appear to be isolated buildings, more like those of western monasteries of the same period, rather than elements of larger ranges such as those which are now being recovered by Rosemary Cramp at Monkwearmouth and Jarrow. It is difficult to imagine a better example of the misinterpretation of archaeological evidence.

I have therefore produced a new version of the plan, redrawn from originals kindly supplied by the Directorate of Ancient Monuments of the Department of the Environment (Drawings 126/20A and 126/43A2, made respectively in November 1924 and October 1925 at a scale of 1 : 96, the latter with spot levels marked).

The area excavated was that north of the medieval abbey church. It was suggested[2] that this was not the nucleus of the monastery but an area of about 0.5 ha in the northern part of the monastic precinct. The north-eastern limit might be indicated by the remains of a roadway running from north-west to south-east, which may have indicated the course of the monastic boundary.[3] It may alternatively have been the foundation of a wall or bank, which might itself be the remains of the *vallum monasterii*.[4] Features shown on the 1943 plan beyond this road were all believed to be medieval.[5] There are, however, three wells among the features in this area, which must be included to bring the total of the Anglo-Saxon wells from the site up to the '10 or 11' mentioned.[6] There are in fact thirteen wells shown on the plan (excluding one shown as medieval), of which five lie beyond the 'road'. These features are accordingly included in the new plan, except those specifically labelled as medieval. Those in the extreme north-east corner are probably medieval, since they are aligned on the wall separating the site from the modern road, and are drawn rather differently; they are not however labelled medieval, so they are included in the new plan. Since some of the features north-east of the boundary seem to be Anglo-Saxon (see p. 457), if the boundary is really the *vallum monasterii*, then they must either be 'extra-mural' features, or of a date earlier than that of the definition of the limits of the monastery. Among the 250 or more graves, shown on the plan, there is one which is said to be of Anglo-Saxon date; the rest are dated to the twelfth century or later, cutting through the Anglo-Saxon foundations in a random manner.[7] 'The site of the Anglian cemetery is unknown',[8] yet among the finds are numerous fragments of Anglo-Saxon worked stones, including part of a recumbent slab and other parts of 'funerary crosses … which stood in the cemetery'. Presumably this means that they had originally stood above graves in the monastic cemetery, but had been moved to the area excavated at a later date (see p. 455). Two cross-bases are shown on the north edge of the plan, but no graves are shown near them. A similar confusion about the graves is apparent in the note on the textile remains[9] which are described as having been found 'in the Saxon cemetery at Whitby'; they 'may belong to the Saxon period before 875 when the early occupation of the cemetery ended'. This sounds as though some Anglo-Saxon graves *were* located, and in a well-preserved context. Evidence from the 1943 plan also supports the Anglo-Saxon dating of some, if not most, of the graves. Not only are many graves shown superimposed on (i.e. overlaid by ?) stones and walling not distinguished from those of the Anglo-Saxon monastery (including a drain), but some graves are specifically labelled 'medieval burial(s)', which might be taken to imply that the graves just marked 'burial(s)' were not medieval but Anglo-Saxon. In the new plan, the stones and walls superimposed on graves are included on the assumption that the graves are earlier, or that some burials were so shallow that the Anglo-Saxon foundations survived beneath them. The only stones omitted are these which are coterminous with the grave outline, and therefore likely to be grave-covers. Some graves on the plan (e.g. that at the west end of Building B) are rather isolated from the main graves, and could be Anglo-Saxon graves which are associated with the buildings in which they lie.

The method of excavation was (to judge by pls 19a and b, and the absence of sections) to remove all the stratification and part of the natural clay to leave the stone foundations standing proud on pillars or areas of clay. The record therefore consists of the finds and a mass of foundation which may well, to judge by the dating of the finds, extend over at least two centuries. The authors were not able to define a building sequence, other than separating Anglo-Saxon from medieval walls,[10] but made some comments on building construction.

They suggest that the clay-packed foundations (61 cm wide) carried stone super-structures; some architectural fragments were indeed recovered,[11] and evidence is quoted for the existence of doorways which must have had upright stone jambs in 'long and short' technique on stone sills.[12] It was assumed that the 'fairwork' or superstructure was set with lime mortar though none was found. The numerous fragments of burnt daub recovered are assumed to be from the framework of internal partitions, of which no other evidence was found. It seems possible, in view of the absence of stone rubble and lime mortar, that the superstructure of all or at least some of the buildings was of wattle and daub construction. It is also possible that the daub is all that remains of an early period of construction before stone was used at all. There was no evidence of the material used for roofs.

Apart from the seven buildings whose outline was clear, the 1943 authors recognized that the complex now named I I was a group of buildings with an open hearth. It is apparent from the plan that this was a complex building with several rooms; it appears to have abutted on E on its west side, though there is no obvious connecting doorway. Levels on the plan show that the large stones which comprise the west wall of H survived to a higher level than the east wall of E; either E had been robbed to a lower level, or had been levelled before H was built.

The length of wall with a door-sill (now named J) was believed to be the north wall of a building; this may well have been linked to C and D in one range – the connecting walls are shown on the plan.

There are clearly many other buildings or rooms of buildings. A few of these have been arbitrarily named: K (three walls, ? two periods); L (part of a large complex perhaps of very small rooms); M (another building or room east of G, possibly also joined to F); and N (a possible building east of H). Other foundations shown may indicate further buildings, but the recorded evidence does not allow these to be even tentatively defined or interpreted. It is uncertain from the plans whether most stones are foundations, floors, or drains.

There are many blank areas on the earlier plan. Some of these, indicated as those lying beyond dotted lines in the new plan, are clearly large unexcavated areas; others, such as that containing only wells on the north side of the plan, appear to have been only partly excavated – there are some 'cut off' lines on the north edge of H. But most importantly, there are linear areas where no foundations are shown. These are not apparently unexcavated baulks or modern paths, as some graves are shown in the one south of E.

They may therefore be paths or roadways, and are shown as 'paths' on the new plan. Oddly there was no comment on these in 1943. If this is indeed the correct explanation, then the buildings can be seen as lying along the edges of paths or roadways on a roughly rectilinear layout, very similar to that of an urban complex. One of the possible roads or paths appears to run behind the ? *vallum monasterii*, in the same way as that behind a town wall circuit. A gap with drains on its east side could link this with the path system running between the buildings.

The redrawing of the plan was done by tracing from drawing 126/43A2, using rather thicker lines so that the drawing could be more satisfactorily reduced; this had led to a decrease in the differential between thick and thin lines, but as far as possible features such as wall-edges which were heavily outlined on the originals have been emphasized. A lack of sensitivity in the drawing is deliberate – the use of a mapping pen rather than the stylus pens used would have encouraged minor interpretation which would be unwarranted. Graves and features marked 'medieval' have been omitted; this procedure makes a clearer assessment of the remains possible; but in any closer study of individual buildings or areas, the extent to which graves have destroyed some areas would need to be known and can be found out from the original drawings. Additional detail has been added by comparison of the two original drawings (one of which shows the actual drain-stones in the central areas) and with the published plan (i.e. by putting dotted lines where the 1943 plan is red-shaded).

The foregoing discussion will, it is hoped, have made it clear that in spite of much ambiguity and incompleteness in the record, the evidence points to a complex and almost certainly multi-period site, but one which certainly does not consist of a group of individual buildings with empty areas separating them. The appearance of the plan is far more that of an organized and dense conglomeration of structures, many of which may well be rooms or elements of large and complex ranges of buildings. Of the 'cells' originally defined, only A and B have been isolated; but they are part of a layout which has more in common with that of a developed medieval claustral monastic plan than that of any monastery whose remains have so far been excavated.

Notes

1 Peers and Radford (1943). pl. XXXI.
2 Peers and Radford (1943) 29, 30, 68.
3 Peers and Radford (1943) 29.
4 Clapham (1952) 9.
5 Peers and Radford (1943) 29.
6 Peers and Radford (1943) 33.
7 Peers and Radford (1943) 29.
8 Peers and Radford (1943) 33.
9 Peers and Radford (1943) 86.
10 Peers and Radford (1943) 31.
11 Peers and Radford (1943) 33.
12 Peers and Radford (1943) 31.

List of sources

ABBOTT R. (1963–4). 'Some recently discovered Anglo-Saxon carvings at Breedon on the Hill', *Transactions of the Leicestershire Archaeological and Historical Society*, xxxix, 20–23.

ÅBERG N. (1926). *The Anglo-Saxons in England*, Uppsala.

ADDLESHAW G. W. O. (1959). *The beginnings of the parochial system*, York (St Anthony's Hall Publications, 2nd edn).

—— (1963). *The pastoral organisation of the modern diocese of Durham and Newcastle in the time of Bede*, Jarrow (Jarrow Lecture).

ADDYMAN P. V. (1964). 'A Dark-Age settlement at Maxey, Northants, *Medieval Archaeology*, viii, 20–73.

—— (1965). 'Late Saxon settlements in the St Neots area: I. The Saxon settlement and Norman castle at Eaton Socon, Bedfordshire', *Proceedings of the Cambridge Antiquarian Society*, lviii, 38–73.

—— (1969). 'Late Saxon settlements in the St Neots area: II. The Little Paxton settlement and enclosures', *Proceedings of the Cambridge Antiquarian Society*, lxii, 59–93.

—— (1972). 'The Anglo-Saxon house: a new review', *Anglo-Saxon England*, i, 273–307.

—— (1972a). 'Late Saxon settlements in the St Neots area: III. The village or township at St Neots', *Proceedings of the Cambridge Antiquarian Society*, lxiv, 45–100.

—— (1972b). 'Anglo-Saxon houses at Chalton, Hampshire', *Medieval Archaeology*, xvi, 13–31.

—— (1973a). 'Saxon Southampton: a town and international port of the 8th to the 10th century', *Vor- und Frühformen der europäischen Stadt im Mittelalter* (ed. H. Jankuhn, W. Schlesinger and H. Steuer), Göttingen (*Abhandlungen der Akademie der Wissenschaften: philologisch-historische Klasse*, 3 Folge, Nr. 83), 218–28.

—— (1973b). *Rescue archaeology in York*, Middlesbrough (Teesside Museums and Art Galleries Service. Fourth Elgee Memorial Lecture).

—— (forthcoming). *Current problems in British archaeology* (ed. B. Cunliffe).

—— and BIDDLE M. (1965). 'Medieval Cambridge: recent finds and excavations', *Proceedings of the Cambridge Antiquarian Society*, lviii, 74–137.

—— and HILL D. (1968). 'Saxon Southampton: a review of the evidence. Part I: History, location, date and character of the town', *Proceedings of the Hampshire Field Club*, xxv, 61–93.

—— —— (1969). 'Saxon Southampton: a review of the evidence. Part II: Industry, trade and everyday life', *Proceedings of the Hampshire Field Club*, xxvi, 61–96.

ADDYMAN P., HOPKINS B. G. and NORTON G. T. (1972). 'A Saxon-Norman pottery-kiln producing stamped wares at Michelmersh, Hants', *Medieval Archaeology*, xvi, 127–130.

—— and LEIGH D. (1973). 'The Anglo-Saxon village at Chalton, Hampshire: second interim report', *Medieval Archaeology*, 17, 1–25.

—— and SAUNDERS A. D. (forthcoming). *Lydford, Devon: castle, fort and town* (Royal Archaeological Institute monograph).

—— and WHITWELL J. B. (1970). 'Some middle Saxon pottery types in Lincolnshire', *The Antiquaries Journal*, 1, 96–102.

ÆTHELWULF *De Abb*. See Campbell (1967).

AHRENS C. (1966). 'Vorgeschichte des Kreises Pinneberg und der Insel Helgoland – Die vor- und frühgeschichtliche Denkmäler und Funde in Schleswig-Holstein, VII', *Veröffentlichungen des Landesamtes für Vor- und Frühgeschichte in Schleswig* (ed. K. Kersten), 205–32, Neumünster.

AKERMAN J. Y. (1855). *Remains of pagan Saxondom*, London.

ALCOCK L. (1963). *Dinas Powys*, Cardiff.

—— (1966–7). 'Roman Britons and pagan Saxons: an archaeological appraisal', *Welsh History Review*, iii, 229–49.

—— (1971). *Arthur's Britain*, London.

—— (1972). '*By South Cadbury is that Camelot . . .*' *The excavation of Cadbury castle 1966–70*, London.

—— (1973). *Arthur's Britain* (Pelican edn), Harmondsworth.

ALDSWORTH F. and HILL D. (1971). 'The Burghal Hidage – Eashing', *Surrey Archaeological Collections*, lxviii, 198–201.

ALEXANDER J. A. (1968). 'Clopton: The life-cycle of a Cambridgeshire village', *East Anglian Studies* (ed. L. M. Munby), 48–70.

—— (1972). 'The beginnings of urban life in Europe', *Man, settlement and urbanism* (ed. P. J. Ucko, R. Tringham and G. W. Dimbleby), London, 843–50.

ALLCROFT A. H. (1908). *Earthwork of England*, London.

ALMGREN B. (1955) *Bronsnycklar och Djurornamentik*, Uppsala.

ANDERSEN H. (1951). 'Tomme høje', *Kuml*, 91–135.

ANDERSON I. (1955). 'Transitional forms between the primitive hut and the house proper', *Vallhagar, a migration period settlement on Gotland, Sweden* (ed. M. Stenberger), Copenhagen and Stockholm.

ANDERSSON H. (1971). *Urbanisierte Ortschaften und lateinische Terminologie: Studien zur Geschichte des nordeuropäischen Städtewesens vor 1350*, Göteborg (Acta regiae societatis scientiarum et litterarum: Humaniora, vi).

ANSTEE J. W. and BIEK L. (1961). 'A study in pattern welding', *Medieval Archaeology*, v, 71–93.

APPLEBAUM S. (1966). 'Peasant economy and types of agriculture', *Rural settlement in Roman Britain* (ed. C. Thomas), London, 99–107.

—— (1972). 'Roman Britain', *The Agrarian History of England and Wales i, pt 2, A.D. 43–1042* (ed. H. P. R. Finberg), Cambridge, 5–267.

ARBMAN H. (1939). *Birka, Sveriges äldsta handelsstad*, Stockholm.

—— (1940). *Birka*, i, Stockholm.

—— (1961). *The Vikings*, London.

ARMSTRONG J. R. (ed.) (1971). *Weald and Downland open-air museum*, Chichester.

ARNOLD J. (1968). *The Shell book of country crafts*, London.

ARRHENIUS B. (1971). *Granatschmuck und Gemmen aus nordischen Funden des frühen Mittelalters*, Stockholm (Acta Universitatis Stockholmensis, Studies in North-European Archaeology, series B).

—— (1974). 'Om knivar och knivtypologi', *Fornvännen*, 105–10.

ARTHUR B. V. and JOPE E. M. (1962–3). 'Early Saxon pottery kilns at Purwell Farm, Cassington, Oxfordshire', *Medieval Archaeology*, vi–vii, 1–14.

ATKINSON J. C. (ed.) (1878). *Whitby Chartulary I*, Edinburgh (Surtees Society, lxix).

BAKKA E. (1963). 'Some English decorated metal objects found in Norwegian graves', *Årbok for universitetet i Bergen, humankstisk serie*, i.

BALDWIN BROWN G. (1903–37). *The arts in early England*, London.

—— (1925). *The Arts in Early England*, vol. 2: *Anglo-Saxon Architecture* (1st edn 1903, 2nd edn, much revised, 1925), London.

BARKER P. A. (1968–9). 'The origins of Worcester: an interim survey', *Transactions of the Worcestershire Archaeological Society*, 3rd series, ii, 1–116.

—— (1969). 'Some aspects of the excavation of timber buildings', *World Archaeology*, i, 220–33.

—— (1971a). *Excavations on the site of the Baths basilica at Wroxeter 1966–1971*, Birmingham.

—— (1971b). 'A pre-Norman field system at Hen Domen', *Medieval Archaeology*, xv, 58–72.

—— (1973). *Excavations on the site of the Baths basilica at Wroxeter (Viroconium Cornoviorum) 1966–1973. An interim report*, Birmingham.

—— and LAWSON J. (1971). 'A pre-Norman field-system at Hen Domen, Montgomery', *Medieval Archaeology*, xv, 58–72.

BARLEY M. W. (1964). 'The medieval borough of Torksey: excavations 1960–2', *The Antiquaries Journal*, xliv, 165–87.

—— and HANSON R. P. C. (ed.) (1968). *Christianity in Britain 300–700*, Leicester.

—— and STRAW I. F. (1969). 'Nottingham', *Historic Towns*, i (ed. M. D. Lobel), London and Oxford.

BARR-HAMILTON A. (1961). 'The excavations of Bargham church site', *Sussex Archaeological Collections*, xcix, 38–65.

BARTON K. J. (1959–60). 'Excavations at Hellesvean, St Ives, in 1957', *Proceedings of the West Cornwall Field Club*, new series, ii, 153–5.

—— (1962). 'Settlements of the Iron Age and pagan Saxon periods at Linford, Essex', *Transactions of the Essex Archaeological Society*, 3rd series, i, 57–104.

—— (1964). 'Excavations in the village of Tarring, West Sussex', *Sussex Archaeological Collections*, cii, 9–27.

—— (1964a). 'The excavation of a medieval bastion at St Nicholas's Almshouses, King Street, Bristol', *Medieval Archaeology*, viii, 184–212.

BATEMAN T. (1861). *Ten years' diggings in Celtic and Saxon grave hills in the counties of Derby, Stafford and York*, London.

BATESON M. (1899). 'The origin and early history of double monasteries: The double monastery in England', *Transactions of the Royal Historical Society*, new series, xiii, 137–98.

BATTISCOMBE C. F. (1956). *The relics of St Cuthbert*, Oxford.

BECKWITH J. (1972). *Ivory carvings in early medieval England*, London.

BEHMER E. (1939). *Das zweischneidige Schwert der germanischen Völkerwanderungszeit*, Stockholm.

BELLAMY C. V. (1962–4). 'Pontefract Priory excavations 1957–1961', *Publications of the Thoresby Society*, xlix, 1–139.

BENSON D. and COOK J. (1966). *City of Oxford redevelopment – archaeological implications*, Oxford.

—— and MILES D. (1974). *The Upper Thames valley. An archaeological survey of the river gravels*, Oxford (Oxford Archaeological Unit, survey no. 2).

BENSON G. (1903). 'Notes on excavations at 25, 26 and 27 High Ousegate, York', *Reports of the Yorkshire Philosophical Society*, 64–7.

BERESFORD G. (1971). 'Tresmorn, St Gennys', *Cornish Archaeology*, x, 55–73.

—— (1974). *The medieval clay-land village: excavations at Goltho and Barton Blount*, London (Society for Medieval Archaeology: Monograph series: vi).

BERESFORD M. (1967). *New Towns of the Middle Ages*, London.

—— (1973). *English medieval boroughs: a handlist*, Newton Abbot.

—— and HURST J. G. (eds.) (1971). *Deserted medieval villages*, London.

—— and ST JOSEPH J. K. S. (1958). *Medieval England: an aerial survey*, Cambridge.

BERGQVIST H. and LEPISKAAR J. (1957). *Animal skeletal remains from medieval Lund*, Lund (Archaeology of Lund, Studies in the Lund excavation material, i).

BERISFORD F. (unpublished). Thesis for University of Oxford (in preparation).

BERSU G. and WILSON D. M. (1966). *Three Viking graves in the Isle of Man*, London (Society for Medieval Archaeology: Monograph series: i).

BESSE J. M. (1906). *Les Moines de l'ancienne France*, Paris.

BIDDLE M. (1964). 'Excavations at Winchester 1963', *The Antiquaries Journal*, xliv, 188–219.

—— (1964a). 'The excavation of a motte and Bailey Castle at Therfield, Hertfordshire', *Journal of the British Archaeological Association*, 3rd series, xxvii, 53–91.

—— (1965). 'Excavations at Winchester 1962–3. Third interim report', *The Antiquaries Journal*, xlv, 230–64.

—— (1966). 'Excavations at Winchester 1965', *The Antiquaries Journal*, xlvi, 308–32.

—— (1967). 'Excavations at Winchester 1966', *The Antiquaries Journal*, xlvii, 251–79.

—— (1968). 'Archaeology and the history of British towns', *Antiquity*, xlii, 109–16.

—— *et al.* (1968). 'The early history of Abingdon, Berkshire, and its abbey', *Medieval Archaeology*, xii, 26–69.

—— (1969). *Excavations near Winchester Cathedral 1961–8*, Winchester.

—— (1969a). 'Excavations at Winchester 1968. Seventh interim report', *The Antiquaries Journal*, xlix, 295–329.

—— (1970a). 'Excavations at Winchester 1969. Eighth interim report', *The Antiquaries Journal*, l, 277–326.

—— (1970b). 'Winchester and Deerhurst (with a comment by Edward Gilbert)', *Transactions of the Bristol and Gloucestershire Archaeological Society*, lxxxix, 179–81.

—— (1971). 'Archaeology and the beginnings of English society', *England before the conquest. Studies in primary sources presented to Dorothy Whitelock* (ed. P. Clemoes and K. Hughes), Cambridge, 391–408.

—— (1971a). *Winchester Cathedral record*, 48–55.

—— (1972). 'Excavations at Winchester 1970. Ninth interim report', *The Antiquaries Journal*, lii, 93–131.

—— (1973). 'Winchester: the development of an early capital', *Vor- und Frühformen der europäischen Stadt im Mittelalter* (ed. H. Jankuhn, W. Schlesinger and H. Steuer), Göttingen (Abhandlungen der Akademie der Wissenschaften: Philologisch-Historische Klasse, 3 Folge, Nr. 83), 229–61.

—— (1974). 'The archaeology of Winchester', *Scientific American*, ccxxx, pt. 5, 33–43.

—— (1975). 'Excavations at Winchester 1971. Tenth and final interim report', *The Antiquaries Journal*, lv, 96–126, 295–337.

—— (1975a). 'Hampshire and the origins of Wessex', *Problems in Social and Economic Archaeology* (ed. G. de G. Sieveking), London.

—— (ed.) (1975b). F. Barlow, M. Biddle, O. von Feilitzen and D. J. Keene, *Winchester in the Early Middle Ages. An edition and discussion of the Winton Domesday*, Oxford.

—— (1975c). '*Felix urbs Winthoniae:* Winchester in the age of monastic reform', *Tenth-century studies* (ed. D. Parsons), London and Chichester, 123–40.

—— (1975d). 'Planned towns before 1066', *The evolution of towns* (ed. M. W. Barley) (Council for British Archaeology, Urban Research Committee, Working Party on Town Plans and Topography, Leamington Spa, Nov. 1974), forthcoming.

—— and BARCLAY K. (1974). Winchester Ware', *Medieval pottery from excavations: studies presented to Gerald Clough Dunning* (ed. V. I. Evison *et al.*), London, 137–66.

—— and HILL D. (1971). 'Late Saxon planned towns', *Antiquaries Journal*, li, 70–85.

—— and HUDSON D. M. (1973). *The future of London's past*, Worcester.

—— LAMBRICK H. T. and MYERS J. N. L. (1968). 'The early history of Abingdon, Berkshire, and its abbey', *Medieval Archaeology*, xii, 26–69.

—— and QUIRK R. N. (1962). 'Excavations near Winchester Cathedral 1961', *The Archaeological Journal*, cxix, 150–94.

BINDING G. (1967). 'Bericht über Ausgrabungen in Nieder-rheinischen Kirchen 1964–6', *Bonner Jahrbuch*, clxvii, 357–87.

—— (1971a). 'Bericht über Ausgrabungen in Nieder-rheinischen Kirchen II', *Beiträge zur Archäologie des Mittelalters*, ii, Düsseldorf (Rheinische Ausgrabungen, ix).

—— (1971b). 'Archäologische Untersuchungen in der Christuskirche zu Rheinhausen-Hochemmerich', *Beiträge zur Archäologie des Mittelalters*, ii, Düsseldorf (Rheinische Ausgrabungen, ix).

BINNS A. L. (1956). 'Tenth-century carvings from Yorkshire and the Jellinge style', *Universitetet i Bergen Årbok* (Historisk-Antikvarisk rekke m. 2).

BIRLEY E. (1961). *Research on Hadrian's Wall*, Kendal.

—— (1963). 'The fourth-century subdivision of Britain', *Quintus Congressus Internationalis Limitis Romani Studiosorum, 1961*, Zagreb, 83ff.

BLAKE B. P. (1959). 'Anglo-Saxon site at Hole Farm, Bulmer Tye, Essex', *Medieval Archaeology*, iii, 282–5.

BLINDHEIM C. (1962). 'Smedgraven fra Bygland i Morgedal', *Viking*, 25–80.

BLOCH M. (1965). *Feudal Society*, London (paperback edn).

BLOMQVIST R. and MÅRTENSSON A. W. (1963). *Thule Grävningen 1961*, Lund (Archaeologia Lundensia ii).

BLUNT C. E. (1961). 'The coinage of Offa', *Anglo-Saxon Coins* (ed. R. H. M. Dolley), London, 39–62.

—— (1969) 'The St Edmund memorial coinage', *Proceedings of the Suffolk Institute of Archaeology*, xxxi, iii, 234–5.

BLUNT C. E. and DOLLEY R. H. M. (1968). 'A gold coin of the time of Offa', *Numismatic Chronicle*, cxxviii, 151–9.

BLUNT C. E., LYON C. S. S. and PAGAN H. E. (1963). 'The coinage of southern England 786–840', *The British Numismatic Journal*, xxxii, 1–74.

BOECKELMANN W. (1956). 'Grundformen in frühkarolingischen Kirchenbau des Östlichen Frankenreiches', *Wallraf-Richartz Jahrbuch*, xviii, 27–69.

BÖHNER K. (1966). 'Spätrömische Kastelle und alamannische Ansiedlungen in der Schweiz', *Helvetia Antiqua: Festschrift Emil Vogt* (ed. R. Degen, W. Drack and R. Wyss), Zürich, 307–16.

BOND F. B. (1910). 'The monastic buildings: first excavation', *Proceedings of the Somerset Archaeological and Natural History Society*, lvi, 62–78.

—— (1911). 'Glastonbury Abbey. Third report on the discoveries made during the excavations, 1909–10', *Proceedings of the Somerset Archaeological and Natural History Society*, lvi, 62–78.

—— (1914). 'Glastonbury Abbey. Sixth report on the discoveries made during the excavations', *Proceedings of the Somerset Archaeological and Natural History Society*, lxix, 56–73.

—— (1916). 'Glastonbury Abbey. Eighth report on the discoveries made during the excavations', *Proceedings of the Somerset Archaeological and Natural History Society*, lxix, 128–42.

—— (1926). 'Glastonbury Abbey. Tenth annual report', *Proceedings of the Somerset Archaeological and Natural History Society*, lxxii, 13–19.

BONNEY D. J. (1966). 'Pagan Saxon burials and boundaries in Wiltshire', *Wiltshire Archaeological and Natural History Magazine*, lxi, 25–30.

—— (1968). 'Iron Age and Romano-British settlement sites in Wiltshire', *Wiltshire Archaeological and Natural History Magazine*, lxiii, 27–38.

—— (1972). 'Early boundaries in Wessex', *Archaeology and the Landscape* (ed. P. J. Fowler), London, 168–86.

—— (1973). 'The pagan Saxon period, *c* 500–*c* 700', *Victoria County History of Wiltshire* I, ii (ed. E. Crittall), Oxford, 468–84.

BONY J. (1965). 'Origines des piles gothiques à futs en delit', *Gedenkschrift Ernst Gall*, Munich/Berlin, 95–122.

—— (1967). (Review of) *Anglo-Saxon architecture* by H. M. and J. Taylor, *Journal of the Society of Architectural Historians of America*, xxvi, 74–7.

BOON G. C. (1959). 'The latest objects from Silchester, Hants', *Medieval Archaeology*, iii, 79–88.

BORGER H. (1972). 'Die Neugliederung der Stadt in ottonisch-staufischer Zeit auf Grund archäologischer Quellen', *Kiel Papers '72* (ed. H. Hinz), Kiel, 9–20.

BOSWORTH J. and TOLLER T. N. (1898). *An Anglo-Saxon dictionary*, London.

BOWEN H. C. (1961). *Ancient Fields*, London.

—— (1969). 'The Celtic background', *The Roman villa in Britain* (ed. A. L. F. Rivet), London, 1–48.

BOWEN H. C. and FOWLER P. J. (1966). 'Romano-British settlements in Dorset and Wiltshire', *Rural settlement in Roman Britain* (ed. C. Thomas), London, 43–67.

BRAAT W. C. (1971). 'Early medieval glazed pottery in Holland', *Medieval Archaeology*, xv, 112–14.

BRANIGAN K. (1968). 'The origins of cruck construction – a new clue', *Medieval Archaeology*, xii, 1–11.

—— (1971). *Latimer*, Bristol.

—— (1972). 'Verulamium and the Chiltern villas', *Man, settlement and urbanism* (ed. P. J. Ucko *et al.*), London, 851–5.

BRASCH C. (1910). *Die Namen der Werkzeuge im Altenglischen*, Leipzig.

BREWSTER T. C. M. (1956–8). 'Excavations at Newham's pit, Staxton', *Yorkshire Archaeological Journal*, xxxix, 193–223.

BRIGGS G. W. D., GRAHAM G. and PARSON D. (1961). 'Sculptured Anglian masonry in the tower of Corbridge church', *Archaeologia Aeliana*, 4th series, xxxix, 363–6.

BRODRIBB A. C. *et al.* (1968). *Excavations at Shakenoak Farm*, i, Oxford.

—— (1971). *Excavations at Shakenoak Farm*, ii, Oxford.

—— (1972). *Excavations at Shakenoak Farm*, iii, Oxford.

—— (1973). *Excavations at Shakenoak Farm*, iv, Oxford.

BRØGGER A. W. and SHETELIG H. (1928). *Osebergfundet*, ii, Oslo.

BROMWICH R. (1961). *Trioedd 'ynis Prydein*, Cardiff.

BRØNDSTED J. (1965). *The Vikings*, Harmondsworth.

BROOKE G. C. (1950). *English Coins*, 3rd edn, London.

BROOKS N. P. (1964). 'The unidentified forts of the Burghal Hidage', *Medieval Archaeology*, viii, 74–90.

—— (1965–6). 'Excavations at Wallingford Castle, 1965: an interim report', *Berkshire Archaeological Journal*, lxii, 17–21.

—— (1971). 'The development of military obligations in eighth- and ninth-century England', *England before the conquest. Studies in primary sources presented to Dorothy Whitelock* (ed. P. Clemoes and K. Hughes), Cambridge, 69–84.

BROTHWELL D. (1972). 'Palaeodemography and earlier British populations', *World Archaeology*, iv, 75–87.

BROWN B. J. W. *et al.* (1957). 'Excavations at Grimstone End, Pakenham', *Proceedings of the Suffolk Institute of Archaeology*, xxvi, 188–207.

BROWN P. D. C. (1972). Review of *Excavations at Shakenoak*, iii, in *Britannia*, iii, 376–7.

—— and MCWHIRR A. D. (1966). 'Cirencester 1965', *The Antiquaries Journal*, xlvi, 240–255.

—— —— (1967). 'Cirencester 1966', *The Antiquaries Journal*, xlvii, 185–97.

BROWN R. A. (1965). 'The architecture', *The Bayeux Tapestry* (ed. F. Stenton), 2nd edn, London, 76–87.

—— (1969). 'An historian's approach to the origins of the castle in England', *The Archaeological Journal*, cxxvi, 131–48.

BROWN T. J. (1969). *The Stonyhurst gospel of St John*, Oxford.

BROZZI M. (1968). 'Zur Topographie von Cividale im frühen Mittelalter', *Jahrbuch des Römisch-Germanischen Zentralmuseums Mainz*, xv, 134.

BRUCE-MITFORD R. L. S. (1948). 'Saxon Rendlesham', *Proceedings of the Suffolk Institute of Archaeology*, xxiv, 228–51.

—— (1956). 'A Dark-Age settlement at Mawgan Porth, Cornwall', *Recent archaeological excavations in Britain* (ed. R. L. S. Bruce-Mitford), London, 167–96.

—— (1956a). 'Late Saxon disc-brooches', *Dark-Age Britain*, London, 171–201.

—— (1968). *The Sutton Hoo ship burial: a handbook*, London.

—— (1969). 'The art of the Codex Amiatinus', *The Journal of the British Archaeological Association*, 3rd series, xxxii, 1–25.

—— (1972). *The Sutton Hoo ship burial: a handbook*, 2nd edn, London.

—— (1972a). 'The Sutton Hoo helmet: a new reconstruction', *The British Museum Quarterly*, xxxvi, 120–30.

—— (1974). *Aspects of Anglo-Saxon Archaeology*, London.

BU'LOCK J. D. (1972). *Pre-conquest Cheshire*, Chester.

—— (1974). 'The problem of post-Roman Manchester', in G. D. B. Jones, *Roman Manchester*, Altrincham, 165–71.

BURFORD J. W. (1967). 'A Saxon wall at Brixworth', *Journal of the British Archaeological Association*, 3rd series, xxxii, 1–25.

BURGESS L. A. (1964). *The origins of Southampton*, Leicester (Department of English Local History: Occasional Papers: xvi).

BURROW C. G. (1973). 'Tintagel – some problems', *Scottish Archaeological Forum*, v, 99–103.

CALBERG M. (1951). 'Tissus et broderies attribués aux saintes Harlinde et Relinde', *Bulletin de la Société royale d'archéologie de Bruxelles*, October, 1–26.

CAM H. M. (1963). 'The origin of the borough of Cambridge: a consideration of Professor Carl Stephenson's theories', *Liberties and communities in medieval England*, London, 1–18.

CAMERON K. (1965). *Scandinavian settlement in the territory of the Five Boroughs: the place-name evidence*, Nottingham.

CAMPBELL A. (ed.) (1962). *The Chronicle of Æthelweard*, London.

—— (ed.) (1967). Æthelwulf, *De abbatibus*, Oxford.

—— (ed.) (1973). *Charters of Rochester*, London (Anglo-Saxon Charters, i).

CAMPBELL J. (1975). 'Norwich', *Historic towns*, ii (ed. M. D. Lobel), London.

CAPELLE T. (1969). 'Schiffsformige Hausgrundrisse in frühgeschichtlicher Zeit', *Frühmittelalterliche Studien*, iii, 244–56.

—— and VIERCK H. (1971). 'Modeln der Merowinger- und Wikingerzeit', *Frühmittelalterliche Studien*, v, 42–100.

CARTER A. (1972). 'The Norwich survey. Excavations in Norwich 1971 – an interim report', *Norfolk Archaeology*, xxv, pt 3, 410–16

CARTER A. (1974). 'The history of Norwich', *A Geographical guide to Norwich* (ed. M. J. Moseley for Institute of British Geographers' Annual Conference), Norwich, 5–9.

—— and ROBERTS J. P. (1973). 'Excavations in Norwich – 1972. The Norwich survey, second interim report', *Norfolk Archaeology*, xxxv, pt 4, 443–68.

CARUS-WILSON E. M. (1957). 'The significance of the secular sculptures in the Lane chapel, Cullumpton', *Medieval Archaeology*, i, 104–17.

—— and LOBEL M. D. (1975). 'Bristol', *Historic towns*, ii (ed. M. D. Lobel). London.

CHADWICK S. E. (1958). 'The Anglo-Saxon cemetery at Finglesham, Kent: a reconsideration', *Medieval Archaeology*, ii, 1–71.

CHAMPION B. (1916). 'Outils en fer du musée de Saint-Germain', *Revue archaeologique*, 5th series, iii, 211–46.

CHAPELOT J. (1970). 'L'atelier ceramique carolingien de Saran (Loiret): rapport préliminaire de fouille (1969–72)', *Bulletin Societé Archéologie et Histoire de L'Orleanais*, new series, vi, 49–72.

—— (1971). 'Un atelier ceramique d'epoque carolingienne: Saran Loiret', *Revue Archéologique du Centre*, xxxvii–xxxviii, 3–10.

CHAPLIN R. E. (1971). *The study of animal bones from archaeological sites*, London.

CHARLES F. W. (1967). *Medieval cruck-building and its derivatives*, London (Society for Medieval Archaeology, Monograph series: no. 2).

CHARLESWORTH M. P. (1949). *The lost province, or the worth of Britain*, Cardiff.

CHISHOLM M. (1968). *Rural settlement and land use*, 2nd revised edn, London.

CHRISTIE A. G. I. (1938). *English medieval embroidery*, Oxford.

CLAPHAM A. W. (1928). 'The carved stones at Breedon on the Hill', *Archaeologia*, lxxvii, 219–40.

—— (1930). *English Romanesque architecture*, i, Oxford.

—— (1933). *English Romanesque architecture*, ii, Oxford.

—— (1946). 'Stow', *The Archaeological Journal*, ciii, 168–70.

—— (1952). *Whitby Abbey*, London.

CLARKE H. (1970). 'Excavations on a kiln at Grimston, Pott Row, Norfolk', *Norfolk Archaeology*, xxxvi, 79–95.

CLARKE R. R. (1937). 'An Iron Age hut at Postwick, Norfolk', *Norfolk Archaeology*, xxvi, 271–7.

—— (1957). 'Archaeological discoveries in Norfolk, 1949–54', *Norfolk Archaeology*, xxxi, 395–416.

—— and DOLLEY R. H. M. (1958). 'The Morley St Peter hoard', *Antiquity*, xxxii, 100–103.

CLEMOES P. and HUGHES K. (ed.) (1971). *England before the conquest: Studies in primary sources presented to Dorothy Whitelock*, Cambridge.

COBBETT L. and FOX C. (1922–3). 'The Saxon church of Great Paxton', *Proceedings of the Cambridge Antiquarian Society*, xxv, 50–77.

COGHLAN H. H. (1956). *Notes on prehistoric and early iron in the Old World*, Oxford (Pitt-Rivers Museum, University of Oxford, occasional papers on technology, viii).

COLGRAVE B. (1927). *The life of Bishop Wilfrid by Eddius Stephanus*, Cambridge.

—— (ed.) (1940). *Two lives of St Cuthbert*, Cambridge.

—— (1950). 'Post Bedan miracles and translations of St Cuthbert', *The early cultures of North-West Europe* (ed. C. Fox and B. Dickins), Cambridge.

—— (ed.) (1968). *The earliest life of St Gregory the Great*, Cambridge.

—— and CRAMP R. (1965). *St Peter's church, Monkwearmouth*, n.p.

—— and MYNORS R. A. B. (ed.) (1969). *Bede's ecclesiastical history of the English people*, Oxford.

COLLINGWOOD R. G. and RICHMOND I. A. (1969). *The archaeology of Roman Britain*, London.

COLLINGWOOD W. G. (1907). 'Anglian and Anglo-Danish sculpture in the North Riding of Yorkshire', *The Yorkshire Archaeological Journal*, xix, 267–413.

—— (1915). 'Anglian and Anglo-Danish sculpture in the West Riding', *Yorkshire Archaeological Society*, xxiii, 129–299.

—— (1927). *Northumbrian crosses of the pre-Norman age*, London.

COLLINS A. E. P. and COLLINS F. J. (1959). 'Excavations on Blewburton Hill', *Berkshire Archaeological Journal*, lxvii, 52–73.

COLLINS A. H. and FLEMING L. (1958). 'Beckets Barn, Pagham', *Sussex Archaeological Collections*, xcvi, 135–48.

COLVIN H. M. (1958). 'Domestic architecture and town-planning', *Medieval England* (ed. A. L. Poole), Oxford, i, 37–97.

COLVIN H. M. (ed.) (1963). *The history of the King's works*, i, London.

CONANT K. J. (1959). *Carolingian and Romanesque architecture 800–1200*, Harmondsworth.

CONGREVE A. L. (1937 and 1938). *A Roman and Saxon site at Elmswell* (Hull Museum publications, cxciii and cxcviii).

COOK A. M. (1974). *The evidence for the reconstruction of female costume in the early Anglo-Saxon period in the south of England* (unpublished MA thesis in the University Library, Birmingham).

COOK J. M. (1958). 'An Anglo-Saxon cemetery at Broadway Hill, Broadway, Worcestershire', *The Antiquaries Journal*, xxxviii, 58–84.

COOK N. C. (1969). 'A fifth-century wheel-made sherd from the City of London', *The Antiquaries Journal*, xlix, 396.

COOK R. M. (1969). 'Archaeomagnetism', *Science in Archaeology* (ed. D. Brothwell and E. Higgs), 2nd edn, London, 76–87.

COOTE C. M. (1952). 'An early Saxon and Roman site at Hemingford Grey', *Proceedings of the Cambridge and Huntingdonshire Archaeological Society*, vii, 68–71.

COPPACK G. (1973). 'The excavation of a Roman and medieval site at Flaxengate, Lincoln', *Lincolnshire History and Archaeology*, viii, 73–114.

CORDER P. (1955). 'The reorganization of the defences of Romano-British towns in the fourth century', *The Archaeological Journal*, cxii, 20–42.

COTTON M. A. (1962). 'The Norman bank of Colchester castle', *The Antiquaries Journal*, xlii, 57–61.

CRAMP R. J. (1957). 'Beowulf and archaeology', *Medieval Archaeology*, i, 57–77.

—— (1967). *Anglian and Viking York*, York (St Anthony's Hall publications, xxxiii).

—— (1967b). 'Appendix B' in Jobey, G. (1967) 'Excavations at Tynemouth priory and castle', *Archaeologia Aeliana*, xlv, 99–104.

—— (1969). 'Excavations at the Saxon monastic sites of Wearmouth and Jarrow, Co. Durham: an interim report', *Medieval Archaeology*, xiii, 21–66.

—— (1970). 'Decorated window-glass and millefiori from Monkwearmouth', *The Antiquaries Journal*, 1, 327–35.

—— (1972). In Webster L. E. and Cherry J. (ed.) 'Medieval Britain in 1971', *Medieval Archaeology*, xiii, 148–52.

—— (1973). Anglo-Saxon monasteries of the north', *Scottish Archaeological Forum*, v, 104–24.

CRASTER H. H. E. (ed.) (1907). *The history of Northumberland*, viii, Newcastle and London.

CRAW J. H. (1929–30). 'Excavations at Dunadd and at other sites on the Poltalloch estates, Argyll', *Proceedings of the Society of Antiquaries of Scotland*, lxiv, 111–46.

CRAWFORD O. G. S. (1928). 'Our debt to Rome?', *Antiquity*, ii, 173–88.

—— (1953). *Archaeology in the field*, London.

CROSBY S. MCK. (1942). *The abbey of St Denis*, Newhaven.

—— (1953). *L'abbaye royale de Saint Denis*, Paris.

CROWFOOT E. and HAWKES S. C. (1967). 'Early Anglo-Saxon gold braids', *Medieval Archaeology*, xi, 42–86.

CROWFOOT G. M. (1948–9). 'Textiles from a Viking grave at Kildonan on the Isle of Eigg', *Proceedings of the Society of Antiquaries of Scotland*, lxxxiii, 24–6.

—— (1950). 'Textiles of the Saxon period in the Museum of Archaeology and Ethnology', *Proceedings of the Cambridge Antiquarian Society*, xliv, 26–32.

—— (1952). 'Anglo-Saxon tablet weaving', *The Antiquaries Journal*, xxxii, 189.

CRUDEN S. (1949). *Click Mill, Dounby, Orkney*, Edinburgh.

—— (1950). 'The horizontal water-mill at Dounby on the mainland of Orkney', *Proceedings of the Society of Antiquaries of Scotland*, lxxxi, 43–7.

CRUMMY P. (1974). *Colchester: recent excavations and research*, Colchester.

CUNLIFFE B. (1964). *Winchester excavations, 1949–1960*, i, Winchester.

—— (1966). 'Excavations at Portchester castle, 1963–5', *The Antiquaries Journal*, xlvi, 39–49.

—— (1967). 'Studies in local history – Portchester', *Portchester Papers*, i.

—— (1969). 'Excavations at Portchester castle, Hants., 1966–1968', *The Antiquaries Journal*, xlix, 62–74.

—— (1970). 'The Saxon culture sequence at Portchester castle', *The Antiquaries Journal*, l, 67–85.

—— (1972). 'Excavations at Portchester castle, Hants., 1969–1971', *The Antiquaries Journal*, lii, 70–83.

—— (1972a). 'Saxon and medieval settlement-pattern, in the region of Chalton, Hampshire', *Medieval Archaeology*, xxvi, 1–12.

—— (1974). 'Some late Saxon stamped pottery from southern England', *Medieval pottery from excavations: studies presented to Gerald Clough Dunning* (ed. V. I. Evison, H. Hodges and J. G. Hurst), London, 127–36.

CURLE A. O. (1913–14). 'Report on the excavation of ... the Mote of Mark', *Proceedings of the Society of Antiquaries of Scotland*, xlviii, 125–68.

CURLE J. (1911). *A Roman frontier post and its people*, Glasgow.

CURWEN E. C. and WILLIAMSON R. P. R. (1931). 'The date of Cissbury camp', *The Antiquaries Journal*, xi, 14–36.

DANIELS C. M. (1966). 'Excavations on the site of the Roman villa at Southwell, 1959', *Transactions of the Thoroton Society of Nottinghamshire*, lxx, 13–54.

DANNHEIMER H. (1973). 'Die frühmittelalterliche Seidlung bei Kirchheim', *Germania*, li, 150.

DAVEY N. (1964), 'A pre-conquest church and baptistery at Potterne', *Wiltshire Archaeological Magazine*, lix, 116–23.

DAVIDSON H. R. E. (1962). *The sword in Anglo-Saxon England*, Oxford.

—— and WEBSTER L. (1967). 'The Anglo-Saxon burial at Coombe (Woodnesborough) Kent', *Medieval Archaeology*, xi, 1–41.

DAVIS R. H. C. (1962). 'Brixworth and Clofesho', *Journal of the British Archaeological Association*, 3rd series, xxv, 71.

DAVISON B. K. (1967a). 'The late Saxon town of Thetford: an interim report on the 1964–1966 excavations', *Medieval Archaeology*, xi, 189–208.

—— (1967b). 'The origins of the castle in England', *The Archaeological Journal*, cxxiv, 202–11.

—— (1968). 'Excavations at Sulgrave, Northamptonshire, 1968', *The Archaeological Journal*, cxxv, 305–7.

—— (1972). 'The Burghal Hidage fort of Eorpeburnan: a suggested identification', *Medieval Archaeology*, xvi, 123–7.

DAWE A. (1967). 'The pre-conquest ditch near Bridlesmith Gate', *Transactions of the Thoroton Society of Nottinghamshire*, lxxi, 32–5.

DEANESLEY M. (1943). 'Roman traditionalist influence among the Anglo-Saxons', *English Historical Review*, lviii, 129–46.

—— (1961). *The pre-conquest church in England*, London.

DECAENS J. (1971). 'Un nouveau cimetière du haut moyen age en Normandie, Hérouvillette (Calvados)', *Archéologie médiévale*, i, 1–124.

DEDEKAM H. (1924–5). 'To tekstilfund fra folkevandringstiden', *Bergen Museums Årbok*, 25–9.

DEMOLON P. (1972). *La village mérovingien de Brèbieres*, Arras (Memoires de la commission départmentale des monuments historiques du Pas-de-Calsis, xiv).

DICKINSON T. M. (1973). 'New perspectives on Dorchester-on-Thames: theories and facts', *Council for British Archaeology: Regional Group 9 Newsletter*, iii, 5–6.

—— (1974). *Cuddesdon and Dorchester-on-Thames, Oxfordshire: two early Saxon 'princely' sites in Wessex*, Oxford (British Archaeological Reports, i).

DICKS T. R. B. (1972). 'Network analysis and historical geography', *Area*, iv, pt 1, 4–9.

DODGSON J. M. (1966). 'The significance of the distribution of the English place-name in *-ingas, -inga* in South East England', *Medieval Archaeology*, x, 1–29.

DODWELL C. R. (ed.) (1961). *Theophilus: the various arts*, London.

DOLLEY R. H. M. (1954a). 'The sack of Wilton in 1003 and the chronology of the "Long Cross" and "Helmet" types of Æthelræd II', *Nordisk Numismatisk Unions Medlemsblad*, 152–6.

—— (1954b). 'The so-called Piedforts of Alfred the Great', *Numismatic Chronicle*, cxiv, 76–95.

—— (1955). 'Contemporary forgeries of late Saxon pence', *British Numismatic Journal*, xxviii, i, 185–9.

—— (1957). 'An unpublished Irish hoard of "St Peter" pence', *Numismatic Chronicle*, cxvii, 123–32.

—— (1958a). 'Some reflections on Hildebrand type A of Æthelræd II', *Antikvariskt Arkiv*, ix.

—— (1958b). 'The Morley St Peter treasure trove', *The Numismatic Circular*, lxvi, 113–114.

—— (1960). 'An unpublished Chester penny of Harthacnut found at Caerwent', *Numismatic Chronicle*, cxx, 191–3.

—— (1960a). 'Coin hoards from the London area as evidence for the pre-eminence of London in the later Saxon period', *Transactions of the London and Middlesex Archaeological Society*, xx, pt 2, 37–50.

—— (ed.) (1961). *Anglo-Saxon coins*, London.

—— (1961a). 'A hoard of Anglo-Saxon pennies from Sicily', *Numismatic Chronicle*, cxxi, 151–61.

—— (1961b). 'The degree of contraction of the ethnic as an index of relative date in the case of "Long Cross" pennies of Æthelræd II', *The Numismatic Circular*, lxix, 241–2.

—— (1964). *Anglo-Saxon pennies*, London.

—— (1965). *Viking coins of the Danelaw and of Dublin*, London.

—— (1966a). *The Hiberno-Norse coins in the British Museum*, London.

—— (1966b). *The Norman conquest and the English coinage*, London.

—— (1970). 'The location of the pre-Ælfredian mint(s) of Wessex', *Proceedings of the Hampshire Field Club and Archaeological Society*, xxvii, 57–61.

—— (1971). 'The mythical Norman element in the 1882 Bishophill (York) find of Anglo-Saxon coins', *Yorkshire Philosophical Society Annual Report 1971*, 88–101.

—— (1973a). 'Some evidence for the date of the *Crux* coins of Æthelred II', *Anglo-Saxon England*, ii, 145–154.

—— (1973b). 'Nogle danske efterligninger af irsk-nordiske penninge', *Nordisk Numismatisk Unions Medlemsblad*, 1973, 93–9.

—— and BLUNT C. E. (1961). 'The chronology of the coins of Ælfred the Great, 871–899', *Anglo-Saxon Coins* (ed. R. H. M. Dolley), London, 77–95.

——and ELMORE JONES F. (1955–7). 'The mints "Aet Gothabyrig" and "Aet Sith(m)este-byrig" ', *British Numismatic Journal*, xxvii, 270–82.

—— —— (1961). 'The transition between the "Hand of Providence" and "Crux" types of Æthelræd II', *Commentationes de Nummis Saeculorum ix-xi in Suecia Repertis*, i (ed. N. L. Rasmusson and L. O. Lagerqvist), Stockholm.

—— and METCALF D. M. (1957). 'Two stray finds from St Albans of coins of Offa and of Charlemagne', *British Numismatic Journal*, xxviii, iii, 459–66.

—— —— (1961). 'The reform of the English coinage under Eadgar', *Anglo-Saxon coins* (ed. R. H. M. Dolley), London, 136–68.

—— and PIRIE E. J. E. (1964). 'The repercussions on Chester's prosperity of the Viking descent on Wirral in 980', *British Numismatic Journal*, xxxiii, 39–44.

—— and SKAARE K. (1961). 'The coinage of Æthelwulf, king of the West Saxons', *Anglo-Saxon coins* (ed. R. H. M. Dolley), London, 63–76.

DOLLINGER-LEONARD Y. (1958). 'De la cité romaine à la ville médiévale dans la région de la Moselle et la Haute Meuse', *Studien zu den Anfängen des europäischen Städte-wesens*, Konstanz und Lindau (Reichenau-Vorträge und Forschungen, iv), 195–226.

DOPPELFELD O. (1970). 'Das Fortleben der Stadt Köln von 5. bis 8. Jahrhundert nach Chr.', *Early Medieval Studies*, i (Antikvariskt Arkiv, xxxviii), 35–42.

—— (1973). 'Köln von der Spätantike bis zur Karolingerzeit', *Vor- und Frühformen der europäischen Stadt im Mittelalter* (ed. H. Jankuhn, W. Schlesinger and H. Steuer), Göttingen (Abhandlungen der Akademie der Wissenschaften, philologish-historische Klasse, 3 Folge, No. 83), 110–29.

DOUGLAS D. C. and WHITELOCK D. (1955). See Whitelock (1955).

DOWN A. (1974). *Rescue archaeology in Chichester*, Chichester.

—— (1974a). *Chichester excavations*, ii, Chichester.

—— and RULE M. (1971). *Chichester excavations*, i, Chichester.

DREIHAUS J. (1972). 'Zum Problem merowingerzeitlicher Goldschmeide', *Nachrictung der Akademie der Wissenschaften, Göttingen, Philologisch-historische Klasse*, xxxi, 389–404.

DUDLEY D. and MINTER E. M. (1966). 'The excavation of a medieval settlement at Treworld, Lesnewth 1963', *Cornish Archaeology*, v, 34–58.

DUDLEY H. E. (1949). *Early days in North-West Lincolnshire*, Scunthorpe.

DUNNING G. C. (1932). 'Bronze age settlements and a Saxon hut near Bourton-on-the-Water', *The Antiquaries Journal*, xii, 279–93.

—— (1951). 'The Saxon town of Thetford', *The Archaeological Journal*, cvi, 72–3.

—— (1952). 'Anglo-Saxon discoveries at Harston', *Transactions of the Leicestershire Archaeological Society*, xxviii, 49–54.

—— (1956). 'Trade relations between England and the Continent in the late Anglo-Saxon period', *Dark-Age Britain. Studies presented to E. T. Leeds* (ed. D. B. Harden), London, 218–33.

—— (1958). 'A Norman pit at Pevensey Castle and its contents', *The Antiquaries Journal*, xxxviii, 205–17.

—— et al. (1959). 'Anglo-Saxon pottery: a symposium', *Medieval Archaeology*, iii, 1–78.

—— and WILSON A. E. (1953). 'Late Saxon and early medieval pottery from selected sites in Chichester', *Sussex Archaeological Collections*, xci, 140–50.

DURHAM B., HASSALL T., ROWLEY T. and SIMPSON C. (1973). 'A cutting across the Saxon defences at Wallingford, Berkshire 1971', *Oxoniensia*, xxxvii, 82–5.

DYER J. (1972). 'Earthworks of the Danelaw frontier', *Archaeology and the landscape* (ed. P. J. Fowler), London, 222–36.

EAGLES B. N. and EVISON V. I. (1970). 'Excavations (of prehistoric and Anglo-Saxon sites) at Harrold, Bedfordshire, 1951–53', *Bedfordshire Archaeological Journal*, v, 17–55.

ECKSTEIN D. (1969). *Entwicklung und Anwendung der Dendrochronologie zur Altersbestimmung der Siedlung Haithabu*, Hamburg.

—— and Lisse W. (1971). 'Jahrringschronologische Untersuchungen zur Alterbestimmung von Holzbauten der Siedling Haithabu', *Germania*, xlix, 155–68.

EDDIUS STEPHANUS. See Colgrave (1927).

ELGEE F. (1930). *Early man in north-east Yorkshire*, Gloucester.

ELISSÉEFF N. (1970). 'Damas à la lumière des theories de Jean Sauvaget' *The Islamic city* (ed. A. H. Hourani and S. M. Stern), Oxford, 157–77.

ELLISON A. and HARRIS J. (1972). 'Settlement and land use in the prehistory and early history of southern England: a study based on locational models', *Models in Archaeology* (ed. D. L. Clarke), London, 910–62.

EMERTON E. (1940). *The letters of St Boniface*, New York.

ENGELHARDT C. (1869). *Vimosefundet*, København.

ENNEN E. (1953). *Frühgeschichte der europäischen Stadt*, Bonn.

—— (1964). 'Das Städtewesen Nordwestdeutschlands von der Fränkischen bis zur Salischen Zeit', *Das erste Jahrtausend* (ed. V. H. Elbern), Düsseldorf, ii, 785–820.

—— (1972). *Die europäische Stadt des Mittelalters*, Göttingen.

ERLANDE-BRANDENBURG A. (1964). 'Le monastère de Luxueil au IXe siècle', *Cahiers Archéologiques*, xiv, 239.

EVANS A. C. and FENWICK V. H. (1971). 'The Graveney boat', *Antiquity*, xlv, 89–96.

EVELYN WHITE H. G. (1933). *The monasteries of the Wadi 'N Natrun*, iii, *The Architecture and Archaeology*, New York.

EVISON V. I. (1951). 'White material in Kentish disc brooches', *The Antiquaries Journal*, xxxi, 197–200.

—— (1955). 'Early Anglo-Saxon inlaid metalwork', *The Antiquaries Journal*, xxxv, 20–45.

—— (1956). 'An Anglo-Saxon cemetery at Holborough, Kent', *Archaeologia Cantiana*, lxx, 84–141.

—— (1963). 'Sugar-loaf shield bosses', *The Antiquaries Journal*, xliii, 38–96.

—— (1968). 'Quoit brooch style buckles', *The Antiquaries Journal*, xlviii, 231–49.

—— (1969). 'A Viking grave at Sonning, Berks', *The Antiquaries Journal*, xlix, 330–45.

—— (1969a). 'Five Anglo-Saxon inhumation graves containing pots at Great Chesterford, Essex', *Berichten van de Rijksdienst voor het Oudheidkundig Bodemonderzoek*, xix, 157–173.

—— (1974). 'The Asthall type of bottle', *Medieval pottery from excavations: studies presented to Gerald Clough Dunning* (ed. V. I. Evison, H. Hodges and J. G. Hurst), London, 77–94.

FARRAR R. A. H. (1962). 'Roman tesserae under the nave of Wimborne Minster', *Proceedings of Dorset Natural History and Archaeological Society*, lxxxiv, 106–9.

FAULL M. L. (1974). 'Roman and Anglian settlement patterns in Yorkshire', *Northern History*, ix, 1–25.

FAUSSETT B. (1856). *Inventorium Sepulchrale*, London.

FELLOWS JENSEN G. (1972). *Scandinavian settlement names in Yorkshire*, Copenhagen.

—— (1973). 'Place-name research and northern history: a survey', *Northern History*, viii, 1–23.

FINBERG H. P. R. (ed.) (1957). *Gloucestershire studies*, Leicester.

—— (1959). *Roman and Saxon Withington: a study in continuity*, Leicester (Occasional Paper no. 8, Department of English Local History, Leicester University).

—— (1964). *The early charters of Wessex*, Leicester.

—— (1964a). 'Yniswitrin', *Lucerna* (ed. H. P. R. Finberg), London, 83–94.

—— (ed.) (1972). *The agrarian history of England and Wales*, i, pt 2, Cambridge.

—— (1972). 'Anglo-Saxon England to 1042', *The agrarian history of England and Wales*, i, pt 2 (ed. H. P. R. Finberg), Cambridge, 385–525.

FISHER C. A. (1962). *The greater Anglo-Saxon churches*, London.

—— (1963). 'Some little known towered Anglo-Saxon churches in Lincolnshire', *Lincolnshire Architectural and Archaeological Society Reports and Papers*, 12–23.

—— (1969). *Anglo-Saxon towers*, London.

—— (1970). *The Saxon churches of Sussex*, London.

FLETCHER E. (1965). 'Early Kentish churches', *Medieval Archaeology*, ix, 11–31.

—— (1966). (Review of) Taylor and Taylor, *Anglo-Saxon Architecture*, *The Antiquaries Journal*, xlvi, 130–2.

FLETCHER E. and MEATES G. W. (1969). 'The ruined church of Stone-by-Faversham', *The Antiquaries Journal*, xlix, 273–94.

FOOTE P. G. and WILSON D. M. (1970). *The Viking achievement*, London.

FORBES J. S. and DALLADAY D. B. (1960). 'Composition of English silver coins (870–1300)', *British Numismatic Journal*, xxx, i, 82–7.

FOWLER P. J. (1969). 'Fyfield Down 1959–68', *Current Archaeology*, xvi, 124–9.

—— et al. (1970). *Cadbury, Congresbury, Somerset, 1968*, Bristol.

—— (1970). 'Fieldwork and excavation in the Butcombe area, North Somerset. Second interim report, 1968–69', *Proceedings of the University of Bristol Spelaeological Society*, xii, 2, 169–94.

—— (1971). 'Early prehistoric agriculture in Western Europe: some archaeological evidence', *Economy and settlement in Neolithic and early Bronze Age Britain and Europe* (ed. D. D. A. Simpson), Leicester, 153–82.

—— (1971a). 'Hill-forts, A.D. 400–700', *The Iron Age and its hill-forts* (ed. D. Hill and M. Jesson), Southampton, 203–13.

—— (ed.) (1972). *Archaeology and the landscape*, London.

—— (ed.) (1975). *Recent work in rural archaeology*, Bradford-on-Avon.

—— and BENNETT J. (ed.) (1973), (1974), (1976). 'Archaeology and the M5 motorway: second, third and fourth reports', *Transactions of the Bristol and Gloucestershire Archaeological Society*, xcii, 21–81; xciii and xciv, forthcoming.

—— and EVANS J. G. (1967). 'Plough-marks, lynchets and early fields', *Antiquity*, xli, 289–301.

—— and THOMAS A. C. (1962), 'Arable field of the pre-Norman period at Gwithian', *Cornish Archaeology*, i, 61–84.

—— and WALTHEW C. V. (eds.) (1971). 'Archaeology and the M5 Motorway: first report', *Transactions of the Bristol and Gloucestershire Archaeological Society*, xc, 22–63.

FOX A. (1968). 'Excavations at the South Gate, Exeter 1964–5', *Proceedings of the Devon Archaeological Society*, xxvi, 1–20.

—— and FOX C. (1958). 'Wansdyke reconsidered', *The Archaeological Journal*, cxv, 1–48.

FOX C. (1923). *The archaeology of the Cambridge region*, Cambridge.

—— (1948). *The archaeology of the Cambridge region* (with supplement), Cambridge.

—— (1955). *Offa's dyke*, London.

FREEMAN E. A. (1876). *The history of the Norman conquest*, iv, 2nd edn, Oxford.

FREND W. H. C. (1968). 'The Christianisation of Roman Britain', *Christianity in Britain* (ed. M. W. Barley and R. P. C. Hanson), Leicester, 37–50.

FRERE S. S. (1960). 'Excavations at Verulamium, 1959. Fifth interim report', *The Antiquaries Journal*, xl, 1–24.

—— (1962a). 'Excavations at Dorchester on Thames, 1962', *The Archaeological Journal*, cxix, 114–49.

—— (1962b). *Roman Canterbury, the city of Durovernum*, 3rd edn, Canterbury.

—— (1964a). 'Verulamium – then and now', *Bulletin of the Institute of Archaeology*, iv, 61–82.

—— (1964b). 'Verulamium, three Roman cities', *Antiquity*, xxxviii, 103–12.

—— (1966). 'The end of towns in Roman Britain', *The civitas capitals of Roman Britain* (ed. J. S. Wacher), Leicester, 87–100.

—— (1967). *Britannia*, London.

—— (1970). 'The Roman theatre at Canterbury', *Britannia*, i, 83–113.

—— (1971). 'Introduction', *Soldier and civilian in Roman Yorkshire* (ed. R. M. Butler), Leicester, 15–19.

FYFE T. (1927). 'Glastonbury abbey excavations', *Proceedings of the Somersetshire Archaeological and Natural History Society*, lxxiii, 86–7.

GAGE J. (1836). 'Sepulchral stones found at Hartlepool in 1833', *Archaeologia*, xxvi, 479–482.

GALBRAITH K. J. (1968). 'Early sculpture at St Nicholas' church, Ipswich', *Proceedings of the Suffolk Institute of Archaeology*, xxxi, pt 2, 172–84.

GALSTER G. (1964). *Sylloge of the coins of the British Isles, royal collection of coins and medals, National Museum, Copenhagen*, i, London.

GARMONSWAY G. N. (trans.) (1955). *The Anglo-Saxon Chronicle*, London.

GATHERCOLE P. W. and WAILES B. (1959). 'Excavations on Castle Hill Thurgarton, 1954–1955', *Transactions of the Thoroton Society of Nottinghamshire*, lxiii, 24–56.

GEIJER A. (1938). *Birka*, iii, *Die Textilfunde*, Uppsala.

GELLING M. (1967). 'English place-names derived from the compound *wīchām*', *Medieval Archaeology*, xi, 87–104.

GEM R. D. H. (1970). 'The Anglo-Saxon cathedral church at Canterbury: a further contribution', *The Archaeological Journal*, cxxvii, 196–201.

GIBB, J. H. P. (1969). 'The Saxon cathedral at Sherborne', *The Shirburnian*.

—— (1972). 'An interim report of Excavations carried out at the west end of Sherborne Abbey in 1964–5', *Proceedings of the Dorset Natural History and Archaeological Society*, 93, 197–210.

—— (1976). 'The Anglo-Saxon Cathedral at Sherborne. Report of excavations carried out at Sherborne Abbey 1964–73', *Archaeological Journal*, forthcoming.

GILBERT E. (1946). 'New views on Warden, Bywell and Heddon on the Wall churches', *Archaeologia Aeliana*, 4th series, xxiv, 115–76.

—— (1947). 'Anglian remains at St Peter's, Monkwearmouth', *Archaeologia Aeliana*, 4th series, xxv, 140–78.

—— (1948). 'Anglo-Saxon work at Billingham', *Proceedings of the Society of Antiquaries of Newcastle-upon-Tyne*, 4th series, xi, 195–204.

—— (1964). 'Some problems of early Northumbrian architecture', *Archaeologia Aeliana*, 4th series, xlii, 65–83.

—— (1965). 'Brixworth and the English basilica', *Art Bulletin*, xlvii, 1–20.

—— (1967). 'The church of St Laurence, Bradford on Avon', *Wiltshire Archaeological and Natural History Magazine*, lxii, 38–50.

—— (1967a). 'St Wystan's, Repton', *Cahiers Archéologiques*, xvii, 83–102.

—— (1968). 'The first stone church at Deerhurst', *Bristol and Gloucestershire Archaeological Society Transactions*, lxxxvii, 71–95.

—— (1970). 'The date of the late Saxon cathedral at Canterbury', *The Archaeological Journal*, cxxvii, 202–10.

GJESSING G. (1934). *Studien i norsk merovingertid*, Oslo (Skrifter ... av det Norsk Videnskaps-Akademi i Oslo, ii, Hist.-Filos. Klasse, 2).

GOLLANCZ I. (1927). *The Caedmon manuscript*, Oxford.

GOODMAN W. L. (1964). *The history of woodworking tools*, London.

GOULD J. (1967–8). 'First report of the excavations at Tamworth, Staffs., 1967: the Saxon defences', *Transactions of the Lichfield and South Staffordshire Archaeological and Historical Society*, ix, 17–29.

—— (1968–9). 'Third report on excavations at Tamworth, Staffs., 1968: the western entrance to the Saxon borough', *Transactions of the Lichfield and South Staffordshire Archaeological and Historical Society*, x, 32–43.

—— (1971–2). 'The medieval burgesses of Tamworth; their liberties, courts and markets', *Transactions of the Lichfield and South Staffordshire Archaeological and Historical Society*, xiii, 17–42.

—— (1972–3). 'Letocetum, Christianity and Lichfield (Staffs.)', *Transactions of the South Staffordshire Archaeological and Historical Society*, xiv, 30–1.

—— (forthcoming). 'Letocetum and Lichfield – a case for continuity', *Journal of the British Archaeological Association*, 3rd series.

GOVER J. E. B. *et al.* (1939). *The place-names of Wiltshire*, Cambridge.

GRACIE H. S. (1958). 'St Peter's church, Frocester', *Transactions of the Bristol and Gloucestershire Archaeological Society*, lxxvii, 23–30.

GRAY H. K. (1915). *The English field systems*, Cambridge (Mass.)

GRAY H. ST G. (1933). 'Trial excavations in the so-called "Danish camp" at Wareham', *The Antiquaries Journal*, xiii, 399–413.

GREBER J. M. (1956). *Die Geschichte des Hobels*, Zürich.

GREEN A. R. and P. M. (1951). *Saxon architecture and sculpture in Hampshire*, London.

GREEN B. and YOUNG R. M. R. (1968). *Norwich: the growth of a city*, 2nd edn, Norwich.

GREEN C. (1962–3). 'Excavations on a medieval site at Water Newton in the county of Huntingdon, in 1958', *Proceedings of the Cambridge Antiquarian Society*, lvi–lvii, 68–87.

—— (1963). *Sutton Hoo*, London.

GREEN C. J. S. (1971). 'Interim report on excavations at Poundsbury, Dorchester, 1971', *Proceedings of the Dorset Natural History and Archaeological Society*, xciii, 154–6.

GREEN H. J. M. (1963). 'Secrets of Whitehall', *Illustrated London News*, ccxlii, 1004–7.

GREEN J. R. (1883). *The conquest of England*, London.

GREENING P. (1971). 'The origins of the historic town plan of Bath', *A second North Somerset miscellany*, Bath, 7–16.

GRIERSON P. (1952–4) 'The Canterbury (St Martin's) hoard of Frankish and Anglo–Saxon coin ornaments', *British Numismatic Journal*, xxvii, 39–51.

—— (1961a). 'Sterling', *Anglo–Saxon coins* (ed. R. H. M. Dolley), London, 266–83.

—— (1961b). 'La fonction sociale de la monnaie en Angleterre aux VIIe–VIIIe siècles', *Moneta e Scambi nell Alto Medioevo*, Spoleto (Settimane di Studio del Centro Italiano sul' Alto Medioevo, viii), 341–85.

GRIFFITH A. F. and SALZMANN L. (1914). 'An Anglo–Saxon cemetery at Alfriston, Sussex', *Sussex Archaeological Collections*, lvi, 16–53.

GRIMES W. F. (1956). 'Excavations in the City of London', *Recent archaeological excavations in Britain* (ed. R. L. S. Bruce-Mitford) London, 111–44.

—— (1968). *The excavation of Roman and medieval London*, London.

GRIMM P. (1968). 'The royal palace at Tilleda', *Medieval Archaeology*, xii, 83–100.

GRODECKI L. (1958). *L'architecture ottonienne*, Paris.

GRUNDY J. E. (1970). 'Notes on the relationship between climate and cattle housing', *Vernacular Architecture*, i, 3–5.

GUÐJÓNSSON E. E. (1962). 'Forn röggvarvefnaður' *Árbók hins íslenzka fornleifafélags*, 12–71.

GUILDAY J. E. (1970). 'Animal remains from archaeological excavations at Fort Ligonier', *Annals of Carnegie Museum*, xlii, 177–86.

GUTHRIE A. (1953–6). 'Dark Age sites at St Ives', *Proceedings of the West Cornwall Field Club*, new series, i, 73–4.

—— (1959–60). 'The Hellesvean dark age house', *Proceedings of the West Cornwall Field Club*, new series, ii, 151–3.

GUYAN W. U. (1952). 'Einige Karten zur Verbrietung der Grubenhäuser in Mittelleuropa im ersten nachchristlichen Jahrtausend', *Jahrbuch der schweizerischen Gesellschaft für Urgeschichte*, xlii, 174–97.

HAARNAGEL W. (1950). 'Das nordwesteuropäische dreischiffige Hallenhaus und seine Entwicklung im Küstengebiet der Nordsee', *Neues Archiv für Niedersachsen*, xv, 79–91.

HABERL J. and HAWKES C. F. C. (1973). 'The last of Roman Noricum: St Severin on the Danube', *Greeks, Celts and Romans. Studies in Venture and Resistance* (ed. C. F. C. Hawkes and S. C. Hawkes), London (Archaeology into History, i), 97–156.

HAIGH D. H. (1846). 'Notes on monumental stones discovered at Hartlepool', *Journal of the British Archaeological Association*, 185–96.

—— (1875). 'On the monasteries of St Heiu and St Hild', *Yorkshire Archaeological Journal*, iii, 349–91.

HALD, M. (1950) *Olddanske tekstiler*, København.

HAMILTON J. R. C. (1968). 'Iron Age forts and epic literature', *Antiquity*, xlii, 103–108.

HAMILTON N. E. S. A. (ed.) (1870). *William of Malmesbury's Gesta Pontificum*, London (Rolls series, lii).

HARBISON P. (1970). 'How old is Gallarus oratory? A reappraisal of its role in early Irish architecture', *Medieval Archaeology*, xiv, 34–59.

HARBOTTLE B. (1966). 'Excavations at the south curtain wall of the castle, Newcastle-upon-Tyne, 1960–61', *Archaeologia Aeliana*, 4th series, xliv, 79–145.

HARDEN D. B. (1956). 'Glass vessels in Britain and Ireland, A.D. 400–1000', *Dark Age Britain* (ed. D. B. Harden), London, 132–67.

—— (1961). 'Domestic window glass, Roman, Saxon and Medieval', *Studies in building history* (ed. E. M. Jope), London, 39–63.

—— (1971). 'Ancient glass III: post-Roman', *The Archaeological Journal*, cxxviii, 78–117.

—— and TOYNBEE J. M. C. (1959). 'The Rothschild Lycurgus cup', *Archaeologia*, xcvii, 179–212.

HARE M. (1971). 'Anglo-Saxon work at Carlton and other Bedfordshire churches', *Bedfordshire Archaeological Journal*, vi, 33–40.

HARRISON A. C. (1970). 'Excavations in Rochester, *Archaeologia Cantiana*, lxxxxv, 95–112.

—— and FLIGHT C. (1968). 'The Roman and medieval defences of Rochester in the light of recent excavations', *Archaeologia Cantiana*, lxxxiii, 55–104.

HARRISON K. (1962). 'The pre-conquest churches of York', *Yorkshire Archaeological Journal*, xl, 232–49.

HARTING J. E. (1880). *British animals extinct within historic times with some account of British wild white cattle*, London.

HASELOFF G. (1973). 'Salin's style I', *Medieval Archaeology*, xvii, 1–15.

HASSALL J. M. and HILL D. (1970). 'Pont d l'Arche: Frankish influence on the west Saxon burgh?', *Archaeological Journal*, cxxvii, 188–95.

HASSALL M. W. C. (1972). 'Roman urbanization in western Europe', *Man, settlement and urbanism* (ed. P. J. Ucko, R. Tringham and G. W. Dimbleby), London, 857–61.

HASSALL T. G. (1970). 'Excavations at Oxford 1969. Second interim report', *Oxoniensia*, xxxv, 5–18.

—— (1971a). 'Excavations at Oxford 1970. Third interim report', *Oxoniensia*, xxxvi, 1–14.

—— (1971b). 'Excavations in Merton College, Oxford, 1970', *Oxoniensia*, xxxvi, 34–48.

—— (1972a). 'Excavations at Oxford, 1971. Fourth interim report', *Oxoniensia*, xxxvii, 137–49.

—— (1972b). *Oxford: the city beneath your feet. Archaeological excavations in the city of Oxford 1967–1972*, Oxford.

HAVIGHURST A. F. (1958). *The Pirenne thesis. Analysis, criticism and revision*, Boston (Problems in European Civilization).

HAWKES C. F. C. (1946a). 'Roman Ancaster, Horncastle and Caistor', *The Archaeological Journal*, ciii, 17–25.

—— (1946b). 'Anglian and Anglo-Danish Lincolnshire: 2. The exhibition', *The Archaeological Journal*, ciii, 89–94.

—— (1947). 'Anglo-Danish Lincolnshire and the deserted villages of the Wolds', *The Archaeological Journal*, ciii, 100–101.

HAWKES S. C. (1958). 'The Anglo-Saxon cemetery at Finglesham, Kent: a reconsideration', *Medieval Archaeology*, ii, 1–71.

—— (1969). 'Early Anglo-Saxon Kent', *The Archaeological Journal*, cxxvi, 186–92.

—— (1974). 'Some recent finds of late Roman buckles', *Britannia*, v, 36–93.

—— and DUNNING G. C. (1961). 'Soldiers and settlers in Britain, fourth to fifth century: with a catalogue of animal-ornamented buckles and related belt-fittings', *Medieval Archaeology*, v, 1–70.

—— —— (1962–3). 'Krieger und Siedler in Britannien Während des 4. und 5. Jahrhunderts', *Bericht der Romisch-Germanischen Kommission*, xliii–xliv, 155–231.

HAWKES S. C. and GRAY I. M. (1969). 'Preliminary note on the early Anglo-Saxon settlement at New Wintles farm, Eynsham', *Oxoniensis*, xxiv, 1–4.

—— MERRICK J. M. and METCALF D. M. (1966). 'X-ray fluorescent analysis of some Dark-Age coins and jewellery', *Archaeometry*, ix, 98–138.

—— and PAGE R. I. (1967). 'Swords and runes in south-east England', *The Antiquaries Journal*, xlvii, 1–26.

HA: BEDE, *Historia Abbatum.* In *Baedae Opera Historica*, ed. C. Plummer (1896), Oxford.

HAA: BEDE, *Historia Abbatum auctore Anonymo.* In *Baedae Opera Historica*, ed. C. Plummer (1896), Oxford.

HE: BEDE, *Historia Ecclesiastica.* In *Bede's Ecclesiastical History of the English People*, ed. B. Colgrave and R. A. B. Mynors (1969), Oxford.

HEARN M. F. (1971). 'The rectangular ambulatory in English medieval architecture', *Journal of the Society of Architectural Historians of America*, xxx, 187–208.

HEARNE T. (ed.) (1727). *Historia de Rebus Glastoniensis*, Oxford.

HEBDITCH M. G. (1967–8). 'A Saxo-Norman pottery kiln discovered in Southgate Street, Leicester, 1964', *Transactions of the Leicestershire Archaeological and Historical Society*, xliii, 4–9.

HEIGHWAY C. M. (ed.) (1972). *The erosion of history. Archaeology and planning in towns*, London.

—— (1974). *Archaeology in Gloucester. A policy for city and district*, Gloucester.

HEITZ C. (1963). *Recherches sur les rapports entre architecture et liturgie*, Paris.

HELLENKEMPER H. (1972). 'Zu archäologischen Untersuchungen in rheinischen Stadtkernen', *Kiel Papers '72* (ed. H. Hinz), Kiel, 21–2.

HENRY F. (1957). 'Early monasteries, beehive huts and dry stone houses in the neighbourhood of Caherciveen and Waterville (Co. Kerry)', *Proceedings of the Royal Irish Academy*, lviii, section C. 45–166.

—— (1965). *Irish art in the early Christian period to A.D. 800*, London.

HERRMANN J. (1971). *Zwischen Hradschin und Vineta, frühe kulturen der Westslawen*, Berlin.

HERRNBRODT A. (1958). *Der Husterknupp*, Köln.

HIGGITT J. C. (1973). 'The Roman background to medieval England', *Journal of the British Archaeological Association*, 3rd series, xxvi, 1–15.

HILDEBRAND B. E. (1881). *Anglosachsiska mynt i Svenska kongliga myntkabienettet funna i Sveriges Jord*, Stockholm.

HILL D. (1967a). 'The Burghal Hidage – Lyng', *Proceedings of the Somersetshire Archaeological and Natural History Society*, cxi, 64–6.

—— (1967b). 'The Burghal Hidage – Southampton', *Proceedings of the Hampshire Field Club*, xxiv, 59–61.

—— (1969). 'The Burghal Hidage: the establishment of a text', *Medieval Archaeology*, xiii, 84–92.

—— (1970). 'Late Saxon Bedford', *Bedfordshire Archaeological Journal*, v, 96–100.

HILL G. F. (1920). 'A find of coins of Eadgar, Eadweard II and Æthelred II at Chester', *Numismatic Chronicle*, lxxx, 141–65.

HILLIER G. (n.d.). *The history and antiquities of the Isle of Wight*, London.

HILTON R. M. (1955). 'The content and sources of English agrarian history before 1500', *Agricultural History Review*, iii, 3–19.

HINTON D. A. (1974). *A catalogue of the Anglo-Saxon ornamental metalwork, 700–1100, in the Ashmolean Museum*, Oxford.

HIRST S. M. and RAHTZ P. A. (1972). 'Hatton Rock, 1970', *Transactions of the Birmingham and Warwickshire Archaeological Society*, lxxxv, 161–77.

HODDER I. R. (1972). 'Locational models and the study of Romano-British settlement', *Models in Archaeology* (ed. D. L. Clarke), London, 887–909.

—— and HASSALL M. W. C. (1971). 'The non-random spacing of Romano-British walled towns', *Man*, vi, 391–407.

HODGES H. (1964). *Artifacts*, London.

HODGES H. W. M. (1954). 'Excavations on Castle Hill, Thurgaton', *Transactions of the Thoroton Society of Nottinghamshire*, lviii, 21–36.

HOFFMAN M. (1964). *The warp-weighted loom*, Oslo (Studia Norvegica, vix).

HOGARTH A. C. (1973). 'Structural features in Anglo-Saxon graves', *Archaeological Journal*, cxxx, 104–19.

HOLDEN E. W. (1965). 'Saxo-Norman remains at Telscombe', *Sussex Notes and Queries*, xvi, 154–8.

HOLMES V. T. (1959). 'The houses of the Bayeux Tapestry', *Speculum*, xxxiv, 179–83.

HOLMQVIST W. (1951). *Tauschierte Metallarbeiten des Nordens*, Stockholm.

—— (ed.). (1972). *Excavations at Helgö*, iv, Stockholm.

HOLST H. (1943). 'Uten- og innenlandske mynter i norske funn, nedlagt før år 1100', *Nordisk numismatisk årsskrift*, 56–112.

HOOD P. (1950). *Whitby Abbey* 5th edn, Middlesbrough.

HOPE W. ST J. (1914–15). 'Recent discoveries in the abbey church of St Austin at Canterbury', *Archaeologia*, lxvi, 377–400 (reprinted in *Archaeologia Cantiana*, xxxii [1917], 1–26).

HOPE-TAYLOR B. (1949). 'A Saxon pot from Thursley', *Surrey Archaeological Collections*, li, 152–3.

—— (1961). *The Site of Ad Gefrin: an investigation of its archaeological and historical significance* i and ii (Cambridge University Ph.D. thesis, Cambridge University library).

—— (1962). 'The "boat-shaped" house in Northern Europe', *Proceedings of the Cambridge Antiquarian Society*, lv, 16–22.

—— (1971). *Under York Minster. Archaeological discoveries 1966–1971*, York.

HOSKINS W. G. (1954). *Devon*, London (A new survey of England).

—— (1955). *The making of the English landscape*, London.

—— (1957a). 'Leicestershire', *The making of the English Landscape*, London.

—— (1957b). *The Midland peasant*, London.

—— (1959). *Local history in England*, London.

—— (1963). *Provincial England*, London.

—— (1967). *Fieldwork in local history*, London.

HUBERT J. (1938). *L'art préroman*, Paris.

—— (1954). 'Les églises à Rotonde orientale', *Frühmittelalterliche Kunst in der Alpen-länden*, Olten and Lausanne (Akten zum III internationalen Kongress für Frühmittel-alterforschung), 309–20.

—— (1963). 'Les "cathedrales doubles" de la Gaulle', *Geneva*, xi, 105–25.

—— PORCHER J. and VOLBACH W. F. (1969). *Europe in the Dark Ages*, London.

—— —— —— 1970). *Carolingian art*, London.

HUGHES K. (1966). *The church in early Irish society*, London.

HUNTER BLAIR P. (1956). *An introduction to Anglo-Saxon England*, Cambridge.

HUNTER M. (1974). 'Germanic and Roman antiquity and the sense of the past in Anglo-Saxon England, *Anglo-Saxon England*, iii, 29–50.

HURST D. G. and J. G. (1967). 'Excavations of two moated sites: Milton, Hampshire and Ashwell, Hertfordshire', *Journal of the British Archaeological Association*, 3rd series. xxx, 48–86.

HURST H. (1974). 'Excavations at Gloucester, 1971–1973: second interim report', *The Antiquaries Journal*, liv, 8–52.

HURST J. G. (1955). 'Saxo-Norman pottery in East Anglia: part I. General discussion and St Neots ware', *Proceedings of the Cambridge Antiquarian Society*, xlix, 43–70.

—— (1956). 'Saxo-Norman pottery in East Anglia: part II. Thetford ware', *Proceedings of the Cambridge Antiquarian Society*, l, 42–60.

—— (1957). 'Saxo-Norman pottery in East Anglia: part III. Stamford ware', *Proceedings of the Cambridge Antiquarian Society*, li, 37–65.

—— (1959). 'Middle-Saxon pottery', *Medieval Archaeology*, iii, 13–31.

—— (1961). 'The kitchen area of Northolt Manor, Middlesex', *Medieval Archaeology*, v, 211–99.

—— (1962a). 'Post-Roman archaeological dating and its correlation with archaeomagnetic results', *Archaeometry*, v, 25–7.

—— (1962b). 'Winchester ware: a new type of Saxo-Norman glazed pottery', *Archaeological Journal*, cxix, 187–90.

—— (1962–3). 'White castle and the dating of medieval pottery', *Medieval Archaeology*, vi–vii, 135–55.

—— (1963). 'Excavations at Barn Road, Norwich, 1954–55', *Norfolk Archaeology*, xxxiii, 131–79.

—— (1963a). 'Post-Roman archaeological dating and its correlations with archaeological-magnetic results', *Archaeometry*, vi.

—— (1965). 'Late Saxon pottery', *The Fourth Viking congress* (ed. A. Small), Edinburgh, 216–23.

—— (1966). 'Post-Roman archaeological dating and its correlations with archaeomagnetic results', *Archaeometry*, ix, 198–9.

—— (1967–8). 'Saxon and medieval pottery from Kirby Bellars', *Transactions of the Leicestershire Archaeological and Historical Society*, xliii, 10–18.

—— (ed.) (1969). 'Red-painted and glazed pottery in Western Europe from the eighth to the twelfth century', *Medieval Archaeology*, xiii, 93–147.

—— (1972). 'The changing medieval village in England', *Man, settlement and urbanism* (ed. P. J. Ucko *et al.*), London, 531–40.

—— and WEST S. E. (1957). 'An account of middle Saxon Ipswich ware', *Proceedings of the Cambridge Antiquarian Society*, 1, 29–42.

—— *et al.* (1959). 'Anglo-Saxon pottery: a symposium', *Medieval Archaeology*, iii, 1–78.

—— (1968). *List of Saxon and medieval imports into Britain* (unpublished, stencilled list).

—— and HURST D. GILLIAN (1967). 'Excavation of two moated sites: Milton, Hampshire and Ashwell, Hertfordshire', *Journal of the British Archaeological Association*, 3rd series, xxx, 48–86.

HUTCHINSON J. and PHILLIPS D. (1972). 'York Minster, the excavations', in Pevsner N. (1972).

JACKSON D. A., HARDING D. W. and MYRES J. N. L. (1969). 'The Iron Age and Anglo-Saxon site at Upton, Northants', *The Antiquaries Journal*, xlix, 202–21.

JACKSON E. D. C. and FLETCHER E. G. M. (1944). 'Long and short quoins and pilaster strips', *Journal of the British Archaeological Association*, 3rd series, ix, 12–29.

—— —— (1949). 'Further notes on long and short quoins in Saxon churches', *Journal of the British Archaeological Association*, 3rd series, xii, 1–17.

—— —— (1951). 'Constructional characteristics in Anglo-Saxon churches', *Journal of the British Archaeological Association*, 3rd series, xiv, 11–26.

—— —— (1953). 'The Saxon church at Bradford on Avon', *Journal of the British Archaeological Association*, 3rd series, xvi, 41–58.

—— —— (1956). 'Porch and porticus in Saxon churches', *Journal of the British Archaeological Association*, 3rd series, xix, 1–13.

—— —— (1959). 'The pre-conquest basilica at Lydd', *Journal of the British Archaeological Association*, 3rd series, xxii, 41–52.

—— —— (1961a). 'Excavations at Brixworth', *Journal of the British Archaeological Association*, 3rd series, xxiv, 1–15.

—— —— (1961b). 'The Anglo-Saxon priory church at Deerhurst', *Studies in building history* (ed. E. M. Jope), 64–76.

—— —— (1962). 'The apse and nave at Wing, Bucks', *Journal of the British Archaeological Association*, 3rd series, xxv, 1–20.

—— —— (1963). 'Aldhelm's church near Wareham', *Journal of the British Archaeological Association*, 3rd series, xxvi, 1–5.

—— —— (1965). 'The pre-Conquest churches of Much Wenlock', *Journal of the British Archaeological Association*, 3rd series, xxviii, 16–38.

—— —— (1966a). 'Barrow: a surviving Saxon oratory in Shropshire', *Journal of the British Archaeological Association*, 3rd series, xxix, 52–60.

—— —— (1966b). 'Bradford on Avon, a reply to Mr Mercer', *Journal of the British Archaeological Association*, 3rd series, xxix, 71–4.

—— —— (1968). 'Excavations at the Lydd basilica 1966', *Journal of the British Archaeological Association*, 3rd series, xxxi, 19–26.

JANKUHN H. (1958). 'Die frühmittelalterlichen Seehandelsplätze im Nord und Osterseeraum', *Studien zu den Anfängen des europäischen Stadtwesens*, Konstanz und Lindau (Reichenau-Vorträge und Forschungen, iv), 451–98.

—— (1963). *Haithabu. Ein Handelsplatz der Wikingerzeit*, 4th edn, Neumünster.

—— (1970). 'Spätantike und merowingische Grundlagen für die frühmittelalterliche nordeuropäische Stadtbildung', *Early Medieval Studies*, i (Antikvariskt Arkiv, xxxviii), 23–34.

—— (1971). *Typen und Funktionen vor- und frühwikingerzeitlicher Handelsplätze im Ostseegebiet*, Wien (Österreichische Akademie der Wissenschaften, philosophisch-historische Klasse, Sitzungsberichte 273. V, Abhandlung).

JANSSEN W. and B. (1973). 'Stand und aufgaben der Archäologie des Mittelalters im Rheinland. Mit einer Bibliographie 1945–1972', *Zeitschrift für Archäologie des Mittelalters*, i, 141–95.

JANSSON S. B. F. (1962). *The runes of Sweden*, Stockholm.

—— (1966). *Swedish Vikings in England, the evidence of the rune stones*, London.

JARRETT M. G. (1970). 'The deserted village of West Whelpington, Northumberland: second report', *Archaeologia Aeliana*, 4th series, xlviii, 183–302.

JARVIS E. (1850). 'Account of the discovery of ornaments and remains ... in the parish of Caenby, Lincolnshire', *The Archaeological Journal*, vii, 36–44.

JENKINS F. (1965). 'St Martin's Church at Canterbury: a survey of the earliest structural features', *Medieval Archaeology*, ix, 11–15.

JESSEN K. and HELBAEK H. (1944). *Cereals in Great Britain and Ireland in prehistoric and early historic times* (Det kongelige Danske Videnskabernes Selskab, Biologiske Skrifter iii, 2).

JOBEY G. (1966). 'A field survey in Northumberland', *The Iron Age in Northern Britain* (ed. A. L. F. Rivet), Edinburgh, 89–109.

—— (1967). 'Excavations at Tynemouth priory and castle', *Archaeologia Aeliana*, 4th series, xiv, 33–104.

JOHN E. (1964). *Land tenure in early England*, Leicester.

JONES G. (1961). 'Settlement patterns in Anglo-Saxon England', *Antiquity*, xxxv, 221–232.

—— (1966). 'The cultural landscape of Yorkshire: the origin of our villages', *Transactions of the Yorkshire Philosophical Society*, 45–57.

JONES G. B. D. (1975). 'The north western interface', *Recent work in rural archaeology* (ed. P. J. Fowler), Bath.

JONES G. R. J. (1971). 'The multiple estate as a model framework for tracing early stages in the evolution of rural settlement', *L'habitat et les paysages ruraux d'Europe* (ed. F. Dussart), Liège, 251–67.

—— (1972). 'Post-Roman Wales', *The agrarian history of England and Wales* i, pt 2, *A.D. 43–1042* (ed. H. P. R. Finberg), London, 281–382.

JONES M. U. *et al.* (1968). 'Crop-mark sites at Mucking, Essex', *The Antiquaries Journal*, xlviii, 210–30.

—— (1969). 'Saxon pottery from a hut at Mucking, Essex', *Berichten van de Rijksdienst voor het Oudheidkundig Bodemondersoek*, xix, 145–56.

JOPE E. M. (1951). 'Medieval and Saxon finds from Felmersham, Bedfordshire', *The Antiquaries Journal*, xxxi, 45–50.

—— (1952). 'Excavations in the City of Norwich, 1948', *Norfolk Archaeology*, xxx, 287–323.

—— (1952–3). 'Late Saxon pits under Oxford castle mound: excavations in 1952', *Oxoniensia*, xvii/xviii, 77–111.

—— (1956). 'A late Dark Age site at Gunwalloe', *Proceedings of the West Cornwall Field Club*, new series, i, 136–46.

—— (1956a). 'Saxon Oxford and its region', *Dark-Age Britain. Studies presented to E. T. Leeds* (ed. D. B. Harden), London, 234–58.

—— (1956b). 'The tinning of iron spurs: a continuous practice from the tenth to the seventeenth century', *Oxoniensia*, xxi, 35–42.

—— (1958). 'The Clarendon hotel, Oxford. Part I: The site', *Oxoniensia*, xxiii, 1–83.

—— (1964). 'The Saxon building stone industry in southern and midland England', *Medieval Archaeology*, viii, 91–118.

KEEN L. (1975). '*Illa mercimonia que dicitur Hamwih:* a study in early medieval urban development', *Archaeologia Atlantica*, i (forthcoming).

KEENE D. J. (1975). 'Suburban growth', *The evolution of towns* (ed. M. W. Barley) (Council for British Archaeology, Urban Research Committee, Working Party on Town Plans and Topography, Leamington Spa, November 1974), forthcoming.

KELLER M. L. (1906). *Anglo-Saxon weapons*, Heidelberg (Anglistische Forschungen, xv).

KENDRICK T. D. (1938). *Anglo-Saxon art to A.D. 900*, London.

—— (1938a) 'Flambard's crozier', *The Antiquaries Journal*, xviii, 236–42.

—— (1949). *Late Saxon and Viking art*, London.

—— *et al.* (1960). *Evangeliorum quattuor codex Lindisfarnensis*, Oltun and Lausanne.

—— and HAWKES C. F. C. (1932). *Archaeology in England and Wales, 1914–1931*, London.

KENT J. P. C. (1961). 'From Roman Britain to Saxon England', *Anglo-Saxon coins* (ed. R. H. M. Dolley), London, 1–22.

KERMODE P. M. C. (1907). *Manx crosses*, London.

KIDSON P., MURRAY P. and THOMPSON P. (1965). *A history of English architecture*, London.

KIRBY D. P. (1967). *The making of early England*, London.

KIRK J. R. (1956). 'Anglo-Saxon cremation and inhumation in the upper Thames valley in pagan times', *Dark Age Britain* (ed. D. B. Harden), London, 123–31.

KLINDT-JENSEN O. (1957). *Bornholm i folkvandringstiden*, København.

—— and WILSON D. M. (1966). *Viking art*, London.

KLINGELHÖFER E. (1975). 'Evidence of town planning in late Saxon Warwick', *Midland History*, iii, pt 1, 1–10.

KNOCKER G. M. (1950). 'Anglo-Saxon Thetford', *The Archaeological News Letter*, ii, 117–122.

—— (1956). 'Excavations at Framlingham castle', *Proceedings of the Suffolk Institute of Archaeology*, xxvii, 65–88.

—— (1967). 'Excavations at Red castle, Thetford', *Norfolk Archaeology*, xxxiv, 119–86.

—— and HUGHES R. G. (1950). 'Anglo-Saxon Thetford, Part II', *Archaeological News Letter*, iii, 41–6.

KNOWLES D. (1963). *The monastic order in England*, 2nd edn, Cambridge.

KNOWLES D. (1966). *From Pachomius to Ignatius*, Oxford.

KNOWLES D. and HADCOCK R. N. (1971). *Medieval religious houses in England and Wales*, London.

—— and ST JOSEPH J. K. S. (1952). *Monastic sites from the air*, Cambridge.

KÖBLER G. (1973). '*Civitas* und *vicus, burg, stat, dorf* und *wik*', *Vor- und Frühformen der europäischen Stadt im Mittelalter* (ed. H. Jankuhn, W. Schlesinger and H. Steuer), Göttingen (Abhandlungen der Akademie der Wissenschaften: Philologisch-Historische Klasse, 3 Folge, Nr. 83), 61–76.

KOLCHIN B. A. (1953). *Chernoe metallurgie v drevnoi rusi*, Moscow.

KRAUTHEIMER R. (1942). 'The Carolingian revival of early Christian architecture', *Art Bulletin*, xxiv, 1–38.

KUBACH E. (1965). 'Architecture', *Encyclopedia of World Art*, x, 874–82.

LAING L. (1969). 'Timber halls in Dark Age Britain – some problems', *Transactions of the Dumfriesshire and Galloway Natural History and Antiquarian Society*, xlvi, 110–27.

LANG J. T. (1973). 'Some late pre-conquest crosses in Ryedale, Yorkshire', *The Journal of the British Archaeological Association*, 3rd series, xxxvi, 16–25.

LATOUCHE R. (1966). *The birth of western economy*, New York.

LAVER H. (1909). 'Ancient type of huts at Athelney', *Proceedings of the Somerset Archaeological Society*, lv, 175–80.

LEE F. (1953). 'A new theory of the origins and early growth of Northampton', *The Archaeological Journal*, cx, 164–74.

LEEDS E. T. (1912). 'The distribution of the Anglo-Saxon saucer brooch in relation to the battle of Bedford, A.D. 571', *Archaeologia*, lxiii, 159–202.

—— (1913). *The archaeology of the Anglo-Saxon settlements*, Oxford.

—— (1923). 'A Saxon village near Sutton Courtenay, Berkshire', *Archaeologia*, lxxii, 147–92.

—— (1927). 'A Saxon village near Sutton Courtenay, Berkshire (second report)', *Archaeologia*, lxxvi, 59–79.

—— (1936). *Early Anglo-Saxon art and archaeology*, Oxford.

—— (1947). 'A Saxon village near Sutton Courtenay, Berkshire (third report)', *Archaeologia*, xcii, 79–93.

—— and SHORTT H. D S. (1953). *An Anglo-Saxon cemetery at Petersfinger, near Salisbury, Wilts.*, Salisbury.

LEHMANN-BROCKHAUS O. (1955–60). *Lateinische Schriftquellen zur Kunst in England, Wales und Scotland vom Jahre 901 bis zum Jahre 1307*, München.

LE PATOUREL H. E. J. (1968). 'Documentary evidence and the medieval pottery industry', *Medieval Archaeology*, xii, 101–26.

—— (1972). 'Medieval pottery: excavations in Low Petersgate, York, 1957–8', *Yorkshire Archaeological Journal*, xliv, 108–13.

—— (1973). 'Excavations at the Archbishop of York's manor house at Otley', *Yorkshire Archaeological Journal*, xlv, 115–41.

LETHBRIDGE T. C. (1927). 'An Anglo-Saxon hut on the Car Dyke at Waterbeach', *The Antiquaries Journal*, vii, 141–6.

—— (1931). *Recent excavations in Anglo-Saxon cemeteries in Cambridgeshire and Suffolk*, Cambridge (Cambridge Antiquarian Society, quarto publications, iii).

—— and TEBBUTT C. F. (1933). 'Huts of the Anglo-Saxon period', *Proceedings of the Cambridge Antiquarian Society*, xxxiii, 133–51.

—— —— (1936–37). 'Southoe Manor', *Proceedings of the Cambridge Antiquarian Society*, xxxviii, 158–63.

LEVISON W. (1940). 'An eighth-century poem on St Ninian', *Antiquity*, xiv, 28–91.

—— (1941). 'St Alban and St Albans', *Antiquity*, xv, 337–59.

—— (1946). *England and the Continent in the eighth century*, Oxford.

LEWIS P. R. and JONES G. D. B. (1969). 'The Dolancothi gold mines, I: the surface evidence', *The Antiquaries Journal*, xlix, 244–72.

LIEBERMANN F. (1903). *Die Gesetze der Angelsachsen*, Halle.

LINDQVIST S. (1941). *Gotlands Bildsteine*, Uppsala.

LINDSAY J. (1842). *A view of the coinage of the heptarchy*, Cork.

LOBEL M. D. (1969). 'Hereford', *Historic towns*, i (ed. M. D. Lobel), London and Oxford.

LOBEL M. D. and TANN J. (1969). 'Gloucester', *Historic towns*, i (ed. M. D. Lobel), London and Oxford.

LOMBARD-JOURDAN A. (1972). 'Oppidum et banlieue. Sur l'origine et les dimensions du territoire urbain', *Annales: économies, sociétés, civilisations*, xxvii, pt 2, 373–95.

LOWE E. A. (1959). *Codices latini antiquiores*, viii, Oxford.

LOWERY P. R., SAVAGE R. D. A. and WILKINS R. L. (1971). 'Scriber, graver, scorper, tracer: notes on experiments in bronzeworking technique', *Proceedings of the Prehistoric Society*, xxxvii, l, 167–82.

LOYN H. R. (1961). 'Boroughs and mints A.D. 900–1066', *Anglo-Saxon Coins* (ed. R. H. M. Dolley), London, 122–35.

—— (1962). *Anglo-Saxon England and the Norman conquest*, London.

—— (1967). *The Norman conquest*, 2nd edn, London.

—— (1971). 'Towns in late Anglo-Saxon England: the evidence and some possible lines of enquiry', *England before the conquest. Studies in primary sources presented to Dorothy Whitelock* (ed. P. Clemoes and K. Hughes), Cambridge, 115–28.

LUCAS A. T. (1965). 'Washing and bathing in ancient Ireland', *Journal of the Royal Society of Antiquaries of Ireland*, xcv, 65–114.

LYON C. S. (1956). 'A reappraisal of the sceatta and styca coinage of Northumberland', *The British Numismatic Journal*, xxviii: 2, 227–42.

—— (1966). 'The significance of the sack of Oxford in 1009/1010 for the chronology of Æthelred II' *British Numismatic Journal*, xxxv, 34–7.

—— and STEWART B. H. I. H. (1961). 'The Northumbrian Viking coinage in the Cuerdale hoard', *Anglo-Saxon coins* (ed. R. H. M. Dolley), London, 96–121.

MACNAB J. W. (1965). 'British strip lynchets', *Antiquity*, xxxix, 279–90.

MAHANY C. (1968). 'Stamford', *Current Archaeology*, i, 266–70.

MAHR A. (1932). *Christian art in ancient Ireland*, i, Dublin.

MAITLAND F. W. (1897). *Domesday book and beyond*, Cambridge (Fontana edn, London, 1960).

—— (1960). See Maitland (1897).

MALMER B. (1966). *Nordiska mynt före år 1000*, Lund.

—— (1968). *Mynt och människor*, Stockholm.

MANN J. C. (1961). 'The administration of Roman Britain', *Antiquity*, xxxv, 316–20.

—— (1963). 'City-names in the western empire', *Latomus*, xxii, 777–82.

MANNING W. H. (1964). 'The plough in Roman Britain,' *Journal of Roman Studies*, liv, 54.

MARSDEN P. R. V. (1967). 'Archaeological finds from the City of London', *Transactions of the London and Middlesex Archaeological Society*, xxxi, 189–221.

MARTIN K. M. (1969). 'A reassessment of the evidence for the *comes Britanniarum* in the fourth century', *Latomus*, 408–28.

MATHEWS C. L. (1962). 'Saxon remains on Puddlehill, Dunstable', *Bedfordshire Archaeological Journal*, i, 48–57.

MATHEWS T. F. (1971). *The early churches of Constantinople: architecture and liturgy*, Pennsylvania.

MCKERRELL H. and STEVENSON R. B. K. (1972). 'Some analyses of Anglo-Saxon and associated oriental silver coinage', *Methods of chemical and metallurgical investigation of ancient coins* (ed. E. T. Hall and D. M. Metcalf), London, 195–209.

MEANEY A. (1964). *A gazetteer of early Anglo-Saxon burial sites*, London.

—— and HAWKES S. C. (1970). *Two Anglo-Saxon cemeteries at Winall, Winchester, Hampshire*, London (The Society for Medieval Archaeology: Monograph Series: iv).

MERCER E. (1966). 'The alleged early date of Bradford on Avon', *Journal of the British Archaeological Association*, 3rd series, xxix, 61–70.

MERTENS J. (1963). 'Quelques édifices religieux à plan central découverts récemment en Belgique', *Genevam* xi, 141–61.

METCALF D. M. (1967). 'The prosperity of North-Western Europe in the eighth and ninth centuries', *Economic History Review*, 2nd series, xx, 344–57.

MICKLETHWAITE J. T. (1896). 'Something about Saxon church building', *The Archaeological Journal*, liii, 293–352.

——(1898). 'Some further notes on Saxon churches', *The Archaeological Journal*, lv, 340–349.

MITCHELL B. (1965). *The Battle of Maldon and other old English poems*, London.

MONTGOMERIE D. H. (1947). 'Old Sarum', *The Archaeological Journal*, civ, 129–43.

MOORE J. S. (1965). *Laughton: a study in the evolution of the Wealden landscape*, Leicester Occasional Paper no. 19, Department of English Local History, Leicester University).

MOORE J. W. (1966). 'An Anglo-Saxon settlement at Wykeham, North Yorkshire', *Yorkshire Archaeological Journal*, xli, 403–44.

MORRIS J. (1959). 'Anglo-Saxon Surrey', *Surrey Archaeological Collections*, lvi, 132–58.

—— (1968). 'The date of Saint Alban', *Hertfordshire Archaeology*, i, 1–8.

 (1973). *The age of Arthur*, London.

MORTIMER J. R. (1905). *Forty years researches in the British and Saxon burial-mounds of East Yorkshire*, London.

MOSS A. A. (1953). 'Niello', *The Antiquaries Journal*, xxxiii, 75–7.

MÜLLER–USING D. (1953). *Über die frühmittelalterlichen Geweihreste von Wollin* (Saugertierkund Mitteilungen, i).

MUSTY J. (1974). 'Medieval pottery kilns', *Medieval pottery from excavations: studies presented to Gerald Clough Dunning* (ed. V. I. Evison, H. Hodges and J. G. Hurst), London, 41–66.

MYRES J. N. L. (1948). *A survey and policy of field research in the archaeology of Great Britain*, London, 116–19.

——(1951). 'The Anglo-Saxon pottery of Lincolnshire', *The Archaeological Journal*, cviii, 65–99.

—— (1956). 'Romano-Saxon pottery', *Dark-Age Britain* (ed. D. B. Harden), London, 16–39.

—— (1968). 'The Anglo-Saxon pottery from Mucking', *The Antiquaries Journal*, xlviii, 222–8.

—— (1969). *Anglo-Saxon pottery and the settlement of England*, Oxford.

—— (1970). 'The Angles, the Saxons and the Jutes', *Proceedings of the British Academy*, lvi, 145–74.

—— and GREEN B. (1973). *The Anglo-Saxon cemeteries of Caistor-by-Norwich and Markshall, Norfolk*, London (Reports of the Research Committee of the Society of Antiquaries of London, xxx).

NELSON P. (1937). 'An ancient box-wood casket', *Archaeologia*, lxxxvi, 91–100.

NEVILLE R. C. (1852). *Saxon obsequies*, London.

—— (1856). 'Description of a remarkable deposit of Roman antiquities of iron, discovered at Great Chesterford, Essex, in 1854', *The Archaeological Journal*, xiii, 1–13.

NEWMAN J. (1969)*The buildings of England: West Kent and the Weald*, Harmondsworth.

NEWTON E. F. (1947). 'Late Saxon sites and a medieval chapel at Weald, Huntingdonshire', *Transactions of the Cambridge and Huntingdonshire Archaeological Society*, vi, 166–75.

NICOLAYSEN B. (1882). *Langskibet fra Gokstad ved Sandefjord*, Kristiania.

NOBLE F. and SHOESMITH R. (1967). 'Hereford city excavations, 1967', *Transactions of the Woolhope Naturalists' Field Club*, xxxix, pt 1, 44–70.

NODDLE N. (1971). 'Animal remains', in Wade-Martins P., 'Excavations at North Elmham 1970: an interim report', *Norfolk Archaeology*, xxxv, 266.

NORDMAN C. A. (1921). *Anglo-Saxon coins found in Finland*, Helsingfors.

NØRLUND P. (1948). *Trelleborg*, København (Nordiske Fortidsminder, iv, 1).

NORMAN E. R. and ST JOSEPH J. K. S. (1969). *The early development of Irish society: the evidence of aerial photography*, Cambridge.

NORTH J. J. (1963). *English hammered coinage*, i, London.

OAKLEY K. P. *et al.* (1939). *A survey of the prehistory of the Farnham district* (Surrey Archaeological Collections).

OHLHAVER H. (1939) *Der germanische Schmeid und sein Werkzeug*, Leipzig.

OKASHA E. (1969). 'Notes of some Anglo-Saxon architectural sculpture', *Journal of the British Archaeological Association*, 3rd series, xxxii, 26–29.

—— (1971). *Hand-list of Anglo-Saxon non-runic inscriptions*, Cambridge.

O'NEIL B. H. ST J. (1944). 'The Silchester region in the 5th and 6th centuries A.D.', *Antiquity*, xviii, 113–22.

ORDNANCE SURVEY (1956). *Map of Roman Britain*, 3rd edn, Chessington.

—— (1966). *Map of Britain in the Dark Ages*, 2nd edn, Chessington.

—— (1974). *Britain before the Norman conquest*, Southampton.

Ó RÍORDÁIN B. (1971). 'Excavations at High Street and Winetavern Street, Dublin', *Medieval Archaeology*, xv, 73–85.

ORWIN C. S. and C. S. (1967). *The open fields,*|3rd edn, Oxford.

OSWALD A. (1955). *The church of St Berthelin at Stafford and its cross*, Birmingham.

OSWALD F., SCHAEFER L. and SENNHAUSEN H. R. (1966–71) *Vorromanische Kirchenbauten*, München (Veroffentlichungen der Zentralinstituts für Kunstgeschichte in München, iii).

OWEN A. (1841). *Ancient laws and institutes of Wales*, London.

OWLES E. and SMEDLEY N. (1957). 'Archaeology in Suffolk 1965', *Proceedings of the Suffolk Institute of Archaeology*, xxvii, 178–85.

OZANNE A. (1962–3). 'The Peak dwellers', *Medieval Archaeology*, vi–vii, 15–52.

PAGAN H. E. (1969). 'Northumbrian numismatic chronology in the ninth century', *British Numismatic Journal*, xxxviii, 1–15.

PAGE R. I. (1970). *Life in Anglo-Saxon England*, London.

—— (1973). 'Anglo-Saxon scratched glosses in a Corpus Christi College, Cambridge, manuscript', *Otium et negotium. Studies in onomatology and library science presented to Olof von Feilitzen* (ed. F. Sandgren), Stockholm, 209–15.

PAGE W. (1920). 'The origins and forms of Hertfordshire towns and villages', *Archaeologia*, lxix, 47–60.

PAINTER K. S. (1971). 'Villas and Christianity in Roman Britain', *Prehistoric and Roman studies* (ed. G. de G. Sieveking), London 156–75.

PARKER H. (1965). 'Feddersen Wierde and Vallhagar: a contrast in settlements', *Medieval Archaeology*, ix, 1–10.

PARSONS D. (1962). 'The west tower of St Andrew's church, Corbridge', *Archaeologia Aeliana*, xl, 171–84.

—— (1969a). 'The pre-conquest church at Canterbury', *Archaeologia Cantiana*, lxxxiv, 175–84.

—— (1969b). 'The Saxon doorways of the church of St Nicholas Worth', *Sussex Archaeological Collections*, cvii, 12–13.

—— (1973). 'Two nineteenth-century Anglo-Saxon finds from Lincolnshire', *The Antiquaries Journal*, liii, 78–81.

PAYNE F. G. (1957). 'The British plough: some stages in its development', *Agricultural History Review*, v, 74–84.

PEACOCK D. (1967). 'Fladbury', *Current Archaeology*, v, 123.

—— and THOMAS C. (1967). 'Class "E" imported post-Roman pottery: a suggested origin', *Cornish Archaeology*, vi, 35–46.

PEARCE F. (1966). 'A textile impression on an Anglo-Saxon pot from Lackford', *Antiquity*, xl, 217.

PEERS C. R. (1902). 'On Saxon churches of the St Pancras type', *The Archaeological Journal*, lviii, 402–34.

—— (1927). 'Reculver: its Saxon church and cross', *Archaeologia*, lxxvii, 241–56.

—— and CLAPHAM A. W. (1927). 'St Augustine's abbey church Canterbury before the Norman conquest', *Archaeologia*, lxxvii, 201–18.

—— —— and HORNE E. (1930). 'Interim report on the excavations at Glastonbury abbey', *The Antiquaries Journal*, x, 24–9.

—— and RADFORD C. A. R. (1943). 'The Saxon monastery of Whitby', *Archaeologia*, lxxxix, 27–88.

PEETERS C. (1969). *De liturgische dispositie van her vroegchristelijk kerkgebouw*, Assen.

PETCH D. F. and THOMPSON F. H. (1959). 'Excavations in Commonhall Street, Chester, 1954–56', *Journal of the Chester Archaeological Society*, xlvi, 33–60.

PETERSSON H. B. A. (1969). *Anglo-Saxon currency, King Edgar's reform to the Norman conquest*, Lund (Bibliotheca Historica Lundensis, xxii).

PETERSEN J. (1919). *De norske vikingesverd. En typologisk-kronologisk studie over vikingetidens vaaben*, Kristiania (Videnskapsselkapet Skrifter, ii, Hist.-Filos. Klasse, 1).

——(1951). *Vikingetidens Redskaper*, Oslo (Skrifter utgitt av de Norske Videntskaps-Akademi i Oslo, ii, Hist.-Filos Klasse, 4).

PETRI F. (1958). 'Die Anfänge des mittelalterlichen Städtewesens in den Niederlanden und dem angrenzenden Frankriech', *Studien zu den Anfängen des europäischen Städtewesens*, Konstanz und Lindau (Reichenau-Vorträge und Forschungen, iv), 227–95.

PEVSNER N. (1963). *The buildings of England: Wiltshire*, Harmondsworth.

——(1972). *The buildings of England: Yorkshire, East Riding*, Harmondsworth.

—— and HARRIS J. (1964). *The buildings of England: Lincolnshire*, Harmondsworth.

PHILIPPS C. W. (1934). 'The present state of archaeology in Lincolnshire, II', *The Archaeological Journal*, xci, 97–187.

——(ed.) (1970). *The Fenland in Roman times*, London.

PHILP B. (1971). 'The discovery of a Saxon *Grubenhaus* at Keston', *Kent Archaeological Review*, xxv, 131–5.

PIRENNE H. (1956). *Medieval cities: their origins and the revival of trade*, New York.

——(1957). *Mohammed and Charlemagne*, Cleveland and New York.

PLANITZ H. (1954). *Die deutsche Stadt im Mittelalter*, Graz–Köln.

PLEINER R. (1962). *Staré evropské kovářistvi*, Praha.

PLUMMER C. (1896). *Venerabilis Bædae Opera Historica*, Oxford.

POCOCK M. and WHEELER H. (1971). 'Excavations at Escomb church, County Durham', *Journal of the British Archaeological Association*, 3rd series, xxxiv, 11–19.

POSNANSKY M. (1956). 'A pagan-Danish barrow cemetery at Heath Wood, Ingelby', *Journal of the Derbyshire Archaeological and Natural History Society*, 40–56.

POSTAN M. M. (ed.) (1966). *The Cambridge economic history of Europe*, I: *The agrarian life of the Middle Ages*, 2nd edn, Cambridge.

POTTS R. U. (1934). 'The plan of St Austin's abbey Canterbury', *Archaeologia Cantiana*, xlvi, 179–94.

PROBERT W. (1823). *The ancient laws of Cambria*, London.

QUIRK R. N. (1957). 'Winchester cathedral in the tenth century', *The Archaeological Journal*, cxiv, 28–68.

——(1961). 'Winchester New Minster and its tenth century tower', *Journal of the British Archaeological Association*, 3rd series, xxiv, 16–54.

RADFORD C. A. R. (1935). 'Tintagel: the castle and the Celtic monastery–interim report', *The Antiquaries Journal*, xv, 401–19.

——(1939). *Tintagel castle, Cornwall*, London.

——(1946). 'A lost inscription of pre-Danish age from Caistor', *The Archaeological Journal*, ciii, 95–9.

——(1950). 'Excavations at Whithorn 1949', *Transactions of the Dumfries and Galloway Natural History and Antiquarian Society*, xxvii, 85–126.

——(1954). 'Trial excavations at Jarrow', *The Archaeological Journal*, cxi, 205–9.

——(1955). 'Excavations at Glastonbury, 1954', *Antiquity*, xxix, 33–4.

—— (1955a). 'The church of St Nicholas, Leicester', *The Archaeological Journal*, cxii, 161–3.

—— (1956). 'Imported pottery found at Tintagel, Cornwall', *Dark-Age Britain* (ed. D. B. Harden), London, 59–70.

—— (1957). 'The Saxon house: a review and some parallels', *Medieval Archaeology*, i, 27–38.

—— (1957a). 'Excavations at Glastonbury Abbey 1956', *Antiquity*, xxxi, 171.

—— (1957b). 'Excavations at Whithorn (final report)', *Transactions of the Dumfriesshire and Galloway Natural History Society*, xxxiv, 131–94.

—— (1959). 'The bishop's throne in Norwich cathedral', *The Archaeological Journal*, cxvi, 115–32.

—— (1961). 'Excavations at Glastonbury Abbey, 1951–4', *Somerset and Dorset Notes and Queries*, xxvii, 21–4, 68–73, 165–9.

—— (1961a). 'The church of St Mary, Stoke d'Abernon, Surrey', *The Archaeological Journal*, cxviii, 165–74.

—— (1961b). 'Repton, the church of St Wystan', *The Archaeological Journal*, cxviii, 241–3.

—— (1962). 'The Celtic monastery in Britain', *Archaeologia Cambrensis*, iii, 1–24.

—— (1968). 'Excavations at Glastonbury Abbey 1962', *Somerset and Dorset Notes and Queries*, xxviii, 114–17.

—— (1968a). 'The archaeological background on the continent', *Christianity in Britain, 300–700* (ed. M. W. Barley and R. P. C. Hanson) Leicester, 19–36.

—— (1970). 'The later pre-conquest boroughs and their defences', *Medieval Archaeology*, xiv, 83–103.

—— (1971). 'Christian origins in Britain', *Medieval Archaeology*, xv, 1–12.

—— (1973). 'Excavations at Cricklade: 1948–1963', *Wiltshire Archaeological and Natural History Magazine*, lxvii, 61–111.

—— (1973). 'Pre-conquest Minster Churches', *The Archaeological Journal*, cxxx, 120–40.

—— and DONALDSON G. (1957). *Whithorn and Kirkmadrine*, London.

RADLEY J. (1971). 'Economic aspects of Anglo-Danish York', *Medieval Archaeology*, xv, 37–57.

—— (1972). 'Excavations in the defences of the city of York: an early medieval stone tower and the successive earth ramparts', *Yorkshire Archaeological Journal*, xliv, 38–64.

RAHTZ P. A. (1960). 'Caistor, Lincolnshire – 1959', *The Antiquaries Journal*, xl, 175–87.

—— (1962). 'Whitby 1958', *Yorkshire Archaeological Journal*, clx, 604–18.

—— (1962–3). 'The Saxon and medieval palaces at Cheddar, Somerset – an interim report of excavations in 1960–62', *Medieval Archaeology*, vi-vii, 53–66.

—— (1964). *The Saxon and medieval palaces at Cheddar* (M.A. thesis, Bristol University).

—— (1968). 'Glastonbury Tor', *The quest for Arthur's Britain* (ed. G. Ashe), London, 111–22.

—— (1968a). 'Hereford', *Current Archaeology*, i, 242–6.

—— (1968b). 'Sub Roman cemeteries in Somerset', *Christianity in Britain, 300–700* (ed. M. W. Barley and R. P. C. Hanson), Leicester, 193–6.

—— (1969). 'Upton, Gloucestershire, 1964–1968, second report', *Transactions of the Bristol and Gloucestershire Archaeological Society*, lxxxviii, 74–126.

—— (1970). 'A possible Saxon palace near Stratford-upon-Avon', *Antiquity*, xliv, 137–143.

—— (1970a). 'Excavations on Glastonbury Tor, Somerset, 1964–6', *The Archaeological Journal*, cxxvii, 1–81.

—— (1971). 'Deerhurst church, interim note on 1971 excavations', *Transactions of the Bristol and Gloucestershire Archaeological Society*, xc, 129–35.

—— (1974). 'Pottery in Somerset, A.D. 400–1066', *Medieval pottery from excavations: studies presented to Gerald Clough Dunning* (ed. V. I. Evison, H. Hodges and J. G. Hurst), London, 95–126.

—— (forthcoming). *The Saxon and medieval palaces at Cheddar*.

—— and FOWLER P. J. (1972). 'Somerset A.D. 400–700', *Archaeology and the landscape* (ed. P. J. Fowler), London, 167–221.

—— and SHERIDAN K. (1971–2). 'Fifth report of excavations at Tamworth, Staffs., 1971 – a Saxon water-mill in Bolebridge Street. An interim note', *Transactions of the South Staffordshire Archaeological and Historical Society*, xiii, 9–16.

RAINE J. (ed.) (1838). *Miscellanea Biographica*, London and Edinburgh (Surtees Society, viii, 2).

RAMM H. G. (1971). 'The end of Roman York', *Soldier and civilian in Roman Yorkshire* (ed. R. M. Butler), Leicester, 179–99.

—— (1972). 'The growth and development of the city to the Norman conquest', *The noble city of York* (ed. A. Stacpoole), York, 225–54.

RASMUSSON N. L. (1961). 'An introduction to the Viking age hoards', *Commentationes de nummis saeculorum ix–xi in suecia repertis*, i (ed. N. L. Rasmusson and L. O. Lagerqvist), Stockholm.

R.C.H.M. (England) (1959). 'Wareham west walls', *Medieval Archaeology*, iii, 120–38.

—— (England) (1960). *A matter of time: an archaeological survey*, London.

—— (England) (1970). *Dorset*, II, pt 2, London, 413–15.

—— (England) (1972). *An inventory of the historical monuments in the city of York*, ii. *The Defences*, London.

—— (England) (1974). *Addendum to the Early Church at Sherborne*, London.

REGEMORTER B. VAN (1949). 'La reliure des manuscrits de S. Cuthbert et de S. Boniface', *Scriptorium*, iii.

REINHARDT H. (1952). *Der karolingische Klosterplan von St Gallen*, St Gallen.

RENN D. F. (1971). *Medieval castles in Hertfordshire*, Chichester.

RICHARDS M. (1962). 'Norse place-names in Wales', *Proceedings of the International Congress of Celtic Studies*, Dublin, 51–60.

RICHARDSON K. M. (1959). 'Excavations in Hungate, York', *The Archaeological Journal*, cxvi, 51–114.

RICHMOND I. A. (1946). 'The four *coloniae* of Roman Britain', *The Archaeological Journal*, ciii, 57–84.

RIGOLD S. E. (1960). 'The two primary series of sceattas', *British Numismatic Journal*, xxx, i, 6–53.

—— (1961). The supposed see of Dunwich', *Journal of the British Archaeological Association*, 3rd series, xxiv, 55–9.

—— (1962–3). 'The Anglian cathedral of North Elmham, Norfolk', *Medieval Archaeology*, vi–vii, 67–108.

—— (1966). 'The two primary series of sceattas: Addenda and Corrigenda', *British Numismatic Journal*, xxxv, 1–6.

—— (1968). 'The double minsters of Kent and their analogues', *Journal of the British Archaeological Association*, 3rd series, xxxi, 27–37.

—— (1974). 'Further evidence about the site of Dommoc', *Journal of the British Archaeological Association*, 3rd series, xxxvii, 97–102.

RIVET A. L. F. (1964). *Town and country in Roman Britain*, 2nd edn, London.

—— (1966). 'Summing up: some historical aspects of the civitates of Roman Britain', *The civitas capitals of Roman Britain* (ed. J. S. Wacher), Leicester, 101–13.

—— (1970). 'The British section of the Antonine itinerary', *Britannia*, i, 34–82.

ROBERTSON A. J. (1939). *Anglo-Saxon charters*, Cambridge.

ROBINSON J. A. (1921). 'The Saxon abbots of Glastonbury', *Somerset Historical Essays*, London.

RODWELL W. (1970). 'Some Romano-Saxon pottery from Essex', *The Antiquaries Journal*, l, 262–76.

RODWELL K. and W. (1972). *1000 years of Rivenhall*, London.

—— (1973). 'Excavations at Rivenhall church, Essex: an interim report', *The Antiquaries Journal*, liii, 219–31.

—— (1973a). 'Rivenhall', *Current Archaeology*, xxvi, 14–18.

ROES A. (1963). *Bone and antler objects from the Frisian terp-mounds*, Haarlem.

ROESDAHL E. and NORDQVIST J. (1971). 'Dedode fra Fyrkat', *Nationalmuseets Arbejdsmark*, 15–32.

ROGERS A. (1972). 'Parish boundaries and urban history: two case studies', *Journal of the British Archaeological Association*, 3rd series, xxxv, 46–64.

ROMANS T. and RADFORD C. A. R. (1954). 'Staindrop church', *The Archaeological Journal*, cxi, 214–17.

ROOSEN-RUNGE H. (1967). *Farbgebung und Technik frühmittelalterlichen Buchmalerei*, München.

ROSS H. (1967). 'Review of Anglo-Saxon architecture', *Wiltshire Archaeological Magazine*, lxii, 141–3.

RUSSELL J. C. (1969). 'Population in Europe 500–1500', *The Fontana Economic History of Europe*, i, ch. 1, London.

RUTTER J. G. and DUKE G. (1958). *Excavation at Crossgates, near Scarborough 1947–56* (Scarborough and District Archaeological Society Research Report: i).

RYAN A. M. (1939). *A map of Old English monasteries and related foundations, A.D. 400–1066*, Ithaca (Cornell Studies in English, 28).

RYDER M. L. (1956). *Kirkstall abbey excavations, seventh report*, Leeds (Thoresby Society).

—— (1957). *Kirkstall abbey excavations, eighth report*, Leeds (Thoresby Society).

—— (1961). 'Livestock remains from four medieval sites in Yorkshire', *Agricultural History Review*, ix, 105–10.

—— (1969). 'Changes in the fleece of sheep following domestication (with a note on the coat of cattle)' *The domestication and exploitation of plants and animals* (ed. P. J. Ucko and G. W. Dimbleby), London, 495–521.

SAALMAN H. (1962). *Medieval architecture*, New York.

SALIN B. (1904). *Die altgermanische Thierornamentik*, Stockholm.

SALIN E. (1957). *La civilisation mérovingienne*, iii, Paris.

SANDERSON W. (1971). 'Monastic reform in Lorraine and the architecture of the outer crypt 950–1100', *Transactions of the American Philosophical Society*, lxi, pt 6, 3–36.

SAWYER P. H. (1957). 'The density of the Danish settlement in England', *University of Birmingham Historical Journal*, vi, 1–17.

—— (1968). *Anglo-Saxon charters*, London (Royal Historical Society Guides and Handbooks, no. 8).

—— (1971). *The age of the Vikings*, 2nd edn, London.

SCARFE N. (1972). *The Suffolk landscape*, London.

SCHAPIRO M. (1959). 'A note on the wall strips of Saxon churches', *Journal of the Society of Architectural Historians of America*, xviii.

SCHIETZEL K. (1968). 'Zur Frage einer wirtschaftlichen und sozialen Gliederung Haithabus', *Studien zur europäischen Vor- und Frühgeschichte* (ed. M. Claus, W. Haarnagel and K. Raddatz), Neumünster.

—— (1970). 'Holzerne Kleinfunde aus Haithabu (Ausgrabung 1963–1964)', *Berichte über die Ausgrabungen in Haithabu*, iv, 77–91.

—— (1974) 'Bemerkungen zur Erforschung der Topographie von Haithabu', *Vor- und Frühformen der europäischen Stadt im Mittelalter* (ed. H. Jankuhn, W. Schlesinger and H. Steuer), Göttingen (Abhandlungen der Akademie der Wissenschaften, philologisch-historische Klasse, 3 Folge, nr. 84), 30–9.

SCHINDLER R. (1973). 'Trier in merowingischer Zeit', *Vor- und Frühformen der europäischen Stadt in Mittelalter* (ed. H. Jankuhn, W. Schlesinger and H. Steuer), Göttingen (Abhandlungen der Akademie der Wissenschaften, philologisch-historische Klasse, 3 Folge, nr. 83), 130–51.

SCHLEDERMANN H. (1970). 'The idea of the town: typology definitions and approaches to the study of the medieval town in northern Europe', *World Archaeology*, ii, 115–27.

SCHMIDT H. (1970). 'Vikingernes husformede gravsten', *Nationalmuseets arbejdsmark*, 13–28.

—— (1973). 'The Trelleborg House reconsidered', *Medieval Archaeology*, xvii, 52–77.

SCHÖNBERGER H. (1973). 'Das Ende oder das Fortleben spätrömische Städte an Rhein und Donau', *Vor- und Frühformen der europäischen Stadt im Mittelalter* (ed. H. Jankuhn, W. Schlesinger and H. Steuer), Göttingen (Abhandlungen der Akademie der Wissenschaften, philologisch-historische Klasse, 3 Folge, nr. 83), 102–9.

SCHOVE J. and LOWTHER A. W. G. (1957). 'Tree rings and medieval archaeology', *Medieval Archaeology*, i, 78–95.

SCHUBERT H. R. (1957). *History of the British iron and steel industry*, London.

SCOTT F. S. (1956). 'The Hildithryth stone and other Hartlepool name-stones', *Archaeologia Aeliana*, 4th series, xxxiv, 196–212.

SEABY P. (1955). 'The sequence of Anglo-Saxon coin types, 1030–1050', *British Numismatic Journal*, xxviii, i, 111–46.

SEDDON D. *et al.* (1964) in Addyman P. V. 'A Dark-Age settlement at Maxey, Northants', *Medieval Archaeology*, xiii, 69–73.

SEEBOHM F. (1905). *The English village community*, 4th edn, London.

SELKIRK A. and W. (1973). 'West Stow', *Current Archaeology*, xl, 151–6.

SELLWOOD D. (1962). 'Medieval minting techniques', *British Numismatic Journ.*, xxxi, 57–65.

SHEPPARD T. (1939). 'Viking and other relics at Crayke, Yorkshire', *Yorkshire Archaeological Journal*, xxxiv, 273–81.   3–81.

SHERIDAN K. (1973a). 'Sixth report of excavations at Tamworth, Staffs. (1971)–a section of the Saxon and medieval defences, Albert Road', *Transactions of the South Staffordshire Archaeological and Historical Society*, xiv, 32–7.

—— (1973b). 'Seventh report of excavations at Tamworth, Staffs–a section through the northern defences excavated by Dr F. T. Wainwright in 1960', *Transactions of the South Staffordshire Archaeological and Historical Society*, xiv, 38–44.

SHERLOCK R. (1963). 'St Editha's church, Tamworth', *Archaeological Journal*, cxx, 295–6.

SHETELIG H. (1940). *Viking antiquities in Great Britain and Ireland*, i–v, Oslo.

—— (1954). *Viking antiquities in Great Britain and Ireland*, vi, Oslo.

SHOESMITH R. (1968a). 'Hereford city excavations. Kings Head site 1968', *Transactions of the Woolhope Naturalists' Field Club*, xxxix, pt 2, 348–53.

—— (1968b). 'Reports of sectional recorders. Archaeology, 1968', *Transactions of the Woolhope Naturalists' Field Club*, xxxix, pt 2, 362–4.

—— (1970–2). 'Hereford City excavations 1970', *Transactions of the Woolhope Naturalists' Field Club*, xi, 225–40.

—— (1972). 'Hereford', *Current Archaeology*, iii (no. 33), 256–8.

—— (1974). *The city of Hereford. Archaeology and development*, Birmingham (West Midlands Rescue Archaeology Committee).

SILVER I. A. (1969). 'The ageing of domestic animals', *Science in archaeology* (ed. D. Brothwell and E. Higgs), London, 283–302.

SIMPSON C. (1973). *Wallingford. The archaeological implications of development*, Oxford (Oxfordshire Archaeological Unit, Survey no. 1).

SIMPSON W. D. (1963). 'The early romanesque tower at Restenneth priory Angus', *The Antiquaries Journal*, xliii, 269–83.

SLICHER VAN BATH B. H. (1963). *The agrarian history of western Europe A.D. 500–1850*, London.

SLOVER C. H. (1935). 'Glastonbury abbey and the fusing of English literary culture', *Speculum*, x, 147–60.

SMEDLEY N. and OWLES E. J. (1963). 'Some Suffolk kilns: iv. Saxon kilns in Cox Lane, Ipswich, 1961', *Proceedings of the Suffolk Institute of Archaeology*, xxix, 304–35.

—— —— (1967). 'A sherd of Ipswich ware with face-mask decoration', *Proceedings of the Suffolk Institute of Archaeology*, xxi, 84–7.

—— —— (1970). 'Excavations at the Old Minster, South Elmham', *Proceedings of the Suffolk Institute of Archaeology*, xxxii, pt 1, 1–16.

SMITH A. H. (1956a). 'Place-names and the Anglo-Saxon settlement', *Proceedings of the British Academy*, xlii, 67–88.

—— (1956). *English place-name elements*, Cambridge (English Place Name Society, xxvi).

—— (1962). *The place-names of the west riding of Yorkshire*, vii, Cambridge (English Place-Name Society, xxxvi).

—— (1965). *The place-names of Gloucestershire*, iv, Cambridge (English Place-Name Society, xli).

—— (1967). *The place-names of Westmorland*, i, Cambridge (English Place-Name Society, xlii).

SMITH C. R. and JENKINS R. C. (1861). 'Lyminge', *Collectanea Antique*, v. 185–200.

SMITH J. T. (1951). 'A note on the origin of the town-plan of Bury St Edmunds', *The Archaeological Journal*, cviii, 162–4.

—— (1957). Appendix in M. W. Thompson, 'Excavation of the fortified medieval hall of Hutton Colswain at Huttons Ambo, near Malton, Yorkshire', *The Archaeological Journal*, cxiv, 69–91.

—— (1964). 'Cruck construction: a survey of the problems', *Medieval Archaeology*, viii, 119–51.

SMITH T. P. (1966). 'The Anglo-Saxon churches of Bedfordshire', *Bedfordshire Archaeological Journal*, iii, 7–14.

—— (1971). 'The church of St Peter Canterbury', *Archaeologia Cantiana*, lxxxvi, 99–108.

—— (1973). 'The Anglo-Saxon churches of Hertfordshire', Chichester.

SPUFFORD M. (1965). *A Cambridgeshire community: Chippenham from settlement to enclosure*, Leicester (occasional paper no. 20, Department of English Local History, Leicester University).

STEAD I. M. (1958). 'Excavations at the south corner tower of the Roman fortress in York, 1956', *Yorkshire Archaeological Journal*, xxxix, 515–37.

—— (1959). 'A sherd of middle saxon pottery from York', *Yorkshire Archaeological Journal*, xl, 426.

—— (1959a). 'An Anglian cemetery on the Mount, York', *Yorkshire Archaeological Journal*, xxxix, 427–35.

STEENSBERG A. (1968). *Atlas over ... Borups Agre 1000–1200 e. Kr.*, København.

STENBERGER M. (ed.) (1943). *Forntida gårdar i Island*, København.

——(ed.)(1955). *Vallhagar, a migration period settlement on Gotland, Sweden*, Copenhagen and Stockholm.

STENTON F. M. (1913). *The early history of the abbey of Abingdon*, London.

—— (1947). *Anglo-Saxon England*, 2nd edn, Oxford.

—— (1957). *The Bayeux tapestry*, London.

——(1970). 'Norman London', *Preparatory to Anglo-Saxon England* (ed. D. M. Stenton), Oxford, 23–47.

—— (1971). *Anglo-Saxon England*, 3rd edn, Oxford.

STEPHENSON C. (1933). *Borough and town: a study of urban origins in England*, Cambridge (Mass.) (The Medieval Academy of America: publication 15).

STEVENS C. E. (1937). 'Gildas and the civitates of Britain', *English Historical Review*, liii, 193–203.

——(1966). 'The social and economic aspects of rural settlement', *Rural settlement in Roman Britain* (ed. C. Thomas), London 108–28.

STEVENSON J. (ed.) (1858). *Chronicon monasterii de Abingdon*, London (Rolls series, ii).

STEVENSON R. B. K. (1951). 'The Iona hoard of Anglo-Saxon coins', *Numismatic Chronicle*, cxi, 63–90.

STEVENSON W. H. (ed.) (1904). *Asser's life of Alfred*, Oxford.

—— (1929). 'Aelfric Bata's colloquies', *Anecdota Oxoniensis*, Oxford.

STJERNQVIST B. (1967). 'Das Problem der Grübenhäuser in Südschweden', *Jahrbuch des Römisch-Germanischen Zentralmuseums Mainz*, xiv, 144–52.

ST JOSEPH H. K. S. (1973). 'Aerial reconnaissance: recent results, 32', *Antiquity*, xlvii, 296–7.

STONE S. (1857). 'Account of certain (supposed) British and Saxon remains recently discovered at Standlake, in the county of Oxford', *Proceedings of the Society of Antiquaries of London*, 1st series, iv, 70–1, 92–100.

—— (1858). 'Recent exploration at Standlake, Yelford and Stanton Harcourt, in Oxfordshire', *Proceedings of the Society of Antiquaries of London*, 1st series, iv, 213–19.

STUBBS W. (1874). *Memorials of St Dunstan*, London (Rolls Series, lxiii).

SUTHERLAND C. H. V. (1942). 'Anglo-Saxon sceattas in England: their origin, chronology and distribution', *Numismatic Chronicle*, cii, 42–70.

—— (1948). *Anglo-Saxon gold coinage in the light of the Crondall hoard*, Oxford.

—— (1973). *English coinage: 600–900*, London.

SWANTON M. J. (1973). *The spearheads of the Anglo-Saxon settlements*, London.

SYMONS T. (ed.) (1953). *Regularis Concordia Angliae Nationes Monachorum Sanctimonialiumque*, London.

SYSON L. (1965). *British water-mills*, London.

TAIT J. (1936). *The medieval English borough*, Manchester.

TALBOT RICE D. (1952). *English art 871–1100*, Oxford.

TAMWORTH RESEARCH COMMITTEE (1971). *Tamworth development. The archaeological implications*, Tamworth.

TANNER L. and CLAPHAM A. W. (1933). 'Recent discoveries in the nave of Westminster Abbey', *Archaeologia*, lxxxiii, 227–36.

TAYLOR C. C. (1967a). 'Whiteparish: a study of the development of a Forest-Edge parish', *Wiltshire Archaeological and Natural History Magazine*, lxii, 79–102.

—— (1967b). 'Strip lynchets', *Antiquity*, xl, 227–83.

—— (1968–9). 'The origins of Lichfield, Staffs.', *Transactions of the South Staffordshire Archaeological and Historical Society*, x, 43–53.

—— (1970). *Dorset*, London (The making of the English Landscape).

—— (1972). 'The study of settlement patterns in pre-Saxon Britain', *Man, settlement and urbanism* (ed. P. J. Ucko, R. Tringham and G. W. Dimbleby), London, 109–13.

TAYLOR H. M. (1959). 'Some little known aspects of English pre-conquest churches', *The Anglo-Saxons* (ed. P. Clemoes), 137–58.

—— (1961). *English architecture at the time of Bede*, Jarrow (Jarrow Lecture).

—— (1962). 'The pre-conquest churches of Wessex', *Wiltshire Archaeological and Natural History Magazine*, lvii, 156–70.

—— (1966a). 'Rediscovery of important Anglo-Saxon sculpture at Hexham', *Archaeologia Aeliana*, xliv, 49–60.

—— (1966b). 'Anglo-Saxon architecture and sculpture in Staffordshire', *North Staffordshire Journal of Field Studies*, vi, 7–11.

—— (1968a). 'Reculver reconsidered', *The Archaeological Journal*, cxxv, 291–5.

—— (1968b). 'Belfry towers in Anglo-Saxon England', *North Staffordshire Journal of Field Studies*, viii, 9–18.

—— (1968c). 'Anglo-Saxon sculpture at Knook', *Wiltshire Archaeological and Natural History Magazine*, lxiii, 54–7.

—— (1969a). 'The Anglo-Saxon cathedral church at Canterbury', *The Archaeological Journal*, cxxvi, 107–30.

—— (1969b). 'Corridor crypts on the continent and in England', *North Staffordshire Journal of Field Studies*', ix, 17–52.

—— (1969c). 'The special role of Kentish churches in the development of pre-Norman (Anglo-Saxon) architecture', *The Archaeological Journal*, cxxvi, 192–8.

—— (1969d). 'Lyminge church', *The Archaeological Journal*, cxxvi, 257–60.

—— (1969e). 'The eighth-century doorway at Somerford Keynes', *Transactions of the Bristol and Gloucestershire Archaeological Society*, lxxxviii, 68–74.

—— (1970a) 'St Giles church, Barrow, Shropshire', *The Archaeological Journal*, cxxvii, 211–21.

—— (1970b). 'The origin, purpose and date of pilaster strips in Anglo-Saxon architecture', *North Staffordshire Journal of Field Studies*, x, 1–27.

—— (1971). 'Repton reconsidered', *England before the Conquest* (ed. P. Clemoes and K. Hughes), Cambridge, 391–408.

—— (1972a). 'Structural criticism: a plea for the systematic study of Anglo-Saxon building', *Anglo-Saxon England*, i, 259–72.

—— (1972b). 'J. T. Irvine's work at Bradford on Avon', *The Archaeological Journal*, cxxix, 89–118.

—— (1973). 'The Anglo-Saxon Chapel at Bradford on Avon', *The Archaeological Journal*, cxxx, 141–71.

—— and J. (1961). 'Problems of the dating of pre-conquest churches', *North Staffordshire Journal of Field Studies*, i, 58–76.

—— —— (1963). 'The Anglo-Saxon church at Edenham, Lincs.', *Journal of the British Archaeological Association*, 3rd series, xxvi, 6–10.

—— —— (1964). 'Herringbone masonry as a criterion of date', *Journal of the British Archaeological Association*, 3rd series, xxix, 3–51.

—— —— (1965). *Anglo-Saxon architecture*, Cambridge.

—— —— (1966). 'Architectural sculpture in pre-Norman England', *Journal of the British Archaeological Association*, 3rd series, xxiv, 3–51.

TEBBUTT C. F. (1960). 'An early twelfth century building at Eynesbury, Huntingdonshire', *Proceedings of the Cambridge Antiquarian Society*, liv, 85–9.

—— (1962). 'An eleventh century "boat-shaped" building at Buckden, Huntingdonshire', *Proceedings of the Cambridge Antiquarian Society*, liv, 85–9.

TESTER P. J. (1956). 'An Anglo-Saxon occupation site at Dartford', *Archaeologia Cantiana*, lxx, 256–9.

THIRSK J. (1967a). *The agrarian history of England and Wales*, IV *1500–1640*, Cambridge.

—— (1967b). 'Preface to the third edition', *The open fields* (C. S. and C. S. Orwin), Oxford, v–xv.

THOMAS A. C. (1958). *Gwithian, ten years' work, 1949–1958*, Camborne, *Proceedings of the West Cornwall Field Club*.

THOMAS A. C. (1959–60). 'Two early ecclesiastical sites, Isle of Whithorn and Ardwall Island', *Transactions of Dumfriesshire and Galloway Natural History and Antiquarian Society*, xxxviii, 71–82.

—— (1959). 'Imported pottery in dark-age western Britain', *Medieval Archaeology*, iii, 89–96.

—— (1967). 'An early Christian cemetery and chapel on Ardwall Isle, Kirkcudbright', *Medieval Archaeology*, xi, 126–88.

—— (1968). 'The evidence from North Britain', *Christianity in Britain, 300–700* (ed. M. W. Barley and R. P. C. Hanson), Leicester, 93–121.

—— (1971). *The early Christian archaeology of North Britain*, Oxford.

—— (1971a). *Britain and Ireland in early Christian times*, London.

THOMAS G. W. (1887). 'On excavations in an Anglo-Saxon cemetery at Sleaford in Lincoln-shire', *Archaeologia*, i, 1–24.

THOMPSON F. H. (1956). 'Anglo-Saxon sites in Lincolnshire: unpublished material and recent discoveries', *The Antiquaries Journal*, xxxvi, 181–99.

—— (1969). 'Excavations at Linenhall Street, Chester, 1961–2', *Journal of the Chester Archaeological Society*, lvi, 1–21.

THOMPSON F. H. and WHITWELL J. B. (1973). 'The gates of Roman Lincoln', *Archaeologia*, civ, 129–207.

THOMPSON M. W. (1957). 'Excavations of the fortified medieval hall of Hutton Colswain at Huttons Ambo, near Malton, Yorkshire', *The Archaeological Journal*, cxiv, 69–91.

—— (1965). Review of R. von Uslar, *Studien zu frühgeschichtlichen Befestigungen zwischen Nordsee und Alpen* (Köln, 1964), *Medieval Archaeology*, ix, 224–7.

THOMPSON T. R. and TAYLOR H. M. (1966). 'St Mary's church, Cricklade. Part II', *Wiltshire Archaeological and Natural History Magazine*. lxi, 38–42.

THOMSEN R. (1963). 'Forsøg på rekonstruktion af en fortidig jernudvindingsproces', *Kuml*, 60–74.

—— (1964). 'Forsøg på rekonstruktion af fortidige smedprocesser', *Kuml*, 62–85.

THORPE H. (1961). 'The green village as a distinctive form of settlement on the North European plain', *Bullétin de la Société Belge d'Études Géographiques*, xxx, 5–133.

THÜMMLER H. (1960). 'Carolingian period architecture', *Encyclopedia of world art*, iii, 82–103, 123–4.

THUN E. (1962–3). 'Die Wassermühlen, ein ökonomischer Entwicklungsfaktor der mittelal-terlichen Städte Schonen', *Meddelanden från Lunds Universitets Historiska Museum*, 224–37.

TISCHLER F. (1952). 'Zur Datierung der frühmittelalterlichen Tonware von Badorf, Ldkr. Köln', *Germania*, xxx, 194–200.

TODD M. (1970). 'The small towns of Roman Britain', *Britannia*, i, 114–30.

—— (1973). *The Coritani*, London.

TOYNBEE J. M. C. and WARD-PERKINS J. B. (1956). *The shrine of St Peter*, London.

TROW-SMITH R. (1957). *A history of British livestock husbandry to 1700*, London.

TURNER H. L. (1970). *Town defences in England and Wales*, London.

Two Lives of St Cuthbert. Ed. B. Colgrave (1940) Cambridge.

TYLECOTE R. F. (1962). *Metallurgy in archaeology*, London.

—— (1967). 'The bloomery site at West Runton', *Norfolk Archaeology*, xxxiv, 187–214.

—— (1973). 'The pit-type iron smelting shaft furnace; its diffusion and parallels', *Anti-kvarisk Arkiv*, liii, 42–7.

URRY W. (1967). *Canterbury under the Angevin kings*, London.

VAN DE WALLE A. L. J. (1969). 'Some technical analogies between building and other crafts in the use of split wood during the Middle Ages', *Chateau Gaillard*, iii, 152–5.

VAN ES W. A. (1965–66). 'Friesland in Roman times', *Berichten van de Rijksdienst voor het Oudheidkundig Bodemonderzoek*, xv–xvi, 37–68.

—— (1967). *Wijster – a native village beyond the imperial frontier*, Groningen.

—— (1969). 'Excavations at Dorestad; a pre-preliminary report: 1967–1968', *Berichten van de Rijksdienst voor het Oudheidkundig Bodemonderzoek*, xix, 183–207.

—— (1973). 'Die neuen Dorestad-Grabungen 1967–1972', *Vor- und Frühformen der europäischen Stadt im Mittelalter* (ed. H. Jankuhn, W. Schlesinger and H. Steuer), Göttingen (Abhandlungen der Akademie der Wissenschaften: Philologisch-Historische Klasse, 3 Folge, nr. 83), 202–17.

VARLEY W. T. (1950). 'Excavations of the castle ditch, Eddisbury, 1935–1938', *Transactions of the Historical Society of Lancashire and Cheshire*, cii, 1–68.

VCH. Victoria History of the Counties of England.

VEECK W. (1931). *Die Alamannen in Württemberg*, Leipzig.

VERBEEK A. (1950). 'Die ottonische Bautengruppe um Essen und Werden und die viergeschosste Wandteederung', *Karolingische und ottonische Kunst*, Wiesbaden (Forschung zur Kunstgeschichte und Christlichen archäologie, iii, ed. F. Gerke).

VERCAUTEREN F. (1969). 'Die spätantike Civitas im frühen Mittelalter', *Die Stadt des Mittelalters* (ed. C. Haase), Darmstadt, i (Wege der Forschung, ccxliii), 122–38.

VERZONE P. (1954). 'Le absidi poligonai del V^e e VIe secolo', *Frühmittelalterliche Kunst in den Alpenländen*, Olten and Lausanne (Akten zum III Internationalen Kongress für Frühmittelalter-forschung), 35–40.

VINOGRADOFF P. (1892). *Villainage in England*, London.

VON PETRIKOVITS H. (1958). 'Das Fortleben römischer Städte Rhein und Donau', *Studien zu den Anfängen des europäischen Städtewesens*, Konstanz und Lindau (Reichenau-Vortrage und Forschungen, iv), 63–73.

VON USLAR R. (1964). *Studien zu frühgeschichtlichen Befestigungen zwischen Nordsee und Alpen*, Köln (Beihefte der Bonner Jahrbücher: xi).

WACHER J. S. (ed.) (1966). *The civitas capitals of Roman Britain*, Leicester.

WADE K. (1972). *The Thetford ware tradition with special reference to Norfolk* (unpublished MA thesis, Southampton University).

WADE-MARTINS P. (1969). 'Excavations at North Elmham, 1967–8: an interim report', *Norfolk Archaeology*, xxxiv, 352–97.

—— (1970). 'Excavations at North Elmham, 1969: an interim report', *Norfolk Archaeology*, xxxv, 25–78.

—— (1971). *The development of the landscape and human settlement in West Norfolk from 350–1650 A.D., with particular reference to the Launditch Hundred* (unpublished Ph.D. thesis, Leicester University).

—— (1971a). 'Excavations at North Elmham, 1970: an interim report', *Norfolk Archaeology*, xxxv, 263–8.

—— (1972). 'Excavations at North Elmham', *Norfolk Archaeology*, xxxv, 416–28.

—— (1975). 'The origins of rural settlement in East Anglia', *Recent work in rural archaeology* (ed. P. J. Fowler), Bradford-on-Avon.

WAKEMAN W. F. (1893). *A survey of the antiquarian remains on the island of Inismurray* (Royal Society of Antiquaries of Ireland. Extra volume for 1892).

WALTON J. (1954). 'The hogback tombstones and the Anglo-Danish house', *Antiquity*, xxviii, 68–77.

WAQUET H. (1942). *Abbon*, Paris.

WARD G. (1949). 'A note on the Mead Way, the Street and Doddinhyrnan in Rochester', *Archaeologia Cantiana*, lxii, 37–44.

WARD J. H. (1973). 'The British sections of the *Notitia Dignitatum:* an alternative interpretation', *Britannia*, iv, 253–63.

WATERMAN D. M. (1959). 'Late Saxon, Viking and early medieval finds from York', *Archaeologia*, xcvii, 59–105.

WATSON P. J. *et al.* (1971). *Explanation in archaeology: an explicitly scientific approach*, New York.

WEBB (1956). *Architecture in England: the middle ages*, Harmondsworth.

WEBSTER G. (1951). 'Chester in the Dark Ages', *Journal of the Chester Archaeological Society*, xxxviii, 39–48.

—— *et al.* (1953). 'A Saxon treasure hoard found at Chester, 1950', *The Antiquaries Journal*, xxxiii, 22–32.

——(1967). 'Excavations at the Romano-British villa in Barnsley Park, Cirencester, 1961–1966', *Transactions of the Bristol and Gloucester Archaeological Society*, lxxxvi, 74–83.

—— (1969a). 'The future of villa studies', *The Roman villa in Britain* (ed. A. L. F. Rivet), London, 217–49.

—— (1969b). 'Barnsley Park villa', *The Archaeological Review*, iv, 38.

WEBSTER L. E. and CHERRY J. (1972). 'Medieval Britain in 1971', *Medieval Archaeology*, xvi, 147–212.

WEIDEMANN K. (1968). 'Die Topographie von Mainz in der Römerzeit und dem frühen Mittelalter', *Jahrbuch des Römisch-Germanischen Zentralmuseums Mainz*, xv, 146–99.

—— (1972). 'Zur Topographie von Metz in der Römerzeit und im frühen Mittelalter', *Jahrbuch des Römisch-Germanischen Zentralmuseums Mainz*, xvii, 147–71.

WERNER J. (1970). 'Zur Verbreitung frühgeschichtlicher Metallarbeiten (Werkstaff–Wanderhandwerk-Handel–Familienverbindung)', *Early Medieval Studies*, i, Stockholm (Antikvariskt Arkiv, 38), 65–81.

WEST S. E. (1963). 'Excavations at Cox Lane (1958) and at the town defences, Shire Hall Yard, Ipswich (1959)', *Proceedings of the Suffolk Institute of Archaeology*, xxix, pt 3, 233–303.

——(1969a). 'The Anglo-Saxon village of West Stow: an interim report of the excavations, 1965–68', *Medieval Archaeology*, xiii, 1–20.

——(1969b). 'Pagan Saxon pottery from West Stow, Suffolk', *Berichten van de Rijkdienst voor het Oudheidkundig Bodemonderzoek* xix, 175–81.

—— (1970). 'The excavation of the town defences at Tayfen Road, Bury St Edmunds, 1968', *Proceedings of the Suffolk Institute of Archaeology*, xxxii, pt 1, 17–24.

—— (ed.)(1973). *Ipswich. The archaeological implications of development*, Bury St Edmunds (Scole Committee).

WHEELER R. E. M. (1927). *London and the Vikings*, London (London Museum Catalogues: no. 1).

—— (1935). *London and the Saxons*, London (London Museum Catalogues: no. 6).

WHITE G. M. (1934). 'A settlement of the South Saxons', *The Antiquaries Journal*, xiv, 393–400.

WHITE L. JR. (1965). *Medieval technology and social change*, Oxford.

—— (1969). 'The expansion of technology 500–1500', *The Fontana Economic History of Europe*, London, i, ch. 4.

WHITELOCK D. (1952). *The beginnings of English society*, Harmondsworth.

—— (1955). *English historical documents, c. 500–1042*, London.

WHITLOCK R. (1953). *Rare and extinct birds of Britain*, London.

WHITWORTH T. (1968). 'Deposits beneath the North Bailey, Durham', *Durham University Journal*, xxx, 18–29.

WILDGOOSE R. H. (1961). 'The defences of the pre-conquest borough of Nottingham', *Transactions of the Thoroton Society*, lxv, 19–26.

WILLIS R. (1845). 'Architectural history of Winchester Cathedral', *Proceedings of the Royal Archaeological Institute*, Winchester.

WILSON D. M. (1955). 'An Irish mounting in the National Museum, Copenhagen', *Acta Archaeologica*, xxvi, 163–72.

—— (1959). 'Almgren and chronology, a summary and some comments', *Medieval Archaeology*, iii, 112–19.

—— (1961). 'An Anglo-Saxon bookbinding at Fulda (Codex Bonifatianus I)', *The Antiquaries Journal*, xli, 199–217.

—— (1962). 'Anglo-Saxon rural economy', *Agricultural History Review*, x, 65–79.

—— (1964). *Anglo-Saxon ornamental metalwork, 700–1100, in the British Museum*, London.

—— (1965). 'Some neglected late Anglo-Saxon swords', *Medieval Archaeology*, ix, 32–54.

—— (1967). 'The Vikings' relationship with Christianity in northern England', *Journal of the British Archaeological Association*, 3rd series, xxx, 437–47.

—— (1968). 'Anglo-Saxon carpenters' tools', *Studien zur europäischen Vor- und Frühgeschichte* (eds. M. Claus, *et al.*), Neumunster, 143–50.

—— (1968a). 'Archaeological evidence for the Viking settlements and raids in England', *Frühmittelalterliche Studien*, ii, 291–304.

—— (1971). *The Anglo-Saxons*, 2nd edn, Harmondsworth.

—— (1971a). 'The Norsemen', *Who are the Scots?* (ed. G. Menzies), London.

—— (1974). *The Viking age in the Isle of Man, the archaeological evidence*, Odense (C. C. Rafn lecture, no. 3).

—— and BLUNT C. E. (1961). 'The Trewhiddle hoard', *Archaeologia*, xcviii, 75–122.

—— and HURST J. G. (1957). 'Medieval Britain in 1956', *Medieval Archaeology*, i, 147–171.

—— —— (1958). 'Medieval Britain in 1957', *Medieval Archaeology*, ii, 183–213.

—— —— (1959). 'Medieval Britain in 1958', *Medieval Archaeology*, iii, 295–326.

—— —— (1960). 'Medieval Britain in 1959', *Medieval Archaeology*, iv, 134–65.

—— and HURST D. G. (1961). 'Medieval Britain in 1960', *Medieval Archaeology*, v, 309–339.

—— —— (1962–3). 'Medieval Britain in 1961', *Medieval Archaeology*, vi–vii, 306–49.

—— —— (1964). 'Medieval Britain in 1962 and 1963', *Medieval Archaeology*, viii, 231–299.

—— —— (1965). 'Medieval Britain in 1964', *Medieval Archaeology*, ix, 170–220.

—— —— (1966). 'Medieval Britain in 1965', *Medieval Archaeology*, x, 168–219.

—— —— (1967). 'Medieval Britain in 1966', *Medieval Archaeology*, xi, 262–319.

—— —— (1968). 'Medieval Britain in 1967', *Medieval Archaeology*, xii, 155–211.

—— —— (1969). 'Medieval Britain in 1968', *Medieval Archaeology*, xiii, 230–87.

—— —— (1970). 'Medieval Britain in 1969', *Medieval Archaeology*, xiv, 155–208.

—— and KLINDT-JENSEN O. (1966). *Viking art*, London.

—— and MOORHOUSE S. (1971). 'Medieval Britain in 1970', *Medieval Archaeology*, xv, 124–79.

WILSON D. R. (1962). 'Silchester in Roman Britain in 1961', *Journal of Roman Studies*, lii, 185–6.

—— (1970). 'Roman Britain in 1969', *Britannia*, i, 269–305.

WILSON J. (1909). *The evolution of British cattle and the fashioning of breeds*, London.

WINKELMAN W. (1958). 'Die Ausgrabungen in der frühmittelalterlichen Siedlung bei Warendorf (Westfalen)', *Neue Ausgrabungen in Deutschland*, Berlin, 492–517.

WORMALD F. (1952). *English drawings of the tenth and eleventh centuries*, London.

WRIGHT D. (trans.) (1960). *Beowulf*, Harmondsworth.

WYLIE W. M. (1855). 'The graves of the Alemanni at Oberflacht in Swabia', *Archaeologia*, xxxvi, 129–60.

ZARNECKI G. (1951). *English romanesque sculpture, 1066–1140*, London.

—— (1955a). 'The Winchester acanthus in romanesque sculpture', *Wallraf-Richartz Jahrbuch*, xvii, 211–15.

—— (1955b). 'Sources of the English romanesque sculpture', *Actes du XVIIe Congrès International d'Histoire de l'Art*, The Hague, 171–5.

—— (1958). *The early sculpture of Ely Cathedral*, London.

—— (1966). '1066 and architectural sculpture', *Proceedings of the British Academy*, lii, 87–104.

ZEUNER F. E. (1963). *A history of domesticated animals*, London.

Index